Advance Praise for *Ascent to Power*

"With a complete mastery of the sources, David Roll takes us on the gripping journey from Harry Truman's election as vice president in 1944 through to his death, rightly concentrating on the crucial years that ended in his stunning reelection as president in 1948. Roll has a fine sense of all the key figures around Truman, but it is his insights into the man himself that are so valuable. Well-researched, well-written, and intensely readable, this book confirms Truman as a giant of American—indeed global—history."

    —Andrew Roberts, Baron Roberts of Belgravia, *New York Times* bestselling author
      of *Churchill: Walking with Destiny*

"The sudden death of Franklin Roosevelt shook the world; the recognition that power would pass to Harry Truman shook it even more. But the untested Truman turned out to be just what America and the world needed as World War II segued into the Cold War. No one has told this vital story more thoroughly or with greater verve and insight than David Roll does in this fine book."

    —H. W. Brands, Pulitzer Prize finalist and author of *The General vs. the President*

"After winning World War II, America rebuilt the world—including its enemies. How that happened is one of the great stories of any age. Equally remarkable is how Harry Truman, a modest man of the people, took over from the great FDR to achieve this miracle. The author of brilliant biographies of Harry Hopkins and George C. Marshall, lawyer-turned-historian David Roll brings a clear and sharp eye for evidence and a deep human understanding to telling this tale. As the global order Truman built teeters at the brink, *Ascent to Power* could not be more relevant."

    —Evan Thomas, *New York Times* bestselling author of *Road to Surrender*

"Did any president inherit so many challenges, and such consequential ones, as Harry S. Truman? After just eighty-two days as vice president—without ever being taken into the FDR's confidence—the Missouri pol was left to deal with the end of a war and the launch of a new world order. David L. Roll's riveting account of that momentous transition shows Truman rising to the occasion and more—forging a Western alliance, containing the Soviet Union, converting to a peacetime economy and supporting pent-up demands for civil rights. Writing with skill and drama, Roll tells us how this accidental president reshaped America and the world."

    —Susan Page, Washington Bureau chief, *USA Today*, and author of *The Rulebreaker*

"Truman wasn't just a great president, he was a great human being—a model of integrity and resilience and duty that we can all learn from. Most people are changed by power, yet Truman somehow changed for the better. David Lee Roll's incredible book shows this process and its timeless lessons."

—Ryan Holiday, #1 *Wall Street Journal* bestselling author of *The Obstacle Is the Way* and *The Daily Stoic*

"A riveting account of Harry Truman's unexpected emergence onto the world scene, written with authority, candor, verve, and a keen eye for piercing and illustrative detail. David Roll has produced a marvelous account of the highs and lows of the consequential Truman Administration—from which so little was at first expected—triumphs and missteps included unflinchingly. Happily, Truman's salty dialogue permeates these pages, flavoring Roll's expert analysis of the leadership this accidental but supremely confident, new president provided so boldly after the death of FDR. We can and should still argue about Truman's legacy, but not about David Roll's major contribution to the debate; this book sets a new standard."

—Harold Holzer, director of the Roosevelt House Public Policy Institute at Hunter College and author of *Brought Forth on This Continent*

"The Cold War demanded fertile statesmanship, which David Roll re-creates with all the drama and credibility that distinguished his biographies of George Marshall and Harry Hopkins. This is history as literature, intensely relevant and a great read."

—Richard Norton Smith, director of presidential libraries and author of *An Ordinary Man*

"In *Ascent to Power*, David Roll again proves himself a master of the immensely consequential years immediately after World War II, this time exploring one of the odder couples of American politics—the patrician Franklin Roosevelt and his everyman successor, the often underestimated Harry Truman. *Ascent to Power* reveals how Truman steered the world's greatest global power through agonizing decisions about atomic weapons, deadly confrontations with recent ally U.S.S.R., and the beginning of a long overdue reckoning with its hateful legacy of racism."

—David O. Stewart, author of *George Washington* and *Madison's Gift*

"Franklin Roosevelt towers over the history of the mid-twentieth-century United States. But David Roll reminds us that it was FDR's sudden successor—plain, unassuming Harry Truman—who, more than any other single individual, consolidated and even defined an emerging American consensus about the organization of the free world and the first big steps toward civil rights at home. Experienced in writing about this period, Roll has a feel for the people and their times. He does a wonderful, readable job of placing readers at Truman's side as he and his colleagues felt their way through the upheavals and partisan crossfire of the great transition from war to peace."

> —Philip Zelikow, Senior Fellow at Stanford University's Hoover Institution, former counselor of the United States Department of State, and coauthor of *To Build a Better World*

"This riveting story examines a pivot point in American history, the transition from the patrician reformer Franklin Delano Roosevelt to Harry Truman, an apparently more ordinary person. David Roll captures the dynamism and resilience of democratic governance and its ability to respond to the most profound crises. He shows that leadership matters, but that democracy can work with leaders of very different sorts. *Ascent to Power* is both an extraordinary work of history and a book full of insights for our time."

> —Austin Sarat, William Nelson Cromwell Professor of Jurisprudence and Political Science at Amherst College and author of *Lethal Injection and the False Promise of Humane Execution*

"An intriguing historical study of a major presidential transition period . . . With solid research, Roll brings to life a short time frame that laid the foundation for the decades to come." —*Kirkus Reviews*

ASCENT
TO POWER

ASCENT
TO POWER

How Truman Emerged from Roosevelt's
Shadow and Remade the World

DAVID L. ROLL

DUTTON

DUTTON

An imprint of Penguin Random House LLC
penguinrandomhouse.com

Copyright © 2024 by David L. Roll

Penguin Random House supports copyright. Copyright fuels creativity, encourages diverse
voices, promotes free speech, and creates a vibrant culture. Thank you for buying an authorized edition
of this book and for complying with copyright laws by not reproducing, scanning, or distributing
any part of it in any form without permission. You are supporting writers and allowing
Penguin Random House to continue to publish books for every reader.

DUTTON and the D colophon are registered trademarks of Penguin Random House LLC.

LIBRARY OF CONGRESS CATALOGING-IN-PUBLICATION DATA
has been applied for.

ISBN 9780593186442 (hardcover)
ISBN 9780593186459 (ebook)

Printed in the United States of America
1st Printing

Map by Jeffrey L. Ward

BOOK DESIGN BY ELKE SIGAL

While the author has made every effort to provide accurate telephone numbers, internet addresses,
and other contact information at the time of publication, neither the publisher nor the author assumes any
responsibility for errors or for changes that occur after publication. Further, the publisher does not have any
control over and does not assume any responsibility for author or third-party websites or their content.

In memory of my parents

"Two such as you . . . Cannot be parted nor be swept away"
—Robert Frost

Contents

Prologue

Death and Rebirth

On the morning of July 9, 1944, a muggy Sunday in wartime Washington, the Hudson Valley patrician and the so-called "common man" from Missouri were getting ready for their respective road trips.[1]

Outside the White House a four-man Secret Service detail was waiting for President Franklin Roosevelt to be wheeled out and assisted into the back seat of an armored Lincoln limousine.

In his apartment at the corner of Connecticut Avenue and Chesapeake Street (the building today is called the Truman House), Senator Harry Truman was finishing a letter to his twenty-year-old daughter, Margaret. He was about to drive alone to St. Louis and then to his home in Independence in his dove-gray Chrysler coupe, one of the last civilian autos produced before the Pearl Harbor attack and the conversion to tanks and warplanes.

The president would not be alone. His Secret Service driver would pick up Lucy Mercer at her sister's house on Q Street. They would travel north through Maryland to Shangri-La (later Camp David), where they planned to spend the rest of the day and early evening at FDR's rustic retreat on a trout stream in the Catoctin Mountains. Franklin and Lucy, as those with even a casual acquaintance with the president's life know, had carried on a love affair, which was discovered in 1918 by Franklin's wife, Eleanor. To avoid divorce and disinheritance, FDR had promised Eleanor and his mother, Sara, to never see Lucy again. Yet more than two decades later, Franklin was still in love with Lucy and she with him.

As the senator and the president took to the road, among their many thoughts were the Democratic National Convention that was scheduled to convene in ten days and FDR's health. In the letter to his daughter that he had just mailed, Truman wrote that "dozens" of people were "plotting . . . to make [me] VP against [my] will" and that he hoped he could "dodge" it at the convention. With a veiled reference to the president's precarious health, an open secret in Washington, he wrote that "1600 Pennsylvania is a nice address but I'd rather not move in through the back door—or any other door at [age] sixty."[2] Based on these comments, it is clear that Truman assumed, like most everyone else, that Roosevelt, after serving as president for almost twelve years, was going to stand for a fourth term, though it had not yet been officially announced.

The staging and content of the public announcement that he would run once again had to have flickered through the president's "heavily forested interior" as he rode with Lucy that Sunday through the Maryland countryside.[3] The previous Friday, in a meeting with Missourian Bob Hannegan, the new chair of the Democratic National Committee and one of Truman's closest associates, FDR had decided that he would announce his candidacy at a press and radio conference two days after returning from the trip to Shangri-La, a little more than a week before the convention.

During the long Sunday he spent with Lucy on the road and at the presidential retreat, Franklin had to have also thought about, and perhaps even discussed with Lucy, whether he was strong enough healthwise to take on another term. According to a jaw-dropping memo that was suppressed until 2007, FDR had been informed by his personal physician, just a day earlier, that due to "heart failure," he would be "unable to complete" a full four-year term and that "he had a very serious responsibility concerning who is the Vice President."[4] Thus, having decided on Friday to make public that he would run again and been told by his doctor on Saturday that he would die in office if he did, the president on Sunday must have been weighing his odds of living against his desire to remain wartime commander in chief. Whether he gave any thought that day as to who would be his vice president will never be known.

Though there is no record of what Franklin and Lucy actually discussed during the time they were together at Shangri-La, it is reasonable to surmise, as some historians have, that it was Lucy who validated Roosevelt's rash decision to launch his final campaign, even though she too feared that he might not survive a fourth term.[5]

A few minutes after 11 a.m. on Tuesday, July 11, before a crowd of some two hundred reporters in the White House, President Roosevelt began reading aloud a letter from him to Bob Hannegan. The letter was his somewhat presumptuous official announcement to the Democratic National Committee that if nominated, he would "reluctantly, but as a good soldier . . . accept and serve in the office if I am so ordered by the Commander in Chief of us all—the sovereign people of the United States."[6] While speaking, his hands shook so much that he could not light his cigarette. There was no hint of who his running mate might be.

In St. Louis, at roughly the same time, Harry Truman, like so many ordinary Americans during wartime rationing, was worried about the condition of his automobile tires. He needed to get home to Independence to pick up summer suits to wear at the convention but all four tires were in terrible condition after the 840-mile drive on old two-lane U.S. 40 from Washington. However, as Harry wrote in a letter to his wife, Bess, he eventually located a "tire man" who, with some maneuvering, skirted the rationing restrictions to get him one new tire and "four Goodyear puncture proof tubes" that had recently been exempted from the ration regulations. The senator, who by that time had befriended the tire man, invited him to have lunch with him and several of his St. Louis political cronies at the Coronado, an art deco hotel built in the 1920s that is in operation today. In his letter to Bess, Truman wrote, "you'd have thought I was making [the tire man] a Knight of the Garter, it pleased him so much."[7] This was vintage Harry Truman—a man of the people.

———

The lives of the world-famous president who was told he would not survive but ran anyway and the obscure senator who claimed he did not want to run as his vice president would soon intersect. This is a riveting slice of history in and of itself. However, it is the final months of Franklin Roosevelt's presidency, the unsteady transition of power to Harry Truman, and the liberation of tens of millions of people who survived the carnage of World War II that form the core of this book. It is a story of death and rebirth.

After eighty-two days as Roosevelt's VP, Truman began his accidental presidency utterly unprepared. FDR made no effort to bring him up to speed on current foreign relations and domestic issues, nor did Truman insist on being informed by FDR or his staff. As vice president, Truman did not try to recruit experienced advisers or initiate a relationship with an outside foreign policy expert. As to Roosevelt's plans for the future, all Truman inherited was the unrealistic hope that he could achieve lasting peace by perpetuating his predecessor's apparent policy of cooperation and accommodation with the Soviet Union. If FDR actually had a vision for the postwar recovery of Europe and Japan, a stable China, and the conversion of the U.S. to a peacetime economy, he kept such thoughts to himself. Truman was left in the dark. It would take almost four years but he managed with the aid of George Marshall, Dean Acheson, George Kennan, and Arthur Vandenberg to fashion a more muscular and confrontational policy that contained the Soviets without escalation to a hot war, revived Western Europe, supported General Douglas MacArthur's surprisingly liberal reforms in Japan, and midwifed the state of Israel, a home for Holocaust survivors.

Framed by the presidential elections of 1944 and 1948, this study captures the illusions of a dying president and the mistakes and triumphs of his successor, an arc of world history that separated those who found freedom from those consigned to live under tyranny for decades to come. Unlike previous histories of the Roosevelt and Truman presidencies, this book focuses on the transition—the long shadow cast by the dead president, Truman's struggle to emerge, and how decisions during the years of transition, 1944 through 1948, impacted the peoples who survived the sword.

The decisions were bold, their impacts profound. The Marshall Plan, backed by Truman, helped restore the economies of Western Europe, notably West Germany—the engine of Europe—while the Truman Doctrine rescued Greece from Communism and Turkey from undue Soviet influence. The president's endorsement of NATO provided security to millions of Americans and Europeans by checking the aggressive designs of the Soviet Union. Truman's support of the Berlin Airlift prevented citizens from the western zones of that city from being driven out by starvation and lack of heat. His courageous decision to recognize Israel paved the way for hundreds of thousands of Jews from Europe and North Africa to flee to that new state, thus doubling its population in less than four years.

On the other side of the globe, the president's appointment of General MacArthur to command the occupation of Japan, combined with Truman's orders to "reverse course" and restore Japan's economy, set the stage for what became known as the "Japanese miracle," acts of enormous significance in East Asia.

Looking back, it is astonishing that instead of punishing its implacable enemies whose people were responsible for the deaths of so many thousands of Americans, the Truman administration, motivated by a mix of altruism, the need for trading partners, and national security, chose to restore the economies of both West Germany and Japan. By the early 1960s, those two countries had once again become industrial powerhouses, key allies of the United States in its quest for world peace.

At home the transition from FDR to Truman, as we shall see, was not smooth. Americans, many of whom had known only Roosevelt as their president for much of their lives, distrusted and ridiculed the scrappy Missourian, an ex-farmer who spoke with a folksy mid-American twang. Rather than being seen as a reasonably competent two-term senator, Truman had a reputation as a failed haberdasher who had been associated with the notorious Pendergast political machine in Kansas City. Though Truman, as president, carried forward the banner of FDR's New Deal, he faced postwar problems that even Roosevelt could not have solved: reconversion of the entire U.S. economy, runaway inflation, and crippling labor

strikes. Truman's job approval percentages dipped into the low 30s. Truman used to say, "Heroes know when to die," suggesting that if FDR had
lived, he would have experienced the same troubles that bedeviled the first
few years of Truman's presidency.[8] However, in one notable respect—civil
rights—Truman reached beyond FDR's New Deal, a move that might have
been responsible for his surprising election victory in 1948. Though his
civil rights proposals were blocked by Congress, he was the first president
since Lincoln to seriously promote a substantive civil rights agenda, a forerunner of the civil rights legislation that was enacted in the 1960s.

————————

Since the focus of this book will be on the years of transition, it is im-
portant to have a basic understanding of the vastly different paths that
FDR and Truman traveled before meeting for the first time in the White
House on St. Valentine's Day 1935.

Their life journeys began in nineteenth-century America but from
birthplaces that seemed worlds apart. In 1882, Roosevelt was born as an
only child into inherited wealth and privilege in a mansion called "Springwood," which was situated on a bluff above the Hudson River. The wealth
was originally derived from sugar refining off the backs of slave labor
in the Caribbean and smuggling opium into China. Two years after Franklin's birth, Truman was born about thirteen hundred miles from Springwood in an unnamed white frame house measuring twenty feet by
twenty-eight feet in the village of Lamar, Missouri. All four of Truman's
grandparents were Southern sympathizers who had owned slaves. His
mother, who never forgot being evicted as a young girl from her parents'
farm in 1863 by the Union Army, refused to sleep in the Lincoln Bedroom
when her son was president. In 1890, Truman's father, whose business for-
tunes as a livestock trader rose and often fell, moved his wife, young Harry,
and his two other children to the "Queen City of the Trails," Independence, Missouri, gateway to the West. The reason? Excellent public schools.

When Harry graduated from Independence High School and began
working in a Kansas City bank because he and his parents could not afford
college, Franklin was at Harvard, having graduated from the exclusive
Groton School. After Harvard, he spent a few years at Columbia Law

School before clerking at a white-shoe law firm on Wall Street. During that time he married Anna Eleanor Roosevelt (known as Eleanor), his distant cousin. In 1910 FDR entered politics and was elected to the New York State Senate, where he gained a reputation as a reformer for fighting to block a Tammany Hall machine candidate. During his second term, he was appointed assistant secretary of the navy by President Woodrow Wilson. He moved with his family to a comfortable house at 1733 N Street in Washington, DC.

In 1906, Truman had to quit his job as a bank teller in order to help his father run the six-hundred-acre family farm near Grandview, Missouri. For the next decade he worked long, hard days on the farm, planting corn, wheat, and alfalfa and stacking hay. When the U.S. entered World War I in 1917, Harry, at age thirty-three, reenlisted in the Missouri National Guard, which was soon sworn into federal service. He shipped out to France in early 1918. As captain of Battery D of the 129th Field Artillery, Truman earned the approval and respect of his rowdy group of Irish and German Catholic soldiers and led them in combat until the armistice, an experience that was a turning point in his life. After the war he married Elizabeth "Bess" Wallace, whom he had courted for years, and opened a men's clothing store (a haberdashery) in Kansas City with his army pal and partner, Eddie Jacobson. For a couple of years the store was able to survive on credit but due to a nationwide depression during which prices broke into a free fall, the store had to close in 1922. Jacobson, who had no assets, was forced into bankruptcy in 1925. Whether it was ethics or the lure of moving into politics, Truman decided to bear his debt burden, negotiate with the creditors, and slowly pay off what was owed.

Franklin's political ambitions and his thirteen-year marriage to Eleanor barely survived the discovery by his wife in 1918 of a stash of love letters from Lucy Mercer, Eleanor's young, wellborn social secretary whose mother, divorced from her second husband, had squandered her inherited fortune. Though no longer as intimate as they had been when first married, Eleanor and Franklin remained affectionate and developed one of the most successful husband-wife political partnerships in American history.[9] In 1920, the Democrats nominated FDR, a rising star in the party, as their vice presidential candidate to run with James Cox. The ticket lost to

Warren Harding and Calvin Coolidge in a landslide but Roosevelt, at age thirty-eight, had burst onto the national scene. The next summer, he experienced symptoms of polio while vacationing at his family place on Campobello Island. At first he ran a temperature; then his legs became numb and sensitive to the touch. Within a few days, he became paralyzed from the waist down, his legs useless. He did not fully comprehend it at the time, but his political future was in grave doubt.

That fall, Thomas Joseph Pendergast (often called "TJ"), the boss of the Kansas City political machine, and his brother Mike, who was Truman's close friend, assured Harry that he would have their full support if he would agree to run for eastern judge of Jackson County, a position that in Missouri was not a legal judgeship but an administrative job, akin to a county commissioner. Because the men's store was failing, Truman jumped at the opportunity. He ran in 1922 and won. Two years later, he lost his reelection bid because a rival political boss in Kansas City, who was feuding with the Pendergasts, switched parties and supported Truman's Republican opponent.

Meanwhile, FDR was fitted with leg braces so he could at least stand, and he focused on swimming three times a day, hoping that he would walk again if he continued exercising his legs. With the encouragement of Eleanor and his political guru, Louis Howe, Roosevelt made his first political appearance during the summer of 1924 at the Democratic National Convention when he was selected to deliver the speech to nominate Al Smith for president. With no noticeable reaction to his disability from the audience, FDR's speech was widely publicized and praised. In 1926 Roosevelt purchased a resort in Warm Springs, Georgia, known for its healing mineral waters, and he turned it into a rehabilitation facility for polio patients, including himself.

The same year, with the Pendergasts having become the "boss of bosses in Kansas City politics" by outmaneuvering their rival, Truman ran for and won the position of presiding judge for all of Jackson County, which he held until 1934—two four-year terms. During those years he turned a blind eye to the money lining the pockets of the Pendergast family that came from government agencies led by people they had placed there. Truman himself questioned whether he "did the right thing" by putting "a lot of no account sons of bitches" on his payroll or paying inflated prices for supplies in order to "satisfy the political powers," while at the same time saving the county millions of dollars. He answered his own question: "I believe I did do right."[10] To those who knew and worked with him, Truman had a reputation for honesty, integrity, and efficiency. His legacy as presiding judge was the construction of a new road and bridge system, "a distinct achievement," wrote the *Kansas City Times*, "that would be creditable to any county in the United States."[11]

As 1928 approached, Roosevelt was being mentioned as a potential Democratic candidate for the presidency but he was shrewd enough to know that he could not possibly succeed without having first held an important elective office—namely, the governorship of New York. Gambling that he could win even though the booming economy and stock market favored Republicans, FDR entered the gubernatorial race. With only four weeks to campaign, he strapped on his braces, gave speeches throughout the state, and put to rest concerns about his health and stamina. He won the two-year term as governor rather handily even though Al Smith, again the Democratic candidate for president, lost by a landslide to Herbert Hoover. With the nation sinking into a depression in 1930, Roosevelt easily won a second two years as governor by blaming lack of leadership in Washington and the failure of Republicans to curb speculation on Wall Street in 1928–29. In 1931, Governor Roosevelt established a program, run by Harry Hopkins, to provide direct relief to poor New York families (chits for food, shelter, and health care) and jobs for the unemployed, a harbinger of the New Deal. This program, together with a speech promising to support "the forgotten man at the bottom of the economic pyramid," catapulted Roosevelt into the front ranks as a Democratic nominee for the presidency.[12] At the Democratic convention Roosevelt secured the nomination on the fourth ballot. Following a whistle-stop campaign in which he laid out his philosophy of government and put the lie to the whispering campaign that a partially paralyzed man did not have the strength to be president, Roosevelt defeated Hoover, carrying forty-two of the forty-eight states. With fifteen million Americans out of work, Roosevelt took office in the midst of the greatest crisis the nation had faced since the Civil War.

In October 1933, Truman's career path for the first time started to bend toward that of the new president. Strongly encouraged by Bennett Clark, Missouri's senior senator, and the Pendergast machine, Judge Truman accepted a second job, director of the U.S. Employment Service in Missouri, which was part of a New Deal work-relief program under the auspices of the Civil Works Administration (CWA). The post was available because Senator Clark and TJ had demanded that the originally appointed director be fired because he was a Republican. They, of course, wanted to take credit for job creation in their state. Truman's new position entailed the placement of unemployed workers into jobs on infrastructure and public works projects in Missouri financed by the CWA. For the first time Truman found himself traveling on government business to Washington, DC, to attend conferences and to confer with Harry Hopkins, administrator of the CWA, whom FDR had hired during his first hundred days as president.

With Washington on his mind, Truman had to decide what to do after his second term as presiding judge expired in 1934. There were no term limits attached to his judgeship but the tradition was to move on after two terms. His first thought was to run for Congress but TJ had selected someone else. On May 8, Truman's fiftieth birthday, fate intervened. He received a call from Jim Pendergast, TJ's nephew, who told him that TJ wanted him to run for a seat in the U.S. Senate that at the time was occupied by a Republican who had decided to run again in the general election. TJ's idea that he should run for the Senate floored and flabbergasted Truman. It left him close to speechless. When he composed himself he told Jim Pendergast that there were several reasons why he couldn't run, including the fact that he had no money to conduct a statewide campaign and that Bess, his wife, did not want to leave Independence. However, when the Pendergasts and the state Democratic Party promised that he would receive their full support, he agreed to give it a shot. The leading Democratic contender in the primary was six-term congressman Jacob "Tuck" Milligan, a World War I hero, but TJ could not support him because if Milligan won, he and his allies would threaten TJ's control of statewide Missouri politics.

The primary was nasty, with Milligan warning that the Pendergasts would rig the election and that if Truman were to be elected to the Senate, he would take his orders from TJ. Truman prevailed, with almost half of his vote total coming from Jackson County. Compared to the primary, the general election was a "pushover," mainly because of Roosevelt's New Deal relief policies, which helped Missourians and the rest of the country survive the Great Depression.

Senator-elect Truman, along with Bess and their daughter, Margaret, arrived in Washington on the last day of 1934. It was an exciting time to be in the nation's capital, especially for members of Congress. The "Second Hundred Days" of Roosevelt's presidency was about to begin with Social Security and a flurry of other legislative proposals for the Senate and House to transform into law during the next three months. It was the high tide of the New Deal.

The paths traveled by Franklin Roosevelt and Harry Truman finally intersected on February 14, 1935, a month and a half after Truman had been officially sworn in. At 11:15 a.m., the junior senator from Missouri was escorted into the Oval Office, where he and Roosevelt laid eyes on each other for the first time. "It was quite an event for a country boy to go calling on the President of the United States," he recalled.[13] There is no evidence of what was said during the seven-minute meeting. It is likely, however, that FDR did most of the talking.

———

Throughout Truman's first term, the president showed little respect for the junior senator from Missouri even though he almost always voted in favor of FDR's legislative agenda. Truman let him know how he felt. When he found out that a White House staffer had asked TJ to order him to change his vote on a Senate leadership matter, Truman was incensed. "I'm tired of . . . having the President treat me as an office boy," he told a reporter. "They better learn downtown right now that no Tom Pendergast or anybody else tells Senator Truman how to vote."[14] Truman got really angry when he was tracked down by a state trooper while driving to Independence and told he must return to Washington to break a tie vote in the Senate. To FDR's press secretary, Steve Early, he complained, "This is the third time I've come back to bail you guys out on a vote. You tell that to the President!"[15]

Near the end of Truman's first six years in the Senate, Missouri governor Lloyd Stark, a wealthy apple grower who was in Washington having a chummy meeting with Roosevelt, dropped by to see Truman. "Everybody keeps telling me that I ought to run for the Senate," he told Truman, "but don't worry, Harry, I wouldn't dream of running against you."[16] To Truman's ears, "everybody" meant FDR and his political advisers. The moment Stark left, Truman said to an aide, "That S.O.B. is going to run against me." He was right. Pursuant to an agreement with Stark, FDR offered Truman an appointment to the Interstate Commerce Commission that paid more than a senator's salary. It was an obvious ploy to get Truman not to run in the primary against Stark. Truman's response: "Tell the president to go to hell."[17] The race was on. Since Truman could no longer count on support from the crumbling Pendergast machine (TJ was incarcerated at Leavenworth for tax evasion), and Stark controlled both the purse strings of and the local organizers on the Missouri Democratic committee, Truman was on his own. For that reason it was the toughest campaign of his career. With the big-city dailies and almost every other newspaper in Missouri having endorsed Stark, the odds were stacked against Truman. Nevertheless, he defeated Stark in the primary by eight thousand votes out of 650,000 cast. The margin of victory came from wards in St. Louis "delivered" by young Bob Hannegan and the Black vote (due to Truman's "Brotherhood of Man" speech). As expected, Truman won the general election, beating the Republican, Manvel Davis, by forty thousand votes.

A few days after Senator Truman was sworn in for the second time, he conducted a thirty-thousand-mile, monthlong inspection tour of the nation's defense plants, which at the time were gearing up for the possibility of war. As soon as he returned, he arranged an appointment with the president in the Oval Office. At noon on February 3, 1941, Truman informed FDR that he intended to propose the establishment of a Senate committee to investigate the awarding of government defense contracts, with the objective of ferreting out and publicizing profiteering, mismanagement, and inefficiencies. Roosevelt was welcoming and cordial but Truman departed without being sure whether the president supported or opposed his idea. For the next three years, as the United States waged a two-front war, Truman led the "Truman Committee," officially designated the Senate Committee to Investigate the National Defense Program. He and his twelve investigators saved the government billions.

As it turned out, Roosevelt found no good reason to object or intervene in the actions of the Truman Committee because Truman was careful to avoid interfering with FDR's conduct of the war. On the second anniversary of the committee, Truman appeared on the cover of *Time* magazine. While noting his past association with the "odors of the Pendergast mob," the article in *Time* paid him the ultimate compliment: "He is scrupulously honest."[18] A year later, when asked about the Truman Committee, Roosevelt responded, "Oh, yes, that was this committee, this investigating committee, that I, ah, er, created back in 1941, was it not?"[19]

Truman's creation and leadership of one of the most successful government agencies of WWII was in part responsible for his choice as Roosevelt's running mate in the summer of 1944. When the president died at Warm Springs nine months later on April 12, 1945, the transfer of power began. As the following pages reveal, the lack of advance planning by Roosevelt handicapped Truman but it was arguably the most productive and consequential transition of presidential power in the history of the republic.[20]

The story of the transition begins with President Roosevelt's trip in late 1943 by battleship and plane to Tehran, the capital of Iran. He and his entourage thought they were traveling in the strictest of secrecy. In Berlin, however, an SS general was already aware of their destination, the dates they would be there, and the names of the two leaders who were to meet with the American president.

Chapter 1

Over the Rainbow

On Armistice Day, November 11, 1943, a year and a half before the abrupt transition of power from the president to the senator, the two of them happened to be traveling on the same day but in opposite directions. Senator Harry Truman again was alone, this time on a westbound train to Chicago, scheduled to deliver a paid speech that evening to the Chicago branch of the American Association of Advertising Agencies. Franklin Roosevelt, in the eleventh year of his presidency, was being driven secretly, under cover of darkness and cold rain, southeast to the marine base at Quantico, Virginia, where he and his entourage of aides and military chiefs would begin a 17,400-mile trip by sea and air to and from Tehran.[1]

Roosevelt, "in good health" and with an "enormous zest for living," could hardly wait to begin the voyage by battleship and C-54 that would take him more than halfway around the world—beyond the rain.[2] For months he had been pressing Premier Joseph Stalin, via top secret cables, to meet with him and Prime Minister Winston Churchill—a meeting of "vital importance," he wrote. "The whole world will be watching us for this meeting of the three of us," Roosevelt declared.[3] Stalin finally agreed but only on condition that the meeting take place in Tehran.

A part of the world, the very worst part, would in fact be watching. On the day FDR departed Washington, he cabled Churchill: "I have just heard that U.J. [meaning "Uncle Joe" Stalin] will come to Teheran . . . now there is no question that you and I can meet him there between [November] twenty-seventh and the thirtieth."[4] Within a few days, a photo of this top secret cable was on a German courier plane from Ankara to Berlin. A valet, code-named "Cicero," who was working for the British ambassador to Turkey, had stolen the cable from his master's safe and sold it to a Nazi undercover intelligence agent for several thousand pounds sterling (skillfully counterfeited).[5]

In Berlin, the arrival of the purloined cable breathed new life into an audacious Nazi plot to assassinate Roosevelt, Churchill, and Stalin at Tehran. The plot, a "priority for Hitler," was already in the planning stages because of solid intelligence that the Big Three would be meeting somewhere in the fall of 1943.[6] Thirty-three-year-old Walter Schellenberg, the SS general in the Reich Intelligence Service (SD) with responsibility for planning the assassination, could scarcely believe his good fortune, because he had previously installed a network of agents in Tehran. They were put there to sabotage the Trans-Iranian Railroad, which was carrying forty thousand tons of Lend-Lease war supplies to the Soviet Union every month. These agents would provide safe houses in the city for assassination teams that would be parachuted into areas surrounding Tehran.*

Roosevelt knew nothing about the leaked cable, much less the plot. For him, the summit in Tehran was critically important not only to nail down once and for all a date in the spring of 1944 for the Allied invasion of

---

* Historians have questioned the very existence of the plot, and there are a host of books with wildly different accounts of how it was implemented. Based on the release in 2003 of previously classified Russian intelligence documents and virtually everything else written about the subject, Howard Blum's *Night of the Assassins*, published in 2020, is by far the most deeply researched and credible account of the plan by the Nazis to assassinate the Big Three. On the following pages, which mostly focus on FDR and the 1943 Tehran summit, Blum's version of the plot is summarized, footnoted, and sourced.

France but also to persuade Stalin to sign on to the president's vision of the United Nations—a postwar world-peacekeeping organization with enforcement powers. It was the achievement of the latter objective that was FDR's most fervent hope. Having paid homage the morning before leaving DC at the World War I Tomb of the Unknown Soldier, FDR was keenly aware that President Wilson had failed miserably to secure the Senate's advice and consent to the League of Nations and in doing so had suffered a complete breakdown in his health. As Pulitzer Prize winner Robert Sherwood wrote, "The tragedy of Wilson was always within the rim of [FDR's] consciousness. Roosevelt could never forget Wilson's mistakes."[7]

The first leg of what Roosevelt called in his diary "another Odyssey" began a few minutes after midnight on Saturday, November 13, when the spanking new steel-gray battleship USS *Iowa*, the navy's largest and fastest, weighed anchor, emerged from Chesapeake Bay into the Atlantic, and then steamed east toward Gibraltar at a cruising speed of 25 knots.[8] By then the president was asleep in the captain's cabin, which had been refitted to accommodate his disability with a small railed bathtub and two portable elevators, one that would lift him in his wheelchair up to the bridge and the other down to the main deck. Vice Admiral John McCrea, former head of FDR's Map Room in the White House and captain of the *Iowa*, vacated his quarters and moved up to his small cabin in the conning tower. In addition to the president; his physician, Vice Admiral Ross McIntire; aides Harry Hopkins and Edwin "Pa" Watson; as well as the joint chiefs and their staffs, the monstrous ship was home to a crew of 2,700 sailors and marines.

On McCrea's shoulders rested an awesome responsibility. Aboard his battleship was invaluable human cargo—the American commander in chief and his entire military team, who were in the midst of an existential global war. Though they were protected by 157 guns, a screen of six destroyers, fighter planes that could be summoned from a nearby aircraft carrier, and three scout planes, not to mention that the *Iowa* had a top speed of 32 knots, the ship was vulnerable. It was no secret that the Germans had developed guided missile technology capable of directing radio-controlled glide bombs and torpedoes, and that they had begun using them to sink enemy naval vessels. Plus, the new German "snorkels," which allowed U-boats to remain submerged for much longer periods, had led to a resurgence of the U-boat menace in the Atlantic. Given the risk and the stakes, airtight security and absolute secrecy were McCrea's watchwords.

On the second day at sea, during an afternoon gunnery exercise, the *Iowa* and the American high command narrowly escaped disaster, possibly death, but not at the hands of a German U-boat or a guided missile. As the president, seated in his armless wheelchair on the port side of the promenade deck, was enjoying the sights and sounds of antiaircraft guns firing at target balloons, Captain McCrea shouted into the conning tower, "Right full rudder." An officer on the bridge announced, "Torpedo on the starboard beam," and a sailor roared, "This ain't no drill." The gigantic battleship, almost three football fields in length, surged to flank speed and began to vibrate as it heeled over to starboard, heading straight toward "the broaching 'fish'" so it would present the narrowest possible target. The president called out to his valet, Arthur Prettyman, to wheel him "over to the starboard rail." John Driscoll, a young navy officer who was watching the president from the bridge above, recalled that FDR, grasping a lifeline on the starboard side, "was facing the rear of the ship . . . his head was held high, intent, curious and fearless."[9] Seconds later, the torpedo plowed into the *Iowa*'s churning wake a half mile astern and exploded with such force hammering the hull that many aboard thought the ship had been struck a mortal blow.

A mile away, the escort destroyer USS *William D. Porter*, ever after known as the *Willy Dee*, broke radio silence to conditionally confess, "the torpedo may be ours."[10] Roosevelt later dictated a note explaining that the crew of the star-crossed destroyer had been "holding a torpedo drill, using the *Iowa* as a spotting target." A live torpedo had been accidentally fired "and the aim was luckily bad."[11] Either guns from the *Iowa* or the force of its wake caused the torpedo to explode. At dinner that evening, Hopkins tried to make light of it, joking that the torpedo "must have come from some damn Republican."[12]

During a meeting in his cabin on November 15, FDR's military chiefs presented a unanimous recommendation that he should reject once and for all Churchill's "Balkans–Eastern Mediterranean" strategy for defeating

Germany, which the prime minister had been promoting for months, and in so doing implicitly confirm his support for Operation Overlord, the massive cross-Channel invasion of France that was planned to take place in the spring of 1944. As if the president were answering their prayers, and he most certainly was, the minutes recorded FDR as simply saying, "Amen." The chiefs were relieved. They had reason to believe that this time their commander in chief would not accede, as he had in the past, to Churchill's seductive eloquence.

Addressing the next item on the meeting agenda, Roosevelt announced that it was his "idea" that General George Marshall should command not only Overlord but all "British, French, Italian and U.S. troops involved" in defeating Germany.[13] This was the first time the president had gone on record as favoring the appointment of Marshall to be supreme commander in Europe.

In his many hours out on the sun-splashed deck as the *Iowa* raced from Bermuda to the Azores, Roosevelt's thoughts drifted beyond the war and often fixated on Joseph Stalin: whether and if so how he could establish a personal relationship with him, a relationship both friendly and cooperative. FDR was obsessively interested in learning about Stalin's background and personality, having read extensively about him and questioned those who knew him well. The president was under no illusions. He knew that Stalin was a ruthless tyrant, responsible for the indiscriminate murder of tens of thousands of innocent victims in Ukraine and elsewhere. Nevertheless, since only two superpowers—the U.S. and the Soviet Union—would remain after the war, there would be no international peacekeeping organization without buy-in by the Soviet premier and the membership of his empire. In FDR's mind, Joseph Stalin, the absolute dictator of the Soviet Union, was the key to his plan for postwar peace.

Supremely confident that Stalin was "getable," as Roosevelt and Hopkins used to say, the president remarked one afternoon to Doc McIntire, who had accompanied him on the *Iowa*, "If I can convince [Stalin] that our offer of cooperation is on the square, and that we want to be comrades rather than enemies, I'm betting that he'll come in." Roosevelt reasoned that because Stalin and the vast Soviet Union would be faced with daunting challenges after the war, it would be in the best interests of the

Russians to remain friendly with the United States. "I bank on his realism," he told McIntire. "He must be tired of sitting on bayonets," meaning the calls for the restoration of his war-torn country, the demands of his people for humanitarian relief, and the grumblings of his satellite nations, which would soon yearn for freedom.[14] He was convinced that Stalin needed the U.S. as much as FDR needed him.

William Bullitt, former ambassador to the Soviet Union, was skeptical. He had warned Roosevelt in three private letters against "the vice of wishful thinking."[15] The president responded with disdain, saying he was "going to play my hunch," gambling that if he asked Stalin "for nothing in return, *noblesse oblige*," he "will work with me for a world of democracy and peace."[16] George Kennan, who emerged after the war as the leading expert on Soviet intentions, believed FDR was naive. He wrote that Bullitt's letters "deserve a place among the major historical documents of the time."[17]

As the *Iowa* neared the narrow Strait of Gibraltar, where the huge battleship would become exposed to lurking U-boats and bomber-launched Hs-293 glide torpedoes, Admiral Kent Hewitt, the naval commander in the area, was ordered to call upon his destroyers, subs, and aircraft to clear the strait and keep it clear. With all of its lights blacked out, the *Iowa* began sliding through the strait under cover of darkness. Suddenly, its superstructure was silhouetted by beams of powerful searchlights situated on the nearby Spanish shore. Hewitt's task force, however, had done its job. The *Iowa* emerged unscathed at dawn into the broad, sunlit Mediterranean Sea. After the eight-day voyage, Captain McCrea anchored the *Iowa* in the harbor of the great Mers-el-Kébir naval base, six miles west of the Algerian city of Oran.

The American commander in chief had weighed anchor in a war zone, the southern edge of the Mediterranean theater. For the next few days, he and his entourage would fly with fighter escorts in his comfortably fitted Douglas C-54 transport along the North African littoral to Tunis and then Cairo, where they would confer with Chiang Kai-shek and Churchill for four more days before departing for the flight over the Middle East to Tehran and the long-sought meeting with Stalin.

On the eve of departure from Cairo, November 26, 1943, reports from the world's battlefields were mixed. In Italy, the battle closest to Roosevelt, savage fighting by the Anglo-American troops in San Pietro was taking place at what was called "the Winter Line." Plagued by mounting casualties, outbreaks of trench foot, and supply shortages, General Mark Clark gathered the senior commanders of his Fifth Army and ordered them to pause and "hold to [their] present positions" for two weeks.[18] The defending forces of German field marshal "Smiling Al" Kesserling enjoyed a natural advantage in the mountainous terrain. General Lucian Truscott, one of the war's most successful combat generals, drawled, "There's still a lot of fight left in the old son of a bitch."[19]

Eight thousand miles to the east, dispatches from the Pacific in November were encouraging but progress was terribly slow. General Douglas MacArthur and Admiral William "Bull" Halsey had worked out a plan to isolate, starve, and bypass Rabaul, a strategically located Japanese bastion at the eastern end of the island of New Britain, the most heavily defended position by Japan in the South Pacific. By the time Roosevelt had departed Cairo for Tehran, the noose was beginning to be draped around Rabaul's neck. But it would take weeks for MacArthur to encircle Rabaul, cut its supply lines, and deprive the hundred thousand Japanese infantrymen on the base of an opportunity to fight and die for their emperor.

By far the most optimistic reports in late November 1943 came from the Eastern Front, some two thousand to thirty-five hundred miles northeast of Cairo. Having paid a terrible price in military and civilian casualties—an estimated twenty million dead—the Red Army had regained more than half of the territory lost to the Germans since 1941. While Leningrad was still under siege, the cities of Smolensk, Kyiv, and Kharkiv, among many others, had been recaptured. After crippling defeats at Stalingrad and the Kursk salient, an epic battle in which two million men fought for fifty days, the once vaunted Wehrmacht was no longer capable of sustained offensive action. In the south, the German 17th Army had been forced to withdraw across the Kerch Strait into the Crimean

Peninsula. Though its land-based connection and its communications were severed by the Soviets, the Germans were able to hang on to Crimea for the next several months. Nevertheless, Hitler's dream—a nightmare for the Allies—of capturing the oil fields in the Caucasus and linking up with the Japanese in the Middle East would never come to fruition.

Over Berlin, beginning in mid-November, hundreds of Royal Air Force bombers, night after night, indiscriminately carpeted the city with high explosives, killing thousands of citizens and destroying the national opera house, art gallery, theater, and zoo. RAF marshal Arthur Travers Harris, known as "Bomber" or "Butcher" Harris, announced that the bombing would continue "until the heart of Nazi Germany ceases to beat."[20] Hitler's propaganda chief, Joseph Goebbels, tried to persuade the führer to negotiate a separate peace with the Soviets or possibly even the British before the Western Allies invaded France. He reasoned that it was the one strategy that might save the Reich from utter destruction and defeat. However, Goebbels's entreaties were flatly rejected by Hitler. The führer believed that as long as Roosevelt, Churchill, and Stalin were alive, negotiations would be futile.

———

In Joseph Stalin's judgment, the capacity of his armies and the will of his people were approaching a breaking point. To achieve complete victory, a second front in Europe was essential. That conviction, together with the fact that the Germans were no longer able to launch offensive operations, caused him to finally decide that he could trust his generals to run the war for a few days and travel to Tehran to meet with Roosevelt and Churchill. His main goal in Tehran would be to nail down once and for all a firm commitment from Roosevelt and Churchill to open a second front in Europe in May 1944.

With fighter escorts overhead, Stalin's camouflaged train, plagued by breaks in the rails and communications failures, rolled slowly south from Moscow past the rubble surrounding Stalingrad to Kilyazi station in Azerbaijan, fifty miles from Baku on the Caspian Sea. From there, Stalin and his party were driven to an airport where American C-47s, courtesy of

Lend-Lease, would fly them to Tehran. There was no way to get there other than to fly.

Stalin hated to travel. He had not been out of the Soviet Union since 1913. Moreover, he was terrified by the prospect of flying. This would be his first time. As he approached the plane assigned to him, which was to be piloted by a general, he abruptly turned and began walking toward another C-47, which he knew would be flown by a lower-ranking colonel. "Don't take it badly," he called out to the general. "Generals don't often pilot aircraft, we'd better go with the Colonel."[21] Actions like this were typical of Stalin. He was obsessed with his personal safety. He trusted no one.

The plane Stalin chose on the spur of the moment had been assigned to Lavrenti Beria, the sinister head of the Soviet NKVD (secret police, forerunner of the KGB and FSB) who was in charge of Stalin's personal security during the conference. Those flying in the other C-47s included Vyacheslav Molotov, Stalin's stone-faced commissar of foreign affairs; Marshal Kliment Voroshilov, a blond, blue-eyed ex-cavalryman whom Stalin described as "a good fellow but not a military man"; and a general who was responsible for keeping Stalin up-to-date on battlefield developments.[22] Unlike Roosevelt, who would arrive in Tehran with a bevy of high-powered military and diplomatic advisers, Stalin had no one but Molotov. He was the only one in Stalin's entourage with the experience and stature to advise him on policy and strategy, the only one he relied upon. Other than Vladimir Pavlov, Stalin's interpreter, Molotov, whose adopted name meant "hammer" in Russian, would be the individual who would sit next to Stalin at all of the Big Three plenary sessions in Tehran.

Stalin's 335-mile, two-hour flight to Tehran, surrounded by fighter aircraft, was uneventful, except when his C-47 suddenly dipped into air pockets. On those occasions, Stalin clutched his armrests, knuckles whitening, with "an expression of utter terror on his face."[23] The Soviet delegation landed at Gale Morghi aerodrome near Tehran at around noon on Saturday, November 26. American P-39s with red stars could be seen in the distance arrayed wing to wing on the tarmac. Among the ten cars waiting to take them to the Soviet embassy were a Packard, a Lincoln, and a Cadillac, each armored.

Within a few hours, Stalin, his bodyguard of twelve huge Georgians, and the rest of his party had settled in at the embassy. Built by a wealthy Persian years before, the estate consisted of villas, several cottages, a park, and gardens, all surrounded by a high wall. The walled-in British legation was next to the Soviet compound, separated only by a narrow road, while the American legation was some four miles distant through the dusty, teeming streets of Tehran.

———————

Shortly after Stalin arrived, two teams of Nazi-led commandos took off from Simferopol in the Crimea in separate Ju-290 transports, headed for Iran. The South Team, clad in Russian uniforms, consisted of fifteen former Russian soldiers who had defected to Germany, led by Hans Ulrich von Ortel, an SS major who had helped massacre thousands of Jews in the Rovno ghetto in western Ukraine. By midnight the team had parachuted onto a dry lake outside the city of Qom.[24]

In Tehran, local NKVD intelligence agents and Soviet soldiers stationed in and around the city were on high alert to be on the lookout for Nazi infiltrators. They did not know that the Big Three were about to meet, but they had been warned by the Moscow Central Intelligence Directorate that "something big" was being planned and that it would take place in their city.[25] By midmorning on November 27, Ortel, his team, and their gear were inside a "safe" rug warehouse near the western border of the bazaar in Tehran, believing they had arrived undetected. Ortel was at his radio transmitter, reporting to Berlin, when a group of heavily armed Soviet soldiers and NKVD agents burst through the door. Ortel had time to transmit the code word for "abort mission" before bullets knifed through him and the transmitter. He and some of his team were shot dead; the rest surrendered. The scene was witnessed by nineteen-year-old Gevork Vartanian, an NKVD volunteer who would repeat what he saw at a press conference in Moscow in 2003. It was his night patrol that discovered Ortel's caravan wending its way through Tehran's streets as dawn broke. And it was Vartanian who reported his suspicions to the NKVD station on Syroos Street and accompanied the assault force into the warehouse.[26]

Meanwhile, the second assassination team was still at large. Due to pilot error they had parachuted miles from the drop zone near Qom. This team, led by Major Rudolf von Holten-Pflug, an ambitious aristocrat who was experienced in espionage and assassination techniques, had been assigned to command the infiltration and murder of the Big Three. In addition to Holten-Pflug, the group consisted of four highly skilled SS commandos and an Iranian by the name of Gorechi who had emigrated to Germany. Because their radio had been damaged following a hard landing, it was almost daylight by the time they reached the place where they were to rendezvous with Ortel's South Team. Hans-Pflug gave Gorechi the address of the so-called safe warehouse in Tehran and instructed him to make his way into Tehran and borrow a truck from Ortel. With an assist from gossipy Iranians at a café near the warehouse, Gorechi learned of the violent attack and the demise of Ortel's South Team.

When Gorechi returned on the afternoon of November 27 and informed his leader of the South Team's fate, Holten-Pflug could have scrapped the mission but he calculated that there was still at least a chance of success. After all, no one knew where he was and the survivors of Ortel's South Team, now subject to certain torture and execution, had never been told the plan for getting access to the Big Three nor the time and place for killing them all at the same time. Holten-Pflug was the only one in Iran who had this vital information.[27]

———————

By 4 p.m. on the same day, Roosevelt and his party were just settling in at the American legation in Tehran after the thirteen-hundred-mile flight from Cairo. Mike Reilly, the head of FDR's Secret Service detail, was called downstairs to meet with General Dmitry Arkadiev, an NKVD intelligence officer. Arkadiev had unsettling news for the man whose sole responsibility was to protect the president with his life. The general informed Reilly that his men had located, captured, and killed a number of heavily armed Nazi parachutists (Ortel's South Team) and that the survivors had confessed after interrogation—a euphemism for torture—that six more had probably been dropped outside Tehran. To calm Reilly's evident concerns, Arkadiev confidently predicted that with the element of surprise having been eliminated, the mission to assassinate the Big Three had surely been aborted. There was no way, he argued, that six commandos, however skilled, could penetrate the ring of tight security, augmented by thousands of Soviet troops, that would surround the Big Three throughout the conference. Instead, the six would most likely be caught by border patrols within the next few days as they fled north to escape Iran.

Mike Reilly was still skeptical, unable to rule out the possibility that the six-man team possessed both an ingenious plan and the fanaticism to lay down their lives for the fatherland—a slim chance to change the course of history.

Late that Saturday evening, November 27, the Soviet embassy telephoned Averell Harriman and Sir Archibald Clark Kerr, the U.S. and British ambassadors to the Soviet Union, who were at the American legation. They were told that foreign minister Molotov needed to see them immediately. It was after midnight when they arrived. Though he declined to provide specifics, Molotov informed them that Soviet intelligence had just learned that Nazi operatives were in or near Tehran and that assassination attempts were possible. To prevent Roosevelt and his party from exposure while being driven across town for the conference, Molotov urged that they move into the Soviet compound, which adjoined the British legation. Harriman and Kerr spent the next forty-five minutes or so inspecting the proposed quarters for the president, which were in a two-story house attached to the main building where the plenary sessions of the Big Three would take place.

Harriman was not sure that Molotov was on the level. However, first thing in the morning, the day the Big Three conference was set to begin, Harriman huddled with Hopkins, Reilly, and other aides to debate the truth of Molotov's assertions, his motives, and whether a move by the president to the Soviet embassy might alienate Churchill. Reilly, the dominant voice, and all but one of the others believed that Molotov's warning of danger should be given the benefit of the doubt. After all, if the Americans found out that the Russians were lying before the conference had even begun, Stalin's credibility would be destroyed and the conference could founder. The Americans could threaten to deny Stalin the one thing he so desperately needed—a commitment for a second front in 1944. The stakes were too high for lying to make sense. At that point, as Harriman wrote in his memoir, "Hopkins disappeared to see the President, who readily agreed and was delighted with the prospect" of moving into the Soviet compound.[28]

Roosevelt and Reilly were savvy enough to be aware that if the president moved into the Soviet compound, he would be subject to electronic surveillance (i.e., "bugging"). But that possibility, if not a certainty, was outweighed by the priceless prospect of FDR having one-on-one access to Stalin throughout the days and evenings of the conference, during which the president planned to build a close personal relationship with him. As Hopkins explained that day to Lord Moran (Sir Charles Wilson, Churchill's personal physician), FDR had "spent his life managing men [and] he has come to Teheran determined . . . to come to terms with Stalin, and he is not going to allow anything to interfere with that purpose."[29] Hopkins was not explicit, but the first among those the president would not allow to "interfere" was Winston Churchill. Early in the war Roosevelt had bluntly warned the prime minister: "I know you will not mind my being brutally frank when I tell you that I think I can personally handle Stalin better than either you or your Foreign Office or my State Department. Stalin hates the guts of all of your people. He thinks he likes me better, and I hope he will continue to do so."[30]

Protected by jeeps filled with American soldiers both leading the way and guarding the rear, the president's armored limousine departed the American legation for the trip across the city to the Soviet embassy. Mike Reilly's Secret Service agents, brandishing tommy guns, stood on the running boards of the limousine as the motorcade began to move slowly through the main streets of Tehran, lined with cheering Iranians. As soon as the caravan left, Roosevelt was lifted into the back seat of an inconspicuous army sedan. His driver, accompanied by a lone jeep, hit the accelerator and sped through side streets to the Soviet embassy. Since the six assassins were still on the loose, Reilly was taking no chances. The man inside the president's limousine waving at the crowd was Secret Service agent Bob Holmes. "The Boss, as always, was vastly amused by the dummy cavalcade trip," recalled Reilly.[31]

———

"It was a beautiful Iranian Sunday afternoon, gold and blue, mild and sunny," wrote Charles "Chip" Bohlen, the thirty-nine-year-old Russian-speaking State Department officer who would serve as interpreter for the Americans.[32] At a little after 3:00 p.m. on November 28, not long after Roosevelt had arrived, Marshal of the Soviet Union Joseph Stalin, clad in a mustard-colored tunic and red-striped trousers, with the Order of Lenin on his chest, strode "clumsily, like a small bear," across the Soviet compound to Roosevelt's villa. He was led into a tiny sitting room decorated with "Tsarist gilt and Communist red stars."[33] A photo of Stalin smoking a pipe hung on the wall. Seated on a couch, FDR was waiting for him.

To the dismay of Churchill, the meeting of the American president and the leader of the Soviet Union was about to take place and he was not there. All morning Churchill had pressed FDR to get together so they could discuss beforehand the war strategy he hoped to present to Stalin at the first plenary session of the Big Three. Roosevelt refused. He made it clear that "he wanted to see Stalin first and to see him alone except for the two interpreters, Bohlen and V.N. Pavlov." Thus, the so-called Big Three conference at Tehran would actually begin with a meeting of the Big Two, a portent of the future. Harriman was warned by General Hastings "Pug" Ismay, Churchill's military chief of staff, that "storm signals were flying in the British legation."[34]

The historic first meeting between Roosevelt and Stalin lasted forty minutes, though half was taken up by the translators. Yet the brief exchange of views deftly orchestrated by Roosevelt revealed his strategy for "coming to terms" with Stalin and his vision for the postwar world. Its importance cannot be overstated.

It began with a hearty "I am glad to see you" and the offer of an American cigarette.[35] The president casually asked Stalin how things were going "on the Soviet battlefront," knowing that this was a touchy subject because Stalin had been demanding a second front in the west for more than a year. FDR let him respond, "Not too good." But before Stalin could criticize him for the delay, FDR said that drawing away "30 or 40 German divisions from the Eastern Front" was one of the main subjects to be discussed at the forthcoming conference.[36] It was an oblique way of signaling Stalin that the Americans were committed to launching a second front in Western Europe by the summer of 1944. Stalin thanked him, saying that "it would be of great value."[37]

To further ingratiate himself, Roosevelt abruptly pivoted to the postwar period, offering up the prospect that a portion of the "American-British merchant fleet" could be made available to the Soviet Union (although there is no evidence that he discussed this beforehand with the British). Stalin responded with gratitude, adding that he hoped "the development of relations between the Soviet Union and the United States after the war" would be "greatly expanded" through the sale of "raw materials" by the Soviets to the U.S.[38] A postwar trade deal with the U.S.? Roosevelt could not have been more pleased.

Much of the rest of the tête-à-tête ranged over postwar decolonization, with Roosevelt making it obvious to Stalin that he disagreed with Churchill's imperialist views and that he disliked the "attitude" of both Charles de Gaulle and those who were participating in the "present French Government." Stalin concurred, adding that "the French ruling classes" should not share in "the benefits of the peace." As to Indochina (now Vietnam, Cambodia, and Laos), Stalin "completely agreed" with Roosevelt that its people should be prepared for independence after the war under a United Nations trusteeship, which meant that French colonial rule would not be restored.[39]

While dwelling on the injustices of colonial possessions, Roosevelt advised Stalin that it would be a mistake to discuss India, the largest colonized nation in the world, during the conference because it was a "sore point" with Churchill and he "had no solution to that question." It would be preferable, said FDR, for the two of them to discuss India "at some future date."[40]

The president could have ended the discussion of India at that point. Instead, he added that the "best solution [for India's future] would be reform from the 'bottom,' somewhat along the Soviet line."[41] FDR's reference to "the Soviet line" was intended to curry favor with Stalin. However, Chip Bohlen, his interpreter, who was a student of Russian history, believed the remark was "a striking example of Roosevelt's ignorance about the Soviet

Union" and that Stalin would see right through FDR's shameless pandering. As Bohlen wrote later, the Russian Revolution did not come from "the bottom." Rather, it "was based on the ideology of the minority Bolsheviks, and not on the demands of the majority of the Russian people."[42]

Because it was four o'clock, time for the first plenary session of the conference to begin, Roosevelt concluded his private talk with Stalin, saying he was "glad" to be staying in the Soviet compound because it afforded the two of them opportunities to meet "more frequently in completely informal" settings.[43]

Unaware of his gaffe, Roosevelt had every reason to be pleased with the outcome of his first encounter with Stalin. By distancing himself from Churchill, telegraphing his commitment to a second front, and focusing mostly on how they and their two nations would work cooperatively on decolonization and trade after the war, the president had forged the beginnings of a bond of trust, possibly even a friendship with Stalin. He had painted a picture that after the war their two nations would be the world's two great powers, responsible for shaping the destinies of millions. And that they would have to work together to maintain world peace.

During the twenty minutes of actual conversation there was not a hint of conflict or cynicism. Having been treated as an equal, Stalin agreed with everything FDR said. He had gained respect for the American president.

Roosevelt was joined by Stalin and Churchill as he was wheeled into the high-ceilinged boardroom in the main building of the Soviet embassy, which adjoined his house. Flanked by three key advisers and an interpreter, they each took their seats in armchairs upholstered in striped silk around a large circular oak table covered with green baize. Heavy curtains hung over the windows. On a balcony above, Soviet secret police paced and watched. Outside, the entire compound was ringed by upwards of two hundred armed Soviet soldiers, almost all of them over six feet tall.

Having been selected in advance by Churchill and Stalin to preside at the first plenary gathering of the Big Three, the president, who was youngest of the three, set the tone. He began by welcoming those around the table to the "family circle," stressing that they should feel free to speak "with complete frankness" as "between friends," but that nothing said was "to be made public." He added that he was confident that "our three great nations would not only work in close cooperation for the prosecution of the war but would also remain in close touch for generations to come."[44] Postwar peace was ever on his mind.

Mindful that Churchill was peeved at having been left out of the earlier meeting with Stalin and was the most eloquent of the three, Roosevelt called on him first, so he could speak "about matters pertaining to the years to come." The prime minister was brief. "We represent here a concentration of great worldly power," he intoned. They had in their hands not only the responsibility for ending the war but also "the future of mankind. I pray that we may be worthy of this God-given opportunity."

Stalin agreed. "Now let us get down to business."[45]

Roosevelt had decided on his own, probably at the last moment, that the "business" of this first plenary would be "military problems." Thus, as the minutes recorded, he began with "a general survey of the war."[46] The only problem, however, was that two of his three principal military advisers—General George Marshall, chief of staff of the American army, and General Hap Arnold, commander of the U.S. Army Air Forces—were not even in the room. Through an unforgivable snafu, they had been assured before lunch, possibly by the president himself, that there would be nothing scheduled for the rest of the day. As a consequence, they were hiking in the snowcapped mountains high above Tehran, where they became fascinated with their discovery of the ancient Persian water system— the qanats system—that carried fresh water for miles through channels, shafts, and underground tunnels down to the streets of the city.[47]

What followed were more than three hours of talk, mostly by Churchill, and a handful of highly influential pronouncements on grand strategy by Stalin. As most everyone in the room knew, Stalin held the trump cards on strategy in Europe. Because it was obvious that Roosevelt and Churchill disagreed on when and even whether the cross-Channel invasion of France should be launched, Stalin was positioned to be the arbiter. It was his Red Army that had fielded the greatest number of divisions (310) and sustained by far the most casualties (millions).

Lacking assistance from Marshall and Arnold, the president delivered a respectable overview of the war, first in the Pacific and then in Europe. He made it clear that depending on the size and scope of "operations in the Mediterranean" that were being promoted by Churchill, it would be necessary to either "give up" Operation Overlord, the massive cross-Channel invasion of France, or "delay" it "for one month or two or three."[48] Also, for the first time, the president formally revealed to Stalin the date on which Overlord was to be launched—May 1, 1944.

If Bohlen's minutes are correct, Churchill intervened at this juncture with an assertion that Stalin knew to be untrue or at best misleading. Asking Stalin for advice on what "we can do" to help the Soviets on the Western Front, Churchill had the temerity to say, "There are no differences between Great Britain and the United States in point of view except as regards 'ways and means.'"[49] However, at the Moscow conference a month earlier, Churchill had instructed Foreign Secretary Anthony Eden to inform Stalin that the May 1 date for Overlord "must be modified by the exigencies of battle in Italy."[50] When Roosevelt learned of this treachery, he directed Marshall to get a message to Stalin that there was not any chance of having Overlord delayed. Churchill's "ways and means" caveat could have given him some wiggle room but Stalin would have been justified in concluding that the prime minister was lying.

Nevertheless, Stalin was unfazed. He did not react. Instead, he ignored Churchill and focused his attention on the president. Casually, in a barely audible voice, he said, "We Soviets welcome your successes in the Pacific. Once Germany is finally defeated, it would then be possible to send the necessary reinforcements to Siberia and then we shall be able by our common front to beat Japan."[51] Roosevelt was overjoyed to hear this gratuitous gesture, which seemed to come out of nowhere. He knew it was not easy for Stalin to make such an offer because at the time the Soviet Union was bound by a peace treaty with Japan. The president might have flashed a smile or otherwise mouthed a silent "thank you" to Stalin across the table. The minutes, however, do not reflect any spoken response.

Once Churchill regained the floor, he gave lip service to the importance of Overlord, but said that he and "the President" did not want allied forces "to remain idle" during the six months leading up to the cross-

Channel invasion. Those forces, he argued, should capture Rome and hold the Pisa–Rimini line across Italy, which would free them for "other operations" in the Adriatic, Yugoslavia, and the islands in the Aegean Sea.[52] While admitting that these moves could delay Overlord, Churchill asked Stalin whether any of them were of interest to the Soviet Union.

Stalin looked up from his doodling of wolves' heads on a notepad. According to both sets of minutes of the meeting, he remarked that it "was not worthwhile to scatter the British and American forces." Rather, he proclaimed that Operation Overlord should be the *"basis for all 1944 operations and that the other operations should be considered as diversionary."*[53] Instead of pushing back, Churchill argued in favor of a scheme to pressure Turkey to enter the war on the side of the Allies, which he believed would open up the Black Sea to supply Russia. Stalin flatly stated that he "was convinced that she"—that is, Turkey—"would not enter the war."[54]

The president was in total agreement with Stalin's pronouncements prioritizing Overlord but he did not weigh in, perhaps reluctant to openly side with Stalin and against Churchill in front of the others. He concluded the session at 7:20 p.m. by suggesting that "it would be desirable to have a military conference in the morning."[55] It was agreed, therefore, that the Soviet, British, and American military chiefs would meet at 10:30 a.m. the following day, Monday, November 29. They were to discuss and make recommendations to the Big Three concerning further operations in France, Italy, the Adriatic, and the Aegean—presumably recommendations that would help resolve the strategic debate between Stalin and Roosevelt on the one hand and Churchill on the other. The scheduling of this military conference was the only firm decision made during the first plenary at Tehran.

————

During a steak and potato dinner for the Big Three that Sunday evening, "Roosevelt was about to say something," recalled Bohlen, "when suddenly, in the flick of an eye, he turned green, and great drops of sweat began to bead off his face; he put a shaky hand to his forehead." Harry Hopkins immediately jumped to his feet, wheeled FDR to his nearby room, and summoned his doctor, Vice Admiral McIntire. Several minutes later,

Hopkins returned to the dinner. "To the relief of everybody," wrote Bohlen, he reported that it was "nothing more than a mild attack of indigestion."[56] Maybe it was. Or perhaps it was a harbinger of the more serious health issues that would begin to surface a month later.

Late that night an American intelligence officer contacted Mike Reilly. The officer informed him that a German major named Winifred Oberg, who Reilly knew had been arrested a few days earlier at a house in Tehran, had decided, or more likely was persuaded, to talk. Oberg confessed that he had been ordered by General Schellenberg to parachute alone into Iran, help arrange safe houses for German agents, and find a way to access the embassies of the Big Three. Reilly was told that Oberg did find a way to penetrate the British, American, and Soviet embassies: through an underground water tunnel that had been dug in 1942 by American engineers assigned to the Persian Gulf Command. This two-mile-long concrete tunnel that provided clean water from the mountains to each of the embassies was large enough to accommodate three men walking through knee-deep water. Oberg admitted to the U.S. intel officers that he had communicated his discovery via radio to Schellenberg in Berlin. However, because Schellenberg had kept each aspect of the mission compartmentalized, Oberg had no clue that Holten-Pflug's six-man assassination team had been dropped into Iran and was still at large. Moreover, he was under the impression that the mission, whatever it was, had been aborted, which was the reason he was talking in the first place.

By Monday morning, dozens of Russian and American soldiers stood guard outside the city at the entrance to the water tunnel that eventually branched into the grounds of each of the three embassies. Unaware that access to the embassies through the tunnel would be barred, Holten-Pflug, his Iranian interpreter, and four commandos focused on their mission. The plan was to gain entrance to the British legation through its branch of the tunnel and kill the Big Three on Tuesday night, when they could be certain they would all be together at a dinner celebrating Churchill's sixty-ninth birthday. The team realized it was probably suicidal but Holten-Pflug had convinced them that it was worth dying to change the course of history.[57]

On that same morning the president awoke "fully recovered from the attack of indigestion," wrote Bohlen, and seemed "alert as ever."[58] While FDR devoted the early hours to working through pouches packed with mail, Stalin was being briefed by Beria's son, Sergio, on the previous day's eavesdropped conversations of Roosevelt and Hopkins. Stalin must have suspected that the Americans knew they were being bugged because Sergio told him that Roosevelt always spoke positively of him, always revealing "great sympathy and respect."[59] In a separate building in the Soviet compound, the American, British, and Soviet military chiefs spent three hours debating whether Overlord could be launched on schedule, on May 1, 1944, or whether it needed to be delayed to allow for "auxiliary operations" in the Mediterranean, as Field Marshal Allen Brooke, the British chief of the Imperial General Staff, doggedly maintained. If Roosevelt thought they would reach a consensus, he was badly mistaken. They remained hopelessly deadlocked—"no further advanced," as Brooke wrote in his diary.[60]

Having heard of the stalemate from Admiral William Leahy, Roosevelt turned down Churchill's request that he join him for lunch at the British legation. He had had enough of British efforts to delay Overlord. Spurned again, the prime minister was "plainly put out," wrote his physician.[61]

At 2:45 that afternoon Stalin, accompanied by Molotov, arrived at Roosevelt's quarters for another confidential tête-à-tête. It began, as before, with a cigarette, this time a Russian cigarette with a two-inch cardboard holder that Stalin offered to the president. Then, after FDR handed Stalin a sheaf of papers on proposed military operations that he asked him to read later, he brought up his vision for "the future of the world," which he had been mulling over for many months—an "organization based on the United Nations." The president proposed, as outlined in a sketch of three circles accompanied by a few words, the creation after the war of a general assembly of "40" nations that he called "U.N."; a smaller "Executive," akin to today's Security Council, that could issue nonmilitary "recommendations for settling disputes"; and a third entity entitled the "4 Policemen," which consisted of the Soviet Union, the United States, Great Britain, and China. According to Bohlen's minutes, FDR said that these four nations would "have the power to deal immediately with any threat to the peace and any sudden emergency which requires this action."[62]

As Bohlen observed, Stalin "never showed any antagonism to the general idea of a world body" to resolve disputes and keep the peace.[63] However, he was quick to raise the vexing issue of sovereignty—that is, whether decisions of the executive could be "binding on the nations of the world." To that question, Roosevelt answered that while the executive would not be empowered to issue binding decisions (Congress would never "accept"), he "had in mind" certain "machinery" that would enable "the Four Policemen" to enforce and implement its decisions.[64] The minutes do not disclose the enforcement "machinery" that FDR envisioned, although Bohlen indicated that it was "summarized briefly" by the president. Whatever Roosevelt said about enforcement, Stalin was skeptical, suggested several alternatives, and was dubious about the inclusion of China as one of the four policemen. During the remainder of the discussion, the two of them danced around but never came to grips with the issue that had crippled the League of Nations and would eventually hamstring the United Nations.

With the benefit of hindsight, Bohlen wrote years later that Stalin was open to FDR's proposal for a United Nations organization, provided "the Soviet Union could block actions it did not like and could not be forced to take any action against its will." In other words, the Soviet Union would be willing to join a world body like the United Nations as long as it did not infringe upon the Russian concept of sovereignty.[65]

———————

At about 3:30 p.m. Roosevelt was brought into the great hall of the Soviet embassy with Stalin and Churchill standing on either side of him. Staged meticulously with a keen eye for drama, British soldiers with fixed bayonets and Soviets with tommy guns marched into the room. A Red Army band played "The Internationale" and "God Save the King." Prime Minister Churchill, wearing the blue uniform of an RAF officer with pilot's wings, presented Marshal Stalin with the Sword of Stalingrad, a fifty-inch, two-handed sword of tempered steel with a silver hilt sheathed in a crimson scabbard. Reading from the inscription on the sword, Churchill presented it to Stalin: "To the steel-hearted citizens of Stalingrad, a gift from King George VI, as a token of the homage of the British people."[66] Stalin bent and kissed the sword. He appeared to be genuinely moved. "Roosevelt said there were tears in his eyes." Churchill's doctor wrote that for the first time "this hard-boiled Asiatic thawed and seemed to feel the emotions of ordinary people. For a moment it seemed we were meeting as friends."[67]

—————

Perhaps the Soviet leader had softened during the ceremony. However, moments after the second plenary meeting of the Big Three convened, Joseph Stalin, whose assumed name derived from the Russian word for steel, proceeded to ruthlessly eviscerate Churchill, his military chiefs, and the British war strategy. Roosevelt was little more than an observer.

With a hint of sarcasm, Stalin began quietly with a simple question: Has "the military committee completed its work?" He knew the answer. The military chiefs had argued for three hours that morning and achieved nothing. Nevertheless, Stalin lit his curved pipe and patiently listened as first Brooke and then Marshall held forth at length. When Voroshilov, Stalin's own military adviser, was explaining that the "date for Overlord" and "details of that operation" were to be discussed at the next meeting of the military advisers, Stalin cut him off.[68] He had had enough. "Who will command Overlord?" he demanded. The president responded that "it has not yet been decided." Stalin abruptly declared, "then nothing" will "come out of the operation unless one man" is "responsible not only for the preparation but for the execution of the operation."[69] While Stalin's remarks were being translated, Roosevelt leaned toward Admiral Leahy and whispered, "That old Bolshevik is trying to force me to give him the name of the Supreme Commander. . . . I have not yet made up my mind."[70]

Churchill took the floor and talked for a solid half hour on several military operations in the Eastern Mediterranean as well as political questions concerning Turkey, the Balkans, and Bulgaria. Stalin gave him plenty of rope. But at last, when he saw an opening, he returned to Overlord.

Stalin said a date for Overlord must be set in May 1944. He didn't care whether it was the "1st, 15th or 20th, but that a definite date was important." To emphasize the overriding importance of Overlord, he looked across the table at Churchill. Choosing his words carefully, he said that "operations in the Mediterranean have a value but *they are only diversions*."[71]

Despite this devastating put-down, the prime minister persisted, arguing that in the months before Overlord, it would be necessary to continue to press the enemy from all directions. Stalin was running out of patience. On the verge of anger, he said that he wished to ask an indiscreet question: "Do the British really believe in Overlord or are you only saying so to reassure the Russians?" According to Bohlen, "Churchill glowered [and] chomped on his cigar."[72] He replied that if "the conditions" specified at the recent foreign minister conference in Moscow were met—that is, battlefield successes in Italy and adequate landing craft for Overlord— then "it would be the duty of the British Government to hurl every scrap of strength across the channel" at the Germans.[73] What he didn't say was that the achievement of success in Italy would deprive Overlord of landing craft, as General Marshall had pointed out. Thus, Churchill's answer to Stalin's question meant that in his view Overlord would have to be delayed. Precious landing craft were needed for what Churchill and his generals regarded as success in Italy.

The president observed that within an hour a "very good dinner" awaited them.[74] The Big Three adjourned without an agreement on a date certain for Overlord. FDR and Stalin assumed it would be in the early part of May. Churchill believed that the date for Overlord would need to be "modified by the exigencies of the battle in Italy."[75]

The Russian-style dinner that followed, hosted by Stalin, might have been "very good" if measured by the abundance of food and drink. However, it was singularly unpleasant for Winston Churchill. Bohlen wrote later that "Stalin overlooked no opportunity to needle Churchill, implying that he nursed a secret affection for Germany and desired a soft peace."[76] Toward the end of the alcohol-fueled banquet, Stalin and then Roosevelt ganged up on Churchill. In a toast to "swift justice for all Germany's war criminals," Stalin proposed that they drink to the execution by "firing squad" of "at least fifty thousand German officers."[77] Bohlen thought Stalin was not serious, that his toast was made in a "quasi-jocular fashion with a sardonic smile and wave of the hand."[78] Churchill, however, took him at his word. He was red-faced angry. "The British Parliament and people," he growled, "will never tolerate mass executions. . . . The Soviets must be under no delusions on this point."[79] In a lame attempt to break the tension, Roosevelt suggested a compromise—not fifty thousand should be shot, but "only forty-nine thousand." No one laughed. When Roosevelt's son Elliott, who had been invited at the last minute to join the dinner, rose to say that he agreed with Stalin, Churchill, in a fury, left the table and stalked off into an adjoining room. As he wrote later, within seconds "there was Stalin, with Molotov at his side, both grinning broadly, and eagerly declaring that they were only playing." Years later, Churchill still believed "there was serious intent lurking behind Stalin's words."[80]

In a rare criticism, Bohlen thought that FDR's "transparent attempt to disassociate himself from Churchill," was "not fooling anybody and that in all probability aroused the secret amusement of Stalin."[81] As history would judge, he was probably right. The president, however, with his boundless confidence in his ability to manage men, would believe till the day he died that this was the way to win his "bet" that Stalin would "come in," that is, work cooperatively to help maintain peace after the war.

———

After midnight, probably at FDR's request or at least with his approval, Harry Hopkins walked over to the British legation to meet with Churchill alone. It was time to deliver a message, a tough message that Hopkins was in the best position to deliver, given his close friendship with Churchill. With utmost tact, he explained that the Americans and Soviets were adamant about launching Overlord in May and that the prime minister was "fighting a losing battle" in trying to postpone the inevitable. "Yield with grace," Hopkins urged.

Churchill grudgingly yielded but probably not until around noon on Tuesday, November 30, the day of his sixty-ninth birthday. The record shows that throughout much of that morning, the British military chiefs, led by Field Marshal Brooke, were still refusing to agree with the American chiefs on a date certain for Overlord. However, at some point in the late morning, Brooke and his British colleagues relented, no doubt because of a message or phone call from Churchill. Shortly before lunch, the president received a recommendation, agreed to by the Joint Chiefs of Staff, that Overlord and a supporting operation in southern France would be launched "by June 1st." FDR proceeded to cross out "by June 1st" and inserted in his own handwriting "during the month of May."[82] Churchill approved. As amended, the recommendation was read to Stalin. It was not the date certain that he had demanded but it wasn't worth another day or two of wrangling.

At the 1:30 p.m. luncheon of the Big Three, Stalin "expressed his great satisfaction." Then he announced that the Red Army would launch an offensive in the east to coordinate with the Overlord invasion in the west.[83]

Mike Reilly spent part of that Tuesday personally inspecting access to the dining room at the British legation, where the prime minister's birthday celebration would be held that evening. The night before, he could hardly sleep because he had come to believe that Churchill's birthday party, which Roosevelt and Stalin would surely attend, was the perfect place for the still at-large six-man team of commandos to stage an assassination attempt against the Big Three. As Reilly surveyed the sparkling crystal and silver already set out on the long tables, he focused on the place cards for the Big Three. They were to be seated near unlocked French doors that opened onto the garden. Reilly of course knew that access to the legation grounds via a branch of the water tunnel had been barred. Nevertheless, he was still extremely apprehensive. A well-trained, heavily armed group of fanatics with nothing to lose might find a way in or get close enough to blow up the dining room.

Reilly instructed the staff to lock the garden doors and rearrange the seating of the Big Three. He asked General Arkadiev to beef up NKVD security in and around the British embassy. His own Secret Service detail and American troops from the Persian Gulf Command were ordered to be strategically placed in and around the building and on high alert.[84]

———————

On the night of Churchill's birthday, the candlelit dining room in the British legation resembled "a Persian temple," wrote Brooke. "Persian waiters were in blue and red liveries with white cotton gloves."[85] From the shadows Reilly scanned the room, keeping a close watch on the French doors that were being guarded by turbaned Sikhs.

Churchill, with his daughter Sarah, arrived in an "exuberant mood," puffing away on a huge cigar as he received his guests.[86] As soon as everyone was seated, he announced that the party should feel free to "propose a toast at any time during the meal" in what he called "the Russian manner."[87] Anna Roosevelt's husband, Lieutenant Colonel John Boettiger, who was taking notes, wrote that "the champagne consumed would float a battleship."[88] For the most part the dozens of toasts throughout the evening were warm and witty, although Stalin could not "resist a jab at Churchill," recalled Bohlen. After referring to Roosevelt and Churchill as "my fighting friends," he added with a twinkle in his eye, "if it is possible for me to consider Mr. Churchill as my friend."[89] Unlike on the previous evening, Churchill did not take the bait. With magnanimity, he proclaimed that the Soviet leader "was worthy to stand with the great figures of Russian history and merited the title 'Stalin the Great.'"[90]

As the hour was approaching midnight, Churchill raised his glass for a concluding toast but Stalin asked for the privilege of making one more. "I want to tell you," he began, "what the President and the United States have done to win the war. The most important things in this war are machines. . . . The United States . . . is a country of machines. Without the use of these machines, through Lend-Lease, *we would lose this war*."[91] For Stalin, this was a stunning admission, a statement that he would not have dared to make to his own people. If he was sincere, and it appeared that he was, his tribute was an acknowledgment that the United States would emerge as the preeminent economic power after the war and that he and his nation would be indebted to President Roosevelt. FDR had to have been greatly pleased to hear Stalin's words.

Roosevelt was moved to respond: "We have proved here at Tehran that the varying ideals of our nations can come together in a harmonious whole, moving unitedly for the common good of ourselves and the whole world. So as we leave this historic gathering, we can see in the sky for the first time, the traditional symbol of hope, the rainbow."[92]

Following this lofty message of unity and hope, Roosevelt departed the dinner. Several, however, including the guest of honor, stayed on until 2 a.m. The prime minister recalled that he "went to bed tired out but content, feeling sure that nothing but good had been done."[93] Bohlen agreed, writing that the birthday dinner was "the high-water mark of Anglo-American-Soviet collaboration during the war."[94]

Reilly ended the evening with a tremendous sense of relief. There had been no attack. What he didn't know was that the planned assault on the British legation by Holten-Pflug and his team had been averted not because entry to the water tunnel had been denied. Rather, it was due to the fact the would-be assassins, except for Gorechi, had been captured and temporarily detained in a *zurkhaneh*, a gymnasium, by a motley group of Iranian wrestlers. The wrestlers did this so they could demand a large reward from the NKVD in exchange for their German hostages. While two of the wrestlers remained behind to prevent Holten-Pflug and his four comrades from escaping, the rest of them went to the NKVD station to extort money from the Russian agents. When they were gone, Gorechi returned to the gymnasium and shot the two guards in the back. By the time the birthday dinner was over, the assassins had found refuge late that night in another safe house to rest and recoup. The next morning Holten-Pflug knew he would have to change the plan. The only plausible alternative was much less ambitious but it at least stood a chance: ambush one or more of the Big Three while they motored through the city to the airport at the conclusion of the conference.[95]

Because of snowstorms predicted in the mountains that might delay homeward flights, the last day of the Tehran conference would be Wednesday, December 1, a day earlier than planned. It was a long day for Roosevelt, beginning with time-sensitive mail from Washington, followed by a plenary meeting and lunch with Churchill and Stalin of no great consequence. However, it was a frank midafternoon discussion with Stalin, not including Churchill, that would have long-term effects. The subject, as Bohlen's minutes indicated, was "internal American politics," meaning the 1944 presidential election. Roosevelt began by saying that "if the war was still in progress, he might have to" run again. Astonishingly, it was Joseph Stalin who was probably the first person to be told by Roosevelt that he would likely run for a fourth term. The third term had broken precedent; the fourth would shatter it.

FDR explained that while he favored ceding Polish territory in the east to Russia after the war, he did not wish to lose the votes of "six to seven million" Americans of Polish extraction (a vast overstatement). Thus, he asked Stalin to "understand that for political reasons" he could not participate in decisions at Tehran or thereafter concerning Polish postwar borders. Stalin replied that he understood, resisting the urge to say that in exchange for ceding territory in the east to Russia, the restored Polish nation would gain German territory in the west.

As to the postwar restoration of the three Baltic republics, which had been reoccupied by the Soviet Union, Roosevelt made reference to "a number" of American voters who had roots in Lithuania, Latvia, and Estonia, in that order. According to Bohlen's notes, FDR "jokingly" said "he did not intend to go to war with the Soviet Union" if it continued to occupy those states. However, citing the "right of self-determination," he urged Stalin to give substance to the "will of the people" through "future elections" in the Baltics. Stalin gave short shrift to Roosevelt's requests, saying that "there would be lots of opportunities for that to be done." His ominous caveat, however, was that those "elections" would have to be conducted "in accordance with the Soviet constitution."[96]

When the final plenary session was about to begin at a little before 6 p.m., Roosevelt had made up his mind "to do something desperate," as he later confided to Secretary of Labor Frances Perkins. To Churchill, as they were gathering outside the conference room, FDR said, "Winston, I hope you won't be sore at me for what I am going to do." Churchill "shifted his cigar and grunted." Moments later, the president struck up a "chummy" conversation with Stalin at the conference table. Others joined to listen. Then, as Roosevelt further recounted to Perkins, he whispered to Stalin that "Winston is cranky this morning, he got up on the wrong side of the bed." As the translator's Russian words rolled out, "[a] vague smile passed over Stalin's eyes and I decided I was on the right track," recalled FDR. "I began to tease Churchill about his Britishness, about John Bull, about his cigars, his habits" and "it began to register on Stalin. Winston got red and scowled, and the more he did so, the more Stalin smiled. Finally, Stalin broke out into a deep, hearty guffaw, and for the first time in three days I saw light. I kept it up until Stalin was laughing with me, and it was then that I called him 'Uncle Joe.' From that time on our relations were personal . . . the ice was broken and we talked like men and brothers."[97] Or so he believed.

Because the president's conversation was told to Perkins more than two weeks later, there is reason to believe that it was exaggerated or perhaps even fabricated. John Gunther in his book *Roosevelt in Retrospect*, wrote that he "asked someone who was present if this episode had actually taken place as described." His unnamed source replied, "You bet it did, and it wasn't funny either."[98]

Once the final plenary session began, Roosevelt brought up Poland— not its boundaries but the "re-establishment" of relations with the Polish government in exile in London, an event that would appeal to his voters of Polish extraction. Expressing doubt that the London Poles were capable of leading the Polish people, Stalin said he "was prepared to negotiate with them" but only if they "would go along with the partisans" (i.e., the Communists) and "sever all connections with German agents in Poland."[99] Stalin's doubts and conditions concerning Poland's future foreshadowed the disagreements that would bedevil President Truman at the beginning of his presidency and lead to the Cold War. On the issue of Poland's boundaries, Roosevelt watched passively as Churchill opened the discussion, declaring that the "the British Government wished to see a Poland strong and friendly to Russia." Then, using a map supplied by Bohlen, Stalin and Churchill "virtually agreed on the future borders of Poland."[100]

By remaining silent and not taking a firm position on Poland, not to mention his so-called joke about not going to war over the Baltics, the president effectively conveyed the acquiescence of the United States. As Foreign Secretary Eden later pointed out, his silence on Poland "was hardly calculated to restrain the Russians."[101] He could have said the same thing about the president's careless remark about the Baltics.

———————

The last meeting of the Big Three, a dinner that began at 8:30, was long and tedious because it involved the study, careful reading, discussion, and translation in Russian and English of two important documents. The first, a Declaration on Iran, grew out of the facts that in August 1941 the British and the Soviets had invaded Iran and that a year later the Americans had established the Persian Gulf Command outside Tehran. The Allies made these moves mainly to protect a land corridor through which war matériel and Lend-Lease supplies could be safely shipped from the Persian Gulf into Russia. Though Stalin at first resisted, the declaration, signed by all three, formally "guaranteed the [postwar] independence, sovereignty and territorial integrity of Iran."[102] As events unfolded, the violation of this agreement by Soviet encroachment into Iran's northern province of Azerbaijan would provide the Truman administration with one of its first crises, the beginning of what would be called the Cold War.

The second document, a communiqué called the "Declaration of the Three Powers," was initially drafted by Lieutenant Colonel John Boettiger, but finalized by Roosevelt himself. Released on December 6, it began by recognizing "the supreme responsibility" of the three powers and "all the United Nations, to make a peace which will command the good will of the overwhelming mass of the people of the world, and banish the scourge and terror of war for many generations."[103] It was a "brave document," wrote Harriman, "filled with ringing words about working together in peace and war."[104] The final two sentences were almost certainly penned by the president: "We came here with hope and determination. We leave here, friends in fact, in spirit and in purpose."[105]

At 10:30 p.m., it was time to leave. Roosevelt was wheeled out to the portico, smiling with his cigarette holder tipped up, cold wind rustling the leaves, his trademark dark blue cape draped over his shoulders. He was lifted into a waiting car. To Stalin and Churchill, who came out to say goodbye, he said, "I think we have done some great work here." Stalin replied, "No one can doubt now that we shall win." Four Secret Service men jumped on the running boards.

"If there was any supreme peak in Roosevelt's career," wrote Robert Sherwood, "it might be well fixed at this moment, at the end of the Tehran conference."[106]

———

Along with Hopkins and Reilly, Roosevelt spent the night of December 1 with American troops at a camp in the desert outside Tehran. After addressing the soldiers first thing in the morning, the president was scheduled to leave about 9 a.m. for the airport, a twenty-minute ride.

Sometime before midnight, General Arkadiev of the NKVD called Reilly at the camp and told him to commandeer a jeep and return to the city as quickly as possible. NKVD agents had located the so-called safe house where Holten-Pflug's six-man team was hiding. It was almost 1 a.m. when Reilly arrived at the scene. Russian soldiers had surrounded the house. Many were positioned on rooftops with rifles. According to a prearranged plan with the NKVD, a lone man approached the door to the house and was let in. Reilly learned later that his task was to convince the men inside to lay down their arms and surrender or be slaughtered. Seconds after the man entered, the building exploded a with flash of light and a terrific boom. No one survived.[107] Holten-Pflug and his team were killed instantly.

———

"Homeward bound," Franklin cabled to Eleanor on December 9. His plane was about to take off for Dakar, Senegal, where he would board the *Iowa* for the return voyage across the Atlantic to Chesapeake Bay. Two days earlier, near Tunis, Roosevelt had just been deposited into the back seat of an army sedan at the airport when he turned to the man with the four stars beside him and said, "Well, Ike, you are going to command Overlord."[108] This meant that General Dwight Eisenhower would fly to London, where he would command the cross-Channel invasion of France, his springboard to the presidency. It also meant that General Marshall, up to then the front-runner for the post, would remain as army chief of staff in Washington for the rest of the war.

Referring to his trip to Tehran, Franklin's cable to Eleanor went on to say, "On the whole it has been a real success . . . Lots to tell you about and lots and lots of love."[109]

On December 17 at 9:30 a.m., the president, having slept the previous night aboard the *Potomac*, which had motored him from the *Iowa* to the Washington Navy Yard, was greeted in the White House Diplomatic Reception Room by his cabinet, congressional leaders, and a few agency heads. His speechwriter Sam Rosenman wrote that he had never seen FDR "look more satisfied and pleased than he did that morning." He believed that he had brought "Russia into co-operation with the Western powers in a formidable organization for the maintenance of peace." And he was happy to be "the champ who brought home the prize."[110]

Later that day Roosevelt called a press conference. Around one hundred reporters, starved for firsthand news, jammed the Oval Office. The president began by saying that the Tehran and Cairo conferences, he hoped, would "have definite and very beneficial effects for the postwar period." When asked what Stalin was like, he responded, "I would call him something like me—a realist." Another journalist asked, "Does he share your view that there is hope of preventing another war in this generation?" FDR replied, "Very definitely," but only "if the people who want that objective will back it up." Since Roosevelt could never forget Woodrow Wilson's failure, this caveat could be interpreted as a veiled reference to those in Congress and their supporters who would oppose a world-peacekeeping organization such as the one he was preparing to advocate.

Curiously, without any prompting from the reporters, Roosevelt decided to bring up the fact that he had gotten word of the existence of a "German plot" in Tehran and that his Secret Service had "pleaded" with him to move into the Soviet embassy. "So the next morning," he told the reporters, "I moved . . . down to the Russian compound." He went on to elaborate, again gratuitously, that "in a place like Tehran there are hundreds of German spies . . . and I suppose it would make a pretty good haul if they could get all three of us going through the streets." He added that "there was no use going into details." With that, as the transcript indicated, there was general laughter, presumably from the press as well as the president. Despite the tasty bait, there was no recorded follow-up by the reporters.[111]

There is no evidence that Roosevelt, after this press conference, ever again discussed or mentioned the so-called German plot. And the only possible reference to the assassination attempt by either of the other two principals at Tehran was made by Stalin to Roosevelt shortly after he had returned to Moscow. "I am glad," he wrote FDR, "that fate has given me an opportunity to render you a service in Tehran."[112]

Did the word "service" mean Stalin's unswerving support of Operation Overlord or a world-peace organization? Or did it imply something much more personal, namely the defeat by his NKVD of Operation Long Jump, which arguably saved the president's life?

Chapter 2

Go All Out for Truman

On Monday afternoon, December 20, 1943, three days after the president had returned from Tehran, General Brehon Somervell was on the hot seat. Senator Truman, who was chairing a hearing on Capitol Hill, was grilling Somervell on the need for a huge defense contract to build an oil pipeline from Canada to Alaska. At the same time, Roosevelt was meeting in the Oval Office with Robert Hannegan, the commissioner of Internal Revenue. While Somervell came close to perjuring himself during the four-hour Truman Committee hearing, the fifteen minutes FDR spent with Hannegan would alter the course of history.[1]

With a world war going on, a national railroad strike imminent, and a packed schedule following his five-week absence from Washington, why was the president meeting with the IRS commissioner? The answer: politics. It had nothing to do with taxes. As events unfolded, however, it had much to do with Truman's future.

Bob Hannegan, who would later become co-owner and president of the St. Louis Cardinals, was in Roosevelt's office because Truman had a hand in setting the meeting up. Fellow Missourians Truman and Hannegan were close political friends. Four years earlier, in the summer of 1940, Hannegan, then the athletic young chair of the St. Louis Democratic Party, had delivered blocs of votes, roughly eight thousand, from several city wards that were instrumental in helping Truman win his second term as senator. As Truman's stature in Washington ascended after Pearl Harbor because of his high-profile investigations of defense contract fraud and waste, the senator's newfound political clout was responsible for the meteoric advancement of Hannegan's career. Due in part to Truman's influence, Hannegan was appointed IRS commissioner in October 1943. Shortly thereafter, Truman was asked to take on the chairmanship of the Democratic National Committee (DNC). He declined and recommended Hannegan for the post. Hannegan said he didn't want the job. He asked Truman what he should do if it was offered. According to Harry Vaughan, Truman's close friend from WWI days, the senator responded, "Tell them you won't take it unless the President asks you directly."[2]

Evidently, the president asked. The timeline and the White House log indicate that the president summoned Hannegan to the White House, squeezed him into his busy schedule on December 20, and asked him to chair the DNC. There is no other plausible explanation for why he was there at that point in time. Afterward, according to Vaughan, "Hannegan called Truman back and asked sarcastically, 'what do I do now Coach?' Truman laughed. 'You take it,' he said." On January 22, 1944, Hannegan resigned as IRS commissioner after serving for only three months. The next day he took over the DNC, just as speculation over who would run for president in 1944 was beginning to ramp up.

The president had no way of realizing it at the time, but the foresight of his eldest child and only daughter, thirty-seven-year-old Anna Roosevelt Boettiger, during the weeks after he returned to the White House from Tehran would prolong his life for another year. It happened because Eleanor Roosevelt invited Anna and her three children, who were living in Seattle, to travel east to Washington and Hyde Park for the Christmas season (at the time, Anna's husband, John Boettiger, was serving as an army officer in North Africa). The morning after the president returned from his trip to Tehran, Anna—called "Sis" by everyone in the family—was in her father's bedroom, having a "good old chin-fest," which meant the latest juicy gossip about the marriages and sexual escapades of her two roguish brothers, Franklin Jr. and Elliott.[3] FDR dished it back. They laughed like a couple of teenagers. The distance that had grown between them over the years had begun to melt away.

Of the Roosevelts' five children, Anna was by far the most attractive in both personality and looks. "Father could relax more easily with Anna than with Mother," recalled Elliott.[4] FDR adored Anna. And she genuinely loved being around her father. With no advance discussion, Anna selflessly took on all manner of tasks and responsibilities for the president, instinctively sensing what he wanted and how he wanted it to be done. When he said, "Sis, you handle that," she consistently delivered. Anna was highly intelligent and competent, a stunning presence. The random projects she took on for her father would quickly grow "into a full-time job."[5]

Anna's arrival partially filled the void left after the third week in December, when Harry Hopkins and his wife, Louise Macy, departed the Lincoln suite in the White House to live in their own rented house in Georgetown (there is a plaque on a house at the corner of Thirty-fourth and N indicating that Hopkins lived there). While Anna would never replace Hopkins as a behind-the-scenes operator and strategist for Roosevelt, she would become the one person with whom he most liked to spend his time. Like Hopkins, Anna satisfied the paralyzed president's emotional needs. "It was immaterial to me," remembered Anna, "whether my job was helping to plan the 1944 campaign, pouring tea for General de Gaulle or filling Father's cigarette case. All that mattered was relieving a greatly overburdened man of a few details of work and trying to make his life as pleasant as possible when a few moments opened for relaxation."[6]

Though the families of two of Roosevelt's four sons who were serving overseas—Jimmy, the oldest, and Elliott, the second son—would not be there, Christmas 1943 at Springwood was still a boisterous and busy affair. When FDR arrived with a Secret Service detail and a gaggle of reporters in tow, he was greeted by First Lady Eleanor, along with Anna and her three children: Anna (another "Anna"), known as "Sistie"; Curtis, called

"Buzzie"; and Johnny, age four. Also in the big house were the Roosevelts' third oldest son, Franklin Jr.; his wife, Ethel; their toddler; and a five-year-old. Frank Jr., a navy lieutenant, was able to get up to Hyde Park for Christmas only because his destroyer, the USS *Mayrant*, had been bombed during the invasion of Sicily and had to be returned to the U.S. for repairs (he was to be awarded a Silver Star and a Purple Heart). In addition, John, the youngest son; his wife, Anne; and their two children were there. Also a navy lieutenant, John had just finished a shakedown cruise with the newly commissioned aircraft carrier USS *Wasp* and would shortly be transferred to the fast carrier *Hornet*, on which he would see action in the Pacific—New Guinea, Palau, Truk, and the Marianas Turkey Shoot. Finally, cousin "Daisy," FDR's favorite though distant sixth cousin, a frequent presence at Springwood, was on hand. Daisy's given name was Margaret Suckley. A self-described "prim spinster," Daisy, age fifty-two, lived nearby in a Victorian mansion named Wilderstein with a sweeping view of the Hudson River.[7] It was Daisy who had gifted Fala, the renowned Scottish terrier, to FDR. He christened his companion "Murray the Outlaw of Falahill."

Remembering past Christmases at Springwood, when her grandmother Sara ruled the house and her father read from Dickens, Anna wrote that she "loved the old place."[8] In the mornings she shared breakfast with her father. She attended to his needs when he worked in his study in the afternoon. At 3 p.m. on the day before Christmas, with the temperature outside at 20 degrees, the family gathered in FDR's presidential library building to hear him deliver his twenty-seventh "fireside chat" to the nation and to the 3.8 million servicemen and -women on duty overseas. Cousin Daisy wrote in her diary that "Mrs. R."—the First Lady—"sat on the floor behind the P.'s desk" and that Anna "moved over by her."[9] The president's physician, Vice Admiral McIntire, wrote that Roosevelt "looked in the pink."[10]

In contrast to his "Dr. New Deal / Dr. Win-the-War" press conference that would take place in the White House a few days later, the president spent most of the time during his Christmas Eve chat talking about his vision of a durable postwar world peace. The subtext, however, was a not too subtle message that it was his own "personal" relationships, and his alone, with the leaders of Britain, the Soviet Union, and China that caused them to "completely agree" that they would "use force if necessary in the future to keep the peace." (There is nothing that documents the existence of such an agreement.) Throughout his fireside chat, Roosevelt used the word "I" several times to explain how well "I" got along with "Mr. Churchill," "Marshal Stalin," and "Generalissimo Chiang Kai-shek."[11] It was as if he were more than just the president of the United States. He believed he was destined to lead the nations of the world.

While Anna and her children stayed on at Springwood, Daisy rode with the president to Highland Station on Sunday night, December 26, for the midnight train down to Washington aboard the *Ferdinand Magellan*, an armored railcar specially designed for FDR. But for "the servants & the striking clocks," wrote Daisy, she and FDR, just the two of them, spent the next day together "in the deserted [White] House," though "Lincoln, once in a while, makes a sound—in some corner of the room."[12] Daisy actually believed that the ghost of Lincoln frequently made its rounds in the house of the presidents.

From the beginning, the Dr. New Deal / Dr. Win-the-War press conference on the afternoon of December 28 was a clever setup, an opportunity for the president to deliver his first speech of the 1944 campaign—an early pitch to the professional pols, the delegates to the Democratic convention, and the voters. It opened with a preplanned question from a reporter by the name of Donaldson. "Mr. President," he began, it has been said that "you no longer like the term 'New Deal.' Would you care to express any opinion to the rest of us?" Roosevelt fielded the softball, saying, "I supposed somebody would ask that." With the skill and timing of a Broadway actor who had rehearsed his lines, FDR proceeded to introduce a character named Old Dr. New Deal, a mythical physician, namely the president. "Old Dr. New Deal," explained FDR, had supposedly treated and cured a "sick patient," called the United States, who had been suffering from a "grave internal disorder." The president deployed this metaphor to remind the reporters and, more important, their readers, how he, as Old Dr. New Deal, had cured the nation of the Great Depression by setting up a sound banking system, saving farms and homes from foreclosure, "putting in" Social Security and unemployment compensation, and getting citizens back to work via relief programs like the Civilian Conservation Corps.

Enter Dr. Win-the-War. On December 7, 1941, continued Roosevelt, the "patient," that is the nation, had had a "very bad accident." Dr. Win-the-War, an "orthopedic surgeon," had to step in and get "the patient back on his feet." Of course, the hero who came riding to the rescue as Dr. Win-the-War was once again the president. Speaking to the White House reporters and their readership, this time with the new Win-the-War slogan, FDR promised a postwar "plan" to bring about an "expanded economy" that would result in more and better "security," "employment," "recreation," "education," "health," and "housing" for all citizens.

Roosevelt's message was meant to convey the idea that while many of the benefits and reforms of the New Deal would continue, times had changed. Thanks to the war, jobs were plentiful and the economy was roaring. To fit the needs of the postwar years, FDR planned to soon announce the details of new and better government programs and an even more robust economy. It was time for Old Dr. New Deal to retire. The unspoken implication was that he would step in, win the war, and keep the economy humming.

When the president finished his allegory, an unnamed reporter asked the obvious question: "Does that all add up to a fourth-term declaration?" According to the transcript, laughter filled the room. While the president demurred, he did not back off plans for his postwar "program."[13] A headline a few days later on the front page of the *New York Herald Tribune* proclaimed, "Fourth-Term Drive Is Seen as Under Way."[14]

That evening, Daisy wrote in her diary that the president was "feeling a *little* miserably—it is probably a touch of the flu for the both of us."[15] Thus began the first of a series of setbacks in FDR's overall health that would gradually worsen and intermittently afflict him for the remainder of his life. For the next nine days, racked with coughing spells and occasional mild fevers, Roosevelt stayed mostly in bed and took his meals on trays. The White House log showed that he had very few outside visitors, though one of them, budget director Harold Smith, recalled, "I have never seen him so listless" and "so groggy."[16]

At 8 p.m. on January 11, the president felt well enough to be dressed in a suit and tie and wheeled into the Diplomatic Reception Room, where he faced a phalanx of microphones, cameras, and bright lights. Except for speechwriters Sam Rosenman and Robert Sherwood, no one knew that Dr. New Deal, now with a transformative facelift, was about to come out of retirement. After apologizing for not going "up to the Capitol" for his State of the Union speech due to his bout with the "flu," Roosevelt laid out a stunningly progressive legislative agenda. The centerpiece was a proposed "Second Bill of Rights," a guarantee that all citizens regardless of race, color, or creed would have a right to: a useful and remunerative job with earnings adequate enough to provide food, clothing, and recreation; decent housing; adequate medical care; a good education; and protection from the economic fears of old age, sickness, accident, and unemployment.

While Roosevelt implored Congress to "explore the means for implementing this economic bill of rights," he knew that the Southern Democrats, in league with the Republicans, would almost certainly reject his proposal, especially because it was tied to a tax increase and a National Service Act, and would be made available to everyone, not just white people.[17] Nevertheless, the president was "in a fighting mood," wrote Rosenman.[18] With a nationwide radio audience listening, FDR was hoping to circumvent the negative coalitions in Congress, by trying to forge a new alignment of political power with the American citizenry. He believed his bill of rights would appeal not only to liberals and the poor but also to the majority of voters.

Tall, handsome, impeccably dressed Ed Flynn of the Bronx, arguably the most powerful political boss in the country, was not at all sure. To him, FDR's proposed economic bill of rights was not only progressive; it bordered on the radical. Flynn was sure that if Roosevelt insisted on having Vice President Henry Wallace on the ticket, as he did in 1940, the bill of rights proposal, combined with Wallace's reputation as an eccentric farleft mystic, would lead to defeat in 1944. Moreover, Flynn was convinced that Wallace was much too liberal to serve the nation as president, should FDR win the election and then die, an increasingly plausible possibility. Therefore, as far as Flynn and a group of Democratic Party insiders were concerned, Roosevelt had to be persuaded to dump Wallace as his VP candidate in the coming election.

Less than two weeks after FDR's State of the Union message, when Bob Hannegan was taking over the chairmanship of the Democratic National Committee, Flynn, along with Hannegan, Frank Walker, and other members of the DNC, met with Roosevelt in the White House to discuss Wallace's shortcomings as FDR's running mate in 1944.[19] Several names were suggested as promising alternatives, including Senator Truman; James "Jimmy" Byrnes, head of War Mobilization; Sam Rayburn, Speaker of the House; and William O. Douglas, associate justice of the Supreme Court. It was Bob Hannegan who had the most to say about Truman, but he also expressed enthusiasm for Byrnes. However, the group did not settle on any particular candidate; instead, the overwhelming consensus was that Wallace should not be on the 1944 ticket. Roosevelt seemed engaged in the conversation but he did not agree to dump Wallace, nor did he signal a preference for Truman or one of the other alternatives.

———

Over the next two and a half months, Daisy's diary was peppered with words describing the president's declining health—"feels tired," "constant headache," "feverish and generally miserable," and "in bed again."[20] Encouraged by Eleanor and Franklin, by the end of February, Anna and her husband, John, who had been reassigned to the War Department in Washington, moved into the Lincoln suite on the second floor of the White House. Their three children slept in rooms on the third floor. By moving in, Anna and her family replaced ailing Harry Hopkins; his daughter, Diana; and his third wife, Louise Macy. Knowing that FDR had come to rely on her, Anna was committed to staying with him for the rest of his life, taking on a variety of assignments, handling paperwork, serving as his hostess, and dispensing advice. Of course, she could not help noticing his trembling hands, the dark pouches under his eyes, and the occasions when she caught him staring blankly with his mouth hanging open. She became more and more concerned about his declining health.

On Friday, March 24, following what Daisy described to Anna as a "very miserable day" for her father, the president was still "not looking so

well," but he managed to preside at a late-morning press and radio conference in the Oval Office.[21] His aim was to give the broadest possible news
coverage to a "proclamation" that he would be issuing later that day,
"promising to help rescue the Jews of Europe from Nazi brutality" and
from "wholesale systematic murder." Instead of speaking extemporane-
ously, as he usually did, he read it aloud, word for word. In essence, he
wanted to make it clear to the American people that while Hitler would be
held accountable for committing "these crimes against humanity," it was
also his "German functionaries and their subordinates" who were taking
part in the "deportation of Jews to their death." They would be judged
equally guilty. Until victory was won, he said, "this Government" would
"rescue" and "aid the escape of all intended victims of the Nazi and Jap
executioner—regardless of race or religion or color."[22] His remarks summarized the mandate of the War Refugee Board, which he had created by
executive order in January. Though the vastly underfunded and short-
staffed board would manage to rescue an estimated two hundred thousand Jews, it was too little and far too late.

That evening, the president, along with Daisy, took the night train to
Hyde Park, where he planned to spend the weekend, with a long-overdue
visit from Lucy Mercer on Sunday, her first ever to Hyde Park. He knew he
had to be back by Monday because he was scheduled to be examined at the
Bethesda Naval Hospital at 11:30 a.m. on Tuesday.

Why the appointment out at Bethesda Naval? Days earlier, in mid-
March, Anna had finally confronted Vice Admiral McIntire, an ear,
nose, and throat specialist who had been selected by FDR to be his physician because of his sinus condition. In the spacious room where Lincoln
had once had his office, Anna subjected McIntire to a withering cross-
examination on the state of her father's health and what to do about it. Did
he regularly check her father's blood pressure? she asked. He took it when
"I think it is necessary," he glibly responded. His answers were not reas-
suring. Anna thought he did not "know what he was talking about," but
against her better judgment she agreed with McIntire's recommendation
of a seven-day trial period of complete rest and a strict diet.[23]

The president's condition did not improve. In fact, it got worse. In her
diary on March 23, Daisy wrote that "the P. has felt miserable all day" and

"falls asleep, sometimes, sitting bolt upright."[24] This time Anna insisted. She begged McIntire to bring in one or more doctors who could give her father a "thorough checkup. McIntire was annoyed at her interference but reluctantly agreed."[25] He telephoned U.S. Navy lieutenant commander Howard Bruenn, a young cardiologist at the Bethesda Naval Hospital who had been a resident at Columbia Presbyterian Hospital in New York City before enlisting. McIntire informed Bruenn that the president was recovering from "an upper respiratory infection," had not quite regained his strength, and needed to be examined.[26] The appointment needed to be on the following Tuesday, Bruenn was told, because the president would be away for the weekend. Until then, everything about his visit to Bethesda Naval had to be kept in strict confidence.

After resting all day Saturday at Springwood, Roosevelt summoned enough energy on Sunday to greet Lucy Mercer when she arrived around noon with a warm smile and embrace. Six days earlier, Lucy's husband had died at age eighty-two. She and FDR had not seen each other for many months. Lucy, thirty years younger than her late husband, feared that Franklin, whom she had never stopped loving, was also nearing death. Daisy recalled that FDR "showed her around the place," including the library and Top Cottage, both of which he had had a hand in designing. He probably drove her around the estate in his Ford Phaeton with its special hand controls. After Lucy left, the president's fever was "up over 100," wrote Daisy.[27]

On Tuesday morning, Mike Reilly entered the Oval Office. The president looked up from the papers on his desk and said, "Ten-thirty. We go to Bethesda."[28] Along with Anna, Secret Service cars were waiting on the South Lawn. Reilly helped FDR into the back seat and Anna sat beside him for the ride out Wisconsin Avenue to the hospital. When they arrived, she waved goodbye as Arthur Prettyman, the president's valet, wheeled him into the main entrance. Anna had promised her mother that she would meet her at National Airport when she returned in a few hours from her Caribbean tour.

One look at the president on the examining table in the hospital's electrocardiograph department and Dr. Bruenn knew that his famous patient was afflicted with something much more serious than what McIntire had said was "an upper respiratory infection." His "face was pallid," recalled Bruenn, and "there was a bluish, discoloration of his skin, lips and nail beds," which meant that he was oxygen deprived.[29] Bruenn also noted that FDR's slightest movements while being examined "caused breathlessness and puffing."[30] But it was when Bruenn began listening to the sounds of his heart and thumping his chest that he realized that the president's condition was life-threatening. Fluoroscopy and X-rays showed that the president's heart was "markedly enlarged" and its "apex" had moved to the left.[31] His blood pressure that day was a dangerous 186 over 108. Bruenn's quick review of FDR's past medical records, which had just arrived by messenger from the White House, revealed that his blood pressure had been consistently high since 1941—the obvious cause of his enlarged heart. Bruenn's diagnosis was unassailable: the president was suffering from "acute congestive heart failure," specifically, "left ventricular heart failure."[32] (The left ventricle is the pumping chamber.) Bruenn later told an interviewer that the president's condition was simply "God-awful."[33] Without treatment, he could have died at any moment.

Bruenn had been ordered by Dr. McIntire, his superior, not to inform his patient of his diagnosis or any hint of his dangerous condition. The president was not the least bit curious about his condition. He never even asked. But he had to have known that there was something wrong with his heart. After all, he was examined in the electrocardiograph department and Bruenn was a cardiologist. Yet that evening, when FDR called Daisy, he merely told her that the doctors "found nothing drastically wrong, but one sinus clogged."[34]

The next day, Bruenn presented his written findings and recommendations for treatment to McIntire. His prescription included absolute bed rest with nursing care for weeks, no smoking, two hours of work in the morning, naps during the day, a diet to lose weight and restrict salt, and less tension. Plus, digitalis, a plant-based substance for treatment of heart conditions, including congestive heart failure. Bruenn's regimen was dead on arrival. McIntire was appalled. His reaction was "unprintable," recalled Bruenn.[35] "You can't do that!" he almost shouted.[36] "The President can't take time off to go to bed," he said in disbelief.[37] Digitalis? Too risky. Less tension in the middle of a global war? He had to be kidding.

Bruenn was willing to cut back on many of his recommendations but he held the line on digitalis, even though it could have had dangerous side effects. He told McIntire he would not "have anything to do" with treating the president unless digitalis was administered.[38] In the face of this ultimatum and being unwilling to assume the risk himself, McIntire brought in big guns from out of town for a second opinion—Frank Lahey, the Boston surgeon who would later make sure FDR knew he likely would not live through a fourth term and that he should choose his VP with care, and James Paullin, an Atlanta internist and former president of the American Medical Association. After they examined the president and offered their diagnosis with much "beating around the bush," it was finally agreed that the president would start taking digitalis, so long as his heart was monitored frequently by electrocardiogram to make sure the drug was working.[39]

It was Anna's insistence that her father be examined by specialists and Bruenn's stubborn belief in the value of digitalis that would extend the president's life for another year.

Reporters who covered the White House were aware that Roosevelt's health had declined, that he looked sick and his voice was weak, but they could not find any inside sources to provide confirmation. Regarding the outcome of FDR's visits to Bethesda Naval Hospital, *Time* magazine reported that he had a "mild case of bronchitis" that the president "pooh-poohed," while continuing to "smoke from his long cigarette holder."[40] At a press conference on April 4, Vice Admiral McIntire admitted that the president had suffered "influenza, or 'respiratory infection' and a sinus disturbance." However, "when we got through," asserted McIntire, "we decided that for a man of sixty-two-plus we had very little to argue about." As to the reason that the president had not been seen in public for days, McIntire claimed to be "completely responsible." The "bronchitis had made him a little hoarse," he said, "and I felt if we could hold him in his study for his work . . . we would clear this thing up."[41] McIntire's approach was to hide the truth by disarming the press and deluding the American public. There were words he would never utter, like "heart" and "cardiology," and matters he would not disclose, such as the fact that he had just turned day-to-day management of the president's health over to thirty-nine-year-old cardiologist Howard Bruenn.

———

It was Easter Sunday 1944 in the Low Country when the president, seated in his wheelchair, was lowered by a specially designed elevator from the rear of the *Ferdinand Magellan*. Azaleas were blooming. The air was intoxicatingly warm as the president's motorcade rolled slowly up the long, curved driveway to Hobcaw Barony, home of Bernard Baruch, a wealthy financier who had known the Roosevelts for years. Beginning with President Woodrow Wilson, Baruch had had a penchant for befriending and advising presidents. He had let it be known that his South Carolina mansion and sixteen-thousand-acre former plantation were available for FDR to rest and recuperate in peace and quiet for as long as he wished to stay. During the previous week the digitalis had done its job with the result that Roosevelt's enlarged heart was starting to shrink and his color had improved, though his blood pressure remained alarmingly high. Still, as Lieutenant William Rigdon, one of the naval aides in FDR's official party, recalled, "The President felt miserable upon arrival."[42] Fatigue was in his eyes. After exchanging greetings with his host, the president said to him, "I want to sleep and sleep. Twelve hours every night."[43] He had an "early dinner" and went "immediately to bed."[44]

For the next six or seven days, FDR retired by 9:30 and slept until 9 the next morning in a corner bedroom on the first floor. He napped after lunch and ate from a tray, never appearing at the dinner table. Eventually, however, he became more sociable, often joining Baruch, Bruenn, and Pa Watson, Roosevelt's military adviser and appointments secretary, for a cocktail and dinner. During the afternoon Roosevelt would sit out on a pier beneath a grassy bluff, casting a baited hook into the waters of Winyah Bay, hoping to catch a channel bass. After a couple of weeks he ventured out onto the open sea aboard a Coast Guard patrol boat and landed seven bluefish.

The president did little work, although he occasionally had to sign bills into law or answer critically important letters and cables that arrived in the daily pouch from Washington. Meanwhile, there was a war going on. In all theaters, combat was raging at sea, on the ground, and in the air, notably the April 1944 massive night-and-day carpet-bombing of the German aircraft industry by British and American air forces. But it was not combat but *preparation* for war-ending battles that dominated the period when Roosevelt was resting at Hobcaw. In England, the Allies were rehearsing for Operation Overlord, the invasion of Normandy scheduled for early June. Across Europe to the east, the Red Army was gearing up for Operation Bagration, its most powerful strike of the war, which would support the Allied invasion of France in the west, thus forcing the Wehrmacht to fight on two broad fronts. In the Mediterranean, General Mark Clark's Fifth Army was preparing to break out of the Anzio beachhead in Italy, where it had been stalemated for months. Similarly, in the Pacific, the Joint Chiefs of Staff ordered Admiral Chester Nimitz and General MacArthur to prepare plans: MacArthur was to land and occupy Hollandia on the north coast of New Guinea in April with the objective of establishing bases for heavy bombers to strike the Palau islands; Nimitz was to invade the southern Marianas in June (D-day in the Pacific) and seize the Palaus in September; and MacArthur, with the aid of the Pacific Fleet, was to occupy Mindanao, the southern island of the Philippines, in November.[45]

Mercifully for the president, the global war made few demands on him during the month he spent at Hobcaw, though General Mark Clark, who was in the U.S. to see his wife before the Anzio breakout, made a brief visit to Hobcaw to inform the president of his plan to take Rome. The only real breaks from FDR's routine of rest, fishing, and light socializing occurred when Eleanor and Anna (back from a trip west with her children) visited with him for a single afternoon and three days later Lucy Mercer drove over with her daughter-in-law from her horse farm in nearby Aiken. During lunch with Lucy, a message was handed to Roosevelt; it said that Frank Knox, his Republican secretary of the navy, who had been Alf Landon's running mate in 1936, had died of a heart attack, his third. After Lucy departed, the president summoned reporters to Hobcaw so he could express his sympathies, emphasizing that Knox was a "casualty of the war." His words were the first of his to be released to the public in three weeks. The *New York Times* report of the interview commented that the commander in chief was "bronzed and obviously in improved health."[46] That evening, however, he suffered severe abdominal pains (later diagnosed as a gallbladder attack). His blood pressure rose to 230 over 120.

Two days before FDR was scheduled to return to Washington, Daisy, who had been staying with friends in Florida, arrived at Hobcaw. She "was so glad to see him," she wrote in her diary, "but, under his tan, he looks thin & drawn & not a bit well."[47] When she was in Florida, Daisy had received a telephone call from the Secret Service saying that "the boss" wanted her to come to Hobcaw and then return with him to the White House. "He is feeling much better," she was told.[48]

With Daisy and Fala, the president departed Hobcaw by train and they were all back in the White House by 9:30 a.m. on Sunday, May 7. Though the First Lady was traveling and not there to greet him, FDR was delighted to be reunited with Anna, her husband, and their children. Anna believed her father looked better than when she had seen him for a few hours at Hobcaw. However, she was still very concerned about his health. During the month they were apart, she had "read up on cardiovascular disease," recalled Bruenn, and she was determined to prevent her father from "fall[ing] back into his old habits." It was Anna, said Bruenn, "who became his protector." It was she who would "enforce the new regime" of diet, rest, no more than "one and a half cocktails," and only "five or six" Camels, "down from twenty or thirty a day."[49] Lots of luck with that.

McIntire decreed that Bruenn was not to be seen visiting the White House, much less photographed going in and out. In his press briefing on the president's health, McIntire asserted that his patient had "shaken off his sniffles and bronchitis" and declared, "I am perfectly satisfied with his physical condition . . . excellent shape . . . and [the fact that he is] as strong as he was a year ago."[50] These statements were bald-faced lies.

Ed Flynn, Bob Hannegan, and the other party bosses and kingmakers were getting nervous. The Democratic National Convention was set to begin in a little over two months. While none of them had had access to the president while he was at Hobcaw, they assumed that despite his precarious health, FDR was still intent on running for a fourth term. They

also believed that the Republicans would most likely nominate Thomas
Dewey, a formidable candidate who at age forty-two was governor of New
York following a hugely successful career as a racket-busting district attorney in New York City. Flynn and his compatriots were reasonably confident that Roosevelt, the most prolific Democratic vote getter since
Andrew Jackson, could beat Dewey but not with Wallace on the ticket; the
president had to replace him with a veep candidate who would not be a
political liability.

Flynn's political allies were not only nervous; they were frustrated because they could not get Roosevelt to focus on the choice of a running
mate. He was devious and manipulative. Byzantine. He enjoyed keeping
them off-balance. Anna, who knew FDR better than most anyone other
than Harry Hopkins, told one of Wallace's friends that her father was
"cold, calculating, shrewd and you can't tell what he will do."[51] It is also
likely that Roosevelt regarded his choice of a vice president as neither urgent nor important because, as Anna recalled, he "never had the idea that
his health was going downhill the way it was," and he refused to believe
that he would die in office.[52]

The last three weeks of May and most of June flew by with virtually no
opportunities for access by political operatives to the president. In the
White House, the Allied advances in Italy and the capture of Rome, combined with the tense buildup for D-day and the ferocious battles in the
Normandy bocage, captured FDR's attention. All the while Anna was
monitoring her father's schedule, cutting back his working time, and encouraging him to take extended personal trips to Hyde Park, Shangri-La,
and Pa Watson's farm in Charlottesville, for a total of twenty-four full days
out of Washington. Finally, in late June and during the first week of July,
less than three weeks before the convention, the White House log shows
that Hannegan and Flynn managed to schedule brief meetings with FDR,
though not together. There can be little doubt that each of them forcefully
argued that Roosevelt needed to abandon Wallace. However, while
Hannegan told an interviewer in 1946 that he was the one who persuaded
the president to choose Truman as his running mate, Flynn wrote in his
memoir a year later that it was he who convinced FDR to drop Truman
"into the slot" as the only plausible candidate who would do the least harm

to the ticket.[53] There is no hard evidence to support either claim. Indeed, it is conceivable that Roosevelt had had his eye on Truman for months and was just playing his usual long game of keeping everyone guessing.

Time was running out. The Democratic convention in Chicago was set to begin on July 19. Despite what Hannegan and Flynn chose to believe, the president still had not indicated to them his choice of a running mate. Moreover, during the entire convention, FDR would be on the West Coast and then on his way to Hawaii, where he planned to mediate a dispute between Admiral Nimitz and General MacArthur over grand strategy in the Pacific. Because he would be departing Washington by train on July 13, Roosevelt asked Flynn to arrange for the key party officials to meet and discuss with him the VP decision before he left town. Flynn's aim and that of the others was to force FDR to reach a firm decision.

On the sultry evening of Tuesday, July 11, the party bosses shed their coats and ties. In shirtsleeves they gathered in the Oval Study on the second floor of the White House. Earlier in the day, the president, having returned from his Sunday trip to Shangri-La with Lucy Mercer, had publicly announced his decision to run for a fourth term. That night, in addition to Roosevelt, Flynn, and Hannegan, those in attendance included Chicago mayor Ed Kelly, California oil tycoon and party treasurer Edwin Pauley, party secretary and fundraiser par excellence George Allen, and U.S. postmaster general Frank Walker, former head of the DNC.

To the dismay of his guests, Roosevelt began by praising his vice president, Henry Wallace, saying he would be happy to run with him again. However, what he didn't tell them was that the day before, and again that same afternoon, he had informed Wallace that he wanted him to be on the ticket and planned to release a statement to that effect (which he later did, although it was less than an outright commitment). In any event, there was not a touch of enthusiasm from the politicos. Not one of them expressed support. Consequently, FDR did not persist. Those gathered around FDR's desk were relieved, under the impression that Wallace had been buried.

Next, Roosevelt held forth at length on the strengths of his so-called assistant president, the suave former South Carolina senator and Supreme Court associate justice Jimmy Byrnes, who as head of War Mobilization operated from an office in the East Wing. But this suggestion was almost as quickly quashed. Several in the room reminded Roosevelt that Byrnes had left the Catholic Church to become an Episcopalian when he married. They argued that the large Roman Catholic population would have a reason not to vote for the ticket if Byrnes was on it. Plus, chimed in Flynn from the Bronx and Kelly from Chicago, Byrnes was a Southern segregationist who was on record as opposing an anti-lynching bill and would therefore alienate the Black vote.

The group went on to discuss and then dismiss Kentucky senator Alben Barkley (too old; had crossed FDR), House Speaker Sam Rayburn (lost support of conservative Texas Democrats), former ambassador John Winant (New Hampshire Republican), and even West Coast shipbuilder Henry Kaiser (favored national sales tax).

It was Roosevelt who spoke up for William O. Douglas, the rugged young associate justice of the Supreme Court and former chair of the Securities and Exchange Commission. Douglas, he argued, would offset the youthful appeal of Tom Dewey. "He has a nice crop of hair," FDR observed. "He looks like a Boy Scout . . . plays an interesting game of poker and would appeal to the people."[54] Except for Mayor Kelly, there was dead silence from the party leaders. Some had reason to think that the president wasn't serious, that he was playing with them. Yet even if FDR were serious, Douglas was relatively unknown and had no political experience. He would have been too much of a heavy lift, they felt.

Roosevelt broke the awkward silence and said, "All right, Bob—start talking," cuing Hannegan to deliver his pitch for Harry Truman.[55] Hannegan began by pointing out that Truman had attained a national reputation fighting against fraud and waste in war contracts, which saved the government billions, and that he was considered incorruptible, notwithstanding his past association with the Pendergast political machine in Kansas City. Truman was respected by labor leaders and the Black community, he argued. Plus, as a seasoned Senate insider from a border state, he could deal with the Southern senators and convention delegates but not join them and their cause, namely opposition to civil rights. Having a straight shooter like Senator Truman on the ticket, said Hannegan, would give the president someone who could actually help FDR persuade other senators to approve future peace treaties and vote in favor of a UN peacekeeping organization. Unlike other candidates under consideration, he claimed, Truman would be an asset, definitely not a liability.

The president was listless, said little. He commented that Truman and his Senate committee had done an excellent job ferreting out wasteful defense contracts. He asked about Truman's age and was told that he was sixty. In the presence of Roosevelt, there was scarcely any discussion among the politicos as to whether any of the candidates were actually prepared for the office, probably because such talk would have implied that FDR would not survive a fourth term. It was Roosevelt, however, who stated at some point during the evening that he thought Byrnes was the most qualified.

It was getting late. FDR was tired. He could sense that a consensus had coalesced. Accounts vary, but according to Ed Pauley, Roosevelt turned to Hannegan and said, "Bob, I think you and everyone else want Truman." And before anyone could respond, he added, "If that's the case, it's Truman."[56]

Perhaps more important than what the president allegedly said is what he actually did as the meeting came to a close. Since he was about to be gone for more than a month to the West Coast and the Pacific, FDR wanted to make sure that negative messages would be delivered to the two candidates who had made it known that they desperately wanted to be on the ticket. He deputized Hannegan to inform Henry Wallace that the convention delegates would not renominate him. And he assigned Frank Walker the task of administering the "coup de grâce" to the hopes of Jimmy Byrnes.[57] Unless FDR changed his mind, it appeared that Truman would be on the ticket.

When most of the bosses were downstairs retrieving their suit jackets, Frank Walker, who correctly suspected that Roosevelt might waffle, pulled Hannegan aside and told him to "go back and get it in writing."[58] On the pretext that he had left his jacket upstairs, Hannegan went up and found that Pauley was in the Oval Study with the president looking for his own jacket. Pauley heard Roosevelt say to Hannegan that he understood that the Truman choice "makes you boys happy," but "I still think Douglas would have the greater appeal."[59] In response to Hannegan's request the president handed him a note "scribbled on an envelope in pencil."

Hannegan put it in his pocket and returned downstairs. According to George Allen, who was there, the note simply read, "Bob, I think Truman is the right man. FDR."[60] This note has never been found, though Truman later described the dimensions of the note ("two inches by eight") and claimed that Hannegan had shown it him.[61]

Near the end of the week, what the political bosses thought had been settled—"it's Truman"—seemed to have completely unraveled. After Wallace flatly rejected Hannegan's request that he "withdraw" from the VP sweepstakes because he would be a detriment to the ticket, he had lunch with the president on Thursday the thirteenth.[62] As he was getting ready to leave, Roosevelt told him he intended to send to the chairman of the convention a letter saying something like "If I were a delegate I would vote for Wallace."[63] Then, as Wallace recalled, FDR "drew me close and turned on his full smile and a very hearty handclasp" and said, "'While I cannot put it just this way in public, I hope it will be the same old team.'"[64] In fact, Roosevelt had no intention of running with Wallace.

Like Wallace, Jimmy Byrnes had also refused to withdraw. Frank Walker's effort to dash his hopes for the vice presidency had failed. On Thursday, the day Wallace had lunch with the president, Byrnes managed to cop a half-hour appointment with FDR in the Oval Office. Byrnes knew, from his conversations the day before with Walker and others, that the consensus choice was Truman first and perhaps Douglas second, and that he, Byrnes, had been "passed over" because the boss could not afford to lose the "Negro" vote. Byrnes came prepared. He was armed with a photograph of the First Lady addressing a group of rapt Blacks from the South, which he showed to Roosevelt. "You can't tell me," argued Byrnes, "that because you have a Southerner on the ticket that these people are going to turn against Mrs. Roosevelt and the President who have done more for them than anybody else in the history of the world." To this vast overstatement, Byrnes added that if he were VP and thus had the power to preside over the Senate, he would have the stature as a former senator from the South to curtail filibusters over anti–poll tax and other civil rights bills by his fellow Southerners. FDR was persuaded. "I believe you are right," he responded. Were it not for "the Negro issue," the president said, "all of us agreed you were the best qualified man and all of us would rather have you than anyone else."[65] According to Byrnes's memoir, FDR then said, "You must not get out of the race. If you stay in you are sure to win."[66] To Byrnes, this was his green light. He was back in the game. That evening FDR departed by train for Hyde Park, the first leg of his journey to Hawaii, with stops along the way in Chicago and San Diego.

Friday morning, around 9:00 Washington time, Byrnes telephoned Harry Truman, who was staying at the President Hotel in Kansas City (Bess and Margaret were in Denver visiting family). Truman was getting ready to drive to the Chicago convention.[67] According to most accounts, Byrnes asked him if he was serious about not wanting to be nominated as vice president. When Truman said yes, Byrnes got to the point. He explained that "the President" had given him "the go sign for the Vice Presidency" and that he was calling to ask if Truman would nominate him at the convention.[68] Truman accepted on the spot, believing that Byrnes was the president's choice.

Byrnes had deliberately trapped Truman, who was thought to be the front-runner, and took him out of the VP race, at least for the time being—"a neat, though unethical, move," wrote Margaret Truman.[69] Byrnes was whip-smart. He suspected that Truman protesteth too much about not wanting the vice presidency—that he might have had a hidden ambition to be president. As Truman said later of Byrnes, he was a "slick conniver."[70]

On Friday, with the president in Hyde Park, Byrnes arranged to have lunch with Hannegan and Walker in a suite at the Mayflower. After the two of them again told Byrnes that Walker had been instructed by Roosevelt on Tuesday to tell him he was not under consideration, Byrnes quoted what the president had told him just the day before—that "he was the best qualified" and that "he must not get out of the race." Hannegan and Walker were gobsmacked. "I don't understand it," said Hannegan, "but I can't call the president a liar."[71]

Byrnes was determined to get a straight answer from the boss—good luck with that—or at least an answer that satisfied his ambitions. He returned to his White House office and put a call through the switchboard to Roosevelt at Springwood in Hyde Park. Byrnes, who had been trained as a court stenographer, recorded the substance of the conversation in shorthand and had his secretary on an extension phone to back him up. When FDR came on the line, Byrnes opened by saying that Hannegan and Walker had told him earlier that day that "you"—that is, the president— preferred "Truman first and Douglas second" as vice president, and that "either would be preferable to me because they would cost the ticket fewer votes than I would." Happily for Byrnes, Roosevelt replied, "Jimmy, that is all wrong." Byrnes pressed him to explain. "We have to be damn careful about language," admonished FDR as he began reimagining the truth and ignoring his actions. "They asked if I would object to Truman and Douglas and I said no. That is different from using the word 'prefer.' . . . You know I told you I would have no preference."[72] This so-called explanation differed from the recall of everyone else who had been there on Tuesday evening, July 11. Nonetheless, since Byrnes had not been at the meeting on July 11, he was pleased to accept and take advantage of the president's clever dodge on what was actually said.

For Byrnes's purposes the conversation ended on an even more positive note. The president asked him if he intended to stay in contention for the nomination. Byrnes said he was seriously considering it but needed to know FDR's views. Roosevelt responded by disparaging the competition: "After all, Jimmy, you are close to me personally and Henry is close to me. I hardly know Truman. Douglas is a poker partner. He is good in a poker game and tells good stories."[73]

Not exactly a straight answer but it was more than enough for Byrnes.

On Saturday afternoon, July 15, the president and the Missouri senator were only a few miles apart. Truman had checked in to his room on the seventeenth floor of the Stevens Hotel in Chicago. Within the maze of rails and ties in Chicago's Fifty-first Street railroad yard, POTUS's train, on the way to San Diego, was being serviced. FDR was seated in the dining compartment of the *Ferdinand Magellan*, expecting DNC chairman Bob Hannegan and Chicago mayor Ed Kelly to come aboard. While the Democratic National Convention would not officially convene for another four days, the hard work was about to begin. Given the president's fragile health, the party leaders and delegates who were already in or on their way to Chicago believed that they would likely have the unique distinction in the coming days of nominating not one but two presidents. Roosevelt's nomination for a fourth term, of course, was a foregone conclusion. But the choice of his running mate would become one of the most capricious and unpredictable political dramas in the annals of American politics.

Hannegan and Kelly boarded the air-conditioned *Ferdinand Magellan* at about 3 p.m. It was 86 degrees outside. After conferring with the president in his sitting room for almost an hour, they emerged with two conflicting messages, each cunningly designed to leave the president blameless. First, Mayor Kelly was instructed to immediately call Byrnes in Washington, inform him that he had the green light from FDR to declare his candidacy for VP, and thereafter "Clear it with Sidney." Clearance from Sidney meant that Kelly or Hannegan should get the approval of Sidney Hillman, a powerful labor leader who controlled the purse strings of the Congress of Industrial Organizations (CIO). When Kelly made the call to Byrnes, he delivered the green-light message but neglected to mention what sounded to him like an innocuous condition. FDR's second message was a "Dear Bob" letter to Hannegan, signed by Roosevelt, that stated that he would be "glad to run" with either Truman or Douglas because they would bring "real strength to the ticket."[74] Notably, that letter did not indicate that the president actually intended or preferred to run with either of them. Hannegan pocketed the letter, suspecting that FDR gave it to him so it could be disclosed to the convention delegates at the appropriate time.

When Byrnes received the call from Kelly informing him that the president had given him the "the green light" and that "he wants you in Chicago," he booked a night train.[75] He spent Sunday with Kelly and Hannegan in Chicago organizing his nomination celebration, including the ordering of signs that read "Roosevelt and Byrnes" for the delegates to brandish on the convention floor. That evening, the party leaders, sans Flynn, who would arrive on Monday, hosted what amounted to a victory celebration for Byrnes. It was the high-water mark of Byrnes's relentless quest for what he dreamed would be a first-class ticket to the presidency. At the end of the dinner, when everyone was preparing to depart,

Hannegan remarked to Kelly, "Ed, there is one thing we forgot. The President said, 'Clear it with Sidney.'"[76] They regarded doing so as a formality.

———————

On the same night, at his suite in the Stevens Hotel, Truman was having a few drinks with Ed Harris, a reporter with the *St. Louis Post-Dispatch*. Harris asked Truman, supposedly off the record, whether he was in the running for the vice presidency. Having already committed himself to Byrnes, Truman bragged that he was sure he could "win the nomination" if he tried, but he did not want it. When the subject of Roosevelt's failing health came up, Harris recalled that Truman said, "The plain fact is, I don't want to be president." After a pause, he went on. "You want to know why?"[77] He reeled off a number of reasons, including being vilified for his previous association with the Pendergast machine, the failures of previous VPs who had succeeded to the presidency through death, and a vague statement that it would not be fair to his family.

Though Truman was not specific, it was the last reason—family—that explains why he was so emphatic about not vying for the vice presidency. To Truman, "family" was code for his wife, Elizabeth "Bess" Wallace Truman. Bess was by far the most important person in his life, and Truman could not afford to let his ambition for higher office harm her or his relationship with her. Mrs. Truman was deathly afraid that if her husband sought and captured the vice presidency, the secret she had harbored so long would become public. In 1903, Bess's father, David Wallace, a heavy drinker, had committed suicide by shooting himself in the temple when she was eighteen. In those days and up through the 1940s, suicide was considered a shameful sin, an act that disgraced the entire family. Truman knew that if the suicide story came out, he would be blamed, not only jeopardizing his cherished marriage to Bess but also endangering the health and perhaps the life of her elderly mother, who had been living with them in Washington.

Another secret that would likely be disclosed if Truman ran for the vice presidency was the fact that Bess and his sister, Mary Jane, were on his Senate payroll. When Bess was in Washington, she showed up at Truman's office two or three times per week and did little work. Mary Jane, who lived with and cared for Truman's mother in Grandview, Missouri, did virtually no work for the senator and had never been to Washington. Truman was very concerned that if the payroll issue surfaced, Bess's name would be sullied in the press and on radio and he would be blamed for his ethical lapse. To his close friends, Truman cited this as a justification for not wanting the vice presidency, though as it turned out nothing much came of it.

Beyond the secrets that might have been revealed, Truman knew that Bess abhorred the publicity that would surround them if her husband became vice president and then president. Probably because of the spotlight on and tabloid gossip about the Roosevelts for the past dozen years, she had come to dislike them and their patrician lifestyle, often criticizing their unconventional marriage and the serial divorces of their children. As if living in the White House might somehow spread a disease that would cause these moral shortcomings, Bess had come to dislike the presidency itself.

By all accounts Bess Truman had a much stronger emotional hold over her husband than he did over her. As their daughter, Margaret, wrote, her father craved her mother's "approval."[78] And by withholding her approval, as Bess did in the case of the vice presidency, she restrained his underlying political ambitions. Were it not for Bess, it is likely that Truman would have signaled a willingness to be considered for the vice presidency. Indeed, when the president at last made his decision and stuck to it, Truman's ambition would override his wife's resistance. He could have turned down the vice presidency, as Bess fervently desired, but as events unfolded, he would not do so. His decision would eventually result, as Margaret wrote, in "an emotional separation."[79]

For Byrnes, Roosevelt, and Truman, Monday, July 17, 1944, was a turning point. That morning, as Truman was working on his nomination speech for Byrnes, Ed Flynn arrived in Chicago and was told, "It's all over. It's Byrnes." As Flynn recalled, he was extremely upset, swearing and almost shouting, "The boss wanted Truman and Truman is the man." Later in the day, Bob Hannegan and Frank Walker met with Sidney Hillman in his suite at the Ambassador East Hotel. Their aim was to "clear" the Byrnes nomination with Sidney, as FDR had requested. It didn't take long for Hillman to make it clear that the CIO and the political action committee that he controlled—that is, a large segment of organized labor—were implacably opposed to having Jimmy Byrnes on the ticket. The reason? Byrnes would alienate labor and Blacks. Hillman's veto meant that Byrnes's chances for the vice presidency and his succession to the presidency were doomed. For the rest of his life, Byrnes believed it was Roosevelt who had used Hillman to knife him in the back. He was probably right. The White House log for the previous Thursday, July 13, shows that Hillman met alone with FDR. The president could have suggested or actually told Hillman directly that he should oppose Byrnes.

At about 6:45 that evening, Flynn, Hannegan, and Walker placed a call to the *Ferdinand Magellan*. After informing the president that Hillman would not support Byrnes, FDR pronounced Byrnes a "political liability." With Walker listening, Roosevelt ordered, "Frank, go all out for Truman."[80] Hannegan told Truman that night or perhaps the following morning what the president had said—that Truman was his choice. The senator had had enough experience with FDR to know that he could always change his mind and he often did. Indeed, as Truman had advised Hannegan when he was being considered to head the DNC in late 1943, one could not assume that a job dangled by Roosevelt was secure unless he "asks you directly."

There is no record of who the instigator was, but the next morning, Tuesday, Truman met Hillman for breakfast in the labor leader's suite. According to a 1949 interview, Truman informed Hillman that he intended to nominate Byrnes for vice president and he asked for Hillman's endorsement. Hillman, of course, declined and said labor was for Wallace. Then, seemingly out of nowhere, Hillman said that if it became necessary for Wallace to be passed over, there was another candidate that labor could support, and "I'm looking at the other one" right now. Truman might have been surprised, but as he later recalled, he coolly reacted by saying that he was "not running and that Byrnes was [still] my man."[81]

Why would Hillman have tilted toward Truman? Had he been tipped off by Hannegan or someone else—possibly Truman himself—that the senator was FDR's choice? Or had Roosevelt suggested during their meeting on July 13 that he should opt for Truman? Either explanation is plausible. However, Hillman's papers contain no clues.

Whoever or whatever caused Sidney Hillman to give his nod to Truman, the fact is that after the senator left Hillman's hotel room, he knew that he had labor's support and that he was the president's choice, unless of course FDR changed his mind. It was at this quintessential moment when Truman must have realized that the vice presidency, followed by the presidency, was within his grasp. And with this understanding, he knew he would have to decide either to accept the vice presidency if it was directly offered by the president or choose to remain in the Senate. Truman's concern for "family," meaning Bess, versus his ambition was about to be tested.

———

The day before the opening of the convention, the letter that FDR had promised Henry Wallace was released to the delegates and the press. It caused an uproar. In his letter, Roosevelt wrote that while it was the delegates "that must" make the decision, "I personally would vote for [Wallace's] renomination if I were a delegate to the convention."[82] Cleverly written, the letter was both an expression of loyalty to Wallace and his service as VP and a way of saying that the delegates should feel free to vote their conscience. It was not meant as an endorsement, though many delegates and newspapers treated it as such. Pulitzer Prize–winning author Allen Drury had a different view. He wrote that it was "the coolest and cruelest brushoff in all the long Roosevelt career."[83]

On Wednesday morning, day one of the twenty-ninth national convention of the Democratic Party, Byrnes officially dropped out of the race, citing the "wishes of the president."[84] Henry Wallace, who had just arrived, announced at a press conference, "I am in this fight to the finish." Asked about the letter from Roosevelt to the convention, Wallace confidently said that "the letter did exactly what I suggested."[85]

Since Truman was still refusing to announce his candidacy for the vice presidency, Hannegan made arrangements for a late-afternoon telephone call to the president's train in San Diego and summoned Truman to his rooms at the Blackstone Hotel. It was a setup. Based on his previous experience with Truman, Hannegan knew that Truman would have to hear directly from the president before he made up his mind. When the call was put through, Truman was sitting on one of the twin beds and Hannegan, with phone receiver in hand, was on the other. They were surrounded by Walker, Kelly, Flynn, Pauley, George Allen, and "Boss" Frank Hague of Jersey City. Hannegan held out the receiver so that everyone could hear.

As if it had been rehearsed with Hannegan, and it probably had been, the president began, his well-known voice filling the room, "Bob, have you got that fellow lined up yet?" Roosevelt had been told that Truman would be listening.

"No," replied Hannegan. "He is the contrariest goddamn mule from Missouri I ever dealt with."

"Well, you tell the Senator that if he wants to break up the Democratic party in the middle of the war, that's his responsibility." FDR banged down his receiver.

To Truman, Hannegan asked, "Now what do you say?"

As Truman remembered, he blurted out, "Jesus Christ!" Others who were there reported that he swore, "Oh shit." Truman walked around the room for a minute or so to gather his composure. Having made his decision, he was a bit more careful with his words: "Well, if that's the situation, I'll have to say yes. But why the hell didn't he tell me in the first place?"[86] This last remark was a tell. It suggests that all along Truman had been eager to run as VP if the president had only asked.

When Truman entered the room packed with the party leaders and saw or sensed that Hannegan was about to connect with the president, it would have been awkward, but if he felt strongly enough about his reasons for remaining in the Senate, he could have figured out a way to excuse himself from the gathering. However, once the president was on the phone and playing his "patriotic duty during the war" card, it was too late. Truman had to say yes. Whether he thought about Bess during those tense minutes is unknown.

By the time Truman made his fateful decision, the convention had already officially begun in the old Chicago Stadium, a barnlike venue that seated twenty-four thousand people and had room for about ten thousand more standing. A Gallup poll showed that 65 percent of Democrats supported Wallace for VP with only 2 percent for Truman. During a radio broadcast the day before, all of the pundits had predicted that Wallace would receive the nomination.

That night, Margaret, who had been sitting with her mother in the stadium gallery along with friends from home, wrote in her diary, "Ye gods! The Missouri delegation has decided to nominate Dad for V-P. Vice President Wallace is very strong so I doubt if we win, although the South doesn't want Wallace at all."[87] The words "we win" suggest that both Bess and Margaret, who had been staying in another hotel, were aware by then that "Dad" had decided that he would enter the race for the vice presidency with the objective of winning, notwithstanding all of his denials. The phrase "Ye gods!" with its exclamation point indicates that they were astonished at the prospect but does not reveal if they disapproved.

The next morning, Thursday, July 20, as the presidential nomination speeches were about to begin in Chicago, Roosevelt was getting ready to leave his train at Camp Pendleton, a marine base near San Diego, in order to observe amphibious-landing exercises. He "suddenly turned white," recalled his eldest son, Jimmy, a marine colonel who was the only one with him. Roosevelt groaned and said, "I don't know if I can make it. I have horrible pains." Jimmy wanted to call a doctor but FDR resisted, saying it was only indigestion. He asked his son to help him out of his bed and let him lie on the flat floor of the railroad car. "So for perhaps ten minutes," recalled Jimmy, "my father lay on the floor . . . his eyes closed, his face drawn, his powerful torso occasionally convulsed as the waves of pain stabbed him."[88] Eventually the pain and shaking subsided and Jimmy helped his father into his wheelchair. Before long, from a high bluff over the Pacific, the commander in chief would be filmed watching his marines storm the beach. The staged footage would be shown in movie theaters across the country, burnishing FDR's image as the only candidate in that election year who could win the war.

Meanwhile, in the cavernous Chicago Stadium, Vice President Wallace seconded FDR's nomination for president with a sensational speech "that riveted the delegates' attention," wrote *Time* magazine.[89] The speech triggered a long and boisterous demonstration that seemed to be more for Wallace than Roosevelt. The president won easily but an anti-Roosevelt group of Southern delegates cast eighty-nine votes for Senator Harry Byrd of Virginia, a harbinger of the future.

Just before the evening session, when the president was scheduled to deliver his acceptance speech via radio from the West Coast, Hannegan released the "Dear Bob" letter from Roosevelt saying that he would be "very glad to run" with either Truman or Douglas because they would bring "real strength to the ticket." Hannegan's objective was to make sure that the delegates and the press would interpret FDR's "strength to the ticket" phrase in the "Dear Bob" letter as more of an endorsement than the letter released to the convention the day before, in which Roosevelt wrote that if he "were a delegate" he would vote for Wallace.

That evening, from an observation car that had been attached to his train, the president delivered his acceptance speech, his disembodied but amplified voice floating in mellifluous tones throughout the stadium, which by then had been packed beyond its capacity by Wallace supporters. The speech was brief. "I shall not campaign in the usual sense, for the office," he intoned. "In these days of tragic sorrow, I do not consider it fitting. And besides, in these days of global warfare, I shall not find the time."[90] He kept this promise until the last month, October, when old Dr. Win-the-War found plenty of time and thought it more than fitting to get out on the hustings and campaign in the traditional way.

Among the many photographs taken of Roosevelt while giving his speech, one depicted him with his mouth hanging open, slack-jawed, haggard, and gaunt, while hunched over the microphone. The photo, which ran in newspapers across the country, made Roosevelt out as a frail old man who could not possibly carry on for another year, much less a four-year term. Moreover, when the photo appeared uncropped in *Life* magazine, a doctor at the Mayo Clinic recognized Dr. Bruenn sitting near the president while he was giving his speech. Within days, Bruenn was outed as FDR's "heart specialist."[91] Republicans exploited the death mask photo, thus undermining the image of FDR high on a bluff above the Pacific, commanding his troops and brilliantly orchestrating the global war.

Seconds after the applause for the president's acceptance speech died down, a preplanned chant took hold on the floor and then spread throughout the stadium, becoming louder and more persistent. "We want Wallace! We want Wallace!" The organ sprang to life, playing "The Song of Iowa," about Wallace's home state. Hundreds of Wallace posters were waved above the crowd. Parades and conga lines began to form. Though the schedule called for the vice presidential nominations to take place the next day, the Wallace supporters had launched what was called, in political convention parlance, a "stampede"—an attempt to ram through an immediate vote of the delegates that would renominate Wallace as FDR's running mate.

The party bosses knew what was happening. Ed Pauley made the first move. "Stop the organ," he bellowed to a convention official.[92] Mayor Kelly informed Hannegan that he had the power to declare that the vastly overcrowded stadium must be evacuated and closed down as a fire hazard. Hannegan deputized the future mayor of Pittsburgh, David Lawrence, to move for adjournment but he first had to be recognized by the convention chair, Indiana senator Sam Jackson, who was on the platform below the podium. Hannegan could see Senator Claude Pepper of Florida, one of Wallace's floor generals, elbowing through the boisterous crowd toward the platform, on his way to move for an immediate vote on the VP nomination. Hannegan screamed at Jackson, "You get up there"—on the podium—"and I mean now, and recognize Dave Lawrence, or I'll do it for you!"[93] As Pepper was mounting the stairs, Jackson obeyed the DNC chair's order. He recognized Lawrence, allowed him to move to adjourn until the next morning, and called for a voice vote by the delegates of the ayes and nays. Though their voices could not be heard above the din, Jackson ruled, "That's it," meaning Lawrence's motion carried. By then, Pepper was at the top step. As Jackson was announcing that the convention would be in recess until 11:30 the next morning, Wallace supporters roared, "No, no, no, no."[94]

That evening there was speculation by the delegates and party bosses over how the news from Japan and Germany might affect voters in November. Earlier that day they had learned that an attempt on Hitler's life had nearly succeeded when a bomb planted by Colonel Claus von Stauffenberg, a highly placed German officer, exploded near the führer while he was conferring with his battle commanders. Hitler suffered burns and minor injuries but was well enough to assure his people by radio broadcast that the "criminally stupid officers" behind the plot would be quickly rounded up and eliminated.[95] Added to this electrifying development was the news from the previous day that the Japanese government had collapsed following the resignation of Hideki Tojo, the militarist Japanese premier, due to the fall of Saipan, which meant that American B-29s would soon be in range of the Japanese home islands. These two incidents fueled hopes among those at the convention that, with the leadership of their enemies in disarray, the war would be over before the end of 1944. While that would certainly have been a happy prospect for most, many of the Democratic politicos at the convention feared that American voters might turn at the last minute to Tom Dewey, their vigorous young opponent. Indeed, it later came out that FDR had confided to General MacArthur in Hawaii that "if the war against Germany ends before the election," he expected to lose.[96]

On the final day of the convention, Friday, July 21, the political bosses were in control. Beginning in the morning and through the midafternoon, they fanned out to the key state delegations. Their message was that Roosevelt wanted Truman not because he was the most qualified or would be the best president. No, their argument was that Franklin Roosevelt, the greatest vote getter in U.S. history, was "convinced that Truman would cost him less votes than any other candidate."[97] Knowing that Wallace would beat Truman on the first ballot, Hannegan and the party leaders wanted to deny Wallace a majority and force a second ballot by urging state delegations to vote for their favorite sons and to otherwise allow Wallace supporters to have their way. Since there were at least a dozen favorite sons, Wallace did not win a majority, but he came close. By the time the first ballot was completed and the votes counted, it was past six o'clock.

Ordinarily the convention, which had been going on for almost seven hours, would have adjourned for dinner, followed by a night session. However, Hannegan made a shrewd move. To prevent another Wallace stampede, he ordered convention chairman Jackson to announce that the second ballot would begin immediately. Hannegan did this so that hundreds of Wallace supporters, who had planned to demonstrate that evening in advance of the second ballot, could not gain access to the stadium because their tickets were valid only for the night session.

There were a couple of blips at the outset, but for the most part, the favorite sons began breaking for Truman on the second ballot. Governor Herbert O'Conor of Maryland was the first, followed by Oklahoma governor Robert Kerr, who had delivered the convention's keynote speech. "Under the unit rule," he declared, "Oklahoma casts twenty-two votes for Truman."[98] At that point, wrote Turner Catledge in the *New York Times*, "word flashed around the hall" that other favorite sons "were to follow in line to the Truman side and the avalanche started."[99] Up in the gallery, Margaret reveled in the pandemonium as the tide turned to her father, "but Mother was barely able to muster a smile," she recalled.[100]

Thanks to Chicago mayor Ed Kelly, who held his state's delegation together, the nomination went to Truman when Illinois abandoned Scott Lucas, its favorite son, and threw all fifty-eight of its votes to the man from Missouri. At 8:13 p.m. Wallace's Iowa delegation moved that the nomination of Harry S. Truman for vice president be made unanimous. The actual tally was 1,031 votes for Truman and 105 for Wallace.

BBC reporter Alistair Cooke found himself standing next to Truman at a concession stand behind the stage when the voice of Samuel Jackson, shouting to be to be heard above the roar of the crowd, called out for the second time, "Will the next Vice President come to the rostrum?" Truman was in the process of ordering a Coca-Cola and a hot dog. According to Cooke, Truman turned around and said, "By golly, that's me!" and he dashed off.

Truman's off-the-cuff acceptance speech was possibly the shortest in convention history, less than a minute. Dressed nattily in a blue double-breasted suit and a polka-dot bow tie, his rimmed glasses glinting in the bright lights, Truman stood before the bank of microphones, waiting patiently for the applause to subside. In a "halting and shy manner," wrote Turner Catledge, Truman said he accepted the nomination with "all humility" and was "perfectly willing" to take on the "great responsibility" that it entailed. Without having the slightest foretaste of all that would be demanded of him, he pledged to do everything in his power to help "shorten the war and to win the peace."[101] It was the *St. Louis Post-Dispatch* that picked up his closing line, the only newspaper that did: "Now give me a chance."[102]

As thousands spilled out of Chicago Stadium that night into the July heat, scores of well-wishers, reporters, and photographers surrounded Truman, Bess, and Margaret, blocking their path to a limousine that was assigned to take them to the Morrison Hotel, where Bess and Margaret were staying. People were trying to grab their arms, shake their hands, even hug them. Flashbulbs popped, temporarily blinding them. Bess was unhappy. Harry had to ask policemen to form a wedge to help them get through to the curb. Once inside the limousine, Bess leaned toward Harry and said, as Margaret later wrote, "Are we going to have to go through this all for the rest of our lives?" Harry said nothing, though he actually enjoyed the adulation of crowds.

On the long drive home to Independence, the mood was "arctic," wrote Margaret. "Dad tried to be cheerful and philosophic simultaneously. Mother said little."[103] The tectonic plates of their marriage had shifted. While Harry was elated over how far he had come and how close he was to reaching the highest office in the land, his partner of twenty-five years was bitter, failing to comprehend why he couldn't have just said no. It was almost as if Bess had caught her husband having an affair, only to her his sin was not another woman but unbridled lust for more power. To Harry, a politician to the core, the lure of the presidency was irresistible even if it meant a measure of emotional distance from Bess.

Chapter 3

Best He Could Do

When Harry Truman was asleep in Chicago around 3:00 on the morning following his nomination, the fourteen-thousand-ton battle-scarred heavy cruiser USS *Baltimore* nosed out of San Diego Bay, bound for Oahu. Always mindful of sailors' superstition about Friday departures, the president had ordered the captain of the warship to delay the voyage until a few minutes after midnight on Saturday, July 22, 1944, Pacific War Time (West Coast time). Roosevelt's party included, among others, Drs. Bruenn and McIntire; Admiral Leahy, the president's chief of staff; speechwriter Sam Rosenman; and Fala, who would not be allowed to leave the ship in Hawaii due to quarantine regulations. The other chiefs of staff—Marshall, Arnold, and Admiral Ernest King—had been left behind. The ostensible purpose of the trip was to afford the commander in chief an opportunity to personally mediate a major strategic dispute between General Douglas MacArthur and Admiral Chester Nimitz and to speak to ground, air, and navy forces on Oahu and later in Alaska on the trip back to the States. Another objective, left unsaid, was to provide the ailing president with five days of shipboard rest before tackling the egos and intellects of his two top commanders in the Pacific.

During the three-thousand-nautical-mile crossing, Fala received unwanted attention from the *Baltimore*'s sailors. They clipped locks of lush black hair from the coat of Roosevelt's famous companion to be displayed as souvenirs to the folks back home. It was Sam Rosenman who was told to put a stop to it. "The poor dog was in danger of being completely shorn," he wrote.[1]

W hile the president rested, read, and slept in the captain's quarters and was rarely seen on deck, Truman, with Bess and Margaret, by then was back at home in Independence delivering speeches and pep talks at campaign rallies for the mayor of Independence, who was running for governor, and for Missouri senator Bennett Clark, who was trying to get reelected. Both lost in the August 1 primaries. On one of those days, an older relative told Margaret that she needed to know that her grandfather had committed suicide, since the story was sure to come out during her father's campaign. Margaret was extremely upset, having never been told the truth. When she went to her father with the story, he was furious, grabbing Margaret's arm and saying, "Don't you *ever* mention that to your mother."[2] And she never did.

R oosevelt was up on the bridge with Dr. Bruenn and a couple of admirals when the *Baltimore* approached the pier at the navy yard in Pearl Harbor at about 3 p.m. on July 26. They had passed by dozens of warships and more than a hundred support vessels, with sailors lining the rails in gleaming whites. Two and a half years after the Japanese attack, FDR was pleased to see that Pearl Harbor had become the epicenter of overwhelming American power in the Pacific. Silver-haired Admiral Nimitz had already come aboard, having arrived by launch to greet the president personally, along with his top officers. After docking at the pier, a half hour passed with no sign of General MacArthur at the quayside, though his B-17 had landed an hour earlier following a twenty-six-hour flight from

Brisbane. "Where's Douglas?" FDR asked Nimitz.[3] Suddenly, a large red open touring car, with sirens wailing, pulled up beside the *Baltimore*. Notwithstanding the heat, MacArthur, attired in a heavy leather bomber jacket, emerged from the auto and charged up the gangplank to greet the president. They had not seen each other for seven years. Roosevelt could not resist ribbing the general: "Doug, what are you doing with that leather jacket on? It's darn hot today." MacArthur replied, "Well, I've just landed from Australia. It's pretty cold up there."[4]

In his memoir, MacArthur wrote that he was "shocked" by the president's "appearance . . . physically just a shell of the man I had known."[5] He would remark to his own physician after he returned to Australia, "Doc, the mark of death is upon him! In six months he'll be in his grave."[6]

The next day, after Roosevelt spent more than six hours touring and inspecting Oahu's military bases and hospitals, with plenty of photo ops for the coming presidential campaign, MacArthur and Nimitz, plus Admirals Leahy and Halsey, dined with the president at his temporary quarters, the palatial Holmes Estate overlooking Waikiki Beach. When coffee was served, the president escorted them to a conference room next door, where a ten-foot-high map of the Pacific had been hung. Once they settled into bamboo chairs, Roosevelt teed up the key question that they had all journeyed thousands of miles to resolve: "Where do we go from here?"[7] In other words, what should be the next major move by the vast armada of American land, air, and naval forces arrayed in the Pacific? Looking at the wall map, Roosevelt aimed a long pointer at New Guinea, where MacArthur's Southwest Pacific forces were clustered, and then moved the pointer north to the Mariana Islands in the Central Pacific, where Nimitz's forces were gathered. Thus began a surprisingly calm and professional discussion, led by the president's astute questioning, that went on until midnight. "It remained on a friendly basis the entire time," recalled Admiral Leahy.[8]

Nimitz's strategy, which was dictated by his boss, Admiral King, was to bypass the Philippines, strike due west across the Pacific, and invade Formosa (today Taiwan). Since Formosa was closer to Japan than the Philippines, argued Nimitz, his forces could take the fight more quickly to the Japanese home islands by airpower, invasion, and blockade. Nimitz's plan, of course, meant that MacArthur's theater would be reduced to nothing more than a backwater.

Speaking without notes, MacArthur delivered an eloquent and persuasive presentation. The Philippine archipelago must be liberated first, he argued. It was both a moral imperative and a military necessity. Because the Philippines had been governed for years by the U.S. and had been promised their sovereignty by act of Congress, the loyal Filipinos looked to America as their "mother country." To bypass and abandon them, along with hundreds of starving American POWs, to the brutal rule of the Japanese army, contended MacArthur, would be a "blot on American honor."[9] Moreover, he argued, the northern Philippine island of Luzon was more important from a military standpoint than Formosa because it would give MacArthur's air and naval forces control over the South China Sea—and the ability to interdict shipments of oil and vital supplies from Japan's southern conquests to their home islands. Also, he added, Luzon had to be invaded and captured because otherwise it would be used by Japanese bombers to launch attacks on Nimitz's task forces on their way to Formosa and elsewhere.

Before adjourning for the evening, MacArthur stole a private moment with the president. He warned Roosevelt that he would pay a price at the ballot box in November if the Filipinos were abandoned and American survivors of the Bataan Death March were slaughtered.

The back-and-forth continued the next morning. Nimitz conceded that MacArthur would have to at least take Luzon in order to protect his flank, while MacArthur gave up the idea of invading the southern Philippine island of Mindanao, where there were more than sixty thousand Japanese troops. MacArthur argued forcefully that the conquest of Formosa would spill more blood and would take much longer than it would take him to conquer Leyte and Luzon. Eventually, Nimitiz's differences with MacArthur narrowed to relative insignificance. Pressed by Roosevelt, Nimitz admitted that he did not disagree with MacArthur's revised plan to liberate the Philippines. By noon when they adjourned, a consensus had emerged. MacArthur would return to the Philippines as he had famously promised to do in 1942. Nimitz would establish airfields on Guam and the Marianas to accommodate the new long-range B-29 bombers, set up a forward headquarters in the Central Pacific, continue to degrade the Japanese fleet, and plan the invasions of Iwo Jima, Okinawa, and possibly Formosa.

The president's handling of Nimitz and MacArthur was masterful. Having conserved his energy aboard the *Baltimore*, he rose to the occasion, remaining focused throughout while tactfully converting the two highly intelligent rivals into teammates who would work together to defeat Japan. MacArthur praised Nimitz for "his fine sense of fair play" and FDR for conducting himself as a "neutral" "chairman." Leahy concluded that FDR had been "at his best."[10]

Before departing Hawaii for Alaska, the president had one of his Secret Service men wheel him through a navy hospital ward that contained several amputees. No photos of FDR in that little bamboo-seated chair with wheels were allowed. When he stopped to smile and offer private words of encouragement at their bedsides, they were astonished to see that their president's legs were lifeless. Sam Rosenman, who accompanied FDR, wrote that Roosevelt wanted the servicemen to know that "he was living proof of what the human spirit could do to conquer the incapacities of the human body." Rosenman had never seen "Roosevelt with tears in his eyes," but that day, "as he was wheeled out of the hospital he was close to them."[11]

———

On the voyage north to the Aleutians, the president received a cable reporting that Marguerite "Missy" LeHand, his totally devoted secretary, trusted adviser, and close companion for almost twenty years, had died at age forty-seven from cerebral thrombosis. Missy had spent two winters in 1926 and 1927 with FDR, living with him aboard a rickety old houseboat that cruised the warm waters of the Caribbean, a time when Roosevelt was still hoping he could restore life to his useless legs. Missy had been "one of the most important people of the Roosevelt era . . . the frankest of the President's associates," wrote Rosenman.[12] FDR mourned in silence, her death undoubtedly taking a toll on his own health.

To navigate the Inside Passage southbound from Juneau along the coastline into the navy yard at Bremerton, Washington, the president and his party left the *Baltimore* and sailed aboard the USS *Cummings*, a much smaller destroyer. During the last two days of the voyage, FDR dictated a speech, a nationwide address that he was scheduled to make upon arrival at Bremerton, the first time Americans would hear his voice since his acceptance speech at the Democratic convention on July 20. Ordinarily, such a speech would have been drafted by Sam Rosenman and revised several times by the two of them. However, because Rosenman had already flown back to the States, Roosevelt had to prepare it himself. FDR revised it only once and did not rehearse. "It deserved more attention than that," wrote Rosenman after he had heard the speech delivered.[13]

On August 12 at about 5 p.m., the president gripped a lectern at the rear of a gun turret on the forecastle deck of the *Cummings*, which was docked in Bremerton. He was standing, his legs and waist encased in loose-fitting heavy steel braces that dug painfully into his flesh. It had been almost a year since he had worn those braces. The *Cummings* was rocking due to a brisk wind that made it difficult for him to maintain his balance and to keep the pages of his speech from blowing off the podium. Mike Reilly, who was there, wrote later that Roosevelt's speech "was the poorest of his life . . . dull and wandering" and "even the magnificent Roosevelt delivery was missing."[14] A *Washington Post* reporter wrote: "It looked like the old master has lost his touch. His campaigning days must be over. It's going to look mighty sad when he begins to trade punches with a young Dewey."[15] FDR's gaunt appearance due to the loss of thirty pounds during the past six months no doubt influenced the negative reporting of his Bremerton speech.

In addition to FDR's rambling delivery and lack of substance, about ten minutes into his thirty-five-minute speech, he began experiencing excruciating chest pains that radiated into his shoulders. A recently discovered grainy photograph shows Anna Roosevelt, who had been summoned from Seattle to attend her father's speech, staring anxiously around the corner of the gun turret at Roosevelt, an unmistakable look of alarm on her face. The pain went on for fifteen minutes but Roosevelt never flinched. Dr. Bruenn later told an interviewer that the president "kept on with the speech," then "came below and said 'I had a helluva pain.' We stripped him down in the cabin of the ship, took a cardiogram." Bruenn's diagnosis: "a transient episode, a so-called angina, not a myocardial infarction," which could have led to death. "It was, nevertheless proof positive that he had coronary disease, no question about it."

————————

W hen the president was touring bases and talking to troops in the Aleutian Islands and on Alaska's mainland, Truman headed back to Washington from Independence. Changing trains at Union Station in St. Louis, he ran into presidential candidate Tom Dewey as he and his campaign aides were arriving. "Not more than ten people" were there to meet him, wrote Truman to Margaret, while "more came and spoke to your dad accidentally. . . . I just now thought of its significance." He warned her that "this is going to be a tough, dirty campaign and you've got to help your dad, protect your good mamma."[16]

But before Truman could focus on the campaign, he had to bid a bittersweet farewell to a closely knit group of senators and staff that he had bonded with since 1941. It was then, before the Pearl Harbor attack, when he had come up with the idea of forming a bipartisan Special Committee to Investigate the National Defense Program. Truman owed his prominence in the Senate and arguably the vice presidential nomination itself to the diligence and support of his committee. His investigators had saved the taxpayers $10 to $15 billion in military spending, though he got most of the credit. As noted earlier, in May 1943, the craggy face of "Investigator Truman" appeared on the cover of *Time* magazine. Based on a survey of Washington journalists, *Look* magazine named Truman one of the ten most valuable civilians to help the war effort, the only member of Congress on the list. Truman knew that his members and staff were responsible for his success and he hated to leave them. But he had little choice. If he stayed on as chair during the coming campaign, he would politicize the committee. He had to resign.

It was an emotional moment for Truman when he gathered the senators in suite 240 of the old Senate Office Building to tell them he had to "quit" the committee. In a letter to Bess, he wrote that the Republican members, particularly Senator Harold Burton of Ohio, urged him not to resign. Truman used the word "blubber" in his letter as a substitute for tears and it is not clear whether he meant his or theirs.[17] A few days later, on August 7, Truman officially announced his resignation with a speech on the floor of the Senate. Truman quipped that the Senate had passed a resolution that "makes me a close relative of Christ."[18] The next day he went down to room 160, where he explained to his staff why he had to resign. A member of his seventeen-person staff, Walter Hehmeyer, recalled that after Truman spoke to the group, "he shook hands with every single person in the room including the office boy. . . . This is the kind of man Truman was. . . . It was just very personal . . . the kind of thing that endeared the people that worked for Truman . . . he was very genuine."[19]

Truman might have been revered by his fellow senators, but he was resented by Black Americans and the Black press because, as the new VP nominee, he had replaced their hero Henry Wallace. For years, Wallace had been publicly denouncing racism and calling for political and economic equality between the races. In an interview reported by the Blackowned *Pittsburgh Courier* on August 5, Truman said that he had always been for "equality of opportunity . . . in working conditions and political rights" and that the "Negro in the armed forces" ought to have the "same treatment and opportunities" enjoyed by white members. His main point, however, was that the election was not about him. Rather, "the real issue is the reelection of the greatest living friend of the Negro people. Franklin Roosevelt."[20]

———

At half past noon on August 18, vice presidential candidate Harry Truman, who had been with Bob Hannegan and others at the Mayflower Hotel, walked the four and a half blocks to the White House front gate. He had been invited to meet FDR for lunch. The morning before, the president, accompanied by his daughter, Anna, had arrived from the West Coast after a six-week absence. Roosevelt had traveled 13,912 miles by train, ship, and auto. Whether it was FDR's idea, Anna's, or a political adviser's, it had been decided that it was time for a photo op and a conversation with his running mate, whom he barely knew. Except for one other occasion near the end of the campaign, this was to be the only face-to-face meeting of FDR and Truman between the convention and the inauguration.

When Truman was greeted by Roosevelt in the Oval Office, "you'd have thought I was the long lost brother or the returned Prodigal," he wrote Bess. "I told him how I appreciated his putting the finger on me for Vice President."[21] Because Truman had not seen FDR for at least a year, he was stunned by the other man's haggard appearance, telling Harry Vaughan afterward that the president was mentally okay, "but physically he's just going to pieces."[22] There is no record of the president's impression of Truman. Most likely he was focused on simply trying to put his third running mate at ease with his legendary charm. Truman was most impressed when FDR presented him with a rose to give to Bess, who was back in Independence. Aside from cabinet meetings "where Roosevelt never discussed anything important," recalled Truman, he saw FDR only twice between the convention and the inauguration.[23]

After a press conference about the campaign, they went outside into what Truman called the "backyard" of the White House, that is, the South Lawn, where a table had been set under an oak tree alleged by Truman to have been planted by "old Andy Jackson." As soon as they shed their coats and sat down in their shirtsleeves, "the flashlight boys," meaning the photographers, swarmed around them.[24] A famous close-up shows Roosevelt in a trim bow tie and a monogrammed white shirt, with a bloodstone signet ring inherited from his father on his left pinkie, dark circles under his eyes. He was gazing pleasantly not at Truman but across the table. Seated to his right, Truman, looking robust and younger than his sixty years, was wearing a striped shirt and a long, wide tie. His warm smile was directed at Anna Boettiger, who had been cropped out of the photo. The contrast in appearance between the aging Northeastern blue blood and the ex-haberdasher from Middle America was striking.

Appearance was one thing, but the differences in life experience that the two politicians brought to the table that day were legion—too numerous to recount. One difference, however, is worth pointing out because it has to do with making major decisions. Noted for his "heavily forested interior," FDR masked his thoughts and feelings. Even his closest advisers did not know what was going on in his head because he often made creative connections among unrelated concepts and ideas. He was an abstract thinker who trusted his instincts without regard to consistency. FDR once described himself as a "juggler," never letting his right hand know what his left hand was doing.[25] His decisions were typically made on his own.

Truman's thought processes were decidedly different. He was a linear thinker, usually predictable and consistent. His strength was his ability to cut through complex problems and view them in simple terms. Except at the beginning of his presidency, when he made snap decisions to appear decisive and tough, Truman was deliberative, using reason and logic to arrive at his decisions. He absorbed information by listening to his advisers whether they agreed with him or not. He rarely moved precipitously. And when he delivered a decision, he was blunt and straightforward, unlike Roosevelt, who was subtle and devious. Truman was all about order, coherence, efficiency, and collegiality.

They were alike, however, in two significant respects—courage and extraordinary optimism. Each had faced struggles with courage: FDR fighting polio and Truman surviving the Argonne, debt, and the Pendergast stigma. And each possessed faith in human progress.

Lunch was prepared by Henrietta Nesbitt, the Roosevelts' White House cook, whose meals were regarded as the worst in Washington. The fare that day was roast sardines on toast, mixed vegetable salad, and pickled clingstone peaches, followed by a demitasse (Truman called it a "teaspoon full of coffee"). In his letter to Bess, Truman wrote that the president "gave me a lot of hooey about what I could do to help in the campaign."[26] In fact, FDR told Truman to go home to accept the official notification of the VP nomination and deliver a Labor Day speech in Detroit but not anything more until they conferred again. According to the diary of Vic Housholder, a close WWI friend of Truman's, Roosevelt asked Truman to "promise" him that he wouldn't "do any flying" until after the fall campaign began. When Truman said he liked to fly because it allowed him to cover more ground, FDR responded, "Harry, I'm not a well man, we cannot be sure of my future."[27] This was the only time when Roosevelt admitted that he might not survive a fourth term.

At some point during the lunch, FDR revealed what he thought was the best-kept secret in Washington. He told Truman about the atomic bomb but not the details. This is at odds with the statement made by

Truman in his memoirs that he knew nothing about the bomb until Secretary of War Henry Stimson informed him after being sworn in as president. In fact, Truman had known about the nuclear bomb project even before his lunch meeting with FDR through his investigators on the Truman Committee.[28] In his oral history, Walter Hehmeyer, one of Truman's investigators, said that "just about every staff member on the Truman Committee knew about the development of the atomic bomb, that such a project was underway."[29]

As instructed by FDR, on August 31 Truman went home to officially receive "notification" of the vice presidential nomination, his first speech of the campaign of 1944. "Home" was Lamar, Missouri, Truman's birthplace, though he had no memory of it because his family had moved north shortly after he was born. Until the civil rights era in the 1960s, Lamar was known as a "sundown town," one of thousands of small cities throughout America where the all-white citizens barred African Americans from entering after dark, often posting warning signs at the city limits. "Everyone who had a few spare gallons of gas for dozens of miles around poured into the little town" to see her father, wrote Margaret Truman, though it is doubtful that any African Americans saw and heard Truman's speech because it was not delivered until darkness had fallen.[30] Accompanied by Senator Tom Connally (D-TX) and no fewer than eight other U.S. senators, Truman stood in front of Lamar's "old red-brick courthouse" and told the crowd of at least seven thousand (estimates went as high as twenty thousand) that they "can't afford to take a chance" on Dewey, the GOP standard-bearer. "You should endorse tried and experienced leadership," he thundered, words that would become the theme of the coming campaign.[31] Truman introduced his mother, Martha Ellen Truman, as "Mamma" and invited her to say a few words. "Am I proud of him?" she began. "Say, I knew that boy would amount to something when he was nine years old. He could plow the straightest row of corn in the county. He could sow wheat so there wasn't a bare spot in the whole field."[32]

Eleven days later Roosevelt was again on the move, demonstrating to American voters that he was busy running the war. Following a visit with

Lucy Mercer at her English manor house in Allamuchy Township, New Jersey, and a five-day rest in Hyde Park, he was on his way to meet Churchill and his military chiefs for a conference at the Citadel and Château Frontenac in Quebec City. Just before his departure, FDR "felt just tired, not up to anything," wrote cousin Daisy.[33] When the prime minister's train pulled into Wolfe's Cove, Quebec, the president, sporting a wide-brimmed panama hat, was waiting in an open car to greet his friend as he stepped off the train wielding a cane. "I'm glad to see you," he called out to Churchill, adding, "Eleanor is here." Clementine Churchill, who had spotted the First Lady, shouted, "Hello there!"[34]

The two wives would shop together and take trips to the countryside but, as Eleanor complained, "our duties are all social . . . it seems like such a waste of time."[35] Referring to her conversations with the prime minister, Eleanor wrote that "he feels women should be seen and not heard on any subject of public interest."[36]

For a change, debates over military strategy did not dominate this conference. The Allies were advancing on almost all fronts. "Victory is everywhere," exclaimed Churchill to the press, although privately he was not as optimistic as the American leaders, who were beginning to believe the war in Europe would be over by the end of 1944.[37] As it turned out, there were two interrelated issues that absorbed the most attention at the conference: the dire financial condition of Great Britain and the treatment of Germany after the war.

Treasury Secretary Henry Morgenthau, Roosevelt's close friend and neighbor in Dutchess County, had returned in August from a trip to meet Churchill and told the president that Britain was virtually bankrupt and needed an extension of Lend-Lease and a major loan "to put her back on her feet" for the sake of "a permanent world peace." Morgenthau called the financial package "Lend-Lease II." Thus, on September 12, the second day of the Quebec conference, FDR was not surprised when Churchill said that "one of the most important things I have to discuss with you is Stage II [the British term for Lend-Lease II]."[38] Since Churchill knew that Secretary Morgenthau supported such relief, he urged Roosevelt to summon Morgenthau to the conference. FDR was happy to do so because he too believed in keeping Britain strong enough to police postwar Europe.

At dinner on the evening of September 13, with Lend-Lease II negotiations yet to be finalized, the "only subject of conversation," wrote Lord Moran, was a plan "to prevent another war with Germany."[39] Weeks earlier, Morgenthau and senior Treasury Department official Harry Dexter White, who would later be accused of being a Soviet spy, had worked up a comprehensive plan that was titled "A Program to Prevent Germany from Starting World War III." Asked by Roosevelt to outline the plan at the dinner, Secretary Morgenthau explained—White was not there—that the program, later known as the "Morgenthau Plan," envisioned the complete deindustrialization of postwar Germany, turning the nation into an agrarian economy so that its people could never rearm. In particular, he said, the steel mills in the Ruhr and Saar, munitions plants, and manufacturing centers throughout Germany should be dismantled, if not already destroyed in the war. Germany's eighty million people should be forced to survive on food produced on their farms. Churchill was violently opposed. He angrily erupted, "I'm all for disarming Germany, but we ought not prevent her from living decently. . . . The English people will not stand for the policy you are advocating. . . . You cannot indict a whole nation." The president "mostly listened." (He had once remarked "that a factory which made steel furniture could be turned overnight to war production.") Because FDR had invited Morgenthau to hold forth, it was apparent to those at the dinner that he supported the Morgenthau Plan. After three hours, the dinner ended with an "absolute cleavage" between Churchill and the Americans.[40]

The next morning, Lord Cherwell, Churchill's adviser, somehow persuaded the prime minister that the Morgenthau Plan would not result in starvation of the German people and that their standard of living in an agrarian economy would actually be higher than it had been under the Nazis. To Morgenthau's "amazement," Churchill agreed to reconsider his opposition, provided some of the plan's draconian provisions were softened.[41] That afternoon, September 14, Churchill met with Roosevelt, expecting that Lend-Lease II was to be finalized. Instead, FDR delayed initialing the memorandum of understanding. It is entirely possible if not likely that the president's delay was due to the fact that Churchill was still trying to soften the Morgenthau Plan and was not yet fully aboard. It appeared that Roosevelt was using Lend-Lease II as a bargaining chip to cause the prime minister to sign on to the Morgenthau Plan. In any event, Churchill, who was desperate for the aid to his people and outraged at FDR's delay, could not contain himself. He burst out, "What must I do? Get on my hind legs and beg like Fala?"[42]

At noon on the fifteenth, in the presence of Morgenthau and Foreign Secretary Anthony Eden, Roosevelt and Churchill closed the deal. After reading the Lend-Lease II agreement and making one change, the president affixed his initials. It consisted of a write-off of Britain's Lend-Lease debt and a $3 billion loan. "Churchill was quite emotional and at one time had tears in his eyes," wrote Morgenthau in his diary, and he thanked Roosevelt "most effusively." Then Churchill proceeded to dictate aloud what became the final memorandum that essentially restated the substance of the Morgenthau Plan with only a few minor revisions. When he finished, Eden was "quite shocked" and said, "You can't do this. After all, you and I publicly have said quite the opposite." They argued at length. It ended when Churchill said, "The future of my people is at stake, and when I have to choose between my people and the German people, I am going to choose my people."[43] Both Roosevelt and Churchill initialed the memorandum.

The life of the Morgenthau Plan was shorter than that left to the president. Back in Washington, when Secretary of War Henry Stimson learned that Roosevelt and Churchill had signed on to the plan in Quebec, he was appalled at the "Carthaginian attitude" of Morgenthau, White, and their colleagues at the Treasury Department. "It is Semitism gone wild for vengeance . . . and will lay the seeds for another war in the next generation." He believed that preservation of the Ruhr and the Saar industrial areas was key to the recovery of Europe and that there was not nearly enough farmland in the new boundaries of Germany to feed its population. [44]

The opinion of Henry Stimson, whom historian David Schmitz called the "First Wise Man," initially annoyed Roosevelt but it could not be ignored.[45] At age seventy-seven, Stimson, a Republican internationalist, had been at the center of American power for forty years as secretary of war under Taft and secretary of state under Hoover before Roosevelt had had the wisdom in 1940 to bring him back to Washington to be his secretary of war.

It did not take long for the Morgenthau Plan to be leaked to the press and for GOP presidential candidate Dewey to begin making it into a campaign issue. Hammered by claims that the plan threatened to starve the German people and prolong the war by stiffening resistance, Roosevelt realized he was in trouble and looked for a way out. In a meeting with War Secretary Stimson on October 3, a month before the election, he blamed Morgenthau, telling Stimson with a "naughty" grin that "Henry Morgenthau pulled a boner," an expression of the day derived from the word "bonehead," meaning a stupid mistake. Stimson was not about to let FDR off so easily. He produced a copy of the Morgenthau Plan memorandum dictated by Churchill in Quebec, read him a few sentences, and pointed to the initials "O.K. F.D.R." The president was "not a man to get flustered," recalled Stimson, but he was "perfectly staggered" and said, "I have not the faintest recollection of this at all."[46]

Whether the president's memory had been affected by his "fatigue and illness," which Stimson had noticed "for the first time," or whether he was lying in order to disassociate himself from what had become an unpopular and ill-advised position will never be known.[47] What is known is that the Morgenthau Plan would be consigned to a dusty file cabinet somewhere in the Treasury Department, as if it had never existed. At a press conference days later, FDR claimed falsely that "every story that came out" about the Morgenthau Plan "was essentially untrue in its basic facts."[48]

———

For Harry Truman, the 1944 campaign began in earnest in early October when he and his small staff boarded a sleeper–dining car and departed on a 7,500-mile tour west through Texas to the Pacific coast, then back east across the Midwest to Boston and New York. The theme of Truman's fifty-four speeches, dictated by the DNC, was that the country needed Roosevelt's experience and leadership to win the war and secure the peace. In other words, the president was indispensable. This was not the time to change horses.

To the press and many observers, Truman's speeches were dull and unexciting, probably because he did not directly attack Dewey and the Republicans. He was not the colorful and pugnacious "Give 'em hell, Harry" campaigner that he would later become. Meanwhile, with more than a hint that FDR might die in office, the GOP opposition mounted vicious attacks against Truman, mainly focusing on his past association with the Kansas City Pendergast machine. The anti-Roosevelt *Chicago Tribune* labeled Truman as "the tool of Boss Pendergast in looting Kansas City's county government . . . and apologist in the Senate for political gangsters."[49] One morning when Truman was in Peoria, Illinois, the Hearst newspapers published a story that he had been a member of the Ku Klux Klan. His advisers were beside themselves. Truman confidently denied the story, knowing that the Klan had opposed him when he was running for Jackson County judge in 1926. While the Klan story soon lost its legs, GOP congresswoman Clare Boothe Luce, the wife of *Time* magazine's publisher, struck a nerve when she began calling Mrs. Truman "payroll Bess" for having received a salary while doing little work on Truman's Senate staff. Fortunately, the fact that Bess's father had committed suicide never came out during the campaign.

When Truman ended his vice presidential campaign with a speech in early November, he delivered a line to the hometown Kansas City crowd that he believed would clinch the election for the president: "Ask yourself if you want a man with no experience to sit at the peace table with Churchill, Stalin, and Chiang Kai-shek."[50] Almost no one in the audience could say yes because they all assumed that the man he was referring to was Tom Dewey, who had had no experience in foreign affairs. Ironically, however, in nine months President Harry Truman, also lacking experience, would find himself sitting at the peace table.

———————

As with most vice presidential campaigns, Truman's was essentially a sideshow. With the GOP circulating rumors of Roosevelt's worsening health and Dewey attacking FDR's longevity indirectly by calling his administration a bunch of "tired, exhausted old men," all eyes were focused on the president. His poll numbers were dropping. When, where, and how would he hit back?

The president and his political advisers decided that his opening salvo would take place on Saturday evening, September 23, in the grand ballroom of the Statler Hotel, just a few blocks from the White House, at the annual gathering of the leaders of the Teamsters Union. The DNC had quietly purchased radio time for a nationwide presidential address to commence at 9:30 Eastern War Time. Seated up on the dais with NBC and CBS microphones and motion picture cameras arrayed before him, FDR beamed at the crowd of one thousand and began what would become known as the most effective campaign speech of his long career.

With wicked humor and impeccable timing, Roosevelt skewered Republicans for trying to restrict the voting rights of soldiers, airmen, and sailors serving overseas and for propagating the big lie—actually, four big lies. Likening the GOP to Hitler in *Mein Kampf*, whose "big" lie was repeating "over and over" that the German Army did not lose WWI, FDR charged the Republicans with adopting the same "technique" by claiming falsely and repeatedly that it was the Democrats, not the Republicans, who were responsible for the Great Depression. The second big lie, claimed FDR, was the GOP's "brazen falsehood" that the Roosevelt administration was going to keep all soldiers in the army after the war was over because "there might be no jobs for them in civil life," when in fact a plan for "speedy discharge" had already been announced. But it was the third big lie that the president thought was "the most ridiculous"—the failure of his administration to "prepare for the war," a "falsification" that "even Goebbels" would not have attempted because it was the Republicans who in fact tried to "block and thwart" efforts to "warn our people and to arm our nation."

By this stage in his speech, the Teamsters and their guests, many of whom had been drinking for hours, were clapping and cheering with gusto at every opportunity. "The Old Master still had it," wrote a reporter from *Time*.[51] However, it was Roosevelt's deft delivery of the fourth big lie that riveted the nationwide listeners, made headlines throughout the country, and brought the raucous crowd to its feet. With deadpan seriousness, the president confessed that while he and his family were accustomed to hearing "malicious falsehoods" from Republican leaders about themselves, his "little dog Fala" *resented* such attacks. With a stand-up comedian's sense of timing, FDR paused while laughter rippled through the audience and morphed into a roar. When the crowd settled down, FDR went on. "You know, Fala is Scotch, and being a Scottie, as soon as he learned that the Republican fiction writers in Congress had concocted a story that I had left him behind on the Aleutian islands and sent a destroyer back to find him— at a cost to taxpayers of two or three, or eight or twenty million dollars— his Scotch soul was furious." The crowd erupted with laughter. In a mournful tone the president added, "He has not been the same dog since." The audience went wild, howling with delight. He concluded: "I think I have a right to resent, to object to libelous statements about my dog."[52] The thunderous applause seemed interminable. Only those within a few yards of the president could see the dark circles of fatigue under his eyes.

Roosevelt's 1944 reelection campaign "had got off to a flying start," reported *Time*. "The Champ had swung a full roundhouse blow. And it was plain to the newsmen on the Dewey Special that the challenger had been hit hard."[53]

In the ensuing weeks, while FDR spent a good deal of time resting at Hyde Park, rumors of his declining heath ran rampant. It was whispered that he had suffered "a brain hemorrhage, a nervous breakdown, an aneurism of the aorta, and cancer of the prostate."[54] In a front-page editorial, the New York *Sun* exhorted its readers to "not be squeamish" in weighing the consequences of FDR's dire condition. After all, it warned, "Six Presidents have died in office."[55]

Roosevelt decided that another radio address would not be enough to offset the rumors. He needed to show the voters that he had the stamina to serve for another term. On October 21, in New York City, he made his point. It was a perfectly miserable day, raining heavily due to an offshore hurricane, with temperatures hovering at 40 degrees. For four straight hours FDR rode in an open Packard, bareheaded and without his navy cape, through the city's four largest boroughs. Though soaked to the skin, he waved and flashed his radiant smile all during the fifty-one-mile trip. He spoke to a crowd of ten thousand at Ebbets Field. An estimated three million New Yorkers saw the president that day.

After Roosevelt's ordeal a reporter asked an associate, "How can they talk about a tired old man now?" Another called FDR's trip through New

York City "one of the most arduous physical fitness tests any campaigner ever met."[56]

Election night 1944, like the first three for Roosevelt, was shaped by tradition and superstition. Dinner at Springwood featured FDR's "lucky dish," scrambled eggs. When the dining table was cleared, the president remained seated in his usual place, a telephone at his elbow. Long tally sheets were brought in so he could tabulate the results. A radio was tuned in to election coverage. AP and UP teletype machines clacked in the next room. By 10 p.m. the president was convinced that the trends indicated a clear victory for the Roosevelt–Truman ticket, though Dewey did not concede until 3:45 a.m. Around midnight, according to ritual, Roosevelt was wheeled out to the portico to greet a torchlight parade of townspeople and girls from Vassar. Anna draped his cape around his shoulders. Addressing the crowd, FDR said, "It looks like I will be coming up from Washington again for another four years."[57] Sadly, he would return for only a handful of occasions before his death.

———————

On election eve the man from Independence who would replace the president had his hands full. He was trying to control a boisterous crowd in the penthouse suite at the Muehlebach Hotel in Kansas City. According to Margaret, her father had "yielded to the pleas of his battery D boys"—comrades from WWI—and his "Missouri friends" and had invited them all to the suite for the anticipated victory celebration.[58] Alcohol was plentiful, though Truman knew how to nurse a bourbon or two for an entire evening. A skilled pianist, he tried to calm them down by playing a rendition of Paderewski's Minuet in G.[59] Before the night ended they had had way too much to drink. Margaret recalled that she was "shocked" by the drunkenness and that Bess, who was also there, must have been disgusted.[60] Harry Easley, an old friend of Truman's from southwest Missouri, stayed on after everyone had left. While Truman stretched out on a bed, the two pals had a long talk. According to Easley, Truman told him that FDR "had the pallor of death on his face and [Truman] knew that . . . he would be President before the term was out. . . . I think it just scared the very devil out of him." Truman said he would "have to depend on his friends . . . people like me," recalled Easley.[61] Margaret wrote that her father must have felt "lonesome" that night, having realized for the first time the "near inevitability" of becoming the president of the United States, which meant that he and he alone would be held responsible for the security and welfare of the American people.[62]

When the votes were counted, the Roosevelt–Truman ticket received 3.6 million more popular votes than Dewey and his running mate, former Ohio governor John Bricker, and it carried thirty-six states with 432 electoral votes. The GOP candidates won twelve states and ninety-nine electoral votes. It was the closest of FDR's four elections and the tightest presidential election since 1916. Due to Truman's future stance on civil rights, it would be the last election for president in which the so-called Solid South remained solid for the Democrats.

Of the ten weeks between the election and the inauguration, Roosevelt spent a total of five in Warm Springs, in Hyde Park, and on Pa Watson's farm. By December, the "exhilaration and energy" that he derived from the campaign had worn off.[63] He was once again fatigued and listless. Having lost ten pounds in the past few months, he looked thin and gray but his mind was "wonderfully active," wrote Daisy.[64] When he was working, which was not often, he was sparring by cable with Stalin over the makeup of the government of Poland and a site for the next Big Three meeting. Stalin was unyielding. He insisted that the Soviet-backed Polish Committee of National Liberation (known as the "Lublin Poles") should govern rather than Poland's exiled government in London and members of the Polish underground. As to the meeting place, the ailing president finally gave in and agreed to travel halfway around the world to Yalta in the Crimea, which Churchill called "the Riviera of Hades."[65] Roosevelt hoped that when he met again with the dictator, he could "handle" him. But at a distance of thousands of miles, he was unable to erode Stalin's intransigence.

———————

After the election, Truman took a few days off to relax in Florida before returning to Washington to resume his duties as senator and vice president in waiting. According to economic expert Derek Leebaert, in November 1944 Truman asked his friend John Wesley Snyder, a St. Louis banker, to "promise to drop everything should FDR die in office" and move to Washington to help him manage the nation's economy.[66] Snyder had worked closely with Truman to help him establish and lead his committee to investigate defense fraud and waste. He would be at Truman's side when he became president and would eventually rise to become treasury secretary. When Truman learned that Roosevelt would be out of the country after the inauguration to meet with Stalin and Churchill and that he would, therefore, become acting head of state, he told Snyder that he would have liked to have been briefed "in some detail" by White House aides about pending national issues before the president departed.[67] It is hard to believe but Truman never pressed for such a briefing, perhaps because he knew that if he did he would be rebuffed. Nor did the VP make an effort to be briefed by others in the Roosevelt administration.

Inauguration Day, Saturday, January 20, 1945, was bitterly cold. A light snow dusted the capital city. Because of the war and no doubt his miserable health, President Roosevelt had shifted the ceremony from the Capitol steps to the South Portico of the White House and canceled the traditional parade ("Who is there to parade?").[68] The crowd at his fourth inaugural was the smallest on record. It would be an austere, no-frills affair.

Along with the Roosevelt family and a hundred or more shivering VIPs, Bess and Margaret Truman were seated on the portico, looking out on several thousand invited guests standing in crusted snow on the South Lawn, including Eddie Jacobson, Truman's haberdashery partner, and a huge contingent of fellow Missourians. One guest who had a special pass was Lucy Mercer. She was seated with Secret Service agents inside an automobile that had been positioned on the lawn to afford her a view of the speakers. By the time the proceedings began, the temperature was 33 degrees Fahrenheit. The sky was slate gray.

The first to be sworn in was Harry Truman. One-term vice president Henry Wallace stepped forward and asked Truman to raise his right hand. Back then it was not unusual for the outgoing vice president to administer the oath to the incoming but this would be last time it was done. Since Wallace had fought hard to get the VP nomination and lost to Truman, it could have been an awkward moment. However, not a trace of bitterness was evident.

After her father completed the oath, Margaret glanced over her shoulder to the French doors that led to the portico. As she later wrote, she could see that Roosevelt was "arriving in a wheelchair, pushed by his son" Jimmy, a uniformed marine colonel, and that he "looked haggard, his face pale, with dark circles under his eyes."[69] Out on the portico, Roosevelt, bareheaded and coatless, was helped to his feet by a Secret Service agent and his son. Under the president's dark suit, he was wearing his steel braces and harness for the last time. Leaning on Jimmy's arm, the president clumped slowly down the narrow aisle to the lectern. The United States Marine Band in scarlet jackets played "Hail to the Chief." After the president shook hands with his new vice president, he raised his right arm and repeated the words of the oath intoned by Chief Justice Harlan Fiske Stone, who was holding the Roosevelt family Bible (printed in 1686). It had been opened to the thirteenth chapter of First Corinthians: "And now abideth faith, hope, charity; these three; but the greatest of these is charity."

Roosevelt's speech, the first in wartime since Lincoln in 1865, lasted less than five minutes, the shortest in inaugural history. Unlike Lincoln in his second inaugural, FDR said nothing about charity, much less charity for all. Instead, he began by speaking of the war as "a supreme test," the resolve to "fight for total victory," and the need for a "durable peace." But the "lessons learned" part of his address was the most visionary. Anticipating a turning point in the history of the nation, FDR concluded that the essential lesson of the war was that Americans would have to become "citizens of the world."[70] It would be Harry Truman, however, who was destined to transform his vision into reality.

When Roosevelt was finished with his speech and the ceremonies were concluded, Jimmy wheeled his chilled-to-the-bone father into the Green Room of the White House to warm up and rest before facing the luncheon crowd of almost two thousand, the largest during the Roosevelt presidency. Accounts differ but apparently FDR had suffered a painful angina attack either during his speech or afterward in the room with his son. The pain was similar but somewhat less than that which he had experienced on the train in San Diego. According to Jimmy, his father gripped his arm and said, "I can't take this unless you get me a stiff drink. You'd better make it straight." So Jimmy brought him a half tumbler of whiskey.

Roosevelt gulped it down and then went into the State Dining Room, where a buffet luncheon of chicken salad (with very little chicken) was being served. There, at the head of the reception line, he joined Mrs. Roosevelt and the Truman trio in shaking hands with the frozen VIPs. After a half hour or so, the president departed to the Red Room to relax with Norway's Princess Martha and friends. Truman also left early, getting a ride with a friend to the Senate Office Building. The paint was hardly dry on the door to suite 240. It read "The Office of the Vice President." Once inside, he remembered to call Mamma. "Now you behave yourself," she told her Harry.[71]

———————

Three days after the inauguration, Roosevelt boarded the heavy cruiser USS *Quincy*, sister ship to the *Baltimore*, and headed across the Atlantic to the island of Malta in the Mediterranean. For some reason FDR insisted that Jimmy Byrnes, head of War Mobilization, join the delegation despite Byrnes's protests that he was needed in Washington. At Malta, the president and his party rendezvoused with Churchill and his delegation before flying for the first time in the specially fitted *Sacred Cow* to the Crimea and motoring to the Soviet resort town of Yalta on the Black Sea. Stalin would arrive a day later. "If we had spent ten years on research," complained Churchill to Harry Hopkins, "we could not have found a worse place in the world than [Yalta]." "[Churchill] feels he can survive it," wrote Hopkins to Roosevelt, "by bringing 'an adequate supply of whiskey,'" which is "good for typhus and deadly on lice which thrive in these parts."[72]

For the next eight days, the Big Three and their key aides would meet in the grand ballroom of the Livadia Palace, a summer home with 116 rooms that had been built in 1911 for Czar Nicholas II. The president, accompanied by his daughter, Anna, had his own bedroom plus a private bathroom and the czar's study for small meetings. Mrs. Roosevelt was terribly disappointed and resentful that FDR chose Anna rather than her to accompany him. To the First Lady, FDR had lamely explained, "If you go, they will all feel they will have to make a great fuss, but if Anna goes it will be simpler."[73] More than two hundred others in the U.S. delegation, including Anna and the daughters of Churchill and Averell Harriman, were shoehorned into the other rooms in the palace. They would share six bathrooms.

Despite elaborate efforts to maintain strict secrecy, by the time the conference was about to begin, the *New York Times* was aware that the Big Three were meeting somewhere. On February 6 radio Berlin was reporting that the conference "was under way either aboard a warship in the Black Sea or in a Black Sea port."[74] This time, there would be no assassination attempt because the Germans had long ago been driven out of the Crimea by the Red Army and their assets were focused on a last-ditch defense of the fatherland. Soviet marshal Georgy Zhukov's armies were less than fifty miles from Berlin. A day or two after the broadcast, FDR ordered the release of a statement indicating that the Big Three were in the "Black Sea area" discussing the "final phase of the war against Nazi Germany" and the making of "a secure peace."[75]

While Roosevelt's overriding priority at Yalta was to reestablish a close rapport with Stalin, he was concerned with only three substantive issues: organization of the United Nations; Soviet entry into the war against Japan; and a free and independent Poland. By the fourth day of the conference, the president had achieved what Admiral Leahy described as a "major victory."[76] Having been assured of an effective veto in the UN Security Council, Stalin agreed to the voting procedures for the council proposed by the U.S. and reduced his claims for seats in the General Assembly from sixteen Soviet republics to two (Ukraine and Belarus). To avoid backlash in the U.S., Roosevelt secured an agreement for two additional votes in the General Assembly, though that provision never made it into the UN Charter. With the structure of the UN in place, it was agreed that the founding conference would be held in San Francisco on April 25.

The next day, in a private meeting, the Soviet dictator confirmed to FDR what he had promised at Tehran—that within two to three months after Germany's surrender, the Soviets would declare war against Japan and invade Manchuria. This time, however, Stalin demanded territorial concessions in the Far East as the price for Soviet intervention. Roosevelt would be severely criticized later, but he readily agreed to the transfer to the Soviet Union of the Kuriles and the southern half of Sakhalin Island. He also agreed to the restoration of leases to the Soviets of warm water ports at Dairen and Port Arthur in Manchuria as well as rights to the railroads leading to those ports. Roosevelt was confident that Chiang Kai-shek would consent because Stalin had agreed to encourage Mao Zedong's Communists to enter into a coalition with Chiang's nationalist government in order to preserve Chiang's position as ruler of China.

By far the most difficult and contentious issue at Yalta was Poland, specifically the composition of its postwar government. After the Red Army, at great cost in lives and treasure, occupied much of the country, Stalin had installed a Communist-dominated provisional government called "the Lublin Poles." For three days Churchill and Roosevelt argued for a new government that would consist of non-Communists from within Poland (members of the underground), plus those from the exiled Polish government in London. Because the Soviets already occupied Poland, FDR and Churchill lacked bargaining leverage, but they still managed to achieve some success. On February 9, Stalin agreed that the Lublin regime would be "reorganized on a broader democratic basis with the inclusion of democratic leaders from Poland and Poles abroad."[77] He pledged that the reorganized government would hold elections as early as a month after Yalta. Then, to give broader substance to this Polish protocol, a day later Roosevelt convinced Churchill and Stalin to sign a "Declaration of Liberated Europe." This declaration called for the right of self-determination to countries liberated from Nazi control through "free elections . . . responsive to the will of the people."[78] Poland was set to be the first test of self-determination via free elections. However, terms like "free elections," "self-determination," and "democracy" were not defined. Plus there were no verification procedures. When Leahy read the words of the Polish protocol against the lofty promise of the declaration, he told Roosevelt, "This is so elastic that the Russians can stretch it all the way from Yalta to Washington without ever technically breaking it." FDR replied, "I know, Bill. I know it. But it's the best I can do for Poland at this time."[79]

It *was* the best he could do. In fact, Poland and indeed all of Eastern Europe had been forfeited by the West not at Yalta but much earlier, when Roosevelt and Churchill decided to invade North Africa, thus delaying the opening of a second front in France until June 1944. This enabled the Soviets to occupy most of Eastern Europe by the time of the Yalta Conference. They could be forced out only by another war, an option that was unthinkable.

By most accounts, FDR's health did not hamper his dealings with Stalin at Yalta. He sometimes rambled and was caught a few times staring into space. And he was occasionally forgetful. But those who sat with him at the conference table agreed with Admiral Leahy: "It was my feeling that Roosevelt had conducted the Crimean Conference with great skill and that his personality dominated the discussions. . . . The president looked fatigued as we left, but so did we all."[80]

On St. Valentine's Day 1945, exactly ten years after FDR's first meeting with Truman, the president was seated in his wheelchair, enjoying the morning sun on the deck of the *Quincy*, which was anchored in the Great Bitter Lake at the midpoint of the Suez Canal. Having departed Yalta a few days before, he was awaiting the approach of the USS *Murphy*, a destroyer that had participated in the major amphibious landings in Europe, including Overlord. As the comparatively small warship loomed into view, the president could see at the rail dozens of men in white flowing Arabic robes, a small flock of sheep nibbling feed on the fantail, and a huge man sitting on a throne up on *Murphy*'s superstructure deck. When *Murphy* was alongside *Quincy* and a gangplank was rigged between the two vessels, six-foot-eight-inch King Abdul Aziz Ibn Saud, weighing well over two hundred pounds, limped up the gangway and was welcomed by President Roosevelt. The king was accompanied by his "court, slaves (black), coffee taster, astrologer & 8 live sheep." The "whole party was a scream!" wrote FDR to Daisy.[81]

The notion of meeting with His Majesty Ibn Saud, the ruler of Saudi Arabia, had taken root in the weeks after the election when Roosevelt knew it was likely that there would be a Big Three summit in Crimea. He had promised during the campaign that if reelected he would help establish a "free and Democratic" homeland for Jews in Palestine.[82] Shortly before leaving for Yalta, FDR informed his cabinet and Zionist leader Rabbi Stephen Wise that he intended to meet with Ibn Saud and "try and settle the Palestine situation," that is, broker a rapprochement between Arabs and Jews.[83] In early January, he had told Ed Stettinius, his new secretary of state, that he was going to bring a map with him to show King Saud the "small size of Palestine in relation to the Arab world."[84]

A homeland for Jews was probably the main reason for getting together with Saud, but Roosevelt had another objective in mind: access to Saudi Arabia's vast oil reserves. Since 1943, FDR had been aware that the "center of gravity in the world of oil production" was shifting from "the Gulf of Mexico–Caribbean area to Saudi Arabia and the Persian Gulf."[85] By late 1944, there was concern in the Roosevelt administration that an oil shortage was imminent and rumors that the British were trying to take control of the Chevron–Texaco partnership, which had established a foothold in the king's domain. Arrangements to guarantee access to Saudi oil had become a matter of national security.

For the first hour of the Valentine's Day meeting on the *Quincy*, the two leaders, with pro-Arab Colonel William Eddy as interpreter, sat in the sunshine, getting acquainted with each other. It was the first time that Ibn Saud had been out of his kingdom. Roosevelt was in "top form as a charming host," reported Eddy.[86] Before long, the king, with a gleaming smile, remarked that he and FDR were like "twin brothers," each dealing with physical disabilities (FDR polio; Saud leg wounds from battle) and each bearing burdens as head of state. Complaining that his legs "grow feebler every year," Saud complimented FDR for having a "reliable wheelchair." FDR responded that he had two wheelchairs, "which are also twins," and asked whether Saud would accept one as a personal gift. "Gratefully," said the king. "I shall use it daily and always recall affectionately the giver, my great and good friend."[87]

Having established a rapport, they went into FDR's private quarters for lunch and a substantive discussion. Roosevelt began by making the case for why Jewish refugees from Europe, who had survived indescribable horrors, should be allowed living space in Palestine. Saying he felt responsible and was committed to finding a solution, he asked for His Majesty's assistance. Ibn Saud was diplomatic and polite, but his responses, despite FDR's persistence, were negative, leaving no room for compromise. Essentially, his consistent position was that the Arabs would rather die than tolerate a homeland for Jews in Palestine and that the U.S. and its allies should force Germany to cede territory for a Jewish homeland. When FDR dangled the possibility that the U.S. might assist with irrigation and other improvements to agriculture in Palestine, Saud responded that he would not accept such improvements "if this prosperity would be inherited by the Jews."[88] Stymied, FDR backed down. He assured the king that personally he "would make no move hostile to the Arab people" and he fell back on the traditional line of the State Department—the Allies would make no decision on Palestine without first consulting both Arabs and Jews.[89]

Thus, while Roosevelt came away from the meeting having failed to persuade Ibn Saud, he achieved a major victory for national security by being the first head of state to forge a close relationship with the king. For generations to come, there would be ups and downs but Saudi Arabia, at least until recently, would remain within America's sphere of influence. And Great Britain would not control Saudi oil.

———————

Four days earlier, February 10, when the last dinner of the Big Three at Yalta was drawing to a close, an intimate evening "which passed away agreeably," Vice President Harry Truman was seated at an upright piano in the crowded National Press Club in Washington.[90] Lauren Bacall, a sultry twenty-year-old movie star who was in love with Humphrey Bogart, was perched atop the high cabinet that housed the piano works, her shapely long legs dangling off the edge at an alluring angle (by 1945 standards). The stunt had been arranged by Bacall's Hollywood press agent. An Associated Press photograph, the most famous photo of Truman ever taken, shows a side view of the VP, fingers on the keyboard, gazing upward into Bacall's amazing eyes, she down into his. He appeared to be having an awfully good time. Margaret wrote that "Mother did not care for it very much."[91] In fact, Mrs. Truman was furious. Yet, as the photo was printed in newspapers across the nation, it provided a first impression to the American public of the relatively unknown vice president from Missouri.

With much more time on his hands than he had when he was running the Truman Committee, Truman was enjoying himself while Roosevelt was at Yalta. His only official duty, presiding over the Senate, allowed him to hang out with his friends during the day either in his "gold plated" office in the Capitol, the Senate cloakroom, or "the Doghouse," a hideaway stocked with bourbon in his old office suite, which he had been allowed to retain.[92] As the new VP, Truman was much in demand socially and he delighted in being the guest of honor at dinner parties, luncheons, and other social occasions. "He was lively and animated . . . a guest among guests," wrote author John Gunther.[93]

Before FDR left for Yalta, the one substantive matter that the president asked Truman to handle was to persuade the Senate to confirm ex–vice president Henry Wallace as secretary of commerce, a powerful job at the time because the cabinet post controlled the heavily funded Reconstruction Finance Corporation (RFC). Republicans and Southern Democrats moved to block the nomination because they had reason to fear that Wallace lacked the ability to responsibly manage the millions of dollars that the RFC was authorized to loan to U.S. businesses. To secure Wallace's confirmation, Truman twisted arms, broke two tie votes, and negotiated a shrewd compromise that involved the transfer of the RFC's assets and powers to an independent Federal Loan Agency (later to be headed by Truman's close friend, John Snyder).

While Truman was telling friends that "if that old man should die," he "would be in one hell of a shape" and that "it scares hell out of me," there is no evidence that he did anything to prepare himself to become president, especially given the fact that he was not that busy.[94] To be sure, the president and some of his top aides were out of town, and even if they had been in Washington, they might have ignored Truman's attempts to prepare. But he could have set up or tried to schedule briefing sessions with members of the cabinet as well as with officials in the War and State Departments and assistants in the White House. Because Truman knew that the president was dying and that he could have become president at any moment, his apparent failure to at least try to prepare to take on the job was malpractice. Similarly, as historian Wilson Miscamble wrote, the president's "failure to brief his vice president" or to arrange to have him briefed by others was "disgraceful."[95]

———

On March 1, as Truman was seated up on the dais in the House Chamber beside Majority Leader John McCormack, he watched President Roosevelt being wheeled down the aisle to the well of the House. A joint session of Congress had been convened to hear Roosevelt's report on the

Yalta Conference. At the base of the podium, Secret Service men helped FDR into a cushioned armchair. Speaking into a row of microphones, the president began by asking the indulgence of the Congress because it relieved him from carrying "ten pounds of steel" on his legs and also because he had "just completed a fourteen-thousand-mile trip."[96] This was both the first time FDR had mentioned his disability and the first occasion on which he hinted at his deteriorating health not only to Congress but to a nationwide radio audience.

The president's delivery was "halting" and "ineffective," recalled speechwriter Sam Rosenman, and his trembling right hand was embarrassingly obvious.[97] As to substance, FDR's speech oversold the achievements of the Yalta Conference. For example, while focusing on favorable interpretations of agreements reached (e.g., Poland), he glossed over "elastic" language concerning elections and self-determination. In addition, he omitted discussion of issues that had to be tabled because of disagreements, failed to mention territories and ports ceded to Stalin in the Far East, and hid the fact that both the Soviet Union and the U.S. would have three votes instead of one in the UN General Assembly. In concluding his speech, he hyped Yalta as "a turning point" in U.S. history and "in the history of the world," claiming that it would end "exclusive alliances . . . spheres of influence . . . balances of power, and all the other expedients that have been tried for centuries—and have always failed."[98]

Having raised expectations, the president came under sharp criticism when details of the agreements and concessions to Stalin were revealed. After he died, the myth that he had sold out to the Russians at Yalta gained traction and has persisted to this day.

In the remaining days of Roosevelt's life, relations with the Soviets deteriorated. Stalin was angered when he learned that Soviet officers were excluded from talks in Bern, Switzerland, between Allen Dulles and a German SS officer, talks that were actually aimed at arranging a conference to discuss surrender of the German Army in Italy that would include the Russians. In cables to FDR, Stalin accused the Americans of negotiating terms that would allow the Germans to shift divisions away from Italy to the east to fight the Red Army while allowing Allied forces to move into Germany and limit the scale of Soviet occupation. In cables drafted by Leahy that used heated words like "bitter resentment," "distrust," and "lack of faith," Roosevelt tried to convince Stalin that he was misinformed.[99] Stalin would not back down. Indeed, he escalated the feud by refusing to send Molotov, his foreign minister, to the April 25 UN organizing conference in San Francisco and insisting on sending representatives of the Lublin government to represent Poland at the conference. At the end of March, Roosevelt wrote Stalin: "I cannot conceal from you the concern with which I view the development of events . . . since our fruitful meeting at Yalta."[100]

During March, when Roosevelt was jousting with Stalin, the decline in his health accelerated. On March 29, the day FDR returned to Washington from Hyde Park before leaving that evening for Warm Springs, the so-called assistant president, Jimmy Byrnes, and General Lucius Clay, the newly appointed head of the military government to be established in Germany, met in the Oval Office with the president. Afterward, Clay remarked to Byrnes that they had been "talking to a dying man."[101] William Hassett, FDR's correspondence secretary, who saw the president that day, wrote in his diary: "[The president] is slipping away from us and no earthly power can keep him here . . . the Boss is leaving us."[102] At some point, also on that day, the Secret Service, either on its own or at the request of some unknown person, increased the security detail assigned to Vice President Truman. Yet no one—Byrnes, Clay, Early, Hassett, the Secret Service, or apparently anyone else in the White House—thought to give Truman an explicit warning that the president's death was imminent. Nor did Admiral Leahy, who was intimately familiar with the breakdown of trust with the Soviet Union, move to brief Truman even though the VP was on the verge of inheriting the nation's most critically important national security issue.

———

For Roosevelt the balmy April weather in Warm Springs was restorative. "Within a week," wrote Dr. Bruenn, "there was a decided and obvious improvement in his appearance and sense of well being which may have been due to the anticipated visit of Lucy Mercer."[103] On April 9, Lucy arrived from Ridgeley Hall, her winter home in Aiken, South Carolina, along with her friend Ukranian-born Elizabeth Shoumatoff, a portrait artist who had been commissioned by her to paint a likeness of the president. Dinner that evening found the president "full of jokes," recalled Madame Shoumatoff, and he was particularly attentive to Lucy.[104] Eleanor, of course, was not there. She had remained in Washington and took trips to Hyde Park and New England.

On the morning of April 11, Roosevelt read, revised, and signed off on two cables, the first to Churchill, in which he advised that they should "minimize" the recent disagreements with the Soviets because in time, "most of them straighten out," as in the case of the talks with the German officer in Bern. Nevertheless, he cautioned that "we must be firm . . . and our course thus far is correct." The second cable, to Stalin, characterized "the Bern incident" as "a minor misunderstanding" that had "faded into the past" and urged that there be no "mistrust" between the two of them.[105] Roosevelt's pandering was an attempt to "manage" Stalin. Yet, by backing down and mislabeling the Bern incident as minor, he was in effect encouraging Stalin to remain firm the next time they had a disagreement.

During a press conference in Truman's Senate office on April 11, a reporter asked him to compare his life as a senator with that of being the vice president. The Senate is "the best place there is," Truman said with a grin. "I was getting along fine until I stuck my neck out too far and got too famous"—an obvious reference to the Truman Committee—"and then they made me V.P. and now I can't do anything. . . . No sir, I can't do anything."[106] Truman might have felt impotent on the eleventh, but near the end of the next afternoon, the eighty-second day of his vice presidency, the U.S. Constitution would confer on Harry S. Truman executive powers to "do things" that he could never have dreamed of accomplishing in the Senate.

In the Little White House in Warm Springs, the morning of April 12 got underway when the president "woke up with a slight headache and a stiff neck," wrote Daisy.[107] Dr. Bruenn massaged his neck and took his blood pressure, which was 180 over 110 to 120. After breakfast FDR received the latest news of the war, which featured reports that elements of General George Patton's Third Army had liberated the Buchenwald concentration camp and the Ninth Army had reached the Elbe River near Magdeburg, just sixty-five miles from Berlin. He telephoned Dewey Long, who handled White House travel arrangements, and instructed him on the itinerary that he preferred for traveling to the UN meeting in San Francisco, which was to take place in thirteen days. Roosevelt seemed confident that he would make the trip.

At one in the afternoon, a quarter of an hour before lunch, FDR was seated in a chair surrounded by four women—Lucy, Daisy, Elizabeth Shoumatoff, and blue-haired cousin Laura "Polly" Delano. After the president had placed the holder of his cigarette in an ashtray, Madame Shoumatoff noticed that he "raised his right hand and passed it over his forehead in a strange jerky way."[108] Daisy heard him say, "I have a terrific pain in the back of my head."[109] He then slumped forward toward a card table and lost consciousness. Shoumatoff screamed. Daisy called the telephone operator and asked her to send for Dr. Bruenn. FDR's valet, Arthur Prettyman, and a Filipino steward carried the president into his bedroom. It seemed like an hour, but within fifteen minutes Dr. Bruenn arrived. He quickly surmised that FDR had suffered a stroke, technically a subarachnoid hemorrhage. Bruenn did everything he could to save him. Amid the shock and confusion, Lucy had the presence of mind to realize that she and Shoumatoff needed to quickly pack their things, fetch their driver, and leave. "The family is arriving by plane and the rooms must be vacant," she said to Shoumatoff, and "we must get to Aiken before dark."[110]

While Roosevelt continued to breathe for more than two hours after he was stricken, he was doomed from the moment he raised his hand to his head. At 4:35 Eastern War Time (3:35 local time), the dreaded yet inevitable moment arrived. The nation's longest-serving president was pronounced dead by Drs. Bruenn and James Paullin, an Atlanta heart specialist. He was sixty-three years old. In her diary Daisy wrote, "Franklin D. Roosevelt, the hope of the world, is dead. . . . What it means to the world, only the future can tell."[111]

Chapter 4

Unprepared

During the last few hours of President Roosevelt's life, Vice President Harry Truman was bored. As president of the Senate, he was seated up on the dais in the Senate Chamber, writing a letter to his mother and sister and listening out of one ear as a debate droned on over a water treaty with Mexico.

From Warm Springs, Bill Hassett called the White House shortly after 4:35 p.m. to inform Steve Early, FDR's former press secretary and confidant, that the president had drawn his last breath. Early asked Hassett to alert no one else until he was able to get in touch with the First Lady and others, including Anna Boettiger and Truman. Knowing that Eleanor was speaking at the Sulgrave Club, a women's club on Massachusetts Avenue at Dupont Circle, Early asked the White House operator to get her on the phone. Eleanor excused herself from the head table to take the call. She later remembered that Early was "very much upset" and that he "asked me to come home at once." Vice Admiral McIntire had called an hour or so earlier to tell Eleanor that the president had merely "fainted," though he must have known that Roosevelt was in his death throes. Now, however, Eleanor knew that "something dreadful had happened."[1]

Seconds later, Anna, who was at Bethesda Naval Hospital with her son Johnny (he had contracted a serious gland infection), received word that she needed to return to the White House immediately. Like Eleanor, she had already been told by McIntire that FDR had fainted. Now she too suspected the worst. A car assigned to the head of Bethesda Naval Hospital rushed Anna to the White House.

At a few minutes before five, the Senate recessed. Truman stopped by the vice president's office to tell one of his secretaries that he was heading over to Speaker of the House Sam Rayburn's hideaway (often called "the Board of Education") to have a "libation" with "Mr. Sam" and his guests. Truman also asked the secretary to get word to Harry Vaughan at the VP's main office suite in the Senate Office Building and explain to him where he would be. After Truman had left, Vaughan answered a call from the White House and told the caller that Truman was on his way to Rayburn's private office and to contact the VP there.

Following a brisk walk over to the House side of the Capitol, Truman arrived at Rayburn's office at about 5:05 p.m. After handing Truman a bourbon and water, Rayburn told him that Steve Early had just called and wanted to speak with him right away. Truman picked up the phone and dialed the White House. Early came on the line. His voice was tense and strained. With no explanation he ordered Truman to get to the White House "as quickly and quietly as possible" and to use the main northwest entrance off Pennsylvania Avenue.[2] Legendary House parliamentarian Lew Deschler, who was in the room, recalled Truman's first words after he hung up: *"Jesus Christ and General Jackson!"* Turning to Rayburn, Truman excitedly said, "Steve Early wants me at the White House immediately. . . . Boys, this is in the room. Something must have happened."[3]

The former vice president, now president, burst out the door and started to run. There was no time to pick up one of the three Secret Service agents assigned to him. Truman's limousine and driver were all the way over on the Senate side of the Capitol, a long block away. Taking the steps downstairs two at a time, he reached the basement corridor and then alternately ran and fast-walked the length of the entire building. The few staffers who Truman passed had no idea that he was president, nor did he. At the end of the passageway, out of breath and gripping a brass banister, Truman charged upstairs to his main office and, of all things, grabbed his hat. Outside in the misty rain, he spotted his car, a black Mercury sedan, and Tom Harty, his driver. By then it was about 5:15 p.m. Truman's Secret Service detail had no clue as to where he was. With no police escort, Harty steered down Capitol Hill and began threading his way through the rush-hour traffic toward the White House.

Truman wrote later that he wouldn't even "allow himself to think" that FDR had died.[4] But if so, why had he run? Why had he exclaimed before leaving Rayburn's office that he had to get to the White House "immediately" because "something must have happened"? By intuition he had to have known.

Upstairs in Eleanor Roosevelt's private study, Early and McIntire had just finished informing her that her husband "had slipped away." Composing herself, Eleanor paused and then said: "I am more sorry for the people of this country and of the world than I am for ourselves."[5] After McIntire left, she dictated a short message for transmittal via cable to her four sons overseas: "Pa slept away this afternoon. He did his job to the end as he would want you to do. All our love."[6] These selfless sentiments at this tragic moment in her life were emblematic of her character.

Ashen-faced, Truman was shown into Eleanor's sitting room on the second floor at 5:30. By then, Anna was there along with her husband. Eleanor rose to greet Truman. Putting her hand gently on his shoulder, she said quietly, "Harry, the President is dead." Truman, who had anticipated the worst, was shaken after hearing and digesting those blunt words. He remained speechless for a few seconds before finding his voice. "Is there anything I can do for you?" he asked at last. Truman later wrote that he never forgot Eleanor's "deeply understanding" reply: "Is there anything *we* can do for *you*? For *you* are the one in trouble now."[7] For the first time, Truman understood that he was president of the United States.

Eleanor too recognized that the transition of power had taken place and she was no longer First Lady. She asked the president if it would be appropriate for her to fly to Warm Springs that evening in a government plane. "Of course," Truman said. "I will arrange it myself."[8] At about that time, white-haired Secretary of State Edward Stettinius, former chair of U.S. Steel, entered her study, tears welling up under his eyes and running down his cheeks. Truman was calm and composed. He asked Stettinius to contact the rest of the cabinet members for a meeting as soon as they could get to the White House, summon the chief justice, and arrange for the swearing in at seven.

At 5:47 Eastern War Time, news of Roosevelt's death was conveyed by former press secretary Early to the wire services and radio networks. A brief announcement was broadcast to the nation and the rest of the world. Not long afterward Lucy Mercer insisted that Mr. Robins, who was driving her and Madame Shoumatoff back to Aiken, stop at a hotel in Macon so they could find out what was going on in Warm Springs. The portrait artist went in for a few minutes. When she returned she told Lucy that the president was dead. She recalled that Lucy "sat motionless and remained utterly silent."[9]

The *New York Times*, a frequent critic of Roosevelt, declared the next day, "Men will thank God on their knees a hundred years from now that Franklin D. Roosevelt was in the White House."[10] In Berlin, news of FDR's demise was regarded by gleeful propaganda minister Joseph Goebbels as a last-minute miracle—a turning point in the war, he predicted to Hitler. In London, Churchill said he was "overpowered by a sense of deep and irrefutable loss." And in Moscow, Stalin was "deeply distressed," suspecting that the president had been poisoned.[11]

Truman left Eleanor's study and went down to the West Wing. From the president's desk in the Oval Office, he telephoned Les Biffle, secretary of the Senate, and asked him to notify the congressional leadership that they should gather in the Cabinet Room by 7 p.m. Next, he called his apartment on Connecticut Avenue. Margaret picked up the phone. "In an odd tight voice," she recalled, "Dad asked to speak to Mother." When Margaret tried to kid around with her father as she often did, he told her "in a voice of steel" to put Mother on the line. She handed the phone to Mrs. Truman.

"Bess," Harry said, "I'm at the White House. President Roosevelt died about two hours ago in Warm Springs. I'm sending a car for you and Margaret. I want you here when I'm sworn in."[12]

By 6:10 most of the cabinet members were assembled in the Cabinet Room. Mrs. Roosevelt stayed upstairs, getting ready to depart for Warm Springs. Truman called the meeting to order. "It was a very somber group," wrote Secretary of War Stimson to his diary.[13] Whether rehearsed or not, Truman's remarks seemed appropriate to the occasion. After repeating Mrs. Roosevelt's statement that her husband had died "like a soldier," Truman said, "I want every one of you to stay and carry on, and I want to do everything just the way President Roosevelt wanted it."[14] However, he made it clear that he was now the president and that he would take responsibility for his decisions. He told them that while he welcomed and valued their advice, once a decision was made, he expected the cabinet to support him.

Outside the White House, a silent crowd of two thousand Washingtonians gathered in the dusk along the fence and in Lafayette Park. They knew that a transition was unfolding and many were worried about the future.

By the time Mrs. Truman, Margaret, and Chief Justice Harlan Fiske Stone arrived, the Cabinet Room was filled not only with cabinet members, but with congressional leaders, the Joint Chiefs, and other top government officials. When Bess entered the room, she "looked sad and a little frightened," recalled press secretary Jonathan Daniels.[15] The chief justice asked Truman whether he had brought a Bible. Of course he had not. A Bible was the last thing on his mind. While a frantic search was being conducted, the swearing-in ceremony was suspended. Finally, Howell Crim, one of the White House ushers, located a cheap Gideon Bible with red-edged pages in Bill Hassett's desk drawer.

Standing at the end of the room in front of a marble mantel beneath a portrait of Woodrow Wilson, with Bess, Margaret, and several others clustered in a semicircle behind him, Harry Truman faced Chief Justice Stone and raised his right hand. His left hand held the Gideon Bible, his thumb pressed on top of an index card on which the oath of office was typed. The hands of the clock on the mantelpiece registered 7:09, almost two and a half hours since Roosevelt had died.

"I, Harry Shippe Truman," the chief justice mistakenly began. "I, Harry S. Truman," the president responded. The single "S" had been a compromise by his parents between the middle name of his paternal grandfather—Shippe or Shipp—and the first name of his maternal grandfather—Solomon. After that correction, Truman repeated verbatim each portion of the rest of the oath intoned by Chief Justice Stone. ". . . do solemnly swear / that I will faithfully execute the office of the president of the United States / and will to the best of my ability preserve, protect and defend the Constitution of the United States." The chief justice added a phrase not in the official oath that Truman repeated: "So help me God." Truman raised the Bible to his lips just as George Washington had done after he spontaneously added the same plea to God in 1789.

The nation's thirty-third president, the seventh vice president to succeed to the highest office upon the death of a president, turned and kissed both Bess and Margaret. While Truman was shaking dozens of hands and receiving assurances of support following the solemn ceremony, assistant press secretary Eben Ayers tactfully interrupted and asked that the new president come with him to the Red Room. Bess and Margaret followed them in. There, Ed Stettinius confronted Truman with an urgent question: In light of Roosevelt's death, should the UN organizing conference that was scheduled to begin in San Francisco on April 25, 1945, be called off or delayed? Truman replied with an emphatic no. It was his first policy decision as president. Truman also reviewed and approved a brief statement that was released to the press under his name at 8:10 p.m. "The world may be sure that that we will prosecute the war on both fronts, east and west, with all the vigor we possess to a successful conclusion."[16]

After Bess and Margaret departed for home, Secretary of War Henry Stimson asked to speak to Truman "about a most urgent matter." As Truman recalled, once they were alone, Stimson told him that he wanted him to know about an "immense project" involving the development of a "new explosive of almost unbelievable destructive power," but he did not feel "free" to provide details. In his memoirs and diary, Truman wrote that he was "puzzled" and "shocked," as if this were the first he had heard of the atomic bomb project.[17] But it was not the first. As noted earlier, he was already aware of the project through his investigators on the Truman Committee and FDR's disclosure when they had had lunch together on August 18, 1944. Why Truman felt he had to deny his knowledge of the project and why he apparently did not press Stimson for details, as he should have, are mysteries. Likewise, Stimson's statement that he was not free to provide details to his boss, who was the president and commander in chief of the U.S. armed forces, is baffling.

That night, when the motorcade pulled up to the entrance to Truman's apartment building, the sidewalks were jammed with people eager to get a glimpse of the new president. Truman was starving. Finding his apartment empty, Harry located Bess and Margaret down the hall with neighbors. There, he wolfed down a turkey and ham sandwich and a glass of milk and announced that he was going to bed. From his bedroom he telephoned his friend John Snyder in St. Louis and offered him his first appointment—federal loan administrator to the largest lending operation in the world. Then he called his mother and told her he was all right but that he would be busy for a few days. "Be good," she said, "but be game too."[18] Within minutes he was asleep.

Later that night Harry awoke "to find Bess sobbing in the bed beside him."[19] He tried but failed to console her. For a moment he thought about how utterly unprepared he was for what he would face in the morning. Then he turned over and went back to sleep.

————

The next morning, Truman's first day as president, he arrived at the West Wing at 9 a.m., nattily dressed in a gray double-breasted suit, a pressed white shirt, a dark tie, and black shoes. Guided by press secretary Jonathan Daniels, Truman walked at a brisk pace through the corridors to the Oval Office. Upon Truman's entering and scanning the room, the first thing he did was try out the wood-and-velvet swivel chair behind the massive desk. Observing that the desk's maple surface was littered with the former president's ashtrays, campaign souvenirs, miniature statues, small flags, and all manner of odd knickknacks, Truman asked Matt Connelly to have someone box up all of FDR's possessions in the Oval, including his ship models and maritime paintings, and take them upstairs to Mrs. Roosevelt. Connelly, who had been the Truman Committee's chief investigator, was the president's first White House staff hire, and he would shortly become the president's appointments secretary. "It was amazing," recalled Daniels, "to see the transition from the aristocrat from Hyde Park" to what those who had been with Roosevelt "thought was this little guy from Kansas City."[20] FDR's skeptical staffers, some of whom had worked for him for twelve years, had "no idea what was going to happen next."[21]

While Truman was leafing through the first batch of memos and correspondence that Admiral Leahy had brought in, the hearse carrying FDR's casket departed the Little White House for the Warm Springs train station. From her car behind the hearse, Mrs. Roosevelt, with Fala in her lap, looked back at the driveway ellipse where soldiers from the different services presented arms. Far ahead, down the narrow clay road, a U.S. Army band led the procession to the station, the muffled drums beating a slow, deadly cadence. Helmeted paratroopers lined the road. The hearse stopped for a moment. Chief Petty Officer Graham Jackson hoisted his accordion and began to play the melody of Antonín Dvořák's "Goin' Home," tears streaking down his black face.

Back in the Oval Office, Truman initiated the first installment of what would become a days-long crash course in foreign affairs. He thought he had a firm grasp on domestic issues but he was painfully aware that he knew nothing about commitments made by FDR to U.S. allies, the status of relations with the Soviet Union, and the grand strategy for ending the global war and winning the peace. At 10:15 a.m. Secretary of State Edward Stettinius, who had been summoned earlier that morning, began Truman's tutorial with a forty-five-minute overview of the key foreign relations issues and plans for the forthcoming UN meeting. They agreed that Truman, like FDR, would start receiving a two-page summary of foreign affairs issues each morning. In addition, Truman requested that Stettinius provide him with an outline by the end of the day on the "background and present status" of the principal foreign relations problems confronting the

U.S. As to the UN meeting that was to convene in less than two weeks, Truman said that he would not attend but was confident that Stettinius would do a fine job of leading the U.S. delegation. The president offered to deliver a message to the UN and Stettinius said he thought that would be appropriate.

At 11 a.m., a few minutes before the train bearing Roosevelt's remains left the Warm Springs station, Stimson, Navy Secretary James Forrestal, and the Joint Chiefs arrived in the Oval Office to report to the new president on the current military situation. "They were brief and to the point," Truman wrote in his memoirs. The war was far from over, they said. It would take at least another six months to finally overcome Germany and "Japan would not be conquered until another year and a half." There appeared to be a consensus among the chiefs that Japan could not be defeated without an invasion of ground forces. They were already planning the invasion, which was code-named Operation Downfall.

Given the uncertainty about development of the atomic bomb, the prediction by the chiefs that it would take that long to defeat Japan seems reasonable. However, the speed of the advances of the Russian, American, and British armies into the heart of Germany, which was plain to see in the White House Map Room, suggests that the military experts were wildly off base as to when Hitler's Third Reich would collapse.

Truman told the group that he planned to send a message to the armed forces about "what they could expect from him" but that he first needed to address a joint session of Congress.[22] When the military leaders were leaving, Truman asked Admiral William Leahy, who had been FDR's chief of staff and liaison to the Joint Chiefs, to remain in the Oval Office. Leahy, with a reputation for being blunt, crusty, and outspoken, had enjoyed a distinguished career in the navy before serving as ambassador to Vichy France. With the doors closed Truman asked Leahy to stay on. Leahy agreed, although he told Truman, "I always say what's on my mind." That was what he needed, responded Truman. "I want the truth and I want the facts at all times."[23]

When Stimson and army chief of staff George Marshall had left the Oval Office and were riding back to the Pentagon, Stimson said that he was favorably impressed by Truman, describing him as a "man who is willing and anxious to learn and do his best" but who was handicapped by not having background information relevant to the challenges he would face as president. Marshall wisely observed, "We shall not know what he is really like until the pressure begins to be felt."[24]

———————

Shattering tradition, President Truman left the White House a little after noon for Capitol Hill. He had asked Les Biffle, with little notice, to arrange a lunch in his office—"Biffle's Tavern"—with Speaker Rayburn, the House and Senate majority and minority leaders, and twelve more of the president's old friends in the Senate and House from both sides of the aisle. It was a move "both wise and smart," wrote Senator Arthur Vandenberg (R-MI) in his diary. While Truman's motive was to begin his presidency by laying a foundation of goodwill, the congressional leaders saw his gesture as an end to FDR's twelve years of "contempt for Congress," as Vandenberg put it.[25] During a lunch of salmon, corn bread, and peas, Truman pleaded for their help and support, though he could not possibly have imagined the fierce battles with Congress on domestic issues that lay ahead. To Senator George Aiken of Vermont, Truman frankly admitted his inadequacies, saying, "I'm not big enough for this job."[26]

When Truman left Biffle's office, a group of reporters was gathered in the hall, and Truman had known most of them for years. "Boys, if you ever pray for me, pray for me now," he told them. "I don't know whether you fellows ever had a load of hay fall on you, but when they told me yesterday what had happened, I felt like the moon, the stars and all the planets had fallen on me. I've got the most terribly responsible job a man ever had."[27] The journalists, who were used to dealing with Truman, were stunned. They had never heard him reveal himself like this. For them it was an unexpected display of both his humility and his authenticity.

In his memoirs, Truman wrote that before he departed the Capitol, he lingered "in the empty Senate Chamber and the silent vice presidential office," cherished places where he had experienced the most "exciting adventure" he "ever expected to have."[28] Later that day, he asked Harry Vaughan to deliver the last box of cigars that he had left in his office to Senator Vandenberg with a note: "Our swan song."[29] Little did he know that in the coming years Vandenberg would become Truman's most indispensable ally in the Senate, helping him revive postwar Europe due to passage of the Marshall Plan and contain the Soviet Union through the creation of NATO.

––––––––

Having learned earlier in the day that Jimmy Byrnes was in Washington, Truman invited him to the White House. (Spurned by FDR for the VP slot at the Democratic convention, Byrnes had angrily resigned as head of War Mobilization on April 2 and moved back to South Carolina.) The former senator and associate justice of the Supreme Court arrived at 2:30, shortly after Truman had returned from the Hill. Truman had always admired and respected Byrnes for his ability and unprecedented experience at the highest levels in all three branches of the federal government (House and Senate, Supreme Court, and "assistant president" in the White House). For the first half hour Truman questioned Byrnes about everything he could recall concerning the substantive discussions and decisions made at Yalta. Then, since Truman knew that Byrnes had personally taken shorthand notes of the conference, he asked him to transcribe the notes for him. Byrnes readily agreed. Truman then pivoted to his second reason for summoning Byrnes to the Oval Office. He informed him that he was thinking about nominating him for secretary of state after the UN meeting in San Francisco. As Truman put it, Byrnes "practically jumped down my throat to accept."[30] The president went on to explain that because he had no vice president, the secretary of state, under the Constitution at that time, would be next in line to succeed him. Thus, if he, Truman, were to die or become incapacitated, he wanted a successor who had been elected by the American people rather than someone, namely Stettinius, who came from the private sector and had never stood for public office. In addition, Truman believed that Byrnes was far better qualified to be president than Stettinius and that his popularity in the Senate would be useful when it came time to secure approval of peace treaties and the UN Charter. Moreover, Truman felt he owed the top diplomatic job to Byrnes because of the shabby way his VP candidacy had been sidetracked by FDR and the political bosses at the Democratic convention. As Truman wrote in his memoirs, he thought that "calling on [Byrnes] at this time might help balance things up."[31]

Truman's inclination to nominate Byrnes as his secretary of state was her father's "first miscalculation as President," wrote his daughter, Margaret.[32] As Truman would soon learn, Byrnes thought and acted as if the presidency should have been his. Before the appointment was even announced, Harold Ickes, FDR's long-serving secretary of the interior, predicted that "Jimmy was willing to take over and tell Truman how to run his job."[33]

At 3:30 Secretary Stettinius was back in the Oval Office, this time accompanied by Russian expert Chip Bohlen. The subject was the deterioration of relations with the Soviet Union, specifically the failure of the Russians to live up to their agreements at Yalta concerning the inclusion of democratic leaders and others in Poland's Communist-dominated government, and the promise of free elections. Bohlen, who had been the interpreter at Yalta, summarized for Truman the discouraging exchanges of cables between Stalin and FDR up until his death and explained why the Russians were so intent on maintaining tight control over Poland. Stettinius came away with the distinct impression that Truman thought "we had been too easy" with the Soviet leader.[34] However, in his memoirs written years later, Truman indicated that he did not want to push Stalin too hard for fear of "a breakdown in negotiations."[35]

After an hour or so of discussing Poland, a cable from Averell Harriman, ambassador to the Soviet Union, was brought into the Oval Office by an aide and handed to Stettinius. It was welcome news. For weeks Stalin had stood by his refusal to send Foreign Minister Molotov to the UN organizing conference in San Francisco. Since most every other nation was sending its top diplomat, Stalin's refusal gave the impression to the world that the Soviets were not interested in creating a world-peacekeeping organization. Now, according to Harriman, Stalin had changed his mind. Appealing to Stalin's high regard for FDR at a meeting in the Kremlin, Harriman had argued that "the most effective way" to perpetuate Roosevelt's legacy would be to support his chosen predecessor and send Molotov to San Francisco.[36] Stalin was persuaded. As an added bonus, he agreed with Harriman's suggestion that Molotov should stop in Washington to see Truman on his way to San Francisco.

On Saturday, April 14, in the late-morning sun, the caisson bearing FDR's remains, drawn by six white horses, arrived at the South Portico of the White House. With Mrs. Roosevelt and Anna Boettiger standing near the bottom step, FDR's bronze casket was lifted by eight noncommissioned officers and carried up the stairs into the mansion. After it had been placed on Lincoln's catafalque in the East Room near the Stuart portrait of George Washington, Eleanor approached. "Can you dispense with the Honor Guard for a few moments and have the casket opened?" she asked J. B. West, a White House usher. "I would like to have a few moments alone with my husband." According to West, "Mrs. Roosevelt stood at the casket, against the east wall, gazing down into her husband's face. Then she took a gold ring from her finger and tenderly placed it on the president's hand. She straightened, eyes dry, and she left the room. The casket was never opened again."[37]

The gold ring was likely her wedding ring. Perhaps she had placed it in his hand with the thought that it would restore their marriage vows for eternity. Daisy wrote the night before that Eleanor "loved him more deeply than she knows herself and his feeling for her was deep & lasting."[38]

Accounts differ, but most say that as soon as the casket was closed, Mrs. Roosevelt went upstairs to Anna's room to confront her. Eleanor was seething with anger. She had been bluntly informed by FDR's cousin Polly Delano, either at Warm Springs or on the train to Washington (again, there are differing accounts), that Lucy was present when Franklin Roosevelt had died. As if that revelation were not shocking enough, Polly also told her, not without cruelty, that Lucy had been seeing FDR in recent years, that Anna knew all about it, and that Anna had arranged for and acted as hostess at dinners in the White House involving Lucy when Eleanor was not there. It was as if a knife had been plunged into Eleanor's chest. "The wound was deep," wrote journalist Jim Bishop.[39]

Eleanor burst into Anna's room. With a withering look that "dripped disapproval," she accused Anna of betraying her.[40] There is no firsthand account of her exact words but she must have peppered Anna with questions: How long had this been going on? Dinners in the White House with her hosting? Why didn't she tell her mother? As a justification, Anna tried to explain to her mother the emotional trap she felt she had been in when her beloved father first asked whether she would object if he invited Lucy to the White House. She knew he could die at any moment. How could she refuse his request and at the same time preserve her relationship with her mother? To Anna, it had been an impossible situation. She thought she could assuage her mother's rage by saying that "there were always people around," but Eleanor sensed it was a lie and it was (the White House log discloses that the two of them had spent countless hours alone).

Anna believed she would never be forgiven. However, "after two or three days that was all," she recalled. "We never spoke about it again."[41] And for the rest of Eleanor's life, "she did not tell anyone" about Lucy's presence in Franklin's life during his last years.[42]

––––––––––

While Eleanor was confronting Anna upstairs, Harry Hopkins, Roosevelt's closest adviser and confidant, and the new president were pecking at sandwiches in the Oval Office on trays ordered from the White House kitchen. Knowing that Hopkins had returned from his sickbed at the Mayo Clinic to attend the afternoon funeral, Truman had asked him to come to the White House early so he could pick his brain—the fourth installment of Truman's crash course. More than anyone else in or out of government, Hopkins was in the best position to tutor the new president because he had attended all but one of the wartime conferences (he had missed the Quebec conference in 1944 due to recovery from illness) and he was intimately familiar with Roosevelt's thinking with regard to both domestic and foreign policy issues. The two Harrys were old acquaintances, having met in 1933 or 1934 when Truman, as Missouri director of the Federal Reemployment Service and presiding judge in Jackson County, worked with Hopkins in directing unemployed laborers in Missouri to jobs on federal public works projects. Over the years, Hopkins had always been accessible and helpful to Truman, traits that he would never forget. He trusted Hopkins implicitly.

When Hopkins entered the Oval, Truman asked him how he felt. "Terrible," he replied.[43] Hopkins had had half—some say two-thirds—of his stomach removed due to cancer in 1937, and he was suffering from malnutrition. For two hours Truman mostly listened as Hopkins described and characterized the world leaders he had met, and explained the policies advocated and deals made by Roosevelt in Casablanca; Washington, DC; Cairo; Quebec (1943); Tehran; and Yalta. For Truman, Hopkins was an invaluable resource with an eye for telling details and keen insights on personalities. "Stalin," he told Truman, "is a forthright, rough, tough Russian. He is a Russian partisan through and through, thinking always first of Russia. But he can be talked to frankly." These remarks, recorded by Truman in his memoirs, suggest that some of the optimism Hopkins had expressed in the immediate aftermath of Yalta regarding future dealings with Stalin had faded. Expressing confidence that Truman would "continue to carry out the policies of Franklin Roosevelt," Hopkins said that he would offer Truman "all the assistance [he could]."[44]

A few minutes before four, Hopkins, "looking like death," was guided by an usher into the East Room, where the funeral service for FDR was about to be held. Mourners had already filled the room. The walls were covered from floor to ceiling with flowers, their thick scent overpowering. Robert Sherwood, one of FDR's speechwriters, wrote that when Truman came in, "nobody stood up, and I'm sure this modest man did not even notice this discourtesy or, if he did, understood that the people present could not associate him with this high office; all they could think of was that the President was dead."[45] Two minutes later, Mrs. Roosevelt entered. Everyone stood up until she was seated by her son Elliott in the front row on the aisle. The Episcopal service began with the singing of "Eternal Father, Strong to Save," the navy hymn, the hymn that Roosevelt loved more than any other. The ritual was poignant but brief, lasting about twenty minutes.

———

After spending Sunday at Hyde Park for the burial service, Truman faced his first test as the new leader of the United States—a speech to a joint session of Congress and a nationwide radio audience. From the gallery in the chamber of the House of Representatives, where she sat with her mother, Margaret Truman could see that her father was "terribly nervous" as he mounted the rostrum.[46] During a twenty-minute speech that was interrupted seventeen times by applause, Truman checked all the boxes.

He began by saying that he could never fill the "tremendous void" left by Roosevelt's passing, but with the help of all Americans he would "support and defend" FDR's New Deal values, namely to "improve the lot of the common people." Without mentioning the Soviet Union by name, he stressed the need for the postwar "cooperation of the nations" and called for a "strong and lasting United Nations." As to his war policy, and the defeat of Germany and Japan, two words sparked the loudest and longest ovation—"unconditional surrender." Truman concluded with a prayer for wisdom and understanding, asking "only to be a good and faithful servant of my Lord and my people."[47]

While Truman could never match FDR's eloquence and sense of timing, he spoke plainly and directly, albeit with a flat, clipped, slightly nasal accent. His voice was that of an ordinary man from the middle of America. In the days after the speech, letters of support from the American people deluged the White House, evidence that Truman had delivered the reassurance that they desperately wanted. The new president had not only passed his first test as the nation's leader. "He had scored a triumph," wrote biographer Alonzo Hamby.[48]

That afternoon, Bess, Margaret, and Bess's mother, Mrs. Wallace (who never liked Harry), moved from their apartment on Connecticut Avenue to Blair House, diagonally across the street from the White House. Harry and Bess had decided that it was impossible to remain in the apartment because of the noisy crowds of tourists, Washingtonians, reporters, and photographers who surrounded the building at all hours and invaded their privacy. Plus, the Secret Service had warned them about security. Blair House, which was owned by the government and used to host visiting VIPs, was a magnificently furnished four-story yellow stucco house built in 1813. The Trumans planned to live there until Mrs. Roosevelt was able to pack twelve years of belongings and move out of the White House. The best thing about Blair House, wrote Margaret, was that "the food matched the surroundings."[49]

———

The next morning, Tuesday, April 17, the new president faced another major test—his first press conference. By 10:30, an unprecedented number of reporters and visitors, 348 men and women, had checked in and were gathered in the "fish room" off the main lobby. The large crowd of visitors was escorted outside to the terrace while the regular correspondents were crammed into the Oval Office.[50] Everyone who could see Truman could not resist comparing his vitality to that of the ailing, wheelchair-bound Roosevelt. The *New York Times* implicitly gave voice to the contrast. "[Truman] stood behind his desk, a compact, active, vigorous figure with a complexion which glowed a healthy pink."[51] At the beginning, Truman laid out the ground rules: no quotes without express permission, and off-the-record statements were to be kept in strict confidence. Then he announced that Foreign Minister Molotov would "pay his respects to the President of the United States" before going to the UN conference in San Francisco. To questions from the reporters, Truman's answers were crisp and direct.[52] One reporter who was not familiar with Truman's background asked whether "Negroes" in America could expect his support for "fair employment practices and the right to vote." Truman's response: "All you need to do is read the Senate record of one Harry S. Truman."[53] Many if not most of the reporters in the room were not aware of the Missouri senator's pathbreaking 1940 "Brotherhood of Man" speeches in the city of Sedalia, where he called for equal rights under the law for African Americans.[54] Nor were they aware that Truman had consistently supported voting rights and anti-lynching legislation when he was in the Senate. The new president, whose grandparents on both sides had been slave owners and one of whom had been held in a Union concentration camp, was ahead of his time. His stance bordered on the radical. At this, his first press conference, Truman gave notice that as president he would promote civil rights.

The fact that Truman sought civil rights and equal opportunity for Blacks did not absolve him of racism. Privately, in letters to Bess, family, and friends, Truman often used the word "nigger," in one instance referring to Harlem congressman Adam Clayton Powell as that "damn nigger preacher."[55] During poker games and behind closed doors in the Senate, he told and enjoyed racial jokes. However, after the Sedalia speeches, he remained dead serious about the need for legislation to guarantee civil rights and economic equality for Black Americans—but not "social equality," which in effect meant that he sanctioned a nonlegal form of segregation. In one of his Sedalia speeches, he put it this way: "Their social life will, naturally, remain their own."[56]

On the sixth day of his presidency, Truman summoned his old friend Charlie Ross to the Oval Office. Ross, who was head of the Washington bureau of the *St Louis Post-Dispatch*, had been Harry's classmate at Independence High School. They had kept in touch for the past forty-five years. Even though FDR's press secretaries, Steve Early and Jonathan Daniels, had volunteered to stay on, the moment Truman became president, he wanted Ross to serve as his press secretary and more than that—one of his principal advisers. At first, Ross said he must decline for financial reasons. Truman persisted, knowing that Ross was interested in the job. When Ross was finally convinced that he had a duty to accept the appointment, they telephoned their favorite high school teacher, Miss Tillie Brown. When they had her on the line, Harry said, "This is the president of the United States. Do I get that kiss?" He was referring to the fact that at graduation in 1901 she had kissed Charlie because he was class valedictorian, but she refused Harry's request for a kiss, saying he did not deserve one "until he had done something worthwhile." Miss Tillie, despite her age, had lost none of her wit. She responded to Harry's question: "Come and get it."[57]

Over the next week, as the Allies gained the upper hand in the war in Europe and the Pacific, issues concerning the liberation of the tens of millions around the world who would survive the carnage began finding their way to the office of the new president. Tens of thousands of refugees were clogging the roads in Germany as they fled from the oncoming Red Army horde that was already in Berlin's suburbs. Skeletal humans who could barely walk, mostly Jews, had been liberated that week from the hell of the Bergen-Belsen and Buchenwald concentration camps but they had nowhere to go. From the Po Valley in Italy, American and British troops were pushing north but they and the Germans had left behind a trail of devastation and homelessness that reached all the way down the spine of Italy to the boot. In the Pacific, General MacArthur's Philippine liberation campaign had finally ended; the survivors were scarred for life due to memories of the atrocities committed on their loved ones and fellow citizens by the Japanese forces. On the Japanese home islands, paper-thin houses in Tokyo and other major cities were being firebombed nightly by the Americans, the starving survivors clinging to life under railroad bridges amid the ruins.

The first to reach Truman's office with a plea for liberated survivors was Rabbi Wise, chair of the American Zionist Emergency Council. He arrived in the Oval Office at 11:45 on April 20 for a fifteen-minute appointment. Basing his appeal on photos and firsthand descriptions of the horrors of Buchenwald, which foreshadowed the enormity of Hitler's atrocities against the Jews, Wise told Truman it was time to seriously consider providing U.S. support for a homeland for Jews in Palestine. Having previously endorsed the Zionist goal as senator, Truman was inclined to help. However, he had already received a memo from Stettinius saying that the U.S. had vital interests in the Middle East and that the subject should be handled carefully. Truman likely told Wise that he would try to assist but there is no evidence that he made a commitment.

At noon Averell Harriman, the fifty-three-year-old ambassador to the Soviet Union, was introduced to Truman for the first time. Knowing that Truman was scheduled to meet with Foreign Minister Molotov in two days, Harriman had flown from Moscow to Washington in record time, a little over forty-nine hours. Harriman's aim was to persuade Truman that in his sessions with Molotov, it was time for the U.S. to stand firm with the Soviets—that is, to insist that they live up to their agreements at Yalta concerning self-determination for the liberated people in Eastern Europe, with a particular focus on democratization of Poland's government and the scheduling of free elections. Harriman believed that the new administration should back off the policy of accommodation that FDR had followed until shortly before his death.

Truman had never worked with anyone having a background like that of Harriman. As the son of a railroad baron, Harriman had inherited fabulous wealth, attended elite schools (Groton, Yale), become a nationally ranked polo player, and served as chairman of the Union Pacific Railroad and a partner in Brown Brothers Harriman, a lucrative investment banking firm. He was also tall, dark, and handsome. A glamor photo of Harriman on skis at his Sun Valley resort appeared on a magazine cover in the late 1930s.

In the presence of Ed Stettinius, Chip Bohlen, and Undersecretary of State Joseph Grew, Harriman began by explaining to his new chief that "the Soviet Union had two policies which they thought they could successfully pursue at the same time—one, the policy of co-operation with the United States and Great Britain, and the other, the extension of Soviet control over neighboring states through unilateral action."[58] Harriman told Truman that in his judgment the Soviets were engaged in "a barbarian invasion of Europe."[59] Our policy—meaning FDR's policy—of "generosity" and "cooperation," Harriman said, had been "misinterpreted" as weakness, but the U.S. "had nothing to lose by standing firm on issues that were of real importance. . . ." He reasoned that the Soviets would need American help in postwar reconstruction and would not risk a break with the U.S. Truman agreed, saying that he "intended to be firm with the Russians and [to make] no concessions from American principles or traditions for the fact of winning their favor."[60]

Harriman questioned Truman on the relationship of two issues of "real importance"—the composition of the Polish government and the establishment of the UN. Truman replied that the Senate's approval of U.S. entry into the UN would be dependent on satisfactory resolution of the Polish issue and that without the U.S. there would be no UN. Truman said he would stress this critical point with Molotov "in words of one syllable."[61]

When the others left the room, Harriman took Truman aside and told him that he was "relieved to discover" that in his limited time as president he had managed to read all of FDR's cable traffic with Stalin and "that we see eye to eye on the situation."[62] By this he meant that Truman fully understood that Stalin was breaking his agreements at Yalta.

Molotov arrived in Washington on Sunday, April 22, and met briefly and amicably with Truman after dinner at Blair House. They exchanged platitudes about friendship and their confidence that present and future difficulties could be resolved. Truman was restrained. He encouraged

Molotov to adhere to the agreements at Yalta, including "the Polish matter." They departed with the understanding that Molotov would meet with Stettinius and British foreign secretary Anthony Eden the next day with the objective of resolving the Polish question.

"Stony arse" Molotov, as Eden called him, remained immovable. As a result it was decided that Truman would meet Molotov late that afternoon "and explain to him in blunt terms the effect of his attitude on future co-operation between the great powers."[63] But before seeing Molotov again, Truman wanted reassurance from his top diplomatic and military advisers, all of whom he had inherited from FDR. A surprise meeting was convened at 2 p.m. on April 23. The "consensus of opinion," wrote Admiral Leahy, "was that the time had arrived to take a strong attitude toward the Soviet Union and that no particular harm could be done to our war prospects if Russia should slow down or even stop its war effort in Europe or Asia."[64] Henry Stimson and George Marshall, however, expressed reservations about confrontation with the Soviets, fearing that Stalin might not follow through on his promise to declare war against Japan after Germany was defeated. Truman was not persuaded. He adjourned the meeting, vowing to take a firm stand. Averell Harriman's advocacy from the outset had turned out to be determinative.

The expected showdown with Molotov began at 5:30 p.m. when Truman received him, this time in the Oval Office. Almost immediately he zeroed in on the Polish matter. According to Chip Bohlen's minutes, Truman informed Molotov that "the United States Government could not agree to be a party to the formation of a Polish Government which was not representative of all Polish democratic elements."[65] He went on to say, however, that the U.S. intended to go forward with organization of the UN despite their differences on other issues but he warned that lack of progress on the Polish question could undermine American support for economic assistance to the Soviet Union. Though not exactly a threat, the latter point was not lost on Molotov.

When Molotov sought to explain, Truman interjected more than once, saying he merely wished that the Soviet government would live up to its agreements at Yalta. According to Bohlen, Molotov "turned a little ashy" and tried to divert the discussion but Truman cut him off again. He concluded the interview with a curt "That will be all, Mr. Molotov. . . . I would appreciate it if you would transmit my views to Marshal Stalin."[66]

In his memoirs written years later, Truman claimed that the meeting ended on a much more acrimonious note, with Molotov complaining, "I have never been talked to like that in my life," and Truman sharply responding, "Carry out your agreements and you won't get talked to like that."[67] Since there is no mention of Truman's version in the contemporaneous notes and minutes prepared by Bohlen and in the written accounts by the Soviet interpreter and others in attendance, there is reason to believe that Truman, prone to embellishment, imagined this angry dialogue in order to emphasize his own firmness in dealing with Molotov. Nevertheless, several historians have suggested that this exchange signified a "sharp reversal" by Truman of FDR's conciliatory policy toward the Soviet Union, the "beginning of the postwar divergence that led to confrontation."[68]

This interpretation of the Truman–Molotov meeting exaggerates its significance. Indeed, Bohlen wrote later that "Truman merely said what Roosevelt would have said had he been alive."[69] Rather than a dramatic "reversal" of policy, Truman's tough talk with Molotov, if it happened at all, was a mere blip in Truman's slow and halting movement away from his predecessor's belief that a policy of cooperation and faith in the UN was the best way to check the aggressive designs of the Soviets.

Wednesday, April 25, turned out to be momentous. For it was on this day that President Truman caught a fleeting yet positive glimpse of the future—an end to the war, liberation of the survivors, and the establishment of a world organization to keep the peace.

The important part of the day began at noon, when Henry Stimson arrived in the Oval Office. The elderly but wise war secretary, who was approaching the age of seventy-eight, handed the president a top secret two-and-a-quarter-page memorandum, which he asked Truman to read while he waited in silence. In hindsight, it ranks as one of the most farsighted foreign relations documents in the annals of American diplomacy, a paper that accurately predicted a looming threat to civilization, a threat that should be immediately addressed by U.S. policymakers and the president. The first sentence riveted Truman's attention: "Within four months [August 1945] we shall in all probability have completed the most terrible weapon ever known in human history, one bomb of which could destroy an entire city." From his days in the Senate and from FDR himself, Truman had known that there was an atomic bomb project but not that such a bomb would likely be ready in August, nor that it could be "the most terrible weapon" in history. Instead of focusing on the short-term use of the weapon for purposes of ending the war in the Pacific, Stimson's memo pointed out that "world civilization" would eventually be at the mercy of other nations or groups that would take advantage of widely known nuclear technology and produce atomic bombs. For that reason, he wrote, the United States had a "moral responsibility" to prevent proliferation and control use of such weapons so that "the peace of our world and our civilization can be saved." He declared that "the question of sharing [the atomic bomb] with other nations and, if so shared, upon what terms, becomes a primary question of our foreign relations." Since Stimson had made a point in his memo that "Russia" was the only nation other than the U.S. capable of producing an atomic bomb "in the next few years," he was suggesting by implication that the president and his foreign policy team should take up the question of whether to share U.S. nuclear know-how with the Soviet Union.* He asked that a committee be established to recommend a course of action to the president and other branches of government.

As soon as Truman finished reading, General Leslie Groves, head of the "Manhattan Project," as the U.S. atomic bomb project was called, slipped into the Oval Office through a side door. To avoid being seen by reporters who hovered near the West Wing entrance, he had been told to come into the White House through a back door. Truman immediately recognized Groves, a large man with a luxurious mustache who was about six feet tall and weighed 250 pounds. Groves had earlier overseen the construction of the Pentagon in record time. Like Stimson, Groves

---

* Memorandum discussed with the president, April 25, 1945, National Security Archives online, https://nsarchives.gwu.edu/document/28505-document-6b-memorandum-discussed -president-april-25-1945.

brandished a memorandum, which he handed to Truman. In contrast to Stimson's policy paper, Groves's memo concisely described the genesis of the Manhattan Project, the power of a nuclear explosion (between five thousand and twenty thousand tons of TNT), and the potential of the bomb for "winning the war more quickly with a saving in American lives."[70]

Truman's questions and comments during and after his meeting with Stimson and Groves suggest that the president was more interested in using the atomic bomb to win the war, save lives, and liberate the survivors than in grappling with the moral responsibility to control its use and deciding whether to share it with the Soviet Union. Referring to the possible use of the weapon on Japan, Truman confided to a White House staffer right after Stimson and Groves left, "I am going to have to make a decision which no man in history has ever made."[71]

At a few minutes after 2 p.m. on this extraordinary day, Truman's motorcade pulled up to the entrance to the Pentagon. The president had received a report from his ambassador in Stockholm that Heinrich Himmler, the head of the Gestapo and implementer of "the final solution," had submitted a proposal via the Swedish Red Cross to surrender German forces on the Western Front to the Anglo-American allies but not those fighting the Red Army on the Eastern Front. It was unclear exactly what forces Himmler proposed to surrender and whether he had authority to speak for the German government. However, the fact that he had made some kind of a surrender offer meant that Hitler's Third Reich was probably beginning to collapse.

Accompanied by the Joint Chiefs, Truman was taken to a secure communications room to discuss Himmler's offer with Prime Minister Winston Churchill. A call was patched through. According to a transcript of the conversation, Truman, who was speaking to Churchill for the first time, said, "If [Himmler] is speaking for the German government as a whole," he must "include the surrender of everything, and it ought to be all three governments," meaning the U.S., Great Britain, and the Soviet Union. Churchill agreed, declaring that once Stalin signaled his approval, the Red Cross in Stockholm should inform Himmler that all German forces must surrender unconditionally and simultaneously to the three powers.[72] Turning to other matters, Truman and Churchill spoke of having a face-to-face meeting "some day soon." As to the "Polish situation," Churchill said he agreed with all that Truman had done. "In fact," he said, "I am following your lead, backing up whatever you do on the matter."[73]

That evening, in a speech broadcast by radio from the White House to the delegates at the United Nations organizing conference in the San Francisco Opera House, President Truman envisioned a future in which the nations of the world would "live together in peace." Since he was speaking at the opening session of the conference, his hopes "for cooperation of the nations" were high, perhaps too high, as he called for the "establishment of a world organization for the *enforcement of peace*."[74]

Truman's euphoria was short-lived. By the end of the UN conference, tensions among the delegates had been aggravated rather than alleviated, mainly due to Molotov's request that the Lublin Poles be recognized as Poland's representatives at the conference and the arrest by the Soviets of sixteen non-Communist Poles who had been promised safe passage to Moscow to discuss "reorganization" of the Lublin regime. U.S. delegates Averell Harriman and influential Republican senator Arthur Vandenberg did not hide their hostility toward the Soviets, nor did they hesitate to spread the word at the conference that everything should be done to impede Soviet attempts to dominate Poland. In his diary, Vandenberg wrote that "we should stand our ground against the Russians and quit appeasing Stalin and Molotov."[75] For the first time, Americans blamed the Soviet Union more than Britain for causing difficulties in cooperation among the Big Three.

———

Thousands of miles to the east, on the same day that Truman was told about the bomb and delivered his UN speech, American and Red Army soldiers linked up at the Elbe River as comrades in arms. "Once they recognized us, we were all buddies," recalled Corporal James J. McDonnell, among the first to meet elements of a Soviet rifle regiment on a destroyed bridge at Torgau.[76] It was a historic moment because it meant that Nazi Germany had been almost split in half, with the Red Army occupying the

east and the Western Allied forces overrunning the west. Known thereafter as "Elbe Day" by the liberated citizens of Torgau, the linkup has been
celebrated annually there since April 25, 1945.

Two days later Truman issued a statement: "The last faint, desperate
hope of Hitler and his gangster government has been extinguished. This is
not the hour of final victory in Europe, but the hour draws near. . . ."[77] Truman was kept advised almost hourly as events in Europe flashed by. On
April 28, Benito Mussolini, the fascist dictator of Italy, was shot by partisans along with his mistress, his bullet-riddled body hung upside down
from a gantry above a petrol station in Milan. The next day, German officials surrendered to the three allied powers in Caserta, ending the war in
Italy. Ten miles north of Munich, the U.S. 45th Infantry Division liberated
thirty-two thousand prisoners in the Dachau death camp, mostly Jews.
There the sickened and outraged soldiers found piles of emaciated corpses
and railroad cars packed with decomposing bodies. Rampaging prisoners
clubbed SS guards and informers, beating them to death and tearing their
bodies apart. American soldiers machine-gunned guards until officers
stepped in.

On the morning of April 30, Hitler tested an ampule of cyanide on his
beloved Alsatian canine named Blondi to make sure the poison worked. It
did. That afternoon, after lunch, he entered his study, which was in the
Führerbunker's thirty-room office-and-living complex located below the
old Reich Chancellery garden in central Berlin. He was joined there by Eva
Braun, whom he had married in a private ceremony the previous day. Apparently, none of Hitler's aides heard the single gunshot. Just after 3:15
Heinz Linge, Hitler's valet, entered the study and found Braun dead from
biting into one of Hitler's cyanide ampules. Slumped on a sofa next to her
sat the führer. He had shot himself in his mouth with a Walther PPK
7.65 mm pistol. Truman received word of Hitler's death while getting a
massage in the White House.

On the day Hitler committed suicide, Truman spent hours listening
to Joe Davies, a wealthy Washington lawyer who had served as ambassador
to the Soviet Union from 1936 to 1938. He was married to cereal heiress
Marjorie Merriweather Post. An unabashed supporter of Stalin and an
advocate of Soviet–American amity, Davies defended the Soviet position

on Poland and counseled Truman that he should avoid a "get tough" attitude when dealing with Molotov and Stalin. As British historian Wilson Miscamble wrote, "Davies proved a crucial influence on Truman's following the more cautious and even conciliatory approach," the same strategy that FDR had employed. "It was just plain horse sense," argued Davies, "to exhaust every possible means" to preserve unity.[78]

As if triggered by Hitler's death, the final collapse of the Third Reich began to accelerate at midafternoon on Wednesday, May 2, when Soviet artillery shells suddenly stopped falling on Berlin. An ominous quiet descended upon the city. Fear of Red Army revenge was in the air. Berlin's commandant, General Karl Weidling, had surrendered what was left of his troops earlier in the day to Soviet general Vasili Ivanovich Chuikov. Powerful loudspeakers across the city had announced the end of hostilities. The big red flag could be seen fluttering in the breeze at the top of the Reichstag.

In Washington on the same day, Truman approved Stimson's recommendation to create what would become known as "the Interim Committee," a group of eight civilians, including three prominent scientists associated with the Manhattan Project. The mandate of the committee was to formulate postwar atomic policy concerning the control and sharing of nuclear technology, but the committee spent most of its time developing recommendations concerning the use of the bomb against Japan. Truman appointed Stimson as chair and approved his request that Jimmy Byrnes should be on the committee as the president's personal representative (Stimson likely knew that Truman was going to replace Stettinius with Byrnes as secretary of state).

Over the next four days, the president received reports that hundreds of German submarines were being scuttled, that German ground forces in the Netherlands and northwest Germany had stopped fighting, and that formal surrender negotiations were taking place at General Eisenhower's headquarters in Reims. From the Far East and the Pacific, Truman was advised that the capital city of Rangoon in Burma had been liberated, kamikazes had scored major successes against American ships off Okinawa, and Japanese fire balloons had reached Oregon on the U.S. West Coast.

At 2:15 on the morning of May 7, General Alfred Jodl and Admiral

Hans-Georg von Friedeburg climbed the stairs to the second floor of a redbrick school building in Reims, the "war room" of Eisenhower's headquarters. In the presence of Ike's chief of staff, Walter Bedell "Beetle" Smith, a Soviet general, several Allied officers, and seventeen reporters and photographers, Jodl and Friedeburg, on the behalf of the German government, signed the unconditional surrender documents. Jodl was led into Eisenhower's office. By this time, Ike had toured Ohrdruf, a liberated Nazi death camp, where he viewed more than "3,000 naked, emaciated bodies" that had been flung into shallow graves or lay in streets where they had fallen.[79] Seated at his desk, Eisenhower looked up at Jodl. "Do you understand the terms of the document of surrender you have just signed?" Jodl answered, *"Ja. Ja."* Ike added a warning: "You will be personally responsible if the terms of the surrender are violated. That is all." Eisenhower cabled his last war report to Washington. "The mission of this Allied Force was fulfilled at 0241 local time, May 7, 1945."[80]

Truman had to hold off officially announcing the surrender on the seventh even though thousands had gathered in Times Square to celebrate. He had agreed with Churchill and Stalin that their three governments would announce the unconditional surrender simultaneously. Since Stalin was receiving reports that the Wehrmacht and the Red Army were still fighting, the dictator insisted that the announcement be delayed until he was satisfied that the fighting had stopped.

That night Truman slept in the White House for the first time. Earlier in the day, Harry, Bess, Margaret, and Mrs. Wallace had moved clothing and furniture from their apartment and some newly purchased pieces into the freshly painted second-floor living quarters. "We had moved from the Blair House with very little commotion," wrote Truman, "except that Margaret's piano had to be hoisted through a window of the second-floor living room."[81] A half-full truckload of possessions was all that the Trumans required, whereas it had taken twenty army trucks to haul the Roosevelts' twelve years of accumulated belongings to Hyde Park.

The White House the Roosevelts left behind was "a mess," complained Margaret, with carpets threadbare and draperies rotting.[82] "Mrs. Roosevelt told Bess and me," wrote Truman to his mother, that the White House was "infested with rats!"[83]

The next morning, May 8, it was not only Truman's birthday, his sixty-first. It was also Victory in Europe Day, known thereafter in America as V-E Day. Before going downstairs, Truman wrote a letter to his mother and sister, Mary Jane. "So far luck has been with me," he wrote. "I hope it keeps up."[84] From his desk in the Oval Office at 8:30 a.m., the president broke the news of Germany's surrender to the press. When he was finished, the reporters stampeded out of the room to get to the phones. Merriman Smith, one of the most respected journalists, was in such a rush that he fell and broke his arm. Truman waited until they were gone and then calmly headed to the Diplomatic Reception Room, where a battery of twelve microphones and a flock of photographers awaited him, along with Bess, Margaret, the Joint Chiefs, Stimson, Forrestal, Byrnes, the cabinet, and several others. "The guests murmured quietly," wrote George Elsey, as Truman took his seat at "the battered old desk that F.D.R. had used for years."[85]

At 9 a.m. Truman began reading his speech to a record-setting radio audience. "This is a solemn but a glorious hour," he began. "I only wish that Franklin D. Roosevelt had lived to witness this day. General Eisenhower informs me that the forces of Germany have surrendered to the United Nations. The flags of freedom fly over all Europe." Nevertheless, he cautioned, "We must work to finish the war. Our victory is but half-won. The West is free, but the East is still in bondage to the treacherous tyranny of the Japanese." He concluded by proclaiming the following Sunday "a day of prayer" for an end to the war against Japan and guidance "into the ways of peace."[86]

At the instigation of Stimson and Forrestal, who were concerned that U.S. insistence on "unconditional surrender" would cause the Japanese never to give up and to fight to their deaths, Truman released a separate message to their government and to their citizens. "Unconditional surrender does not mean the extermination or enslavement of the Japanese people," proclaimed the president. What it did mean, he promised, was returning "the soldiers and sailors to their families, their farms, their jobs" and an end to the "suffering of the Japanese in the vain hope of victory." It is up to you, declared the president, either "utter destruction" or the end of the war.[87] Tens of millions of leaflets containing a photo of Truman, together with his message translated into Japanese, were dropped from B-29s over the Japanese home islands. The government in Tokyo did not respond.

At some point during that busy day, Truman telephoned Eleanor Roosevelt. "I told her," Truman wrote in his memoirs, "that in this hour of triumph I wished that it had been President Roosevelt, and not I, who had given the [surrender] message to our people."[88]

The day ended with a birthday party for Harry and some of his pals, including Tom Evans, a drugstore magnate and owner of radio station KCMO, one of Truman's best friends from Kansas City. After more than a few old-fashioneds and dinner, the president was presented with a large white frosted cake that had been prepared by Elizabeth Moore, one of the White House cooks. Apparently, a slice had slipped off Truman's plate, because a photo shows him beaming while one of his inebriated friends pretends to be a dog licking frosting off the floor. After the dinner party was over, Truman went into the kitchen to thank Ms. Moore. Alonzo Fields, a tall African American who had served as head butler since the presidency of Herbert Hoover, observed that this was the first time since President Coolidge that a president had entered the White House kitchen. "I always felt that [Truman] understood me," wrote Fields, "not as a servant to be tolerated. . . . President Roosevelt was genial and warm but he left one feeling, as most aristocrats do, that they really do not understand one."[89]

Thanking the staff, whether Black or white, and treating them as fellow human beings were second nature to Harry. He was thoughtful, considerate, and just plain kind, character traits that engendered loyalty and devotion. Ms. Moore, the African American who had baked the cake, went home that night with a warm feeling.

Chapter 5

Second Coming in Wrath

In contrast to Franklin Roosevelt, who was prone to delay important decisions until events forced his hand, Truman seemed eager to make decisions on the spot during the early months of his presidency. "You could go into his office with a question and come out with a decision from him more swiftly than from any man I have ever known," recalled Averell Harriman.[1] Truman's tendency to make hasty decisions is perplexing because he was so new to the job. Perhaps he thought that snap decisions rather than deliberation and delay would demonstrate strength of conviction while masking his insecurities.

Barely a month after taking office, Truman proudly told British foreign secretary Anthony Eden during his first meeting with him, "I am here to make decisions, and whether they prove right or wrong I am going to take them."[2] Truman of course didn't grasp it at the time, but just a few days earlier, he had made two "shoot from the hip" decisions that would prove to be major mistakes. On May 10, he signed off on a directive on how postwar Germany was to be governed by U.S. occupation forces. In fact, it was nothing more than a watered-down version of the discredited

Morgenthau Plan, which had been designed to turn Germany into a nation of farmers on land that could never feed its eighty million citizens. During the last months of his administration, FDR, having been advised by Stimson and Assistant Secretary of War John J. McCloy, abandoned his support of the Morgenthau Plan. If FDR had briefed Truman on his policy or put him in touch with Stimson or McCloy, he would never have signed the directive. When Stimson learned what Truman had done, he bluntly informed the new president that he had made a mistake in approving the directive because it still placed strict limits on the revival of German industry and specifically banned "the economic rehabilitation of Germany."[3] Stimson explained that the directive would subject millions of Germans who had survived the war to a starvation diet and hinder the recovery of Europe itself. Truman almost immediately agreed with his secretary of war, later saying that he was "never in favor of that crazy plan."[4] General Eisenhower, the initial commander of occupation forces, insisted that the directive be suppressed. Thereafter, it was circumvented by Ike's successors and eventually replaced. Nevertheless, Henry Morgenthau, whom Truman had inherited as treasury secretary, continued to advocate for implementation of the directive as written until he resigned on the eve of the Potsdam Conference in July.

The next day, Friday, May 11, Truman made another mistake, this one even more consequential because it resulted in a further deterioration of relations with the Soviet Union. The issue involved the curtailment of Lend-Lease deliveries of supplies and war matériel to the Soviet Union following the cessation of hostilities in Europe (as required of all U.S. allies by the Lend-Lease legislation). Truman's mistake was that he signed a memorandum presented to him without reading it. "[Acting Secretary of State Joseph Grew and Foreign Economic Administrator Leo Crowley] asked me to sign it. I reached for my pen and, without reading the document, I signed it."[5] Truman neglected to add that Grew and Crowley had warned him in advance that the cutbacks authorized by the memo would cause serious "difficulty with the Russians."[6] Though the document signed by Truman allowed continuation of military supplies to the Soviets for use in the Pacific theater on the assumption that they would declare war against Japan, essentially all other Lend-Lease deliveries were to be "cut off

immediately as far as physically possible."[7] The next day federal bureau-
crats implemented the provisions of the memo by ordering that the load-
ing of ships bound for the Soviet Union and other countries receiving
Lend-Lease aid be immediately halted and that vessels at sea carrying Lend-Lease supplies be recalled to the U.S.

Truman blamed Grew and Crowley for his mistake but it was he who
bears responsibility for what turned out to be a major diplomatic blunder.
If Truman had been schooled by Roosevelt, he would have been told to
beware of the State Department, to avoid hasty decisions, especially when
they involved the Soviet Union, and if he did not have time to read a document himself, to place it in the hands of a trusted adviser to review and
recommend. Warned in advance that the document would cause "difficulty with the Russians," FDR would have toned it down and handled the
matter tactfully through personal diplomacy.

Though the Soviets had been told that the law required a curtailment
of Lend-Lease supplies after the defeat of Germany, and were therefore not
"completely surprised" as many historians have asserted, it was the suddenness of the cutoff that riled the Soviet leadership.[8] When word of Truman's decision reached Stalin and Molotov, they quickly concluded that
the new president had weaponized Lend-Lease, using it as leverage to pressure them to yield on the two major issues pending from the UN conference in San Francisco—the composition of the Polish government and
voting procedures in the Security Council. Both Ambassador to the Soviet
Union Harriman and Secretary of State Stettinius had helped draft the
memo that Truman signed, but they believed the communication of its
substance had been badly mishandled. Harriman tried to stem the Soviet
outrage by obtaining authority from Truman to order the ships at sea to
turn around and deliver their cargoes to Soviet ports and to resume load-
ing on U.S. docks. But the Soviet leaders were not appeased. Stalin later
told Harry Hopkins that Truman's decision was "brutal." If it had been
"designed as pressure on the Russians in order to soften them up," he said,
"then it was a fundamental mistake."[9]

Later, as Truman settled into the job, he was much more deliberative
in arriving at important decisions. Just as Harry Hopkins had been the
trusted adviser who helped FDR avoid mistakes, Sam Rosenman and then

Clark Clifford would become Truman's most trusted and capable trouble-shooters.

————

S tung by the criticism and uproar over the Lend-Lease fiasco, Truman was grateful to receive a phone call from Joe Davies at four on the afternoon of the second Sunday of May, Mother's Day. He was grateful because the former ambassador to the Soviet Union, a confirmed Sovietophile, expressed grave concern over the deterioration of relations with the Russians and offered to advise him on how to restore peace and understanding in a "spirit of 'give and take.'"[10] Even though Truman's mother and sister, Mary Jane, had just arrived for a week's stay in the White House, the president asked Davies to come right over for a "family supper," after which the two of them would discuss the restoration of relations with Soviet leaders. Davies did not hesitate. At supper he ingratiated himself with Truman by charming his "mamma," whom Davies described as a "dear old lady—93—bright as a 'squirrel' and 'All American!'"[11]

Truman and Davies retired to the library and talked until midnight. Davies began by reading a letter he had written the day before in which he again discouraged Truman from using a "get tough" approach with the Soviets, urged tolerance, and warned that threatening the Soviets or trying to isolate them would prove "disastrous."[12] Like Roosevelt, Davies advocated a policy of cooperation and accommodation. He blamed "anti-Soviet bias" on the part of State Department officials for the hostility that pervaded relations with the Russians at the UN meetings in San Francisco. Truman heartily agreed, only too happy to shift responsibility to the "striped pants boys." He told Davies in confidence that Byrnes would soon replace Secretary Stettinius, implying that Byrnes would shake things up at the State Department. At one point Truman asked Davies if he could travel to Moscow and arrange a face-to-face meeting for him with Stalin. Davies declined, citing his poor health and doctor's orders, but he offered to write to Marshal Stalin (through Molotov) and suggest that if Stalin would agree to have a "frank, personal, heart-to-heart talk" with Truman, many of "these misunderstandings could be cleared up."[13] A cable to that effect was sent the next day through the Soviet embassy.

Since Davies could not travel to Moscow to try to restore amicable relations with Stalin, Truman searched for an alternative. It turned out that Harriman had in mind the ideal candidate—Harry Hopkins. It was Hopkins whom Roosevelt had sent to Moscow in the summer of 1941 to establish a collaborative relationship with Stalin. As a result of that and subsequent encounters at Tehran and Yalta, Hopkins was held in high regard by Stalin. Along with Chip Bohlen, Harriman sounded out Hopkins in the bedroom of his house in Georgetown. His response to Harriman's request that he fly to Moscow and meet again with Stalin "was wonderful to behold," wrote Robert Sherwood. "Although he appeared to be too ill to get out of bed and walk across N Street, the mere intimation of a flight to Moscow converted him into the traditional old fire horse at the sound of the alarm."[14]

Truman was at first hesitant. But the more he thought about it, the more Hopkins seemed the logical choice. By sending Hopkins, Truman would signal to the Soviets that he intended to continue the Roosevelt policy of friendship and cooperation. At the same time Truman had been persuaded by Harriman that Hopkins, based on his relationship with Stalin, stood the best chance of convincing him to keep his word and adhere to the Yalta agreements.

On May 19 Truman cabled Marshal Stalin via navy channels that Hopkins would join Harriman on his return to Moscow to meet with him personally on "complicated and important questions with which we are faced."[15] There was no mention of hot-button issues such as Lend-Lease, the Polish question, or the UN. Instead, his message was purposely vague, suggesting that all aspects of U.S.–Soviet relations would be up for discussion. On the same day, Truman summoned Hopkins from his sickbed to the White House to be briefed on his mission. In his instructions to Hopkins, Truman was equally vague, saying only that Hopkins should feel free to use "diplomatic language or a baseball bat" to achieve a "fair understanding" with the Soviet government and that he should invite Stalin to come to the U.S. to meet with the president.[16] However, a private note concerning his instructions to Hopkins, which Truman wrote on May 23, was both specific and deeply revealing. There, he made it clear that

Hopkins should not be concerned with Soviet influence and control over the Eastern European and Baltic states (he named each one). As to "free elections" in Poland, Truman instructed that Hopkins should settle for a face-saving arrangement, something akin to how political bosses in some large U.S. cities dictate electoral outcomes. Truman also charged Hopkins with persuading "Uncle Joe to make some sort of gesture—whether he means it or not" to indicate to the American public that he intended to abide by the agreements he had made at Yalta. "Any smart political boss would do that," he wrote. [17]

Given the leeway accorded Hopkins, it is apparent that in order to achieve amicable relations with the Soviet Union, Truman was willing to give up on the fate of Eastern Europe and even the Baltic states. Moreover, he would have been satisfied with something substantially less than Western-style democracy in Poland.

After three weeks and six amiable sessions with Stalin in Moscow, Hopkins returned to Washington on June 12 with a series of commitments and agreements. A surprising number of the pending issues had been rather quickly settled. As early as the second session, Stalin pronounced that he was "fully satisfied" with Hopkins's explanation that the Lend-Lease debacle was due to bureaucratic "confusion" and was of no "fundamental policy significance." He accepted a suggestion by Harriman (who participated in most of the sessions) that he and Molotov would discuss "the whole Lend Lease matter" the following day.[18] After that breakthrough, Stalin agreed with Hopkins that his Red Army would join the fight against Japan and be prepared to invade Manchuria by August 8, 1945. He pledged to support the unification of China under Chiang Kai-shek's leadership, and he committed the Soviet Union to a four-power trusteeship for Korea. When Hopkins advised Stalin that the Western Allies had been waiting for the Russians to appoint a member of the Allied Control Council for Germany, Stalin appointed Marshal Georgy Zhukov on the spot. Regarding a Big Three meeting, Stalin said he had already agreed with Truman and Churchill that such a meeting (later known as the Potsdam Conference) would take place on July 15 near Berlin.

As to the most contentious issue—the Polish question—Hopkins returned to Washington with a conditional understanding, which he and Stalin managed to finalize on the last day of their meetings. The "agreement," which was not spelled out in a single document, was designed to reorganize and partially democratize the Soviet-sponsored Lublin regime (Communists) in Warsaw by adding to it a minority group consisting of five non-Communist Poles residing in Poland and three living in England. It took long hours for Hopkins and Stalin to agree on the names of the eight outsiders and secure the approval of Churchill and Roosevelt. These eight and three of the majority Lublin Poles were to be invited to "consult" with a three-member commission in Moscow chaired by Molotov. If all three members of the commission were to agree that the eight were acceptable, that group would become a minority voice in forming a new Polish provisional government that would presumably in due course call for free elections as agreed at Yalta. Hopkins reported to Truman that, during the negotiations for this agreement, he had pressed hard for Stalin to release from prison sixteen Polish underground leaders who Stalin claimed had been involved in "diversionist" activities (the U.S. regarded them as political prisoners).[19] Stalin would not budge. Hopkins promptly backed down and later advised Truman that it would have been a "mistake" to condition the release of the dissident prisoners on "the starting of the consultation in Moscow promptly."[20] Truman agreed, praising Hopkins for doing "a grand job," even though the deal Hopkins had struck with Stalin was little more than window dressing.[21] The Moscow commission, which was chaired by Molotov, might have allowed the eight non–Lublin Poles to consult with it, but Molotov, acting for Stalin, would never have allowed Poland to become truly independent, much less permitted free elections. In a June 4 letter to Truman, Churchill warned that the Hopkins–Stalin agreement would not solve the Polish problem.[22] He was right. However, his alarm fell on deaf ears in Washington.

Perhaps to mollify Hopkins and Truman for flatly refusing to release the prisoners, Stalin gave Hopkins a gift to take home to the president. Near the end of the last of his six sessions with Stalin, Hopkins brought up the fact that the UN convention in San Francisco had reached an impasse that threatened to doom approval of the UN Charter. The problem was that the Soviet delegates at the convention, instructed by Molotov, were insisting that the veto provision in the Security Council should apply not only to decisions and actions, as previously agreed, but also to mere discussions. In the presence of Hopkins and Bohlen, Stalin reprimanded Molotov, calling his position "nonsense."[23] The delegates were ordered to reverse the Soviet position and side with the Americans. In doing so Stalin was repeating a pattern he had followed at Yalta: conceding on a UN issue that was not that important to him in exchange for preserving a virtually free hand in Poland, which he regarded as vital.

The day after Hopkins returned, Truman held a press conference. Despite having been warned by Hopkins not to be overly optimistic, Truman nevertheless announced that the Hopkins mission was "completely satisfactory and gratifying," and he predicted a path forward to "a just and durable peace." Asked about the Polish situation, he said that it was "on the road to a complete settlement," though no details as to the deal Hopkins negotiated with Stalin were discussed or released.[24]

Virtually all of the U.S. media assessments of the Hopkins mission pronounced it to have been successful across the board. However, with respect to Poland, the *Times* of London was more nuanced, writing that the mission contributed "to the better prospects of a Polish settlement."[25] No doubt this statement was influenced by Churchill's misgivings.

Hopkins's mission to Moscow was his last, thus ending a lifetime of service to the American people. He resigned from the government in early July and moved with his wife to a six-story town house in New York City across from Central Park, which was most likely financed by his friend Averell Harriman. Hopkins returned to Washington only once, when in September Truman presented him with a Distinguished Service Medal in the Rose Garden. Beginning in mid-October his health began to deteriorate even further but he continued to smoke incessantly. He never recovered. A week after dictating a short but affectionate note to Churchill, Hopkins lapsed into a coma and died.

Truman owed a debt of gratitude to Hopkins. The favorable publicity that resulted from the Hopkins mission boosted the president's approval rating in June to 87 percent, three points higher than ever recorded for Franklin Roosevelt. In part because of his decision to send Hopkins to

Moscow but mainly due to the prospect of troops coming home after the surrender of Germany, Truman's approval ratings, though beginning to decline, remained just above 80 percent for the rest of 1945. Of course, there were other factors that contributed to Truman's popularity during his first six months in office. People felt comfortable referring to him as "Harry." They liked his modest, unassuming, down-home Midwestern style—an ordinary next-door-neighbor kind of fellow they could relate to. Referring to the contrast between Roosevelt and Truman, Harry Vaughan quipped, "After a diet of caviar, you like to go back to ham and eggs."[26]

With the signing of the UN Charter set for June 25, Truman flew to the West Coast to spend a day with his former Senate friend Mon Wallgren, governor of Washington state, before going on to San Francisco to particpate in the signing ceremony and address the closing session. When he arrived in Washington, he was informed that the Soviet delegates were insisting that there should be limits in the charter on what could be discussed in the General Assembly. It took three days to settle the issue. As a result, the ceremony had to be delayed. Truman spent the weekend salmon fishing in Puget Sound with the governor. The local papers heaped criticism on him for going fishing while WWII raged.

After proudly watching Ed Stettinius and the other forty-nine foreign ministers sign the charter, Truman spoke to the closing session in the opera house. He characterized the charter as a "new structure of peace," and "an instrument for peace." Invoking Roosevelt, he said the charter had "set up machinery" to foster "cooperation" and avoid "conflict." All well and good, though the terms were vague. But what about the five permanent members of the Security Council, each of which had veto power? On that point, the most Truman could say was that the "strong nations" had a "duty" to lead toward world peace and international justice.[27] In hindsight, the structure of the Security Council was the elephant in the room.

———

Weeks before departing on his mission to Moscow, Hopkins gave Truman advice that he was only too pleased to receive. It was a mistake to ask FDR's cabinet to stay on, said Hopkins. The president should have his own people around him, not Roosevelt's, and he should start with the cabinet.

Since Truman already had a "very poor opinion of many" of FDR's ten cabinet members, some of whom had submitted pro forma resignations, he did not hesitate to act.[28] The first to go was Frank Walker, the postmaster general, who had expressed a desire to retire. In his place Truman nominated DNC chair Bob Hannegan, the person largely responsible for Truman being in position to assume the presidency upon FDR's death. On May 23, the president announced three more changes: Texas lawyer Tom Clark, head of the Justice Department's criminal division, to replace aristocrat Francis Biddle of Philadelphia as attorney general; Truman's Senate friend and confidant Lewis Schwellenbach for Frances Perkins as secretary of labor (Truman had told his staff that he did not want a woman in the cabinet);[29] and former House member Clinton Anderson of New Mexico for Claude Wickard as agriculture secretary.

On June 30, Truman made good on his mid-April promise to former Senate majority leader Jimmy Byrnes that he would be nominated to replace Ed Stettinius as secretary of state. Around this time Sam Rosenman warned the president about Byrnes. "I don't think you know Jimmy Byrnes," he said. "You think you do. In the *bonhomie* of the Senate, he's one kind of a fellow; but I think you will regret this, and if I were you, I wouldn't do it." Later, Truman told Rosenman he should have taken his advice.[30]

Byrnes was sworn in on July 3 at a brief ceremony on the East Portico of the White House. A few days later, Treasury Secretary Morgenthau insisted on announcing his resignation because Truman refused to include him in the forthcoming Big Three conference at Potsdam and would not commit to keeping him on as head of treasury until the end of the war against Japan. Truman later said Morgenthau's plan for Germany "wasn't worth a hoot."[31] To close friends he described Morgenthau as a "nut" and a "blockhead" who didn't "know shit from apple butter."[32] On the afternoon of July 6, just before leaving for Potsdam, the president accepted Morgenthau's resignation and announced that former congressman Fred Vinson, head of the Office of War Mobilization, would be nominated to replace Morgenthau (Truman wanted to make sure that if he and Secretary of State Byrnes were both killed during the journey abroad, Morgenthau would not succeed to the presidency, as the law at the time prescribed).

Thus, on the eve of the Potsdam Conference with Stalin and Churchill,

all that was left of the Roosevelt cabinet were two New Dealers—
curmudgeon Harold Ickes, secretary of the interior, and ultraliberal Henry
Wallace, secretary of commerce—and the secretaries of war and navy,
Henry Stimson and James Forrestal. Truman wanted to retain Ickes since
he had been doing a good job, Wallace because he felt he owed it to him
and to FDR, and Stimson and Forrestal because he could not risk replacing
them with the nation still at war.

––––––––

While the president was in the midst of transforming his cabinet, prominent nuclear physicist Dr. Leo Szilard was desperately trying to get an
appointment with him and "those members of Truman's cabinet who are
responsible for formulating policy."[33] Born in Hungary and educated at the
Institute of Technology in Berlin, where he met Albert Einstein, Szilard fled
to London in 1933 and then to the U.S. in the late thirties. At the University of Chicago, he and Enrico Fermi had built the world's first nuclear
reactor (Chicago Pile-1) capable of achieving a self-sustaining nuclear
chain reaction, which enabled the development and production of atomic
bombs. Knowing that the president and his military advisers were contem-
plating use of the bomb to destroy one or more Japanese cities, Szilard
believed it was vitally important for Truman and members of his cabinet
to understand that use of the bomb would trigger an atomic arms race with
profound implications for world peace and civilization itself. Instead of
being the first nation to "set a precedent for using atomic energy for purposes of destruction," wouldn't it be prudent, he surmised, for the American
government to consider whether avoiding an arms race might be "more
important than the short-term goal of knocking Japan out of the war?"[34]

Though Szilard had plenty of connections to the Roosevelt administration, he was at a loss when it came to knowing those who could get him
into the Truman White House. Finally, through a University of Chicago
mathematician who had worked for Tom Pendergast in Kansas City,
Szilard scored a meeting with Matt Connelly, Truman's new appointments
secretary. At the outset of the meeting, Szilard handed Connelly a letter of
introduction from Albert Einstein and a memorandum explaining Szilard's
concerns about using the bomb against Japan.[35] When Connelly finished

reading these documents, he declared, according to Szilard, "I can see that this is serious business."[36] Apparently, Connelly had already mentioned Szilard's mission to Truman because he told the physicist that the president would like him to travel to Spartanburg, South Carolina, and discuss his concerns with Jimmy Byrnes. Connelly scheduled the appointment with Byrnes for the next day. Szilard had no way of knowing but he was about to get a meeting with the future secretary of state, who would also serve as the president's representative on the Interim Committee, the body that would make recommendations to the president on the use of the bomb and postwar atomic policy.

Having taken the night train to Spartanburg, Szilard and two colleagues arrived the next day, May 27, 1945, at the front porch of a grand neoclassical house in the Converse Heights neighborhood of Spartanburg owned by Donald Russell, Byrnes's law partner, who would soon become assistant secretary of state and later governor of South Carolina. From Szilard's perspective the meeting with Byrnes was a disaster. Instead of focusing on his moral concerns, Szilard tried to make the case that use of the bomb would inevitably endanger national security—namely that by initiating a nuclear arms race with the Soviets and other powers, the U.S. would rather quickly lose its "initial advantage," leaving "most of our major cities" open to a sudden attack in which millions of Americans would perish and perhaps "both countries" would be destroyed. Why didn't the Truman administration pause and consider, with the aid of scientists who "have first-hand knowledge of the facts," whether a policy could be developed to "cope with the problem that the bomb would pose," not only to America but "to the world"?

Byrnes would have none of this. He was immediately put off by Szilard's egocentric attitude and his attempt to meddle in government policy. As incoming secretary of state, Byrnes told Szilard that sole possession of the bomb, albeit for a limited time, would give the United States leverage over Russia's expansionist designs in Europe and the Far East. Moreover, with his eye on domestic politics, Byrnes was convinced that the bomb must be used as soon as possible to end the war with Japan, stop American casualties, and bring the boys home. Since the Japanese people were prepared to fight until their last breath, he argued, the bomb was the only plausible option. Finally, as to the future of postwar atomic research and controls over proliferation, Byrnes's "complete indifference" astonished Szilard and his colleagues.[37]

Notably, there is no evidence that Szilard or Byrnes mentioned, much less discussed, the moral responsibility that the U.S. would bear should it be the first to use the bomb to incinerate noncombatants and open the door to an atomic arms race. However, for Szilard it was the paramount concern. Two months later, he made his position explicit. In a petition to President Truman, Szilard, with sixty-nine Manhattan Project cosigners, urged the president to make public the terms of surrender to the Japanese, and if they still refused to surrender, then he must consider his "moral responsibilities" in deciding whether to use atomic bombs on Japanese cities.[38]

Szilard later recalled that for him the meeting with Byrnes marked the end of an "illusion" about American exceptionalism.[39] He and many of his colleagues had come to believe that the United States was different, that it would take and hold the moral high ground in its foreign relations. If the U.S. did become the first nation to use the bomb against innocent civilians, however, it would cede the moral argument. After the war, any attempts by the American government to persuade the Soviets and other nations on moral grounds to rid themselves of atomic weapons or subject themselves to international control would ring hollow.

———

Shortly after a disillusioned and depressed Leo Szilard departed Spartanburg, Byrnes returned to Washington for a two-day meeting of the Interim Committee at the Pentagon. Though chaired by Secretary of War Stimson, it would be Byrnes, as Truman's personal representative on the committee, who would play a critical role in shaping American policy on the use of the atomic bomb. When U.S. Army chief of staff George Marshall, in the interest of maintaining harmony with Soviet allies, suggested that two Soviet scientists be invited to observe a test of the plutonium bomb in New Mexico, Byrnes nixed the proposal, saying that once information about the bomb was disclosed to the Russians, Stalin would demand "to be brought into the partnership."[40] He also blocked proposals to share atomic research with the Soviets and even the British ("politically untenable in Congress," he said).[41] At lunch on May 31, when Ernest Lawrence, a University of California Nobel laureate, who had invented the cyclotron, proposed that the bomb be detonated in a bloodless demonstration designed to shock the Japanese into surrendering, Byrnes lowered the boom. "If the Japanese were told that the bomb would be used on a given locality," he said, "they might bring our boys who were prisoners of war to that area."[42] Using the same reasoning, Byrnes shot down the idea of giving the Japanese an advance warning that the weapon would be detonated over one of their cities so they could evacuate their citizens. Moreover, Byrnes and others worried that the bomb might not work and that failure would encourage the Japanese to fight on even harder.

The Interim Committee, aided by a panel of handpicked scientific advisers, finalized its recommendations on the use of the bomb on Friday, June 1. Late that afternoon Byrnes rushed from the Pentagon to the White House to brief Truman. The Interim Committee recommended "that the bomb should be used against Japan as soon as possible," reported Byrnes. "To make a profound psychological impression on as many inhabitants as possible," it "should be used on a war plant surrounded by workers' homes," and it should "be used without warning." The idea, Byrnes explained, was to create such a tremendous shock that the Japanese leadership would conclude that the Americans possessed and would use the power of the bomb to destroy the empire and that therefore there was no alternative but to surrender unconditionally. Byrnes pointed out that Dr. Robert Oppenheimer, who was responsible for the research and design of the atomic bomb, had assured the committee that the "visual effect" of the bombing would be otherworldly, an unimaginably "brilliant luminescence which would rise to a height of 10,000 to 20,000 feet."[43]

"With reluctance," recalled Byrnes, the president agreed with the unanimous recommendations of the Interim Committee concerning use of the bomb, never questioning its moral legitimacy as a combat weapon or considering the prospect that its use might spark an arms race or the fact that such bombs would kill tens of thousands of Japanese civilians.[44] Instead, Byrnes and Truman, both seasoned politicians, focused on the hope that one or more atomic bombs could cause the Japanese to surrender, save American lives, and end the Second World War.

Truman never wavered. Indeed, if this was the moment when the "decision" was made to use the bomb against Japan, it was foreordained. As distinguished Stanford historian Barton Bernstein wrote, up until FDR's death, it had been assumed by his key advisers and those directing the Manhattan Project that their commander in chief would deploy the bomb when it was ready. This assumption was regarded by Truman as FDR's legacy, an unspoken bequest to his successor. "For Truman," Bernstein wrote, "the question had never been how to openly challenge this legacy, it was only how to fulfill it, how to remain true to it."[45] General Leslie Groves put it differently but the thought was similar: Truman's "decision was one of noninterference—basically, a decision not to upset the existing plans."[46]

Whether Roosevelt, had he lived, would have decided differently will never be known. The evidence of his thoughts on this question is ambiguous and conflicting.[47] But most historians speculate, with little conviction, that he probably would have used the bomb against Japan.

For the president the nights in the White House during June were long and lonely. On the first of that month, the night before Bess would be leaving Washington, along with her mother and Margaret, to spend the entire summer at home in Independence, Truman wrote in his diary, "I hope—sincerely hope, that this situation (my being president) is not going to affect her adversely."[48] It is obvious from this entry that Bess was not happy. Was it Harry's all-consuming new job, lack of privacy, depression, her role as First Lady, or the creaky old house? Bess's evident unhappiness combined with her monthslong absence from the White House caused tongues to wag in Washington concerning the state of the Truman marriage, just as they had gossiped about the relationship of Franklin and Eleanor. Yet the source of Bess's bouts of unhappiness would remain a mystery.

Since it would not be known for another month if the atomic bomb would actually work, Truman needed to be briefed on whether Japan could be defeated by conventional bombing and naval blockade or whether it would be necessary to launch a ground invasion of the two main Japanese home islands (Kyushu and Honshu). At a meeting of senior military and civilian advisers with Truman on the afternoon of June 18, it was concluded that bombing and a blockade should continue but these actions would not be enough to force the Japanese to surrender. General Marshall pointed out that no nation had ever been bombed as extensively as Germany yet the Germans remained in the war until the Allies invaded and occupied the fatherland. As to whether a naval blockade would cause the Japanese to surrender, none of Truman's advisers except Admiral Leahy believed it would be effective, and even so, it would take far too long to starve the millions of Japanese into submission.

The plan for invading Japan proper, code-named Operation Downfall, would proceed in two phases, explained Marshall. The first phase, Operation Olympic, would be launched on November 1 against Kyushu, the southern island, by an American force of 766,700 combat soldiers. Once the island was secured, at least in part, Kyushu would provide "maneuver room," said Marshall, and would be "essential both to tightening our strangle hold of blockade and bombardment on Japan, and to force capitulation by invasion of the Tokyo Plain."[49] The second phase, the invasion of the main island of Honshu and its Tokyo Plain, called Operation Coronet, would not take place until March 1946. Planners estimated that Coronet would require twenty-four divisions and more than a million soldiers. In answer to Truman's questions concerning casualties, Marshall told the president that U.S. forces would suffer no more than thirty-one thousand casualties during the first thirty days of the battle to take Kyushu (based on the percentage of casualties incurred during the conquest of Luzon). Admiral King, chief of naval operations, said they should not exceed forty-one thousand (based on percentages at Luzon and Okinawa). These casualty estimates were intentionally lowballed by Marshall and King.[50] Other casualty figures were tossed around during the meeting, including the horrific casualties thus far incurred during the ongoing battle to take Okinawa, but as events unfolded all estimates became obsolete because within the next month U.S. intel revealed that actual Japanese troop and air strength (particularly kamikazes) for the defense of Kyushu would be far greater than projected.

After "weighing all the possibilities," Truman accepted the unanimous recommendation of the Joint Chiefs "that the Kyushu operation was the best solution under the circumstances."[51] Consequently, planning for

Operation Olympic was given the green light and a decision on Coronet would be reserved for "final action later."[52]

Another topic raised at the meeting is worth noting. In response to Admiral Leahy's proposal to soften the "unconditional surrender" demand, Truman ducked the issue, saying that "he had left the door open for Congress to take appropriate action with reference to unconditional surrender."[53] He also implied that American public opinion would be against any change. Assistant Secretary of War John J. McCloy later asserted that during the meeting he brought up the idea of warning the Japanese leaders that the U.S. was prepared to use a "terrifyingly destructive weapon" and at the same time informing them that they could retain their emperor. Though there is no mention in the official minutes of this proposal or of the president's reaction, McCloy claimed that Truman instructed him to discuss it with Byrnes. According to McCloy, Byrnes told him that an advance warning would strengthen America's moral position but that revising the unconditional surrender demand to allow retention of the emperor was a nonstarter. Rather than an inducement to surrender, declared Byrnes, the Japanese would regard this concession as a weakness.[54]

—————

On the first leg of his journey by train, ship, and plane to the summit with Churchill and Stalin at Potsdam near Berlin, Harry Truman penned a letter to Bess after having had an unpleasant telephone conversation with her the night before. "I am blue as indigo about going," he wrote. "You didn't seem at all happy when we talked. I'm sorry if I've done something to make you unhappy. All I've ever tried to do is make you pleased with me and the world."[55]

Bess's attitude only added to Truman's considerable stress. He was already worried about how he would get along with the two iconic leaders at Potsdam and whether he would be able to achieve success in negotiations concerning the occupation and future of Germany, Soviet demands for reparations, and Polish borders. He was also most anxious to hear about an atomic bomb test in the New Mexico desert, the results of which could end the war against Japan without a bloody invasion and profoundly alter U.S. relations with the Soviet Union

The test site, code-named "Trinity," was in the isolated Jornada del Muerto ("Dead Man's Journey") desert, 230 miles south of Los Alamos. Robert Oppenheimer, the director of the Los Alamos Laboratory, had named the site after a poem by John Donne that he cherished in which the logic-defying Christian concept of the "glorious Trinity" ("bones to philosophy, but milk to faith") mysteriously imparted to the poet the power "to love" and "to know."[56] Given the purpose of the bomb and the message of the poem, it is impossible to understand why Oppenheimer chose the name Trinity. Some writers, however, believe it was simply a tribute to his lover, Jean Tatlock, who had introduced him to Donne's poetry.[57]

On July 6, the day Truman wrote his letter to Bess, a 140-ton steel sphere containing a plutonium bomb (nicknamed "Gadget"), absent its active components and explosive lenses, was loaded onto a truck for a dry run, and transported to the Trinity site next to a hundred-foot steel tower with a corrugated steel shed on top. The procedures for final assembly at the base of the tower were followed and notes were made for "desirable changes for the hot run." Over the next nine days, changes would be made and the hot run of Gadget would begin. When properly assembled, Gadget would be winched up into the shed at the top of the tower.[58]

After departing his train at the army port of embarkation in Newport News, Virginia, at 6 a.m. on the morning of July 7, the president and his immediate party of fifty-three advisers and newsmen were welcomed aboard the ten-thousand-ton heavy cruiser USS *Augusta* for the next leg of their journey to Potsdam. That night, ensconced alone in the admiral's cabin, Truman wrote in his diary, "How I hate this trip!" A few days earlier, in two separate letters to Bess and then another to his mother and sister, he expressed essentially the same thought—"I hate to go"; "Wish I didn't have to go"; "I'm on the way to the high executioner." Truman's multiple and emphatic expressions about hating the trip suggest that he doth protest too much.[59] While he would have liked Bess and others to believe he was genuinely intimidated or scared, the truth was that he was a self-confident, ambitious politician eager to play on the world stage. His protestations about going to Potsdam were akin to those he made to mask his ambition when he repeatedly said that he did not want to be vice president.

Rather than loathing the trip, Truman thoroughly enjoyed the eight-day ocean cruise to Europe. Each morning, and often during the day with Jimmy Byrnes, the president would take brisk walks up and down the cruiser's long forecastle deck. To his diary Truman referred to Byrnes, his closest adviser, as his "able and conniving Secretary of State," an "honest man" with a "keen mind."[60] The president enjoyed chatting with the sailors as he stood in line with them at chow time carrying an aluminum tray. Though Truman had plenty of time for rest and relaxation, he spent hours alone digesting briefing papers in red binders prepared by the State Department. Almost every day he attended meetings in Byrnes's cabin to discuss issues likely to come up at the Potsdam summit and how to interact with Stalin and Churchill. Key advisers in these sessions included, in addition to Byrnes, Admiral Leahy and Chip Bohlen, who had been at Yalta with Roosevelt. Truman "took advantage of the [shipboard] conferences," wrote Bohlen, "absorb[ing] information and asking pertinent questions. . . . He stuck to business."[61]

The evenings were the best. At six o'clock Truman and his party were entertained before dinner by a thirty-six-piece band. After dinner, the latest movies were shown in the captain's cabin, where Byrnes was billeted. Quite often Truman and his old pals Brigadier General Harry Vaughan and U.S. Marshal Fred Canfil, a few others in his intimate circle, and a couple of reporters would sneak out to play low-stakes poker in the president's cabin. "A most restful and satisfactory trip," wrote Truman to Bess.[62]

As *Augusta* passed Lyme Bay near the western entrance to the English Channel, she was joined by a British escort force of seven destroyers and a light cruiser, each flying the American colors at their foremasts. *Augusta* was well known to the Royal Navy. She had hosted the historic shipboard conference between Roosevelt and Churchill off the coast of Newfoundland in the summer of 1941, joined the British Fleet at Scapa Flow to prevent German battleships from entering the Atlantic Ocean, and supported the Anglo-American amphibious invasions of North Africa, Normandy, and southern France. When Her Majesty's British warships passed

Augusta in July 1945, their crews shouted, "Three cheers for Mr. Truman, President of the United States."[63]

Early on the morning of the fifteenth of July, *Augusta* entered the Westerschelde Estuary, which led through Holland and then Belgium to the great port of Antwerp. The weather was clear and warm. Though Hitler had targeted half of his V-2 bombs on the estuary and his troops had occupied the area as late as the previous November, Truman could see "little evidence of damage."[64] As *Augusta* cruised by small towns, "the President was cheered by hundreds of wildly enthusiastic Belgians and Hollanders lining the south banks."[65] They viewed his arrival in war-torn Europe as the symbol, if not the promise, of rebirth.

Once *Augusta* was moored at Antwerp's municipal dock, "many wrecked buildings and gaping holes" could be seen. "Antwerp was battered, but the greater part of her many docks were still serviceable."[66] The president and his party embarked in a forty-car caravan bound for an airfield several miles northwest of Brussels. The route, lined with recently liberated Belgians, was guarded by soldiers from Truman's old outfit in the First World War, the 137th Infantry Regiment (First Kansas), as well as white-helmeted U.S. Army MPs, Belgian gendarmes, and British soldiers. Along the way, Truman observed bombed-out factories and homes. When his armored car passed Fort Breendonk, Truman was told that it was "the most feared concentration camp for Belgians during the war."[67]

From the Brussels–Evere airport, Truman and his group of advisers boarded FDR's *Sacred Cow* and two other C-54s for the three-hour flight to Berlin. Protected by twelve P-47 Thunderbolts, Truman asked the pilot to fly low over Germany so he could see from his window seat the appalling devastation below. Over the "cities of Kassel and Magdeburg [he] could not see a single house that was left standing." Piles of rubble were the only things that remained. Roads were clogged with displaced persons and refugees. Starvation and pestilence stalked the land. Still, there were hopeful signs—occasional patches of green indicating that fields "seemed to be under cultivation."[68] While flying over the Soviet zone of occupation, Truman was told that the "Red Army soldiers had 'torn up' the factories and taken 'everything out of them. . . . They destroyed everything they could get their hands on.'"[69]

———

Following a ten-mile drive from the airfield near Berlin, Truman and his housemates—Byrnes, Leahy, Bohlen, Vaughan, and press secretary Charlie Ross—arrived at 2 Kaiserstrasse, the president's villa, a three-story stucco house on Lake Griebnitz in the thickly wooded Babelsberg neighborhood of Potsdam. Courtesy of the Secret Service, Truman's bags were already unpacked, waiting for him in his second-floor quarters, which featured a bedroom, crude bathroom and bathing facilities, large office, sitting room, sunporch, and views of the lake through windows without screens. The house had been stripped of furnishings at the end of the war but had been refurnished by the Russians. Though the villa was painted yellow and was quite large, it soon became known as "the Little White House."

Soviet officials told Truman that the house had been owned by a Nazi film mogul who had been sent to Siberia. In truth, as Truman learned in the mid-1950s, it had belonged to a prominent publisher and his large family. Ten weeks before the president and his party arrived, Russian soldiers had ransacked the house, raped the daughters in front of their parents and younger siblings, and beat up the parents. The family was ordered to pack only their clothes and leave in an hour. Everything else was "smashed with bayonets and rifle butts."[70]

The long day had exhausted Truman, but before he went to bed, he scribbled out a cable message to Bess, telling her that he had "safely landed," that "things are in good shape," and "Please call Mamma."[71] At 11:00 the next morning, July 16, when Truman had been up, shaved, and dressed for more than four hours, a bleary-eyed Winston Churchill, age seventy, called on the president at his villa. He was accompanied by British foreign secretary Anthony Eden, Permanent Undersecretary of State for Foreign Affairs Sir Alexander Cadogan, and Churchill's daughter, Mary. Mary later explained that her father had not been out of bed this early in ten years.

Since Harry Truman and Prime Minister Churchill had met only once for a few minutes in Washington, this presummit meeting was to be a "get to know you" social call. They conversed for two hours. The only substance touched upon was a mention by Truman that he had prepared an agenda for the conference. He asked whether Churchill had done so. "No. I don't need one," replied the prime minister. In his memoirs published a decade later, Truman wrote that he took "an instant liking" to Churchill during this first meeting and that "there was something very open and genuine about the way he greeted me."[72] However, in his diary that night, Truman's impression was almost the opposite and surely more accurate. Churchill is a "most charming and a very clever person," he wrote, but "he gave me a lot of hooey about how great my country is and how he loved Roosevelt and how he intended to love me etc. etc. Well . . . I am sure we can get along if he doesn't try to give me too much soft soap."[73]

Churchill's first impressions of Truman were consistently positive. Walking back the two blocks to their quarters at 23 Ringstrasse immediately after the meeting, he told his daughter that he "liked the President immensely" and was "sure he could work with him." In a letter to her mother, Mary Churchill wrote effusively that "it seemed like divine providence. Perhaps it is FDR's legacy. I can see Papa is relieved and confident."[74] A day later, Lord Moran, the prime minister's personal physician, asked him whether Truman had "real ability." "I should think he has," responded Churchill. "At any rate, he is a man of immense determination. He takes no notice of delicate ground, he just plants his foot down firmly upon it."[75] In *Triumph and Tragedy*, published in 1953, Churchill wrote that when he called on the president, he "was impressed with his gay, precise and sparkling manner and his obvious power of decision."

At the conclusion of their meeting, it was probably Churchill who suggested that the two of them "strike a blow for liberty" by downing tumblers of Scotch whisky. To his diary, Cadogan wrote, "P.M. delighted with Pres."[76]

After Churchill left, Truman met briefly with General Marshall to approve his recommendation that General Douglas MacArthur be appointed commander of all Allied ground, sea, and air forces in the Pacific. That meant that MacArthur would command Operation Downfall, the invasions of the Japanese home islands.

———

Truman was scheduled to meet with Stalin that afternoon but was told that his arrival would be delayed by a day due to "illness." Accounts differ as to the reason for the so-called delay, with some chroniclers claiming that Stalin was recovering from a mild heart attack or ministroke. The fact, however, is that Stalin arrived at his villa a mile from the Little White House sometime that same afternoon and that former ambassador Joe Davies, who had been invited by Truman to the Potsdam Conference, spent time huddling with Stalin and his advisers. Davies would sit next to Truman at several of the plenary sessions.[77]

With the rest of the afternoon free, the president commandeered an army-green Lincoln convertible and a driver and asked Byrnes and Leahy to join him for an impromptu top-down tour of the city of Berlin. The experience would be burned into Truman's memory for the rest of his life. It was not so much the miles of shattered buildings, the mountains of rubble, and the stench of death, but it was "the long, never-ending procession of old men, women, and children wandering aimlessly along the autobahn and the country roads carrying, pushing, or pulling what was left of their belongings" that brought the American president to the depths of despair.[78]

After Truman returned to the Little White House at about half past five, an aide handed him a message from Joe Davies informing him that Stalin was at his villa and would like to meet with him that evening. To Davies's dismay, Truman, a "morning person," responded that he was unable to meet with Stalin that night but would be pleased to see him the next day. Knowing that Davies was disappointed, the president invited him to dinner at eight. The president spent the next two predinner hours alone, working on his mail and jotting down his thoughts and feelings about what he had just witnessed in Berlin. "I hope for some sort of peace," he wrote, "but I fear that machines are ahead of morals by some centuries and when morals catch up perhaps there'll be no reason for any of it."[79] Truman would very soon learn about the status of a particularly diabolical "machine," a nuclear gadget that would be placed ahead of what many would say were moral considerations.

As dessert and coffee were being served, an aide whispered to Truman that Secretary of War Stimson and U.S. Army chief of staff General Marshall were on their way to the Little White House with an urgent message. When they arrived, Davies was invited to stay downstairs if he wished while Truman went upstairs to his office with Stimson and Marshall. Once the president's office doors were closed, Stimson showed him a cable from Washington—the first report on the Gadget at Trinity, which read as if the author, in order to disguise the true facts, was reporting on a surgical operation: "Operated on this morning. Diagnosis not complete but results seem satisfactory and already exceed expectations. . . . Dr. Groves pleased. . . . I will keep you posted."[80]

Though the message was guarded, Truman was delighted. It was the news he had been so anxiously awaiting. Contrary to the pessimistic predictions of Admiral Leahy and others, the atomic bomb actually worked![81] Its use could end the war with Japan and save American lives. Moreover, with the world's most powerful weapon in his hip pocket, Truman would be able to conduct negotiations at the Potsdam Conference with renewed confidence. The three men talked for an hour or so, about the implications of possessing the bomb. Stimson argued that because Tokyo had recently issued peace feelers, this was the "psychological moment" for the U.S. to send a warning to the Japanese, and that if they refused to surrender, "the full force of our newest weapons should be brought to bear."[82] Stimson also advised that in the forthcoming talks, the U.S. should do everything possible to curb Soviet moves for greater influence in the Far East, particularly establishment of trade ports in China and the training of military divisions in Korea. "Korea," Stimson prophesized, "is the Polish question transplanted to the Far East."[83]

When Truman returned downstairs to bid Davies good night, the former ambassador to the Soviet Union must have suspected that something important had transpired. He asked Truman, "Is everything all right?" When Truman said yes, Davies inquired, "Over here or back home?" Truman replied, "Back home. It has taken a great load off my mind."[84]

There is no evidence that Davies overheard or suspected the gist of what Truman had been told by Stimson upstairs. But he might have. And if he did, one wonders whether he alerted Stalin or his advisers.

Earlier that day, at 1:29 p.m. in Berlin, 5:29 a.m Mountain War Time in New Mexico, the detonation of Gadget, the plutonium bomb, at the

Trinity site was far more momentous than the cryptic description in the cable that Stimson had handed to Truman. Observers on Compania Hill, twenty miles from the steel tower, along with those in bunkers as close as 5.6 miles, saw a searing flash of light brighter than the noonday sun, followed by a powerful blast wave and a deafening roar that could be heard for one hundred miles. The force of the explosion was equivalent to twenty thousand tons of TNT. A huge yellow fireball "gradually turned from white to yellow to red as it grew in size and climbed into the sky."[85] Twelve minutes after detonation, a mushroom cloud ascended to an estimated height of forty thousand feet. There could be no question but that the Trinity test had exceeded expectations.

Out at Compania Hill, General Thomas Farrell, chief of Los Alamos field operations, walked over to his boss, General Leslie Groves, and said, "The war is over."[86] Robert Oppenheimer had mixed emotions. He was pleased that the bomb would likely shorten the war. But he could not help recalling a line from Hindu scripture in the *Bhagavad Gita*: "Now I become death, the destroyer of worlds."[87] Harvard physicist Kenneth Bainbridge, director of Trinity, was having similar thoughts. He greeted Oppenheimer with a wry comment: "Now we are all sons of bitches."[88] After the war he committed himself to the control of nuclear weapons.

Coincidentally, at about the time Gadget exploded at Trinity, Truman and Churchill were striking a "blow for liberty" with more than a few drams of Scotch, completely unaware that they were also toasting the dawn of the Atomic Age. The successful test at Trinity would mean liberty for upwards of a million American GIs, but to hundreds of thousands of Japanese citizens, it would mean death, hideous disfiguration from burns, and radiation sickness.

The success of the plutonium bomb at Trinity was crucial. In the time they had, engineers and scientists on the Manhattan Project were able to refine only enough plutonium for two bombs, and to process enough uranium for a single bomb. After Trinity there were two remaining atomic bombs that could be used against Japan, the unexploded plutonium bomb (renamed "Fat Man" by the military) and the uranium gun-type bomb (called "Little Boy"); the engineers knew the bombs would work and did not therefore need to be tested. To convince the Japanese government to surrender, the explosions of at least two nuclear bombs were essential. The first bomb would demonstrate its destructive power, the ability to destroy a large city and most of its inhabitants. The second would prove that there was more than one and at least suggest that the U.S. had produced and could explode many more. Two bombs would convince the Japanese that their situation was completely hopeless, and they would surrender unconditionally, or so the strategists predicted. But if they were wrong, additional bombs could be produced. However, it would be more than a week before a third bomb would be ready for delivery.

The next day at noon, Tuesday the seventeenth of July, Stalin's armored Packard limousine halted in front of the Little White House. Groups of heavily armed bodyguards appeared from nowhere and quickly surrounded the house. Stalin, who had been recently elevated from the rank of marshal to that of generalissimo, stepped out, accompanied by Pavlov, his interpreter, and Foreign Minister Molotov. The "Man of Steel," fearsome dictator of the Soviet Union's 190 million people, was dressed in a fawn-colored military tunic with epaulets, red striped trousers, and the Order of Lenin pinned to his chest. The president, who had been seated at a large wooden desk, "looked up," he wrote in his diary, "and there stood Stalin in the doorway."[89] Truman was surprised to see how short he was—"a little bit of a squirt," he later said.[90]

Generalissimo Stalin began with a fib, apologizing for being a day late when in fact he had arrived the day before. As a prelude to getting down to business, Truman explained that he was "no diplomat," that he intended to give straightforward "yes or no" answers without prevarication, and that he was "here," according to Bohlen's notes, "to be yr friend."[91] Stalin appeared to appreciate Truman's "pledge of frankness," wrote Bohlen, saying that "the Soviet Union would always try to 'meet' the views of the United States."[92]

Invited by Truman to "fire away" on his proposed agenda for the conference, Stalin began by saying he wanted to remove Francisco Franco's fascist government and divide up the Italian colonies. In his notes of the conversation, Truman wrote that Stalin's proposals were "dynamite" but "I have some dynamite too which I am not exploding now," an obvious reference to the atomic bomb. As to the secret Yalta agreements granting Chinese territory and concessions to the Soviets, Stalin told Truman that in their negotiations with T. V. Soong, China's foreign minister, several significant differences over railroads and ports were still unresolved. Yet in Truman's notes he wrote that "most of the big points with Soong had been settled" and that Stalin had assured him—that is, Truman—that the Soviets "would be in the Jap War on August 15th." With this reaffirmation, Truman believed he had achieved one of his main goals before the first plenary session of the Potsdam Conference had even begun. Overjoyed, he wrote that night, "Fini Japs. "[93]

When Truman suggested that Stalin and his party stay for lunch, Stalin at first refused. Truman pressed him, saying, "You could if you wanted to."[94] Stalin relented. Lunch consisted of creamed spinach and liver and bacon. The main subject of conversation revolved around whether Hitler was still alive. Stalin was convinced that "he's loose somewhere," possibly in Argentina or Spain.[95]

Following toasts with California wine and photos out on the porch, Stalin and his aides departed. During the next few hours, Truman jotted down his impressions, the first hopeful, the second naive, and the third accurate. "I can deal with Stalin. He is honest—but smart as hell," he wrote.[96] Stalin's reaction to the president? He was not impressed. Asked later to compare Truman with FDR, Stalin remarked, "They couldn't be compared. Truman's neither educated nor clever."[97]

———————

Later that afternoon, after a short nap and a shower, Truman stepped out of his limo into the inner courtyard of the vast three-storied Cecilienhof Palace, site of the first of thirteen plenary sessions of the Potsdam Conference, aptly code-named "Terminal." The 176-room mansion had been built by Kaiser Wilhelm II during the Great War to resemble half-timber English Tudor houses that he had seen while visiting his relatives at Windsor and Balmoral. To remind Truman and Churchill that the Soviets were hosting the Big Three, a huge star of red geraniums had been planted amid the lush grass in the center of the courtyard.

The conference was held in an oak-paneled reception hall with a bank of floor-to-ceiling windows that afforded a view of the gardens and lake beyond. Once the Big Three and their advisers were seated at the circular conference table, Stalin proposed that President Truman, as the only head of state present, chair the proceedings. Churchill, who had just fired up an eight-inch cigar, seconded the motion.

Expecting that he would be asked to chair the conference, as FDR had done at Tehran and Yalta, Truman was prepared but nervous. Glancing down at a briefing paper, he began by proposing the creation of a Council of Foreign Ministers (CFM), which would later negotiate peace treaties with the defeated powers and, as events would unfold, function as a key vehicle at Potsdam for shaping issues to be presented to the Big Three for decision at the afternoon plenary sessions. The establishment of the CFM would become the first and one of the few substantive proposals to be quickly approved by the Big Three at Potsdam.

Truman's next agenda items were much more controversial, but he addressed each in a businesslike manner. They included democratization of the governments of Rumania, Hungary, Bulgaria, and Greece as pledged in the Yalta "Declaration of Liberated Europe" and admission of Italy into the UN even though it had "stabbed" Britain "in the back" when she stood alone against the Wehrmacht. As soon as Truman had finished, Churchill added Poland's borders and "early holding of free elections" in that nation to the list.[98] Finally, Stalin weighed in, proposing that the conference agenda include the Soviet share of reparations to be extracted from Germany, trusteeships over colonies, the role of China in peace talks, and a plan to end the Franco regime.

Faced with a variety of complex issues that could take weeks to resolve due to the diversity of views, the verbosity of Churchill, and the absence of an efficient way to proceed (the CFM had yet to be tested), Truman, as chair, laid down a few rules. He wanted an agenda to be circulated by the CFM well before each plenary session and he wished to begin the plenaries at 4 p.m. instead of 5. With impatience, he exclaimed, "I don't want just to discuss. I want to decide!"[99]

The first day's conference at Potsdam ended on a note both ominous and humorous, at least to some. Stalin asked Churchill whether he was willing to share the German fleet, which had been surrendered to the

British. Churchill responded that the warships "should be either sunk or divided" but ducked Stalin's question as to his preference. Then "let's divide it," pronounced Stalin. "If Mr. Churchill wishes, he can sink his share."[100] Notes of the meeting do not disclose whether anyone in the room dared to laugh.

Buoyed by the praise of Byrnes and Leahy, Truman was pleased with his performance during the meeting with Stalin and throughout the first plenary with the Big Three. Chip Bohlen, the president's interpreter, wrote that "the successful start raised his confidence. By nature sure of himself anyway, he moved through the conference with the poise of a leader of much greater experience."[101]

———

While the talks droned on for days, Truman was immensely fortified by good news from New Mexico and Washington. On the morning of the second plenary, July 18, he was shown a cable from Groves's assistant confirming with enthusiasm the shock-and-awe power of the explosion at Trinity. At lunch, Churchill agreed with Truman that Stalin should be informed about the existence of the bomb, but none of details. Three days later, in the presence of Truman and Byrnes, Stimson read out loud, word for word, an "immensely powerful" top secret report from Groves, which concluded that the test at Trinity had been "successful beyond the most optimistic expectations of everyone."[102] Truman was "tremendously pepped up" by the report, wrote Stimson. "He said it gave him an entirely new feeling of confidence."[103] When Churchill was informed, his reaction, in a few words, captured the significance of the Manhattan Project: "Stimson, what was gunpowder? Trivial. What was electricity? Meaningless. This atomic bomb is the Second Coming in Wrath."[104]

On the morning of the twenty-fourth, the president approved the final draft of what would become known as the "Potsdam Declaration," an ultimatum to the Japanese that warned them to surrender immediately or face "prompt and utter destruction," an intentionally vague reference to the atomic bomb. The declaration called for the "unconditional surrender of all armed forces," a demand originally made by Roosevelt at Casablanca that the Germans had been forced to accept and that had been publicly reaffirmed by Truman after FDR's death. There was no mention in the declaration of Emperor Hirohito or preservation of a monarchy under the existing dynasty but it promised that the Japanese people would not be "enslaved as a race or destroyed as a nation." This language could be construed to assure them that their emperor would not be imprisoned or executed. On the other hand, the clause stating that "stern justice shall be meted out to all war criminals" certainly did not exempt His Majesty.[105]

Since the declaration needed to be approved by Nationalist China as well as the U.S. and Great Britain before it could be communicated to Japan and the rest of the world, one of Truman's aides immediately arranged for the draft to be cabled via the Map Room in the White House to Patrick Hurley, the U.S. ambassador to China, who had to hand-deliver it to Generalissimo Chiang Kai-shek for his review and approval. Because Hurley had to travel from Chungking (now Chongqing) by boat, auto, and sedan chair to Chiang's mountaintop summer capital of Kuling, it took him three days to secure Chiang's approval of the declaration and get it cabled back to the Little White House, where it had already been signed by Churchill and Truman (Stalin did not sign because the Soviet Union had not yet declared war against Japan).

At 10:30 on the morning of the twenty-fourth, shortly after the draft declaration had been dispatched to China, Stimson climbed the stairs to Truman's office. Once again, he told Truman that it would be a mistake to include the demand for unconditional surrender in the declaration because, he said, it would be interpreted by the Japanese to mean that they could not keep their emperor. Truman explained that it was too late, the declaration was on its way to Chiang. Plus, he and Byrnes were convinced that it would be political suicide to remove the demand.

Next, Stimson showed Truman a "Top Secret" message from Groves's aide that he had just received; it stated that depending on the weather and the "state of preparation," there was a "good chance" that an atomic bomb could be detonated over Japan "August 4 to 5" and "almost certain before August 10."[106] In his diary that night, Stimson wrote, "Truman said that was just what he wanted . . . that he was highly delighted."[107]

In recounting his conversation with Stimson, Truman wrote that he "told the Sec. of War" to "use" the atomic bomb against "a purely military" target and that only "soldiers and sailors" should be in the target area and "not women and children."[108] This assertion appears to be a blatant attempt by the president to memorialize for the record his version of a moral high ground for the sake of his legacy. Based on Groves's detailed report concerning the power and reach of the bomb, Truman had to have known that a single atomic bomb would kill, injure, and irradiate most of the inhabitants of the cities to be targeted, including women, children, and civilians. Moreover, the Interim Committee chaired by Stimson had recommended that the target should be a military installation surrounded by workers' houses. If Truman actually believed that women, children, and noncombatants could be spared, he was delusional. And if he in fact had instructed Stimson to avoid harming them, the secretary of war would have pushed back hard. There is no evidence that he did.

A few minutes after Stimson left, the British and American military chiefs of staff gathered with Churchill and Truman in the dining room of the Little White House behind closed doors. It was the only time all of them had met together at Potsdam. It was not a timid group. If anyone in the room believed the bomb should not have been used against a Japanese city, this was the time to speak up. No one did. Thus, the inevitable "final decision," if it could be called that, was unanimous. It was Truman who summed up the governing rationale: "a quarter of a million of the flower of our young manhood were worth a couple of Japanese cities."[109] When the group adjourned, the operations order, dated July 24, was issued by the acting army chief of staff in Washington. The 509th Composite Group of the 20th Air Force was to "deliver," meaning detonate after being dropped from a high-altitude B-29 bomber, the one and only available uranium bomb (Little Boy) over Hiroshima, Kokura, Niigata, or Nagasaki on or after August 3. "Additional bombs" were to be delivered over the foregoing targets "as soon as made ready," although only one, the plutonium Fat Man, would be immediately available.[110] With this order, the flame was lit. There would be no turning back.

The plenary session at the palace on the late afternoon of July 24 was particularly contentious, with Truman flatly informing Stalin that the U.S. would not recognize Soviet satellite states in Eastern Europe unless their governments were reorganized "along democratic lines."[111] Once again, there would be no agreement, no progress. When the meeting adjourned, Truman walked idly around the conference table toward Stalin and Vladimir Pavlov, his interpreter. "I casually mentioned," Truman wrote in his memoirs, "that we had a new weapon of unusual destructive force. The Russian Premier showed no special interest. All he said was that he was glad to hear it and hoped we would make 'good use of it against the Japanese.'"[112] Pavlov, who recalled Stalin's reaction, said that "no muscle moved in his face." In fact, Stalin had not only been aware of the Manhattan Project since March 1942; he knew that the specifications of the American plutonium bomb were already in the hands of his nuclear scientists (courtesy of Soviet spy Klaus Fuchs), and he had even been told by Lavrenti Beria a few days earlier of the successful test at Trinity. He and Beria had agreed that if the bomb were mentioned during the conference, he "should pretend not to understand."

When Stalin returned to his villa and informed Molotov, the foreign minister said, "They're raising their price," meaning possession of the bomb would make it much more difficult to extract concessions from Truman and Churchill. "Let them," replied Stalin. "We'll have to talk it over with Kurchatov and get him to speed things up."[113] Professor Igor Kurchatov was Russia's leading nuclear scientist, director of the Soviet atomic bomb program. The nuclear arms race predicted by Leo Szilard and others had begun.

Meanwhile, by sunset on July 24, the USS *Indianapolis*, carrying a heavy zinc-lined canister of weapons-grade U-235 uranium and the firing mechanism for Little Boy, was plowing westward through the Pacific toward the tropical island of Tinian, at the time the largest air base in the world. In two days *Indianapolis* would anchor offshore of Tinian and unload the precious cargo. At Hamilton airfield on the U.S. West Coast, five C-54 transports were preparing to take on the "bullet" that would trigger the explosion for Little Boy, the plutonium core and its initiator for Fat Man, and various other pieces of equipment for the two atomic bombs. The C-54s would arrive at Tinian on July 29. Awaiting them would be the secretive 509th Composite Group, a B-29 squadron whose sole mission would be to drop Little Boy and Fat Man on the targeted Japanese cities.

––––––––––

On July 26, after the conference had been suspended for a couple of days because Churchill and Clement Attlee were in London to learn the results of the British elections, Truman spent several hours in Frankfurt, inspecting American troops with Eisenhower. At one point, recalled Ike, Truman suddenly turned toward him and said, "General, there is nothing that you may want that I won't help you get. That definitely and specifically includes the presidency in 1948." Eisenhower said he laughed and responded, "I don't know who will be your opponent for the presidency, but it will not be I." This was a rather odd remark to make because Truman was suggesting that Eisenhower could take his place on the Democratic ticket, not that he would help him become his Republican opponent. Or perhaps this was Ike's clever way of saying he was a Republican, not a Democrat.

Early that evening, back at the Little White House, Truman was stunned to learn that Churchill had been defeated and that Labour Party leader Clement Attlee, the new prime minister, and his foreign secretary, Ernest Bevin, would be returning to the conference. The British voters, tired of wartime privations and fearing a return to unemployment, had responded to Attlee and his party's promises of social reform, full employment, and government benefits.

At 9:20 p.m., press secretary Charlie Ross released the Potsdam Declaration to the news media. At the same time he instructed the Office of War Information (OWI) in Washington to get the message out to Japanese government officials that unless they surrendered unconditionally, their people would face "prompt and utter destruction." Rather than relying on diplomatic channels, OWI used powerful radio transmitters on the West Coast to broadcast the declaration to the Japanese home islands. Some three million leaflets summarizing the declaration were dropped from bomb bay doors of U.S. bombers flying over mainland Japan.

Two days later, July 28, Japanese prime minister Kantaro Suzuki responded to the Potsdam Declaration by calling a press conference that was broadcast to the world by Radio Tokyo. "The government does not think it has serious value," announced Suzuki. "We must [*mokusatsu*] it. We will do our utmost to complete the war to the bitter end." Depending on context, the word *"mokusatsu"* can mean either "treat with silent contempt" or something like "wait in silence until we can speak with wisdom."[114] As events unfolded, this was Japan's last opportunity to avoid the wrath of the atomic bomb.

————————

Having returned from London, Prime Minister Clement Attlee and Foreign Secretary Ernest Bevin called on Truman and Byrnes at the Little White House on the evening of the twenty-eighth. In a letter to his mother and sister about his first impressions, Truman called Attlee and Bevin a couple of "sourpusses."[115] Attlee, a bald, pipe-smoking Oxford man, was mild-mannered and unassuming—"a modest man with much to be modest about," as Churchill had remarked.[116] Nevertheless, because Attlee had served as deputy prime minister under Churchill and had been a member of the war cabinet, he was fully informed when he replaced Churchill as prime minister, unlike Truman when he had suddenly been thrust into the presidency. Similarly, Bevin, the new foreign secretary, was well briefed on international affairs because he too had served in Churchill's war cabinet. However, in contrast to Attlee, Bevin had an outsize personality with a rotund 250-pound body to match. He was a rough, gruff, "blue collar" kind of fellow who spoke with a cockney accent and possessed only a few years of formal education. As it turned out, however, Bevin was to be Attlee's best appointment.

Since the tenth plenary session was to begin in forty-five minutes, Byrnes briefed Attlee and Bevin on a negotiating strategy that he planned to use with Molotov and Stalin to break the deadlock on the major issues in dispute, which had existed when Attlee and Churchill left for London. At the suggestion of Joe Davies, Byrnes had decided to package the key issues of "Reparations, the Satellite States, the Polish border and Italy together" into a single proposal and try to "secure an agreement" on all of them "through simultaneous concessions."[117]

Over the next three days, with the go-ahead from Truman, Attlee, and Bevin, Byrnes seized the lead in a series of "horse trading" meetings with

Molotov and Bevin under the umbrella of the Council of Foreign Ministers. In his first move, Byrnes proposed to trade a movement of Polish
borders to the west for a reduction in Soviet reparations from Germany.
The U.S. would agree that Poland, by then a Russian satellite state, could
swallow up a Massachusetts-size chunk of prewar Germany, including
precious coal mines and farmland. It was a major concession. In exchange,
Molotov would have to drop the Soviet demand for a fixed dollar amount
of war reparations ($10 billion) to be extracted from all four occupation
zones of Germany because it would cripple the recovery of the German
economy, as had happened after WWI. Instead, proposed Byrnes, Soviet
reparations would have to be limited to the removal of industrial equipment from its zone only, plus removal of 15 percent of such equipment
from the other zones in return for East German food, coal, and other natural resources. Molotov agreed to consider this trade. As to the diplomatic
recognition of Italy and the other Soviet satellite states, Byrnes and Molotov fashioned a tentative "kick the can down the road" agreement whereby
those nations would be recognized by the three powers but only after
peace treaties had been concluded and provided that Italy's treaty would
be "the first among the many important tasks to be undertaken by the new
Council of Foreign Ministers."[118]

By the morning of July 31, Byrnes and Molotov had worked out a
framework for a three-cornered proposal concerning the borders of Poland,
reparations, and the delayed recognition by the Big Three of the governments of Italy and the Soviet satellite states of Rumania, Bulgaria, Hungary, and Finland. "I told him," Byrnes later wrote, that "we would agree to
all three parts of the deal or none and that the President and I would leave
for the United States the next day."[119] In other words, take it or leave it.

At the plenary conference that afternoon, Truman asked Byrnes to
explain the three-part package. Stalin groused about "the tactics of Mr.
Byrnes," meaning the linkage of the three issues, and he haggled over
wording but he eventually accepted the Byrnes proposal.[120] Once Stalin
gave the green light, a number of other issues—including "free and unfet-
tered elections" in Poland, war crimes trials, the purge of Nazism, control
of the German economy, trusteeships, and the German fleet—were settled.
However, notwithstanding Byrnes's threat, Truman could not leave on

August 1 because it would take most of that day for aides to reduce the oral understandings to words.

The agreement at Potsdam providing that the Western Allies and the Soviets could extract most of their reparations from Germany only out of their own respective zones would have profound strategic and tactical implications. It meant that Germany would not be unified. Stalin himself foresaw this when he proposed, and Truman and Attlee agreed, that with regard to German investments in Europe, "everything to the west of the Soviet zone would go to the [Western] Allies and everything east to the Russians."[121] As a consequence, Germany would eventually be divided into the nation states of West and East Germany, an "economic iron curtain splitting Europe in two."[122] To put it another way, it was a "spheres of influence" peace, not the kind of lasting peace that Truman and Byrnes had envisioned when they arrived at Potsdam. And certainly not the peace that Roosevelt had dreamed of in his dying days.

Ironically, it was the Rooseveltian policy of achieving a cooperative relationship with the Soviets that resulted in a spheres of influence peace at Potsdam. To reach a genuine settlement and maintain a cooperative postwar relationship with the Soviets, Truman had to insist on limiting most of the Soviet reparations to those extracted from their own zone, a decidedly uncooperative move that eventually resulted in the division of Germany. As Professor Marc Trachtenberg aptly put it, "The way to get along was to pull apart."[123] As an incentive Truman allowed Stalin to grab a large swath of German territory to compensate his satellite Poland for the land that Russia had seized from it in the east.

Soviet expert George Kennan criticized the settlement by Truman at Potsdam, arguing that since Stalin's motives should have been clear, "it was time for a showdown."[124] By that he meant that Truman and Byrnes should have refused to acquiesce in Stalin's land grab and should have put greater pressure on him to allow free elections and democratization of his satellites in accordance with the agreements at Yalta. But Truman, who was advised by Joe Davies at Potsdam, was still beholden to Roosevelt's policy of continued cooperation with the Soviets as the best way to achieve peace. Such was FDR's power and influence that well after his death, Truman felt compelled to work under his shadow and to pursue his illusions.

_____

At 10:30 p.m. on August 1, the Big Three and their key advisers gathered in the palace for the thirteenth and final plenary meeting to flyspeck and sign the Potsdam Protocol and the associated communiqué.[125] After midnight Truman moved to adjourn with the "hope that the next meeting would be at Washington." Stalin, the former seminarian, replied, "God willing." The generalissimo went on to pay special tribute to Jimmy Byrnes, who, he said, had "worked harder" than anyone to help "us to reach agreements. Those sentiments, Secretary Byrnes, come from my heart."[126] It was the high-water mark of Byrnes's service as secretary of state. Yet, while it was Byrnes who broke the deadlock, leading to an agreement, "Truman acquitted himself well at Potsdam," wrote Chip Bohlen, and "Roosevelt's presence would not have made any difference."

Truman awoke before 6 on Thursday morning, August 2, anxious to leave the Little White House before the day got underway. By 7:15 he and his motorcade sped off, bound for a flight in the *Sacred Cow* from Gatow airfield to Plymouth, England, where he would board the *Augusta* for the trip home. The timing of his departure was dictated by an order concerning the atomic bomb that he had issued two days earlier. "Release when ready," he had written with a lead pencil, "but not sooner than August 2." The president did not want to be anywhere near Stalin when the bomb was detonated over Japan. "I don't want to have to answer any questions" from him about sharing atomic bomb technology, he explained.[127]

_____

Potsdam was to be Truman's last involvement in international summitry. Moreover, despite Stalin's invocation of the Father Almighty when Truman invited him to come to Washington, the president would never see or speak with the generalissimo again.

Chapter 6

Bearing the Unbearable

"This is the greatest thing in history!" Harry Truman blurted out.[1] Shortly before noon on August 6, somewhere south of Newfoundland on his fourth day at sea aboard the *Augusta*, the president was seated elbow to elbow with the ship's crew in the aft mess, eating his lunch from a tray. Captain Frank Graham had just handed him a radio telegram from Washington that caused his spontaneous outburst. Referring to the atomic bomb, it said in part, "Hiroshima bombed visually . . . Results clear cut and successful in all respects. Visible effects greater than in any test."[2] A few minutes later, a second message—this one from Secretary of War Stimson, who had returned to Washington ahead of the president—was delivered to Truman by Graham. "Big bomb dropped on Hiroshima August 5 at 7:15 p.m. Washington time," it began. "First reports indicate complete success which was even more conspicuous than earlier test."[3] Truman leaned across the table to Jimmy Byrnes and exclaimed, "It's time for us to get on home!"[4] Then he stood, called for quiet, and announced to his messmates, "We have just dropped a bomb on Japan which has more power than 20,000 tons of TNT." (Actually it was twelve to fifteen kilotons.) "It was an overwhelming success."[5] They stood and applauded. With tears in their eyes, the young American sailors believed that the war would soon be over, that they would live to return home to their families and loved ones.

In Washington, assistant press secretary Eben Ayers released to the press and radio networks a previously prepared statement from the president. "Sixteen hours ago," it began, an American airplane dropped "an atomic bomb" on Hiroshima. Although Hiroshima, the seventh-largest city in Japan, was full of noncombatants, the message characterized it not as a city but as "an important Japanese Army base." In several paragraphs Truman's statement described the Manhattan Project for the first time, calling it "the greatest scientific gamble in history," and he thanked the British for their contributions. He made it clear that the technology to produce the bomb would be kept secret "to protect the world from sudden destruction" and that the British would be in on the secret but no one else. Though the Soviet Union was never mentioned, the fact that they were not included was noted by the press. "Let there be no mistake," Truman's message continued, "we shall completely destroy Japan's power to make war. . . . If they do not now accept our terms they may expect a rain of ruin from the air, the like of which has never been seen on this earth."[6] If this sentence threatening a "rain of ruin" sounds familiar, it is because it was borrowed by another American president more than seventy years later to threaten North Korea.

––––––––––

As Truman would soon learn, it was 8:15 a.m. Japan time on August 6 (across the dateline from the U.S.) when the *Enola Gay*, a B-29 bomber named for its captain's mother, suddenly lurched upward. Seconds before, the restraining hook holding the ten-foot long, five-ton Little Boy had been released. Through the open bomb bay doors, the first atomic bomb to be used in war hurtled toward a target six miles below, the T-shaped Aioi Bridge over the Ota River near the center of the city of Hiroshima. For forty-three seconds the bomb descended before being detonated at 1,870 feet, about a third of a mile above Hiroshima and its estimated 255,000 residents, not counting approximately forty thousand soldiers and workers who commuted from surrounding areas.

The nuclear chain reaction created a blinding flash of light and a temperature at ground zero of 5,400 degrees Fahrenheit. The resulting fireball killed virtually everyone within a kilometer of its surface, roasting them into unrecognizable black char. The shock waves that followed tore clothing from bodies, scattered streetcars like matchsticks, and turned to rubble an estimated seventy thousand of Hiroshima's seventy-six thousand houses and buildings. Fires broke out amid the flammable ruins, mainly caused by cookstoves and live wires.

Three-quarters of a mile from the epicenter of the explosion, Mrs. Hatsuyo Nakamura, a thirty-four-year-old widow, had been standing at her kitchen window when "everything flashed whiter than anything white she had ever seen."[7] She came to, buried beneath the debris of her collapsed house, and heard the cries of her three children, ages five, eight, and ten. After struggling free, she crawled over and frantically dug each of them out from under the wreckage. Amazingly, the children were bruised and filthy but none of them, including Mrs. Nakamura, had been injured. Urged by a neighbor, the Nakamura family set off to Asano Park, an estate on the Kyo River that had been designated as an evacuation area. They joined a procession of wretched humanity, many naked and horribly burned, their skin literally sloughing off their red or blackened bodies in sheets. Some were blind, the fluid from their hollow eye sockets running down their cheeks. As the Nakamura family passed hundreds of swollen, putrid corpses along the way, they could hear the cries for help from those still trapped beneath houses and those unable to walk because of crushed limbs, nausea, or sheer exhaustion. Among the first to arrive in leafy Asano Park, the Nakamuras settled in a bamboo grove and thirstily drank from the river, soon to be a mass grave. They almost immediately began vomiting and lay prostrate, retching for the rest of the day. As if this were not enough, it began to rain and suddenly "a whirlwind ripped through the park," downing trees and whipping up flat pieces of detritus from the piles of destroyed wooden buildings in the burning city.[8]

For the Nakamura family and so many others, the night of August 6 in Asano Park was apocalyptic. They were so sick that none of them were able to sleep, and they were terrified of approaching fires. Mrs. Nakamura, whose husband, a tailor, had been killed in the war, would soon learn that she had lost her mother, brother, and sister to the bomb, yet she found solace in the fact that she and her children were survivors. A year later, son Toshio, age eleven, seemed to have forgotten, or probably sublimated, the horror of that night. Instead, he chose to write about beauty on the river and the excitement and sorrow of a new day. In a school essay, Toshio wrote, "At night a gas tank burned and I saw the reflection in the river. We stayed in the park one night. The next day I went to Taiko Bridge and met my girlfriends Kikuki and Murakami. They were looking for their mothers. But Kikuki's mother was wounded and Murakami's mother, alas, was dead."[9]

Somewhere in the park that night, Kiyoshi Tanimoto, pastor of the Hiroshima Methodist Church and a 1940 graduate of Emory University in Atlanta, was preaching the lesson of Psalm 90 to the burned, maimed, and dying. Their lives, in the sight of the Lord, would last no longer than "a watch in the night," he quoted. "They quickly pass and fly away." Though their time on earth had been "consumed by the wrath of God," Tanimoto asked the survivors to pray to the Almighty, as Moses had, that "the beauty of the Lord will rest upon us."[10] Three years later, Reverend Tanimoto would tour the United States, raising money to rebuild his church and promoting a world peace center in Hiroshima. He devoted the rest of his life to working for peace.

An accurate number of those who perished as a result of the bomb is unknowable. Estimates from several organizations range from a low of seventy thousand to a high of 140,000 deaths. The wide variance is due to a number of complex factors, including uncertainty as to the number of people in Hiroshima at the time of the explosion, how soon death occurred after the explosion, judgments as to causes of death, and the bias of those who wished to emphasize moral concerns and the suffering of the victims as against those who stressed the necessity of ending the war and saving American lives.

Truman's motorcade from Newport News did not arrive at the White House until 11 p.m. on August 6. By that time, almost midday on August 7 in Tokyo, Truman's "rain of ruin" statement, which was broadcast by radio, had been picked up by the Japanese government, and an investigation team was dispatched to Hiroshima. In addition, 131 B-29 Superfortresses had attacked the Toyokawa ammunition plants with conventional weapons, killing fourteen hundred Japanese, many of whom were female workers. Based on initial reports of the power of the bomb, the reactions of many of the Japanese military leaders were skeptical, some suggesting that "countermeasures" could be taken to minimize casualties and others predicting that the U.S. was not capable of producing more than another bomb or perhaps two.[11] However, in a meeting with Emperor Hirohito on the morning of the eighth, Foreign Minister Shigenori Togo, who had prepared a report on the Hiroshima catastrophe, advised that it was time to accept the Potsdam Declaration and terminate the war. According to Togo, the emperor agreed and said that Japan "must make such arrangements as will end the war as soon as possible."[12] He asked Togo to convey his wishes to Prime Minister Kantaro Suzuki.

Suzuki tried to convene "the Big Six," his supreme decision-making council, but some were unable to attend due to prior commitments. As a consequence, he had no quorum. Thus, Suzuki was unable to carry out the emperor's request that day, even though he knew by then from the investigating team that it was a nuclear bomb that had destroyed Hiroshima two days earlier. The most the prime minister was able to do on August 8 was to cable Ambassador Naotake Sato in Moscow and ask him if the Kremlin was prepared to offer assistance by helping to arrange a truce. Sato cabled back and said Molotov would receive him at 5 p.m. Moscow time, 11 p.m. in Japan.

———

As soon as Sato arrived in Molotov's office at the Foreign Commissariat, the foreign minister interrupted Sato's usual greetings and asked him to sit down. He withdrew a one-page document from a folder and began slowly reading its six short paragraphs, pausing every so often for translation. Molotov stated that because Japan had refused to surrender unconditionally as demanded in the Potsdam Declaration, the U.S., Britain, and China had asked the Soviets to join the war against Japan and "thus shorten the duration of the war, reduce the number of casualties and contribute toward the most speedy restoration of peace." The final line was a stunner. "In view of the above," intoned Molotov, "the Soviet Government declares that from tomorrow, that is, from August 9, the Soviet Union will consider herself in a state of war against Japan."[13]

The declaration of war did not specify a time zone and Sato was perhaps too shocked to ask. It is likely that he simply assumed that "tomorrow, that is, from August 9" meant Moscow time, which would be dawn in the Far East, plenty of time for him to at least send an encrypted telegram to warn Japan and its armed forces hours before the Russians attacked. But that was not what Molotov intended. For him and the 1.5 million Red Army troops poised on the Siberian–Manchurian border, "tomorrow" meant the Transbaikal time zone (six hours ahead of Moscow), which would leave Sato less than an hour to dispatch a warning before the onslaught began.

Not long after Sato left Molotov's office, Red Army tanks, troops, and warplanes crossed the Manchurian border from the north, east, and west on August 9, a few minutes after midnight Transbaikal time. Their aim was to occupy not only Manchuria but also northern Korea, the southern half of Sakhalin Island, and the Kurile Islands. Sato's coded telegram never arrived in Tokyo, but even if it had, it would have been too late. Molotov and his comrades had made certain that the attack would be a complete surprise.

In the White House Map Room, shortly after noon on August 8, George Elsey received a message that the Soviet Union had declared war on Japan (Moscow time was seven hours later than DC). As he and Admiral Leahy were on their way to the Oval Office to inform Truman, Elsey said, "They're jumping the gun, aren't they, Admiral?" Leahy replied, "Yes, damn it. It was supposed to be the fifteenth. The bomb did it. They wanted to get in before it's all over."[14] Leahy was right. Stalin was intent on acquiring "war trophies," which to him meant acquiring "shares of Japanese enterprises," dominating Manchuria, and stripping the region of its industries, as well as taking possession of the Kuriles and the remaining half of Sakhalin.[15] Nevertheless, when Truman heard the news of the declaration, he was jubilant. At a hastily called press conference at 3 p.m., the president began by explaining that he didn't have time to "hold a regular press conference today; but this announcement is so important I thought I would call you in." He paused for emphasis and simply said, "Russia has declared war on Japan! That is all!" The transcript indicated, "Much applause as the reporters raced out."[16]

Earlier that day Stimson had met with Truman and showed him aerial photographs of the devastation in Hiroshima and reports of estimated casualties. In his diary that night, Stimson wrote that Truman spoke to him of the "terrible responsibility that such destruction placed upon us here and himself."[17]

W hile the president's press conference was winding up in Washington and the Red Army attack was well underway in Manchuria, *Bockscar*—a B-29 named after its pilot, Captain Frederick Bock—was going through its preflight checklist at Tinian air base in the western Pacific. Fat Man, the plutonium bomb whose twin brother had been tested at Trinity, was secure in the belly of *Bockscar*. The size of a VW, Fat Man weighed five tons and had been painted mustard yellow. Early on the morning of August 9 (the late afternoon of August 8 in Washington), the heavily burdened B-29 made an unusually long takeoff run, climbed to an altitude of seventeen thousand feet, and headed toward its primary target in Japan, the city of Kokura. Truman was aware that a second atomic bomb was to be detonated over Japan but there was no need for an express "decision" to be made or an order to be issued by him. Two weeks earlier, on July 24, when Truman had agreed with Churchill and the British and U.S. military chiefs to the use of the first atomic bomb, he had implicitly approved a directive by the acting army chief of staff to "deliver"—that is, detonate—"additional bombs" over the four targeted cities in Japan.[18]

At thirty-one thousand feet, *Bockscar* circled three times over Kokura but the bombardier could not see the aiming point through his Norden bombsight. Accordingly, *Bockscar*'s pilot that day, not Bock but Major Charles Sweeney of Quincy, Massachusetts, was forced to fly to the secondary target, Nagasaki, and he did not arrive over the city until 10:50 a.m.

Japan time. Sweeney and his crew had been in the air for eight hours. Fuel was dangerously low, enough for only one bomb run. When Sweeney began his run at twenty-nine thousand feet with the bomb bay doors opening, the bombardier could not see the aiming point, the Mitsubishi Steel and Arms Works. Suddenly, he shouted, "I got it! I got it!" Fat Man plunged through the open doors and detonated at about eighteen hundred feet over Kyushu's third-largest city, with an estimated population of 195,000.[19]

As with Hiroshima, blinding light bathed the flight deck and shock waves hammered *Bockscar*'s fuselage, although the shocks were more powerful than those that had emanated from Little Boy. A sphere of pink light punched through the cloud cover. After that, Sweeney recalled, "All we could see was a blanket of thick, dirty, brownish smoke with fires breaking through sporadically."[20]

Due to the hills, valleys, and steep ridges that shielded large parts of Nagasaki from heat, shock waves, and radiation, the explosion over the city caused far fewer casualties per capita than at Hiroshima, even though Fat Man packed a more powerful TNT punch than Little Boy. Estimates of deaths at Nagasaki range from a low of forty thousand to a high of seventy-five thousand, about half of those for Hiroshima. The wide variances were caused by the same factors that influenced the range of death estimates for Hiroshima.

In Tokyo, August 9 was to become, in the words of Foreign Minister Shigenori Togo, "the day that [Japan's] future course was charted."[21] That historic day began early, several hours before Nagasaki was bombed, when Togo was awakened before 5 a.m. to hear the startling news that the USSR had declared war against Japan and that several divisions of the Red Army had invaded Manchuria. After meeting with his advisers, Togo concluded that it was necessary to accept the terms of the Potsdam Declaration (unconditional surrender) and quickly terminate the war, provided "the Emperor's position" could be preserved. He conveyed his opinion to Prince Takamatsu, the emperor's younger brother, and Prime Minister Suzuki. Hirohito granted a brief audience at 10 a.m. and expressed his "wish"— that is, his demand—that Suzuki assess the views of his government.[22]

For the rest of the day, Suzuki's Supreme War Leadership Council (the Big Six) and then his entire cabinet met and intensely debated whether and, if so, how to respond to the Potsdam Declaration. The atmosphere was fraught with tension. Around half past noon, they were interrupted by a report from the governor of the Nagasaki prefecture that downplayed the power of the explosion there and minimized casualties. Nevertheless, the report destroyed the belief that the Americans could not produce more than one atomic bomb and added to the participants' fear that Tokyo would be the next to experience the wrath of the atomic bomb. By 8 p.m. they had reached an impasse. One faction, led by Togo, was adamant that the declaration should be accepted, subject to only one condition (preservation of the emperor), while another, led by army minister General Korechika Anami and a group of hard-liners, insisted on three additional conditions (self-disarmament, control of war crimes trials, and a ban on occupation forces). Anami acknowledged that Truman would initially reject these additional conditions; his audacious plan was to stage an epic bloodbath on the beaches of the Japanese homeland that would beat back the American invaders, inflict enormous casualties, and force President Truman to agree to his conditions at the bargaining table.

In view of the deadlock, Emperor Hirohito agreed to Suzuki's unprecedented request for an imperial conference. At a few minutes before midnight on August 9, Suzuki, the Big Six, Baron Hiranuma (president of the privy council), and five aides gathered in a small underground air-raid shelter adjoining the Imperial Library where the emperor had been living. When Hirohito quietly entered the room, everyone stood and bowed. All were attired in formal suits or dress uniforms and the military officers were wearing white gloves. With the emperor seated at the head of a table, copies of Togo's one-condition and Anami's four-condition acceptances of the Potsdam Declaration were distributed to the participants. After listening for two hours to Suzuki's summary of the events of the day that led to the impasse and to the arguments of everyone else in the room who wished to speak (except aides), the emperor was respectfully asked by Suzuki to decide "which proposal should be adopted—the one stated by the Foreign Minister or the one containing the four conditions."[23]

With no hesitation, His Majesty rose to respond. After his first few

sentences, it was apparent that Hirohito lacked confidence in Anami's plan
to extract concessions from Truman by prolonging the bloodshed, especially in light of the destructiveness of the atomic bomb (he made no mention of the Soviet attack). Therefore, he concluded that "the time has come
when we must bear the unbearable. I swallow my tears and give my sanc-
tion to the proposal to accept the [Potsdam] proclamation on the basis
outlined by the Foreign Minister."[24]

Suzuki concluded the conference by declaring, "The Imperial decision
has been expressed."[25] By then, it was about half past two in the morning,
Friday, August 10. Hirohito exited the room, leaving it to the Big Six to
ratify the decision. Thereafter, Togo's foreign ministry drafted the formal
surrender message that accepted the Potsdam Declaration, subject, however, to Togo's one condition.

———————

At about 6:30 on Friday morning in Washington, DC, also the tenth of
August, Truman was about to leave the White House living quarters for
his morning walk when a War Department messenger arrived bearing
Togo's decrypted surrender message. Addressed to Secretary of State
Byrnes, the diplomatic note stated that Japan would accede to the Potsdam
Declaration "with the understanding that the said declaration does not
comprise any demand which prejudices the prerogatives of His Majesty as
a Sovereign Ruler." Truman realized at once that he was confronted with
a grave problem. "Could we even consider a message with so large a 'but'
as the kind of unconditional surrender we had fought for?"[26]

The president summoned Byrnes, Stimson, Leahy, and Navy Secretary
James Forrestal to the Oval Office to advise him on how best to answer his
question. For political reasons, Byrnes was opposed to preserving the position of the emperor. Keenly aware that the American people wanted to
hold Hirohito accountable for Pearl Harbor, Japanese atrocities, and the
long, savage war that had killed so many young Americans, Byrnes warned
Truman that accepting Togo's condition would mean "the crucifixion of
the president."[27] Stimson argued forcefully that preservation of Hirohito
would serve the national interest. First, his symbolic authority could be
used to effect an organized surrender of Japanese armed forces. Without

His Majesty to order his forces to lay down their arms, the U.S. would be compelled to fight bloody battles throughout China, Korea, Indonesia, and the Japanese home islands. Second, it was profoundly important, asserted Stimson, to quickly end the war before the Soviets could lay claim to participate in the occupation and rule of Japan and before they could extend their influence throughout East Asia. Leahy agreed with Stimson.

Forrestal broke the deadlock with a brilliant suggestion. There was no need to accept or reject the Japanese condition, he counseled. Instead, they should make an "affirmative statement" setting out their "intent and view" concerning the emperor's postwar status.[28] Truman liked that idea. In his diary, he simplified the thought: if the Japanese wanted to keep their emperor, "then we'd tell 'em how to keep him."[29] This would take the sting out of Togo's only condition, reasoned Truman.

Wordsmithed by Byrnes, and with one minor revision, Truman's official response to the Japanese government, which was approved by the British, the Chinese Nationalists, and reluctantly by the Soviets, included the following key passages:

> From the moment of surrender the authority of the Emperor and the Japanese Government to rule the state shall be subject to the Supreme Commander of the Allied powers who will take such steps as he deems proper to effectuate the surrender terms. . . .
>
> The Emperor will be required to authorize and ensure the signature of the Government of Japan and the Japanese [military] Headquarters of the surrender terms . . . [and] to issue orders to all the armed forces of Japan to cease hostilities and to surrender their arms. . . .
>
> The ultimate form of government of Japan shall be . . . established by the freely expressed will of the Japanese people. . . .
>
> The Armed forces of the Allied powers will remain in Japan until the purposes set forth in the Potsdam Declaration are achieved.[30]

The American response to Togo's offer was transmitted via Bern, Switzerland, to Tokyo on Saturday, August 11, but not until after Molotov had

backed down from his attempt to have a Russian general share in the capitulation and governance of postwar Japan. On the same afternoon Truman advised Attlee, Chiang Kai-shek, and Stalin that General Douglas
MacArthur would be appointed supreme commander for the Allied powers
(SCAP), and they endorsed him the next day.[31] Like a shogun, MacArthur
was destined to oversee the surrender and occupation of postwar Japan.

"We are all on edge waiting for the Japs to answer," wrote Truman in
his diary on Saturday night. "Have had a hell of a day."[32] With no word
from the Japanese government on Saturday and then Sunday, the president
recalled in his memoirs that "large crowds gathered outside the White
House and in Lafayette Park," expecting an announcement at any moment. "The place"—meaning 1600 Pennsylvania Avenue—"was beleaguered by press and radio people," hoping to be among the first to write or
broadcast the story of the century.[33] Upstairs in the living quarters, Truman enjoyed his time to relax with Bess, who had returned from Independence after a two-month absence, but he remained on tenterhooks. On
Sunday he devoted a quarter hour to his sister, Mary Jane, writing that
"things are going all right. Nearly every crisis seems to be the worst one
but after it's over it isn't so bad."[34] On Monday the thirteenth, with still no
word, Truman ordered a resumption of conventional bombing by B-29s to
signal the Japanese government that U.S. patience was running out. The
next day, a fleet of 828 B-29s (with 186 fighter escorts) bombed two military installations, a railway yard, and two cities in Japan.

On Monday evening in Washington, it was Tuesday morning in Tokyo.
At about 11 a.m., Emperor Hirohito, wearing a uniform and white gloves,
entered the same air-raid shelter where the first imperial conference had
been held five days earlier. His Majesty had already decided to accept the
Allied reply drafted by Byrnes, but he patiently listened to War Minister
Anami and two other hard-liners argue that unless the U.S. elevated the
emperor's status, Japan should fight on to the end. Then he announced his
sacred decision. I "have concluded," he declared, that "the terms of the Allied reply . . . constitute a virtually complete acknowledgement" of our
position. "In short, I consider the [Allied] reply to be acceptable." He

requested that Suzuki and his cabinet "prepare at once an imperial rescript" announcing the surrender so that he could read it over the air in a radio broadcast to the nation.[35]

Every member of the cabinet, some in tears, ratified and signed on to Hirohito's decision. In Togo's name the foreign ministry transmitted the Japanese surrender note to the U.S. and its three allies through the neutral embassies in Stockholm and Berne.

Notwithstanding the emperor's decision, a substantial number of field-grade army officers and one high-ranking admiral spent the day plotting an insurrection—a military takeover of the government with the objective of fighting on to victory or extinction. The key to their success would be Anami, who had the power as war minister to order the Eastern Army headquartered in Tokyo to back the revolt. In the early evening of August 14, Anami met with the conspirators and listened to their plans. Though he declined to express in writing a definite commitment to support them, he left the impression that he could change his mind and join them.

Hours later, the last night of the Second World War, fanatical rebel officers, led by Major Kenji Hatanaka, murdered the commander of the Imperial Guard and forged an order in his name. Hatanaka used the order to convince a regiment of the guard to support the coup, occupy the emperor's palace, and seal it off to anyone outside the moats. Once they were inside the palace, the immediate objective of the insurrectionists was to find and seize the recording of the emperor's speech announcing the surrender so that they could prevent it from being broadcast to the nation while they tracked down and eliminated the emperor's most influential supporters. Brandishing rifles with fixed bayonets, the fanatics raced through the labyrinth of catacombs and archaic passageways in and under the palace, trying to find the room or bunker where the recording had been made. As they banged on doors, they called out to Marquis Koichi Kido, the emperor's closest adviser and keeper of the privy seal, warning him wherever he was hiding to produce the recording on penalty of death (he was hiding in a bank vault underneath the palace).

Major Hatanaka and his gang never found the recording. Plus, support for the insurrection from Anami and other higher-ups never materialized. As dawn broke, it was apparent that the coup had collapsed. Hatanaka committed suicide (*seppuku*) with a bullet to his forehead. His principal coconspirator killed himself with a dagger and a shot through his brain. Anami was found at his residence, where he had committed ritual suicide, the samurai's way, by slicing open his belly, carving through the viscera, and allowing his intestines to slide out. He left behind two scrolls, one of which read, "Believing firmly that our sacred land shall never perish, I—with my death—humbly apologize to the Emperor for the great crime."[36] What "crime" was he referring to? Historian Richard Frank in *Downfall* suggests that "the great crime involved Anami's flirtation with and defiance of the Emperor's command."[37]

While coded diplomatic intercepts (called Magic) and other reports of the Japanese surrender reached Truman around four on the afternoon of August 14, it wasn't until 6:10 that Secretary Byrnes received the official surrender document from a messenger sent to the State Department by the Swiss chargé d'affaires. Charlie Ross got the word out to the White House press corps that a press briefing was in the offing. A few minutes before seven, reporters, broadcasters, and cameramen were allowed into the Oval Office. Expecting what was coming, they were buzzing with excitement. Truman, attired in a snappy dark blue double-breasted suit with matching accessories, entered the room with Bess on his arm, followed by Byrnes and Leahy (Cordell Hull, FDR's secretary of state who had accepted the Japanese declaration of war in 1941, was invited but he did not arrive until after the conference was over). The service chiefs and most of the cabinet were already in the room. Standing behind his desk with the surrender document in his hand, Truman announced that he had received what everyone had been waiting for, a reply from the Japanese government, and that copies would be handed out to everyone when he concluded his remarks. Then, enunciating each of his words slowly and clearly so that everyone could hear, he said, "I deem this reply a full acceptance of the Potsdam Declaration which specifies the unconditional surrender of Japan. In the reply there is no qualification." Truman's words were accurate but masked the fact that the imperial system, though subordinate, would be preserved. He went on to explain that he had appointed General

MacArthur as supreme Allied commander and that he would preside over the signing of the surrender documents, but nothing was said about plans for the occupation of Japan. After reading the full text of Togo's reply, in which he wrote that the emperor had pledged to order his military forces to lay down their arms, Truman simply said, "That is all." The transcript indicates that a voice from the audience congratulated Truman and that Joe Fox of the *Washington Star* thanked the president. No questions were asked.[38] The reporters climbed all over one another to grab copies of the surrender document, and raced out of the office to tell the world. It was finally over. The Second World War had ended.

Outside in the steamy August heat, a growing crowd of thousands who had gathered beneath the trees in Lafayette Park spilled out onto and across Pennsylvania Avenue and pressed against the iron fence that surrounded the White House. Sailors were climbing atop cars, and streetcars were stranded in the middle of the avenue. A conga line consisting of the young, old, and middle-aged snaked through the crowd. Teenagers had climbed trees to get better views. A chant started by a few of the inebriated in the crowd gathered volume, growing louder and ever louder. "We want Harry! We want Harry!" Harry and Bess ventured out onto the White House front lawn near the fountain. Borrowing from Winston Churchill's playbook, Truman rather clumsily flashed a "V for victory" sign with his index and middle figure. The crowd responded with roars each time he repeated the gesture. Bess looked like she was actually happy, even breaking into an occasional smile.

After several minutes the two of them retreated into the mansion. Truman went to his office to call Eleanor Roosevelt, who had supported his decision, if it could be called that, to drop the atomic bomb. "I told her," he recalled, "that in this hour of triumph I wished that it had been President Roosevelt and not I, who had given the message to our people." She responded with appreciation the next day, predicting that, from an "economic standpoint," Truman was about to "face pressures from every side" in the coming days, yet assuring him that his "wisdom and experience and faith in God" would guide him "aright."[39] He also called his aging mamma. "That was Harry," she said after hanging up. "Harry's a wonderful man. . . . I knew he'd call. He always calls me after something that happens is over."[40]

But it wasn't over. The boisterous crowd outside was still chanting "We want Harry!" So Harry and Bess went out again and stood beneath the North Portico. Speaking into a microphone, Truman delivered what the crowd wanted to hear. "This is a great day," he said, "the day we've been waiting for. This is the day that we've been looking forward for since December 7, 1941. This is the day for free government in the world. This is the day that fascism and police government ceases in the world."[41]

The next day, August 15, as headlines across America heralded the Japanese surrender, accounts of the sinking of the USS *Indianapolis* appeared well below the fold on page one and more often three or four pages inside the nation's newspapers. A few minutes after midnight on July 30, after having off-loaded components of Little Boy at Tinian four days earlier, *Indianapolis* was torpedoed by a Japanese submarine. It took only twelve minutes for the heavy cruiser to capsize and sink, entombing about three hundred of its crew of twelve hundred. The other nine hundred abandoned ship. Over a period of five days, they fell victim to a nightmare of drowning, saltwater poisoning, and vicious shark attacks. Almost six hundred perished. Only 316 survived. To cover up or perhaps minimize its blunders in taking so long to rescue its sailors, the navy imposed a news blackout for twelve days and then decided to lift it on the day that Truman's announcement of the end of the war would dominate the news. Correspondents who had been forced by the navy to embargo their stories about the catastrophe and the delays in rescue were outraged. The *New York Times* called it "one of the darkest pages of our naval history."[42]

As upwards of seventy-five thousand citizens in Washington continued their wild celebration into the night of August 14, it was a few minutes before noon on August 15 in Tokyo. The streets were empty and silent. Except for American POWs, the survivors throughout Japan—some eighty million of them—were huddled around radios, waiting to hear for the first time the "jeweled" voice of "His Imperial Highness," a man-god known to most not as Hirohito but simply as "Tenno." At noon a technician placed a needle on a vinyl record, and the voice of the emperor tremulously began, "To our good and loyal subjects." For a few the voice was jeweled but to most it was very difficult to understand because he spoke in an obscure Japanese court dialect. Without using the words "surrender" or "defeat," the emperor explained with almost laughable understatement that "the war situation has developed not necessarily to Japan's advantage" and that therefore the government had decided to "effect a settlement," namely acceptance of a "Joint Declaration" that most Japanese people had never heard of. Nevertheless, everyone eventually caught the drift. The war was over. Japan had capitulated to the United States, Great Britain, China, and the Soviet Union. Based on the emperor's words, the people were led to believe that the defeat was due not to battlefield losses but to deployment by the enemy of "a new and most cruel bomb" that would lead not only to the "obliteration of the Japanese nation," but to "the total extinction of human civilization." An oblique reference was also made to the Soviet invasion—the "world" had "turned against" Japan—but nothing explicit was said in that regard.

When a translation of the emperor's statement was published in newspapers across the U.S. the next day, many Americans, especially those whose loved ones had fought in the Pacific, were incensed by the emperor's self-righteous justification for starting and waging the war. In his recorded statement, Hirohito argued that it had been necessary to "declare war on America and Britain out of a sincere desire to insure Japan's self-preservation and the stabilization of East Asia" and that his nation never intended to "infringe upon the sovereignty of other Nations or to embark upon territorial aggrandizement."[43] In hindsight, it is arguably true that the U.S. oil embargo in the summer of 1941 threatened Japan's economy and caused her to declare war. However, to the citizens of China, Korea, the Philippines, and all the other nations that Japan had occupied and brutalized, the statement by the emperor that Japan had never intended to infringe on their sovereignty was a flat-out falsehood.

From the commander in chief in Washington down the chain of command to the lowest-ranking sailors, soldiers, and airmen in the Pacific, the burning questions were whether the Japanese forces would stop fighting and lay down their arms and if so when. No one knew how long it would take for the emperor's surrender order to reach the far-flung Japanese troops and, when it did, whether it would be obeyed. General MacArthur, the supreme commander, anticipated this problem. On the morning of August 15, SCAP radioed the government in Tokyo from his headquarters in Manila and demanded that he be "notified at once of the effective date and hour of the cessation of hostilities" and that the government send a "competent representative" to his headquarters in Manila to receive instructions for effecting "the terms of surrender." Within twenty-four hours Tokyo responded to SCAP's initial assertion of authority with a report that the emperor had issued a second order requiring the "entire armed forces" to "cease hostilities," along with details as to the time it would take to fully effectuate cease-fires in the various theaters (e.g., forty-eight hours in Japan, eight days in China).[44]

It was apparent from the outset that the upper echelons of the Japanese government and military were committed to compliance with the emperor's orders and MacArthur's instructions. However, there remained pockets of fanatic resistance, especially at the heavily bombed Atsugi Airdrome on the Kanto Plain, thirteen miles west of Yokohama and Tokyo Bay. Atsugi, which had been the training base for kamikaze pilots, was to serve as an initial staging area for the occupation of Japan, the place where Supreme Commander MacArthur planned to land and take control of the defeated nation. During the week of August 14, hothead pilots at Atsugi, under the command of Captain Yasuna Kozono, were threatening to launch kamikaze suicide attacks against the U.S. Third Fleet and incoming American cargo planes, which would be carrying supplies and troops for the occupiers. They had held the base captive for seven days. It took a personal visit to the airfield by Prince Takamatsu, the emperor's brother, to persuade the seditionists to stand down. Navy minister Mitsumasa Yonai sent a select detachment of naval security troops armed with clubs to occupy Atsugi and disable Japanese warplanes by stripping them of their propellers. Yonai later admitted, "I probably never worried so much as I did during the period from the 14th to the 23rd of that month."[45]

The occupation of Japan began on August 28, when a U.S. Army vanguard of engineers and technicians landed at Atsugi with communications equipment. As they set up a control tower to guide in the occupiers' aircraft, not a shot was fired. For the next two days, a force of forty-two hundred heavily armed U.S. paratroops in the 11th Airborne Division deplaned from more than a hundred C-47s to secure the twelve-hundred-acre base. However, they were far outnumbered by some thirty thousand grounded kamikaze pilots near the base and 150,000 Japanese soldiers stationed out on the Kanto Plain, many of them still armed.

On the afternoon of August 30, *Bataan II*, the silver C-54 Douglas Skymaster bearing General MacArthur and his top aides, banked and prepared to land at Atsugi. The mood inside was tense. General Courtney Whitney recalled that "he held his breath." Below, he could "see numerous anti-aircraft emplacements. . . . Here was the opportunity for a final and climactic act," he feared—an assassination of SCAP before he could set foot on Japanese soil. After a "rubbery landing," MacArthur ordered everyone to leave their sidearms in the plane.[46] They would all arrive unarmed. When the cabin door opened, MacArthur stood, or rather posed, on the second step of the steel ladder leading to the tarmac. Dozens of cameras caught him at his most photogenic—dark aviator glasses, crushed cap at a rakish angle, corncob pipe in clenched teeth, and not a single decoration pinned to his khaki shirt. "It was a masterpiece of psychology," recalled historian Kazuo Kawai, "which completely disarmed Japanese apprehensions. From that moment, whatever danger there might have been from a fanatic attack on the Americans vanished in a wave of Japanese admiration and gratitude."[47]

As supreme commander, MacArthur was about to exercise viceregal authority—dictatorial control—over eighty million Japanese citizens. Undaunted by the sight of armed Japanese soldiers in the distance, MacArthur and his staff descended the steps and took control. In typical overstatement, Winston Churchill wrote "that of all the amazing deeds of the war, I regard MacArthur's personal landing at Atsugi as the greatest of the lot."[48]

———

In his memoirs Truman wrote that shortly after receiving word on August 14 that the Japanese had accepted the Potsdam Declaration, he "suggested, without hesitation" that the formal surrender ceremony should take place in Tokyo Bay aboard the USS *Missouri*, the nation's newest battleship, which at the time was headed north to the coast of Honshu with Admiral William "Bull" Halsey's Third Fleet. With a political plus on his mind, Truman wrote that he chose the *Missouri* because it was named after his home state, his daughter had christened her, and he "had spoken on that occasion." News coverage of the historic event, he directed, was to be "open . . . and competitive."[49]

While MacArthur was preparing to occupy Japan and preside at the surrender proceedings, President Truman approved General Order No. 1, an August 17 directive that would establish fault lines having far-reaching implications for his presidency, American foreign policy, and the balance of power in East Asia. Order No. 1 required Japanese commanders in Korea to surrender all of their armed forces located north of the thirty-eighth parallel to the Red Army and those south of that arbitrary line to the U.S. troops who would be rapidly dispatched into the southern half of Korea. Secretary Byrnes, backed by Truman, did not want the Soviets and Korean Communists to control all of Korea. In addition, Order No. 1 required Japanese commanders in Vietnam Indochina to surrender their forces located north of the sixteenth parallel to the Chinese Nationalists and those south of that line to British soldiers, a proxy for France. In fact, the British would hand southern Vietnam back to France without objection by the U.S. State Department. No consideration was given to the unification and independence of Vietnam. With respect to Manchuria (North China), a region dominated by the Chinese Communists, Order No. 1 mandated that the Japanese surrender to the Chinese Nationalists even though few of their troops were there.[50] To accept the surrender of the Japanese in the north, the Nationalists called upon the U.S. to transport their troops to the region and dispatch fifty thousand American marines to assist in repatriation. With Truman's concurrence, the U.S. complied.

In the midst of celebrating victory and an end to the Second World War, little thought was given to whether arbitrary lines dividing Korea and Vietnam and the temporary support by the U.S. of one political or military party over another in Manchuria might encourage armed attempts to reunify territories and the resumption of civil wars. Truman could not possibly have imagined that he would eventually intervene in the Korean civil war, that his support of the Nationalists in Manchuria would undermine his efforts to broker an end to the Chinese civil war, and that his successors would be drawn into the Vietnamese civil war.

———

With "the waste of war and the ignominy of surrender" on his mind, Toshikazu Kase, age forty-two, climbed slowly up the starboard gangway of the forty-five-thousand-ton battleship *Missouri* on the surprisingly cool morning of September 2, 1945.[51] Out on Tokyo Bay history's greatest fleet of warships was arrayed. Kase, a high-ranking foreign ministry official, was the youngest member of a delegation of eleven Japanese civilian and military officers who were about to participate in the carefully choreographed formal signing of the Instrument of Surrender. Kase was to play a passive role. A graduate of Amherst College and research fellow at Harvard who had returned to Japan in the early 1930s, he was fluent in English. As secretary to Foreign Minister Mamoru Shigemitsu (Togo's successor), who would actually sign the surrender documents, Kase had been ordered to prepare a report on the proceedings that would be delivered personally to Emperor Hirohito.

Led by Shigemitsu, who had to lean on a cane to steady his wooden prosthetic leg, the Japanese delegation marched across the polished teak quarterdeck and stood at attention before their former enemies. Shigemitsu, in the front row, stood out. He was wearing a black frock coat, white gloves, and a tall silk hat. Describing the scene, Kase wrote, "The gallery of spectators seemed numberless, crowding every inch of available space on the giant ship: on the mast, on the smokestacks, the gun turrets— everything and everywhere."[52]

At precisely nine o'clock, General MacArthur, followed by Admirals Chester Nimitz and Bull Halsey, stepped forward on the veranda deck to a table covered with green baize and two copies of the surrender documents, one in green leather for the United States and the other in cheap black binding for Japan. All wore "suntans," open-collared khaki uniforms without neckties and decorations. Speaking slowly into a bank of microphones, MacArthur offered a lofty vision for the consequences of the agreement they were about to sign. "It is my earnest hope and indeed the hope of all mankind," he proclaimed, "that from this solemn occasion a better world shall emerge out of the blood and carnage of the past—a world dedicated to the dignity of man and the fulfillment of his most cherished wish—for freedom, tolerance and justice."[53]

Kase, "who expected the worst humiliation . . . was thrilled beyond words, spellbound, thunderstruck," he wrote. "For the living heroes and dead martyrs of the war [MacArthur's] speech was a wreath of undying flowers."[54]

Ordered by MacArthur to come forward to sign the surrender documents, Shigemitsu hobbled to the table with Kase holding his left arm for support. Hands trembling, the foreign minister signed in Japanese kanji on behalf of the Emperor of Japan and the Japanese government. After MacArthur and all of the Allied representatives added their signatures, MacArthur returned to the microphones. "Let us pray that peace be now restored to the world and that God will preserve it always," he intoned. The supreme commander paused for effect, then proclaimed: "These proceedings are closed."[55]

––––––––––

When Truman made his decision in early August to appoint MacArthur as supreme commander, he had a host of reservations. Though he had never met the famous general, who had been out of the U.S. since 1937, the president had heard all the stories and rumors about MacArthur's imperious manner, his narcissistic self-promotion, the "Dugout Doug" myth, the enormous sum of money he had secretly received from the president of the Philippines when he left Corregidor, and his abortive quest for the 1944 Republican presidential nomination, which was championed by Senator Vandenberg.* In June 1945, when Truman was anguishing over whether to confer the appointment, he confided to his diary that MacArthur was nothing more than "a play actor and bunco man." What should he do with "Mr. Prima Donna, Brass Hat, Five Star MacArthur?" the president wrote

––––––––––

* "Dugout Doug" was a derogatory nickname that some of MacArthur's troops saddled him with after he took shelter in Malinta Tunnel on the island of Corregidor in 1942, following the Japanese invasion of the Philippines. In truth, there were instances when he showed extraordinary bravery under fire.

to himself. "He's worse than the Cabots and the Lodges—they at least talked with one another before they told God what to do. Mac tells God right off. It is a very great pity to have stuffed shirts like that in key positions."[56]

Given his personal reservations, plus a telephone call from Senator Tom Connally, chair of the Foreign Relations Committee, warning Truman that he "was making a mistake," why did he go ahead with the appointment?[57] Five-star admiral Nimitz was well qualified and known to have wanted the job. Why MacArthur? Most likely the answer had much to do with the shadow cast by Franklin Roosevelt. It was FDR who had chosen MacArthur over Nimitz as chief strategist in the Pacific when he traveled to Hawaii during the Democratic convention in 1944. Truman, who had been president for a mere four months, was reluctant to appear to be questioning his predecessor's political and military judgment. Secretary of the Interior Harold Ickes, one of the few FDR cabinet members whom Truman retained, grudgingly agreed with the appointment of MacArthur. "Politically, [Truman] couldn't do anything else," Ickes wrote in his diary. "The blame is due to Roosevelt," he said, because it was FDR who had made MacArthur into a national hero by ordering him to leave Corregidor, awarding him the Medal of Honor, and choosing him over Nimitz. Moreover, if Truman had denied MacArthur the appointment, he would have played into the hands of Republicans, who wanted to "make a martyr" out of the general and a "candidate for president" in 1948.[58]

Both Truman and Ickes reasoned that by consigning MacArthur to the Far East for at least the next three years and probably more, they could keep him away from more important policy issues, namely those involving how to handle Soviet aggression in Europe. Moreover, they harbored some hope that if they issued strict, unambiguous rules to govern the occupation of Japan, MacArthur's tendency to find ways to ignore or skirt policies that he disagreed with could be curbed.

Within the first month MacArthur managed to ignite a bonfire in Washington that foreshadowed policy conflicts that would cause Truman to fire him six years later in the midst of the Korean War. It began on September 17, when MacArthur was quoted in press reports as saying that he planned to make a "drastic" cut in his occupation forces from four hundred thousand to two hundred thousand, drawing them down in six months "as rapidly as ships can be made available."[59] In addition, MacArthur's top subordinate, General Robert Eichelberger, issued a shocking statement that morning, saying that "the occupation of Japan will be unnecessary after 1 year."[60] These remarks outraged Truman and U.S. Army chief of staff Marshall because, in the face of immense pressure from the American public to demobilize, they were fighting to maintain a sizable peacetime draft so that they would have enough troops not only to meet occupation objectives in Japan but also to garrison hot spots elsewhere in the world, namely Western Europe, Berlin, Korea, China, and parts of the Middle East. In addition to being premature, the troop reductions suddenly announced by MacArthur and Eichelberger threatened to sabotage the national security policy that Truman, with Marshall's aid, was trying to implement through maintenance of adequate draft levels.

It turns out that MacArthur's announced drawdowns were politically motivated. His West Point classmate Robert Wood, CEO of Sears, Roebuck—at the time the largest retailer in the world—warned MacArthur on September 4 that unless he made dramatic cuts in his occupation forces, he would fall into a trap set by his Democratic enemies in Washington. These adversaries, said Wood, were spreading the word that MacArthur had demanded an excessively large army of occupation that would make him, rather than Truman, the object of criticism by the American public for perpetuating the need for a draft, which would jeopardize his presidential aspirations in 1948.[61] MacArthur followed Wood's advice. This was the reason why SCAP announced a cutback of half of his allotted occupation force and had his subordinate claim that he could achieve the reforms described in his occupation instructions within a year.

When news of the troop cutbacks hit the press, Truman complained to his staff that MacArthur's statement was "wholly uncalled for" and would do a "great deal of damage." He vowed to "do something about that fellow who's been balling things up," but he did nothing.[62] Instead, he left it to Acting Secretary of State Dean Acheson to release a statement, a "sharp and unmistakable rebuke," that characterized the announcement by MacArthur as rash and violative of administration policy.[63] Nobody "can see at this time the number of forces that will be necessary" to maintain order in Japan, declared Acheson. "The occupation forces are instruments of policy and not the determination of policy," he stated.[64] To emphasize the significance of his statement, Acheson authorized the press to quote it verbatim.

Aside from the troop-cutback announcements that touched off a political storm in Washington, Truman had reason to be satisfied with MacArthur's initial performance as SCAP. To prevent starvation, which "breeds mass unrest, disorder and violence," MacArthur immediately imported 3.5 million tons of surplus food from army stockpiles to feed at least some of the starving and homeless survivors. "The effect upon the Japanese was electrical," he wrote. His first order as supreme commander was to have food and provisions shipped into the country for his occupying forces and to ban them from taking or eating any food produced in Japan. When later questioned by the House Appropriations Committee about the expense, MacArthur replied, "Give me bread or give me bullets."[65] Eventually, the U.S. delivered more than $100 million of food supplies per year to the Japanese people.

During his first full year, MacArthur managed to implement many of the demilitarization and democratization reforms that had been drawn up in Washington by the Truman administration, approved by the president in early September and outlined in an operating document by the Joint Chiefs of Staff dated November 3.[66] Exercising authority, usually through the existing Japanese government, SCAP established war crimes tribunals, dismantled the Japanese military establishment, released political prisoners, abolished the secret police, reformed the education system, strengthened labor unions, and broke up large landholdings to benefit tenant farmers. At the same time, MacArthur issued a "Bill of Rights" directive requiring the Japanese government to repeal laws restricting political, civil, and religious freedoms and to enact legislation guaranteeing free elections and the right of women to vote (the most radical of his reforms). To make it difficult to repeal these reforms after occupation ended, MacArthur ordered that the existing constitution be substantially revised. Written by American lawyers under the direction of MacArthur, the new constitution incorporated MacArthur's bill of rights; granted universal suffrage for every citizen, including women; and outlawed Japan's right to make war. On April 10, 1946, thirty-seven million Japanese men and women went to the polls to cast their votes, a new experiment with democracy. Voter turnout was 72 percent. The constitution was passed. Ninety-five percent of the candidates competing for the legislative body, called the Diet, ran for the first time.

The scope and magnitude of the reforms that MacArthur initiated were nothing short of astonishing. The "greatest reformation of a people ever attempted," he bragged.[67] The irony, however, is that while the reforms liberated the people, SCAP's authority could not be challenged. MacArthur promoted progressive change but his governance was authoritarian.

As to the fate of Emperor Hirohito, MacArthur "stoutly resisted" the demands of the Russians, British, Australians, and some in Washington that the emperor be hanged as a war criminal, reasoning that he would have to have a "million reinforcements" to prevent guerrilla warfare from breaking out. After their first meeting, on September 27, 1945, MacArthur wrote that the emperor made a "tremendous impression" on him when he purported to take "sole responsibility for every political and military decision" during the war.[68] On New Year's Day 1946, Hirohito issued an imperial rescript that many Westerners regarded as a renunciation of his divinity. However, revisionist historian Marc Gallicchio wrote that it was at best a halfhearted renunciation that was "shrouded in ambiguity" and designed to placate the Americans. "A key element of the speech," wrote Gallicchio convincingly, "was that in asserting continuity with the Meiji Constitution, [Hirohito] seemed to make democracy a matter of imperial will, not the will of the people."[69] The new constitution, which became effective in 1947, relegated the emperor to a figurehead, "a symbol of the State and of the unity of the people," but until then Hirohito tried to maintain a semblance of his authority.[70]

All of these achievements burnished MacArthur's reputation and enhanced his political aspirations in America. However, there was one economic reform pushed by the Truman administration during the fall of 1945 that MacArthur doggedly resisted—a breakup of the zaibatsu, the giant family-owned industrial and banking conglomerates that controlled

Japan's trade and industry. When Truman sent envoys to Tokyo to persuade MacArthur to relent, he flatly refused, arguing that the idea of dissolving the oligopolies, which had existed since the Meiji period, was "too idealistic" and would not revive the faltering Japanese economy. Truman suspected that MacArthur had decided to put trust-busting on the back burner, preferring instead to focus on democracy and the kinds of political reforms that would play well back in the USA.

The president sputtered and fumed privately to his aides but he tolerated MacArthur's defiance. Truman, like MacArthur, was also motivated by political considerations. If he picked a public fight with SCAP over economic reform in Japan, it would only strengthen MacArthur's chances of securing the GOP nomination in 1948. Truman was worried that if he had to run against MacArthur, he could lose and that MacArthur as president, among other things, would endanger national security.

The president and MacArthur would spar over occupation policy for the next five years. But what about the quality of the lives of the Japanese people, who were consigned to exist in a devastated land? Would survivors of the sword like Toshio Nakamura and his mother find grace in the wilderness of postwar Japan?

In 1948, the Truman administration offered a measure of grace. It "reversed course," turning away from further reforms and shifting into a full court press to revitalize Japan's lagging economy. The goal was to rebuild Japan into a sustainable industrial powerhouse so that it would serve as an anti-Communist bastion able to resist Soviet influence, in essence the strategic linchpin of U.S. national security policy in the Far East. The story of the Truman administration's "reverse course" in occupation policy, a forerunner of the "Japanese miracle," and how it improved the lives of the Japanese people, will unfold in subsequent pages.

Chapter 7

Had Enough?

During the white-tie and tails Gridiron Club dinner at the Statler on Saturday, December 15, 1945, the first since the beginning of the war, Truman, who was the main target of the night's lampoonery, could not stop laughing. One of the newsmen on stage, dressed like Truman in a double-breasted suit jacket with a neatly folded handkerchief protruding from his breast pocket, was crooning the popular song "Wanting You" to "Veto M. Molotov," who was attired in an ill-fitting black suit. Molotov, known in Washington as a stone ass who always said no, first replied, "What is it you want of me?"[1] The audience expected that Truman would tell Molotov that he wanted peace with Russia. Instead, the president riffed off William Tecumseh Sherman, who famously said, "War is hell." Truman quipped, "I want you to know that I find peace is hell."[2] The crowd of Washingtonians roared, knowing that for himself Truman spoke the truth.

As he left the dinner that night, four-star admiral Ernest King, the hard-nosed chief of naval operations throughout the war who was on the verge of retiring, approached Truman and said, "Mr. President, we're not going to quit you; we'll do anything you want."[3]

I n September 1945, as the ink was drying on the surrender documents in Tokyo Bay, Truman's version of hell was figuring out how to deal with the daunting challenges of rapidly converting the arsenal of democracy to peacetime production and of the demobilization of sixteen million servicemen and -women who would be returning home. In the first ten days of peace, 1.8 million wartime workers lost their jobs. Roosevelt and then Truman had been almost completely preoccupied with ending the war. There had been some reconversion planning prior to August 1945 but little urgency because the military had predicted that the war would not end for another year. Thus, the Truman administration, as journalist Robert J. Donovan wrote, "had to begin the reconversion program practically from scratch."[4]

At first there was fear of depression and deflation as the Pentagon canceled huge war contracts and the nation's defense contractors, such as Boeing and Ford, laid off millions of workers. However, when some of the price controls were relaxed, American consumers, with pent-up demand for scarce goods and unprecedented levels of savings, touched off an inflationary spiral that was to bedevil Truman for the next three years.

The initial reconversion policy developed by Truman's advisers allowed for wage increases through collective bargaining on the condition that such increases not be used as a basis for seeking the lifting of price controls. Most price controls were slated to be ended but those that were needed to smooth the transition and curb inflation were to be continued.[5] This meant that several important price controls would remain in effect but only for limited periods of time.

To effectuate this policy, the administration needed to persuade labor and management to quickly agree to renew their no-strike, no-lockout pledge, which had expired at the end of the war. To avoid a breakdown in industrial relations, the pledge had to remain in effect until such time as a national labor-management conference to develop a process for settling disputes could be organized and convened in early November. Absent such an agreement, it was widely understood that relations with organized labor would sour and strikes could ensue. Union leaders were already under enormous pressure from their members (nearly fifteen million in 1945) to compensate them for being forced by the government to hold the line on wage increases during the war while their employers raked in tens of millions. Massive work stoppages were in the offing.

Instead of personally dealing with the leaders of labor and management, Truman delegated to his labor secretary, former senator Lewis Schellenbach, the task of convincing labor and management to renew their no-strike, no-lockout pledge. However, for the next few weeks, Schellenbach devoted his energies to a turf war against William Davis, director of the Office of Economic Stabilization, who he believed had overstepped his authority by predicting in a leaked off-the-record press conference that there were going to be substantial wage increases in the coming year. Schellenbach went to Truman and complained (misleadingly) that Davis's statements would provide support to those who were attacking him and his administration for being prolabor, antibusiness, and inflationary. Truman impulsively fired Davis on September 17. Schellenbach apparently made little, if any, effort to broker a renewal of the no-strike, no-lockout pledge. According to historian Barton Bernstein, the "failure to secure a renewal of this agreement" was "at the root" of the administration's subsequent "difficulties" with both labor and management.[6]

Union leaders could not have cared less about turf wars and backbiting in the Truman administration. The heads of the CIO and AFL, the two largest unions, were angry that the president had not given them a voice in his reconversion policy. Workers were seething, all too ready to walk off their jobs for pay equity. By late October, with demands for wage increases of up to 30 percent remaining unmet, more than seven hundred thousand coal, oil, and auto workers were on strike. A *Time* magazine columnist wrote, "The President is in deep and serious trouble," and accused his administration of "muddling through" the looming labor-management crisis.[7]

In a radio address to the nation on October 30, Truman unveiled an amended wage-price policy, which had been laid out in an executive order issued earlier that day. Truman explained that since workers were currently being paid less than during wartime, when their compensation had been boosted by time-and-a-half overtime pay and a longer workweek (forty-eight hours versus forty hours), "wage increases are therefore imperative." Any wage increase to "correct a maladjustment or inequity which would not interfere with effective transition to a peacetime economy," whatever that meant, would be approved. At the same time, he warned the labor movement that its "demands for wage increases" must be "reasonable," even though no such limitation appeared in his executive order.[8] With regard to existing price controls, Truman said that in determining whether increases in price ceilings would be allowed, increases in wages might be taken into account, a significant concession to the interests of business, albeit inflationary. [9]

Reactions to the president's speech were predictable. Labor regarded it as a full-scale endorsement of their demands for substantial wage increases. On behalf of the business community, the *Wall Street Journal* criticized Truman for "encouraging unions to strike out immediately for whatever wage increases they can get."[10] An industrialist warned that "increased wages can only be met by increased prices."[11]

Truman's amended reconversion plan did little to limit wage and price increases, prevent strikes, and curb inflation. Indeed, given postwar demand for consumer products, the enormous savings built up during the war, and pressure from unions for wage increases to reward workers for their wartime sacrifices, virtually no administration, whether Republican or Democratic, could have succeeded in stabilizing the nation's economy. For the sake of FDR's place in history, "it was fortunate that he died when he did."[12] A period of adjustment, perhaps two or three years, would be and was necessary.

————

For Truman it was not enough to advocate a short-term reconversion policy. With the war over, the president decided that the time was ripe to set the "tone and direction" of his administration. Aided by New Dealer Sam Rosenman, an FDR holdover, Truman composed a twenty-one-point series of progressive proposals that he planned to promote through legislation and executive actions in the coming months. As historian Alonzo Hamby wrote, the idea was to explain to Congress and the American public "just who he was ideologically and politically."[13] Although most of his advisers agreed with the lengthy message Truman intended to deliver to

Congress and the American public, John Snyder, director of the Office of War Mobilization and Reconversion, told him in the "frankest and most explicit terms" that he should not feel bound to FDR's New Deal policies and that his message would at best be a political nonstarter.[14] Nevertheless, on September 6, just four days after MacArthur declared that "these proceedings are closed," Truman's sixteen-thousand-word manifesto was released to the public and deposited with a thud on each congressperson's desk.

If the American public and the nation's political parties thought that Harry Truman, their unelected president, was going to be a moderate placeholder until the 1948 election, they were in for a rude awakening. Assuming the mantle of Franklin Roosevelt's first hundred days, the president called Congress into an emergency session. His twenty-one-point message urged members to take up and pass full-employment legislation and to adopt FDR's "economic bill of rights," a breathtaking set of progressive proposals to confer upon "all" citizens—presumably including African Americans—rights to a job, housing, health care, and an expanded Social Security system. Included among the twenty-one points were requests that the Democratically controlled Congress take action to significantly enhance unemployment compensation, minimum wage, aid to farmers, and public works programs. In addition to these hugely expensive initiatives, Truman called for universal military service and to make permanent the Fair Employment Practices Committee with a mandate to eliminate discrimination by employers on the basis of "race, religion, and color."[15]

Truman, a savvy politician, must have known that as the Great Depression finally ended because of the war, the American people had become much more conservative, and that the vaunted Roosevelt coalition was crumbling as Southern Democrats were aligning with Republicans in increasing numbers. Since the 1937 attempt to pack the Supreme Court, Democrats from the Deep South along with Republicans had blocked FDR's domestic initiatives and brought the New Deal to a standstill. After skimming Truman's twenty-one-point message, Representative Charles Halleck, chair of the House Republican Campaign Committee, jubilantly declared, "This is the kickoff" to victory in the 1946 midterms, the return of Republicans to power in Congress after decades of languishing in the minority.[16] Halleck was convinced that the country would not buy in to Truman's radical agenda and that it would turn out to be a political albatross for Democratic officeholders.

Truman understood that many if not most of his twenty-one points would not become law and that he risked alienating blocs of voters, but he set those concerns aside. He believed that at the outset of his postwar presidency, it was essential that everyone in America—liberals, conservatives, labor, business, and Blacks, whether they agreed with him or not—knew exactly where he stood on issues of importance to them. In his memoirs he wrote that his twenty-one-point message to Congress and the American people expressed the "political principles and economic philosophy" that he had followed throughout his "political life."[17] Very few picked up on it at the time, but Truman's stance on the Fair Employment Committee and his inclusion of "all" citizens in his proposed reforms set the stage for the beginning of what would become his courageous positions in support of civil rights and equal opportunity, arguably his most enduring domestic legacy.

Six weeks after introducing his twenty-one-point program, Truman wrote that "the Congress are balking" at—that is, resisting—most of the program's legislative proposals.[18] By late November 1945, his calls for legislation to guarantee full employment, increases in unemployment compensation, and national health insurance had been rejected or tabled by Congress. To the war-weary legislators, his advocacy of universal military service was dead on arrival. Legislation to make permanent the Fair Employment Practices Committee, with its mandate to prohibit racial discrimination, was stonewalled by threats of Southern senators to launch a filibuster.

The only proposals in Truman's message that gained near-term traction with Congress were his recommendations to liberalize and expand the education and loan guarantee benefits of the Servicemen's Readjustment Act, commonly known as the GI Bill. The original GI Bill had been signed into law by President Roosevelt in June 1944.[19] FDR deserves credit for promoting the general idea of benefits for returning veterans, but the driving forces behind the enactment of the GI Bill were the American Legion and Senator Ernest McFarland of Oklahoma, a progressive Democrat.

In a short speech, Roosevelt claimed paternity for the GI Bill even though he neither introduced nor expressly endorsed the legislation when it was making its way through Congress. During that winter and spring, he had had more pressing concerns, including his wretched health and the lead-up to the Normandy invasion.

Scarcely a year after it was passed, the 1944 GI Bill, although broad and generous, was seen as something of a disappointment, having been criticized as underutilized by vets and ineffective. The unemployment compensation and job placement services were regarded as less important because after the war, jobs had become plentiful. Educational benefits were widely recognized as "faulty, loosely drawn . . . make-shift," and in need of revision.[20] Aware that House and Senate committees would be holding hearings during the fall of 1945, the president, in the "VETER-ANS" section of his twenty-one points, expressed his full-throated endorsement of the amendments to the GI Bill recommended by General Omar Bradley, whom Truman had appointed in mid-August to head the Veterans Administration (VA). Bradley, a soldier's general who commanded the loyalty and respect of virtually all veterans, was one of Truman's outstanding appointments. From 1945 to 1947, he reorganized and revitalized the Veterans Administration before departing to replace Dwight Eisenhower as army chief of staff. However, he did nothing to improve access for African American and female veterans to the bill's benefits.

When President Truman signed the amended GI Bill on December 28, 1945, it contained two sets of significant improvements backed by Truman and Bradley. The first was the government-financed education program, which was amended to further liberalize subsidies by allowing the VA to pay the "customary cost" of tuition and related fees for each vet, provided they did not exceed $500 for the school year, and to increase education subsistence allowances from $50 to $65 per month for vets with no dependents and from $75 to $90 if "he" had dependents. The word "he" meant that female vets with dependents would not be eligible for anything more than $75 per month. In addition, Congress lengthened the period for when a vet could begin studies after discharge from the service.

With regard to VA loan guarantees for purchases of homes, farms, and businesses, the amended law raised the limit on automatic VA guarantees from $2,000 to $4,000. Loans were to be appraised on the basis of "reasonable value" to account for inflation. Interest rates could not exceed 4 percent. Home loans had to be paid off within twenty-five years, farm loans within forty years. Vets could also obtain guaranteed loans for "working capital" needed for farms or businesses that they had purchased.[21]

The amended GI Bill did not change the mandate in the original legislation that the benefits were to be made available to all American veterans regardless of their "race, creed, color or national origin." Nevertheless, as African American GIs returned to seek education, loans, and employment benefits from mostly all-white VA administrators and local lending officers, they encountered hostility and systemic racial prejudice, especially in the South. There were no provisions in the original or amended GI Bills to enforce the antidiscrimination mandate. Moreover, the VA was barred from control or supervision over state education agencies, colleges, lending institutions, and real estate brokers, each of which served as gatekeepers of benefits provided in the GI Bill. One of the most insidious mechanisms that deprived Black Americans of benefits was the creation of "onerous and subjective tests for determining need."[22]

Likewise, GI Janes were disadvantaged. Unlike men, female vets were not entitled under the amended GI Bill to the extra $15-per-month education subsistence allowance for dependents (remember the word "he"). In addition, while their husbands were in school or when they were raising children, female vets tended to delay their education, which often meant that they would run afoul of the nine-year limit on eligibility to obtain GI Bill benefits. Widows of deceased vets felt that they too had sacrificed for their country and deserved government assistance. Organized as Gold Star Wives, they petitioned Congress to extend the benefits of the GI Bill to more than a hundred thousand WWII widows. On behalf of the VA, General Omar Bradley urged Congress to reject the widows' request because of the "tremendous additional cost to the government."[23] Congress agreed.

Except for veterans of color and women, the GI Bill, as amended, evolved into an enormous success, although its democratizing impact is still debated. It certainly wasn't grace in the wilderness for all American veterans, but for many it eased their transition to civilian life. Millions of returning soldiers, almost all of whom were white males, were able to use the benefits to go back to school and purchase homes, farms, and businesses. They would later say, "The GI Bill changed my life."

Whether Truman was aware of the discriminatory potential of the amended GI Bill when he signed it is unknown. It would be another year before he began to address civil rights in America.

––––––––––

Truman's long-anticipated national labor-management conference was finally convened in Washington on November 5. The objective, as Truman lectured at the outset, was for the two adversaries to agree on a wage-price policy and a process to avert crippling strikes. Instead of offering a plan and his personal leadership, Truman left it to the two sides to hammer out an agreement. However, even if he had inserted himself, it was probably too late. By then, the labor-management relationship had been poisoned and labor itself was hopelessly divided. In the midst of the conference, Walter Reuther's United Auto Workers (UAW), having demanded a 30 percent increase in wages, shut down General Motors (GM), the largest automaker in the country, at a time when consumers were clamoring for new cars. In addition, steelworkers were threatening a nationwide strike against U.S. Steel over a $2-per-day wage increase.

After the labor-management conference adjourned at the beginning of December without accomplishing anything, Truman made moves that were harshly criticized by both sides. On December 3 he asked Congress to enact legislation modeled after the Railway Labor Act to head off strikes by invoking a thirty-day no-strike cooling-off period, pending a report and proposed solutions by a federal fact-finding board. Philip Murray, president of the CIO, was furious. He declared that Truman's request would "weaken and ultimately destroy labor organizations."[24]

Then, in an effort to settle the GM strike, the president proceeded to alienate management. Having appointed a fact-finding board, he announced at a press conference that this board would have authority "to examine the books" of GM in order to determine whether the UAW's proposed wage increase could be absorbed by GM without raising its prices.[25]

Alfred P. Sloan Jr., the legendary chair of GM, issued a statement on December 29 claiming that Truman's action would lead to "the death of the American system of competitive enterprise." GM "will not participate," he announced, in "a regimented economy."[26]

Thus, by the end of 1945, Truman had been charged with both the destruction of the labor movement and the death of capitalism. A two-count indictment. From a high of 80 percent in the early fall, the president's approval rating began a steady decline. And still the strikes would not abate.

———

Consumed by domestic issues after the surrender of Japan, the president was content to allow Secretary of State Jimmy Byrnes to take the lead in managing the nation's foreign policy. They both understood that the main focus would be addressing major problems caused by the Soviet Union's aggressive attempts to expand its influence in Europe, Turkey, the Iranian province of Azerbaijan, and East Asia. Their goal was to maintain world peace by achieving a cooperative relationship with Joseph Stalin. But there was no new grand strategy. Rather, Truman and Byrnes remained wedded to FDR's vision of resolving differences amicably over time through offers of friendship, collaboration, compromise, and concession if necessary. Their tactic, as the press parodied on the night of the Gridiron Club dinner, was "wanting you [Joseph Stalin], nothing else in the world will do."[27]

After an unsuccessful Council of Foreign Ministers conference in London during September and early October, in which Byrnes found Molotov impossible to deal with, the secretary did not give up hope. Convinced that "Stalin wants peace," Byrnes organized a less formal meeting of just the Big Three foreign ministers (Byrnes, Bevin, and Molotov), this time in Moscow, where he could go over Molotov's head and appeal directly to Stalin.[28] Truman had no objection, pleased that Byrnes had taken the initiative.

To Byrnes's relief, Generalissimo Stalin cut short his vacation at Sochi and agreed to meet with him in Moscow. Whether or not his presence made a difference, the fact is that Byrnes returned to Washington from the ten-day conference on Saturday, December 29, with a briefcase full of agreements. At the top of the list of what Byrnes regarded as his accomplishments was a pledge by Molotov to cosponsor a UN resolution to establish a commission for international control of atomic energy. In addition, Byrnes brokered a deal to allow a Soviet representative (whom MacArthur would likely ignore) to have an advisory role in the occupation of Japan, and he acceded to Molotov's demand that the U.S. recognize Rumania and Bulgaria, provided the Soviets added one or two token opposition figures to those governments. With respect to China, the Soviets agreed to support Chiang's government and to remove their troops from Manchuria in exchange for a conditional U.S. commitment to withdraw their forces from North China. Envisioning a unified Korea, Byrnes persuaded the other two foreign ministers to join him in calling for the creation of a joint commission to assist in setting up a Korean provisional government.

While the secretary was cutting deals in Moscow, back in Washington, the president had begun sniping to his aides about Byrnes's failure to cable daily reports and to consult with him. Speechwriter Sam Rosenman told Joe Davies that Truman was going "sour on Jim" and that he might have to replace him before long.[29] It was not a matter of substance. After all, Truman had heard nothing of substance from Byrnes. Rather, Truman's hackles were aroused because he felt his conniving, "too smart" subordinate was treating him with disrespect.[30] Plus, the fact that he was alone in the White House during the holidays added to his foul mood. On December 20, Bess, her mother, and Margaret had departed for Independence. On Christmas Eve, when Truman finally received a so-called progress report from Moscow, he scoffed with anger at Byrnes's arrogance and condescension, calling the report nothing more than an assurance that Byrnes's "business trip was progressing well and not to worry."[31]

On Christmas morning 1945, Truman recklessly risked his life by insisting that his pilot, Hank Myers, take off from National Airport in a driving wind and snowstorm. Fortunately, after an hour of deicing, the *Sacred Cow* and its precious cargo were aloft and headed west to Kansas City, from where the president would be driven home to Independence. The *New York Times* wrote that "it was one of the most hazardous 'sentimental journeys' ever undertaken" by a head of state.[32] Under the prevailing law, if Truman had not survived the rough takeoff and flight, Byrnes would have succeeded him as president because the office of the vice president was vacant. If that had happened, Byrnes would have mourned Truman's demise while being more than pleased to assume the presidency, which he had felt was his due ever since FDR passed him over for VP in 1944. Given his self-confidence and years of experience in the three branches of the federal government, Byrnes believed he was capable of being a far better president than Truman.

When Truman finally arrived home at 219 North Delaware Street on the evening of Christmas Day, Bess was extremely upset. She had worried all day about his dangerous flight and was convinced he had manufactured excuses to delay his departure until the last minute. Instead of welcoming Harry with a warm embrace, she berated him. In a letter written two days later and apparently never sent, Truman described his emotions:

> When you told me I might as well have stayed in Washington so far as you were concerned, I gave up. . . . You can never appreciate what it means to come home as I did the other evening after doing 100 things I didn't want to do and have the only person in the world whose approval and good opinion I value look at me like I'm something the cat dragged in and tell me that I've come in at the last because I couldn't find any reason to stay away. . . . You, Margie and everyone else who may have any influence on my actions must give me help and assistance; because no one ever needed help and assistance as I do now. . . . [33]

This letter, which was discovered in a desk drawer soon after Harry's death twenty-seven years later, reveals the extent of his dependence on Bess, her hold over him, and his feelings of insecurity.

The night before Truman left Independence and flew back to Washington, Thursday, December 27, he received the text of the communiqué by the three foreign ministers describing the results of the Moscow conference. However, it arrived a full hour *after* it had been released to newspapers and radio networks. Truman's temper flared not only because he had not been given an advance copy by Byrnes before the communiqué was broadcast to the nation, but more important because "there was not a word about Iran or any other place where the Soviets were on the march."[34]

On Friday, before boarding the presidential yacht *Williamsburg* for a six-day trip down the Potomac to work on a radio speech and play poker at night with his cronies, Truman met briefly in the Oval Office with Senator Arthur Vandenberg, ranking Republican member of the Foreign Relations Committee. Vandenberg was up in arms. Based on ambiguous language in the foreign ministers' communiqué, the senator believed Byrnes might have agreed to share atomic secrets with the Soviets without having provided for an effective international inspection system. Truman assured Vandenberg that he was mistaken. Nevertheless, it was necessary to issue a statement clarifying the Moscow agreement on the sharing of atomic energy. Truman once again had reason to be annoyed with his secretary of state.

During an early-morning refueling stop in Newfoundland on December 29, Byrnes cabled Undersecretary Dean Acheson that he would be arriving in Washington later that day and asked him to arrange time with the radio networks for a report on the Moscow conference. According to Acheson, "in view of the President's state of mind," he thought it would be wise for Byrnes to report first to Truman and then, presumably "with the President's blessing," speak to the nation on the day after his return. Acheson took it upon himself to suggest this to Truman. "The President agreeing, we arranged it this way," he later wrote.[35]

Shortly after Byrnes landed in Washington, he was handed a telegram from Truman. "Suggest you come down today or tomorrow to report your mission. . . . We can then discuss among other things the advisability of a broadcast by you."[36] According to Acheson, who had met his boss at the airfield, Byrnes was exhausted after the long flight from Moscow and was understandably irritated with having to take yet another flight to meet the president at Quantico, where the *Williamsburg* was anchored just offshore in the Potomac River. When Acheson explained as gently as possible that the president was not pleased with Byrnes's failure to report and consult, the secretary was "disbelieving."[37]

Byrnes flew down to Quantico that afternoon and met with Truman in his stateroom aboard the *Williamsburg*. Truman wrote in his memoirs that he bluntly told Byrnes that he "did not like" being "left in the dark" about both the Moscow negotiations and the communiqué and that he "would not tolerate a repetition of such conduct."[38] Byrnes's recollection of their meeting could not have been more different. Byrnes wrote that rather than a confrontation, it was a pleasant conversation during which Truman expressed his "hearty approval" of the secretary's accomplishments in Moscow and had no objection to the radio broadcast that Byrnes planned to deliver on the evening of December 30. Byrnes also recalled that Truman invited him to stay for dinner that evening and insisted that he come back and spend New Year's Eve on the *Williamsburg*, which he did.[39]

It is likely that Byrnes's account, though self-serving, is closer to the truth than Truman's, which was written at least five years later. Truman had a reputation for being extremely sensitive to others' feelings and rarely uttered a harsh word to a subordinate. As Acheson, who knew both men well, speculated, the president had a tendency to "vastly" exaggerate his "bark," whereas thick-skinned Byrnes would not "take as personal criticism Mr. Truman's desire to be kept more fully informed."[40]

A week later, when Byrnes was about to depart for the first session of the UN General Assembly in London, the president summoned him to the Oval Office. There, according to Truman, he read aloud a long letter he had written to "My dear Jim" that sharply rebuked the secretary. This time Truman claimed that he criticized Byrnes not only for leaving him "completely in the dark" regarding the Moscow negotiations but also for compromising with the Soviets on the recognition of Rumania and Bulgaria and for his failures to confront the Russians "with an iron fist and strong language" on a host of issues involving Iran, Eastern Europe, and Asia. Assuming Truman read every word of the letter, he concluded by saying to Byrnes, "I'm tired of babying the Soviets."[41]

Because Truman filed the letter away, having never shown nor sent it to the secretary, Byrnes did not read the letter until it surfaced in 1952.[42] By then, the former secretary, who had broken with Truman politically, was governor of South Carolina. In his memoir *All in One Lifetime*, Byrnes swore that Truman never read the letter to him. "Had this occurred," he wrote, "with my deep conviction that there must be complete accord between the President and his Secretary of State, I would have resigned immediately."[43]

Whether Truman read the letter to Byrnes or not, the question to Cold War historians was and is whether the president's statement that he was "tired of babying the Soviets" signaled a "get tough" turning point in U.S.–Soviet relations beginning in the early days of 1946. Some believed it did. The record, however, belies such a development. Throughout 1946, Truman never called for nor attempted to implement a new and consistent approach toward the Soviets. In fact, even though his relationship with Secretary Byrnes had frayed, the president remained dependent on him to manage foreign policy. A major transformation—a clear departure from FDR's policy—would not take place until 1947.

In *All in One Lifetime*, Secretary Byrnes wrote that in the fall of 1945, Truman asked him to find an appointment for Eleanor Roosevelt in the field of foreign affairs. The president told Byrnes that he had to have her on his political team because of her "influence with the Negro voters."[44] Since the second week of May, Truman and the former First Lady had carried on a lively correspondence, in which she felt free to express her opinions on issues of the day as she had done with her husband. On Truman's part, he valued her judgment and suggestions, although he was not always in agreement. According to Byrnes, within a week he presented Truman with a slate of individuals who he recommended should be the U.S. delegates to the first meeting of the United Nations General Assembly, which would be held in London in January. Mrs. Roosevelt was at the top of his list. Truman liked the idea and immediately called her at her Washington Square apartment in New York City. At first she demurred, claiming that she had no background or experience in foreign policy. Deep down she feared that she would fail. Truman gently persisted. Eleanor consulted friends and family, including her son Franklin Jr., who urged, "You have to do it."[45] Finally, she came around, after convincing herself that she owed it to her deceased husband, who had placed so much faith in the UN as a guarantor of world peace. After Truman sent the nomination to the Senate for confirmation, a few senators, including Arthur Vandenberg, expressed reservations, but when the vote was taken on December 22, only Theodore Bilbo (D-MS), an outspoken white supremacist, dissented.

On Sunday, December 30, 1945, Eleanor Roosevelt stepped out of a taxi at Pier 90 on the Hudson River. Carrying a typewriter and briefcase, she avoided her eventual colleagues, who were surrounded by reporters, and boarded the RMS *Queen Elizabeth* alone. She was headed to the first session of the General Assembly in London. In the coming years Mrs. Roosevelt would become even more famous and respected, serving as chair of the UN Commission on Human Rights and overseeing the drafting and adoption of the Universal Declaration of Human Rights.

———

At the beginning of his first speech to the nation in the new year, President Truman announced that for the future of the economy, "1946 is our year of decision." A close reading of the text reveals that Truman was actually appealing not to the American people but to Congress, imploring that body of decision-makers to address labor-management strife and enact laws to help his administration stabilize the economy.[46] Yet, as the months slipped by, Congress for the most part failed to act. It became apparent that an increasingly conservative Congress preferred to leave it to Truman to try to manage the economy through executive powers and persuasion. The result was inflation, massive work stoppages, product shortages, indecision, and the appearance of a president not in control. His weakness as a public speaker added to the impression that he was out of his depth. According to Gallup polls, Truman's approval ratings plunged from a high of 87 percent in the weeks after he was sworn in to below 40 percent. In the fall of 1946, with the midterm elections looming, Karl Frost, a clever ad executive from Swampscott, Massachusetts, coined a slogan for the Republican opposition, which had been out of power since 1930: "Had enough?"[47] The glib slogan resonated with voters. Though Truman would not be on the ballot, the November 1946 midterms would be a referendum on his presidency.

———

During the first five months of 1946, with millions of workers on strike or threatening to strike, Truman was compelled to spend an inordinate amount of his time on labor-management issues. Not only was he brought in at various stages to meet with union leaders and corporate executives but he also had to listen to and resolve countless disputes among strong-willed advisers responsible for holding the line on prices to consumers and those advocating the lifting of controls, which would increase production and stimulate the economy. The little sign that was on the president's desk for a time, "The Buck Stops Here," which was a gift from his old friend Fred Canfil, said it all. Harry Truman was the decider, which meant that at least one side and sometimes both would end up criticizing him after they left his office.

Because the production of steel, an essential raw material, was so important to the health of the American economy, the strike by 750,000 workers on January 19, which shut down more than a thousand mills of the United States Steel Corporation, was by far the most worrisome. It was the largest strike ever recorded in the U.S. With Truman's reluctant support, Philip Murray, head of the steelworkers' union, was demanding a wage increase of 18.5 cents per hour while Benjamin Fairless, CEO of U.S. Steel, was insisting that an increase of that magnitude would force him to raise steel prices beyond that allowed by the price control regulations. The president had no choice but to become personally involved because if the steel industry breached price controls, then other industries throughout the economy would follow. Chester Bowles, who was administrator of price controls in the Truman administration and thus responsible for curbing inflation, adamantly opposed any steel price increase of more than $2.50 per ton, warning Truman that if he agreed to more, then Bowles could not hold the line on rents, farm products, and other items. John Snyder, Truman's pro-business friend and director of the administration's economic reconversion program, commissioned an expert report. The report concluded that without a price increase of more than $4 per ton, U.S. Steel would lose money if it agreed to a wage increase of 18.5 cents per hour. In a private meeting with the president, Snyder laconically advised, "We need the steel," which meant that to end the strike and resume production, he should be authorized to offer up to $5 per ton.[48] Truman, the decider, agreed.

When Bowles, who was in the South playing golf with his wife, read in the newspapers that he had been overruled, he rushed back to Washington and tried to change Truman's mind. According to Bowles, the president, who "seemed harassed and tired," said he had to support Snyder.[49] Bowles resigned. After the steel strike ended on February 15 and the wage and price increases were put into effect, another spiral of inflation reverberated throughout the economy.

Distracted by the U.S. Steel and GM strikes, Truman failed to personally intervene or appeal to the public as the House and Senate gutted the full-employment bill that he had been advocating for months. Gone were its provisions guaranteeing a "full employment budget" and the right to a job. When the Employment Act of 1946 was sent to his desk, it was a shadow of what it had been. But it was better than nothing because it at least authorized the government to "use all practical means" to achieve "maximum employment" and it established a Council of Economic Advisers.[50] Truman signed the bill into law on February 20. Liberal Democrats and labor unions criticized Truman for his ineffective leadership.

Liberals also blamed Truman for mishandling the nomination of his friend Ed Pauley, a California oilman, to be navy undersecretary, which resulted in the resignation of Harold Ickes, a New Dealer who had served as secretary of the interior from the beginning of the Roosevelt administration. When Ickes suggested during Pauley's Senate confirmation hearings in 1946 that Pauley had attempted to bribe him in September 1944, Truman should have withdrawn the nomination. Instead, he backed Pauley to the hilt and proclaimed at a press conference that Ickes was "mistaken."[51] With his honor impugned, Ickes announced on national radio that he could no longer remain in Truman's cabinet. Truman promptly accepted Ickes's resignation and told him he had three days to vacate his office. The entire messy affair, including editorials lamenting Truman's incompetence, was chronicled in the nation's newspapers. With the departure of Ickes, Henry Wallace was the last of FDR's New Dealers in Truman's cabinet.

———

Though Truman remained focused on strikes and the economy, a linkage of events involving the Soviet Union in February and early March led to him being criticized by the media as "remarkably inept."[52] It began with

British foreign minister Ernest Bevin. Encouraged by former prime minister Churchill, Bevin became the first prominent statesman to publicly confront the Soviet Union for its occupation of Azerbaijan in northwest Iran and to challenge its expansionist moves in Turkey and Eastern Europe. Bevin's concerns were amplified by Comrade Stalin in a speech he delivered on February 9 in Moscow's Bolshoi Theatre to his so-called voters (this was the first "election" for the Supreme Soviet in eight years). In an effort to rally his war-weary constituents to support another five-year plan that would emphasize production of capital goods and armaments, Stalin predicted that "capitalist countries" would attempt to "redistribute 'spheres of influence' . . . by employing armed force." As a result, he said, it would be "impossible" to avoid "catastrophic wars . . . under the present capitalistic conditions of world economic development."[53] His language was elliptical, his intent perhaps lost in translation. Did he mean that a shooting war with the Soviet Union was inevitable? Supreme Court associate justice William O. Douglas certainly thought so. He told Navy Secretary Forrestal that Stalin's speech was tantamount to "the Declaration of World War III."[54]

Freeman Matthews, director of the State Department's Office of European Affairs, wasn't sure what Stalin had in mind. A couple of days after Stalin's speech, he drafted a message, signed by Secretary Byrnes, to forty-two-year-old Russian-speaking George Kennan, the chargé d'affaires at the U.S. embassy in Moscow, asking him to provide "an interpretive analysis of what we may expect in the way of future implementation of [Stalin's] announced policies."[55] Kennan, who had been discouraged and on the verge of quitting because he felt that no one at State was listening to him, was only too pleased to oblige. "They had asked for it. Now by God, they would have it," he wrote.[56] From his upstairs bedroom in the embassy, suffering "a cold, fever, sinus, tooth trouble," Kennan dictated a 5,540-word telegram—the longest in State Department history—that was wired on February 22 to Kennan's superiors at State, the Pentagon, and the White House.[57] It was the most influential analysis of Soviet postwar intentions and how the U.S. should react that was ever written.

Setting aside Kennan's brilliant explication of Russian history and Soviet motivation, his long telegram answered the key question raised in

Stalin's speech: Was a shooting war with the U.S. inevitable? Kennan's answer was no. "Soviet power," he wrote, "does not take unnecessary risks." It responds to the "logic of force," and "for this reason it can easily withdraw—and usually does when strong resistance is encountered at any point." The policy of the United States, therefore, should be to maintain "sufficient force" and to make clear its "readiness to use it." Kennan concluded that as long as this policy was implemented through diplomacy, determination, patience, and courage, the U.S. could cope with the problem of Soviet aggression "without recourse to any military conflict." The word "containment" did not appear in the long telegram, but that is the policy Kennan meant to convey.[58]

While Truman and Byrnes had read enough of Kennan's telegram to absorb its essence and were aware that it raised serious doubts about their FDR-inspired policy of compromise and accommodation toward the Soviet Union, Kennan's views did not trigger an immediate shift.[59] Still, in the days after the telegram electrified official Washington, Senator Vandenberg and one day later Secretary Byrnes delivered speeches that signaled a hardening of the U.S. attitude toward the Soviet Union. "If we are a great power," declared Byrnes, "we must act as a great power."[60] Pundits dubbed Byrnes's speech the "Second Vandenberg Concerto."[61]

Winston Churchill, who was out of power in March 1946 but deeply concerned about Communism's ascendancy, had decided that this was the moment to harden policy toward the Soviet Union even more. Having accepted Truman's offer to introduce him at a speech he had been invited to deliver at tiny Westminster College in Fulton, Missouri, Churchill planned to urge America, the UN, and his own country to relentlessly confront the Soviets with the only thing they would respond to—military strength or, as Kennan put it, "the logic of force."

The tale of the eighteen-hour, all-night train trip to the quaint village of Fulton by Churchill, Truman, and his aides—replete with descriptions of drinks (for Churchill, water "made palatable by the addition of whiskey"), Churchill's apparel (looking "like a bunny" in his "zippered blue siren suit"), and poker (while Churchill was losing $250, the two world leaders called each other "Harry" and "Winston")—has been told too many times to bear repeating in full.[62] According to White House acting naval aide Clark Clifford, by the time they arrived in Fulton on the morning of March 5, Truman had read the final draft of Churchill's speech and pronounced it "brilliant and admirable."[63] However, Truman would claim later that he had neither read nor approved the speech in advance and that his presence at Westminster College was not to be interpreted as an endorsement of Churchill's address.

Clark Clifford, movie-star handsome and suave at age thirty-nine, was destined to become one of Truman's most influential political advisers. In a few months he would be named "special counsel" by the president, replacing Sam Rosenman, who had decided for financial reasons to return to his law practice. During the night on the train to Fulton, Clifford was part of the group that played poker with Truman and Churchill. Commenting later on Churchill's prowess at the card table, Clifford pronounced him "a lamb among wolves."[64]

Churchill began his "iron curtain" speech, which Russian historians date as the beginning of the Cold War, by saying that Truman's presence dignified and magnified the occasion, thereby undermining the president's subsequent attempts to distance himself from the substance of Churchill's remarks.

The substance was sobering. Though Churchill spoke broadly of the need to defend against the twin threats of war and tyranny, he zeroed in on the dangers to liberty of Soviet expansionism and its attempt to spread Communism around the world. "Nobody knows" what the Soviets "intend to do in the immediate future," he ominously said. Then came the most famous and oft-quoted words of Churchill's entire speech, "the facts" as he saw them:

From Stettin in the Baltic to Trieste in the Adriatic, an iron curtain has descended across the Continent. Behind that line lie all the capitals of the ancient states of Central and Eastern Europe. Warsaw, Berlin, Prague, Vienna, Budapest, Belgrade, Bucharest and Sofia, all these famous cities and populations around them lie in what I must call the Soviet sphere, and all are subject in one form or another, not only to Soviet influence but to a very high and, in many cases, increasing measure of control from Moscow.

Having said that nobody knew Soviet intentions, Churchill suggested that he knew: "I do not believe that Soviet Russia desires war," he declared. "What they desire is the fruits of war and the indefinite expansion of their power and doctrines." Kennan's long telegram in which he discounted the prospect of war could have been the source of Churchill's belief but there is no evidence to support such a conjecture.[65]

How best to deal with this situation? The solution, Churchill was convinced, should be based on the premise that there is nothing the Soviets "admire so much as strength, and there is nothing for which they have less respect than for weakness." Accordingly, his recommendations to his audience at Westminster and to the world at large were to form an Anglo-American military alliance, equip the UN with "an international armed force," and establish a union of the Western democracies. With a show of strength "by the English-speaking world and all its connections," Churchill advised, peace could be achieved through negotiations with Russia under the authority of the UN. In other words, the policy going forward should be strength and diplomacy.[66]

In America the reaction to Churchill's speech was divided. The *Wall Street Journal*, reflecting conservatives' views, lauded Churchill for dramatizing "a hard core of indisputable facts" about the Soviet threat.[67] Southern senator Burnet Maybank (D-SC) agreed with Churchill that "Russia seemed bent on 'indefinite expansion' of 'its power and doctrines' and needed to be reined in."[68] Moderate to left-leaning newspapers and leaders criticized Churchill's call to entangle the U.S. in a military alliance with the British Empire. The *Nation* declared that Churchill had added "a sizeable measure of poison to the already deteriorating relations between Russia and the Western powers" and lambasted Truman as "inept" for publicly associating himself with the speech.[69] Walter Lippmann, one of the nation's leading columnists, labeled Churchill's iron curtain speech "an almost catastrophic blunder."[70]

Truman himself was somewhat divided. Clark Clifford, who was intimately familiar with Truman's views, wrote that Truman admired the speech but was "not yet ready to embrace it." While the president, Clifford continued, "was torn between a growing sense of anger at, and distrust of, the Soviet Union," he held out "a residual hope that he could still work with Stalin."[71] In other words, he was not yet prepared to emerge from FDR's shadow. For this reason, Truman did everything he could to disassociate himself from Churchill's views. He lied to reporters and others about not having read the speech in advance of its delivery and he ordered Undersecretary Dean Acheson not to attend a reception honoring Churchill in New York City. When asked what he thought about the speech, he pleaded "no comment."[72] To mollify Stalin, the president sent a message "emphasizing that he still held out hope for better relations," and he actually invited the Soviet leader to the University of Missouri, where he could deliver a response to Churchill's speech."[73] Thus, as of the spring of 1946, Truman was still singing "Wanting You" to the Soviet autocrat.

On Thursday evening, May 23, 1946, Harry Truman confronted the most serious domestic crisis of his presidency. His ability to govern hung in the balance. Six days earlier, negotiations to end a nationwide coal strike had failed. Though Truman had seized control of the coal mines by using his executive powers, the shutdown persisted. Since coal was America's major source of energy, the economy was grinding to a halt. Factories were shuttered and electrical dimouts proliferated as coal supplies dwindled. As if that were not enough, at 5:00 that afternoon, 250,000 railroad workers across the country walked off their jobs, which meant that virtually all of America's freight and passenger trains halted in place or were shunted off into rail yards. Together, the vast work stoppages were about to paralyze the entire nation.

Enraged, betrayed, frustrated, exhausted, and alone, Truman sat down at his desk that evening. Bess had retired. He began writing what Clark Clifford later described as "surely one of the most intemperate documents ever written by a President."[74] It was styled as a speech he would give to the American people but in actuality it was an explosive yet cathartic release of emotion. Some said that Truman "went off the rails." With hate and pent-up fury, he accused the labor leaders by name of being liars, egomaniacs, and

Communists and of "holding a gun at the head of the Government." He labeled Congress as "weak-kneed" and senators and representatives as "Russian." As to the "Wall Street crowd," Truman put them in the same class as the union leaders but curiously he never mentioned the role of corporate management in prolonging the strikes and work stoppages.

As the old "sticks and stones" saying teaches, "names will never hurt you," but what Truman suggested near the end of his so-called speech was downright dangerous. He called on the recently discharged veterans, his "comrades in arms," to *eliminate* the named union leaders and "Russian" congressmen. His last two sentences, again invoking the vets, were beyond the pale. "Let's put transportation and production back to work, *hang a few traitors*, make our own country safe for democracy, tell the Russians where to get off and make the United Nations work. Come on, boys [that is, the vets], let's do the job."[75]

The following morning, having summoned an emergency meeting of his cabinet, the president, his eyes blazing and his jaw set, took his place at the head of the long table. "He was mad," recalled Clifford, who was seated in a chair along the wall, feeling "oddly out of place" in his naval uniform.[76] Truman began by informing the group that he had called Congress into a special session for the next day (Saturday). He explained that since he had already nationalized the railroads by Executive Order 9727, he planned to demand that Congress take immediate action, as a matter of national security, to empower him to draft striking railroad workers into the armed forces so they could keep the trains running—a breathtakingly audacious and arguably unconstitutional ultimatum. To explain the crisis and prepare the American people for what he intended to do, Truman said that he would be addressing the nation at 10:00 that evening.

According to Clifford, after the cabinet meeting adjourned, press secretary Charlie Ross, who by that time had read the intemperate "speech" that Truman had scrawled out the night before, spoke with the president alone in the Oval Office. He convinced Truman that he could not possibly speak that way to the American people. "The President," wrote Clifford, felt "better after having let off some steam" and asked that Clifford "draft a message more moderate in tone but still tough enough to make the point."[77]

For Clark Clifford the assignment was a turning point. Up until then, the tall naval aide from St. Louis with the resonant voice was regarded as a capable assistant. But after producing Truman's speech under pressure that afternoon and evening, he emerged as a rising star in the West Wing, eventually becoming Truman's wisest and most trusted counselor.

The message to the American people that the president delivered on the night of Friday the twenty-fourth was not as bombastic as the one he had written the night before (not a word about hanging and eliminating), but because it amounted to a personal attack directed by the president of the United States against two union leaders—Alvaney Johnston and A. F. Whitney—it was probably more effective in shaping public opinion and softening the attitudes of the two targeted individuals. Truman claimed in his speech that due to the intransigence and selfishness of Whitney and Johnston, the transportation shutdown would cause veterans to be stranded at discharge centers and barred from returning to their loved ones. He warned that it would result in "starvation and death" at home and abroad, constitute a danger to "health and safety," cause millions of workers to be "thrown out of their jobs," and so on. "I am a friend of labor," Truman pleaded, but now is the "time for plain speaking." This strike was "not a contest between labor and management," he declared. It was a contest between Whitney and Johnston, on the one hand, and their government, on the other. "It is inconceivable that in our democracy any two men should be placed in a position where they can completely stifle our economy and ultimately destroy our country." Truman closed by announcing that he would speak at a joint session of Congress at 4 p.m. the next day. If the striking workers did not return by then, he promised as commander in chief to order the army to operate the trains.[78] However, he said nothing about drafting the strikers. Ross and Clifford had convinced him to save that extraordinary move until the following afternoon when he addressed Congress.

At 3:30 p.m. on Saturday, May 25, a half hour before Truman was scheduled to address the joint session in the House Chamber, the tension in the East Wing of the White House was palpable. Clifford, who had been working on the president's speech with Sam Rosenman (summoned from his law office), was waiting for a telephone call from Dr. John Steelman, the president's preferred labor negotiator. Steelman, a large, gum-chewing Arkansan who had taught labor economics, was closeted at the Statler Hotel with Johnston and Whitney. Steelman had reported earlier that due to "mounting public pressure," a settlement of the strike was possible.[79] At 3:35, with the presidential motorcade idling outside, Steelman called to say that he was making progress but as yet there was no agreement. Clifford got on the line. He told Steelman that he was on the way to the Capitol, and if a settlement was reached, Steelman should call him at the office of Les Biffle, secretary of the Senate, so that Clifford could get the word to the president. With the latest draft of the president's speech in hand, Clifford dashed out of his office and rode with Truman up to the Hill.

At a few minutes after four, Truman entered the House Chamber and was greeted by a standing ovation as if he were a hero. Meanwhile, Clifford was stationed in Biffle's office, waiting for Steelman's call. When Truman was well into his speech, beseeching Congress to "work fast" with him to stop the railroad strike against the government before it "cripple[d] the entire economy of the Nation," Steelman called. *"We have reached an understanding!"* he shouted into the phone. *"The strike is broken!"*[80] Clifford jotted a note, hurried into the House, and handed it to Biffle, who, as secretary of the Senate, was seated below the podium. At that moment, applause was echoing throughout the chamber because Truman had just asked for "emergency legislation" to "draft into the Armed Forces of the United States all workers who are on strike against their Government." It was an unprecedented power grab. Biffle handed Clifford's note up to Truman. The president silently read the note and waited for the noise to subside. "Word has just been received," he announced, "that the railroad strike has been settled, on terms proposed by the President!"[81] The "House chamber erupted," wrote Clifford, "louder, louder and more sustained than any [Truman] had experienced before or was ever to experience again in Congress."[82]

Hours later, Senator Wayne Morse (R-OR) charged publicly that the timing of the dramatic moment had been staged. According to Clifford, Truman called Morse and explained the facts. Morse apologized to the president and said that "he was awfully sorry that he had gone off half cocked."[83]

Though the strike had ended, the House nevertheless debated into the evening and passed by a vote of 306–13 the legislation recommended by the president, including his request for authority in the future to draft strikers. In the Senate the bill was stalled by Senator Robert Taft (R-OH), who argued, among other things, that it was unnecessary because the strikers had gone back to work. By amendment, the Senate removed the draft provision from the House bill by a vote of 70–13. A watered-down version was eventually approved and sent back to the House. However, it never gained traction there and eventually died at the end of the session.

For the most part, newspapers throughout the country praised Truman for his courage and bold action in his handling of the railway strike, revealing himself to be tough and decisive when it mattered. On the other hand, liberals and major labor leaders, including of course Whitney and Johnston, were furious, pledging to defeat the president if he ran in 1948. Some union officials even threatened to withdraw their support for Democratic candidates in the 1946 midterms. Clifford wrote that Truman had "calculated correctly" that this opposition "would pass in time."[84] He was right about the 1948 election, but as events unfolded, the labor movement was not as supportive of Democrats in the 1946 midterms as it had been in past elections.

Throughout the crisis Truman leaned heavily on Clifford for his advice and his ability as a speechwriter to reflect the president's manner of thinking and speaking. In early June, as Clifford recalled in his memoir, Truman called him into the Oval Office and said that "it was about time for me to get out of [my navy] uniform and become Special Counsel in name as well as in fact."[85] The next day Clifford showed up in an impeccably tailored pin-striped suit.

To describe the Truman administration during the summer of 1946, Clark Clifford used the word "wallowing," which suggests rolling about in pleasure or luxury.[86] Based on actual events, however, the more accurate descriptors of that summer are "lack of progress" and "constant worry." From the contentious meeting of foreign ministers in Paris in June and July, Jimmy Byrnes reported making "no progress at all" on peace treaties with Germany and Austria.[87] Moreover, due to a diagnosis of "coronary sclerosis," Byrnes felt it necessary to submit his resignation that summer. Truman requested him to stay on until the treaties and other matters had been negotiated and expressed his support, notwithstanding his concern for Byrnes's health and reservations about his performance.[88] Knowing that he would have to replace Byrnes before long, Truman cabled Dwight Eisenhower, who as army chief of staff was inspecting troops in the Far East. Truman asked Eisenhower to meet with George Marshall in Nanjing, China, and inform him that the president wanted him to become secretary of state when he ended his mission. (Marshall responded, "Great Goodness, Eisenhower, I would take any job in the world to get out of this place."[89]) Truman had sent Marshall to China in early 1946 with the virtually impossible mission of settling the civil war between Chiang Kai-shek's Nationalists and Mao Zedong's Communists, and negotiating a coalition government with Chiang as head. Though Marshall came close to a breakthrough in March, by the summer of 1946, there was little hope of success, which was a source of constant worry to Truman and his State Department, not to mention Marshall himself.[90]

The president was alone in the White House (Bess and Margaret were in Independence, Margaret working with a voice teacher), with plenty of time to brood. His main worries were twofold: how to tame inflation at home and whether to stand up to the Kremlin abroad. With publicly stated reluctance, Truman signed an extension of the price control law on July 24, 1946.[91] Though it was tougher than a bill that he had vetoed in June, it contained a provision that exempted livestock, the source of the nation's meat, from price controls for a month. As will be seen, for Truman it was a major mistake because the farmers who raised livestock gamed the system. During the period of exemption, they increased prices and rushed virtually every unfattened and mature animal to slaughterhouses. Then, when controls were reimposed, the farmers in effect went on strike by keeping livestock on their farms, a move patterned after the steelworkers to force the government to again lift controls. The result was a massive meat shortage and skyrocketing prices on the eve of the fall midterms. Truman would be blamed, his effort to curb a major cause of inflation having failed.

As to administration policy toward the Soviet Union, Truman was torn, far from resolved, and worried. He was tired of hearing from Byrnes and Senator Vandenberg about Soviet recalcitrance in Paris. Was it time to get tough? If so, was war a possibility? At a staff meeting on July 12, Truman revealed his "frustration with Soviet behavior" and asked Clifford to prepare a record of Soviet violations of agreements with the U.S.[92] Clifford turned the project over to George Elsey, his only assistant. According to Elsey, a mere list of violations "would serve no useful purpose."[93] What the president needed, he told Clifford, was an in-depth assessment of Soviet intentions and a series of policy recommendations based on the views of senior advisers and Kennan's long telegram. Clifford agreed. At a meeting on July 16, Truman authorized Clifford and Elsey to expand the scope of the project. Elsey did virtually all of the work but Clifford insisted that the final product be called the "Clifford–Elsey report."

Elsey was content to work behind the scenes. In his memoir he cited the lament of a Washington bureaucrat: "No one signs a paper that he writes, nor does he write a paper that he signs."[94] Nevertheless, he was pleased when Margaret Truman, in her biography of her father, pronounced that his report was "immensely perceptive."[95] At the time, Elsey was only twenty-eight years old, but in his few years as an adult, he had worked in the Map Rooms of both FDR and Truman, and as a navy intelligence officer during the war, he had been the eyes and ears of prominent naval historian Samuel Eliot Morison. On D-day, off the coast of Normandy, with further landings at a standstill, Elsey had volunteered for a trip on a small scout boat to report on the extent to which American assault teams in designated beach areas were able to reach the tops of the bluffs.

It would be another month before Truman would receive the so-called Clifford–Elsey report, which recommended that the U.S. "must maintain sufficient military strength," including atomic and biological weapons, "to restrain the Soviet Union."[96] The significance of the report was that it went beyond Kennan's long telegram by arguing for a policy of *military* containment, though the word "containment" was never used, and that it was a summary of what the key national security advisers in the Truman administration were already thinking. It is no coincidence, therefore, that six months later the Truman Doctrine and the Marshall Plan would be announced. After Truman read the report on the night of September 24, he told Clifford that "it was powerful stuff" and requested that all copies be given to him for safekeeping. He feared that if it got out, it would "blow the roof off" the White House and Kremlin and that Henry Wallace would accuse him of warmongering.[97]

Meanwhile, as the summer was ending, Truman blundered into a diplomatic and political firestorm of his own making. It began on September 6 at the opera house in Stuttgart, where Secretary Byrnes promised the starving and homeless German people in his "Speech of Hope" that the U.S. would help them "win their way back to an honorable place among the free and peace-loving nations of the world," and declared that "we do not want Germany to become the satellite of any other power," an obvious reference to the Soviet Union. Byrnes's speech marked the first step away from the policy of dismantlement to one of economic reconstruction. At the suggestion of General Lucius Clay, deputy military governor of Germany (U.S.), Byrnes added another pledge to the final draft of his address: so "long as there is an occupation army in Germany"—another oblique reference to the Soviet Union—"American armed forces will be part of that occupation army."[98] According to Clay, Byrnes tried "very, very hard" but could not get Truman on the phone to approve this promise (at Yalta, FDR had told Stalin and Churchill that U.S. troops would return home within two years).[99] Whether Truman approved any other part of the speech before it was delivered is unknown.

Six days later, charismatic Secretary of Commerce Henry Wallace, rightful heir to FDR's legacy and the last New Dealer in Truman's cabinet, addressed a rally of twenty thousand far-left liberals in Madison Square Garden. His speech, which Truman had earlier approved, by either reading each page or skimming for three minutes—diary accounts differ—contained lines that were at odds with the new and more aggressive policy toward the Soviets that Byrnes had just unveiled in Stuttgart.[100] A "Get Tough" policy with the Soviets was counterproductive, Wallace proclaimed in his speech. "Get tough never brought anything lasting. . . ." He warned that "the tougher we get, the tougher the Russians will get." The pro-Soviet audience roared. Then, invoking the fear of another war, he ad-libbed: "I realize that the danger of war is much less from Communism than from imperialism."[101] To many in the audience who conflated British imperialism with that of the U.S., Wallace appeared to be accusing the Truman administration of warmongering. At the end of his remarks the former VP told his audience that Truman had approved every word.

When asked at a press conference whether he thought Wallace's speech was "a departure from Byrnes's policy toward Russia," Truman briskly replied, "I do not. They are exactly in line."[102]

The press had a field day, mocking the president for being the only person in Washington who could not tell the difference between two plainly different foreign policies, let alone articulate his own. Truman tried to disassociate himself from Wallace but the ruse did not placate Byrnes. With the backing of Vandenberg, Byrnes threatened to resign, cabling Truman, "When the administration is divided on its own foreign policy, it cannot hope to convince the world that it has a foreign policy."[103] Truman had put himself in a box. Because of Wallace's substantial political base, he wanted to keep him in his cabinet but he was unable to prevent him from speaking out again. On the other hand, given the delicate negotiations with the Soviets, the bipartisan support of Vandenberg and other Republicans, and the upcoming congressional elections, he could not afford to lose Byrnes.

"Never was there such a mess," wrote Truman to his mother and sister. "But when I make a mistake it is a good one," he confessed.[104] By the morning of September 20, he had made his decision: Wallace had to go. In doing so, he knew that the dismissal of Wallace would split the Democratic Party. Yet he was also aware that a large swath of Wallace's supporters were Communist sympathizers and that some were even card-carrying Communists. In a revealing diary entry, Truman wrote that the "Reds, phonies and 'parlor pinks'" who followed Wallace were "becoming a national danger," and he was "afraid that they are a sabotage front for Uncle Joe Stalin."[105] By firing Wallace, Truman reasoned, he might be paving the way for a third party, but in the end it would be a positive move because Wallace's association with Communism and the far left was becoming a liability to his administration and to Democratic politicians who were facing charges by Republicans in the midterms that they were "soft" on Communism.

When news broke that Wallace had "resigned" due to a "fundamental conflict" with the administration, the "crackpots," wrote Truman, were having "conniption fits. I'm glad they are. It convinces me I'm right."[106]

While Truman was right to rid his administration of Henry Wallace, his clumsy handling of the affair added yet more substance to the jokes and slogans about him that proliferated during the 1946 midterm congressional campaigns. The cutting slogan "To err is Truman," which was first uttered at a Georgetown party by Martha Taft, the wife of the Republican senator, was picked up by the press and trumpeted from coast to coast. A close second was "I'm just mild about Harry," followed by a joke about the housing shortage allegedly caused by Truman: "Two families in every garage." Plus, there were countless variations on the popular anti–Truman administration slogan "Had Enough?" such as "Had Enough Inflation?" and "Had Enough Strikes?"

Congressional elections are usually dominated by local issues and concerns, but voters are always influenced, as they were in the fall of 1946, by the state of the economy and the perceived performance of the administration in power. Surprisingly, the economy at that time was doing quite well. As of October, postwar unemployment stood at slightly less than 4 percent, close to a record low. Business profits, after taxes, were at their highest average level in history. Consumer spending and business investment added seven points to the GDP. Personal income rose to a new peak. However, there were two major problems that voters blamed on the Truman administration, whether warranted or not: inflation and shortages. Since the end of 1945, the average rate of inflation had shot up by 8 percent. In the weeks before the November elections, there were persistent shortages of housing and consumer products, such as new cars, refrigerators, coffee, sugar, and, most notably, meat.

In addition to the woes of inflation and shortages, the Truman administration's job performance was harshly and often unfairly criticized, especially in the realm of labor-management relations. Voters simply could not understand why there were so many disruptive strikes, why they went on so long, and why the administration could not settle them sooner. After the president's threat to draft striking workers into the army, the labor movement had lost confidence in Truman, believing he had distanced himself from FDR's record of solid support and was no longer fighting as hard as he could for them. As a result, unions were apathetic about getting out the vote for Democrats in the midterms. Moreover, Southern voters were wary of Truman, not sure where he stood on racial issues and disgusted with him for asserting federal jurisdiction over offshore oil in the Gulf of Mexico instead of respecting states' rights.

In the first week of October, polls showed that Truman's job approval rating had sunk to below 40 percent. Bob Hannegan, chair of the Democratic Party, advised Truman to avoid endorsing congressional candidates and to stay off the campaign trail. Out on the hustings, Democrats rarely invoked his name.

Truman's steep slide in voter approval was due to intangibles beyond job performance and the economy. The plain fact is that voters tended to look down on him as insufficiently "presidential," a so-called little man, a failed haberdasher. Along with his Midwest twang, tales of his poker, bourbon drinking, cussing, and Missouri cronies were not appealing, especially when compared to the genteel habits of his patrician predecessor. Truman's precipitate drop in popularity was bound to have an influence on voters' choices at the ballot boxes in November.

It turned out, however, that the decisive influence—the tipping point— on voters' choices on November 5, 1946, was the meat shortage. As House Speaker Sam Rayburn had predicted weeks before Election Day, "This is going to be a damn *beefsteak* election."[107]

Ever since price controls on meat had been restored in late August, farmers had been withholding their livestock from slaughterhouses in an effort to force the Truman administration to lift controls. Knowing that if he abandoned price controls on meat, he would be criticized by consumers for adding to inflation, Truman resisted. As a result, beef and pork gradually disappeared from America's grocery stores. With fewer than three weeks before Election Day, Truman was being blamed for creating a national meat famine. American consumers had been demanding the impossible—low prices and at the same time plenty of meat on the table. Since one of the two had to give, consumers and politicians abruptly turned against controls and overwhelmingly opted for an end to the shortage. In an October 8 letter to the president, four Democratic House members, facing defeat at the polls, pleaded with Truman to "do something about meat," meaning to end the shortage by lifting controls. Democratic voters, they wrote, were telling party canvassers, "No meat—no votes."[108]

Truman responded to the pressure. In a nationwide address on October 14, he reluctantly announced, "There is only one remedy left—that is to lift controls on meat." He blamed Congress for creating a one-month exemption from price controls in August, when unfattened livestock were rushed to market and prices rapidly rose. And he excoriated an unnamed "reckless group of selfish men who, in the hope of gaining political advantage, have encouraged sellers to gamble on the destruction of price control." This "same group," the president claimed, "hated Franklin D. Roosevelt and everything he stood for."[109]

In the days after Truman's speech, meat-packers were back in business as controls were lifted and prices started to rise. However, even if Truman's decision changed a few thousand votes in favor of Democrats, an announcement by John L. Lewis that he was once again taking his coal miners out on strike, just four days before the election, enraged the American electorate into voting against dozens of prolabor Democrats.

By Election Day, November 5, Truman's approval rating had reached an all-time low of 32 percent. His elderly mother, who was a "keen political observer" with "a tart sense of humor," was asked on election morning whether she had voted at her home in Grandview before being driven to Independence to be with her son and his family. "I certainly did," she replied, "and I am thinking of voting again on my way home."[110]

Anticipating that the election results would be devastating, Truman, along with Bess and Margaret, boarded the train back to Washington long before the polls closed in Independence. That evening, United Press reporter Merriman Smith was invited with other reporters to join the president for a late-night poker game. As Smith recalled, the election "returns had been arriving in a steady stream since 9 p.m. Not once did Truman look at them, nor did he refer to the elections."[111]

For the Democratic candidates, it was a bloodbath. They lost fifty-four seats in the House and eleven in the Senate. For the first time since 1928,

Republicans ran the table, taking control of both houses of Congress—majorities of 246 to 188 in the House and 51 to 45 in the Senate.[112] Republicans occupied 75 percent of the seats outside the South. New faces in the House included two future presidents: Republican Richard Nixon of the 12th District in California, then a thirty-three-year-old navy veteran who beat a highly respected incumbent; and 11th District Massachusetts Democrat John F. Kennedy, age twenty-nine, a Pacific war hero whose father bought off rivals and torpedoed the candidacy of a popular city politician. In the Midwest, Joseph McCarthy of Appleton, Wisconsin, emerged as a new face in the Senate. A highly intelligent Republican, McCarthy would achieve national prominence as a Red-baiting demagogue. At age thirty-seven, he would become the youngest senator.

It had probably dawned on Truman that the election of 1946 revealed fault lines in the Democratic coalition. As distinguished FDR scholar William Leuchtenberg pointed out, Republican congressional candidates had begun to attract African American voters by reminding them that "Democrats were the party not only of Franklin and Eleanor Roosevelt but also of Southern racists" and white supremacists, such as Mississippi Klansman Theodore Bilbo, who ran and won his third six-year term as senator, and Eugene Talmadge, who was elected to his fourth term as governor of Georgia. "Though most African Americans in the North held fast to the party of FDR," wrote Leuchtenberg, "considerable numbers in Harlem and other predominantly black neighborhoods gravitated toward the party of Abraham Lincoln."[113] Within a month the president would take action to address this problem.

———

A fter being up the half the night playing poker, Truman awoke on Wednesday morning, November 6, in his private railroad car with "a bad cold and a Republican Congress," wrote his daughter, Margaret.[114] When her father stepped onto the platform at Union Station in Washington with a book under his arm, there was one person in his administration waiting to greet him—Undersecretary of State Dean Acheson. Since it had been the custom for key aides to meet FDR's train when he returned from elections, Acheson was surprised and horrified to be the only one on the

Senator Truman with TJ Pendergast in 1936, the notoriously corrupt boss of the Kansas City political machine who controlled Democratic candidates and influenced election outcomes in much of Missouri. It was TJ who persuaded Truman to run as "judge" (administrator) in Jackson County and then Senator in 1934. In Washington, Truman became known as the "Senator from Pendergast." *(AP Photo)*

Tehran conference, November 30, 1943. Roosevelt, Churchill, and Stalin, seated together in the British legation at Churchill's sixty-ninth birthday dinner. Nazi commandos had parachuted into Iran with a plan to assassinate the Big Three during the birthday celebration, which was thwarted by the Soviet NKVD. *(Imperial War Museum)*

Eleanor Roosevelt with Anna Roosevelt Boettiger, her daughter. Anna and her children lived in the White House from Christmas 1943 until FDR's death. Anna's attention and care helped extend her ailing father's life by more than a year. Though Eleanor was angry and hurt when she learned that her daughter had facilitated liaisons between FDR and Lucy Rutherfurd, within a few days she resumed her close relationship with Anna. She never spoke of it again. *(Franklin D. Roosevelt Presidential Library and Museum)*

Portrait of Lucy Mercer Rutherfurd painted in the 1930s by Russian artist Elizabeth Shoumatoff. After Eleanor Roosevelt discovered that her husband was having an affair with Lucy, he promised never to see her again. FDR broke that promise whenever Lucy visited her sister in Washington. Beginning in July 1941, Lucy was the president's guest at the White House on countless occasions when Eleanor was out of town. *(Rutherfurd Hall, Hackettstown, NJ)*

Truman's daughter, Margaret, and his wife, Bess, hoist a sign during the balloting at the 1944 Democratic convention when Truman is nominated as vice president. Bess was not happy. Jostled by the crowd and blinded by flashbulbs as she exited Chicago Stadium into a waiting car, she said to Truman, "Are we going to have to go through this all for the rest of our lives?" *(Harry S. Truman Library and Museum)*

Having been nominated in July of 1944 to run for his fourth term, FDR stages a photo op on the South Lawn of the White House with his vice-presidential nominee whom he barely knew. They are both gazing across the table at Anna Roosevelt Boettiger, who has been cropped out of the photo. During their tête-à-tête at lunch, Roosevelt discloses the existence of the atomic bomb. Senator Truman feigns surprise, but he already knows a good deal about the Manhattan Project. *(Office of War Information, Harry S. Truman Library and Museum)*

With little to do except preside over the Senate, VP Harry Truman tickles the ivories at the National Press Club while movie star Lauren Bacall, perched atop the upright piano, locks eyes with the president. When the photograph of the two appeared in almost every newspaper, "Mother did not care for it," wrote Margaret. Truman was utterly unprepared for what he would face when FDR died on April 12, 1945. *(AP photo)*

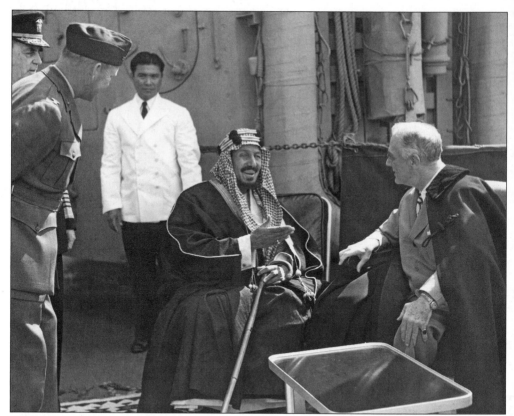

Following the Yalta Conference in the Crimea, FDR tries to establish a rapport with King Ibn Saud, the ruler of Saudi Arabia, aboard the USS *Quincy*, which was anchored in the Suez. Asked by Roosevelt whether Jewish refugees in Europe could be allowed a homeland in Palestine, Saud's response was an emphatic no. FDR backed down, assuring Saud that he and his allies would make no decision on Palestine without first consulting Arabs and Jews. *(Franklin D. Roosevelt Presidential Library and Museum)*

Seated in the well of the House Chamber at a joint session of Congress, Roosevelt, looking exhausted, delivers a speech in which he oversells his achievements at the Yalta Conference. It is the first time that he mentions his disability and hints at his deteriorating health. *(Franklin D. Roosevelt Presidential Library and Museum)*

Facing Chief Justice Harlan Fiske Stone (out of the photo), Harry S. Truman, his left hand holding a Gideon Bible, is sworn in at the White House as the nation's thirty-third president, with Bess and Margaret in the foreground. It is about 7:10 p.m. on April 12, 1945, two and a half hours after Roosevelt's death. Eleanor Roosevelt was upstairs getting ready to fly to Warm Springs. *(Harry S. Truman Library and Museum)*

After Franklin Roosevelt's casket is lowered and the lingering notes of "Taps" hang in the air, Anna consoles Eleanor as they walk out of the Rose Garden with son, Jimmy, cradling a carefully folded American flag. Above and to the left at the edge of the crowd, President Truman, wearing sunglasses, grips his gray fedora in his left hand. The last words of Reverend Dr. Anthony, rector of St. James in Hyde Park, were, "Father in Thy gracious keeping, Leave we now our brother sleeping." *(Franklin D. Roosevelt Presidential Library and Museum. Credit: Abbie Rowe, National Park Service)*

On August 1, 1945, the final night of the summit in Potsdam, Germany, Churchill and Stalin join hands with Truman in an act of supposed solidarity. In fact, they had just entered into an agreement that would lead to the division of East and West Germany. Truman expressed the hope that their next meeting would be in Washington. It was the last time he saw Stalin. *(Harry S. Truman Library and Museum)*

At the annual convention of the NAACP on June 29, 1947, Truman proclaims his commitment to civil rights on the steps of the Lincoln Memorial. Seated to his left in the front row are Walter White, head of the NAACP; Eleanor Roosevelt; and Senator Wayne Morse (R-OR). In Navy whites, five-star Admiral Chester Nimitz is in the second row behind Truman, while two chairs over at the end of that row Attorney General Tom Clark is focused on the president. *(Harry S. Truman Library and Museum)*

Further up the steps of the Lincoln Memorial, the Howard University chorus amplifies Truman's message by singing a rendition of "Lift Every Voice," a song of faith and hope that had been promoted by the NAACP as "the Negro national anthem." The presence of Old Abe deep in the shadows above them could be felt but not seen. *(Harry S. Truman Library and Museum)*

The ex-president is having a laugh with his old friend Eddie Jacobson on the sidewalks of Kansas City after Truman had been presented with a certificate for trees planted in his honor in Israel. Jacobson was a key intermediator in helping to persuade President Truman to be the first head of state to diplomatically recognize the new state of Israel. The two had become fast friends in 1917 when they served in the army together, and they had remained such until Truman's death. *(Harry S. Truman Library and Museum)*

During his 1948 whistle-stop campaign through Iowa, Truman delivers his "farm speech" to an enormous crowd of between 75,000 and 100,000 and a nationwide radio audience. Waving his arms wildly in the air, he ripped into the Republican-controlled Congress, claiming that it had stuck a "pitchfork in the farmer's back" and warning, without evidence, that Republicans, the "gluttons of privilege," were hell-bent on destroying price supports for farm products. In terms of electoral votes, it was probably Truman's most effective performance of the campaign—and a performance it was. *(AP photo)*

Smooth-talking, movie-star-handsome Clark Clifford relaxes in Key West with the president after the stunning victory in 1948. It was Clifford who was responsible for persuading Truman and his speech writers to adopt the most important strategic insight of the campaign—that the president should run not against his opponent Tom Dewey but against the Republican Party's record in the "do nothing" 80th Congress. *(Harry S. Truman Library and Museum)*

platform other than the stationmaster and a few reporters. On his part, Truman was not expecting much of a welcome because he knew that he would be held responsible for the Republican landslide. Nevertheless, as diplomat Karl Inderfurth wrote, Acheson's "gesture of loyalty and respect" was something that Truman "would never forget."[115] It marked the beginning of a bond of friendship and mutual regard between the two men that lasted until Truman's death. Referring to the president as "My Captain with the mighty heart," Acheson would come to believe that Truman ranked up there with the greatest of American presidents.[116]

Ironically, the disaster at the polls had the effect of liberating Truman from the long shadow cast by FDR. With the last of the New Dealers out of his cabinet, Truman felt free to be himself. Press secretary Charlie Ross echoed the mood. "Nobody here in the White House is downhearted," he wrote to his sister. "The consensus is that President Truman is now a free man and can write a fine record in the coming two years."[117] From the warm sunshine in Key West, where the president went to rest and cure his persistent cough, Truman pledged to do "as I damn please for the next two years and to hell with all them."[118]

"The real Truman administration," Ross told reporters, "began the day after [the 1946] elections."[119]

Chapter 8

Transformation

Charlie Ross was right. The president had become a free man. Shortly after the November elections, Truman decided to take on John L. Lewis, the "Lord of Labor." It would be a celebrated "fight to the finish," a courageous move that Roosevelt would never have dared to make. FDR had "toadied to him time and again," recalled Clifford.[1]

As head of the United Mine Workers (UMW), Lewis was "a figure of almost unbelievable power" and he spoke with "the measured cadence of a nineteenth-century Thespian," wrote Cabell Phillips of the *New York Times*.[2] Sporting a mane of white hair and immense black eyebrows, and projecting a menacing demeanor, Lewis had nothing but contempt for Truman. The previous May, Lewis's coal strike had ended after Truman, having nationalized the mines, approved a contract between the government and the UMW that was highly favorable to the miners. Around the time of the November elections, Lewis, with maximum leverage due to the approach of winter, began demanding that the government and the UMW enter into an entirely new contract with higher wages. He issued an ultimatum, threatening to strike if his demands were not met by November 20.[3]

By all accounts, Truman's decision to "fight to the finish" was made at midnight on Saturday, November 16, after the president had returned from a black-tie dinner and asked Clark Clifford, John Steelman, Attorney General Tom Clark, and Interior Secretary Julius Krug to meet him in his study on the second floor of the White House. Clifford arrived at the gathering convinced that Lewis's ultimatum "constituted a direct threat to the President's political survival." Armed with an opinion from the attorney general that Lewis's breach of contract followed by a nationwide strike would be unlawful, Clifford argued forcefully that Truman should stand firm and beat Lewis not only in a court of law but also in the court of public opinion. At the conclusion of his pitch, Clifford recalled saying, "Mr. President, you have to take him on." Truman agreed. He ended the meeting by authorizing Clark's Justice Department to file suit and to seek a temporary restraining order and injunction against the strike. Clifford recalled that Steelman, who claimed that he could negotiate a settlement and avoid a strike without litigation, "was openly furious at losing the President's support."[4]

After a federal district judge issued an order enjoining Lewis from going ahead with the strike, Lewis "respectfully" refused to comply. His UMW members walked off their jobs on November 20 and closed the mines. The next day, Lewis was convicted of civil and criminal contempt. The judge imposed an extraordinarily high $3.5 million fine on the UMW and ordered Lewis to pay a fine of $10,000.

Lewis had gambled and lost. As the days and nights got colder, the effects of the coal strike were starting to be felt. Public opinion turned against Lewis. He and his UMW colleagues tried to telephone Truman and his aides in frantic attempts to reach some kind of a settlement. Clifford counseled that no one in the White House should speak to Lewis and the UMW while their members were still out on strike. Finally, at 4 p.m. on December 7, 1946, the seventeenth day of the strike, with the pressure unbearable, Lewis called a news conference that was broadcast live by radio. Truman and Clifford listened to it in the Oval Office. Lewis ordered

his workers "to return to work immediately under the wages and conditions of employment in existence on and before November 20, 1946."[5] It
was akin to Japan's unconditional surrender. Like Emperor Hirohito, Lewis
could keep his job but he had lost a great deal of power while Truman's
prestige with the press and his standing in the polls sharply rebounded.
"Harry S. Truman stood fast, whereas Franklin D. Roosevelt had met
[Lewis] halfway," editorialized *Newsweek*. "The mild-looking, often inde-
cisive man from Missouri was stubborn in his determination that no
man, not even John L. Lewis, could push the United States of America
around."[6]

Truman was proud of the fact that he had rebuffed Lewis's telephone
calls for more than two weeks, forcing the labor king to publicly capitulate.
While savoring his victory in the Oval Office, Truman reportedly said,
"The White House is open to anybody with legitimate business but not to
that son of a bitch."[7]

On March 7, 1947, Chief Justice Fred Vinson issued an opinion up-
holding the convictions of Lewis and the UMW for contempt, although
the fines were reduced.[8] A ballad sung at the Gridiron Club's spring dinner
two months later included the following stanza:

> When John L. Lewis said, "no coal"
> And put the country in a hole
> Our Harry said, "I'll find support
> For I put Vinson on the Soo-preme Court."[9]

———

Two days before John L. Lewis tossed in the towel, Truman made a
second courageous decision. Delivering on his pledge to the National Association for the Advancement of Colored People (NAACP) to "do something" about the most controversial domestic issue in America, he signed
Executive Order 9808, which established the President's Committee on Civil
Rights. The mandate of this fifteen-member committee was to study and
make recommendations for legislation and other measures to "safeguard
the civil rights of the people," principally African Americans.[10] This 1946
executive order was the first postwar step in what would become a long

and still ongoing quest to address the ugly history of race relations and discrimination in the United States.

Truman's promise to "do something" had been made to Walter White, executive secretary of the NAACP, during a meeting in the Oval Office on September 19, 1946. In an effort to persuade Truman to back laws to stop lynchings and mob violence against Blacks in the South, White began the meeting by describing the lynchings of four Black Americans and the brutal details of what had happened to Isaac Woodard, a decorated African American veteran who had unloaded ships under fire in the Pacific. Three days after Woodard had been honorably discharged from the army and was on a Greyhound bus home to rejoin his family, he got into an argument with the driver about access to a bathroom. He was ordered off the bus in Batesburg-Leeville, South Carolina. There, he was seriously beaten by white policemen and his eyes were deliberately gouged out by a nightstick. He was permanently blinded in both eyes. "The Mayor of the town," Truman was told, "had bragged about committing this outrage."[11] According to White, Truman stood, his face bright red, and "exclaimed in his flat Midwestern accent, 'My God, I had no idea it was as terrible as that! We've got to do something!'" David Niles, Truman's assistant in charge of minority issues (mainly Jews and Blacks), was in the meeting. It was Niles who suggested that a committee be appointed "to investigate the entire subject of the violation of civil liberties and to recommend a program of corrective action."[12]

Thus began the modern civil rights movement.

The day after the meeting, Truman wrote Tom Clark, the attorney general, to inform him of the Woodard incident and to let him know that he was giving serious consideration to the establishment of a commission to present remedies to Congress to deal with the "increased racial feeling all over the country."[13] He also solicited Clark's views on a policy to prevent violence against Blacks. Truman forwarded to Niles a copy of his letter to Clark, adding a note to Niles that he "was very much in earnest on this thing and I'd like it very much if you would push it with everything you have."[14] A week later the Department of Justice filed criminal charges against Woodard's principal assailant, police chief Lynwood Shull. Although Shull admitted that he was the one who had blinded Woodard, it took thirty minutes for an all-white jury to acquit him.

Over the next several weeks, as Niles and his thirty-six-year-old assistant, Philleo Nash, hammered out the language of an executive order and recruited those who would serve on the commission, the story of Isaac Woodard's fate became widely known and was used to ignite a postwar civil rights movement, just as George Floyd in 2021 became the symbol of Black Lives Matter. For his record album *The Great Dust Storm*, Woody Guthrie recorded "The Blinding of Isaac Woodard." He wrote the song, he said, "So's you wouldn't be forgetting what happened to this famous Negro soldier less than three hours after he got his Honorable Discharge down in Atlanta."[15]

Since Niles, a Jew, had wide contacts within the Jewish community and his assistant, Philleo Nash, was an expert in race relations, Niles assigned Nash "the staff work" involved in developing the executive order and figuring out who should serve on the commission. Nash was uniquely qualified. His odd first name had been passed down to him through his family from a couple of Connecticut abolitionists, Prudence Crandall Philleo, who had been jailed for founding an "all-Negro school" in the 1830s before she married Calvin Philleo, a Quaker preacher who was a distant relative with the same surname. Fleeing from persecution, the two of them moved to the Midwest, founded an integrated girls' school, and eventually traveled to Kansas, where they were associated with John Brown. Nash himself grew up in Wisconsin, attended Alexander Meiklejohn's experimental college in Madison, and earned a PhD at the University of Chicago. There he met his future wife, Edith Rosenfels, also a progressive, who cofounded Georgetown Day School, the first racially integrated school in Washington. During the war Nash "was the eyes and ears on racial tensions" for Jonathan Daniels in FDR's Office of War Information.[16] After Daniels became temporary press secretary for Truman, Nash was assigned to work for Niles in the White House on what he called "the Negro-white thing," as well as a few other groups, including the Native American community.[17]

In an oral history Nash pointed out that during the course of his "staff studies," he found that the term currently used by Niles and others to describe the subject of the committee's mandate was "civil liberties." He believed, however, that it would be much better to find a "fresh" term, a term not then widely used, a term that carried more of a punch. It was Nash who decided that the new executive order should be called the President's Committee on *Civil Rights*. Both Niles and Truman agreed. Nash said that "as soon as we created a President's Committee on Civil Rights," the term "acquired its own meaning."[18]

Once the official title of the committee was announced, pundits came up with a less formal title—"the Noah's Ark Committee"—because, said Nash with a bit of exaggeration, "We wound up with two of everything": two women, two Southerners, two businessmen, two labor leaders, two Blacks, and two university presidents—and a few others, including FDR's son Franklin Jr., who would reflect the views of his mother. The recruitment of uncompromising civil rights lawyer Sadie Tanner Alexander, who filled two slots in the Noah's Ark Committee (female, African American), was one of Nash's proudest accomplishments. She was nationally known and highly regarded by the African American leadership. The chair of the committee, Charles E. Wilson, president of General Electric Corporation, was recommended not only by Nash, but by Walter White. As White was leaving the meeting with Truman on September 19, he repeated to the president and Niles what a friend had told him: Wilson "was convinced that the race question was the most important of all American problems and that someday he hoped to be able to do something about it."[19]

Given the racism of the vast majority of white Americans in 1946, the president's establishment of a committee on civil rights, though motivated in part by perceived political gain, was nevertheless courageous. In fact, however, Truman's personal views on civil rights and justice for African Americans were ambivalent. While he genuinely believed there should be laws to protect Blacks from violence and to embrace equal opportunity and voting rights, he rejected laws and policies designed to achieve "social equality." To put it another way, Truman's notion of constitutionally guaranteed civil rights did not include many of the rights that Blacks were claiming for themselves, such as the right to live in white neighborhoods. Between the president and Black leadership, there was bound to be a divergence of expectations.

Sixty-six-year-old George Marshall finally got his wish, but, as the saying goes, he should have been careful what he wished for. As noted earlier, in the summer of 1946, Marshall told General Eisenhower, tongue partially in cheek, that he would "take any job in the world to get out of this place," meaning China. A half year later—at noon on January 21, 1947, to be precise—Marshall found himself in the Oval Office. He had accepted not just "any job," but a high post as the nation's fiftieth secretary of state, next in line for the presidency, should Truman die in office. Marshall was happy to be out of China after his yearlong mission to stop the civil war and persuade Chiang Kai-shek to form a coalition government with Mao's Communists had failed. When the president pressed Marshall in early January to take the job, Marshall felt it was duty to answer in the affirmative. However, he confided enigmatically to his chief military aide, Colonel Marshall (Pat) Carter, that "my personal reaction is something else."[20]

George Marshall could not have realized it at the time, but under Truman's leadership and with the support of the Senate Foreign Relations Committee, he was destined to implement a profound transformation in U.S. foreign policy, a level of engagement in the world beyond anything that FDR had envisioned. Marshall was not selected because Truman intended to revolutionize America's international relations. Rather, he was chosen because of his stature, judgment, and ability—a "great one of the age," as Truman used to say.[21] It would be the actions of the Soviet Union, not proactive moves by Truman, that would soon drive the administration's transformative foreign policy.

As fate would have it, Truman's decision to recall Marshall from China and nominate him as secretary of state was the most important and consequential personnel decision of his presidency. A photograph taken in the Oval Office after the official swearing in captured the portent of the moment. With his hand literally clutching Marshall's elbow, Truman can be seen absolutely beaming as his revered idol is being cordially greeted by the outgoing and incoming chairs of the Senate Foreign Relations Committee, Tom Connally and Arthur Vandenberg (R-MI). Connally, who would become ranking member of the committee, was a segregationist who advocated Jim Crow laws and filibustered anti-lynching legislation, yet he would work tirelessly with Vandenberg, a reformed isolationist, to ensure bipartisan support for Truman's forthcoming foreign relations policies. Jimmy Byrnes, who had departed office on surprisingly good terms with the president, is seen standing at Truman's left, nearly out of the photo, as he gazes with a serious expression at his successor being welcomed by the two powerful senators. Byrnes was about to exit the national stage, pleased to have ended his career in the federal government by being named *Time* magazine's "Man of the Year" for 1946.

After lunch in the soon-to-be-renovated White House, Marshall walked with Undersecretary Dean Acheson across to his office in the old State, War, and Navy Building (today, the Eisenhower Executive Office Building or EEOB). Aware that Acheson expected to return to his law practice, Marshall asked, "Will you stay?" Acheson answered, "Certainly, as long as you need me, though before too long I ought to get back to my profession, if I'm to have one."[22] They agreed that Acheson would stay on for another six months and function as Marshall's chief of staff.

Within his first day or two as secretary of state, Marshall discovered that the department "had no planning agency at all."[23] As Marshall had learned when he was chief of staff of the army, the operations officers of any large organization needed a separate group that stayed out of the day-to-day crises and was able to step back and think about policy, direction of effort, and reappraisal of what was being done. He asked Acheson to create a new section within the State Department to be called the "Policy Planning Staff (PPS)," and to track down George Kennan to head it. Marshall chose Kennan because during his year in China, he had read several of Kennan's dispatches from Moscow, including the "long telegram." In addition, one of Marshall's former advisers, the ambassador to the USSR Walter "Beetle" Smith, had sent him from Moscow a convincing recommendation: "I know all of the Russian experts here and in Washington," wrote Smith, "and they are all good, but Kennan is head and shoulders above the lot, and he is highly respected in Moscow because of his character and integrity."[24] On January 24, Acheson asked Kennan whether he would be willing to lead the new Policy Planning Staff at State. Kennan, who had been recalled to Washington to teach at the National War

College, accepted the offer, but due to commitments at the war college, he could not report for duty until an undetermined date in the spring.

While Marshall was settling in at State, Truman's nomination of David Lilienthal as chair of the newly established Atomic Energy Commission was facing serious opposition by Republicans in the 80th Congress. The son of Jewish immigrants, Lilienthal was a graduate of Harvard Law School and a protégé of Felix Frankfurter. Because of Lilienthal's years as head of the Tennessee Valley Authority, which was regarded by conservatives as a New Deal experiment in socialism, several senators impugned his loyalty, accused him of harboring Communists, and even raised questions about Soviet influence based only on the fact that his parents were born in Eastern Europe. Senator Robert Taft, "Mr. Republican," was quoted as saying that Lilienthal was "'too soft' on issues connected with Communism and Soviet Russia."[25] A whiff of antisemitism was in the air.

Sensing that his nomination was in deep trouble, Lilienthal offered to withdraw if the president viewed him as a political liability. Through Clifford, Truman let Lilienthal know that he "was in this fight to a finish . . . if it took 150 years . . . and if they wanted to make an issue of this matter, he would carry it to the country."[26] Thanks to Truman's firm stand; an eloquent statement by Lilienthal about his "deep belief" in the "democratic ideal"; and strong advocacy by Senator Vandenberg, Truman's nominee was eventually confirmed.[27]

————————

On Friday afternoon, February 21, 1947, the same day that Taft attacked Lilienthal, Truman received a call from Undersecretary Dean Acheson. After explaining that Marshall was out of town for the weekend, Acheson told the president that he had just received from Archibald Kerr, the British ambassador, two diplomatic notes (aide-mémoires). The notes bluntly informed the U.S. that in view of Great Britain's dire financial situation, His Majesty's government would no longer provide financial aid and military equipment to Greece and Turkey as of March 31—scarcely five weeks away. The notes explained what Acheson and Truman already knew. Without a continuation of financial assistance, Greece was in grave danger of being taken over by Communist insurgents and forces of Soviet puppet governments along Greek borders. Turkey was also in need of aid because of persistent demands by the Soviet Union for the revision of the Montreux Convention, which governed the Turkish straits, and because of other threats by the Soviets to Turkish sovereignty that had kept the country's army mobilized, thus putting a drain on its economy and endangering its financial viability. The British expressed the hope that the U.S. would be willing to assume their burden, which they estimated at between $240 million and $280 million for Greece, $150 million for Turkey, and additional sums for both countries in 1948. These amounts seem small in today's dollars but in 1947 they represented around 1 percent of the federal budget. The stakes were high, the British claimed. The entire Middle East was in danger of coming under Soviet domination.[28]

Suspecting that the first foreign policy crisis of 1947 was in the making, Acheson informed Truman that he and his staff would prepare position papers over the weekend for Marshall to consider when he returned the following Monday morning. According to Clifford, who was with the president when Acheson called, Truman was inclined to provide some aid to Greece and Turkey and he knew that he would need Congress to act fast in order to enact legislation and appropriate the funds.

On Monday morning, Marshall approved Acheson's recommendations that aid be provided to Greece and Turkey. Since Marshall had to devote much of his time to preparing for a meeting of foreign ministers in Moscow, he authorized his undersecretary to take principal responsibility for moving the initiative up through the hierarchy to Truman. It did not take more than a day or two for Acheson to bring the War and Navy secretaries on board. On Wednesday afternoon, he and Marshall met with Truman, who had read the State Department's report and recommendations the night before. If Truman had any doubts, they were resolved in favor of providing aid to Greece and Turkey. He understood that standing up to Stalin and his comrades entailed serious risks, including the possibility of armed conflict. But the alternative, he wrote, would have been "disastrous to our security and to the security of free nations everywhere." The president was convinced that "this was the time to align the United States of America clearly on the side . . . of the free world."[29]

The final hurdle was Congress. It would not be easy. In light of the

Republican takeover, Congress was more inclined to cut foreign aid, defense spending, and taxes than to rush in once again to help fund the obligations of the British to preserve their crumbling empire.

At 10 a.m. on Thursday, February 27, the critical meeting with the Senate and House leadership on both sides of the aisle, plus the chairs and ranking minority members of the Senate Foreign Relations Committee and the House Foreign Affairs Committee, was convened in the White House. After Truman began the session with brief remarks, he invited Marshall, his new secretary of state, to make the case for supporting the Greek–Turkish aid package. According to Acheson, Marshall "flubbed his opening statement."[30] Reading from a three-page script, Marshall mouthed all the right words about "crisis" and "Soviet domination" that might extend to the Middle East and so forth, but his delivery was flat, cryptic, and uninspiring. When he finished by saying that the "choice is either to act or lose by default," it was clear that many of the Congressmen were unimpressed. Why should they pull "British chestnuts out of the fire?" one asked. Another: "What are we letting ourselves in for?"[31]

Realizing that the meeting was rapidly going downhill, Acheson whispered to Marshall, "Is this a private fight or can anyone get into it?" Without hesitation, Marshall yielded and told Truman that Acheson had something to say. Acheson seized the floor. His passion for the cause apparently electrified the room. He did it by framing the Greek–Turkish aid initiative as both a moral crusade and a necessary move to protect America's security. Their choice, he proclaimed, was between democracy and dictatorship. The issue at hand had nothing to do with British chestnuts. Rather, it had everything to do with supporting free peoples against Communist aggression, which in turn would protect their national security. "The Soviet Union [is] playing one of the biggest gambles in history at minimal cost," he declared.[32] If Greece should fall into the hands of Soviet-inspired Communism, then "like apples in a barrel infected by one rotten one," Turkey, the oil-rich Middle East, and even Italy and France would fall prey.[33] Those consequences would endanger national security and democracy itself. Eventually, he said, the Soviets could control two-thirds of the world's surface and three-fourths of its people. "We and we alone," Acheson concluded. "We're in a position to break up the [Soviet] play."[34]

According to Joseph Jones, a State Department special assistant who wrote a detailed account of the meeting, the president went around the room and invited comments after Acheson finished his pitch. "No one registered opposition. All had apparently been deeply impressed," he wrote.[35] Senator Vandenberg, who of course was at the meeting, separately wrote that "no commitments" were made by any of the participants.[36] However, according to Jones, the next day the State Department staff was given "the very definite impression that the Congressional leaders would support whatever measures were necessary to save Greece and Turkey, *on the condition*, made by Senator Vandenberg and supported by others present," that the president should lay it all out frankly in a speech to Congress and the nation. In a note that Vandenberg wrote to one of his congressional colleagues, he advised that the issue of aid to Greece and Turkey should not be viewed in isolation. Rather, he said, it was "symbolic of the world-wide ideological clash between Eastern communism and Western democracy." The president concluded the meeting with a promise to deliver a speech advocating Greek–Turkish aid in its "broadest context," which meant that it would be "enveloped in a statement of global policy that picked up the ideological challenge of communism."[37]

Taking his cue from Vandenberg and Truman, Acheson assembled Jones and sixteen other State Department officials in his conference room the next morning. With "unusual gravity," he sketched the broad outlines of a bold presidential speech to a joint session of Congress that he believed would spur, if not scare, the American people and the Congress into supporting the administration's aid proposal. The speech must persuade listeners that there existed an ongoing "struggle between freedom and totalitarianism," instructed Acheson, and if not stopped now, it could eventually threaten the security of the United States. Above all, the president's speech, he stressed, must proclaim a commitment to protect "Democracy everywhere in the world."[38] To those present, wrote Jones, it seemed "that a new chapter in world history had opened."[39]

Over the next week Acheson and his State Department speechwriters churned out drafts of a proposed speech by Truman that not only made the case for aid to Greece and Turkey but also advocated a much broader U.S. policy of providing economic and financial aid to "free peoples" anywhere who were trying to resist "subjugation by armed minorities or outside forces," a veiled reference to the Soviet Union and Soviet-sponsored Communists.[40] More than anyone else, the author of this expanded policy was Dean Acheson, who, as historian John Acacia wrote, "instantly recognized the opportunity to seize the initiative and the threat if it did not."[41]

When George Kennan, still with the National War College, was shown a draft of the speech, he was appalled. Although he supported aid to Greece and eventually to Turkey, he opposed placing it "in the framework of a universal policy," rather than addressing it to a "specific set of circumstances."[42] Moreover, as economic and diplomatic historian Benn Steil wrote, "He thought it dangerously confrontational," since everyone would know that the new policy was aimed at the Soviet Union.[43] When Marshall landed in Paris on his way to Moscow, he reviewed a draft of Truman's speech. According to Chip Bohlen, Marshall objected to the tone of the address to Congress, believing there was "too much flamboyant anti-Communism in the speech."[44]

Except for technical word changes, the objections of Kennan and Marshall were not reflected in the State Department's draft that reached Clifford and his assistant George Elsey on March 9. They were satisfied with the content, but they thought the speech would not sound like Truman and lacked punch, that is, memorable phrases that the newspapers would likely quote. Elsey came up with a solution. He broke up the key paragraph that had been written by Acheson—two long and unwieldy sentences that proclaimed the new foreign policy—into three dramatic declarative statements. He set each apart as a separate paragraph for emphasis. Each began with the words "I believe that . . ." Clifford and Elsey called these sentences "the credo," from a Latin word for "I believe," which are the first words of the Christian Apostles' and Nicene creeds. Truman loved the idea of the credo except that he personally substituted the word "must" for "should" in the beginning statement so that it read: "I believe that it *must* be the policy of the United States to support free peoples . . ." In his view, this change strengthened the sacred core of what would soon become known as "the Truman doctrine."[45]

At a few minutes after one o'clock on Wednesday, March 12, 1947,

President Truman opened a black folder and began his historic speech before a joint session of Congress. Clark Clifford was up in the Executive Gallery of the House Chamber, accompanied by his wife, Marny, and Bess Truman. Dean Acheson, as always perfectly tailored, was seated in the front row on the floor of the House, looking up at the rostrum.

Given the amount of effort that went into the crafting of the nineteen-minute speech, the first half was surprisingly uninspiring. It was not because of Truman's delivery. He spoke slowly and forcefully. It was the structure. Instead of beginning with a powerful sentence or two that foreshadowed the announcement of a lofty new foreign policy to defeat totalitarianism—code for Communism and the Soviet Union—Truman descended into the weeds, devoting almost half of his address to details concerning the plight of Greece and its need for aid before devoting a few lines to Turkey. The online sound recording of the Truman Doctrine speech reveals that only once during the first eleven minutes did a few seconds of scattered applause break out: when Truman promised that his administration would "supervise" the use of U.S. funds by the Greek government.

When Truman finally pivoted from the specifics of Greek–Turkish aid and linked America's national security to helping free peoples protect themselves from totalitarian regimes, the politicians applauded for the second time, though again for just a few seconds and with little gusto. Declaring that this was the "moment in world history" when every nation must choose between freedom and oppression, Truman paused for dramatic effect at minute 12:29 before launching into the credo, his precedent-shattering foreign policy of global engagement:

> I believe that it must be the policy of the United States to support free peoples who are resisting attempted subjugation by armed minorities or by outside pressures.
>
> I believe that we must assist free peoples to work out their own destinies in their own way.
>
> I believe that our help should be primarily through economic and financial aid which is essential to economic stability and orderly political processes.

There was not even a smattering of applause. Looks of surprise or disbelief might have been exchanged, but the chamber remained silent.

Truman concluded by asking Congress to authorize $400 million in aid to Greece and Turkey but he suggested that before long he might ask for more. "The free peoples of the world look to us for support," he declared. "We must keep that hope alive.... If we falter in our leadership, we may endanger the peace of the world. And we shall surely endanger the welfare of our own nation."[46]

The reaction from those in the well of the House as Truman finished was restrained. Members of both parties rose in applause, but, as Acheson perceptively wrote, "it was more in tribute to a brave man rather than unanimous acceptance of his policy."[47] Some said that the congressmen and -women (one woman in the Senate, seven in the House) were stunned, others that they were bewildered. The *New York Times*, however, picked up on the significance of the speech, calling it a "radical change" in foreign policy: "President Truman [has] called for action which will launch the United States on a new and positive foreign policy of world-wide responsibility for the maintenance of peace and order."[48] Truman had promised a level of postwar international commitment by the United States beyond anything that FDR had contemplated.

While editorials in the nation's major newspapers and newsmagazines were for the most part positive, pockets of criticism emerged on Capitol Hill. To those who worried that Truman's new policy was open-ended, both Acheson and Vandenberg assured them that each request for support would be individually evaluated according to hard evidence of need, effectiveness in addressing the problems of each country requesting relief, and consistency with U.S. foreign policy. A case that illustrated their point was Chiang Kai-shek's Nationalist government in China. When Congressman Walter Judd (R-MN), a former medical missionary in China, asked why aid should go to Greece and Turkey but not to Chiang's Nationalists, Acheson responded that hundreds of millions of dollars had already been provided, yet Chiang's military was still engaged in the same self-defeating practices and China's preindustrial economy remained stagnant.

Another criticism leveled at the Truman Doctrine was that it bypassed the UN, a point that Acheson's ally Senator Vandenberg decided to take seriously even though the Soviets would possess veto power in the UN Security Council. As Acheson observed in *Present at the Creation*, this was typical of Vandenberg. He would find a "comparatively minor flaw" in a legislative proposal, "make much of it," and propose a change that he would incorporate into an amendment dubbed the "Vandenberg brand."[49] To solve the so-called problem of bypassing the UN in the Greek–Turkish aid legislation, Vandenberg, true to his past practice, introduced what Robert Donovan characterized as a "meaningless" amendment "paying obeisance to the U.N."[50] According to Acheson "it was a cheap price for Vandenberg's patronage."[51]

Once Vandenberg was fully on board, passage of the Act to Provide Assistance to Greece and Turkey was almost inevitable. Many Republicans and liberal Democrats had reservations but they, along with American public opinion, feared the spread of Communism. "They are all on the spot now," remarked Representative Carl Vinson (D-GA), and "they have to come clean."[52] They would have to vote aye on the bill or risk the dire political consequences of being labeled soft on Communism.

By early May, the Senate and the House, by decisive Republican majorities of more than three to one, approved the bill to provide $300 million in aid to Greece and $100 million to Turkey (a total of $5.8 billion today). Senator Taft voted in favor of the legislation even though he had initially opposed it, falsely claiming that Truman's aim was to dominate the affairs of Greece and Turkey, which he said was equivalent to Stalin's push for hegemony in Eastern Europe. The signing ceremony was scheduled to take place at the White House on May 20. However, word that Truman's ninety-four-year-old mother was in serious condition following a hip fracture caused him to fly to Missouri to be at her bedside. During the six days the president stayed at her home in Grandview, he took part of the day off on May 22 to travel by auto to and from the Muehlebach Hotel in Kansas City to sign the Greek–Turkish aid bill into law.[53] Truman later said that it was his "All-Out Speech" that caused Congress to act.

Was the Truman Doctrine the opening shot of the Cold War? Some historians have argued that it was. But if so, it missed its mark. The fact is that the State Department had miscalculated. Stalin had little interest in Greece and Turkey. Moreover, he understood that Truman's grandly universalist rhetoric, which impressed most of Congress but not Moscow, was unlikely to have any effect on the countries within the Soviet sphere of influence. As British American historian Tony Judt wrote, the Truman Doctrine had "remarkably little impact on Soviet calculations."[54]

Although the Cold War more likely began in March 1946 when the British joined Truman in successfully pressuring the Soviets to withdraw from Iran, the Truman Doctrine speech was nevertheless historically significant. After the incident in Iran, it was the next concrete step toward Truman's mobilization of the Western world to confront and contain Soviet-inspired Communism. To be sure, there was as yet no overall plan and the way forward would be gradual. Inspired by Churchill's speech at Fulton, Kennan's long telegram, the Clifford–Elsey report, and Acheson's "rotten apple" metaphor (which mutated into the "domino effect"), the principles undergirding the Truman Doctrine would guide U.S. foreign policy, for better or worse, over at least the next two decades.

———————

The spring of 1947 was an exhilarating time for the president and his tightly knit White House staff of thirteen (two more than FDR). Truman's approval rating had shot up to 60 percent. Morale had never been higher. With their boss having decided to take on the two most important causes of his time—Soviet aggression abroad and civil rights in America—the team worked with an intense moral fervor, believing that they were not only saving the free world, but striving to guarantee equal rights for Black citizens.

In an assessment of the Truman presidency after his first two years, *Time* magazine pronounced that the "biggest change" was that Truman had "new confidence" and "a new sense of the dignity of the office."[55] With a voice of authority, he had become president in fact, not just in name. Gone were the days of snap decisions. Instead, he would delegate one or more of his four top advisers—Clark Clifford (all-purpose, political), John Steelman (labor, assistant to the president), Charlie Ross (press), and Matt Connelly (agenda)—to study a matter and get back to him with a recommendation. "He likes his job," wrote *Time*, "and he no longer asks anyone to pray for him."[56]

To a man and one woman, Rose Conway, Truman's staff was devoted to him. They respected him, admired his courage, and genuinely liked his company as well as his sense of humor. In an oral history, Clifford's assistant George Elsey described the president as "an extremely thoughtful, courteous, considerate man . . . never too busy to think about members of his staff."[57] Dean Acheson wrote of how in the darkest of times, Truman "brought bounce and cheerfulness . . . which kept us all going." To underscore his point, Acheson quoted lines from Shakespeare's *Henry V* about the night before the battle of Agincourt when King "Harry" walked from tent to tent, looking strong and self-assured, instilling in his soldiers—the frightened wretches—confidence that they would live and achieve victory the next day.

> . . . every wretch, pining and pale before,
> Beholding him, plucks comfort from his looks. . . .
> His liberal eye doth give to every one . . .
> A little touch of Harry in the night.

Harry Truman's touch was not little, nor was it light. It sprung, wrote Acheson, "from an inexhaustible supply of vitality and good spirits."[58]

———

On March 9, 1947, three days before the Truman Doctrine was announced to the world, Secretary George Marshall's C-54 landed at Moscow Central Airport. His flight across Europe with stops in Paris and Berlin had been sobering. The winter of 1946–1947 was the coldest since 1880. Coal shortages in the UK and throughout the Continent resulted in unheated houses, frozen pipes, and deaths from exposure. People were starving, especially in the cities, due to abysmal harvests and bottlenecks in rail and motor transportation. Mountains of rubble still blocked the streets. The bombed-out shells of millions of homes, factories, bridges, churches like St. Columba's in Knightsbridge, and the gates of Moscow could be seen from the air. Nothing had been rebuilt.

During Marshall's layover in Paris, his delegation had been joined by John Foster Dulles, a conservative Wall Street lawyer who functioned as a shadow secretary of state for the Republican Party. Before leaving Washington, Marshall, with Truman's approval, had invited Senator Vandenberg to join him because he valued the other man's advice and wanted the American delegation to be viewed as nonpartisan. However, Vandenberg was unable to attend due to Senate business. Therefore, Dulles took his place.

Backed by Truman, Acheson, and Lucius Clay, Marshall's principal objective in Moscow was to negotiate with the Soviets a peace treaty that would result in a resurgent and unified German economy. Having lobbied along with Clay to set aside the vindictive occupation policy inherited from FDR, Marshall had come to view Germany's capacity to produce coal, steel, and machinery as the key to Europe's recovery, which would lead to an end of its suffering and provide a market for American products. Secretary Marshall's task was to convince his Soviet counterpart, "Veto M." Molotov, that if the economy of a unified Germany were unleashed, then virtually everyone in Europe would prosper, including Russia. Molotov, instructed by Stalin, refused to see it that way. He continued to assert that Germany must be deprived of most of its industrial capacity in order to prevent another world war. Moreover, the rural American zone had been merged at the beginning of 1947 with the more industrialized British occupation zone, which meant that the U.S. shared control of the Ruhr. Consequently, Stalin and Molotov feared the emergence of a capitalist West German state.

Marshall tried to break the impasse by revisiting the fractured reparations settlement at Potsdam. He offered to increase war reparations to the Soviets in exchange for their agreement to cooperate on the economic unification of Germany. In response, Molotov insisted that the Soviets were entitled under the Yalta accords to extract $8 billion of in-kind reparations from Germany's *current* production (they claimed to have already extracted $2 billion, a vast understatement). Marshall was flatly opposed to reparations from current production. The U.S. was pouring funds into Germany so that its economy would be self-supporting in three years. If Marshall and his counterparts in the UK and France were to accept Molotov's position as the price for a unified Germany, the German economy would not be able to recover without subsidization by American taxpayers. In a report to Truman and Acheson, Marshall said he told Molotov that "[we] cannot accept a unified Germany under a procedure [by] which . . . the American people would pay reparations to an ally," that is, the Soviet Union.[59] They were at loggerheads. Compromise was impossible. Marshall was beginning to believe that Molotov was deliberately trying to consign Germany to remaining a "congested slum or an economic poorhouse in the center of Europe."[60]

When they were well into the fifth week of the conference, with no progress on the main issues having been made, it was time to meet with Stalin. Perhaps an appeal to him could break the stalemate. At 10 p.m. on April 15, Secretary Marshall, Ambassador Beetle Smith, and translator Chip Bohlen arrived at Stalin's paneled conference room in the Kremlin. Stalin, age sixty-eight, greeted Marshall with a disarming comment. "You look just the same as when I saw you the last time" at Yalta, he said, "but I am just an old man."[61]

After small talk, which made Marshall uneasy, he told Stalin that he wanted to speak frankly—not as a diplomat but as a soldier. He explained that he was "very concerned and somewhat depressed" by the depth of the misunderstandings and differences with the Soviet Union over reparations from current production and other matters.[62] The moment had come, said Marshall, to end the economic deterioration of Germany and work to re-store the economies of Europe. The consequences of inaction would be tragic, he said.

Stalin responded with "seeming indifference," content "to let matters drift," wrote Bohlen.[63] With reluctance, Marshall came to the conclusion that the cynical goal of the Soviets was to allow Germany and the rest of Western Europe to slide further toward economic ruin and chaos, thus rendering the region ripe for Soviet influence, if not domination.

The conference went on for another week. Nothing of substance was decided. At the final session, the forty-third fruitless meeting with Molo-tov that Marshall endured, all pending matters were referred to various entities for further study until a November meeting in London. "It was the Moscow Conference," recalled Ambassador Robert Murphy, the top dip-lomat in Germany, "which really rang down the Iron Curtain."[64]

On the morning of April 25, Marshall and his delegation departed for the flight home. "All the way back to Washington," wrote Bohlen,

"Marshall talked of the importance of finding some initiative to prevent the complete breakdown of Western Europe."[65]

———

In his memoirs the president wrote that Marshall arrived at his upstairs study in the White House on Sunday evening, April 27, "in a pessimistic mood." Waiting there to hear his report from Moscow were Vandenberg, Taft, three other senators, Speaker Joe Martin, Minority Leader Sam Rayburn, five additional representatives, and, of course, Truman and Acheson. According to Truman's summary, Marshall told them that the Russians "were coldly determined to exploit the helpless condition of Europe to further Communism rather than cooperate with the rest of the world." His report confirmed Truman's "conviction that there was no time to lose in finding a method for reviving Europe."[66]

The next day, following a luncheon meeting with Truman and his cabinet during which Marshall revealed that George Kennan would be heading a policy and planning group in the State Department, the secretary addressed by radio not only the nation but also the Soviet Union, courtesy of a Russian translation delivered by the Voice of America. He conceded that his efforts at the Moscow conference to reach a pact to administer and demilitarize Germany and to agree on a peace treaty for Austria had largely failed. "The recovery of Europe has been far slower than expected," he observed. "Disintegrating forces are becoming evident." Borrowing a medical metaphor, Marshall concluded with a call for immediate action that presaged his Marshall Plan speech at Harvard. "The patient is sinking while the doctors deliberate. Action . . . must be taken without delay."[67]

Scarcely a moment was to be wasted. The next morning, April 29, Marshall summoned Kennan to his office for their first one-on-one conversation. George Frost Kennan was six feet tall, slight, and balding, and he had a huge forehead. His eyes were his most impressive feature—clear blue, intense, wide set. Behind them lay a highly perceptive brain and a first-class intellect. The subject of Kennan's initial meeting with the secretary was a plan for the recovery of the European economy. Something must be done, Marshall told Kennan. "I don't want to wait for Congress to beat me over the head." He gave Kennan and his yet-to-be-assembled Policy Planning Staff two weeks to review the question of Europe's future and to tell him "what you think I ought to do." Did the general have any further instructions? asked Kennan. Marshall's legendary response: "Avoid trivia." "With this instruction," wrote Kennan in his memoir, "and with the weight of the world on my shoulders, I went to work."[68]

So did Undersecretary Acheson. With Truman's blessing, on May 8, in the sweltering gymnasium of Delta State Teachers College in Cleveland, Mississippi, he delivered a speech that picked up where Marshall had left off in his radio address to the U.S. and the Soviet Union. Truman called Acheson's speech "a prologue to the Marshall Plan."[69] Speaking in shirt-sleeves to the Delta Council, an organization of farmers and small businessmen, Acheson began by explaining "the facts of international life" and what that meant for U.S. foreign policy. The fundamental fact, he said, was that unless war-devastated foreign countries could obtain emergency financing so that they could purchase the commodities they needed to sustain life and rebuild their economies, they would continue to disintegrate. Another fact of life, said Acheson, was that even though the U.S. was the only nation in the world able to provide such financial assistance, its resources were not unlimited. It must, therefore, concentrate its financial assistance in areas, namely Europe, where it would be most effective in preserving freedom and democracy against totalitarian pressures. He reminded his audience that this was what Secretary Marshall had meant when he reported to the nation on April 28 that action for European recovery must take place without further delay. "A fundamental objective of our foreign policy," he emphasized, was "the achievement of a coordinated European economy," working "in a harmonious whole," that would not only assure peace and stability but eventually provide markets for the United States. In conclusion, declared the undersecretary, restoration of the European economy "is necessary if we are to preserve our own freedoms and our own democratic institutions." It was not just a matter of humanitarian relief; "it is necessary for our national security."[70]

The audience stood and politely applauded when Acheson finished. It was doubtful, however, that more than a few appreciated the historic implications of what he had just said. Though Acheson referred to "totalitarianism" twice, he never uttered the words "Soviet Union," "Russia," or "Communism," nor did he specify the magnitude of the financial assistance that would be necessary to revive the European economy.

At a press conference in Washington, James "Scotty" Reston of the *New York Times* asked Acheson whether he was announcing a new policy or "just a bit of private kite flying." Acheson responded, "You know this town better than I do. Foreign policy is made at the White House." Reston later asked the president whether Acheson spoke for him. Truman said, "Yes, it certainly was Administration policy."[71]

B ow-tied, ample-bellied Arthur Vandenberg, said to be "the only Senator who can strut while sitting down," needed some stroking.[72] Apparently, Marshall heard from Truman that the Republican chair of the Senate Foreign Relations Committee became irate when he read about Acheson's Delta Council speech and realized that he'd have to push through Congress a huge new foreign assistance package to revive the European economy. Marshall was aware that Vandenberg did not like surprises, that he wanted to be "in on the takeoff," not "the crash landing" of new foreign policy initiatives, as he had told Truman.[73] According to Acheson, he and the Michigander were invited by Marshall to the seclusion of Blair House on the edge of Lafayette Park for a "quiet and very private talk." As soon as they sat down, Vandenberg fulminated about "opening the Treasury to every country in the world." Waving his ubiquitous cigar at the other men, he asked, "Where was this all to end?" Marshall let him carry on for a time. He "visibly relaxed," wrote Acheson, when Marshall told the senator that he would be consulted at every step along the way and that the administration had no intention of asking for the bulk of the foreign aid in the current session of Congress (though Marshall might have to request a small amount of emergency funding before the end of 1947 to carry over to the next session). The security of the U.S. was imperiled, the two of them explained to Vandenberg. "Now as never before national unity depended upon a purely nonpartisan policy," especially because the heavy lifting in Congress would have to take place in a presidential election year. Vandenberg relished the idea of leading a high-stakes legislative challenge.

"At the end of the meeting conversion had been accomplished and a search for the Vandenberg brand had begun."[74] Both Marshall and Acheson knew that before Vandenberg would fully support a legislative initiative, he needed to stamp it with an amendment or proviso uniquely his own—the "Vandenberg brand."

───────────

It took more than three weeks, not two, for Kennan to articulate a policy, but certainly not an operational plan, for the recovery of Europe. The objective, he wrote, was not to combat Communism as such but to "restore the economic health and vigor of European society," which had become vulnerable to exploitation by totalitarianism and "Russian communism." To achieve this goal, wrote Kennan, the U.S. would furnish financial and other assistance, provided the European recipients agreed to abide by two fundamental principles: first, the "initiative must come from Europe; the program must be evolved in Europe; and the Europeans must bear responsibility for it." And second, the request for U.S. support must come "as a joint request . . . not as a series of isolated and individual appeals." This requirement for joint action was a critically important first step toward the integration of Western European economies.

As to the tricky question of whether U.S. assistance should be extended to "Russian satellite countries," Kennan essentially answered in the affirmative. If the Soviets decided to block their Eastern European satellites from participating, he wrote, then the countries of Western Europe should act together without the participation of Russia and its satellites. This, of course, was exactly what happened. Indeed, the fact that Kennan titled his first Policy Planning Staff paper "PPS/1: Policy with Respect to American Aid to Western Europe" indicates that he was quite sure that Russia and its satellites would not participate.[75]

While the policies recommended by Kennan were strategically important, his written views exhibited no real sense of urgency, no bold action plan. Fortunately, six-foot-three, square-jawed teetotaler Will Clayton, undersecretary of state for economic affairs, had just returned from a six-week inspection trip in Europe. Unlike Kennan, Clayton was action personified. Having founded and run the largest cotton-trading company in the world before the war, he was experienced in international trade and practical economics.

Clayton "was genuinely alarmed that Europe was on the brink of disaster," recalled Paul Nitze.[76] In a memo delivered to Acheson and then Marshall on May 27, Clayton wrote, "It is now obvious that we grossly underestimated the destruction of the European economy by the war. . . . Europe is steadily deteriorating." The revival of capitalism, the source of Europe's prewar strength, was imperative, he urged. For an initial action plan, Clayton proposed that the U.S. should provide a "grant of $6 or $7 billion worth of our surplus goods for three years [about $93 billion today]," based on a request worked out by a "federation" of European nations headed by the UK, France, and Italy. Other countries could pitch in with food and raw materials, he said, "but from beginning to end the *United States must run this show*."[77] Clayton pulled no punches. "Let us admit right off that our objective has at its background the needs and interests of the U.S. We need markets—big markets, in which to buy and sell."[78]

The next morning, May 28, Marshall assembled all of his advisers—Acheson, Kennan, Clayton, Bohlen, Ben Cohen, and a few others—who had been working on a plan for Europe's recovery. Everyone who trooped into his office had reviewed Kennan's PPS/1 and Clayton's memo. Marshall began by saying that they could not "sit back and do nothing" while Europe disintegrated.[79] What should they do? As was his custom he said little as the other participants held forth because he preferred to direct the flow with pointed questions. Historians John Agnew and J. Nicholas Entrikin wrote that the discussion that morning "might have been one of the most brilliant political strategy sessions of all time" because it laid out a "simple yet effective plan" for European recovery and provided a "vision of a 'new' Europe to serve as a basis for more specific American military and economic policies toward the region."[80] Marshall's principal concern was whether the offer of U.S. assistance should be made to all of Europe, including Soviet Russia and its satellites. What if they accepted? Kennan responded as only he could. Stalin would never accept the plan, he said, because a condition of the plan would entail cooperation with other European nations and exposure of the Soviet economy to Western inspection. Plus, the Soviets were bound to be deeply suspicious of their motives and opposed to a resurgence of the German economy. "Play it straight," he advised.[81] Make the plan available to all of Europe and the UK. If satellite nations were tempted, Stalin would block them from accepting because he needed them as security buffers and trading partners. They should let the Soviet Union take responsibility for dividing Europe. Bohlen said later that "it was a hell of a gamble."[82] But Kennan, who had met with Stalin several times, knew his man.

Notwithstanding the risk, Marshall seized the moment. Over the next seventy-two hours, he cabled yes to a standing invitation for an honorary degree at Harvard, decided to make the case for a European recovery plan in a brief speech to the Harvard alumni, and asked Bohlen and then Kennan to independently produce drafts for his consideration. The speech was set to take place in Harvard Yard at midafternoon on Thursday, June 5. As Marshall later recalled, he "got impatient" and dictated his own draft. When Bohlen's and Kennan's drafts came in, Marshall found that "they were quite apart." Consequently, he "cut out" parts of each draft and blended all "three together."[83]

On June 2, while Marshall was still massaging the text of his Harvard speech, the White House log indicates that Truman and Marshall met at 12:30 for a half hour, "their usual Monday appointment."[84] In light of Marshall's habit of keeping the president fully informed, there can be little doubt that he discussed the substance of the speech with Truman, as well as when and where it would be delivered. Two days later, Truman hosted a 10 a.m. gathering of the top leaders of Congress at the White House—Senator Vandenberg, who had canceled an engagement to get there; the Senate and House majority and minority leaders; and House Speaker Joe Martin.[85] There was only one reason to summon that group at that time: Truman provided them with an advance summary of Marshall's speech, stressed its importance, and informed them that it would take place at Harvard the next day.

Marshall had made it clear to Truman, Acheson, and his staff that he did not want advance publicity for the speech. No fanfare, he said. His address would not even be broadcast on network radio. Acheson was on board with that, except that he wanted to make sure European leaders appreciated the significance of Marshall's urgent call for action as soon as it was delivered. Accounts vastly differ, but suffice it to say that a day or three before Marshall's speech, Acheson hosted a lunch at the United Nations Club for BBC radio correspondent Leonard Miall and two of his colleagues. Based on what Acheson disclosed during that long and liquid lunch, Miall came away suspecting that an announcement about a plan for the recovery of continental Europe was imminent—and that it would probably be made by George Marshall.[86]

Before leaving on the afternoon of June 4 for a flight to Boston, Marshall managed to get the text of his speech to Acheson so that it could be included in a midday embargoed press release, although the secretary would add introductory and concluding paragraphs and other last-minute edits. Alerted by the press officer at the British embassy, Miall picked up a copy of the text from the embassy press office and spent the evening and following morning drafting a summary of the speech and his opinion as to its significance. He knew he was in possession of highly significant breaking news. Although Miall wasn't sure when Marshall would speak, he recorded his piece at 12:45 p.m. EST on June 5 for a popular BBC weekly news program titled *American Commentary*, which was scheduled to be broadcast in Great Britain at 10:30 p.m. London time.

According to the *Harvard Crimson*, on the afternoon of June 5, "a crowd of 15,000 showed up in the Yard not so much in expectation of seeing history made, as simply in awe of the man." A few minutes before three, well after Miall had recorded his piece, Marshall began with customary humility, noting that he was "overwhelmed" by the words of the honorary degree conferred on him by Harvard's president that morning. Then he donned one of his many pairs of "dime-store" glasses, put his head down, and moved quickly to the subject of his talk: the urgent need to rehabilitate the European economy. Marshall was certainly not a great orator, but one of the only two recordings of his famous speech reveals a clipped tone with a timbre that comes through to the listener as powerful and persuasive. "The truth of the matter," Marshall declared, was that Europe must have substantial outside assistance or "face economic, social and political deterioration" that would adversely affect the American economy and her national security. Thus, "it is logical," he said, "that the United States should do whatever it is able to do to assist in the return of normal economic health in the world, without which there can be no political stability and no assured peace." Stressing that the aid "should provide a cure rather than a mere palliative," Marshall made it apparent that he was advocating a massive infusion of economic assistance by the U.S.

Because Marshall followed Kennan's advice, his most quoted statement of who in Europe would be entitled to assistance and who would not was articulated without ever mentioning the Soviet Union or Communism by name. "Our policy," proclaimed Marshall, "is directed not against any country or doctrine but against hunger, poverty, desperation and chaos." Its aim was to revive working economies wherever "free institutions can exist" and to make aid available to any government that was willing to assist in recovery efforts. These lines were the first to attract a few seconds of applause. After pausing, Marshall went on. "Furthermore, governments, political parties or groups that seek to perpetuate human misery in order to profit therefrom politically or otherwise will encounter the opposition of the United States." This time, more applause. Everyone who was in the audience or who read the speech later knew whom Marshall was talking about when he referred to certain "governments" and "political parties."

Marshall's final words of substance embodied Kennan's two guiding principles, which had been endorsed by Clayton. "It would be neither fitting nor efficacious," he said, "for our Government to draw up unilaterally a program to place Europe on its feet economically. This is the business of the Europeans." The U.S. would provide "friendly aid" in the drafting and support of a program, but the "initiative, I think, must come from Europe." Second, Marshall made clear that "there must be some agreement among the countries of Europe" as to the nature and amount of assistance they required. "The program should be a joint one, agreed to by a number, if not all European nations."

As Marshall ended his prepared speech, he reached into his breast pocket and drew out a piece of paper on which he had written a few closing remarks. It was a final plea, delivered with a level of passion and force that those in the audience and those who have since listened to the audio version could not have missed. "The whole world," he concluded, "hangs on a proper judgment" by the American people. It was they who must decide "What is needed? What can best be done? What must be done?"[87]

Marshall had told his aides that he wanted a speech of less than ten minutes. The recorded version lasted for ten minutes and fifty-one seconds.

Reaction to the speech in the U.S. was muted. The lead story in the *New York Times* was a report of Truman's press conference in which he denounced a Soviet-backed coup in Hungary. Marshall's address at Harvard was reported on the front page but the headline was tepid: "Marshall pleads for European unity."[88] It would be weeks before the American press and the pundits picked up on the historic significance of the Truman administration's offer to do whatever was necessary to assist in the recovery of Europe—a cure, not a palliative.

Thanks to the prerecorded broadcast by Leonard Miall, the reaction in the capitals of Europe was to be quite different. At 10:30 p.m. on June 5, British foreign secretary Ernest Bevin, at his home in London, switched on the little radio near his bed. Within minutes he was riveted by Miall's words: "An hour and a half ago an exceptionally important speech by the American secretary of state was made. George Marshall propounded a totally new continental approach to the problem of Europe's crisis," similar to the "grandeur of the original concept of Lease-Lend." In his measured non-Oxford accent, Miall proceeded to quote at length the vital passages of Marshall's speech, followed by his newsman's analysis of the politics in America that could affect the ability of the Truman administration to deliver on its offer. Miall said there was talk in Washington that Congress could call a special session in the autumn if the UK and European nations could get together and agree on an overall program for assistance over the summer. He warned his listeners that there was no time to lose. "Congress is in a mood" for tax cuts and economizing measures, he said. Bipartisan initiatives would be more difficult as the two parties looked toward the presidential elections, Miall observed. "Whether Congress assembles in the fall depends on Europe's reactions."[89] To Bevin's ears, Marshall's words and Miall's analysis were exhilarating. "It was like a life-line to sinking men," he later said to the National Press Club in Washington. "It seemed to bring hope where there was none. The generosity of it was beyond our belief."[90]

According to Christopher Mayhew, Bevin's parliamentary private secretary, Bevin "came striding into the Foreign Office the next day, saying, 'Get me Marshall's speech.'"[91] Those who heard him had no idea what he was talking about. Later, Bevin rang up Georges Bidault and Vyacheslav Molotov, the foreign ministers of France and the Soviet Union. The three of them agreed to meet in Paris on June 27 to "discuss how Europeans might devise a European recovery plan, its requirements, and the parts they would play in it."[92]

It would be months before Marshall's speech was turned into a fully developed plan. Yet, within a few weeks, journalists and virtually everyone else referred to it as "the Marshall Plan." In his memoir, Clifford suggested to his boss that the plan be called "the Truman Concept" or "the Truman Plan." Keenly aware that 1948 would be an election year and that Congress would be asked to enact the plan into law, Truman responded, "We have a Republican majority in both Houses. Anything going up there with my name on it will quiver a couple of times, go belly up, and die. . . . The worst Republican on the Hill can vote for it if we name it after the General."[93]

Though Marshall was the spokesperson, it was the president who authorized the speech and backed the development of the Marshall Plan. Senator Vandenberg called the Harvard speech a "shot heard round the world."[94] It was surely revolutionary, marking a sharp departure from America's retreat into isolationism after WWI. And it ran against the long-standing policy of George Washington, who warned in 1796 that the republic should "steer clear of permanent alliance with any portion of the foreign world." The speech laid the groundwork for a new order in Europe, arguably a new world order.

Chapter 9

Lift Every Voice

In his memoirs, Harry Truman proudly observed that "for the first time in the history of the world a victor"—namely the United States—"was willing to restore the vanquished."[1] The "vanquished," of course, were Hitler's Nazi Germany and Hirohito's militarist Japan, implacable enemies that for years had engaged in unspeakable atrocities resulting in the deaths of millions. It is beyond astonishing that the American people, led by the Truman administration, pivoted from all-out war to an offer of their treasure, know-how, and friendship to foreign foes who only two years earlier had sought to kill, wound, and imprison their sons and daughters. It was as if their magnanimity had been inspired by Abraham Lincoln's "malice toward none." And perhaps it was.

While lauding the beneficent spirit of his fellow Americans, Truman noted that the Soviets, "one of our allies," adhered to "the conqueror's [traditional] approach to victory." The Russians insisted on seizing billions in war reparations from Germany's current production, which would prevent that formerly industrialized country from recovering unless U.S. taxpayers came to the rescue and subsidized Germany for at least a decade.[2] This was a major problem that the president had to face shortly after the Marshall Plan speech at Harvard. Among other things, he was worried that Stalin might use his demand for reparations to scuttle implementation of the Marshall Plan.

There were a host of other questions, both domestic and foreign, that Truman needed to confront during the remaining months of 1947. Could a penny-pinching Congress be persuaded to appropriate funds for the Marshall Plan? How far should he go in pushing for civil rights in a speech he was to deliver near the end of June? Would he veto the anti-union Taft–Hartley Act, which was about to be passed? Ought the U.S. weigh in on advocating a homeland for the Jews in Palestine? Last, would he dare to run in 1948?

———

Within ten days after Marshall's June 5 speech at Harvard, the "Vandenberg brand" emerged. During a meeting with Marshall at Blair House, the senator told the secretary that he would support the plan and work to push it through the Senate, *provided* Truman agreed to appoint a high-level "bipartisan advisory council" that would assess the ability of the U.S. economy to meet Europe's needs. Through Marshall, Vandenberg made it known "to the White House that he would not touch the plan until this had been done."[3] He believed that the council's recommendations, if positive, would play a critical role in persuading Congress to vote for the Marshall Plan even though many had run on a platform of cutting taxes and spending. Truman endorsed the idea, saying that Vandenberg's call for a bipartisan council "was really a good thing coming at the time it did from him."[4]

Undersecretary of State Acheson, who would return to his law firm, Covington & Burling, at the end of June, thought that a bipartisan council would be a positive step. However, he felt it was of "greatest importance" that Truman move quickly to appoint members of his own choosing.[5] With Marshall's approval, Acheson assembled a nineteen-member blue-ribbon council consisting of several prominent industrialists (e.g., Owen Young of General Electric; Paul Hoffman of Studebaker), labor leaders (George Meany of the AFL; James Carey of the CIO); academic and think tank leaders, and public officials.[6] Acheson recommended that Averell Harriman—his former Groton schoolmate and Yale rowing coach, who was then serving as commerce secretary—be designated chairperson. On the afternoon of June 22, Truman summoned Marshall, Vandenberg, Senate majority leader Wallace White, two Democratic senators, and select members of his cabinet to his upstairs study. After making sure that Vandenberg received full credit for his idea, Truman ticked through the list of nominees and their qualifications. At Vandenberg's suggestion, former Wisconsin senator Robert La Follette Jr., a colorful, progressive New Dealer–turned-Republican, was added to the list. Known as the "Harriman Committee," the council was officially charged with finding facts and providing a report on the "limits within which" the U.S. could "safely and wisely plan to extend" economic assistance to the Europeans.[7] Truman also ordered that two additional reports be prepared: one by the Council of Economic Advisers, headed by Edwin Nourse, on how the foreign aid proposed to be extended would affect domestic production, consumption, and prices; and the other by Secretary of the Interior Julius Krug on whether U.S. resources and physical capabilities could adequately support a large new foreign aid program.

While the U.S. experts began assessing the feasibility of the Marshall Plan, all eyes were on the Europeans, including the Russia-based Soviet Union. Could they come together and make a joint request for assistance? Would the Soviets agree to participate in the Marshall Plan and try to sabotage its effectiveness from within? Or would they simply decline the offer? From the White House, Truman could only watch and wait

It didn't take long. On July 2, after five days of discussions with the foreign ministers of Britain and France at the Quai d'Orsay in Paris, Molotov rejected the Marshall Plan and walked out. The main reason? Reparations. Through intelligence reports, Stalin had learned that the U.S. and Great Britain were about to suspend all prior agreements for payment of reparations from Germany's current production. Since those reparations were the Soviet Union's only source of foreign capital, the Marshall Plan was "totally unacceptable."[8]

Molotov's staged walkout was regarded as good news by Truman. Averell Harriman later commented that if Molotov had not withdrawn, he "could have killed the Marshall Plan."[9] Subsequently, Stalin forced the six Eastern European satellite nations under his control, as well as still independent Czechoslovakia, to reject the plan.

———————

A few minutes after noon on Friday, June 20, 1947, the House of Representatives visitors' gallery was jammed, mostly with labor union sympathizers. Down on the floor the representatives were tense with excitement. They had waited ten days for President Truman to make up his mind. Now copies of a message from him were being distributed to the members as a staffer broke the seal on the original and began reading the opening line: "I return herewith, without my approval, H.R. 3020, the Labor Management Relations Act of 1947."[10] Despite the technical wording and the dry delivery, everyone in the chamber understood that Truman had just vetoed what was known as the Taft–Hartley Act, a piece of Republican-sponsored labor legislation that had passed the House and Senate by three-to-one margins, with more House Democrats (mainly Southern) voting for the bill than against it.

As *Time* pointed out, union supporters in the gallery cheered Truman's veto message when it was read. "Some Congressmen looked up and yelled 'Boo.'"[11]

Ten days earlier, when the Taft–Hartley bill arrived on the president's desk, Truman had had genuine objections. Because of a widespread belief by Republicans and many Democrats that the nation's unions had become too powerful, the legislation was aimed at tipping the balance of power away from labor and toward management. While Truman favored restraints on union power, he was convinced that the complex, interwoven provisions of the Taft–Hartley bill would go way too far and inject the government into the collective bargaining process, cause more strikes, not fewer, and enable employers to engage in endless litigation that would bankrupt the unions. Specifically, Truman opposed provisions in Taft–Hartley that severely restricted the ability of unions to bargain for "closed shops" (requiring all workers in a bargaining unit to join the union if a majority voted for one). And he objected to a section of the act that encouraged states to pass legislation prohibiting closed-shop agreements, known as right-to-work laws. He also opposed provisions that made unions liable in federal court for breach of contract and prevented them from making contributions to candidates in federal elections.

When the president sought advice on whether he should sign or veto the bill, his cabinet, with the exception of Labor Secretary Lewis Schwellenbach, advised him to sign it. Clifford, however, urged him "to strike for new high ground."[12] In other words, take a stand against the 80th Congress: veto the bill. Clifford's advice came straight out of a playbook by Jim Rowe, a brilliant Harvard-educated lawyer from Butte, Montana, who had clerked for Supreme Court associate justice Oliver Wendell Holmes. Rowe's strategy had been endorsed by the Wardman Park Group, a Monday night gathering of subcabinet liberals, including Clifford, who had been meeting unofficially since the midterms to shape Truman's campaign strategy on the assumption that he would run in 1948. According to Leon Keyserling, a charter member of the Wardman Park Group, it was he, not Rowe, who initiated the veto strategy. Keyserling said that "Clifford deserved eighty-five-percent of the credit [for] persuading the President."[13]

From a political perspective, a decision to veto Taft–Hartley was low-risk, close to a no-brainer. Given Truman's high-profile showdowns with the coal and rail strikers, if he signed the bill, he might permanently lose the support of the labor movement and even jeopardize the alliance of labor and the Democratic Party that FDR had forged. The Republicans, of course, would have welcomed the president's support but they would never vote for him. On the other hand, if he vetoed the bill, he would probably regain labor's backing and perhaps capture votes of liberals who were leaning toward Henry Wallace and a third-party run in 1948. Moreover, even if his veto were to be overridden by two-thirds of the Congress and Taft–Hartley therefore became law—a distinct possibility—he would still garner labor's support. The president had nothing to lose.

Accordingly, Truman followed Clifford's advice. He vetoed the bill. As soon as the clerk finished reading the president's veto message in the House Chamber, the representatives voted overwhelmingly to override the veto, 331 to 83, well beyond the necessary two-thirds. Only 71 Democrats, including John F. Kennedy, voted to support Truman, while Lyndon Johnson and 105 others opposed.

When the Senate reconvened at midafternoon to vote on the override issue, a group of five senators organized an old-fashioned filibuster that featured Senator Glen Taylor, a country-western entertainer from Idaho. Taylor had established a reputation for showmanship shortly after he arrived in Washington in 1945 as a freshman senator. Encountering difficulty finding a house for his family, Taylor, after alerting the press, camped out near the Capitol, singing, "Give me a home near the Capitol dome, with a yard for two children to play" to the tune of "Home on the Range."[14] Thereafter, the eccentric senator, always wearing a homemade black toupee (the "Taylor topper"), became known as the "Singing Cowboy."

The objective of the filibuster was to delay the vote, with the hope that Truman's radio speech that night might sway public opinion and persuade uncertain senators to support the president's veto and vote against the override. Senator Claude Pepper (D-FL) kicked off the filibuster at 3:10 p.m. He droned on for four hours, at which point the Singing Cowboy took the stage. According to *Time*, Senator Taylor entertained those who could stay awake until 3 a.m., carrying on about the "difficulties of living in a truck," "sallies at Senators," "how he once ate jack rabbits," and the iniquities of Wall Street. As other members of the filibuster team took over, senators drifted out of the chamber to sleep, shave, and shower. Some passed around a bottle of bourbon. At 4:29 p.m. the next day, a Saturday, the last performer, Senator Wayne Morse of Oregon, a Republican maverick, slumped into a chair. He "had been on his feet" for "nine hours and 59 minutes" before hurrying "to the men's room," wrote *Time*.[15] Following a long discussion about whether it would be Christian to let the debate continue into the next day, Sunday, the filibuster ended at 6:52 p.m. with an agreement to adjourn and vote on Monday.

If the president and his supporters harbored hopes that his nationwide radio address on Friday night during the filibuster would change minds, they were dashed before he said a word. For some unknown reason, the speech was not scheduled to begin until 10 p.m.—on a Friday night, no less! The timing had to have led to a significantly diminished audience. And even if Truman's speech had been delivered in prime time on a weekday, it probably would not have caused listeners to bombard senators with enough telegrams to persuade them to side with the president and support his veto. The speech was long, boring, and larded with pejorative words—"bad bill," "shocking piece of legislation," "unfair to the working people," "dangerous."[16] But listeners were not left with a concrete example or a memorable phrase that would motivate them to send telegrams supporting the veto to their senators.

Before the vote was taken on Monday afternoon, Senator Alben Barkley, the Democratic leader, read a "Hail Mary" letter from Truman in which he wrote that enactment of Taft–Hartley, "this dangerous legislation," would "do serious harm" not only "to this Nation but to the world."[17] Like the president's radio address, his letter was futile. The Senate overrode the veto by a surprising sixty-eight to twenty-five, six more than the necessary two-thirds. Twenty Democrats voted against Truman.

While it is arguable that Taft–Hartley had the effect of weakening labor unions, mainly due to its role in the proliferation of right-to-work laws, there could be little question that Truman's failed veto of the legislation would strengthen his position as a candidate should he decide to run in 1948. A. F. Whitney, former head of the Brotherhood of Railroad Trainmen, declared that Truman's veto "vindicated him in the eyes of labor." An article in the *Nation* proclaimed that the president had given American liberalism "the fighting chance that it had seemed to have lost with the death of Roosevelt."[18]

Truman emerged from the battle as a warrior for the workingman, a president who the unions believed would act to repeal the "dangerous" Taft–Hartley Act, though he never did. Ironically, in twelve separate instances the president took advantage of provisions in that so-called bad bill.

———

T he Sunday after his Taft–Hartley defeat, Truman's motorcade pulled up to the rear of the Lincoln Memorial. There, he was greeted by Walter White, head of the National Association for the Advancement of Colored People, and Eleanor Roosevelt, who had become chair of the UN Human Rights Commission after Truman appointed her as a delegate to the UN General Assembly. Trailed by Secret Service and aides, the three of them walked around to the front of the memorial. Each was scheduled to speak but Truman's speech would be the main event, the first occasion in which an American president would address the NAACP since its founding in 1909. An expectant crowd of ten thousand—a sea of black, brown, and white faces—awaited them, arrayed along both sides of the Reflecting Pool and stretching over half the distance to the Washington Monument.

The idea for the president's speech to the NAACP was originated by Walter White, who had managed to score a thirty-minute appointment with Truman in the Oval Office on April 9, 1947, two and half months before the Lincoln Memorial event. Having had a role in persuading Truman to establish the Civil Rights Committee, White sensed that the president was ready to take another step forward toward the promotion of civil rights legislation, though he knew that if Truman did so, he could shatter the Democrats' hold on the Solid South. According to White's autobiography, he told the president that a speech to the NAACP at the Lincoln Memorial would tell the world that America was committed to narrowing the margin between "our protestations of freedom and our practice of them." The NAACP leader was surprised when Truman accepted on the spot, asking only that White send him a memorandum of "points to emphasize" in his speech. They both laughed, wrote White, when he said that if the NAACP included only half of what they wanted Truman to say, "the Southern Democrats" would "run him out of the country."[19]

It is an understatement to say that White was an unusual individual. The opening line of his autobiography states, "I am a Negro." In the next two sentences he writes, "My skin is white, my eyes are blue, my hair is blond. The traits of my race are nowhere visible upon me." In other words, he could pass for white and he did. White's parents were both pale-skinned African Americans who were descended from enslaved families in Georgia. His maternal great-grandmother had given birth to six light-skinned children, whose father was William Henry Harrison, future president of the United States. Born in 1893, White was raised as a Black child, attended an all-Black university, became an activist for racial equality, and joined the NAACP in New York City as an investigator. He worked his way up in the organization and was promoted to acting secretary (CEO) in 1929 and permanent secretary in 1931.

For Walter White, his success in convincing the president of the

United States to address the NAACP at the Lincoln Memorial on the subject of civil rights was an incredible coup, probably the crowning achievement of his professional life. In a press release announcing that the event
would take place on June 29, 1947, no doubt approved in advance by the
White House, the NAACP promised that Truman would deliver "a major
declaration of government policy" before "100,000 spectators," and credited White with organizing the "most significant" assembly "in the Association's 38 years." (The hundred thousand prediction turned out to be a
vast overstatement.)

During the weeks leading up to June 29, Robert Carr, executive secretary of the Committee on Civil Rights, was assigned to work with Truman
on his speech rather than David Niles, who was responsible for minority
issues, or his assistant Philleo Nash. This was deliberate. Truman trusted
Carr, a nationally known expert on civil rights, to help him develop the
strongest possible message to advance civil rights in America without watering it down to accommodate Southern Democrats. Truman's faith in
Carr was vindicated. Miffed at having been passed over, Niles, who was
less concerned with Blacks than with organized labor and Jews, recommended that the subject of civil rights in Truman's speech should be limited to "the closing paragraph of the speech not to exceed one minute."[20]
His suggestion was ignored. Truman had no intention of minimizing his
message.

By the afternoon of June 29, 1947, a hot and humid Sunday, the rain
had stopped and the skies had cleared when President Truman, Walter
White, and Eleanor Roosevelt took their seats on the stage partway up the
steps of the Lincoln Memorial. The presence of old Abe, deep in the shadows above them, could be felt but not seen. A Howard University chorus
began the program with a rendition of "Lift Every Voice and Sing," a song
of faith and hope that had been promoted by the NAACP as "the Negro
national anthem." Mrs. Roosevelt wrote eloquently of that moment: "The
sun made the top of the Washington Monument glisten before us, and
somehow it seemed as though years of our history lay between the two
monuments. In my heart I said a prayer that this meeting might be the
symbol that we really would lead the world in justice and brotherhood."[21]

At about 4:30 p.m., President Truman approached the podium, which was topped with the microphones of all four radio networks that would broadcast his speech to the nation. Because there was criticism from abroad, mainly from the Soviet Union, that the United States preached democracy while discriminating against and mistreating its Black citizens, the State Department had arranged a special broadcast to dozens of countries overseas.

Truman's delivery was for the most part ordinary, nothing like the cadence and timing of FDR, but his words conveyed a commitment to civil rights that no president since Abraham Lincoln had ever made to the American people. "It is my deep conviction," he said, "that we have reached a turning point in the long history of our country's efforts to guarantee a freedom and equality to all our citizens. Recent events in the United States and abroad have made us realize that it is more important today than ever before to insure that all Americans enjoy these rights." Then Truman, with evident passion, followed with an applause line that he had penciled into Carr's draft: "And when I say all Americans—I mean all Americans." There could be no doubt that this sentence was aimed at the rights of Black Americans.

The power of Truman's speech lay in his vision of the rights "all Americans" are entitled to, how those rights could be guaranteed, and the urgency of the task. Regarding the rights to which Truman "pledged [his] full and continued support," they ranged from the most immediate (that is, freedom from discrimination and the right to a fair trial) to the most expansive (rights to education, housing, medical care, and equal opportunity). The most oft-quoted lines in Truman's speech were: "There is no justifiable reason for discrimination because of ancestry, or religion. Or race or color." These words attracted the second-longest sustained applause. (The first was his promise to guarantee the "right to a fair trial in a fair court.")[22]

Stressing the urgency of addressing discrimination and equal rights, Truman said, "We cannot, any longer, await the growth of a will to action" by the states. And then came the words that Walter White and his NAACP members were waiting for: *"Our national government must show the way."* This was the most important pledge in Truman's speech. It meant that the federal government would act to guarantee minority rights. Truman

elaborated by saying that his Committee on Civil Rights would soon recommend a "vigorous" action plan that would involve "Federal laws and
administrative machineries."[23]

When the president finished his twelve-and-a-half-minute speech
with a quote from Lincoln that he knew his mother would not like, he returned to his seat. The "applause was hearty but not overwhelming," wrote
White, which made him recall the "cool response" to Lincoln's Gettysburg
Address. "I did not think Truman's speech possessed the literary quality
of Lincoln's speech but in some respects it had been a more courageous
one in its specific condemnation of evils based upon race prejudice." As
the applause subsided, Truman asked White how he liked the speech.
White told him that he thought it was "excellent." Truman apparently felt
the need to assure White of his sincerity. "I said what I did because I mean
every word of it—and I am going to prove that I do mean it."[24]

Did he really mean every word? A letter that Truman wrote to his
sister, Mary Jane, the day before his Lincoln Memorial address is revealing.
In the third paragraph he wrote in longhand, "I've got to make a speech to
the Society [sic] for the Advancement of Colored People tomorrow and I
wish I didn't have to make it. . . . But I believe what I say." Together, the
words suggest ambivalence, as if he weren't sure he believed in all-out
equality and civil rights for Black Americans. Later that day, when he fly-
specked the typed version, he deleted the phrase "I wish I didn't have to
make it." However, he left intact his lament that "I've got to make" the
speech tomorrow (forced against his will?), which meant that he still harbored reservations.[25]

The president's principal reservation, which he had made clear in previous speeches, was that he was opposed to policies and laws that would
lead to "the social equality of the Negro." Speaking to a group of Black
Democrats in Chicago, Truman had the temerity to inform them that "Negroes" preferred "the society of their own people" and desired "justice, not
social relations."[26] Thus, while the president in his address to the NAACP
professed that he was all for racial equality, in fact he was against it if it
meant mixed neighborhoods, clubs, and sports teams or, heaven forbid,
integrated schools where white girls would sit beside Black boys (the pri-
mordial fear of Southern segregationists). Consequently, there were

unspoken limits to Truman's assurance to Walter White that he would take action to "prove" that he meant "every word" of his speech. As revisionist historian Carol Anderson wrote in *Eyes off the Prize*, because of Truman's "Confederate-leaning, slaveholding roots," he was not "philosophically or psychologically equipped to accept true Black equality."[27]

As events unfolded, the only effective action that Truman initiated to prove his sincerity to Walter White was to issue two executive orders in 1948: one to afford "Equality of Treatment and Opportunity" to members of the armed forces and the other to protect federal employees from racial discrimination (the words "desegregation" and "integration" were nowhere mentioned in either of the orders).[28] Despite fierce resistance, a committee appointed by the president eventually succeeded in integrating all four armed services but not until 1953. With respect to federal employees, integration was accomplished but only in the State Department and the Bureau of Engraving and Printing. The rest of the agencies were "almost impervious to change."[29] Therefore, to the extent that Black servicemen and federal employees were integrated, they achieved a measure of social equality in their workplaces and Truman did not push back. Nevertheless, African American servicemen and federal employees and their families still had to cope with segregation and rampant discrimination outside their military bases and workplaces, especially in the South.

While Truman is to be lauded for these groundbreaking executive actions, he could have done much more if he had elevated racial justice and nondiscrimination in America to his top priority, equal to or even above his administration's focus on providing massive relief to millions of white Europeans. For example, since the Civil Rights Section of the Justice Department had only six attorneys by 1950, Truman could have instructed Attorney General Tom Clark and his successor, J. Howard McGrath, to transfer attorneys from other parts of the department to beef up the prosecution of lynching and voting rights cases. There is no evidence that he did so. Similarly, he could have pressed the Federal Housing Administration to take action to eliminate its lending practices that discriminated against Blacks and perpetuated racially segregated neighborhoods, but he declined to act because of his opposition to his version of social equality. Simply put, except for two executive orders, Truman failed to keep his promise that the federal government would lead the way by intervening to protect Blacks from violence, denial of voting rights, housing discrimination, and other inequities.

Truman complained that he had tried time and again to persuade Congress to enact his civil rights agenda but was blocked by Republican control of Congress and filibusters of Southern Democrats. This was of course true. However, it does not excuse his failure and that of his administration to do more with the agencies and personnel subject to their control.

Truman had a narrow view of racial equality and some say his civil rights accomplishments— the two executive orders—were meager. Yet his speech at the Lincoln Memorial in 1947 mattered. It gave hope to the African American community. It laid the groundwork for the historic legislation that was enacted in the 1960s. And for Truman it was an act of courage because at the time 80 percent of Americans opposed his civil rights agenda. In his Farewell Address, Truman wrote that his racial equality advocacy caused a "tremendous awakening of the America conscience on the great issue of civil rights."[30] Walter White's NAACP applauded Truman's efforts but his constituents would have to struggle for another two decades before conscience would yield concrete results.

On June 11, 1947, the day Truman approved a directive to German military governor Lucius Clay that the revival of a "stable and productive" German economy was to be the primary goal of U.S. occupation policy, a boatload of 4,506 mostly Jewish displaced persons, including 655 children, who had survived the Holocaust was departing France, bound for Palestine.[31] (In 1947, the territory of Palestine was administered by Great Britain pursuant to a League of Nations mandate.) That evening, Mossad l'Aliyah Bet operatives—Jewish intelligence agents—in France informed their headquarters in Tel Aviv that from that point forward the ship, a dilapidated Chesapeake Bay pack steamer, would be known as *Exodus 1947*. The highly publicized voyage of *Exodus* and its human cargo of illegal immigrants had been sponsored by the Jewish Agency, the de facto "government" of Jews in Palestine, with the objective of embarrassing the British and shifting U.S. opinion in favor of supporting a homeland for the Jews, a goal that Truman would, within a few months, embrace.

It seems ironic that the nation that had helped to liberate the Jews in Europe from Nazi atrocities had decided to restore the living standards of German citizens who had stood by while Jews in the millions were being starved and exterminated in concentration camps. Yet the change by the Truman administration from an initial post-defeat policy of deindustrialization and subsistence living for Germans to one of robust revival of their economy was regarded as essential to the recovery of Europe itself, as well as a bulwark against the spread of Soviet-inspired Communism. Ever since Byrnes's speech at Stuttgart in the fall of 1946, Clay had been pushing Washington for authority to reindustrialize Germany. The fact that the people who had tormented the Jews would benefit from restoration of the German economy did not deter Clay's crusade. His cause was supported by Will Clayton, Secretary of State Marshall, and the Joint Chiefs of Staff, and endorsed by the president. And by the summer of 1947, it was assumed that Germany's western zones would be eligible for Marshall Plan assistance to aid in their restoration.

Twenty miles off the coast of Gaza, on the early morning of July 18, *Exodus 1947* was bracketed by two British destroyers and rammed by one of them. At the time, the British government's policy was to strictly limit Jewish immigration into its Palestine mandate and the quota had already been filled. Royal Marines boarded *Exodus* to prevent it from landing. Following a melee, in which a twenty-four-year-old American seaman and two passengers were killed, the Marines overwhelmed passengers and crew, transferred them to Haifa, and then shipped them on three vessels back to France. A few days later, the first chapter of the modern Exodus story was recounted in newspapers across America. Alone in the White House, worried that the end was approaching for his elderly mother, Truman took a call from FDR's former treasury secretary Henry Morgenthau, author of the plan designed to turn postwar Germany into a vast pasture of farmers. Morgenthau, who was serving as chair of the United Jewish Appeal, told Truman that the U.S. was obliged to find a home for the stateless Jewish immigrants aboard the *Exodus*. That evening, July 21, Truman wrote about his reaction to Morgenthau's plea in a diary that was not discovered until 2003. "He'd no business, whatever to call me," Truman complained. "The Jews have no sense of proportion nor do they have any judgement on world affairs." He followed with a shockingly uninformed rant. "The Jews, I find, are very, very selfish. They care not how [others in Europe] get murdered or mistreated . . . as long as the Jews get special treatment. Yet when they have power . . . neither Hitler nor Stalin has anything on them for cruelty or mistreatment to the under dog." As will be seen, Truman's subsequent pro-Israel stance would seem to overshadow his privately expressed virulent antisemitism. Nevertheless, his words in 1947 should not be dismissed simply because, as the director of the U.S. Holocaust Memorial Museum observed, they were "common at that time in all parts of American society [as] an acceptable way to talk."[32] The truth is that even though Harry Truman throughout his adulthood had Jewish friends, he never rid himself of the deep-rooted prejudices against Jews that he grew up with. In 2003, William Safire, a columnist for the *New York Times*, asked Robert Morgenthau, the legendary Manhattan DA, about Truman's angry diary entry. Morgenthau replied, "I'm glad my father made that call."[33]

By "turnip day," the twenty-sixth of July, when farmers in Missouri were to sow turnips "wet or dry," the three ships bearing the passengers and crew of the *Exodus* were two days from Port-de-Bouc in France, where they had been ordered by the British Admiralty to land. Most of the passengers, however, decided that they would only disembark in Palestine. They vowed to refuse to set foot again anywhere in Europe.

That morning, a Saturday, Harry wrote to Bess a letter reminiscing about the summer they graduated from high school, when he worked as a timekeeper for a "railroad construction outfit," and about their classmate Tasker Taylor, who "drowned in the Mo. River."[34] About an hour later, he received a call from his sister in Grandview saying that Mamma had had a "sinking spell and probably would not live through the day."[35] However, before the president could fly to Missouri, he had to sign the National Security Act and nominate James Forrestal as the new secretary of defense because Congress was about to go into recess. The National Security Act, which attempted to unify the army, air force, and navy under a cabinet-level secretary of defense and created both the CIA and the National

Security Council, had been passed by Congress the previous day but had yet to be signed by the president pro tempore of the Senate, as required by law. In addition, Truman had to take time to meet personally with Forrestal to persuade him to agree to become defense secretary. The meeting needed to be deftly handled because Forrestal knew that he was not Truman's first choice. Nevertheless, he agreed to serve. As soon as the session was concluded, Truman and his entourage departed the White House for National Airport. The enrolled National Security Act arrived at the airport shortly after noon. Aboard the *Sacred Cow*, with its engines warming up, Truman signed it into law.

As he winged westward, somewhere over Ohio, Truman knew instinctively that Mamma had passed on. In his diary, he wrote, "I'd been dozing and dreamed she'd said, 'Goodbye, Harry. Be a good boy.' When Dr. Graham came into my room on the *Sacred Cow* I knew what he would say."[36] She died at home in the old house in Grandview at 11:09 a.m. Central Standard Time. "Well, now she won't have to suffer anymore," said Truman.[37]

The president's mother, Martha Ellen Young Truman, born in 1852 during the presidency of Millard Fillmore, was buried next to her husband at the Forest Hill Cemetery. During the nine decades of her life, she had been evicted from her home during the Civil War by the Union Army, witnessed the onset of electric power and automobiles, survived the Great Depression, and lived to see her adored son sitting in the Oval Office. Her philosophy, as Margaret recalled, was to do right and always do your best. "That's all there was to it."[38]

"I wanted to remember [her] alive when she was at her best," wrote Truman. As president, he felt he could not weep "in public" but he was free to "shed tears" as he pleased when "no one's looking."[39]

Soon after he returned to Washington, Truman asked Charlie Ross to summon to the Oval Office the White House press, many of whom had covered his mother's funeral. "I wanted to express to you all," began Truman, "and to your editors and your publishers, appreciation for the kindness to me during the last week. . . . I have no news to give you or anything else to say to you, except just that . . . you have been exceedingly nice to me all during the whole business and I hope you will believe it when I say to you that it is from the heart when I tell you that."[40] Even the most hardened and cynical reporters must have been touched to hear Truman speak to them like that.

––––––––––

On the last day of August 1947, the president, along with Bess, Margaret, and a number of his aides, flew to Brazil, where Truman was to deliver a speech at the Rio Conference of Western Hemisphere nations. By the time he and his group arrived, the Inter-American Treaty of Reciprocal Assistance, called "the Rio Pact," had already been signed by Secretary of State Marshall and the rest of the foreign ministers. Among its provisions was the forerunner of Article 5 of the NATO treaty—an attack against one of the nations in the Western Hemisphere was to be regarded as an attack against all. Instead of flying back to Washington after his speech, Truman had arranged to spend leisure time with his family and friends aboard the battleship *Missouri*, "the Mighty Mo," for the five-thousand-mile return trip. Hours before boarding, the president was handed a top secret radiogram from Robert (Bob) Lovett, Acheson's replacement as undersecretary of state, asking him to approve a press release concerning funds for the Marshall Plan.

At sundown, the evening before Truman and his party crossed the equator for the first time, a sailor dressed as Davy Jones climbed aboard the *Missouri*, supposedly through a hawser pipe, and indicted the president as a "vile landlubber and a pollywog." Jones told Truman to get ready because in the morning he would be initiated into the Royal Order of Shellbacks by King Neptune's court. Harry joined the fun. Completely relaxed, he looked forward to the navy's traditional "crossing the line" ceremony.

The next morning, the president—Pollywog No. 1—was the first to be initiated by full-bearded Neptunus Rex himself, who was enthroned on the fantail with attendants Davy Jones and a tall Marine sergeant dressed as Queen Amphitrite. Truman allowed himself to be photographed wearing a baker's cap, a sleeveless white undershirt, baggy shorts, and a big grin. It was his idea of what a pollywog was supposed to look like.

According to *Time* magazine, Pollywog No. 2, the president's daughter, had it easy, although the reporter could not resist a dig. Margaret was directed by Neptune "to lead a group in [singing] Anchors Aweigh, which she did falteringly and off key."[41] Bess observed but did not participate. The others who did volunteer to become Shellbacks were plastered with paint, dropped into a dunking pool, and forced to run through a paddle-wielding gauntlet of veteran Shellbacks.

As to the origins of the top secret radiogram from Lovett to Truman, Bob Lovett had spent the summer of 1947 transforming the ideas undergirding Marshall's speech at Harvard into a program of economic recovery acceptable to both the Europeans and Congress, while assiduously courting Senator Vandenberg. In contrast to Acheson, who could be brusque and acerbic, Lovett was tactful, genial, and soothing—qualities that were particularly important when dealing with American and European politicians. By early September, Lovett, assisted by the deft diplomacy of Kennan and the dogged persistence of Clay, had persuaded the European supplicants for Marshall Plan aid that they needed to substantially reduce their collective $28 billion request (over a four-year period). Meanwhile, however, time was running out. The economic situation for a handful of countries in Europe was deteriorating so rapidly that the U.S. had no alternative but to provide "interim aid" so that their citizens could survive the winter. The message that Lovett sent to Truman asked that he approve a press release announcing that the European recovery program would have two phases: first, the provision of interim assistance so that certain European governments could get through the winter; and second, the general program for rehabilitation of Europe, which would have to await the feasibility reports of the Harriman and other committees that Truman had appointed. The proposed press release advised Congress that the Truman administration would probably be asking for it to act in the late fall to provide food and fuel to certain European governments.[42]

After Truman radioed his approval of the press release to Lovett, it was released by Secretary Marshall on September 10, though he was preoccupied at the time with preparations for the forthcoming meeting of the UN General Assembly, where the fate of Palestine and a homeland for the

Jews would be considered. Several months earlier, the British had officially turned the future of Palestine over to the UN. A special UN committee on Palestine thereafter produced a majority report recommending that the Palestine mandate be divided into two states, one Jewish, the other Arab, and a minority report proposing a Swiss-style federated state for both Arabs and Jews. Under the two-state plan, the Jewish settlers, with one-third of the population and ownership of less than 10 percent of the land, would receive 55 percent of the land in Palestine. The U.S. delegation to the UN, which Marshall headed, was expected to take a position and choose which proposal the General Assembly should vote on in November. Truman, who was at sea, was ambivalent. He preferred to stay out of the fray. He believed that under either of the options, an all-out war between Arabs and Jews would break out and American troops needed in Europe would be called upon to keep the peace in the Middle East. He also thought it was wrong for the Arabs to be forced to cede land that they had occupied and owned for centuries. Without direction from Truman, Marshall had to make the decision himself.

As the date for the secretary to address the second annual session of the UN General Assembly approached, newspapers were reporting that the Jews from the *Exodus*, who had refused to land in France, had been transported to Hamburg, Germany, of all places, where many had been forcibly removed from their ships by British soldiers and all had been entrained to displaced persons camps.[43] Mindful that opinion in the U.S. favoring partition had been stoked by the *Exodus* affair and with a desire to avoid arousing the Arabs during the first ten days of the General Assembly, Marshall essentially punted. When he addressed the General Assembly on September 17, he announced that he and the American delegation "gave great weight" to the majority report favoring partition, but that a "final decision" by the U.S. on the matter would have to await further deliberations and debate.[44] The Jewish Agency, an external arm of the Zionists, was frustrated by the lack of an explicit endorsement of partition by the Truman administration. The Arabs were not only aroused; they were outraged that Marshall had tipped the scales in favor of the Jews. Moreover, Loy Henderson, director of the Office of Near Eastern and African Affairs, and others in the State Department who opposed partition were alarmed.

While Truman was still in the Atlantic aboard the *Missouri*, the representatives of the sixteen European nations seeking Marshall Plan assistance, who had been meeting in Paris since the second week in July, finally arrived at a tentative $17 billion, four-year relief package that came much closer to what Lovett and Marshall regarded as acceptable. On September 24, four days after Truman had returned to the White House, the two-volume, 690-page general report from the coalition of European nations (including Western Germany), which "hailed the advent of a new stage in European economic cooperation," was placed on the president's desk for study. It was encased in green manila folders and bound with shocking pink ribbons.

The selling of the Marshall Plan to Congress and the American people was going to require a heavy lift. The first step began at 10 a.m. on Monday, September 29, when the president convened in the Cabinet Room a meeting of eleven key leaders of Congress, plus Marshall, Lovett, Harriman, and a few others, to discuss the critical economic situation facing three European countries (France, Austria, and Italy) and the immediate need for "emergency aid" so that they could have adequate food and fuel for their people to survive the winter. Referring to a written analysis that had been distributed to each participant, Truman said that those countries would require an appropriation of $580 million to take care of immediate needs until March 31, 1948—the earliest date by which comprehensive legislation providing for recovery of all sixteen nations could be enacted.[45] (A draft of the comprehensive legislation was to be delivered to Congress in December.) This meant that Congress would need to adopt a two-part legislative strategy—enact emergency relief by Christmas 1947, followed by hearings and passage of the main recovery plan (the Marshall Plan) in the spring of 1948. In a letter to his wife, Hazel, Senator Vandenberg characterized the reaction to the strategy as "harmonious," and remarked that if interim relief was not provided to the three countries, the "Commies will be completely back in the saddle."[46] House majority leader Charles Halleck, a conservative Republican from Indiana, was pessimistic. "Mr. President," he said, "you must realize there is growing resistance to these programs. I have been out on the hustings and I know. The people don't like it."[47] The next day Truman wrote to Bess that he expected "violent opposition in Congress whose committees with few exceptions are living in 1890.... But I've got a job and it must be done—win, lose, or draw."[48]

Truman knew that opposition to the first stage—the request for almost $600 million in interim relief—could be just as fierce as opposition to the $17 billion European recovery plan. That was because a vote for emergency funds would be tantamount to a vote in favor of the entire Marshall Plan, whereas a vote against could doom the plan before it got out of the starting gate. Sensing the gravity of the matter, Truman sent to the appropriate Senate and House committees letters urging them to get to work on shaping the emergency legislation. A few weeks later he called for a special session of Congress to meet on November 17.

Meanwhile, Marshall and Lovett spent countless hours courting Senator Vandenberg, the Republican chair of the Foreign Relations Committee, who possessed the stature and ability to blunt the opposition. In the late 1940s Vandenberg was known on the Hill as chief advocate of the idea that "politics stops at the water's edge," though a version of the adage had been coined as early as 1812 by Daniel Webster. At the Rio Conference in August, Marshall, Vandenberg, and their respective spouses had established an unusually close relationship, playing Chinese checkers together and sharing meals in their free time. After returning to Washington in September, the senator became Marshall's full partner in "the adventure" (Marshall's term) of trying to persuade Congress to vote for interim aid and to pass the main plan for European recovery. To avoid media attention, they met twice a week, on average, at Blair House through the fall and winter. "We couldn't have gotten much closer together," joked Marshall, "unless I sat in Van's lap or he sat in mine."[49] Similarly, Bob Lovett, with his wicked sense of humor and self-deprecating manner, forged a genuine friendship with Vandenberg during the autumn of 1947. On weekdays he would stop by Van's Wardman Park apartment for drinks after work. To demonstrate the urgency of persuading Congress to approve emergency relief before the onset of winter, Lovett would show the senator classified cables indicating, for example, the progress of the Communist party in France or the threat of a coup in Italy.

As the November date for the special session of Congress approached, reports on the feasibility of the Marshall Plan by the three committees that Truman had established were delivered to the White House and Congress and widely publicized. The bipartisan Harriman Committee, originally proposed by Vandenberg, released its unanimous endorsement of aid for Western Europe on November 7, making the case in its 286-page report that the U.S. could afford the four-year, $12 billion to $17 billion program, that America had a moral duty to help, and that U.S. assistance would halt the spread of Communism in Europe. As economic historian Benn Steil wrote in *The Marshall Plan*, "The Harriman report became Truman's and Marshall's intellectual armor in jousting with Republican opponents."[50] The other two committees, headed by Julius Krug and Edwin Nourse, issued reports in October concluding that a recovery plan costing up to $17 billion would not endanger America's national security and vital resources, nor was it likely to cause inflation or necessitate a tax increase.

A fourth committee, established in July by Representative Christian Herter (R-MA), was arguably the most influential, at least in the House, because it was conducted by those who would actually be voting on interim aid and the Marshall Plan. The House Select Committee on Foreign Aid of course had bipartisan membership. Most of the representatives toured Europe from August to October to investigate relief and rehabilitation requirements in Western Europe. Almost every Herter delegate, including Richard Nixon (R-CA), supported interim relief and later the Marshall Plan, deeply convinced of the "peril of Communist expansion" and the "necessity of American leadership and aid."[51] The firsthand reports by those on Herter's committee, as well as those from other House and Senate members who flocked to Europe in the summer and fall of 1947, were highly persuasive in the halls of Congress when it was time to vote. The main motivating factor? Stopping the spread of Communism.

The opposition was led by fifty-eight-year-old Mr. Republican, Senator Robert Taft of Ohio. Having recently announced his campaign for the presidency, Bob Taft delivered a speech to the Ohio Society on November 10, a week before the opening of the special session of Congress. Complaining darkly about "planned propaganda for the Marshall Plan" and "secret meetings of influential people," Taft opposed interim relief and the

plan itself on grounds that they would be inflationary and require tax increases.[52] A couple of days later, in a letter to his wife, Vandenberg wrote
that he expected "trouble with Bob Taft" and lamented that "the presidential election next year . . . must be what's biting Robert."[53]

Since Taft was rightfully complaining about inflation (it was raging)
as a reason to oppose interim relief, Truman decided to put the Ohio senator and his Republican majority on the spot. In his address to the joint
session of Congress on November 17, which everyone expected would be
limited to a clarion call to legislate funds for emergency aid, Truman instead devoted most of his speech to a demand that Congress enact into law
a long list of anti-inflation measures, including the reimposition of price
and rent controls.[54] Knowing that Republicans would never approve his
program to reduce inflation, Truman advocated it in order to shift blame
for high prices to the Republicans and to undermine Taft's argument for
opposing both interim relief and the Marshall Plan itself. He might have
also done it so he could later allege that the 80th was a do-nothing Congress. Whatever his motive, he was too clever by half. The president's
speech was a dud.

Fortunately for Truman, the reports from the four fact-finding committees, the testimony of Marshall and Lovett before the Senate Foreign
Relations Committee and the House Committee on Foreign Affairs, and
the work of outside lobbying groups had effectively conveyed to Congress the need for interim funds. It was up to Vandenberg to deliver the
votes in the Senate. He had no trouble with the Democrats. To parry arguments by Republican opponents that a vote for interim aid presaged a later
vote for the Marshall Plan, Vandenberg announced that it would carry no
such obligation. Eventually the opposition melted away. Even Taft, who
believed there was no economic justification, was persuaded by Marshall
and Lovett that it was "absolutely necessary in the world battle against
communism."[55] The final vote in the Senate was eighty-three for interim
aid and only six opposed.

Interim aid had a much rougher road in the House. The bill reported
out of the House Committee on Foreign Affairs drastically reduced the
$540 million passed by the Senate. Sixteen floor amendments resulted in

a disappointing authorization of only $509 million, $60 million of which was earmarked for China. The legislation then threaded its way through House–Senate conferences and appropriation committees, resulting in a final amount of $522 million for the three European countries and $18 million for China.[56]

With interim funds on the way to Europe, Truman, on December 19, 1947, sent to Congress a message titled "A Program for U.S. Aid to European Recovery"—the Marshall Plan. His proposal called for an appropriation of $6.8 billion for the first fifteen months (April 1, 1948, to June 30, 1949) and $10.2 billion in the three succeeding years, a total of $17 billion.

In mid-September 1947, while Truman was at sea, Secretary Marshall informed the UN General Assembly that his delegation wished to await "further deliberations and debate" on whether to support the partition of Palestine into two states, although he "gave great weight" to the two-state recommendation by the UN Special Committee on Palestine. At the time, Truman had been content to let Marshall handle the matter according to his judgment. However, on the fifth or sixth of October, the president received a letter from Eddie Jacobson, a Jewish pal whom he had befriended during WWI and partnered with after the war in managing a downtown Kansas City clothing store—Truman & Jacobson Haberdashery. Late in life, when asked how he would describe his relationship with Jacobson, Truman said that "it would be hard to find a truer friend."[57] In his letter, Jacobson referenced Marshall's equivocal "great weight" statement and implored Truman to express his unambiguous support for partition. "Harry," he wrote in closing, "my people need help and I am appealing to you to help them."[58] On October 8, Truman replied rather coldly, writing that "General Marshall is handling the thing," and that he did not "think it right or proper to interfere at this stage."[59] Jacobson must have been disappointed to receive such an abrupt rebuff. But what he didn't know was that the very next day, October 9, Truman expressly authorized the release by Marshall or his designee of a statement in favor of partition, provided Marshall and his UN delegation understood that the U.S. would not take the lead in enforcing partition or providing economic aid to Palestine.[60] In his memoirs Truman put it this way: "I instructed the State Department to support the partition plan."[61]

Given the timing, it is more than likely that Jacobson's letter influenced Truman to direct the State Department to support partition. Yet the president declined to publicly express his support. The reason? He wanted to lie low while Marshall and his UN delegates, including Mrs. Roosevelt, and Jewish Agency representatives discreetly assessed the opinions of UN members. Pursuant to the UN Charter, a two-thirds vote would have been required to approve a resolution supporting the partition plan.

On October 11, Herschel Johnson, deputy U.S. ambassador to the UN, formally announced the Truman administration's support for partition along with a call for increased immigration. However, as directed by Marshall, Johnson said the U.S. delegation would be proposing certain "amendments and modifications" to the partition plan.[62] The changes that Marshall had in mind were of a "pro-Arab nature."[63] The most controversial amendment provided for the transfer of a large inverted triangle of rocky desert (forty-seven hundred square miles) out of the Jewish territory and into the Arab state. Called the Negev, the region extended south to the city of Eliat on the Gulf of Aqaba. Marshall hoped that the transfer of the Negev, along with other pro-Arab boundary changes, might entice the Arabs to negotiate rather than wage all-out war against the Jews. Why Marshall thought his proposal to offer more territory had the slightest chance of bringing the Arabs to the table is difficult to understand. King Ibn Saud of Saudi Arabia, without even mentioning territorial concessions, had warned Truman that the U.S. decision to support establishment of a Jewish state in the midst of Arab territory would result in "violent and long-lasting" conflict, "more shedding of blood," and a "death blow to American interests" in the Arab world. The king also reminded Truman that partition would be "inconsistent" with personal assurances to him by President Roosevelt. According to Chip Bohlen, who had sat in on the conversation between FDR and the king at the Great Bitter Lake in 1945, the president assured Ibn Saud that "he would make no move hostile to the Arab people."[64] To the king, this meant that Truman, honoring the promise of his predecessor, should not support a homeland for Jews in Palestine.

When Moshe Shertok (later Sharett), the political and foreign policy director of the Jewish Agency, found out about Marshall's plan to turn the Negev over to the Arabs, he was, to put it mildly, alarmed. He and David Ben-Gurion, the chairman of the Jewish Agency, attributed critical strategic importance to possession of the Negev because the Gulf of Aqaba at the Negev's southern terminus led to the Red Sea and beyond it to trading ports in East Africa and Southeast Asia. If Egypt or another Arab country should bar the new Jewish state from access to the Suez Canal, the gulf would be the only outlet to the eastern half of its world. With only days before the UN General Assembly was scheduled to vote on partition, Shertok and his political representative in Washington, Eliahu Epstein (later Elath), found a way to persuade Marshall to withdraw his territorial giveaway. Through David Niles, Truman's specialist on Jewish affairs, they arranged for the president to meet with seventy-two-year-old Chaim Weizmann, the grand old architect of the 1917 Balfour Declaration, which promised a national home for the Jewish people in Palestine. In the Oval Office at noon on November 19, Weizmann, a former president of the World Zionist Organization with a PhD in chemistry, spread out a map of Palestine on the president's desk. With eloquence and charm, Weizmann proceeded to eviscerate assertions made by Marshall that the Negev was suitable only for "marginal cultivation and seasonal grazing" and lacked a deepwater port (Weizmann had been briefed before the meeting by Felix Frankfurter).[65] Pointing to the Negev on the map, Weizmann explained how the Jews would make the arid desert bloom with new desalination and irrigation technology and dredge a port in the Gulf of Aqaba off the town of Eliat that would accommodate large cargo ships. Weizmann touted the importance of the port at Eliat as a trade route and a "parallel highway to the Suez Canal."[66]

According to most accounts Weizmann's explanations were persuasive. Any lingering doubts Truman might have had about retaining the Negev in the proposed Jewish state were likely dissipated by a political strategy memorandum he received that day; it dealt in part with the importance of the New York Jewish vote in the 1948 election. The memo—which had been conceived and mostly written by Washington lawyer Jim Rowe, a member of the Wardman Park Group, and signed by Clifford—advised that the "Jewish bloc" centered in New York City was "critical of the Truman administration" and that its resentments had been intensified by the "bungling of the British in the <u>Exodus</u> case." Truman's political strategists warned, therefore, that "unless the Palestine matter is boldly and favorably handled" by the president, he was bound to lose Jewish votes to his probable opponent, New York governor Tom Dewey.[67]

Truman got the message. At 3:30 that afternoon, with Niles in the Oval Office, he telephoned UN delegate John Hilldring to inform him that he had decided to reverse Marshall's instruction—the Negev was to remain in the proposed Jewish state. Accounts conflict, but either Truman was not explicit or Hilldring was reluctant to act until he heard from Marshall or Lovett. For a day or two, confusion reigned. Since Marshall had departed Washington on the morning of November 20 for the foreign ministers conference in London, Lovett, as acting secretary of state, stepped in. Once he had confirmed the president's decision, Lovett ordered the American delegation to withdraw the amendment proposing that the Negev be transferred to the Arab state. Shertok, Epstein, and Ben-Gurion were immensely relieved.

Moshe Shertok's biographer, Gabriel Sheffer, wrote that his subject's "mettle was tested" in the ten days of unprecedented lobbying leading up to November 29, two days after Thanksgiving, when the vote on partition, once deferred, was scheduled to take place. The entire Jewish delegation "experienced excruciating anxiety" while they and their opposition, the Arabs and the British, conducted intense campaigns in New York hotels; in buildings that housed the temporary headquarters of the UN in Flushing Meadows, just south of LaGuardia Airport; and in the UN-leased Sperry plant at Lake Success, twelve miles to the east.[68] The British regarded the partition proposal as a hodgepodge that would never work because the population of Arabs to be included in the planned Jewish state was at least 40 percent of the total and their birth rates exceeded those of the Jews. Foreign Secretary Ernest Bevin told Marshall that "the anti-Jewish feeling in England . . . was greater than it had been in a hundred years," due in part to vicious attacks against British soldiers by Jewish terrorists "that will never be forgotten."[69] Arab leaders in the Middle East, whose countries' populations far outnumbered the Jews in Palestine, called for jihad, a holy war of fire and blood, if the UN voted to approve partition.

With jihad in the offing, the British amped up the pressure on Truman and the UN to again postpone a vote on partition. Just a few days before the vote, the British announced that their mandate over all of Palestine would end at midnight (six p.m. Washington time) on May 14, 1948, much earlier than their original deadline. Not only that, but the British stipulated that if the vote went ahead and favored partition, the UN commission sent to assist in governance should not plan to arrive until May 1, thus leaving little time for the UN to set up new administrative machinery before the British pullout.[70]

Neither the president nor the UN leadership was deterred.

Truman had originally discouraged his administration from actively lobbying UN members to vote for partition or to abstain. His feeling was that they should be free to vote their consciences. Yet, as the day for the vote approached, there is evidence, albeit secondhand, that David Niles called Herschel Johnson and told him that the president wanted the U.S. delegation to "By God, get busy" and dig up all the votes for partition they possibly could, and that there "would be hell" to pay if the voting went the wrong way.[71] In light of Niles's relationships with several Jewish groups in New York, it is virtually certain that he encouraged lobbying by the Truman administration, but whether the president allowed him to invoke his name is unknown.

At last, November 29, the day for the vote, arrived. Out in Flushing Meadows, the UN delegates gathered in a large neoclassical structure that had been built as New York City's pavilion for the 1939 World's Fair. Speaking for the Americans, Herschel Johnson called for the vote on partition. In a rare show of support, the motion was seconded by the Soviet Union's Andrei Gromyko. Each delegation was polled by the president of the General Assembly, Dr. Osvaldo Aranha from Brazil. The final vote, announced by Secretary-General Trygve Lie, was thirty-three to thirteen, with ten abstentions and one absentee. Since more than two-thirds of the votes cast were in the affirmative, the proposal to partition Palestine into two states, one Jewish and the other Arab, was approved. When the Arab delegates heard the results, they began to walk out, "faces twisted with anger," wrote journalist Ruth Gruber. Azzam Bey of Egypt shouted, "Any line of partition drawn in Palestine will be a line of fire and blood."[72]

That Saturday night Jews across the world were said to be attached to their radios, counting each vote as it was announced at the UN. Newspapers reported that when victory was declared, Jewish crowds in Tel Aviv and Jerusalem celebrated through the night and "great bonfires" at the collective farms were "still blazing" at dawn.[73] In New York City, thousands of Jews jammed the streets. One of the many speakers, Dr. Emanuel Neumann, was quoted by the *New York Times* as saying that the vote for partition was "due in very large measure, perhaps the largest measure, to the sustained interest and unflagging efforts of President Truman."[74] While this was a vast overstatement, Truman was happy to accept the credit, notwithstanding his reservations about partition and his irritation toward Jewish leaders who had relentlessly pressured him.

After the vote Truman repeatedly stressed that the resolution by the General Assembly approving the partition plan was only a statement of "principle." Before partition could be implemented, it needed to be translated into a concrete action plan and approved by the Security Council.[75] Nevertheless, the vote was a watershed moment. For the first time the United Nations, the world's peacekeeping authority, recognized the validity of a sovereign Jewish state. The UN vote for partition in November 1947 was a significant step along the rocky road to Jewish statehood.

———

In his memoirs Harry Truman wrote that his motive for supporting a homeland for Jews was "redemption" and "rescue"—redemption of a promise made by Lord Balfour and rescue of the displaced Jews in Europe. Similarly, he wrote that his purpose in appointing the President's Committee on Civil Rights in late 1946 was to redeem the promise of the Bill of Rights and to rescue African Americans from a postwar "revival of terrorism."[76] Undergirding Truman's motives that drove each of these two risky initiatives were an abiding sense of fairness and decency and, of course, a dose of domestic politics.

On October 29, 1947, after nine months of work, Truman's Committee on Civil Rights issued its long-awaited report titled *To Secure These Rights*, a phrase from the Declaration of Independence. Unlike the president's support of a homeland for European Jews, which attracted little public controversy in America, the release of his commission's 178-page report was a "political bombshell," wrote Robert Donovan, "that catapulted the civil rights question to the forefront as never before . . . , led to a split in the Democratic Party in 1948, and 'served for a generation as the basic statement of most of the goals of civil-rights advocates.'"[77]

Briefly summarized, the report began by outlining what it considered to be the basic civil rights possessed by all Americans and, in graphic detail, the ways in which those rights had been denied to Blacks and other minorities. Thereafter, it laid out thirty-five ambitious recommendations, including a call for Congress to enact federal laws that would punish lynching and police brutality; protect voting rights; and ban employment discrimination, poll taxes, and restrictive housing covenants. Citing the failure of the "separate but equal legal doctrine," which authorized segregation, the commission implicitly suggested that the Supreme Court should act to reject or modify that precedent while explicitly recommending the enactment of state education laws that would prohibit discrimination in the admission and treatment of students based on race, color, creed, or national origin. The commission also recommended the establishment of a separate civil rights division in the Justice Department. [78]

In his autobiography, Walter White described the commission's "explosive Report" as bringing "down upon [Truman's] head vilification and denunciation from the South as great as that heaped upon Abraham Lincoln." For that reason, he declared that the president's report was "without doubt the most courageous and specific document of its kind in American history."[79]

Reaction to the report from the Northern all-white press was largely favorable, although some reporters wrote that Truman was simply catering to the Blacks to avoid losing votes to Henry Wallace, who was expected to run against Truman as an independent. Predictably, the president's report won the unanimous approval of the Black press. The so-called Solid South was solidly opposed both to the report and to Harry Truman. In his inaugural address, Fielding Wright, the new governor of Mississippi, known as a reformer because he advocated paved roads, claimed that "Truman's proposals were designed to do nothing less than to wreck the South and its institutions." He warned ominously, "Vital principles and eternal truths transcend party lines and the day is at hand when determined action must be taken."[80]

Knowing that he risked fraying FDR's alliance with Southern conservatives, Truman asked Clifford in early December to prepare civil rights legislation based on the report's recommendations. His aim was to send a package of proposed civil rights laws to Congress in early 1948. Clifford assigned the project to George Elsey. No one realized it at the time, but Truman's decision to knowingly alienate white voters in the South by acting on his commission's recommendations would mark the beginning of a fundamental realignment of American politics that would evolve over the next twenty years.

As 1947 came to a close, Truman had not yet let it be known that he would run for the presidency in 1948. But as far as his staff was concerned, "We just assumed it," recalled George Elsey.[81]

Chapter 10

Politics of 1948

I f Harry Truman was still deliberating whether to run for a second term in 1948, the announcement by former vice president Henry Wallace in late December that he would enter the race as a third-party independent settled the issue. Without mentioning Wallace by name, the president convinced himself that he had a "duty to get into the fight." His objective was to prevent those who "campaigned for peace at any price"—code for Wallace and his Communist supporters—from reaching the White House, where they would surely endanger national security and the freedoms for which Americans had fought so hard.[1] Gone were Truman's feelings of inadequacy as he greeted the new year. No longer did he complain so often of not wanting the job or of being imprisoned in the "Great White Jail." By the end of 1947, the president decided that it was not only his duty to enter the race to fulfill the promise of the Marshall Plan in Europe but that he and only he could preserve the social justice principles underlying Roosevelt's New Deal, which were being threatened by the Republican-controlled Congress. To accomplish these goals he needed to get elected in his own right by the American people. This was "the greatest ambition Harry Truman had," recalled Clark Clifford.[2]

———————

A s events unfolded, smooth-talking Clark Clifford, Truman's most trusted adviser, would be credited as the political genius who enabled his boss to realize his greatest ambition. A month earlier, on November 19, 1947, Clifford had signed and circulated to the president and members of the White House staff a remarkable memorandum entitled "The Politics of 1948." In essence, the lengthy memo outlined a strategy for how Truman should conduct his campaign to achieve victory in the 1948 election. With one glaring exception, the document was incredibly prescient, predicting that Dewey, not Taft, would be the GOP nominee; that Truman needed to concentrate on courting farmers, Blacks, and Jews; and that he should relentlessly attack the Republican House and Senate, thus foreshadowing Truman's famous campaign speeches railing against the do-nothing Congress.

For decades, praise was heaped on Clifford for authoring the road map that led to Truman's surprising victory. In Democratic circles he became a celebrity. After he left the Truman administration and established a legal practice in Washington, Democratic presidents John Kennedy and Lyndon Johnson, as well as dozens of presidential aspirants, sought his advice. Clients flocked to his small law firm, eager to pay top dollar for wisdom dispensed by the so-called mastermind of Truman's against-all-odds campaign.

Over the next forty years, Clifford was content to receive and claim sole credit for writing "The Politics of 1948," although there were rumors that he was not the author. When Clifford's memoir was being written in the late 1980s, the truth finally emerged. Except for a couple of substantive revisions and a number of edits, the memo signed by Clifford was actually authored by Jim Rowe. After serving as an important adviser to President Roosevelt and then as an aide in the Nuremberg trials, Rowe conceived and wrote the famous memo during the summer of 1947 while he was practicing law in Washington with lawyer-lobbyist Thomas Corcoran ("Tommy the Cork"), a former member of FDR's brain trust. Clifford claimed in his memoir that he felt he could not reveal the fact that Rowe had written most of the memo because of his close association with Corcoran, whom Truman intensely disliked. Clifford's explanation was that the president would have refused to read the memo if he knew that Rowe had had a hand in drafting it.[3]

There are some who recall that Truman kept a copy of the Rowe–Clifford memo in his top desk drawer and that he consulted it throughout the campaign. Others say that given Truman's acute political instincts and resourcefulness, the extent to which the memo actually influenced his conduct of the campaign is open to debate. But whether or not the president was influenced, it was Clifford who emphasized Rowe's most important strategic insight—that "the President should run not against his opponent but against the Republican Party's record in Congress."[4] Thus, while Clifford might be faulted for taking credit for the work of another, he should be praised for adopting and even improving Rowe's road map. As Truman's chief political adviser throughout the coming campaign, Clifford, not Rowe, was in a position to see that the recommendations in the memo were actually implemented.

The first of the two substantive revisions that Clifford added to Rowe's original memo was a new section titled "Civil Rights." There, he urged that Truman should "go as far as he feels he could possibly go" in recommending measures "to protect the rights" of Black citizens. This aggressive new strategy, which obviously contemplated anti-lynching legislation, went far beyond the tepid "Negro" section of the memo written by Rowe. Clifford must have felt confident in adding the "as far as you can go" plan of action because he agreed with Rowe, as set forth in an earlier section of both memos, that the South would remain "safely Democratic" and could, therefore, "be safely ignored." This misjudgment by Rowe, which was endorsed by Clifford, turned out to be the most significant flaw in the entire memo.

The other important improvement that Clifford made was in the section titled "The Jew." Clifford agreed with Rowe that the Jewish vote was only important in New York and that it could deliver the state to the president. However, with respect to the U.S. position on the partition of Palestine and the early recognition of Israel, Clifford recommended that those policies should be based on their "intrinsic merits," not on "political expediency" as Rowe had implied. A few months later, in May 1948, Clifford would be able to point to these words—"intrinsic merits"—as a rebuttal when Secretary Marshall accused him, in the presence of Truman, of favoring the immediate recognition of Israel as a sovereign state solely for political reasons.

Except for the aforementioned additions, a few cuts, and some nonsubstantive edits, the final pages of the memo submitted by Clifford to the president and his staff were virtually identical to those of Rowe. Each stressed that the "Land of Electoral Votes"—that is, the progressive West—was the "Number One Priority for the Democrats" and each recommended that Truman should come up with a reason to visit the West, not to go on a "political tour" but to conduct official presidential business such as inspections of atomic energy plants and dams. The final section, titled "The Mechanics for 1948," recommended the formation of a "working committee," forerunner of today's "war room." But amazingly, neither Clifford nor Rowe touched on the need, structure, and composition of a fundraising operation.[5] As will be seen, the shortage of funds for radio time and travel would be a critical problem for the president when the campaign heated up in the fall of 1948.

Truman's unofficial election campaign began with his State of the Union address before a joint session of Congress on the afternoon of January 7, 1948. When Truman and Clifford were waiting outside the door to the House Chamber, they heard a loud, sustained roar. It was occasioned by the presence of Secretary of State George Marshall, who had already entered and was standing next to his seat in the front row at the head of the cabinet. Moments later, as Truman walked down the aisle to the rostrum, the applause "was noticeably milder," recalled Clifford.[6]

Staring out at the largely hostile 80th Congress, which was dominated by Republicans and Southern Democrats, Truman announced that his "first goal" was the enactment of federal legislation to protect the civil rights of all citizens and that he would be sending "a special message to the Congress on this important subject."[7] While he knew that this would infuriate the Southerners and many of the Republicans, he expected at least a smattering of applause from a few of the progressive Democrats. Instead, he was met by deafening silence. Undaunted, he plunged on, laying out a liberal agenda for congressional action that FDR would have envied. He called for universal health insurance (as he had done since 1945), additional Social Security and unemployment benefits, federal housing and education assistance, the extension of rent control, the continuance of the school lunch program, and a generous tax credit for each taxpayer and his or her dependents that would be offset, he said, by a tax on corporate profits. Moreover, in a transparent bid to win back the votes of labor, as recommended in the Rowe–Clifford memo, Truman demanded a doubling of the minimum wage to seventy-five cents an hour and he reiterated his opposition to Taft–Hartley (though not its repeal). For the Western states and Midwest farmers—whose votes, the Rowe–Clifford memo stressed, were essential—Truman said he would press Congress to appropriate funds for dams, water projects, rural electrification, price supports, and crop insurance.

In essence, the speech was a setup. Despite the popularity of most of his legislative program with average Americans (the exception was civil rights), Truman was convinced that the House and Senate would never act on his proposals. Yet he put his agenda out there so he could lambaste the 80th throughout his campaign as the do-nothing Congress. Truman could not have cared less about the chilly reception he received on the Hill or about the criticisms of Scotty Reston and other reporters that his speech was a just a "catalogue" of proposals and not a report on the state of the union.[8] Back in the Oval Office with George Elsey and other staffers, the president celebrated the fact that he had just broadcast to the nation a blueprint for his campaign. Raising their glasses of bourbon and Scotch, they drank to "Success in '48!"[9]

In the week after the State of the Union speech, attacks by Republicans and Southern Democrats were drowned out by one of those brouhahas involving alleged presidential excess that have erupted in Washington from time to time ever since John Adams took up residence in the White

House. The so-called excess was Truman's decision to construct a second-floor eliptical balcony, which would rest within the six columns on the south side of the White House, thus providing a private place for the family to relax outdoors as well as a spectacular view of the South Lawn and the Jefferson Memorial. His move to add the balcony became controversial not due to the expense but because the U.S. Commission of Fine Arts, which was only an advisory body, had disapproved. Plus, there were complaints from indignant citizens that the balcony reminded them of those from which speeches had been delivered by Mussolini and Hitler to adoring crowds. Editorials in Washington and New York newspapers suggested that because Truman was only a temporary tenant who would be defeated in November, he lacked authority to change the facade of the people's White House. Today, the kerfuffle would be called "Balcony-gate."

At a raucous press conference on January 15, Truman fielded numerous questions about his rationale for installing the balcony. At first, the president tried to make light of the matter, claiming that the opposition was akin to the uproar during the Millard Fillmore administration (1850–1853) when First Lady Abigail Fillmore had been attacked in the press for installing bathtubs in the White House. Under repeated questioning he turned serious, arguing that a balcony at the second-floor level would provide shade below, thereby eliminating the need for the unsightly summertime awnings over the first-floor windows that "ruined the looks and proportions of the columns."[10] To put it simply, the balcony was necessary, he said, in order to improve the architectural integrity of the White House.

When a reporter inquired with a grin whether the president intended to have a rocking chair on his new porch, Truman demurred, but later in the press conference, he said, "I anticipate using [the porch] during the next 4 years." Whether planned or not, the four-year remark caused the reporter to ask whether Truman was "predicting victory." No, responded Truman, "I predicted victory here the other day."[11] There is no record of him having predicted victory that early in 1948, but if he did, it would have been regarded as presumptuous because a Gallup poll that month registered his approval rating at a dismal 38 percent.

Within a few weeks, the criticism subsided. After construction was completed in March 1948, the balcony became a tourist attraction but only for a few years. It is known today as the Truman Balcony.

———

S carcely a month after his State of the Union speech, Truman sent up to Congress a groundbreaking "Special Message" on civil rights that committed the Democratic Party to a cause "from which there would be no turning back." So wrote Clark Clifford.[12] The February 2 message was a call by the president for the 80th Congress to enact into law most but not all of the recommendations of his Committee on Civil Rights, including protections against lynching, an end to the poll tax and other voting restrictions, and a prohibition against "discrimination and segregation" on interstate trains, planes, and buses. He also asked Congress to make permanent the Fair Employment Practices Committee, which was charged with preventing employment discrimination, and to create a civil rights division in the Justice Department. Notably, except for interstate transportation, in which the Supreme Court had already paved the way, Truman's message did not address segregation, probably because he opposed policies that might lead to social equality.[13]

Given the racism of most white Americans in 1948, Truman's plea for legislative action on behalf of African Americans was brave, risky, and unprecedented, at that time the boldest such program ever proposed by a president. Even FDR, with his legendary political skills, would not have dared to risk alienating Southern Democrats by acting to redress racial inequality. In fact, during his presidency Roosevelt did not weigh in on any of the anti-lynching or other civil rights bills introduced by progressive members of Congress.

Southern Democrats were by far the most vociferous in their opposition to the president. In a Gallup poll of citizens across America, a whopping 82 percent opposed the president's civil rights legislative proposals, while only 9 percent approved. Members of Congress from the North would find it hard to ignore the attitude of their constituents.

In his diary on the morning the special message was delivered, Truman wrote that Congress, no doubt, would "receive it as coldly as they did the State of the Union" speech, but still "it needs to be said."[14] The reaction, however, was anything but cold. It was white-hot fury, especially among the senators and House members in the Deep South. Truman would shortly be accused of "stabbing the South in the back" and "lynching" the Constitution.[15]

Two weeks after the special message arrived on his desk, South Carolina senator Olin Johnston and his wife, Gladys, staged a "crude but cleverly executed rebuke of the President," a sign that the Solid South was threatening to bolt from the Democratic Party.[16] After they alerted the press, their plot played out before an audience of close to a thousand Democrats at the annual Jefferson–Jackson Day fundraising feast in the Mayflower Hotel, a celebration of the hundredth anniversary of the DNC. When Harry, Bess, and Margaret took their seats in the crammed ballroom, a large table with ten settings directly in front of them was conspicuously empty. It had been purchased by Senator Johnston, "a coon-shouting white supremacy man," wrote *Time* magazine, whose wife was vice chair of the $100-per-person event. *Time* published a photograph of Johnston and Gladys having dinner that night at home with their two daughters and wrote about the snub. Johnston told reporters that his wife and their guests could not risk attending the dinner because they feared being seated beside or near a "Nigra."[17] Another group of Southerners also boycotted the dinner because "of the presence of Negroes." (In fact, three Black Democrats were in the ballroom, seated together at a table in the rear.)[18]

After the dishes were cleared, Truman ignored the empty table as he approached the podium. There was no sign that it had struck a nerve. Speaking via a radio hookup to the crowd in the ballroom and to Democrats attending similar dinners throughout the country, Truman delivered a straightforward message: the heirs to Thomas Jefferson, he claimed, were the party of "progressive liberalism," whereas the party of "reactionary conservatives"—he never called them Republicans and never dared to mention Lincoln—stood for the benefit of the privileged few at the expense of many. "Progressive liberals will rally to the Democratic Party," he said, "because they know that the Democratic Party is the best fighting force for the triumphant achievement of worthy goals."[19] Although he uttered not a word about "civil rights" or their equivalent, half of the crowd of 850 who were listening to Truman's broadcast in Little Rock, Arkansas, were said to have walked out. *Time* panned the president's speech, writing that "the attitude of the audience was one of polite, bored tolerance toward the man they are stuck with in 1948."[20]

From the two Jefferson–Jackson Day dinners in Washington (there was another at the Statler) and those in cities around the country that night, the DNC collected more than a half a million dollars. Nevertheless, the party that year took a hit due to a falloff of contributions by Democrats from the South.

On the Monday after the dinners, Truman's unofficial campaign for the presidency suffered a body blow from Dixie that was much more serious than a decline in donations. At 2:30 in the afternoon, a delegation of six Southern governors, led by forty-five-year-old South Carolina governor Strom Thurmond, was ushered into the offices of Senator Howard Mc-Grath, former governor of Rhode Island. McGrath had recently succeeded Bob Hannegan as chair of the DNC. Thurmond, a tall, handsome World War II combat veteran who had served in the 82nd Airborne Division, had made a name for himself not only because he had bested nine others in the race for governor but also for marrying the queen of the Palmetto State's azalea festival during his first year as governor. Twenty-four years younger than Thurmond, she had just graduated from Winthrop College. While the other governors were seated, Thurmond, a lawyer, took the floor, pacing in front of McGrath as if he were addressing a jury. It didn't take him long to get to the point. "Will you use your influence," he said to McGrath, "to have [Truman's] highly controversial civil-rights legislation, which tends to divide our people, withdrawn from consideration by the Congress?" In light of Truman's firm stance on civil rights, McGrath had to say no, though he wanted to find some way to keep the Southern governors in the fold. They could tweak language in the party platform, he offered, but as to withdrawing the president's legislative program from Congress, that was a nonstarter. "There'll be no compromise," he said. With that, the meeting adjourned.

Alone in his office with Jack Redding, the public relations director of the DNC, McGrath said that the Southern governors believed that they had leverage over the DNC because of the threat caused by Wallace's third-party candidacy and "the Palestine situation," meaning a recent statement to the UN Security Council indicating that the administration was backing away—that is, receding—from the full-throated support for partition that it had advocated before the General Assembly in November 1947. This apparent change in position, if it held, meant that most Jews in New York would not support Truman, thus dooming the chances that the Democrats could capture the state's mother lode of forty-seven electoral votes. Turning to Redding, McGrath shrugged and said, "What is going to happen will happen to them, not to us. President Truman will be nominated. And he will be elected, elected without the solid South and without New York!"[21] Meanwhile, Thurmond was out in the hall announcing to the waiting press contingent that "the present leadership of the Democratic party will soon realize that the South is no longer in the bag."[22]

W hile Southern outrage was building, Wallace's Progressive Party movement had been gaining momentum by making a "highly emotional appeal to the very poor [a euphemism for Blacks], the huddled minorities, and the tightly knit Communists," wrote *Time*.[23] To the astonishment of the White House and New York Democratic operatives, an attractive young Wallace supporter and labor leader by the name of Leo Isaacson won a special congressional election in a predominantly Jewish district of the Bronx by a landslide, beating a candidate backed by Boss Ed Flynn's Democratic machine. Isaacson prevailed by claiming that Truman's civil rights program was just talk and that the president was waffling on whether to advocate for partition of Palestine and a Jewish homeland. Like Wallace, Isaacson also made it clear during his campaign that he was "dead set against the Marshall Plan," which was about to be debated in the Senate.

Given Wallace's momentum, reports that members of the Roosevelt family and others were trying to draft Dwight Eisenhower to enter the race as a Democrat, and rumors that the powerful Americans for Democratic Action (ADA) organization was searching for an alternative to Truman, McGrath decided it was time for the president to officially announce that he was a candidate. His objective was to discourage others from running against Truman and to garner the ADA's endorsement. At midafternoon on March 8, McGrath, Redding, and Gael Sullivan, executive director of the DNC, met with Truman in the White House. After explaining why Truman should publicly declare his candidacy, the president reportedly said, "If you think this is the time, you can tell [the press]." McGrath then brought up the Palestine issue, saying that "Zionist Jews" were in his office every day pressuring the Democratic Party and Truman to step up their advocacy for the partition of Palestine into two separate states, a home for the Jews in lands later to be called "Israel" and a separate but divided state for Palestinian Arabs (Gaza and the West Bank). McGrath and the others should tell them that "it's no use putting pressure on the [DNC]," Truman declared. "The Palestine issue will be handled here" in the White House. "And there'll be no politics involved," he said, repeating the point that Clark Clifford had added to Rowe's original campaign memo.

A few minutes later McGrath stepped out of the Oval Office. After he surprised reporters in the West Wing with the official announcement that "if nominated" Truman would accept and run for the presidency, McGrath added that in the interim Truman would "stand fast" on civil rights and that he would personally "handle" the "Palestine issue."[24] The DNC chairman had no reason to know it at the time, but the president had misled him. Truman had already outsourced the handling of the Palestine issue to the State Department. Three hours earlier, at a noon session with Secretary of State George Marshall, Truman approved a statement to the UN Security Council on Palestine. That statement, to be delivered "when necessary" by Warren Austin, his UN ambassador, would inform the council that the U.S. was withdrawing its support for partition and was instead recommending that Palestine should be placed under a UN "trusteeship" in order to afford Jews and Arabs an opportunity to reach agreement on a future government.[25] Assuming Truman understood what he was approving, he must have been persuaded by Marshall, whom he revered, that rather than partition, a temporary cooling-off period, with the hope of avoiding all-out war between Jews and Arabs, was the prudent course of action.

Meanwhile, political and foreign policy operatives associated with the Jewish Agency, the de facto government of what would become the nation of Israel, were acutely aware that Marshall and his State Department had been pressing for a reversal of the administration's position on partition and that Truman was vacillating. Though those in the agency did not know that Truman had actually approved a statement withdrawing support for partition, they enlisted via Frank Goldman, president of B'nai B'rith, Truman's old friend Eddie Jacobson to once again persuade Truman to meet with Chaim Weizmann, who had previously changed Truman's mind on the Negev issue. It was thought that Weizmann was the only person who could stiffen Truman's resolve in favor of partition and the prompt establishment of a Jewish state.

On a quiet Saturday, March 13, fifty-six-year-old Eddie Jacobson showed up in the West Wing unannounced. Jacobson had known Truman since they served together in the fall of 1917 at Fort Sill, Oklahoma, during World War I. One of Lieutenant Truman's duties was to manage the regimental canteen. To make it a financial success, he assigned Sergeant Edward Jacobson, who had clerked for years in a Kansas City clothing store, to run the day-to-day operation of the canteen. "I have a Jew in charge of the canteen by the name of Jacobson and he is a crackerjack," wrote Truman to Bess Wallace, his future wife.[26] After the Great War, the two men opened a haberdashery that was initially successful but eventually had to close due to the 1921 recession. Like Truman, Jacobson bounced back. By 1948, Jacobson was a respected Kansas City businessman. Most biographers say that Truman and Jacobson were best friends, but for some unknown reason, Margaret downplayed the friendship, writing that Jacobson was just "one of the hundreds of army friends" that her father made during the war and that the idea that Jacobson influenced Truman's "stand on Israel" was "absurd."[27]

Matt Connelly, Truman's appointments secretary, showed Jacobson into the Oval Office. After a few minutes of small talk, Jacobson broached the subject of Palestine. According to a fifteen-page letter written by Jacobson in 1952, he told Truman that he could not understand why the president refused to meet with Dr. Weizmann, by then an "old and sick man," who had traveled thousands of miles to the U.S. "just to see you and plead the cause of the Jewish people." Jacobson recalled that Truman immediately became tense, abrupt, and bitter. He complained about "how disrespectful and how mean certain [American] Jewish leaders" had been toward him when pestering him incessantly to come out foursquare for partition. His "dear friend, the President," Jacobson wrote, "was at that moment as close to being an anti-Semite as a man could possibly be."

When Truman said he "was satisfied" to have the Jews and Arabs "take their cause through the United Nations," an oblique reference to trusteeship that suggested he would not support partition, Jacobson was "crushed"—on the verge of giving up. It was at that point that he glanced over at a small bronze sculpture of Andrew Jackson mounted on a horse atop a table. Knowing that Truman was a great admirer of Jackson, a student of Jackson's life and Jacksonian democracy, Jacobson pointed to the statue and said, "Harry, all your life you have had a hero. . . . Well, Harry, I too have a hero, a man I never met but who is, I think, the greatest Jew who ever lived." Just because "you have been insulted by some of our American Jewish leaders," said Jacobson, "you refuse to see" Weizmann, "even though you know [he] had absolutely nothing to do with these insults."

Jacobson stopped talking. Truman said nothing. He drummed his fingers on his desk. Then he swiveled his chair around and began looking out the window into the garden. Jacobson recognized the sign. "I knew he was changing his mind," he wrote. Truman swung back and looked straight into Jacobson's eyes. "You win, you baldheaded son of a bitch. Tell Matt [Connelly] to arrange this meeting as soon as possible after I return from New York on March 17."

Jacobson was so emotional that when he returned to the Statler on Sixteenth Street, he downed two double bourbons in the bar—"something I never did before in my life," he wrote.[28]

To avoid being seen by reporters, Dr. Chaim Weizmann, whose seventy-plus years had been dedicated to science and the Zionist movement, entered the White House through the East Gate at noon on March 18. The president had ordered that the meeting be kept secret and off the record. No one in the State Department, including Marshall and Austin, was informed. Truman and Weizmann talked for forty-five minutes. Weizmann spoke about the possibilities for "industrial activity" in Palestine and "the need for land," including the Negev, if the Jewish refugees from Europe were to have enough room to raise their families, support themselves, and establish a homeland.[29] As to the critical question of whether Truman would go all out for partition when the British mandate expired at midnight on May 14, the record is muddled. On the one hand, Weizmann wrote in his 1949 autobiography that Truman "indicated a firm resolve to press forward with partition."[30] On the other hand, in the second volume of his memoirs, published in 1956, Truman wrote that he "felt" Weizmann left the meeting "with a full understanding" of his policy. Yet the president was not at all clear on whether he supported vigorous implementation of partition at the time or whether he backed the expedient of a "temporary trusteeship for Palestine," as he suggested in the very next paragraph of his memoirs.[31] By describing what he felt Weizmann understood, instead of the words he remembered using, it appears that Truman chose to deliberately gloss over his actual policy stance.

Whatever Truman said or didn't say, there is no doubt that Weizmann left the White House with the impression that Truman was a resolute supporter of partition. When he informed Moshe Shertok, political and foreign policy director of the Jewish agency, and others in New York, they eagerly accepted his assessment. They were in for a shocking surprise.

Having already received approval from Truman (on March 8) to inform the UN Security Council "when and if necessary" that the U.S. government was in favor of a temporary trusteeship as an alternative to immediate partition, Secretary Marshall decided it was time to pull the trigger. Believing that all-out war between Jews and Arabs in Palestine was imminent and that a trusteeship would give him time to negotiate a truce, Marshall ordered UN ambassador Warren Austin to deliver the message to the Security Council at its next meeting, which happened to be on Friday, March 19, the day after Weizmann's secret meeting with Truman. However, Marshall neglected to provide Truman with advance notice of Austin's announcement. Similarly, the president chose not to tell Marshall about his meeting with Weizmann. These twin oversights led to anger, embarrassment, and charges of gross incompetence.

Believing he had been blindsided by Austin's message, Truman was at first furious. He either forgot about his prior approval or was angry because he had not been given a heads-up. And he was embarrassed about having misled Weizmann. "The State Department pulled the rug out from under me," he wrote in his diary. Referring to Weizmann and perhaps others, he wrote, "I am now in the position of being a liar and a double-crosser."[32] Clark Clifford was livid. He blamed Marshall. "Marshall didn't know his ass from a hole in the ground," he said.[33] Shertok and David Ben-Gurion, chair of the Jewish Agency, as well as Jews and their leaders everywhere regarded the reversal of policy as a stunning betrayal. March 19 quickly became known as Black Friday.

By Monday, Truman had calmed down. He was initially angry because he thought he had never endorsed the trusteeship alternative. However, over the weekend, Clifford, or possibly his assistant George Elsey, persuaded the president that he had in fact approved the substance of Austin's announcement. When Marshall, having returned from the West Coast, met with Truman in the White House, the president admitted to him that he had previously "agreed" with Austin's statement to the Security Council. However, he was "exercised" because no one had told him in advance that the statement was about to be delivered. If he had been given notice, Truman said that "he could have taken certain measures to have avoided the political blast of the press."[34] What those measures would have been was never explained.

With the *New York Times* and other newspapers condemning the Truman administration for unmatched "ineptness," it was obvious to White House staffers and the DNC that the adverse press would reduce Truman's favorability percentage even further and could cost him the presidency.[35] At the time, his approval rating hovered at around 36 percent. On March 24, Truman called a meeting in the Cabinet Room for the purpose of developing a statement to the press that would contain the damage. According to *Time*, the session "exploded into violent argument" between David Niles, who was pro-partition, and Loy Henderson of the State Department, who was for trusteeship. Truman walked out, "bitterly complaining: 'This gets us nowhere. All I want is a statement I can read tomorrow at my press conference.'"[36]

Truman's press statement the next day tried to have it both ways. "Trusteeship" was not "proposed as a substitute for the partition plan," it said, but merely as a temporary "effort to fill the vacuum" that would be created when the British mandate expired. This was intended to convey the thought that partition—establishment of a sovereign Jewish state and a separate state for Palestinian Arabs—remained the ultimate goal. In the next sentence, however, the statement said that "trusteeship does not prejudice the character of the final political settlement." This point obviously opened the door to a one-state solution or some other political settlement that would not involve partition and a separate Jewish state. *Time* concluded: "Now no one in the world could be expected to know where the U.S. stood on Palestine. Harry Truman's comic opera performance had done little credit to the greatest power in the world."[37]

Truman's blunder is reminiscent of FDR's failure to recall that he had endorsed the Morgenthau Plan. The difference was that Roosevelt, by saying that it was Morgenthau who had made a mistake, got away with it, whereas Truman paid a price.

While the Palestine fiasco was playing out, rapid changes were taking place in Europe and Asia that affected U.S. national security and the Truman administration's foreign policy. All eyes were focused on aggressive moves by Joseph Stalin and the spread of Communism. On February 25, 1948, when Truman was vacationing in Key West, Czechoslovak Communists, with Stalin's encouragement and approval, seized power in the only Eastern European nation that still had a democratic government. Americans were outraged and feared further power grabs, particularly in Italy, where elections were scheduled in April. They remembered that only a decade earlier, it had been Hitler's invasion of Czechoslovakia that triggered the Second World War in Europe. Soon after the Soviet-inspired coup in Czechoslovakia, the broken body of Jan Masaryk, the non-Communist foreign minister who was the son of the nation's first president, was found dead, dressed in pajamas, forty-seven feet below his bathroom window in the courtyard of Czernin Palace (the Foreign Ministry) in Prague. The cause of his death, despite four investigations, remains in dispute but agents with ties to the Kremlin are prime suspects. There was a sarcastic joke told by those who discounted the suicide story: "Jan Masaryk was a very tidy man. He was such a tidy man that when he jumped, he shut the window after him."

On February 27, Americans learned that Stalin had delivered to the president of Finland a letter urging (demanding?) that he sign a mutual assistance pact with the Soviet Union. And during that month there were reports that Russian soldiers were stopping, boarding, and "inspecting" trains passing through the Soviet zone into the U.S. and British occupied sectors of Berlin. Soon to be a hot spot in the Cold War, Berlin was like a small Western island in the middle of a Soviet sea. Because of the coup in Czechoslovakia, the letter pressuring Finland, and the sporadic railroad harassment, Truman's concern about Soviet expansion deepened. His National Security Council suggested that Stalin was like Hitler, warning that "Stalin has come close to achieving what Hitler attempted in vain."[38] Similarly, parallels are drawn today between Vladimir Putin and both Hitler and Stalin.

At a briefing by Secretary Marshall on March 5, the day Truman returned from Key West, the president was told of a now famous cable from General Lucius Clay, in which he wrote that a "subtle change in Soviet attitude" made him feel that war *may come with dramatic suddenness.*"[39] According to Secretary of Defense James Forrestal, the cable struck Washington "with the force of a blockbuster bomb."[40] At the bottom of a memo from Marshall, Truman scrawled: "Will Russia move first? Who pulls the trigger? Where do we go?"[41] There is no record of a response. However, the Pentagon reacted by ordering Clay and MacArthur to review "current emergency plans" so as to be ready for an attack or provocative incident by the Soviets. Clay was to be vigilant in the Western zones of Germany and Berlin, MacArthur in Japan, Korea, and Manchuria.[42]

The next day, Saturday, March 6, Truman was briefed at noon by Bob Lovett, undersecretary of state, on a highly significant communiqué sent by a group of ambassadors from the United States, Britain, France, and the Benelux countries (Belgium, the Netherlands, and Luxembourg), who had been meeting in London to discuss the future of Germany. The meeting became known as "the London six-power conference." The communiqué announced an agreement by the six ambassadors that would serve as a bulwark against the spread of Communism and enable economic recovery in the Western nations of Europe. The diplomats recommended to their respective governments that the three Western-occupation zones in Germany should be merged into one, that the unified zone must participate in the Marshall Plan, and that a West German government with "adequate central authority" should be formed.[43] In essence, it was recognition that the economic revival of West Germany, which possessed the resources and people to again become an industrial powerhouse, would be the key to the recovery of all of Western Europe, a concept that had been advocated by Marshall and Clay. The communiqué was good news for the U.S. and Western Europe, very bad news for Moscow.

As policymakers in Europe and the U.S. were concluding that restoration of the economy of Western Germany was essential to the recovery of Western Europe, George Kennan, head of policy planning in the State Department, was in Tokyo meeting with General Douglas MacArthur and his aides. Kennan was of the view that the Japanese economy, like that of Western Germany, needed to be stabilized and reindustrialized so that it could resist Soviet influence or control. The eastern borders of the Soviet Union were not far from Japan. Kennan was convinced that because China did not have the capacity to develop major military strength, it was Japan, America's former archenemy, not China, that was the country in the Far East most vital—indeed, the linchpin—to U.S. national security. Though MacArthur resisted, Kennan's views prevailed. Eventually, Kennan's new policy for Japan—aptly called "reverse course"—was approved by Marshall and Truman, though they personally devoted little attention to Japan in 1948. In his memoir Kennan wrote that aside from the Marshall Plan, his contribution to policy in Japan was the most constructive and significant of his career in government.[44]

For the people of the United States, the Second World War would not really be finished until they had reckoned with revenge and restored the vanquished. Now that half of Germany was set to be revived by inclusion in the Marshall Plan and all of Japan would be guided by American experts to "reverse course" and reindustrialize, the end was in sight.

W ith "rumors and portents of war" in the night air, at five past midnight on Sunday, March 14, 1948, the Senate, having defeated a crippling amendment by Senator Bob Taft, voted sixty-nine to seventeen to approve the Marshall Plan (officially titled the European Cooperation Act of 1948).[45] Thus far, Truman had taken a low profile in the selling of the plan, leaving it to Republican senator Vandenberg and Secretary Marshall to take the lead. Now, as the scene shifted to the House of Representatives, Truman's advisers decided that the time was ripe for the president to demonstrate his leadership and urge the House to act quickly. Their hope was that a forceful speech by the boss would kick off his uphill campaign for a second term.

The speech that Truman delivered to a joint session of Congress on St. Patrick's Day went well beyond a plea to the House for speedy ratification of the Marshall Plan. As Benn Steil, senior fellow at the Council on Foreign Relations, wrote, for the first time the president called out the Soviet Union by name "as the villain of the new Cold War."[46] Truman's words were direct and unmistakably hostile, a sharp break from FDR's policy of friendship and cooperation, which Truman had sought to follow. Since the end of the war, he declared, the "Soviet Union and its agents have destroyed the independence and democratic character of a whole series of nations of Eastern Europe and Central Europe. It is this ruthless course of action, and the clear design to extend it to the remaining free nations of Europe, that have brought about the critical situation in Europe today." Prompt passage of the Marshall Plan was essential, Truman insisted, but "not enough." They must boost their "military strength as a means of preventing war," he implored. To meet this challenge, the president urged Congress to temporarily restore the draft and enact a universal military training program. As to the "growing menace" to freedom in Europe, Truman praised the signing that very day of the "Brussels Pact," a fifty-year common defense alliance of Britain, France, Belgium, the Netherlands, and Luxembourg.[47] Truman stressed that the U.S. fully supported the pact, which foreshadowed the NATO alliance. With this speech Truman cast aside FDR's long shadow. He did not ask himself what Roosevelt would have done.

That evening, after shaking hands and being photographed at New York City's annual St. Patrick's Day Parade with Tom Dewey, Truman's chief rival for the presidency, he attended the Friendly Sons of St. Patrick dinner at the Hotel Astor. In his after-dinner speech to an audience of three thousand, Truman repeated his call for quick action on the Marshall Plan, reinstitution of the draft, and universal military training. However, compared to his earlier speech to the joint session of Congress, his rhetoric concerning the Soviet Union and its aggressive actions in Europe was strangely understated, perhaps because of the large waves of Russian émigrés who populated sections of New York City. Truman omitted pejorative terms he had used in his earlier speech to describe the Soviet Union, such as "ruthless" and "growing menace." In fact, throughout his St. Patrick's Day speech, the president never even uttered the words "Soviet Union" as the source of his call for action, instead referring to "that nation" or "one nation." This was especially odd because the only name that he called out for opprobrium in his after-dinner talk was "Henry Wallace." Near the end of that speech, Truman added to the advance copy a few lines (to which he had alerted reporters) stating that he would "not accept the political support of Henry Wallace and his Communists" because "any price for Wallace and his Communists is too much for me to pay. I'm not buying."[48] Apparently, Truman could not resist scoring a political point in retaliation for Wallace recently telling voters in the Bronx that Truman "still talks Jewish but acts Arab."[49]

When Cardinal Francis Spellman, the archbishop of New York, who was seated next to Truman on the dais, began to speak, his bellicose imagery was in sharp contrast to that of Truman. "In this hour of dreadful desperate need," he intoned, "we are permitting Soviet Russia to continue her policy of persecution and slaughter and dooming our neighbor-nations and ourselves to reap a rotted harvest of appeasement." The popular Catholic leader incited his followers to oppose "the killing and enslavement of whole peoples by the Communists."[50]

Congress responded to Truman's call at the joint session for prompt passage of the Marshall Plan, but it wasn't until June that the draft was reimposed (Truman's expensive universal military training proposal was dead on arrival).[51] On the last day of March, the House, in a voice vote, approved the first-year phase of the Marshall Plan by a lopsided bipartisan margin of 329 to 74. Ominously, on that same day, the Soviets stepped up pressure on access routes through the Soviet zone to Berlin from the U.S., British, and French occupation zones. According to Secretary of Defense James Forrestal, the Soviets announced that as of April 1, they had the right to inspect "material" coming into the Soviet zone "by either train or truck" and "the right to examine the credentials and the belongings of personnel." Truman was consulted, and "on his own initiative," he decided not to notify congressional leaders because it would add to "war hysteria." With Truman's approval, Clay was ordered to prevent the Soviets from boarding the trains, but when he did so, they "retaliated by stopping the trains themselves" from entering the Soviet zone en route to Berlin. Rather than risking a shooting war, Clay orchestrated a "baby airlift," flying "cargoes of food" into the Western sectors of Berlin, a forerunner of the famous Berlin Airlift. The Soviets claimed that the new restrictions were imposed in the interest of "greater efficiency," but they were actually designed to deter the Western powers from going ahead with plans for a West German government and to eventually drive them out of Berlin.[52]

Differences between the House and Senate versions of the Marshall Plan were resolved in conference. On April 3, 1948, after returning to Washington from the College of William and Mary, where he had received an honorary degree, Truman signed the Foreign Assistance Act of 1948 (formerly the European Cooperation Act of 1948) into law. It authorized a total of $6.2 billion for the first twelve months—$5.3 billion for European recovery (the Marshall Plan) and the rest for China, Greece, and Turkey and for international child relief. In today's dollars, the $5.3 billion for the initial year of the Marshall Plan would be approximately $66 billion.

The conception, passage, and implementation of the Marshall Plan were a singular triumph for the Truman administration, arguably the greatest diplomatic achievement by the United States since the Louisiana Purchase. In memory and myth it endures today because it speaks to the moment in the American story when it was the right and honorable thing to do. Though President Harry Truman deserves credit for his support and encouragement of the remarkable team that made it happen, he had little to do with the design and shape of the plan. The statement that he issued when he signed the plan into law heaped praise on "constructive statesmanship" and the "bipartisan foreign policy" of Congress.[53] When asked by a group of editorial writers whether he would ever "get any credit . . . for sending this stuff to Europe," Truman responded, "I'm not doing this for credit. I am backing it because it's right. I am doing it because it's necessary to be done, if we are going to survive ourselves."[54]

***

Near the end of a long letter to his sister, Mary Jane, dated April 8, Truman could not resist gloating over General MacArthur's surprising loss in the Wisconsin presidential primary. During the preceding week, the *New York Times* and a raft of other newspapers had predicted on their front pages that the world-famous, photogenic five-star general, the viceroy of occupied Japan, would easily win the GOP primary in Wisconsin, his home state, over Harold Stassen, the "boy governor" of Minnesota, and Tom Dewey, governor of New York. Stories making the rounds, Truman wrote, were that the "Almighty" had disappointed "his boy Mac" and that MacArthur wanted it kept secret "that he couldn't walk on water." Truman was not only pleased that MacArthur had been soundly defeated by Stassen, but he must have been ecstatic that Tom Dewey, who he thought would receive the Republican nomination, came in a distant third. Unlike MacArthur, who had not set foot in Wisconsin for more than ten years, Dewey "had scoured the state in a fierce struggle for the leavings," wrote *Time.*

***

Meanwhile, Truman's acquiescence in the decision to delay the partition of Palestine in order to give Marshall and Lovett time to arrange a truce and trusteeship came to naught. They were informed by Moshe Shertok of the Jewish Agency that no truce between Jews and Arabs was possible so long as Arab troops remained in Palestine. Shertok advised Marshall that even if the Arab forces withdrew, the Jews would still move to take over governance of the lands allocated to them under the partition plan approved by the UN General Assembly.

By the first week in April, questions of whether Jews of the Yishuv, the Hebrew name for the Jewish community in Palestine, would be able to defend themselves and conduct offensive operations against Arab forces that vastly outnumbered them were answered. Faced with an arms embargo by the U.S. and other Western democracies, the Jewish armed forces in Palestine, called the Haganah, had been receiving from Communist Czechoslovakia (with the approval of the Soviet Union) substantial shipments by air and sea of tanks, planes, artillery, small arms, ammunition, and trucks. In addition, "400–500 young male Jews of military age with records of service in the Soviet Army or the Soviet-sponsored Polish army" were shipped to Palestine.[55] David Ben-Gurion, the leader of the Jewish Agency, reported to Shertok that "the military situation has changed radically in favor of the Jews."[56] As a result, the attitude in Washington shifted from truce and trusteeship to the issue of whether to recognize the Jewish state when the British mandate expired at midnight on May 14, 1948. Partition through force of arms appeared inevitable. On April 9, Chaim Weizmann, the soon-to-be president of Israel, put the matter to Truman in stark terms. "The choice for our people, Mr. President, is between statehood and extermination," he wrote. In other words, truce and temporary trusteeship were off the table. "I am confident that you will yet decide in the spirit of the moral law."[57]

After speaking face-to-face with Dr. Weizmann in New York, Eddie Jacobson took a night train down to Washington. With Weizmann's moral case for statehood on his mind, Jacobson was quietly admitted through the East Gate of the White House for a secret conversation with his friend the president. "It was at this meeting," Jacobson later wrote, that he "discussed with the President the vital matter of recognizing the new [Jewish] state, and to this he agreed with his whole heart" (this last phrase was underlined in Jacobson's letter).[58] Twelve days later, Truman reportedly sent a message to Weizmann through Judge Sam Rosenman that "he would recognize the Jewish state as it was proclaimed."[59]

While it certainly appeared that Truman had firmly decided to grant diplomatic recognition to the new Jewish state when or before the British mandate expired, he once again seemed to vacillate and muddy the waters. According to Dean Rusk, head of the State Department's Office of UN

Affairs, Truman instructed him to inform Marshall and the State Department "to take whatever steps Secretary Marshall thought would hasten the completion of a truce." When Rusk asked Truman what he would do if the Arabs accepted a truce but the Jews would not, Truman "replied that 'if the Jews refuse to accept a truce on reasonable grounds they need not accept anything from us.'" Four days later the Jewish Agency rejected the State Department's latest truce proposal, making it even more clear that the Jews intended to establish a "separate state by force of arms." Having just provided assurance to Rusk—which he presumably shared with Marshall—that the "Jews could not expect anything else from us," Truman was once again caught in a bind of his own making. He had already decided to grant a critically important something "else" to the Jews—U.S. recognition of their new state. Now Truman would have to walk back his assurance to Rusk and Marshall. But until he did so, Marshall would have reason to believe that Truman would not grant immediate recognition to the new Jewish state. It was the second bungling of "the Palestine question" by the president.

In his book *The Arc of a Covenant*, Walter Russell Mead argues that Truman was a consistent supporter of the Jewish cause for partition and recognition and that Jacobson's influence on Truman was a "myth" that the president "was eager to promote." He claims that Truman's Palestine policy was always "rooted in his own settled convictions."[60] The record does not support these conclusions. Instead, it indicates inconsistency and vacillation as if Truman did not know his own mind on what to do about Palestine.

———

At the beginning of the second week in April, Stalin decided to ratchet up the pressure on access to Berlin. Having previously halted civilian rail traffic into Berlin from Hamburg and Nuremberg, the Soviets announced that "all traffic on the remaining rail line between Hanover and Berlin would require additional clearances" from Soviet authorities.[61] During an April 10 teleconference between U.S. Army chief of staff Omar Bradley and General Clay, who was in Berlin, Bradley suggested that since it appeared that the Soviets would continue to intensify the pressure on Berlin, wouldn't it be prudent "to minimize the loss of prestige" by withdrawing from the city before being forced out? Clay responded, "If we mean to hold Europe against communism, we must not budge. . . . If we move out [of Berlin], our position is threatened." And if the Truman administration and its military brass did not believe "that the issue is cast now," said Clay, "then it never will, and communism will run rampant." Bradley dropped his proposal. Clay had convinced him.

General Clay was a formidable character "with a huge ego, inflated further by his position as Military Governor of Germany," wrote Walter Isaacson and Evan Thomas in *The Wise Men*.[62] A West Pointer who had rebelled against the discipline, Clay was a skilled bureaucratic infighter who often got his way by threatening to resign—no fewer than eleven times. He played a pivotal role at the beginning of the Cold War by pressuring his superiors to revive German industry, backing Truman's decision to stay in Berlin, and supporting the airlift.

In Washington, momentum was building toward a security alliance with the free nations of Europe. It will be recalled that in the president's speech to the joint session of Congress on March 17, he hailed the signing of the so-called Brussels Pact, a joint defense agreement between five Western European nations to "protect themselves." Referencing the "significance" of the Brussels Pact, Truman announced in his speech that it would be "matched by an equal determination on our part to help them protect themselves," a telltale sign that the U.S. might seek to join the Brussels Pact or establish something like it.[63] Due to the president's intriguing suggestion, which had been inspired by Jack Hickerson, head of State's Division of European Affairs, and backed by Secretary Marshall, the State Department's Policy Planning Staff (sans Kennan, who was in Japan) and a separate group of high-level American, British, and Canadian diplomats reached agreement on a paper recommending a "collective defense treaty for the North Atlantic area."[64] On April 7, Bob Lovett, as acting secretary of state because Marshall was abroad, explained the proposed treaty to Truman and left him a copy, the first time the president or anyone in the White House had been consulted about discussions between the two groups. Truman gave him the "green light."[65] Six days later, the substance of this proposal, called NSC 9, was approved by the National

Security Council. In summary, NSC 9 proposed that the U.S. enter into an alliance of "organized force"—that is, a military alliance—with members of the Brussels Pact and other non-Communist European nations for the purpose of deterring Soviet aggression, which was said to threaten peace, national security, and the success of the Marshall Plan. NSC 9 made clear that the proposed alliance would be within the framework of the UN Charter but outside the Security Council veto, because it was based on Article 51's inherent right of "collective self-defense against armed attack." NSC 9 purported to "strengthen the UN" by avoiding the certainty of a Soviet veto. Notably, the proposed alliance agreement provided that "an armed attack against any party" should "be considered an armed attack against all," a stipulation almost identical to that in the 1947 Rio Pact.[66]

To lay the groundwork for acceptance of the North Atlantic alliance described in NSC 9 and revised in NSC 9/1, George Kennan, back from Japan, was adamant that a "resolution" favoring the proposed alliance should be introduced by the Senate Foreign Relations Committee and approved by a bipartisan majority of senators.[67] Once that was accomplished, then, and only then, Truman was to step in, make the case for the alliance to Congress and the American people, and invite the free nations in Europe to discuss and conclude a defense agreement for the North Atlantic area.

At this juncture, the action moved from the fifth floor of the State Department to apartment 500G in the Wardman Park Hotel, Senator Vandenberg's home away from home. There, for the next two weeks, Vandenberg, chair of the Senate Foreign Relations Committee, worked privately and quietly with his good friend Bob Lovett to shape a draft resolution, the shorter the better (the senator became known as "one-page Vandenberg"). On April 27, Vandenberg, Lovett, Marshall, and John Foster Dulles met at Blair House. According to Arthur Vandenberg Jr., editor of his father's papers, the senator "fished inside his coat pocket" and pulled out a single-page resolution.[68] In essence, the resolution advised the president that it was "the sense of the Senate" that he be authorized to pursue "collective self-defense" arrangements under Article 51 of the UN Charter. Furthermore, Truman was to assert "Maximum efforts" to obtain agreements to provide the UN with a police force. The resolution was broad, speaking of self-defense agreements, in the plural, although it was really aimed at a single military alliance for the North Atlantic area. Moreover, while the resolution gave lip service to the need to curb excessive use of the Security Council veto, it was obvious but unstated that collective-self-defense agreements under Article 51 would remain outside the Security Council veto power, which had been so often invoked by the Soviet Union.[69]

It would take another month and a half, but on June 11, after a single eight-hour day of floor debate, the Vandenberg Resolution (Resolution 239) was approved by the Senate sixty-four to six. The resolution was important because it "gave the State Department political cover" to begin preliminary talks with its counterparts in the Brussels Pact.[70] Those discussions would lead to the 1949 North Atlantic Treaty, a security alliance that became an essential corollary to the Marshall Plan.[71] As Arthur Vandenberg Jr. wrote of his father's momentous accomplishment, "Rarely in our nation's history has such a small egg hatched so quickly into such a large chicken."[72]

On May 7, with Truman's job approval rating at a low of 36 percent, Clark Clifford and the president sat down in the Oval Office for their customary "day-end chat."[73] The subject was Palestine. Since late November 1947, civil war between Arabs and Jews had been raging on and off in Jerusalem and at settlements in Galilee, the Jordan Valley, and the Negev. The British mandate was set to expire in seven days—midnight on May 14—leaving Palestine without a government and police forces. Truman and Clifford were aware that David Ben-Gurion intended to declare the existence of a new Jewish state in Palestine during the first minute of May 15. Because Truman had made clear that he would neither lift the arms embargo nor send U.S. troops to help defend the Jews, Clifford urged the president to at least issue, at his next scheduled press conference on May 13, a statement that the U.S. would be the first to diplomatically recognize the new state. His rationale, based on notes that were almost certainly prepared by Max Lowenthal, his brilliant assistant, was that a Jewish state was "inevitable"—that partition was about to become an undeniable fact.[74] Why shouldn't the United States be the first to recognize the new nation?

According to Clifford's 1991 memoir, the president was "sympathetic" to his proposal but sensed that Secretary Marshall had "strong feelings" against immediate recognition. In fact, virtually every member of Truman's national security team was opposed. They still clung to the hope that a truce and a trusteeship could be negotiated. In addition, there was concern that American forces would be drawn into the conflict, that the Jews would be outnumbered and annihilated on the battlefield, and that the U.S. would be denied access to Middle East oil. They suspected that election year politics was the main reason behind the rush to be the first to recognize the new Jewish state.

In the presence of Clifford, Truman phoned Marshall to ascertain his views. Listening to Truman's end of the conversation, Clifford "could tell that Marshall objected strongly" to recognition. The president expressed no opinion. He ended the conversation by asking Marshall, along with Lovett, to meet with him in the Oval Office on May 12.

After Truman hung up, he swiveled his chair around to Clifford and said, "Clark, I am impressed with General Marshall's argument that we should not recognize the new state so fast." Truman told Clifford that he would like him to "make the case in favor of recognition" at the meeting on May 12 with Marshall and Lovett. "You know how I feel," he said. "I want you to present it just as though you were making an argument before the Supreme Court of the United States. . . . I want you to be as persuasive as you can be."[75] During an interview in 1977, fourteen years before the publication of his memoir, Clifford recalled that Truman ended his instructions by saying, "You will be addressing all of us present, of course, but the person I really want you to convince is Marshall."[76] Because of the respect that Truman had for Marshall's judgment, an enormous burden had been placed on Clifford's shoulders. However, Clifford off-loaded much of that burden to Max Lowenthal, who fashioned the arguments for recognition that Clifford would use.[77]

The evening after Clifford was asked to prepare for verbal battle with Marshall, Attorney General Tom Clark hosted a celebration of the president's sixty-fourth birthday at the F Street Club, a yellow brick Greek re-

vival house a few blocks west of the White House that is today the residence
of the president of George Washington University. "It was a grand birthday," Truman wrote to Clifford, "in spite of Palistine [*sic*] and the Damn
Republicans."[78] In addition to the birthday boy and Bess, Clark had invited
about forty of their friends and supporters, including Marshall and his
wife, Katherine, who rarely dined out in Washington. Clark knew that the
president needed an emotional lift. His job approval numbers were in the
tank. His own party was imperiling his effectiveness, having overridden
his veto of what he termed a "rich man's" tax bill. Truman trailed in the
polls behind every plausible nominee except Taft. Columnist Arthur
Krock had written that Truman's "influence is weaker than any President
has been in modern history."[79]

After-dinner toasts were delivered by Clark and others, but it was
Marshall's deadly serious tribute that silenced the room, leaving the president almost speechless. Marshall stood, pushed his chair out of the way,
leaned forward with hands on the table, and locked eyes with Truman. "I
cannot recall that there has been a President in our history who has more
clearly demonstrated courageous decision and complete integrity in his
decisions than the Birthday guest of honor tonight," he said. Raising his
glass, Marshall asked "all to drink to the health of the President and to the
courage with which he has fought for peace and good of all mankind."[80] A
Time magazine reporter wrote that Truman "rose to respond but was unable to compose himself." Seconds passed. Finally, he "gestured toward
Marshall and said simply: 'He won the war.'"[81]

At four o'clock on Wednesday, May 12, Marshall, Lovett, and two State
Department aides trooped into the Oval Office. Chairs had been arranged
in a semicircle facing the president's desk. Clifford took the center seat,
with two White House staffers taking seats to his left, while Marshall and
Lovett sat to his right, their aides seated behind them. In his memoir, Clifford later called the meeting "Showdown in the Oval Office," an hour when
"the Truman administration faced a decision whose consequences are still
with us today."[82]

Without mentioning the issue of recognition, Truman calmly opened
the meeting, calling on Marshall and Lovett to bring the group up-to-date
on talks with members of the Jewish Agency. Lovett began by reporting

that "on the basis of recent military successes, the Jews were confident that they can establish their sovereign state without any necessity for a truce with the Arabs of Palestine." Marshall "interrupted," recalled Clifford, and said that four days ago he had met with Moshe Shertok, and told him that "it was dangerous to base long-range policy on temporary military success." If the Jewish armed forces faced setbacks, he warned Shertok, "and came running to us," they could not "expect help from the United States."[83] He concluded by recommending that the U.S. should continue to support UN trusteeship and defer recognition.

Truman signaled Clifford that it was his turn to take center stage. They needed to be realistic, the counsel to the president asserted. The efforts of the State Department to broker a truce and establish a trusteeship had failed. "Partition into Jewish and Arab sectors," he pointed out, "has already happened." Given these facts, Clifford argued that the president should recognize the Jewish state immediately after termination of the British Mandate on May 14 because "this would have distinct value in restoring the President's firm position for support of the partition in Palestine." Moreover, Clifford added, the president should announce his intention to recognize the new Jewish state "at his press conference tomorrow [May 13]" before "the Soviet Union or any other nation does so."[84]

To Marshall's sensitive ears, the press conference that Clifford envisioned would have been nothing more than a thinly disguised effort to squeeze maximum political value from the president's recognition decision—an attempt to repair the damage done on Black Friday, influence New York voters, and steal a march on the Soviets.

Clifford's final arguments were his most eloquent. He invoked the horrors of the Holocaust and the "great moral obligation" of Americans "to oppose discrimination such as that inflicted on the Jewish people."[85] In rich, honeyed tones, he cited the verse from Deuteronomy that Jews regard as the biblical validation of their claim to a homeland in Palestine.

> Behold, I have set the land before you: go in and possess the land which the Lord sware unto your fathers, Abraham, Isaac, and Jacob, to give unto them, and to their seed after them.[86]

While the special counsel was finishing his presentation, he "noticed Marshall's face reddening with suppressed anger." Suddenly he interrupted, sounding, as Clifford recalled, "like a righteous God-damned Baptist."[87] "This is just straight politics," said Marshall. "I don't even understand why Clifford is here. This is not a political meeting."

Truman calmly responded, "General, he is here because I asked him to be here."[88]

Lovett jumped in, pouncing on Clifford's recommendation that Truman should announce his recognition decision at a press conference the next day, twenty-four hours before the new Jewish state existed. And even after its existence was announced on May 14, he contended, why should they then recognize the new state before knowing what kind of a government "would be set up?" In an effort to prove his point, Lovett read excerpts from intel reports "regarding Soviet activity in sending Jews and Communist agents from Black Sea areas to Palestine." Immediate recognition, Lovett said, would be like "buying a pig in a poke."[89]

With his temper barely under control, Marshall piled on. According to a written account of Marshall's words, which he insisted be inserted into the official record, he warned the president that that recognition would be seen as a "transparent dodge to win a few votes." Clifford's recommendation, said Marshall, was "based on political considerations" and would "diminish the great dignity of the office of the President." The secretary looked directly at Truman, just as he had when he lauded his "complete integrity" during his birthday toast. He said, *If [you] follow Mr. Clifford's advice and if in the elections I were to vote, I would vote against the President.*[90]

According to Clifford, "everyone in the room was stunned." Marshall's rebuke to a president of the United States was unprecedented, yet Truman showed no emotion. He broke the uncomfortable silence by saying that it was his responsibility to deal with the political factors. Then, signaling an end to the meeting, the president rose from his chair and walked over to Marshall, the person whom he revered above all others, the "indispensable symbol of continuity" in his administration that he could not afford to lose. Truman could see that Marshall was still seething. "I understand

your position, General, and I'm inclined to side with you in this matter."
Clifford guessed that the remark was disingenuous, a harmless fib that
Truman told to defuse the situation, but he couldn't be certain. The pres-
ident had backtracked on Palestine twice before.

Truman and Clifford lingered in the Oval Office for a few minutes
after everyone else had gathered their papers and left. Sensing Clifford's
disappointment over having lost the argument, Truman sought to cheer
him up. "Well, that was rough as a cob," he quipped, invoking an old Missouri farmers' expression. "I never saw the General so furious." Clifford
asked for approval to "test the waters" with Marshall "one more time."
Truman responded, "Suppose we let the dust settle a little—then you can
get into it again. . . . I still want to do it [that is, recognize the Jewish state].
But be careful."[91] Truman knew that if Marshall went public with his opposition or resigned, his election prospects would be doomed and the
Marshall Plan might never be implemented.

Fortunately, within an hour after the disastrous showdown in the
Oval Office, Bob Lovett telephoned Clifford and offered to help find a way
to avoid the unthinkable, a public break between Truman and Marshall
over the recognition issue. During drinks that evening at Lovett's house in
Kalorama, Clifford made the first concession, admitting that it would be a
mistake for Truman to promise recognition at his press conference the
next day before statehood had even been declared. However, Clifford said
that the president remained adamant: he intended to recognize the new
state as soon as it came into existence. "The thing for you to do," said Clifford to Lovett, "is to persuade General Marshall that he's wrong" to oppose
immediate recognition.[92]

Knowing that he could not possibly persuade Marshall that he was
wrong, Lovett came back on the thirteenth with a proposal to at least delay
recognition for a few days until the State Department could be assured
that the definition of boundaries and other details of the recognition proclamation conformed with the conditions of the UN General Assembly
resolution of November 29. Clifford said Truman would not agree to any
delay. His explanation, according to Lovett, was that the timing of recognition was of the "greatest possible importance to the President from a

domestic point of view."[93] If these were the words Clifford actually used, election year politics was clearly behind the president's decision for early recognition.

On the morning of the fourteenth, with no resolution in sight, Clifford compromised again. He informed Lovett that all Truman was asking was that Marshall agree to refrain from publicly opposing the president's decision. Lovett said he would take this proposal to Marshall. Time was running out. At six p.m. in Washington, which was midnight in Tel Aviv, the mandate would expire and the provisional government would promptly declare the existence of a new state—the name "Israel" had not yet been decided upon.

It wasn't until four o'clock that afternoon when Lovett finally called. "Clark, I think we have something we can work with. I have talked with the General. He cannot support the President's position, but he has agreed that he will not oppose it."[94] When asked later what he said to Marshall to persuade him, Lovett said, "I told him it was the president's choice."[95] Thereafter, Marshall continued to serve as secretary of state. He never spoke publicly of his rift with the president.

Israel's Declaration of Independence was proclaimed to the world by David Ben-Gurion from the Tel Aviv Museum of Art at 12:01 on May 15 (May 14 in Washington). Among its provisions was a promise of "complete equality of social and political rights of all of its inhabitants, irrespective of religion, race, or sex," a promise that has since been repeatedly broken in the case of Palestinian Arabs.[96] Truman's statement was read to the White House press corps at 6:11 p.m. "The United States recognizes the provisional government as the de facto authority of the new State of Israel."[97] De facto as opposed to de jure recognition meant that the U.S. acknowledged the existence of the new state and that its provisional government could carry out its obligations, whereas de jure status would have recognized borders and permitted ambassadors to be exchanged. De jure status would be conferred in due course.

Truman's announcement surprised almost everyone. At the UN in Flushing Meadows, the American delegates, who were still pursuing truce and trusteeship, were shocked and thoroughly disgusted that they had not been told in advance. Delegate Eleanor Roosevelt complained to Secretary Marshall that the U.S. policy of "going it alone" without consultation had undermined the UN and eroded trust in the leadership of the United States. In his letter of reply, Marshall wrote that he regretted the effect that Truman's announcement had on the UN delegates, but "more than this I am not free to say."[98] While the savvy former First Lady probably guessed from Marshall's remark that domestic politics had played a role, Bob Lovett revealed his true feelings concerning the recognition decision in a May 17 memorandum that remained classified for thirty years. "My protests," wrote Lovett, "as to the consequences" of Truman's decision "were outweighed by considerations unknown to me, but I can only conclude that the President's political advisors, having failed [at the showdown on May 12] to make the President the father of the new state, have determined at least to make him the midwife."[99] From this, it seems obvious that Lovett went to his grave believing that Truman's chief political adviser, Clark Clifford, was mainly responsible for Truman's recognition decision and that it was made, at least in part, for political reasons.

While the extent to which domestic politics influenced Truman will never be known, his decision to recognize Israel, and to make the United States the first nation to do so, boosted his standing with Jewish as well as thousands of other voters in America who sympathized with the quest for a homeland. On May 14, the evening in the U.S. that Israel was born, the president spoke to the Young Democrats at the Mayflower Hotel. With restored confidence, "Candidate Truman" announced that "for the next four years there will be a Democrat in the White House. And you're looking at him!"[100]

In the early hours of Saturday, May 15, the last British official boarded the cruiser *Euralysus* at Haifa harbor and departed Palestine. As dawn broke on the Sabbath, the day of rest and worship, Egyptian bombers appeared over Tel Aviv. The second phase of the Arab–Israeli War began, thus transforming it from a civil war to a war between Arab states and the state of Israel. Equipped with tanks, armored cars, artillery, and planes, the armed forces of Egypt invaded Israel, heading north through the Negev and along the coast leading to Tel Aviv. The armies of Syria, Iraq, and Lebanon invaded from the northeast with the objective of cutting Galilee off from the rest of Israel. Advancing from the east, Jordanian king Abdullah's British-trained Arab Legion planned to seize control of the West Bank but stop short of entering Jewish territory, a move by the king that would undermine the Arab war strategy.

By morning, on Washington's Embassy Row, a handmade flag was displayed outside the Jewish Agency's headquarters. It was emblazoned with a Star of David against a white background and bordered by two blue stripes symbolizing the stripes of the tallit, the traditional Jewish prayer shawl. Inside the White House, Truman walked into a roomful of jubilant aides who had gathered in Matt Connelly's office for their regular Saturday meeting. The president spotted Max Lowenthal, who had drafted several memos for Clifford arguing that recognition of Israel was in the national interest. Truman asked why he was looking so happy. Lowenthal replied, "I am smiling because you are going to win the election."[101]

S hortly before his death, President Roosevelt confessed to his only failure as president—his inability to solve the "problem" of a home for the Jews in Palestine. Knowing from his talks with King Ibn Saud at the Great Bitter Lake in February 1945 that a major holy war would surely erupt if he supported the Zionists, FDR said a decision either for or against their cause would have to wait until "some future time."[102] Though Harry Truman also did not solve the problem, he at least stepped into the arena and made a decision—a decision opposed by Marshall, the State Department, and the military brass. As we have seen, the president's actions leading up to his decision were halting and disjointed. At times he appeared to be ambivalent. But he eventually got there. His decision conferred legitimacy on the new state and thus was essential to Israel's "Caesarean birth."[103] Years later, David Ben-Gurion brought Truman to tears when he told him that his "courageous decision to recognize our new state so quickly and his steadfast support since then had given him an immortal place in Jewish history."[104]

Like Roosevelt, Truman knew there would be war. However, he could never have dreamed that there would be no end to the fighting.

Chapter 11

Pour It On, Harry

By the spring of 1948, Harry Truman still had not fully emerged from FDR's long but fading shadow. Two months before the Democratic convention was to convene in Philadelphia, party leaders, delegates, and prominent New Dealers were complaining that Truman was a "lousy" speaker, meaning that his voice went flat as soon as he began reading his speeches and that he seemed to be merely mouthing the words written for him. "Too bad we don't have Roosevelt," they were saying. DNC chair Senator Howard McGrath asked Jack Redding, his perceptive publicity director, what could be done. Redding responded that the problem was that the speechwriters and advisers were trying to "picture the President as FDR" while Truman himself was perhaps unconsciously attempting "to force himself into the Roosevelt mold." This was a mistake, Redding advised. "Roosevelt was an Eastern aristocrat, educated at Groton and Harvard. Truman is a Midwestern farmer."

As Redding recalled, he composed a memorandum to McGrath recommending that "for campaign purposes the greatest assets Mr. Truman had were his forthright manner and his smile. Put him on the rear end of a train," he advised. "If people see him in person . . . his personality, his smile, his manner of approach, his sincerity [will] all come through perfectly." The people, argued Redding, would sense that Harry Truman was authentic to the bone. They "will trust him. Trusting him they will vote for him."[1] McGrath wholeheartedly endorsed Redding's memo, especially the part about Truman speaking from the end of a train. He immediately forwarded it to the White House.

———

During May 1948, the idea of putting Truman on the rear end of a train so that the people could see and hear him in person blossomed into a concrete plan that had two objectives: first, to allow the president to practice and hone an off-the-cuff, extemporaneous speaking style that would play to his strengths; and second, to dispel the gloom and pessimism about Truman's electability that was being spread by the polls and the press and picked up by Democratic Party leaders. Following the Rowe–Clifford "Politics of 1948" memo, the plan called for a train trip that would take the president through the West, the region described in the script as the "Land of Electoral Votes" and the "Number One Priority for the Democrats," where he would take his case directly to the people.[2] The pretext for this "nonpolitical" inspection tour was an invitation, arranged by Clifford, for the president to receive an honorary degree and deliver the commencement address at the University of California. Because the trip would be regarded as "official business," it would be financed out of Truman's $30,000 annual travel allowance (the DNC did not have the funds).

Truman's "shakedown cruise," as Clifford called it, was not only aimed at improving his speaking style and electability; it was also designed to head off a looming threat to his nomination at the forthcoming Democratic convention.[3] As if the president did not have enough problems with the Southern revolt, the far-left New Dealers, and the Wallace candidacy, a "Dump Truman" movement was gaining traction. It had been organized in March by union leaders, big-city bosses, the California Democratic Party, chairman of Americans for Democratic Action (ADA) Leon Henderson, Hubert Humphrey, and, most worrisome of all, three of Franklin and Eleanor Roosevelt's sons. Members of the movement were convinced that Truman could not possibly win in the general election against Governor Tom Dewey, who was almost certain to be the GOP nominee. Polls showed that in a head-to-head race against Dewey, Truman would lose by 9 percentage points. The main effort of the Dump Truman alliance was to convince Dwight Eisenhower, then serving as Columbia University president, to enter the race as a Democrat before the convention. At the time, Truman appeared to have the nomination well in hand against any conceivable Democratic opponent. However, Eisenhower would have been a game changer.

Of the three Roosevelt sons promoting the Dump Truman movement, thirty-three-year-old Franklin Jr., "the party's golden hope" in the eyes of many Democrats, was the most influential.[4] He had become a player in New York politics and would be elected to Congress in 1949. Despite being told by Eisenhower that he would not enter the race, Franklin Jr. persisted. He called his mother, a UN delegate appointed by Truman, and read her a "draft Eisenhower" statement that he proposed to make. Because he did not ask her opinion and she did not object, Franklin Jr. went public with his statement. His older brother James ("Jimmy") Roosevelt, age forty, who was chair of the California State Democratic Central Committee and was planning to run for governor, also endorsed Eisenhower, as did their brother Elliott, a businessman and author who was married to actress Faye Emerson.

With three of her sons backing an Eisenhower draft, Eleanor Roosevelt wrote Truman and told him that she "would not presume to dictate" their stance. While she pledged to stay out of preconvention politics, she warned him that "the younger Democrats," meaning her sons and others, believed that the party would go "down to serious defeat" in the 1948 federal elections.[5] It was an indirect suggestion that if Truman became the nominee, he would not only lose, but he would be a drag on down-ballot Democrats. On April 29, when Mrs. Roosevelt came out of Truman's office after a fifteen-minute meeting, she brusquely declined to answer questions from reporters about whether she intended to endorse the president, which caused some of them to draw a negative conclusion. Responding to a letter from May Craig, a sympathetic journalist who asked for clarification, the former First Lady wrote, "I haven't made up my mind."[6] If that weren't enough to discourage Truman and his supporters, there is evidence that she had made up her mind but not in the direction that favored the president. According to Minneapolis mayor and future senator Hubert Humphrey's memoir, *The Education of a Public Man*, which was published in 1991, Mrs. Roosevelt called him several times in the spring of 1948 to promote the draft-Eisenhower campaign.[7] It wasn't until late October, well after Truman had been nominated, that she publicly endorsed him. Even then, she privately felt that he was a "weak and vacillating" leader and that he would be defeated by Dewey.[8]

Given the facts that Truman had tried to do everything he could to perpetuate the Roosevelt legacy and that he had carried on an intimate correspondence with the former First Lady while supporting her work for the UN, it must have been disheartening if not infuriating for the president to know that the Roosevelt family, whose patriarch had selected Truman to be his running mate and successor, would not support him at the convention. However, except for an angry encounter with one of the Roosevelt sons in Los Angeles, the president bit his tongue. Above all, he needed Eleanor Roosevelt on his political team when the campaign heated up in the fall. Aside from Eisenhower, she was the most respected and admired person in American public life.

———

It was almost 11 p.m. on June 3 when Truman arrived at Union Station to board "the Presidential Special" for his two-week shakedown cruise to the West. Most of the working staff and traveling press had already settled down in their staterooms and berths on the train. Accompanied by the Secret Service and a few aides, Truman waved hi and shook hands as he made his way through the group of cabinet members who were there to see him off as well as many others in the station who were attracted by the commotion. Before the train departed, Truman posed for a photo op on the spacious open platform at the rear of the president's 142-ton armored railcar dubbed the *Ferdinand Magellan*, which he had inherited from FDR. Looking dapper and fit in a light double-breasted suit and polka-dot tie,

Truman responded to a question about how he felt, which had been shouted by a reporter over the noise of the locomotive. "If I felt any better I couldn't stand it."[9]

The next morning, as the seventeen-car train descended the last of the Appalachian foothills and raced westward, Truman, as usual, rose early, then shaved and showered in his private stateroom. Before long, the train rolled to a stop on an embankment just outside the village of Crestline, Ohio, which was located near the Sandusky River. In 1948 Crestline was anything but a sleepy village. Since WWI, it had been the site of a major railway crossroads with a huge brick roundhouse that sheltered a turntable, thirty stalls, and machine and repair shops. Adjacent to the roundhouse were sprawling railroad yards that accommodated hundreds of locomotives and freight and passenger cars. Truman could see through the green-tinted bulletproof windows of the *Ferdinand Magellan* that about a thousand railroad workers, county farmers, and their families were seated on the embankment and milling about the canopied rear platform adorned with the presidential seal. More than eighty years earlier, at 4 in the morning, crowds of mourners had gathered at this place to catch sight of Abraham Lincoln's funeral train as it slowly passed through the village on its way home to Springfield.

When Truman stepped through the blue velvet curtain onto the rear platform, the crowd was surprised. Rather than the small, bungling haberdasher portrayed in news articles and cartoons, they saw a rather attractive, normal-size man who had a friendly grin and oozed vitality. Truman's beginning words, the words that kicked off his historic 1948 political campaign—the fight of his life—were plain and personal. As if he were a Crestline neighbor, he drew them into his world. "The President, you know, is virtually in jail." He paused. Laughter rippled through the crowd. "He goes from his study to his office and from his office to his study, and he has to have guards all the time." More laughter. "But when you get out and see people and find out what people are thinking about, you can do a better job as a President of the United States." Some clapped; a few whistled. He was likable. Then, acknowledging that his trip had been publicized as "nonpolitical," the president proceeded to make fun of that characterization. With a wink and a grin, he claimed that his journey west across Ohio was a "nonpartisan, bipartisan trip." Again, he paused. The crowd, mostly Republicans, appreciated the joke and laughed with him. He continued: "I understand there are a whole lot of Democrats present too." At that point, former Ohio governor Frank Lausche, a Democrat who was running for a second term, was said to have come out onto the platform. Truman declared, "I know he is going to be the next Governor of Ohio."[10] Nonpolitical? Hardly.

With stops in Fort Wayne and Gary, Indiana, and a ride in an open car with Chicago mayor Martin Kennelly from the train station in Chicago to the Palmer House, which was witnessed by a crowd of a hundred thousand, Truman's first day on the hustings was a success. They had yet to reach the West but Truman and his advisers could tell from the reactions of the large crowds that the labor vote was solid and that the farmers who voted Republican in 1944 might be open to persuasion, especially because Truman had been a Midwest farmer himself.

Bess and Margaret joined Truman when the Presidential Special arrived in Omaha, often called the "Gateway to the West" (though St. Louis and Independence also laid claim to the phrase). Omaha was surrounded by stockyards and meatpacking factories, and the lengthy packinghouse strike of 1948 had just ended. The citizens were in a celebratory mood. Despite the fact that the city was staunchly Republican, the president "thrilled and charmed" a crowd of 160,000 in the morning, when he marched in a parade through downtown with his old Battery D outfit and waved his Western-style hat right and left to cheering onlookers. He "never looked more pleased," wrote the *Omaha Morning World-Herald*.[11] That evening, it was a different story. Truman was scheduled to deliver a speech on farm issues at the Ak-Sar-Ben ("Nebraska" spelled backward) Coliseum, a venue outside Omaha that seated ten thousand. Due to sloppy advance work by Truman's WWI friend Eddie McKim, when the president walked onstage and approached the microphones, he could see that there were very few there in the vast auditorium except reporters and photographers. Yet Truman didn't seem to care. As he explained later to McKim, since his speech was to be broadcast by radio and the farmers outside Omaha would be at home listening, he "didn't give a damn" about who was in the arena. The farmers "are the ones I am going to talk to," he told McKim.[12]

Accordingly, the president launched into his speech as if the auditorium were packed. He excoriated the failure of the GOP-dominated 80th Congress to act on the farm bill and implored the farmers who were listening to throw the Republicans out of office by voting for Democrats. While Truman was holding forth, flashbulbs popped as photographers took photos of him speaking to a nearly empty hall and reporters scribbled notes. Publication of the photos and news stories of the Truman administration's ineptitude fueled opinion throughout the country that the campaign was a joke and a waste of time. Appointments secretary Matt Connelly probably overstated the impact of the Omaha incident, remarking, "It was almost the death knell for the campaign."[13] On the other hand, Truman later told McKim, "It was one of the best things that happened to me in my whole campaign. It made a martyr out of me."[14]

Except for a few brief stops, the Presidential Special sped in a long arc almost due west across Nebraska and Wyoming to Carey, a city in southern Idaho that had been founded by Mormons and that had grown to more than six hundred residents by 1948. The mayor had invited Truman to speak at the dedication of a new airport. The president was informed by his aide Harry Vaughan that the airport was to be named after a young man who had been killed in the war. Whether he told him that the airport was to be named "Willa Coates" is not known. When Truman, during the ceremony, said he "was honored to dedicate this airport and present this wreath to the parents of the brave boy who fought for his country," he was startled to hear a low murmur emanating from the crowd. A woman, almost in tears, spoke up. "Mr. President, it wasn't my son. It was my daughter Willa" who, she explained, had been killed in a plane crash nearby.[15] Truman, of course, was deeply embarrassed and apologized profusely. The reporters traveling with him gleefully pounced on the mistake. Coming on the heels of the Omaha debacle, the stories of Truman's gaffe that appeared in newspapers across the country added to the impression that his campaign was a clown show. In the motorcade to Idaho Falls, where his train was waiting, Truman rode in silence. He did not lash out at Vaughan or the Secret Service agent who was actually responsible. There would be a few more mishaps along the way, but fortunately for Truman, this was the last major blunder of his Western campaign trip.

That evening, for the first time, Truman "hit his stride," recalled Robert Nixon, a White House correspondent who was on the train as a reporter for the International News Service. "He began to talk instead of orating," stressed Nixon, "using his Missouri dialect . . . natural in every way."[16] The setting was Naranche Stadium in Butte, Montana, a copper mining boomtown two hundred miles north of Idaho Falls as the crow flies. Perhaps it was the enthusiasm and size of the crowd (forty thousand), which were way out of proportion to the city, but whatever it was, reporters and staffers could sense that something was happening. Truman began not by reading a prepared speech but by introducing Bess ("the Boss") and Margaret ("the Boss's Boss"). He complimented the local band and asked it to play "one more piece before I have to speak." The proud band members played Sousa's "Stars and Stripes Forever." The crowd responded positively to Truman's relaxed, folksy touch. "There is a melody in his voice," wrote *Nation's Business*.[17] The president's theme was the do-nothing 80th Congress, which, he made clear, was controlled by the Republicans. "If this Congress," he declared, adjourned "without passing an agricultural bill, without passing a housing bill, without doing something about prices, this Congress has not done anything for the country." With a pace and sincerity that had been lacking in previous speeches, he said in his straightforward Midwestern way, "I am here to tell you the truth, which you haven't been getting."[18]

After an all-night ride over Northern Pacific tracks to Spokane, Washington, Truman made an unscheduled appearance that bolstered his standing with the labor movement. Having been informed early that morning by the state's governor that the Communications Workers of America were meeting in Spokane and had been complaining about the unfairness of the Taft–Hartley Act, Truman decided on the spur of the moment to speak to them from the rear platform of the *Ferdinand Magellan*. He began by confiding that he was keeping a huge crowd downtown waiting (they thought he had gone "AWOL," he said) and that "nobody but you knows I am here." The only way to get rid of Taft–Hartley, he advised, was for them and other Democrats to vote in November 1948. If the union members didn't get others to the polls, he warned, "It's your fault and not mine." His hands were tied, he explained. "I have to enforce" the act until it is repealed.[19] The union leaders and members were impressed. They came away committed and energized. It wasn't so much Truman's words as it was the fact that the president of the United States, while keeping the mayor and townspeople waiting, took time out of his tight schedule to speak bluntly to them.

Before a huge midmorning crowd ("2 or 3 acres of people," said Truman) outside the Spokane Club, Truman started by referring to the fact that he was wearing a hat because his face had been "fried" the day before by the "Western sun" and he did not want it "turned over" like a hamburger and fried again.[20] Noting that large populated areas adjacent to the nearby Columbia River had suffered the most destructive floods in more than fifty years, Truman lamented that the disaster could have been averted if only the 80th Congress had been willing to finance reclamation projects in the Northwest, just as earlier Congresses had stepped up when FDR was president. Back then, Truman added, "I happened to be a Member [of Congress]" and was "in favor of these things." In those days, Truman claimed, the chairmen of the key committees believed "in the theory of Daniel Webster that the West is no good and there is no use wasting money" on flood-control projects, a popular but by no means scholarly interpretation of Webster's views. "You have a chance to remedy" this situation in the fall elections, urged the president, and if you don't vote for Democrats "I won't have any sympathy with you. You will get what you deserve."[21] Again, he was direct and blunt.

Later that afternoon, eighty-six miles from Spokane, the president's motorcade reached the road that traversed the top of the Grand Coulee Dam, one of the marvels of New Deal engineering, which had taken nine years during the Roosevelt administration to complete. The dozens of White House reporters traveling ahead of the motorcade had missed hearing a controversial statement made by Truman to Rhea Felknor, a local reporter, back at the Spokane train station. They were clamoring for confirmation. Was it true, one of them yelled to the president over the sound of roaring water, that he had told Felknor that the 80th was "the worst Congress in the United States" and that his Spokane newspaper and the *Chicago Tribune* were "responsible for it?"[22] Truman shouted back that they could stand on his statement to Felknor since it was already out on the wire services (although Truman subsequently conceded that the Congress during Reconstruction after the Civil War was probably the worst, with the 80th a close second).

Back in Washington, DC, when Truman's "Worst Congress" remark made the headlines, Senator Taft, as the leader of 80th Congress on domestic issues, was not only angry; he was deeply offended. From his point of view, the 80th was a smashing success. After all, he had engineered passage of the anti-labor bill that bore his name. And among other accomplishments, he had organized the override of Truman's veto of the so-called rich man's tax bill. The Ohioan took Truman's attack personally, perhaps too much so. On June 11, Taft decided to hit back with a speech before the ultraconservative Union League of Philadelphia. In a talk that was also broadcast widely by radio, Taft accused "our gallivanting president" of "blackguarding Congress at whistlestops all across the country."[23] In railroad parlance, a whistle-stop was a small city or town so insignificant that it did not warrant regularly scheduled train service. Therefore, trains had to be signaled by a whistle from the community if any passengers wished to board.

At the DNC Jack Redding saw Taft's whistle-stop sentence as a political "opening too good to miss." Almost immediately, the DNC polled the mayors and chambers of commerce of thirty-five cities on Truman's itinerary, asking them to please wire whether they "agree with Senator Taft's description of your city as a 'whistle stop.'" Most of the responses made a mockery of Taft and by proxy the Republican Party. For example, the chamber of commerce of Laramie, Wyoming, wrote, "Characteristically, Senator Taft is confused, this time on whistles." Similarly, the mayor of Eugene, Oregon, responded that Taft "must have the wrong city," while the mayor of Gary, Indiana, wired that "Senator Taft [is] in very poor taste.... 135,000 citizens of America's greatest steel city resent this slur."[24]

After Spokane, Truman spent the rest of the day (June 9) traveling west toward Seattle, delivering down-to-earth rear-platform talks that linked the need for flood control and reclamation projects to the indifference and inaction of the Republican-controlled 80th Congress. In effect, he was using the Columbia River flood disaster as a convenient justification for his attacks on the do-nothing Congress.

The next morning, at Bremerton, near the Navy Yard where FDR had spoken in 1944, Truman was on fire. He tore into the 80th Congress as he had never done before. The president told the crowd that "this Congress" was a "disgrace to this country" because it had done nothing to help the working poor by curbing inflation. The Republican members of Congress, he said, were about to adjourn for the nominating convention, where they would "tell you what a great Congress they have been." Caustically, he added, "If you believe that, you are bigger suckers than I think you are." A voice from the crowd cried out, "Pour it on, Harry!"[25]

And pour it on he did. After Truman took a ferry across Puget Sound to Seattle, a crowd of a hundred thousand, the largest in thirty years, greeted him at the pier, lined the streets as he drove past in an open car, and flooded into Seattle High School's Memorial Stadium. There, the president again invoked the Columbia River disaster, urging those present and a nationwide radio audience to join him in the "battle" to defeat influential Republicans in Congress who "look on the West as some sort of wilderness in which the Nation should invest in as little as possible." Then, on to stops in Tacoma and Olympia, he warned the people that if they "want to continue the policies of the 80th Congress, that will be your funeral."[26]

From the rear platform in Eugene, one of his final stops in Oregon, Truman made careless and uninformed remarks that caused an uproar in Washington, DC. In an extemporaneous riff about his meeting with Stalin in Potsdam, Truman confided to the crowd, "I like old Joe. He is a decent fellow. But Joe is a prisoner of the Politburo. He can't do what he wants to."[27] Robert Donovan, an enterprising reporter for the *New York Herald Tribune* who was traveling with the president, realized that for policymakers in Washington and a growing share of the American public, Truman's bizarre statement about Stalin would be not only newsworthy but highly controversial and damaging, especially in an election year. At the time, Stalin was stoking war anxiety by denying access to Berlin off and on as a prelude to forcing U.S. occupation troops and Berliners to withdraw from the city. Aware that Stalin had been complicit in the murder of millions of his own people during the 1930s, Donovan knew that the Soviet premier was hardly "a decent fellow" who was being manipulated by others. So the reporter dashed off a quick piece on Truman's remarks and paid a woman in the crowd $20 to telephone the story to his editor. It was published the next day in the morning edition. That afternoon, Undersecretary of State Bob Lovett called Clark Clifford to urge that the president repudiate his comments and commit never to repeat them. According to Clifford, he and Charlie Ross had the delicate task of telling the president that he had made a mistake. "The president listened to us quietly," wrote Clifford, and "after a moment, he said, 'Well, I guess I goofed,' and from then on there was no more affectionate talk about Stalin."[28]

At Davis, California, the last stop before Truman's commencement speech at Berkeley, which was the so-called reason for his "nonpolitical trip," Truman provided the fifty-plus hard-drinking reporters aboard the Presidential Special with two memorable lines for a stanza of a farcical ditty that columnist Thomas Stokes and other reporters had composed along the way. The stanza, part of a rollicking theme song for the Western trip, was sung to the tune of "Oh! Susanna."

> They can't prove nothing
> They ain't got a thing on me
> I'm going down to Berkeley
> Fur to get me a degree.[29]

The first two lines of the stanza poked fun at remarks blurted out by Truman from the rear platform in Pocatello, Idaho, which reminded listeners of his past association with the Pendergast machine.[30] The last two, delivered by Truman at Davis, spoke to the disdain of the East Coast educated elite, who regarded Truman as a dumb farmer undeserving of a college degree.[31] Those lines no doubt led to more than a few favorable votes from the millions of Americans who, like the president, had had to work on the family farm and had been unable to afford college.

At the traditional outdoor alumni box luncheon in Berkeley prior to commencement exercises, University of California president Dr. Robert Sproul's opening words were shocking, beyond the pale. According to speechwriter Charles Murphy, Dr. Sproul, a rock-ribbed Republican, began by saying, "It is very difficult to introduce this man"—meaning Truman, who was seated on the dais—"because if I said anything good about him I wouldn't believe it; and if I said anything bad about him it wouldn't be polite." Murphy recalled that "he actually cringed," wondering whether Sproul was serious and being unable to anticipate how Truman would react.[32] Apparently, Sproul was serious because he went on to inform Truman and the alumni that he was going to the Republican National Convention as a delegate in a few weeks.

Truman gave as good as he got. Standing at the podium, he looked over at Sproul and said with a hint of sarcasm, "I don't know how to accept the hospitality of the University of California when it is delivered in that graceful manner." Laughter erupted. Truman went on to say that while he was happy to be there "on a nonpolitical subject," he hoped that Dr. Sproul, when he went to the Republican convention, "will consult with me, because I have got a candidate I would like to see nominated there."[33] Truman grinned and laughed along with the alumni. Murphy later said that the president defused the tension, having done a "most beautiful job" of handling the awkward situation.[34]

Truman's foreign policy commencement speech in the Cal football stadium, delivered with dignity and poise to a capacity crowd of fifty-five thousand and a nationwide radio audience, was the best of his formal speeches during his Western whistle-stop tour, arguably the best of his career. It should have been, because it had been crafted by Pulitzer Prize–winning playwright Robert Sherwood, Judge Sam Rosenman, and Louis Nizer, one of the nation's foremost trial lawyers. The speech went through seven drafts. Attired in cap and gown, Truman asked rhetorically, "Why do we live today in a twilight period between war so dearly won and a peace that still eludes our grasp?" His answer: "The attitude of one nation—the Soviet Union." Its "refusal to work for world peace is the most bitter disappointment of our time." With the worsening situation in Berlin in the headlines, Truman declared, "We are not waging a 'Cold War.' . . . The cleavage that exists is not between the Soviet Union and the United States. It is between the Soviet Union and the free nations of the world." Without once uttering Stalin's name, he warned the USSR that the United States was determined to remain strong, yet "the door is always open for honest negotiation, looking toward genuine settlements. . . . Our policy," he concluded, "will continue to be a policy of recovery, reconstruction, prosperity—and peace with freedom and justice. In its furtherance, we will gladly join with all those of like purpose."[35]

Two mornings later, in Los Angeles, after the Presidential Special had arrived at Union Station, an estimated crowd of one million lined both sides of the flag-draped four-mile route to the historic Ambassador Hotel. They were hoping to glimpse President Truman as he smiled and waved from a slowly moving orange-colored open Cadillac. With skywriters spelling "Welcome President Truman" above the city and confetti showering the streets, Truman was enjoying one of the best days of his shakedown cruise to the West. Journalist Robert Donovan wrote that "[at] one corner a group of blacks displayed a sign: 'The Sixty-second District Republicans Welcome President Truman—Thanks for the Civil Rights Program.'"[36] If Truman had seen that message, he would have been very pleased.

At a packed luncheon, sponsored by the Greater Los Angeles Press Club, in the huge Embassy Ballroom in the Ambassador Hotel, the president, of course, was the keynote speaker. However, before he spoke, Dinah Shore, age thirty-two, the top female vocalist during the 1940s, serenaded Truman with the popular song that began: "You made me love you, I didn't want to do it, I didn't want to do it." Fittingly, the lyrics foreshadowed a political comeback. After Ms. Shore finished, Truman was said to have looked around and grinned.

Knowing that those in the press club audience would appreciate his joking reference to Senator Taft's recent blunder, Truman began his speech by observing that "Los Angeles is the biggest whistlestop." The remainder of his unusually long address was dead serious, a relentless and somewhat monotonous point-by-point attack on the failure of the 80th Congress to act on eight legislative measures that the president had proposed, starting with the most urgent, standby price controls.

As reporter Charles Lucey of the Scripps-Howard newspaper chain observed, each of the president's proposals "carried the banner of Franklin Roosevelt."[37] But neither Lucey nor the other reporters traveling on the Presidential Special noted that Truman failed to mention civil rights, a cause that set Truman apart from FDR. Though significant numbers of Blacks, Hispanics, and other minorities lived in Los Angeles at the time, Truman had apparently decided that bringing up civil rights before an almost 100 percent white audience would not benefit his campaign. In fact, except for an oblique reference during a speech to Swedish immigrants in Chicago, the president never mentioned his civil rights program in any of the seventy-three speeches and talks he delivered on his whirl through eighteen states in the spring of 1948.[38]

An hour or so after the press club luncheon, Jimmy Roosevelt was ushered into the presidential suite at the Ambassador Hotel to meet with Truman. Cocky and full of himself, FDR's eldest son had asked for the meeting, thinking that, as chair of California's Democratic Central Committee, he might persuade Truman to step aside for the good of the party and to allow Eisenhower to accept the Democratic nomination. For his part, Truman, who was well aware that Jimmy was a leader of the draft-Eisenhower movement, had agreed to the meeting hoping that he might make an ally of FDR's powerful son by convincing him that Eisenhower was not ready to run. Given their clashing motives, the meeting quickly turned into a disaster. Secret Service agent Henry Nicholson, the only other person in the living room, watched as the younger man, the alpha male, closed in on the president, using his towering six-foot-four height and broad frame as instruments of intimidation. Truman did not back down. The next thing Nicholson saw was Truman poking his finger into Roosevelt's chest. "Your father asked me to take this job," Nicholson recalled Truman saying. "I didn't want it. . . . But your father asked me to take it and I took it." Truman angrily continued. "If your father knew what you are doing to me, he would turn over in his grave. But get this straight: whether you like it or not, I am going to be the next President of the United States. That will be all. Good day."[39] He walked into an adjoining room, leaving FDR's son speechless.

That evening, June 14, the Presidential Special turned eastward, heading back to Washington, DC. After an unscheduled pause at Barstow in the Mojave Desert, where Truman, in bathrobe and pajamas, greeted a small gathering of citizens, his train barreled into Kansas, the midpoint between the West and East Coasts. From the rear platform in Dodge City, Truman told the crowd that he had "definitely fixed the issues which are before the country."[40] He was sure that his campaign strategy had resonated. Now it was up to the people, an estimated three million of whom had laid eyes on him during his fifteen-day, 9,505-mile trip.

By the time Truman arrived in the nation's capital, three days before the start of the Republican convention, the Washington newspapers had thrown cold water on his shakedown cruise. The *Post* and *Star* wrote that instead of demeaning the office by making a spectacle of himself on a political junket, the president should have stayed at home. Journalists who had been on the train and witnessed the surging crowds were not so sure. Barnet Nover of the *Denver Post* was cautiously optimistic. Referring to Harry Truman, he wrote, "He has begun to make an impression."[41]

While the president was out campaigning, his administration and its counterparts in Britain and France had agreed to merge their three occupation zones in Germany into a single West German state. The plan, approved by Truman, was to integrate the new state into the European community of nations, fit it into the Marshall Plan, and stabilize its economy through currency reform. On June 18, the day Truman returned to the White House, General Clay notified the Soviet Union that in forty-eight hours the virtually worthless reichsmark would be replaced by a new currency, called the "deutsche mark," which would be circulated throughout West Germany at a fixed and stable exchange rate, though initially not in the Western sectors of Berlin. Clay's decision, together with the actions leading up to it, brought the United States and the Soviet Union to the precipice of war.

Because currency is a "symbol of sovereignty and a mechanism for exercising sovereignty," wrote Daniel Yergin in *Shattered Peace*, the Soviets strongly objected to what appeared to be a permanent division between East and West Germany and they feared the takeover of all of Berlin by the Western powers.[42] As expected, the Soviets retaliated by declaring the deutsche mark illegal and announcing that they would introduce their own currency, the ostmark, into East Germany and Berlin, including the sectors in the city allocated to the U.S., Britain, and France. This attempt to exercise sovereignty over West Berlin could not be tolerated. On June 23, the Western Allies hit back by suddenly introducing 250 million crisp deutsche marks into their sectors of Berlin. The following day, the day that Governor Dewey accepted the GOP nomination, Stalin made a decision that he would later regret. He ordered that all overland access to West Berlin from West Germany via roads, rail, and canals be blockaded "because of technical difficulties."[43] In addition, Stalin's minions halted all deliveries of coal and food to the Western sectors of Berlin and cut off supplies of electricity from East Berlin. Overnight, Berliners in the Western sectors were isolated, effectively imprisoned more than one hundred miles inside Soviet territory. Stalin's cynical aim was to rid West Berlin of its 2.5 million people through slow starvation. He gambled that with only a month's worth of food and coal, the citizens and Western occupiers would either stay and die or the Western Allies would be forced to evacuate all of them from the city. It was just a matter of time. Seventy-four years later, Vladimir Putin, the "History Man" who revered Stalin for building a "great country," would take a similar gamble, although instead of starvation he would try to ensure victory by deploying artillery and committing atrocities against civilians to decimate, drive out, and overwhelm the forty-four million people living in Ukraine.[44]

The situation in Berlin was fraught with danger. Clay repeatedly recommended that the Western Allies should break the blockade by sending armed convoys by rail or autobahn to Berlin. Since this risked a shooting war, he was rebuffed by General Omar Bradley and the other Joint Chiefs in Washington. They were against a military operation. The alternative was a humanitarian effort to supply the beleaguered Berliners with food, fuel, and other necessities by air. An airlift was less likely to be challenged by the Soviets because access by aircraft through three twenty-mile-wide air corridors to and from Berlin was guaranteed by a written agreement, whereas overland access was pursuant to an oral understanding that the Soviets claimed was no longer operative. As to who should be credited for originating the airlift idea, Foreign Secretary Bevin deserves to be first in line because it was he who had the vision to immediately order a feasibility study. A three-way tie for second place should go to Air Commodore Reginald "Rex" Waite (RAF), a logistics expert who quickly concluded that it

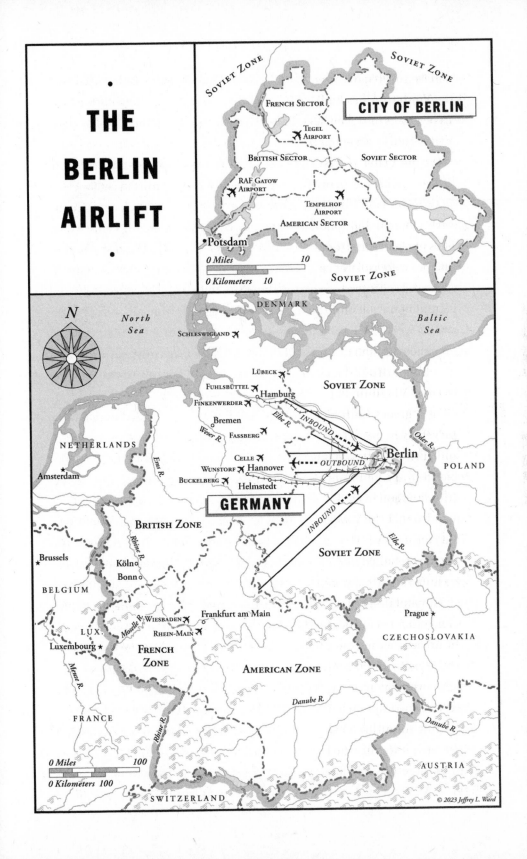

would be possible to supply the city by air, and Generals Lucius Clay and Brian Robertson (Clay's British counterpart), who actually "started" the airlift. "Our primary purpose," said Clay to an interviewer, "was to show that we could make enough landings to do the job."[45]

According to the president's daily appointments calendar, at 11:59 a.m. on Saturday, June 26, 1948, Truman "ordered a Berlin airlift in conjunction with the British."[46] Clay's initial move was to prevail upon General Curtis LeMay, commander of U.S. air forces in Europe, to assign his entire fleet of C-47 transports to the Berlin Airlift. When Clay asked LeMay whether his planes could carry coal, LeMay responded, "We can haul anything."[47] That day, Clay ordered the first flight of thirty-two C-47s, collectively carrying eighty tons of milk, flour, and medicine, to fly from airfields in West Germany over Soviet-occupied East Germany and drop off their cargoes at Tempelhof Airport in West Berlin. Shortly thereafter British Yorks and Dakotas (Douglas DC-3s) joined the airlift, flying their cargoes from Hamburg into Gatow Airport in the British sector of Berlin.

On Monday, June 28, with Marshall out at Walter Reed undergoing tests by kidney specialists, his undersecretary Bob Lovett and the secretaries of defense (Forrestal) and army (Ken Royall) gathered in the Oval Office at half past noon. There was considerable uncertainty among the group as to how long the airlift could be sustained and what the future policy in Berlin and West Germany itself should be. When Lovett mentioned the possibility of withdrawal from Berlin, Truman interrupted: "We are going to stay. Period." Royall suggested that the consequences had not been fully thought through, namely the risk of war. "We will have to deal with the situation as it develops," Truman said. "We are in Berlin by the terms of an agreement, and the Russians have no right to get us out by either direct or indirect pressure."[48] For Truman it was as simple as that. He would look back on his decision as one of his proudest moments.

At the same meeting Truman "expressed affirmative approval" for sending two groups of B-29s to Germany, and "Lovett announced casually that he assumed that two other groups of B-29s would go to England."[49] His assumption was correct. At the time a single group of B-29 heavy bombers consisted of approximately thirty planes. The rationale for increasing the number of B-29s in England and Germany was deterrence.

The Soviets knew that the high-altitude, long-range Superfortresses could easily reach Moscow and other targets deep within Russia, and that they were the type of plane that had delivered atomic bombs to Hiroshima and Nagasaki (they probably did not know, however, that the B-29s sent to Germany and the UK had not been fitted to carry atomic bombs). The purpose of having B-29s in the West was to deter the Red Army from trying to shoot down the C-47s and C-54s or otherwise prevent them from landing in Berlin. On the other hand, because the arrival of the huge bombers at bases in England and West Germany would quickly become known to the public and the Kremlin, there was a risk that their presence would be seen as a provocative act that might backfire and cause the Soviets to initiate hostilities. It was a delicate balance but Truman thought it was the right decision.

After receiving the approval of Truman, Marshall announced to the world on June 30 that the U.S. government expected to "deal promptly" with "questions of serious import" raised by the Soviet blockade but that "meanwhile" it intended to stay in Berlin and make "maximum use of air transport" to "supply [its] civilian population." The final sentence of Marshall's statement was odd. It said that the tonnage of supplies that could be lifted by air was not yet predictable, thus suggesting that the airlift might not work.[50] Why was this caveat added? Because Truman as well as Marshall wanted the Soviets to think that even if the airlift failed—which most experts believed it would—the U.S. had the atomic bomb in its back pocket and was prepared to use it.[51]

––––––––––

With scarcely a week before the opening of the Democratic National Convention, Harry Truman's presidential prospects were bleak. His job approval rating stood at a disappointing 36 percent. Powerful leaders in his own party, convinced that Truman could not win back the presidency, were still trying to persuade Eisenhower, or if not him some other alternative, to jump into the race for the nomination. Southern segregationists were on the verge of abandoning the Democrats, while Truman was concerned about the Wallace movement on the left, which appealed to liberals and Northern Blacks. Preoccupied with the Berlin Airlift and other duties,

Truman was behind schedule, having not yet vetted and chosen a running mate who could improve his chances of winning. Meanwhile, the Republicans had nominated a heavily financed bicoastal ticket of Governor Tom Dewey of New York and California governor Earl Warren, a strong vote-getting pair from electoral-rich states who pollsters and pundits predicted would beat Truman and whomever he selected.

Over the July Fourth weekend, the "Dump Truman / nominate Eisenhower" drive reached its peak even though Eisenhower had repeatedly issued statements of disinterest and little was known about his political views. Big-city bosses Jacob "Jake" Arvey (Chicago) and Frank Hague (Jersey City) announced that they would withdraw their support for Truman and throw the votes of their delegates in Illinois and New Jersey to Eisenhower. Jimmy Roosevelt persuaded eighteen party leaders to send to each of the 1,592 delegates telegrams that urged them to arrive at the convention two days early for a caucus to select Eisenhower. In his diary, Truman labeled Jimmy and the others "doublecrossers all."[52] The *New York Times* reported on July 5 that support for Eisenhower was increasing and that the president was "facing a hard and possibly losing fight for the nomination" because "sentiment for the nomination of General Eisenhower has spread like wildfire."[53]

Three days before the convention began, Truman doused the flames. Following a political "bull session" in the White House about the Eisenhower groundswell, Truman asked Army Secretary Ken Royall, who was close to Eisenhower, to try to talk the general into issuing a statement clarifying once and for all that he was not available. He succeeded. With Ike's consent and Clifford's help, Royall drafted a Shermanesque statement that Eisenhower signed and sent to Senator Claude Pepper, Eisenhower's most active supporter, for public release: "No matter under what terms, conditions or premises a proposal might be couched, I would refuse to accept the nomination."[54] Thus ended the Eisenhower boomlet of 1948.

With Eisenhower out of the picture and time running out, Leon Henderson, a New Dealer who was chair of ADA, attempted to generate enthusiasm for Supreme Court associate justice William O. Douglas as an alternative to Truman. "The Democratic party must choose Douglas or invite a disaster," he proclaimed.[55] Douglas had been covertly angling to have a shot at replacing Truman as president, and he made it known to close associates that he would accept the nomination if offered. Nevertheless, Henderson's effort fizzled because Truman's overall political support for the nomination had begun to stabilize and there wasn't enough time for the ADA New Deal liberals to convince a large enough number of delegates to back Douglas. On Sunday, the day before the convention began, the ADA board voted to endorse Truman, and informed Douglas, who was fishing in Oregon's Wallowa Mountains. He was deeply disappointed. The last person standing in the way of Truman was none other than ultraliberal senator Claude Pepper. On the eve of the convention, Pepper announced that he was running for the nomination in place of Eisenhower. However, because his foreign policy ideas were dangerously close to those of Wallace, his candidacy lasted for less than a day.

Due to the fracturing of the party and doubts about Truman's electability, the 1948 Democratic National Convention opened on July 12 in an atmosphere of despair. "You could cut the gloom with a corn knife," recalled Senator Alben Barkley (D-KY). "The very air smelled of defeat," not to mention the oppressive heat and humidity.[56] Though the Philadelphia Convention Hall had been renovated for both the Democratic convention and the earlier Republican one, it lacked air-conditioning. Around and above the rostrum, the banks of blindingly hot television lights caused temperatures to exceed 90 degrees throughout the three days of proceedings. The 1948 Republican and Democratic conventions were the first ever to be televised. The four networks (NBC, CBS, ABC, and DuMont) reached an audience of ten million.

On Monday, the first day of the convention, while the president was working in the air-conditioned Oval Office, he occasionally looked up and watched the opening speeches on a twelve-inch black-and-white RCA TV set that had been installed on a table to the left of his desk. Around noon the White House operator told the president that Justice Douglas was calling from the Benson Hotel in Portland, Oregon. Truman had been waiting to hear from him. Since the previous Friday, when he had asked Douglas to join the ticket as his vice president and followed up with two more calls over the weekend, Douglas had strung him along by repeating that he needed time to think it over (Truman was not aware that Douglas had been quietly campaigning for the presidential nomination). Convinced that the dynamic forty-nine-year-old justice would add luster to the ticket and help him attract votes from Blacks, labor, and the West, Truman tolerated the delays. He picked up the phone, expecting that Douglas would accept. "I am very sorry," said Douglas, "but I have decided not to get into politics. I do not think I should use the Court as a stepping stone." Truman was furious but all he could say was "I am disappointed. That's too bad."[57]

Douglas's brush-off was disingenuous. As his ADA supporters knew, he was perfectly willing to use the Court as a stepping stone if it led to the presidency. However, he could not throw away lifetime employment by joining what he and most others believed was a losing cause. "It was money and security," wrote his biographer Bruce Allen Murphy, plus a dream that he might one day be president, that dictated Douglas's decision.[58]

For Truman, Douglas's refusal was a personal rebuke and a waste of time. Recalling how he had assiduously courted the justice, Truman remarked to his staff, "I stuck my neck all the way out for Douglas, and he cut the limb out from under me."[59] In his diary on the night of July 12, Truman wrote that he was "inclined to give some credence" to the rumor that Douglas had bragged that "he could 'not' be a no. 2 man to a No. 2 man."[60]

Having been spurned by Douglas, the president and his team decided that "Old man Barkley," as Truman privately called the popular senator, was probably the next best contender for the VP slot. That evening portly Alben Barkley, age seventy, a seasoned orator with a fine sense of humor, delivered the convention's keynote address. By all accounts he roused the delegates, restored a measure of hope to their cause, and summoned memories of "New Deal Glory." After he finished his stem-winder, a so-called spontaneous demonstration erupted when the band began playing "My Old Kentucky Home."[61] Alone in the White House (Bess and Margaret would arrive from Independence the next afternoon), Truman watched the speech on TV in his pajamas, and he noted that Barkley mentioned him only once, "casually by name." At midnight, Truman tried but failed to reach Barkley by phone to congratulate him on his "good speech" and "smooth his feathers."[62] Apparently, Barkley had complained that Truman was down on him for trying to get himself nominated for the presidency and miffed because he had heard that Truman had chosen Douglas instead of him for VP.

The next morning, Tuesday, July 13, Barkley returned Truman's call and made it clear that he wanted to run as his VP. Truman genially but with forked tongue responded, "Why didn't you tell me you wanted to run, Alben? That's all you had to do."[63] With that, Truman had finally secured a running mate but he was far from enthusiastic. In a staff meeting later that day, he remarked that Barkley was not "the best candidate but if the delegates wanted him, let them have him." He also commented adversely on Barkley's age, saying that "a vice president should not be seven years older than the president."

Compared to Douglas, Kentuckian Alben Barkley was certainly not the ideal choice. The electoral potential of Kentucky, when added to nearby Missouri, could hardly match that of the New York–California Republican ticket. Nevertheless, as a border-state centrist, Barkley could help the ticket in the more moderate sections of the South and his immense popularity with the delegates might serve to unify the fractious Democratic Party. Truman's attitude, however, was that he was the one who would win or lose the election and that Barkley would neither help nor hurt the Democratic ticket.

The excitement of Barkley's rousing keynote address was overshadowed by a looming fight over the party's civil rights platform. Still upset over Truman's strong civil rights message in February, the Southern Democrats pressed for a states' rights plank while liberal delegates and big-city bosses lobbied for the strongest civil rights platform possible. As Clark Clifford predicted, "The clash between these two groups was to change the Democratic party—and American politics—forever."[64]

Hoping to prevent a revolt by the South, Truman, at the urging of Clifford and DNC chair McGrath, agreed to soften the civil rights plank, thereby positioning himself and his party between the two warring coalitions, but he made it clear to Clifford that he remained firmly committed to passing the federal legislation he had forcefully advocated in February. Consequently, the 1948 platform committee, which was controlled by the

DNC and the White House, introduced a watered-down, vague civil rights statement, similar to that adopted by the convention in 1944, but it still referenced constitutionally based civil rights and called for Congress to enforce them. The Southerners refused to compromise. Instead, to prevent the federal government from enforcing civil rights, they sought states' rights amendments to the platform, the most serious of which reserved to the states the power to regulate and police all local affairs. Introduced by former Texas governor Dan Moody, it was called, of course, the "Moody amendment."[65]

Moody's amendment sparked a blistering counterattack by scores of progressive delegates, who were led by Andrew Biemiller, a former Wisconsin congressman (Truman referred to him privately as a "crackpot"), and Hubert Horatio Humphrey, the dynamic thirty-seven-year-old mayor of Minneapolis.[66] The two of them introduced to the platform the "Biemiller amendment," which called upon Congress to enact four of the specific guarantees that Truman had advanced in his February message—voting rights, equal employment opportunity, integration of the armed services, and prosecution of lynchings in federal courts.

While Truman worked and watched TV from the Oval Office, the floor fight on the civil rights platform played out in Philadelphia's steamy Convention Hall on Wednesday, July 14. That afternoon, Humphrey, who was running for the U.S. Senate, gave the most inspiring and consequential speech of his life. Risking his political career, he admonished his own party, and implicitly Truman himself, for advocating a mild civil rights plank. "There can be no hedging"—"no watering down," he proclaimed. No "compromise." As to the Southerners and moderates "who say, we are rushing this issue of civil rights, I say to them we are 172 years [too] late." And then came Humphrey's most quoted lines, which were directed to everyone in the hall and to the millions throughout America who were listening and watching: "The time has arrived in America for the Democratic party to get out of the shadow of states' rights and walk forthrightly into the bright sunshine of human rights. People—human beings—this is the issue of the 20th century." Except for the Southerners, most of the delegates stood and roared their approval. As if Truman had not been a party to watering down the platform, Humphrey concluded his speech by demanding "in unmistakable terms that we proudly hail, and we courageously support, our President and leader Harry Truman in his great fight for civil rights in America!" The hall rocked with thunderous applause.[67] Delegates danced in the aisles to tunes played by a forty-piece band.

When the celebrations subsided, voting on the amendments began. The states' rights Moody amendment lost overwhelmingly on a roll call vote, 924 to 310. The vote on the strong civil rights plank, the Biemiller amendment (Truman called it "the crackpot amendment"), was much closer, but with the last-minute help of big-city bosses, it prevailed, 651.5 to 582.5, thus eliminating the watered-down proposal that Truman had been talked into supporting with the hope of holding on to the South.[68]

The South, or at least a part of it, did not hold. Minutes after the "crackpot amendment" was passed, convention chairman Sam Rayburn could see that Birmingham public safety commissioner Bull Connor, a member of the Alabama delegation who would become famous in the 1960s as the symbol of violent white resistance to civil rights, was trying to get his attention. Sensing that Connor wanted to seize the moment to stage a walkout by the Alabama delegation, Rayburn quickly gaveled the late-afternoon session to a close and sent word to the White House that it was time for Truman to come to Philadelphia to accept the nomination. While Truman, with Bess, Margaret, and a group of close aides, was on the presidential train heading to Philadelphia, the convention reconvened. As balloting for the president's nomination was beginning, Handy Ellis, chair of the Alabama delegation, was recognized. Speaking to the delegates in the hall, Ellis explained that his presidential electors had been instructed never to vote for Truman and never to vote for anyone with a civil rights platform like the one just adopted. As half of the Alabama delegation, thirteen members, stood ready to walk out, Ellis also announced that the entire Mississippi delegation would join them. "We bid you goodbye," he shouted. Led by Ellis, they were greeted with mixed boos, hisses, and cheers as the TV cameras showed them waving Confederate flags and marching down the center aisle and out into a summer rainstorm. The rest of the Southerners, looking glum and defeated, remained in their seats, apparently believing that they could do more for their cause by remaining inside the Democratic tent.

Having heard on the train's radio that there had been a walkout and that Missouri governor Philip Donnelly had nominated him for the presidency, Truman arrived in rainy Philadelphia and entered the hall through a rear door at a little before 10 p.m. Unable to bear the stifling heat backstage, he spent the next three and a half hours seated in a straight-backed chair on an outdoor service ramp overlooking the railroad yards. While inside the hall seconding speeches were made and votes taken on nominations for the presidency and vice presidency, Truman enjoyed a "pleasant time" sitting with Alben Barkley.[69] Though Truman's nomination was contested by Georgia senator Richard Russell, he won easily, 947.5 to 263. At 1:30 a.m. Barkley was nominated by acclamation.

Since the nomination process had taken several hours and the TV networks had stopped broadcasting after midnight (though radio continued), Speaker Rayburn suggested to Truman that the convention be adjourned so that he could deliver his acceptance speech the next day. According to Clifford, "Some instinct in Harry Truman told him he should seize the moment" and "deliver fighting words to this deeply wounded convention and party."[70] At 1:45 a.m. Truman and Barkley walked out onto the stage and took their seats below the speaker's platform. Despite the long wait and the heat, Truman looked fresh and unrumpled. After a few moments the eyes of the vast crowd were diverted from Truman's blazingly white double-breasted linen suit to the flapping white wings of a flock of fifty "doves of peace," which had been suddenly liberated from a large floral Liberty Bell. The birds, actually just pigeons, ascended into the rafters and then began dive-bombing the delegates and swooping low over the platform. It was a surreal scene. Truman and Barkley couldn't stop laughing. Jack Redding, in charge of publicity for the DNC, spotted a bird flying toward one of the "big whirring fans." He wrote later that if *Time* magazine had snapped a photo of a chopped-up "dead pigeon" at the convention, it would have become a metaphor for the leader of the Democratic Party.[71]

At 2 a.m. Truman confidently strode to the podium. His opening words, unscripted, achieved the impossible. With the strong staccato voice that he had perfected during his Western trip and his hands punching the air, the president brought the huge audience to its feet. "Senator Barkley and I will win this election and make these Republicans like it—don't you forget that!" Thus far, no one had openly predicted a "win." Daughter Margaret wrote of that moment: "An incredible current of emotion surged through the crowd. People who thought they were too tired even to stand up again were on their feet shouting their heads off."[72]

As recommended in the "Politics of 1948" memo, Truman focused his fighting speech on the Republican-controlled, "worst 80th Congress." Time and again, the president lamented, he had called for legislation to control prices, provide slum clearance and low-rent housing, increase Social Security benefits, protect civil rights, and improve public education. What did he get from the do-nothing 80th Congress? Nothing. Yet, as Truman pointed out, the Republicans had adopted a platform at their recent convention that promised legislative action to address most of the very same reforms that he had been recommending. "I wonder," said the president, "if they think they can fool the people of the United States with such poppycock as that!" The delegates booed with derision.

Having set the bait, Truman sprung his trap. "On the 26th day of July," he announced, "which out in Missouri we call 'Turnip Day,' I am going to call [the Republican-controlled] Congress back and ask them to pass the laws" that they endorsed in "their platform." And "if there is any reality behind the Republican platform, we ought to get some action from a short session of the 80th Congress. They can do this job in 15 days if they want to do it."[73]

"For two solid minutes," wrote Margaret, "the convention hall was drowned in total pandemonium as the delegates roared their support of this daring move."[74] But beyond the applause, Truman's preplanned Turnip Day gambit was a strategic masterstroke. The session would not only focus the nation's attention on the record of the unpopular 80th Congress and its "Neanderthal" leaders; it would expose a schism between the Taft-led conservative Republicans who dominated votes on domestic issues in Congress and the liberal presidential wing led by Dewey, who had dictated the moderate GOP platform. If, as was most likely, the 80th Congress were to refuse to pass laws called for by Truman and endorsed in Dewey's platform, Dewey would be trapped. He would have to either criticize Congress or implicitly admit that his platform "lacked reality," as Truman had insinuated. On the other hand, even if Congress were to pass one or more reforms called for in the Dewey–Warren plank, it would be Truman, fighting for the people on Capitol Hill, who would garner the credit.

The Turnip Day strategy put the Truman campaign on the offensive and changed the dynamic of the presidential race. But it had not been Truman's idea. Rather, it was based on an unsigned memorandum dated June 29, 1948, that had been written by a team led by William L. Batt Jr., director of the DNC's Research Division. Truman was persuaded by Clark Clifford to adopt the memo's game plan. Both he and Truman were confident that the 80th Congress would not pass anything of significance.[75]

Clifford recalled that on the train back to Washington, the president "talked with enthusiasm about how he was going to surprise everyone, especially Dewey, when the campaign got under way." Truman arrived at the White House at 5:30 a.m. After only three hours of sleep, he ordered breakfast and was in the Oval Office by ten o'clock, devouring editorials and columns that "gasped and wondered" about the wisdom of his Turnip Day surprise.[76] At the same time, he was expecting a reaction from the Republican nominee. It didn't take long. That afternoon Dewey refused to comment. However, he had already fallen into Truman's trap because he had just praised the record of the 80th Congress, which meant that his party plank wasn't worth the paper it was written on. A day or two later, Dewey fell deeper. He told Michael Straight of the *New Republic* that Truman's emergency session of Congress would be "a frightful imposition." Straight wrote that this dismissive attitude undermined "the sincerity" of the platform that Dewey had dictated and the "urgency of the problems which Americans face."[77]

————————

While Truman had adopted a strategy to knock Dewey onto his back foot, two more presidential candidates emerged during July, each of whom was a defector from the Democratic Party. On Saturday, July 17, six thousand Southern Democrats from twelve states gathered in Birmingham, Alabama, to form a new party, the States' Rights Party, soon to be popularly known as the "Dixiecrats." The party platform proclaimed, "We stand for the segregation of the races and the integrity of each race," as if the word "integrity" validated the policy.[78] At the convention, which was held in the Birmingham armory and broadcast by the major radio networks, the delegates chose two governors as their standard-bearers: Strom Thurmond of South Carolina for president and Fielding Wright of Mississippi for vice president (the official nomination would take place in August). In his keynote address, Thurmond, a relatively unknown newcomer to the national stage, announced that his campaign strategy was to win enough electoral votes to deny a majority to Dewey or Truman and thereby throw the race into a vote by the House of Representatives, as the Constitution mandated. Then, assuming the Democrats regained control of the House, the South would "hold the balance of power."[79] With delegates waving Confederate battle flags to the tune of "Dixie," Thurmond predicted that in a straight-up contest in the House against Truman, he would win. Asked later why he stayed in the Democratic Party in 1944 when FDR made civil rights promises but deserted it in 1948, Thurmond said the difference was that "Truman really means it."[80]

A week later, Henry Wallace's Progressive Party convened in Philadelphia in the same venue where the GOP and the Democratic conventions had been held. In contrast to the three other parties, the Progressive Party was the party of peace. Its nine-thousand-word platform demanded negotiations with the Soviet Union "to win the peace," and it opposed "anti-Soviet hysteria," the draft, universal military training, possession of the atomic bomb, and the Marshall Plan. On the domestic side, Wallace's platform went well beyond that of the Democrats, calling for desegregation of public schools, food stamps for the poor, and an equal rights amendment for women. Among the convention's attendees were folk singer Pete Seeger, Black entertainer Paul Robeson, writer Lillian Hellman, future presidential nominee George McGovern, and an unknown number of card-carrying Communists. On the opening night, the keynote speech was delivered by an African American, the first at a national political convention to do so. Invoking the policy of FDR at Yalta and Tehran, Charles Howard, publisher of a Black newspaper in Iowa, delivered a strident plea for "cooperation" with the USSR. "What is at stake here is the very survival of Western civilization," he warned.[81] On the last night of the convention—held in Shibe Park, then the home of the Philadelphia Athletics baseball team—Wallace and his running mate, Glen Taylor, the singing cowboy, accepted their nominations before a crowd of thirty thousand. Wallace ignited the audience by telling them what he would have done if he had become president instead of Truman. The Berlin crisis did not just "happen," he said. "Berlin was caused," he thundered, and there he stopped mid-sentence, leaving it to his audience to conclude that the crisis had been caused by Truman's complete failure to reach an understanding with Stalin, an objective that only Wallace could have achieved.[82]

No question, Wallace was a charismatic speaker with a vision of peace and abundance that was seductive. The problem, however, was that a majority of Americans believed that he and his Progressive Party were controlled by a small group of Communist bosses, a belief that was fueled by the press. Moreover, Wallace himself consistently refused to distance himself from the Communist line and Stalinist aggression. After his speech at Shibe Park, a *Time* reporter quoted Wallace as saying "that the communists are the closest thing to the early Christian martyrs."[83] When Truman read or heard about that remark, he commented to Clifford, "Poor Henry. He doesn't know what's happening to him."[84]

————————

In the space of five tumultuous weeks (June 21 to July 25), four presidential candidates had been selected. As the Democratic nominee, Truman could no longer count on the kind of support that FDR had had in the Deep South, nor was there any prospect that such losses could be replaced by the Black vote, portions of which were likely to be drained off by Wallace and even by Dewey, who had a reasonably progressive civil rights record. Although still lagging in the polls, Truman nevertheless was confident that on November 2 he would beat Dewey, the front-runner, and win.

While Truman had been preoccupied with his own convention and monitoring the three others, threats to America's security did not pause. With Stalin's backing and encouragement, Communism continued to be ascendant in Europe, China, Korea, parts of the Middle East, and even in the United States. In Germany, the Berlin Airlift had achieved a measure of initial success, but in the previous few weeks, civilian and military leaders in the Truman administration, including Undersecretary of State Bob Lovett, reasoned that it could not be sustained and that unless more aggressive action was taken, all of Berlin would be controlled by the Soviet Union. However, any such moves by the Western powers risked a shooting war with the Soviet Union. Therefore, Truman would have to conduct his election campaign throughout the fall of 1948 while coping almost every day with the possibility of war.

On the president's first day back from the convention, when he was meeting with Secretary of Defense Forrestal about custody of the nation's stockpile of fifty atomic bombs, U.S. Army chief of staff Omar Bradley was in the Pentagon reading a cable from General Clay. The cable urged Bradley to take more aggressive action to break the Soviet blockade of Berlin, namely by dispatching armed overland convoys of two hundred trucks with engineering battalions for bridging rivers.[85] Since Clay acknowledged that his request carried with it "an inherent risk" of war, Bradley kicked the decision up to Forrestal, his boss, and Forrestal then arranged with Marshall to meet Truman four days later. According to Forrestal's notes of the meeting, Marshall calmly advised the president to stay the course, meaning the airlift but not Clay's armed convoys. If they remained firm, the Soviets would back down, he counseled, just as they had done when the administration's policies managed to contain them in Greece, France, and Italy. Forrestal reminded Marshall that available American ground forces were inadequate to defend Berlin. Truman ended the discussion by saying that "our policy will remain fixed," and he declined to approve Clay's request.[86] In his diary that night, he wrote that Forrestal "wants to hedge—he always does. . . . I reiterate my 'Stay in Berlin' decision. I don't pass the buck, nor do I alibi out of any decision I make." At the conclusion of that evening's diary entry, Truman complained that Bess and Margaret had departed to Independence for the rest of the summer while he had to stay in "the great white jail. . . . It is hot and humid and lonely. Why in hell does anybody want to be a head of state? Damned if I know."[87]

Responding to belligerent provocations by the Soviets not just in Berlin but around the world, Truman informed his cabinet at a luncheon meeting on July 19 that he was reinstituting the draft. The next day, he issued Executive Order 9979, which required almost ten million men to register for military service over the next sixty days. Truman knew that this unpopular move, only three and a half months before the election, could doom his chances but he felt he had little choice.

Meanwhile in Berlin, Clay was beside himself. Since his requests for armed convoys had been rejected in Washington, he feared that without two hundred more transport planes, the airlift would fail and not only would the Soviets occupy all of Berlin, but their policy of aggression, unchecked, would retard the recovery of Europe itself and snuff out democracy. Thus far, Clay's fleet of eighty C-47s and fifty C-54s had achieved miracles, flying 250 round trips each day. However, the lift was bringing in less than half the food, fuel, and supplies required for the survival of the 2.5 million Berliners through the winter. If the airlift were to succeed, Clay needed an immediate addition of seventy-five C-54 Skymasters to his fleet. There is no record of exactly how he pulled it off, but somehow he persuaded Army Secretary Ken Royall to order him to fly to Washington so he could make his case directly to the president and the three Joint Chiefs at a meeting of the National Security Council (it was probably just bluster, but in a letter to Bess, Truman inexplicably said Clay's presence was "not necessary").[88] In the Cabinet Room of the White House on July 22, Clay began his pitch by stressing that failure of the airlift and resulting abandonment of Berlin to the Soviet Union would be a "disastrous blow to the maintenance of freedom in Europe."[89] After telling the president and the generals that he saw no indications that the Soviets would go to war over continuance of the airlift, he launched into what he described later as an "impassioned plea" for more planes.[90] Speaking for himself and the army and navy chiefs, U.S. Air Force chief of staff Hoyt Vandenberg flatly opposed Clay's request for the seventy-five C-54s and more later, warning that "these planes could be destroyed on the ground in the event of war with the Soviet Union," and that "the diversion of so many aircraft to Berlin would seriously impair America's ability to wage strategic warfare."[91] Truman listened but said little. After a few minutes he had to excuse himself for another appointment, but as he left, he asked Clay to drop by his office before he departed for Berlin. The meeting went on but since none of the military chiefs supported Clay's request, he thought he had lost the fight.

When Clay returned to the White House in the morning, Truman said something like "You're not feeling very happy about this, are you?" As he later recalled, Clay responded, "No sir, I'm not." The refusal to grant his request for more planes, he said, "will make our efforts a failure, and I'm afraid what will happen to Europe if it does fail." "Don't you worry," said the president. "You're going to get your airplanes." Truman grinned and explained, "I have just overruled the Joint Chiefs."[92]

Recalling that moment years later, Clay told his interviewer that the president, unlike the Joint Chiefs, decided to go all out for the airlift because he "realized that the Berlin crisis was a political war, not a physical military war." It was a gamble to be sure, but Truman agreed with Clay that Stalin would not start a real war over Berlin, probably because the U.S. possessed the bomb. Having witnessed the debate firsthand, Clay admired the fact that Truman, whom he called a person of "great courage," did not "hesitate to make his own decisions."[93]

As if his cunning Turnip Day ploy had not been enough to shake up the presidential sweepstakes and capture headlines, Truman had another bombshell, actually two, that he planned to unleash on opening day of the special congressional session. On July 16, ten days before Congress was to convene, the president's close friend and strategic adviser Oscar Ewing told him that the time was fast approaching when he should issue two executive orders: one to guarantee equality of treatment and opportunity in the armed services, and the other to protect the nation's civil service employees against racial discrimination in the workplace. Truman was empowered to take both actions without the approval of Congress. Ewing argued that since Congress would not act on civil rights at the special session, it was incumbent on the president to take advantage of his executive powers, preferably on opening day. Truman agreed, having concluded that it was not only the right thing to do, but also, of course, because it would appeal to African American voters, even though the orders would be violently opposed in the Deep South and generally opposed by the vast majority of Americans. As Philleo Nash, who handled civil rights issues for the president, remembered, he received a call from White House aide

George Elsey while vacationing near the town of Wisconsin Rapids and immediately "jumped on the night train" to Washington.[94] At his office in the Dupont Circle Building, it was Nash who drafted the two orders, vetted them with the solicitor general, and obtained Truman's approval.

On Monday afternoon, July 26, as Congress gathered for the special session on Capitol Hill, Truman, with no advance warning, issued the two related civil rights orders.[95] While implementation of those orders would face serious resistance and take time, Truman, with the stroke of his pen, had "assaulted the institution of racism in America as it had not been attacked since Abraham Lincoln issued the Emancipation Proclamation."[96]

Even before the bombshells landed on the Hill, the atmosphere in the House Chamber during the opening hours of the Turnip Day session was hostile. Republicans were angry and divided on what to do. Some wanted to call for adjournment right after Truman addressed them, and then go home. Others believed that the Dewey team should call Truman's bluff by persuading reluctant members of the 80th to enact significant civil rights and anti-inflation legislation. Neither strategy was adopted. Instead, Representative Hugh Scott (R-PA), Republican National Committee chairman, and Herbert Brownell, Dewey's campaign chair, privately asked Senator Bob Taft to corral his conservative colleagues and pass one or two liberal-leaning bills, which would turn the tables on Truman. "No," replied Taft as Scott and Brownell recalled, "we're not going to give that fellow [Truman] anything."[97] Clifford wrote that this "was a serious error: the President gambled that they would not try to pass any significant legislation, and, thanks to Taft, he proved to be right."[98]

The next day, at half past noon, when Truman walked down the aisle to deliver his plea for legislative action to the joint session, the reception was decidedly cool. Most Republican members and Southerners in both parties did not stand or applaud. Yet Truman relished the moment. "Our people," he began, "demand legislative action by their government" to "check inflation" and solve the "acute housing shortage."[99] These were the highest priorities, he stressed. But while these two were being addressed, he added, there would be plenty of time to reconsider and enact "other important legislative measures" that he had previously recommended to the 80th Congress.[100] These liberal proposals, a total of nine, ranged from increases in minimum wage and Social Security benefits to civil rights. The president anticipated that Congress would fail to pass any of his recommendations, including the top priorities, so his aim was to lay it all out so that the voters, especially African Americans and poor whites, would understand how much they stood to lose by electing Dewey and keeping the Republicans in power.

After eleven contentious days, with a weekend break, the Turnip Day joint session ground to an unproductive end. Only three bills were presented to Truman for his signature—restoration of consumer credit controls for a shorter period than recommended to check inflation, more authority to the Federal Reserve to regulate bank credit, and a loan to build the UN its headquarters in Manhattan.[101] Truman signed all three, even though he pronounced the puny credit control adjustments as grossly inadequate and "advantageous to the ends of special privilege."[102] At a press conference after the session concluded, a reporter asked a question that sounded as if it had been planted in advance: "Would you say it was a do-nothing session, Mr. President?" The president swung at the slow pitch: "I think that's a good name for the 80th Congress."[103]

The nickname caught on. As if the 80th were his principal antagonist, Truman would repeatedly attack the do-nothing Congress during the fall campaign. Rarely, if ever, would he utter the names Tom Dewey, Henry Wallace, or Strom Thurmond.

Chapter 12

Now It's My Fight

In early August 1948, while Clark Clifford was outlining a strategy for the fall campaign and the DNC was still searching for a finance chair, Harry Truman, alone at nights in the "Great White Jail," confided to his diary that the White House was "falling down." One of the two pianos in Margaret's sitting room had broken through the floor above the family dining room. Truman's marble bathtub was about to fall into the Red Room—he hoped, he joked, not with him in it while Bess was entertaining the Daughters of the American Revolution (DAR) or the Lady Elks and Eagles downstairs. The foundation of the old building was literally sinking into the swampy ground. For safety's sake, the White House architect (Douglas Orr) and engineer (Richard E. Dougherty) insisted that the president's sleeping quarters be moved into the Lincoln suite since the ceiling below his bedroom "only stayed up from force of habit." To his sister, Truman wrote, "I'm using old Abe's bed and it is very comfortable."[1]

The Truman family wrote and gossiped back and forth about the terrible condition of the executive mansion, often with mordant humor, and they realized that the interior would have to be completely gutted.

Truman cautioned the others, however, to keep the matter to themselves until after the election. As Margaret later wrote, "Can you imagine what the press would have done with this story? The whole mess would have been blamed on Harry Truman. The White House would have become a metaphor for his collapsing administration."[2]

With the DNC coffers virtually empty, the quest for a fundraising chair began in earnest shortly after the Democratic convention adjourned. The White House log indicates that at 8:00 on the evening of July 22, ten men met with Truman "off the record" in the president's study.[3] The purpose was to recruit wealthy individuals to join the DNC finance committee and to select a chairman. According to a reliable witness, at least one individual who was not listed in the log was present. His name was Louis A. Johnson, former commander of the American Legion and assistant secretary of war under Roosevelt. "Colonel" Johnson, as he was called, had been invited to attend by Major General Harry Vaughan, the president's military aide and confidant who had known Truman since the Great War. With Vaughan's encouragement, Johnson had been working over the past five months to build political and financial support for the president among the large cohort of veterans throughout the U.S. Johnson was pleased to have Vaughan as a supporter but he "got into the business of raising money in a cold-blooded way," recalled Jean Kearny, his close associate. "He gambled that if Truman should win and if he raised enough money for the campaign it would advance his standing as a Washington lawyer [cofounder of Steptoe & Johnson], and a national figure."[4]

Bald, beefy Louis Johnson, a heavyweight boxer and big man on campus when he had attended the University of Virginia, made a positive impression that evening. Along with Ambassador William Pawley, a well-to-do aircraft manufacturer who had been involved in organizing and supporting the Flying Tigers in China during World War II, and the fabulously wealthy Cornelius Vanderbilt Whitney, the others present at the meeting believed Johnson could be an effective chairman of the DNC finance committee. In fact, Johnson had come to the meeting with the intention of accepting the chairmanship if offered the position.[5] However, the meeting adjourned with a consensus that Bill Pawley should serve as chair because he was better known and wealthier than Johnson. Pawley was inclined to accept but said he needed to think it over. Matt Connelly remembered that a few days later Pawley backed out after "reading the Gallup polls," which convinced him that his chances of raising enough money for the fall campaign were "a little dim and he didn't want any part of it."[6] The last the DNC heard from Pawley was a telegram from his secretary saying her boss would be in Europe until October.

Throughout August, with polls predicting a Dewey landslide, efforts by the DNC and the president to recruit a finance chair were unsuccessful. Truman personally reached out to Jesse Jones, a Texas real estate tycoon and philanthropist who had been FDR's secretary of commerce, and then Bernard Baruch, a wealthy financier. Each, citing age and other excuses, politely declined to take the job. Members of the DNC's finance committee tried but failed to interest George Killion, who had chaired the finance committee in 1944 and owed to Truman his position as CEO of the American President Lines (the shipping company was owned by the government). At the end of the month Truman vented his frustrations in a letter to Baruch. "A great many honors have passed your way," he wrote, "and it seems that when the going gets rough it is a one-way street."[7] Meanwhile, Louis Johnson kept in close touch with members of the finance committee and Truman himself, while not so subtly hinting that he was available.

With only two months before Election Day, DNC chair Howard McGrath sent telegrams to about eighty potential fundraisers asking them to attend a meeting in the White House with the president, followed by a "business session" in the evening.[8] His objective was to obtain specific monetary commitments from the fundraisers and to select a chairman of the finance committee. At 5 p.m. on Thursday, September 9, forty mostly wealthy men gathered in the Red Room. Based on an interview with a source who was there, columnist Drew Pearson wrote that after tea was served, Truman stood up on a chair. "I am appealing to you to help carry my message to the American people," he began. The president went on to explain that a few days earlier, before a huge Labor Day crowd at Cadillac Square in Detroit, he had had to cut out one of the most important parts of his speech because "we didn't have the money to stay on the air," meaning the prearranged national radio broadcast. Truman said that he planned to launch the opening leg of his fall campaign in a week. He predicted that he would be victorious but only if he had money for trains, radio time, advertising, and professional staff. "Mr. Truman looked pathetic and alone," wrote Pearson.[9]

During the business session that evening (Truman wasn't there), Mc-Grath announced that his goal was to raise $1.5 million. Following discussion and a few telephone calls, he obtained pledges totaling a half million dollars. Colonel Johnson, after pledging $100,000 of his own money, singled out two laggards on the finance committee, bluntly demanding that they either do "some real work" or "get out."[10] Not surprisingly, the decision of the group, having run out of options, was that Johnson should chair the finance committee. Accounts differ but many who were there recalled that Johnson was inclined to take the job but wanted to meet with Truman before accepting it. Assuming these recollections were accurate, the next day, after meeting alone with Truman "off the record," Johnson accepted.[11] According to gossip in the nation's capital, Johnson agreed to serve as chair but only after Truman dangled an eventual appointment as secretary of defense, the position that Johnson had been yearning for ever since FDR had forced him out of the War Department in the summer of 1940. There is no hard evidence to substantiate this speculation. However, in March 1949, shortly after Truman's inauguration, Johnson was appointed and confirmed as secretary of defense. He succeeded James Forrestal, who was mentally ill and committed suicide two months later.

On September 14, just three days before the president started out on the first of three whistle-stop campaigns, Howard McGrath officially announced that Colonel Louis Johnson would serve as the DNC finance chairman. By all accounts, "Louie" Johnson, "a real fireball," did an outstanding job, as Neale Roach, head of campaign headquarters in the Biltmore Hotel in New York City, recalled.[12] Given the polls, pundits, and media that were all predicting an overwhelming victory for Dewey, it was very difficult to raise money for Truman. Sam Brightman, assistant director of publicity at the DNC, remembered that many of the larger Democratic contributors in the past "suddenly had become conservative Republicans." Fortunately, however, Johnson was "a hard man to say 'no' to."[13] And he was most effective in raising money at the last minute to pay for Truman's nationally broadcast speeches, recalled John Snyder, secretary of the treasury during the Truman administration.[14] Based on the 1949 *Congressional Quarterly*, the DNC, under Johnson's leadership, raised $2,308,211, a total amazingly close to that collected by the RNC—$2,507,396—and far in excess of McGrath's goal.[15] Johnson's seemingly miraculous efforts were crucial to Truman's success. As Clifford put it, "Truman owed a very real debt to Louis Johnson"—a debt, he hinted, that the president paid off when he nominated Johnson to become the nation's second secretary of defense.[16]

———————

As the fall campaign heated up, the president would find himself owing another debt—this one to three African Americans (two men and a woman), remarkable individuals whom previous Truman biographers have ignored. In August 1948, a few weeks after the convention, the two most powerful Black men in Chicago, both of whom were convinced that Truman was serious about civil rights, launched the National Citizens Committee for the Re-election of President Truman. This committee would serve as both a fundraising organization and a platform for mobilizing Black people throughout America to vote for Truman. It was the first initiative of its kind in U.S. presidential politics.

The two Chicago-based founders were accomplished and ambitious. John Sengstacke, publisher of the *Chicago Defender*, one of the largest Black-owned newspapers in America, promoted the Citizens Committee in his own newspaper, declaring that the organization planned to raise a million dollars and that it was time for African Americans to "Put Up or Shut Up." Referring to the fact that most of the Deep South was no longer contributing to the DNC, Sengstacke was quoted as saying, "We will raise ten dollars for every one dollar withheld by the Dixiecrats who are fighting Mr. Truman over the Negro issue."[17]

The other founder, Illinois congressman William Levi Dawson, a machine politician who had represented the 1st District on the South Side of Chicago for twenty-seven years, was not as outspoken as Sengstacke, but because he was one of the only two African Americans in Congress at the time (the second was Harlem's Adam Clayton Powell), he was well known by Black activists from coast to coast. As vice chair of the DNC, the highest post in the party that an African American had ever achieved, Dawson recruited a prominent African American woman, his friend and fellow Black activist, to become executive director of the Citizens Committee. Her name was Anna Arnold Hedgeman.

Anna Hedgeman had met Dawson when she was working in Washington, DC, as the director of a lobbying organization aimed at ending discrimination and providing equal opportunity to African Americans in the workplace. Since being the first Black student to graduate from Hamline University in St. Paul, Minnesota, Hedgeman had devoted her professional life to the education and improvement of the lives of Black Americans, especially women, during her years working for the segregated branches of the Young Women's Christian Association in Harlem and several other locations and as the first consultant on racial problems in New York City. From 1946 to 1947, Hedgeman had served as the assistant dean of women at Howard University in Washington, where she mentored young women and worked with them on planning a women's day event.

Despite friends telling her she was joining a losing cause, Hedgeman moved into DNC headquarters in New York, hired a small staff, and went to work as leader and chief strategist of the Citizens Committee to reelect Truman. "Mr. Truman planned his whistle-stop campaign and we planned ours," she wrote.[18] With the help of Congressman Dawson, one of the few people she knew who believed Truman could actually win, Hedgeman assembled lists of African Americans who could afford to make donations to the campaign and targeted large cities in balance-of-power states where the Black vote could swing the election. To whip up enthusiasm for Truman and his civil rights agenda, Hedgeman convened a meeting of the editors of twenty Black newspapers (including Sengstacke) and she booked speaking gigs and organized rallies for Black audiences in urban areas throughout the country. A photo signed by Truman depicted Hedgeman introducing three Black community leaders to the president on the *Ferdinand Magellan* when his train stopped in Des Moines on September 18. She later recalled having "a great time with Truman" aboard his train in Kansas City as he welcomed local politicians "both Negro and white."[19]

While Hedgeman focused in particular on African American donors and voters in Illinois and Ohio, which were critically important "battleground states," Dawson and Sengstacke toured the entire country by train, spreading the word about Truman to Black citizens, raising money, and stressing the need to vote. The two of them started in the Jim Crow South, then traveled all the way out to Los Angeles, and finished back East in New York City, where they participated in the president's huge rally in Harlem. According to *The Defender*, a book chronicling the paper's history, Dawson and Sengstacke recruited "eighty prominent" African Americans from every region of the U.S. to serve as vice chairs of the Committee to Reelect.[20] They were charged with the tasks of soliciting campaign donations large and small and urging African Americans in their communities to vote for Truman in November.

When Dawson and Sengstacke were out in Los Angeles, they touched base with Augustus Hawkins, an African American Democrat who had represented the 62nd District of the California State Assembly since 1935. They wanted to make sure that Hawkins, whose heavily populated district in 1948 was 98 percent Black, got out the vote for Truman and the other Democrats on the ballot. Hawkins told them not to worry. His constituents, he said, would remain solidly Democratic, as would the Blacks in the rest of the state, even though VP candidate Earl Warren, the popular California governor with a decent record on civil rights, was on the Republican ticket. After the 3.8 million California votes were cast in November, Truman prevailed by 18,800 votes and in so doing garnered twenty-five precious electoral votes. Due to the second "great migration" from the South, by 1948 there were close to four hundred thousand African Americans in California, three-quarters of whom lived in or near Los Angeles. It is arguable that the "Negro" vote put Truman over the top in California. As Loren Miller, a prominent Los Angeles civil rights lawyer, wrote, the allegiance of "Negro voters" to the California Democratic Party rested "on pragmatic grounds"—that is, the material benefits to their race conferred by Democratic administrations.[21]

Truman would owe yet another debt of gratitude for his miraculous victory in 1948, this one to a white woman named India Edwards, the colorful and dynamic executive director of the DNC's Women's Division, whose contributions have also been overlooked by presidential historians. Taking the name "India" from her grandmother and mother, Edwards, beginning at age eighteen, had worked her way up to become a prizewinning journalist for the *Chicago Tribune* before moving to Washington and joining the DNC in 1945. Anticipating that substantially more women than men were likely to cast votes in 1948 than in any previous presidential election, Edwards convinced her boss, Howard McGrath, to provide her with resources to create an afternoon radio show for women, mobile trailers with props to demonstrate GOP responsibility for high food prices, and a plan to organize "Housewives for Truman." Edwards believed, correctly, that the number one issue for women in 1948 was the high cost of living, particularly for food. Her strategy was to use the resources at her disposal to convince women voters that the lifting of price controls by the Republican-controlled 80th Congress was responsible for the high cost of groceries. "As a housewife and mother," she planned to say again and again, "I appeal to all American women to join together to bring down the cost of living. . . . Register. Vote. Elect Democrats."[22]

India Edwards's watchword at the DNC was "Pay attention to the women," and by that she meant not only white women but African Americans as well.[23] "We are going to have an integrated Women's Division," Edwards insisted. Her deputy was Venice Tipton Spraggs—"a brilliant, wonderful Negro woman," recalled Edwards—who took a leave of absence from the *Chicago Defender*, for which she wrote about issues facing Black women.[24]

As Truman's fall campaign was about to get underway, the Citizen's Committee for the Re-election of President Truman and the Women's Division of the DNC were poised to deliver. The names of their leaders, however, never made it into Truman's memoirs or histories of his presidency.

For candidate Truman, age sixty-four and bursting with vitality, the first phase of the fall campaign began on the afternoon of September 17, 1948, on track sixteen in Washington's Union Station. As he parted the curtains and stepped out onto the rear platform of the *Ferdinand Magellan*, flanked by his running mate, Senator Alben Barkley, and daughter Margaret, flash-bulbs popped while the crowd below on the tracks and station floor clapped and cheered. As if on cue, when the applause began to die, Barkley turned to Truman. With an orator's voice that echoed off the station's high ceiling, he implored, "Mow 'em down, Harry." Truman replied, "I'm going to fight hard. I'm going to give them hell."[25] The media picked up the memorable exchange and flashed it across the nation.

Back in the presidential suite, Truman's briefcase was full of campaign strategy papers, notably a memo by Clifford stressing that the president should "concentrate" on three groups inclined to vote Democratic that could swing the entire election: "workers, veterans, and Negros."[26] Truman appreciated Clifford's advice but he had in mind a surprise strategy for carrying a critically important fourth group—"the farm vote."[27] At the time, farmers, mostly located in the Midwest, represented 17 percent of the nation's workforce. Confident that his strategy would work, Truman aimed to flip a least three key farm states, Ohio, Wisconsin, and Iowa (a total of forty-seven electoral votes, equal to New York), which had gone Republican in the 1944 election.[28]

The idea for making farm policy an effective campaign issue was originated by Denver-born Charles "Chuck" Brannan, Truman's new secretary of agriculture, a relatively unknown but clever bureaucrat with a flair for brass knuckles politics. It was Brannan who supplied Truman with two arguments for attacking the GOP that were bound to resonate with farmers and put Dewey on the defensive. First, Brannan urged Truman to claim that because Republicans were accusing the administration of deliberately keeping consumer prices high, they in fact were harboring a diabolical plot to destroy farmers' price supports, a highly popular program that had been implemented during the Roosevelt administration. There was no evidence that the GOP actually intended to do away with price supports, but that detail deterred neither Brannan nor Truman. Second, Truman should argue more plausibly that when the Republican-controlled 80th Congress recently renewed the Commodity Credit Corporation's charter, it virtually eliminated the CCC's previous practice of providing storage bins for farmers. Without government-provided storage bins, went the argument, farmers were and would be forced to sell their bumper wheat and corn crops before they spoiled at less than the support prices. Brannan convinced Truman that he could blame the influence of special interests—big grain traders—and the 80th Congress for the storage bin shortage. Truman would brush aside the fact that he had signed the bill renewing the CCC charter, which included the provisions restricting the distribution of storage bins.

When Truman left Union Station for his fifteen-day, seventeen-state swing across the Midwest to California and back, the only major speech in his briefcase was the farm speech, which he planned to deliver at the National Soil Conservation Field Days and Plowing Matches in Dexter, Iowa, forty miles west of Des Moines. The conservation-and-plowing contest venue was selected because that was the place where his advisers expected the largest crowd in the Midwest during September. The speech had been drafted the previous weekend aboard the *Williamsburg* by Albert Z. "Bob" Carr, an economist educated at the University of Chicago, Columbia, and the London School of Economics. Carr was "one of the group that actually could write," recalled Charles Murphy, who was on the Potomac River cruise along with Truman, Clifford, and another speechwriter, David Noyes.[29]

Early on the morning of September 18, when the president's so-called Truman Special crossed the Mississippi River into Iowa, Truman informed the surprisingly large crowds at almost every whistle-stop that he would elaborate on his Democratic farm program when he reached Dexter, "a hotbed of Republicanism." In fact, except for liberal Grinnell, where Truman introduced Margaret to the townspeople, the whole state seemed to be dominated by the GOP—the governor, both senators, and all eight congressmen were Republicans. At the station in Des Moines, Bess quietly boarded the train while Truman, from the rear platform, told the crowd through loudspeakers mounted atop the *Ferdinand Magellan* that when he reached Dexter, he would explain "the policy of the Democratic Party as it affects the farmer . . . and then if you don't take my advice [and vote Democratic] you won't have anybody to blame but yourselves."[30]

Via the Rock Island Railroad tracks, the Truman Special chugged into the Dexter depot at about 11 a.m. The town fathers were delighted to welcome the president of the United States. However, he was not their first choice. Months before, they had invited Tom Dewey but he had declined.

After the plowing match queen and her court were recognized and the Dexter High School band finished playing the "Missouri Waltz," Truman, the First Lady, and Margaret climbed into the back seat of a robin's-egg-blue Cadillac. Its driver, accompanied by the Secret Service, led a dozen other convertibles north of town to the plowing contest site on the R. P. Weesner farm. The roads to the farm were clogged with bumper-to-bumper traffic (a marker commemorating the presidential visit can be seen today along Dexfield Road).

With mercury rising to 100 degrees and the sun blazing at half past high noon, Truman, attired in a suit and dark sunglasses, mounted a five-foot-high broad platform. Behind him, a line of local dignitaries and politicians was seated beneath a gigantic "Welcome to Iowa" scoreboard, which listed the names of those who would compete in four "contouring" and "level land" plowing events. As the president stepped up to the even higher podium, which was adorned with the presidential seal and topped with six microphones, he could see acres of people; thousands of parked trucks, tractors, and automobiles; more than fifty private airplanes; and off to the horizon, endless rows of green corn. Estimates of crowd size ranged from a low of seventy thousand to a hundred thousand.

Truman's twenty-nine-minute "farm speech," delivered to the enormous crowd at the Weesner farm and the millions who listened to the nationwide broadcast, was not his best, but in terms of electoral votes, it was probably his most effective performance—and a performance it certainly was. After the first few minutes, Truman ripped into the "Wall Street Republicans," claiming they were controlled by "big business," which would stop at nothing to "grasp the balance of power and take the country over, lock, stock, and barrel"—"a return of the Wall Street economic dictatorship." He called Wall Street Republicans "gluttons of privilege." No fewer than seven separate times, he hammered home that phrase, which had been coined by speechwriter Bob Carr. The words "Wall Street," "big business," and "gluttons of privilege" were code for New York City's elite Republican Tom Dewey, whose name Truman never uttered.[31]

Having warned his audience of how poorly farmers had fared under previous Republican administrations—Harding, Coolidge, Hoover—Truman proclaimed that the current do-nothing, Republican-controlled

80th Congress had "already stuck a pitchfork in the farmer's back." With the abundant harvest coming, he said, the farmers knew they would need storage bins for their wheat and corn crops. Without storage capacity, they would be forced to sell below support prices. Otherwise, their crops would spoil. But they should get a load of this, he said: "big business lobbyists and speculators" had persuaded the 80th Congress to prevent his administration from "setting up storage bins that you will need in order to get the support price for your grain." Moreover, he went on, "the Republican reactionaries are not satisfied with that. Now they are attacking the whole structure of price supports for farm products."

Truman's "pitchfork" pitch to the huge crowd and the national radio audience, together with his wild attacks against Republicans, which were appropriated from Brannan and wordsmithed by Carr, hit a nerve with farmers all over America. Applause interrupted his speech thirteen times, with cheers breaking out after he excoriated the do-nothing Congress. Today, his extreme rhetoric and unsupported assertions would probably pass for normal campaign talk. But in 1948, it would have been fair to label Truman's farm speech and some of his others as fiery oratory emanating from a demagogue—a leader who gained power by rousing common people against elites through false claims and promises that whipped up the passions of the crowd.

After a dinner of fried chicken on a red-and-white-checked tablecloth, Truman and his entourage headed out to the soil conservation demonstrations to see terraces, ponds, and other conservation practices. Bob Larson, then an eighteen-year-old farmhand who had been recruited to work on the demonstration sites, recalled that Truman jumped off a hayrack, asked a lot of questions, and rode with him for about ten minutes on his bulldozer. "Truman made a good impression on me," remembered Larson. "If I'd been old enough to vote in 1948, I probably would have picked Truman." When Larson was later told that Dewey had been invited to Dexter but turned the Iowans down, he reportedly said, "The Midwest didn't like Dewey because he was an elitist who had no time for Iowa dirt farmers."[32]

When Truman returned to the platform under the scoreboard, the director of the plowing contest asked him whether it was true that he could "plow one of the straightest furrows of anyone in your community." Truman replied that his mother used to say that but of course she was a "very prejudiced witness." Then, in all seriousness, he told the crowd that he had had a reputation in Grandview, Missouri, for "being able to sow a 160-acre wheat field without a skip place showing in it."[33] The crowd was delighted. Truman, once a dirt farmer, was one of them.

After seeing the reactions of the Iowans at the Weesner farm, Truman came away convinced that the farmers were persuadable. He was confident that if he continued to claim on the campaign trail that Republicans planned to undermine price supports, he would capture a major share of the farm vote. To amplify this message, he accepted the support of the National Farmers Union and he sent Chuck Brannan, his agriculture secretary, on a speaking tour to farm communities throughout the nation. For Truman, but not for most of his advisers or the working press, the few hours he spent at the Iowa soil conservation-and-plowing contest felt like a game changer.

Meanwhile, when Dewey heard that Truman had accepted an invitation to speak at Dexter, he invited dozens of farm editors to show off his agricultural expertise at his dairy farm near Pawling in Upstate New York. The well-publicized event took place on the same Saturday that Truman spoke at the plowing contest. Two days later, the fifteen-car Dewey Victory Special, packed with some ninety-two mostly A-list reporters, arrived in Des Moines. Polls showed that Dewey was leading Truman by 51 percent to 37 percent. That evening, before an audience of thirty thousand at Drake Stadium, Dewey began by proclaiming, "Tonight we enter upon a campaign to unite America."[34] The contrast between Dewey's lofty theme of unity and Truman's divisive pitting of farmers against Wall Street Republicans and the 80th Congress could not have been greater. Since Dewey was so far ahead of Truman and had been endorsed by two-thirds of the nation's newspapers, his strategy was to stay above the fray, to avoid saying anything controversial—a strategy that fueled the impression that he was guarded, imperious, aloof, and cool, far from the earthy, emotional, and occasionally hot-tempered man that Truman was. Herb Brownell, Dewey's campaign manager, almost resigned over Dewey's refusal on the night of the Drake speech to attack and refute Truman's allegations concerning price supports and storage bins. Though born in the town of Owosso, Michigan, Truman's principal adversary had become an Easterner while at Columbia Law School in New York City. Since Dewey knew almost nothing about growing wheat, corn, and soybeans, it was impossible for him to connect, as Truman did, with the needs of the nation's dirt farmers.

India Edwards, head of the Women's Division of the DNC, recalled that it was she who "sold" DNC chair McGrath and Bill Boyle, the man who ran Truman's campaign train, on the idea of having the president take Mrs. Truman and Margaret along with him on the *Ferdinand Magellan* for as long as they could stand it. Edwards believed that the crowds would love seeing the First Lady of the nation and her daughter, by then a well-known opera singer. Her instinct was spot-on. Since there would be hardly any other women on the campaign train, it was suggested that Edwards should also go along to look after them, which she did. Aboard the train one morning, Harry and Bess invited India to join them in the *Ferdinand Magellan* for breakfast (Margaret never got up that early). As Mrs. Edwards distinctly recalled in her oral history, the president said, "You know, sometimes, India, I think that there are only two people in the United States who really think I'm going to be elected president. And they're both sitting at this table and one of them is not my wife." There is no evidence that Bess disagreed or otherwise reacted. But Truman was right about India Edwards. An experienced reporter, she would often get off the train after Truman's rear platform speeches and engage people in the crowd. Because of their reactions, "I just *knew* the President was going to be elected," she recalled.[35] Obviously, there must have been more than two who believed Truman would be elected, but in her oral history, Edwards was adamant that neither Howard McGrath, chair of the DNC, nor Jack Redding, head of publicity, thought Truman could win. Furthermore, she claimed that Truman actually knew how those two men, who were supposed to be all in for victory, felt about his chances.

As the Truman Special left farm country and raced across the prairie, sometimes at speeds of 80 to 100 mph, toward the electoral riches of the West, the president knew *how* he could win. Adhering to the Rowe–Clifford memo's number one priority, he must hold the Western states, which FDR had carried in 1944 (103 electoral votes), and he had to replace the unanticipated loss of the South with victories in the Midwest farm states and California. With a total of 214 votes from those states, plus fifteen from his home state of Missouri, he would be only thirty-seven votes shy of the 266 required in 1948 to win the presidency. Truman was certain that with the support of labor, veterans, and African Americans, he could pick up thirty-seven electoral votes from two or more Democratic-leaning Eastern and Midwestern states, which would put him over the top. What's more, he could pull this off while losing New York, New Jersey, Pennsylvania, Massachusetts, and other "big" industrial states. Just as Truman counted cards when he played poker, he memorized the electoral votes of each state and the mathematical combinations that would lead him to 266 and victory.

From dawn to midnight and with short naps in between, Truman campaigned through the West on a ripsnorting, rollicking road show. At almost every stop from the Rockies through Utah and Nevada, across the Sierras to the Pacific, and down California's Central Valley, one or more in the crowd would cry out, "Give 'em hell, Harry!" especially when he tore into the Wall Street Republicans and the gluttons of privilege. His crowds loved to egg him on, delighted to hear him make wild and baseless claims about the GOP and big business. As Robert Donovan, one of the reporters on the train, wrote, Truman "got away with murder" in blaming the Republican-controlled 80th Congress for inflation, the housing shortage, and "any charge that came into his head." For example, without any facts to back it up, he would suddenly blurt out, "The Republicans are trying to sabotage the West!"[36] No one with national stature, least of all Dewey, stepped forth to call Truman out on his false claims.

Up until Truman's train reached Los Angeles, he had virtually ignored Henry Wallace, the standard-bearer for the Progressive Party, the party of peace and accommodation with the Soviets. Nationally, the former VP's popularity had eroded due to the opposition of the labor movement (except for John L. Lewis's mine workers) and his refusal to repudiate the support of Communists. Nevertheless, two of Truman's most aggressive speechwriters—Bob Carr, the economist who could write, and David

Noyes, a small-town newspaper publisher and advertising executive—convinced the president that it was time to take on Wallace and his Progressive Party. Why? Because one of his Los Angeles surrogates had been seducing a cohort of liberal voters away from Truman and into the Wallace tent. No one believed Wallace could actually win by taking votes from Truman but there was fear that he and his surrogate could tip the election in California in favor of Dewey. Truman could not afford to lose California's twenty-five electoral votes.

The Los Angeles surrogate in question was Charlotta Bass, the African American owner of the *California Eagle*, a newspaper catering to a Black readership by focusing on civil rights. After the war, Bass renounced her registration as a Republican. She became a well-known advocate for global peace and an outspoken critic of Truman and his policy of containing both the Soviet Union and Communism itself. She joined the Progressive Party and campaigned for Wallace throughout 1948.

On the evening of September 23, halfway through his speech in Los Angeles at old Gilmore Stadium (demolished in 1952), Truman took aim at Charlotta Bass, Henry Wallace, and the Progressive Party without ever mentioning their names. "It is folly," he began, "for any liberal to put his hope in this third party." It had no power, he alleged, and no chance of acquiring power. Without power, "this third party" could never achieve peace. The Democratic Party was the only party that had the power to fulfill anyone's hopes. "Think again. Don't waste your vote. A vote for the third party plays into the hands of the Republican forces of reaction."[37]

It was a hard-hitting speech but whether it changed any votes is unknown. What is known is that the individual who introduced Truman that night was none other than Ronald Reagan, president of the Screen Actors Guild. A photo of those on the dais with Truman includes Reagan, Congresswoman Helen Gahagan Douglas, movie stars Lauren Bacall and Humphrey Bogart, and comedian George Jessel.

On the way back to Washington, Truman and his advisers decided that they should take a run at capturing Texas's twenty-three electoral votes by spending four full days whistle-stopping across its dry western expanses and into the rolling hills and piney woods of southeast Texas. According to Margaret, her dad, who was not satisfied with the local

Democratic organization, ordered "big, handsome" Don Dawson, a relatively new White House staffer, to fly to Texas and serve as the campaign's
advance man.[38] When Dawson arrived, he was faced with the task of finding a venue in or near Dallas where Truman could deliver a major speech
to a large crowd that would include African Americans. Dawson knew that
Truman wanted Blacks to attend and hear his message even though he did
not plan to mention civil rights to the predominantly racist crowd of white
Texans. Ironically, Dawson picked the "Rebel Stadium" for the president's
speech and he urged Black leaders in Dallas to encourage their people to
attend. He assured them that segregation would not be enforced. In her
book *Harry S. Truman*, Margaret claimed that her dad spoke to "the first
integrated [campaign] rally in the south," a "*very* daring" thing to do in
that part of Texas in 1948.[39] Apparently, a small number of African Americans showed up to see and hear Truman speak but for Margaret to claim
that the crowd was "integrated"—meaning that Blacks actually sat and
mingled with whites at Rebel Stadium—was an overstatement.

The capstone of Truman's campaign in Texas was definitely not integrated. On Sunday morning, September 26, in the now infamous town of
Uvalde, "Cactus Jack" John Nance Garner, former House Speaker and
FDR's first vice president, treated Truman and his entourage at his home
to a gargantuan Texas-style breakfast, "the best Truman had had in forty
years."[40] Garner was an old friend of Truman's whom he had gotten to
know well when Garner presided over the Senate. During breakfast,
Truman presented Cactus Jack with a bottle of fine Kentucky bourbon,
solemnly advising that this "medicine [is] only to be used in case of snake-
bites."[41] The First Lady was so moved by Garner's hospitality that she broke
her usual public silence by stepping up to a microphone and expressing her
thanks to Garner and everyone else for the extraordinary welcome. After
breakfast, Truman posed for photos on the front porch with Garner; Sam
Rayburn, who hailed from Bonham, Texas, and who was soon to be
Speaker of the House; and Texas governor Beauford Jester, from Corsi-
cana, Texas, who died in office less than a year later.

When the Wallace campaign came to Dallas on September 28, Henry
Wallace, in a pitch for Black votes, took pleasure in recounting the anti–
civil rights positions of those standing with Truman on the porch. Ray-

burn, he said, supported the poll tax and opposed anti-lynching legislation. Jester had recently called Truman's civil rights agenda a "stab in the back." And to be polite, since Garner was so widely respected in Texas, Wallace simply said that Garner "was never noted for his support of civil rights." As for Truman, Wallace pointed out that discrimination was rampant in Missouri and "Truman isn't doing anything to eliminate it."[42]

———————

On the train back to Washington, probably in Kentucky or West Virginia, Bob Carr and David Noyes, Truman's enterprising speechwriters, hatched a bold and unorthodox plan that they believed would swing the election in the president's favor. Today, it would be called "an October surprise." Huddling with Matt Connelly, they proposed that the president should schedule a nationwide "non political" radio broadcast to announce that he was sending Fred Vinson, the chief justice of the Supreme Court, to Moscow to meet face-to-face with Joseph Stalin; and that Truman should say to the American people that the purpose of the mission was to persuade the Soviet Union (and to show the world) that the U.S. would spare no effort to achieve peace. The speech and the mission, the speechwriters maintained, would persuade Wallace-leaning voters that the Truman administration was committed to peace, calm fears among voters that the Berlin Airlift would result in war, and demonstrate to Dewey's supporters and the American public that he was the commander in chief best able to deal with Soviet aggression.

Connelly passed the idea on to Truman, who, according to Clifford, liked it "from the moment he heard it."[43] It will be recalled that three years earlier Truman had sent Harry Hopkins to meet with Stalin. Since Hopkins had succeeded in easing tensions, albeit briefly, Truman thought Vinson stood a good chance of achieving a breakthrough as well. On Sunday, October 3, the day after Truman returned from his exhausting two-week campaign trip, he summoned Vinson, his poker-playing pal, to the White House (he had nominated Vinson in 1946). Vinson was at first astonished at what the president asked him to do, protesting for several obvious reasons that he was not the man for the job. No one knows for sure what Truman said, but by the end of the day, Vinson agreed to go to Moscow, possibly having been ordered to do so or perhaps reminded by the president that he had a patriotic duty to try to avert a catastrophic war. As soon as the chief justice left, Truman instructed Charlie Ross to secure a half hour of nationwide airtime on the evening of October 5 "for a public statement of major importance."[44] Ross did so on the condition that the broadcasters maintain secrecy.

Incredibly, it was not until the morning of Truman's proposed address to the nation that the White House notified the State Department. Bob Lovett, acting secretary of state since George Marshall was in Paris, was the first top official at State to get word of Truman's plan to send Vinson to Moscow. Lovett was appalled. He realized at once that the plan needed to be canceled because it would undermine Marshall's efforts in Paris to reach a diplomatic solution to the Berlin crisis via the UN and seriously alienate his British and the French allies. After phoning and telling Truman that he needed to see him "right away, urgent," Lovett, for the first and only time, ordered his driver to turn on the flashing "red light" mounted atop the car, activate "the siren," and get him to the White House as fast as he could.[45] According to Lovett, as soon as the president received him, he bluntly told Truman that his plan was "utterly impossible." Asked to explain, Lovett summarized the diplomatic machinations going on in Paris and said that if Truman announced that evening that he was sending Vinson to meet with Stalin, he would be accused of playing politics, the standing of the United States with its European allies would be irreparably damaged, and Marshall might resign. In other words, it was a bad idea. To his credit, after a teletype conference later that day with Marshall, Truman backed down, even though members of his cabinet argued that it was his last best chance to win the election. "We won't do it," he said.[46]

With the public unaware of the canceled Vinson mission, the president embarked on the second of his whistle-stop campaigns, this one a quick three-day swing through Delaware, eastern Pennsylvania, New Jersey, and upstate New York. On the third day, October 8, Walter Trohan, a reporter with the *Chicago Tribune*, somehow dug up a source, possibly someone with one of the networks or a disloyal White House staffer, who helped him break the story of Truman's planned October surprise. Truman got wind of the news at a stop in Schenectady. Predictably, the rest of the national media picked up Trohan's juicy item and pounced, accusing Truman of staging a desperate election-eve gambit that had to be aborted when Lovett and Marshall found out about it. Truman issued a statement that attempted to frame the episode in terms of a search for peace but it did not quell the outcry. Fortunately, Dewey did not publicly exploit Truman's blunder, confident that he was far ahead and would easily win the election. However, off the record he told reporters that Truman needed to "keep his hands off things for another few weeks . . . particularly . . . foreign policy, about which he knows considerably less than nothing."[47]

In his memoir, Clifford, who claimed that he opposed the Vinson mission, wrote that "it was the worst mistake of the Truman campaign."[48] To be sure, it was a mistake, but there is no evidence that it affected the outcome of the election. Truman was not worried. He believed that the American public would not penalize him for trying to achieve peace.

An article published in the *Atlantic* in 2012 suggests that Truman, a "canny politician," deliberately planned the leak of the Vinson mission in order to keep the Berlin crisis and his role as commander in chief in the news, while pushing Dewey out of the spotlight and demonstrating to potential Wallace voters that he was striving for peace. Such deception is implausible. To pull this off, Truman would have had to dupe his closest advisers or enlist them into going along with this blatantly political scheme. The fact that those who had to have been in the know or those who had initially been deceived never revealed such a fantastic ruse for the rest of their lives is evidence in itself that it never happened.[49]

For the president, Monday, October 11, 1948, was probably the most consequential single day of his entire campaign. On that exhausting fifteen-hour day, Truman whistle-stopped 350 miles across Ohio, seemingly confident that he could flip the hard-core Republican bastion away from Dewey, who had easily carried the state against FDR in 1944. In 1948, Dewey was so certain of winning Ohio's twenty-six electoral votes that he did not bother to actively campaign in the state. As far as Truman was concerned, the Buckeye State was wide open for him to persuade and convert.

After a disappointing start at dawn in Cincinnati—home of the Taft dynasty, where the welcome was tepid, the audience sparse, and the rain cold—the skies began to clear. Once out into rural Ohio, the Truman Special stopped at nine small towns from Hamilton to Rittman, and crowds in the thousands, sometimes tens of thousands, were waiting there to greet the president. Speaking from the rear of the *Ferdinand Magellan*, the president would vary each of his informal talks with an observation unique to the town he was in and he would often introduce Bess as "the Boss" (however, after he called her the Boss in the city of Lima, she told him that if he did it again, she would leave the train). Then he would shift into attack mode, blaming the 80th Congress for high inflation, explaining the evils of the Taft–Hartley law, or warning that if Republicans were elected they would eliminate the farmers' price support program. By this time in the campaign, Truman's whistle-stop talks were spontaneous. The people did not doubt his sincerity.

At his final Ohio stop in the industrial city of Akron, home of the tire industry and its unionized workers, Truman received a tumultuous welcome. It was estimated that sixty thousand people lined the streets of Akron, "the biggest political show in the city's history."[50] Inside the Akron armory, he told the audience, "I have lived a long time, 64 years, . . . but I have never seen such turnouts. . . . The Republicans have the propaganda and the money, but we have the people and the money, and the people have the votes. *That's* why we're going to win!"[51]

Early the next morning, at a stop in Richmond, Indiana, Clifford exited the train to find a newsstand where he could purchase the October 11 issue of *Newsweek* magazine. For days he and those on the campaign train had been awaiting the results of a *Newsweek* survey of the nation's fifty leading political journalists on who would win the elections for the presidency and the 81st Congress. At a newsstand inside the station, Clifford picked up the magazine and leafed through it until he located the headline of the lead article: "Election Forecast: 50 Political Experts Predict a GOP Sweep." As Clifford wrote in his memoir, he was shocked. He had expected that Dewey would be favored, but not by a vote of "fifty to *nothing*." Quickly scanning the article, Clifford noted that based on the survey, *Newsweek* predicted a "landslide for Dewey," and that Republicans would maintain control of the Senate while increasing their majority in the House.

With only three weeks until the election, the article was sobering, to say the least. The survey eclipsed the euphoria of the previous day, when huge crowds from Hamilton to Akron could not stop cheering for "Give 'em Hell" Harry Truman.

Clifford reentered the *Ferdinand Magellan* with the magazine tucked under his suit coat. When he started to pass by the president, who was sitting next to Margaret and reading a newspaper, Truman looked up and said, "What does it say?" Clifford pretended not to understand. According to Clifford's memoir, Truman said something like "Clark, I saw you get off the train just now" and go into the station. "I think you have that *Newsweek* survey under your coat." Clifford reluctantly handed it over.[52] According to Margaret, "Dad stared at the magazine for a moment and then grinned."[53] Then he said, "Don't worry about that poll. I know every one of those fifty fellows, and not one of them has enough sense to pound sand into a rathole."[54]

Negative predictions "seemed to bounce right off of him," recalled Clifford.[55] The next day, October 13, on the train from Duluth to St. Paul, Minnesota, Truman rattled off the names and the number of electoral votes of each of the states that he was convinced he would win and asked George Elsey to add up the votes. "Three hundred forty, Mr. President," responded Elsey, seventy-four more than the 266 required to win. Although Truman's three hundred forty included five states that he would not win and two that he did, the point was, wrote Elsey, that Truman did not "just *think* he would win, he *knew* he would win."[56]

While most of Truman's entourage on the campaign train was treated to a six-day break in Washington so they could sleep in their own beds, take showers, wear fresh clothes, and spend moments with their loved ones, the president, with a skeleton staff, flew south, his only foray into enemy territory other than the one into southeast Texas. According to a new Gallup poll, Truman had narrowed Dewey's lead to six points, close to the margin of error. Something out there "was rolling," recalled Clifford. "We could sense it and the newspapermen could sense it." The pundits and pollsters could have been wrong.

Truman's reasons for flying south had little to do with trying to persuade Southerners to vote for him. He regarded the nine or ten Southern states as lost causes, not worth his time, although, as it turned out, he would lose only four. Rather, the president wanted to explain to the twelve thousand fellow veterans attending an American Legion convention in Miami, as well as a nationwide radio audience, his rationale for the Vinson mission and to rebut claims by the Wallace campaign that he was not trying hard enough to achieve peace with the Soviets. Although obviously biased, Truman wrote in his memoirs that after his Miami speech, "a great many people" began to understand that the prospects for peace in the world were best served by a Democratic administration.[57]

On his flight back to Washington, the president made a brief stop in Raleigh, North Carolina, where, as a favor to an old friend, he dedicated a monument at the state capitol to three former presidents born in North Carolina, one of whom was Andrew Johnson. Johnson, who succeeded to the presidency after Lincoln's death, was a traditional Southern Democrat with pronounced states' rights views. Truman had always prided himself on his knowledge of American history, but his remarks that day to a large all-white audience in Raleigh heaped praise on Johnson, one of the nation's worst presidents, and were at odds with Johnson's actual record. Truman had to have known that Johnson was a racist, a white supremacist whose commitment to obstructing political and civil rights for Blacks led to the failure of Reconstruction. Yet he pandered to his Southern audience, claiming that Johnson—by opposing the Civil Rights Act of 1866 and other measures that Truman said had been designed by radical Republicans to keep the South "in chains"—had been courageously following the "Constitution of the United States."[58] Oddly, Dewey and Wallace neglected to criticize Truman for misstating Johnson's record. Moreover, none of Truman's biographers suggested that the president's effusive praise of Johnson was at odds with Truman's own civil rights agenda, which was then being promoted in Northern cities to attract Black voters. The word "hypocrisy" was never invoked.

Setting aside the campaign for another two days, Harry Truman, having returned to the White House, eagerly awaited General Lucius Clay, who had flown in from Europe to brief him on the Berlin crisis. At precisely 11 a.m. on October 21, Clay, accompanied by James Forrestal, Kenneth Royall, and General William ("Bill") Draper, a banker and former partner in Dillon Read & Co. on Wall Street, trooped into the Oval Office. The news from Clay was encouraging. With winter approaching, more planes would be needed but the airlift of supplies into Berlin should be enough to keep Berliners from freezing and starving. In negotiations by "neutral" members of the UN Security Council to end the blockade, reported Clay, the Soviets had made a concession that appeared to be a clever first step toward their eventual goal of forcing "all hands [to] get out of Germany." Under no circumstances, Clay bluntly told Truman, should the U.S. pull out of Berlin because it would mean "withdrawal from Europe and in the long run the beginning of the third world war."[59] Truman agreed. He authorized Clay to "draw up to 66 additional C-54s" to be used in the Berlin Airlift and to acquire enough aviation fuel to sustain the airlift, as well as a "stockpile for emergency purposes."[60]

The final leg of Truman's come-from-behind whistle-stop campaign began just before midnight on Friday, October 22. This time, there were only a few on the platform at Union Station who had come at that hour to see Harry, Bess, and Margaret board the *Ferdinand Magellan*. Although the national consensus was that Dewey would win, there were signs that the gap was closing. The Gallup poll on October 25, its last before the election, showed the president trailing Dewey by only five points. Truman was full of vigor and vinegar, ready to fight until the end. His itinerary for the next nine days was ambitious, with major speeches scheduled in Pittsburgh, Chicago, Cleveland, Boston, New York, and St. Louis, and dozens of stops at small towns and cities in between (Dewey followed much the same route but stopped only at the big cities). By focusing on open-car parades and speeches in large cities of the Midwest and East, Truman's goal was to appeal to FDR's old New Deal coalition, that is, labor unions, Blacks, Jews, Catholics, and the many voters of East European descent.

In Pittsburgh, Truman entertained an audience of a hundred thousand at Armory Hall by taking a page from FDR's playbook—playing the part of a doctor for the American people and then the role of his patient, as FDR had been wont to do. As a cure for the patient's inflation sickness, Dr. Truman prescribed a dose of "soothing syrup." "I call it unity," he said, thereby mocking Dewey's above-it-all magic cure for the ills of the nation.[61] Truman's timing did not match that of Roosevelt, but he still brought down the house.

Before a crowd of twenty-five thousand in Chicago Stadium, Truman's speech, drafted by Bob Carr and watered down by Clifford and Elsey, was the most unhinged of his entire campaign. With subtle references, Truman likened his opposition, meaning Dewey, to Hitler and Mussolini, warning that shadowy fascist elements in America could get control of the economy and appoint a "front man," that is, Dewey, to run the country for them. Under Republican government, he asserted, "democracy can be destroyed and tyranny born." Invoking Nazi Germany again, and with no evidence whatever, Truman went on to speak of "demagogues among us"—Republicans?—who were trying to win a war on democracy by "attacking Catholics, and Jews, and Negroes and other minority races and religions."[62] Setting aside the question of whether Truman actually believed what he was saying, the fact that he uttered these delusional words indicated that he had come to the point where he would say almost anything if he thought it would help to win the election.

At Cleveland's Municipal Auditorium on the night of October 26, Truman took on what he called "the Republican polls," which the Dewey campaign had been touting. Since the national polls—Roper, Gallup, and Crossley—had all shut down prior to the twenty-sixth, he might have been also referring to "state polls," which showed Dewey winning by wide margins in key states.[63] Speaking to the Clevelanders in the auditorium and a nationwide radio audience, Truman claimed, without evidence, that national and state polls "are part of a design"—conspiracy?—to suppress voter turnout "by convincing you that it makes no difference whether you vote or not." They "do this," said Truman, "because they know in their hearts that a big vote spells their defeat."[64]

Among those in the audience that night was Aaron H. Payne, a Howard-educated African American lawyer known throughout Black America for his famous clients—heavyweight champ Joe Louis, Nat King Cole, and Josephine Baker. According to Margaret Truman, Aaron Payne, who had been traveling and campaigning for the president on the Truman Special at his own expense, exercised his considerable influence in Cleveland's large Black community. (The city was home to James Cleveland "Jesse" Owens of Olympic fame; when he was nine years old, he had migrated with his family to Cleveland—the so-called "Promised Land to colored people in his part of Alabama."[65]) Margaret wrote that Payne was instrumental in helping to "carry four predominantly black wards in Cleveland." Since Truman was to win Ohio by the slim margin of 7,107 votes, Payne's assistance, she said, was "crucial."[66]

With five days to go until the election, Truman pressed on to Boston. where a quarter of a million working-class Irish Catholics lined the streets. At Mechanics Hall that evening, the main subject of Truman's address was Communism. While making it clear to the capacity crowd that he hated Communists and they detested him, Truman claimed that "Republicans in State after State had worked to get Communist-supported [Henry Wallace] on the ballot in order to defeat me." That the Republicans would stoop so low, continued Truman, proved that they would do "anything to get votes" and thus obtain political power. He concluded by proclaiming, "We are engaged in a great crusade for freedom. . . . This fight is Roosevelt's fight. And now it is my fight."[67]

More than a million New Yorkers turned out for a ticker tape parade to catch a glimpse of Truman smiling and waving while perched atop the back seat of an open car moving slowly through Manhattan with loudspeakers blaring "Happy Days Are Here Again." That evening, Thursday, October 28, in Madison Square Garden before a crowd of sixteen thousand, the president delivered a speech directed primarily at appealing to Jewish voters. Reminding listeners that he had been the first to recognize the new state of Israel, he pledged to "help the people of Israel," who, he said, had already demonstrated that they deserve to take their place "in the family of nations" as a "strong, prosperous, free, and independent democratic state."[68] All day and the night before, Truman's sleepless aides had frantically worked to make sure that Secretary of State Marshall, who was in Paris at a meeting of the UN General Assembly, canceled his endorsement of a two-state solution, which had been rejected by the Israeli government because it would have awarded the Negev territory to the Arabs—a complete reversal of the provision assigning the Negev to the Jewish state in the UN resolution adopted in November 1947. "Jewish war veterans and young Zionists," including Eddie Jacobson, who had been praying and singing in the lobby of the Roosevelt Hotel, where the president was staying, were relieved when they got word that night of Truman's uncompromising commitment to support Israel.

The following morning, Truman met for a few minutes with Philleo Nash to go over the latest draft of a civil rights speech that Nash had been working on for weeks. Nash, who had helped create the President's Committee on Civil Rights, had suggested from the outset of the fall campaign that "the President should be silent" on the subject until he reached Harlem, "leaving everybody wondering and guessing until right up to the end," when it would have the most dramatic effect.[69]

At around 3:30 p.m. on Friday, a crisp, sunny day, Nash arrived at Dorrance Brooks Square, the venue in Harlem for Truman's civil rights speech. The square (actually a long, narrow rectangle) was named after Private First Class Dorrie Brooks, a Harlem native who had been killed in action in France near the end of WWI. Situated between West 137th and West 136th streets, the square was bounded on the east by Edgecombe Avenue. To the west, above the bluffs of St. Nicholas Park, the Gothic buildings of the City College of New York (CCNY) overlooked the square.[70] As early as 10 in the morning, the crowd, mostly Black and standing, had begun gathering, and occasionally broke out in song as it awaited the president. According to police estimates, the throng numbered sixty thousand when the Council of Negro Clergymen, sponsors of the event, assembled on the platform to greet the president.

As Truman got up to speak, Nash heard shouts from CCNY students in the distance: "Pour it on, Harry. Give 'em hell, Harry." Then, when their cries did not catch on, the voices faded and the massive crowd became ominously silent. Nash turned around. "Almost everybody in the crowd was praying," he recalled. "They were praying for the President, and they were praying for their own civil rights. And they thought it was a religious occasion."[71]

Sensing the mood of the crowd, the president began by saying, "This . . . is a most solemn occasion." Gazing out at the sea of silent Black citizens, he added, "It's made a tremendous impression on me." And it had. "Eventually," he went on, "*we* are going to have an America in which freedom and opportunity are the same for everyone." From the crowd there were murmurs of "Amen." The use of the inclusive word "we," which he repeated throughout his talk, resonated. The president reminded his audience that exactly a year earlier, on October 29, 1947, his Committee on Civil Rights had issued its report, and he said that after he won the election, he planned to make its recommendations "a living reality for every American, regardless of his race, his religion, or his national origin." To accomplish the report's objectives, he said, the courts and every branch of government—federal, state, and local—must have a role. "For my part," he concluded, "I intend to keep moving toward this goal with every ounce of strength and determination that I have."[72]

The speech was short, lasting less than twenty minutes, applause included. Back at the Roosevelt Hotel, where the exhausted staff was resting before an evening speech in Brooklyn and then the train to St. Louis, Nash encountered Truman walking down the hall, "looking for somebody to talk to." Nash asked him how he felt about the speech. "Well," responded Truman, "that was the high point of the campaign. That was emotional, that was really from the heart." [73]

En route to St. Louis, where the campaign would end, Margaret wrote, her "father for the first time showed that he was at least *capable* of getting tired and took a long afternoon nap."[74] When Truman woke up, he was asked to review the latest draft of a speech that he was scheduled to deliver that evening to a nationwide radio audience at the huge Kiel Auditorium; it was the last campaign speech that he would ever make. Confiding to his friend, Treasury Secretary John Snyder, who had hitched a ride to his hometown, Truman said that the draft lacked "punch." He refused to use it, and informed Snyder that he would speak off the cuff.[75]

At 9:30 that evening, October 30, when the president approached the podium, the roar in jam-packed, standing-room-only Kiel Auditorium (capacity ninety-three hundred) was deafening. Without a rough outline and with only a few notes to remind him of statistics, Harry Truman did what he had done throughout the campaign—he went on the attack. Characterizing the media as "assassins" and the Republicans and their special interests as "saboteurs," he tore into the 80th Congress for passing a "rich man's tax bill" and a "fake housing bill" while rebuffing his national health insurance and education reform proposals. Each of his attacks was met by wild cheering, stomping, and applause. When Truman mocked the "Republican candidate" (read Dewey) for "following me up and down the country" and making "speeches about home and mother and unity" without talking about "the issues," the crowd rocked with laughter and derision. "People are waking up that the tide is beginning to roll," he concluded. "If you do your duty as citizens of the greatest Republic the sun has ever shone on, we will have a Government that will be for your interests."[76]

After the speech, Clark Clifford, who had been with Truman throughout the grueling campaign, bade a warm farewell to Harry, Bess, and Margaret as they boarded the train to Independence. Clifford, who had grown up in St. Louis, would stay there for a few days to vote and spend time with his mother. Reflecting on the campaign, he had mixed emotions. He was proud that he had helped the president close the gap, yet terribly worried that there was still not enough time for his boss to catch up to Dewey. There was one emotion, however, that was crystal clear—"a wave of joyous relief" that he no longer had to live on the train; he felt "as though a prison sentence had been lifted."[77]

———————

Meanwhile, officials at the DNC and the New York Democratic Party believed that voters in the state of New York were teetering between Dewey and Truman and that an endorsement of the president by Eleanor Roosevelt could tip the election in his favor. Thus far, Mrs. Roosevelt had declined to publicly endorse Truman, using the excuse that because she was a delegate to the UN, it would not be appropriate for her to engage in political activities. However, when Jack Redding, the DNC's publicity director, phoned her in Paris, where she had been attending UN sessions since early October, the widely respected former First Lady agreed to deliver a six-minute endorsement of Truman. It was decided that her remarks would be broadcast by ABC over shortwave radio on Sunday night,

October 31, just over twenty-four hours before Election Day. Courtesy of the Greek community in the New York area, Louis Johnson produced a paper shopping bag stuffed with bills of varying denominations totaling $25,721, the amount charged by ABC for clearing airtime and arranging the broadcast from Paris. The bag of cash was delivered to ABC on Sunday afternoon. That night, Mrs. Roosevelt's distinctive voice was heard throughout the U.S. "There has never been a campaign where a man has shown more personal courage and confidence in the people of the United States. Harry Truman needs the people's mandate to help him if he's going to be our president. I still believe in the Democratic party and its leadership."[78]

Oddly, Truman and his White House aides could have acted to save the DNC a bucketload of money by publicizing and hyping a letter from Mrs. Roosevelt to him dated October 4. In that letter, which was quietly released to the public by the White House during the week of October 25 to 29, Eleanor wrote, "I am unqualifiedly for you as the Democratic candidate for the Presidency."[79] Except for the sound of her voice, this was a stronger endorsement than the one on Sunday night that cost more than $25,000, because she wrote that Truman was the best candidate rather than stressing his "need" for "help" in doing his job. *Time* magazine noted the existence of this letter of endorsement and its release in its November 1 issue.

For Truman, Election Day, Tuesday, November 2, began at 5 a.m. with his usual morning stroll along the sidewalks of Independence. Across the nation the weather was generally fair. Nevertheless, voter turnout was expected to be low because newspapers and pundits had continued to predict a GOP landslide. Dewey's victory was a foregone conclusion, the thinking of many Republicans went, so why take the time and effort to vote?

Moreover, because the last Gallup poll—based on a survey conducted during the period from October 15 to October 25—indicated that Truman trailed Dewey by five points, almost no one foresaw the rapid shift in "voter intentions" that would take place during the final week of the campaign, nor did the so-called experts take note of the fact that from August 20 to August 25 until mid-October, the gap had narrowed significantly from twelve to five points.[80] In hindsight, it seems obvious that the turnout and trend lines would not favor Dewey on Election Day.

At 10 a.m., Harry, Bess, and Margaret, who were trailed by reporters, photographers, and neighbors, walked the three blocks to Memorial Hall on West Maple across from Truman's barbershop to cast their votes, the first for Margaret in a presidential election. Truman had helped dedicate the hall on July 4, 1926, when he was running for Jackson County presiding judge as a Pendergast machine candidate. As they left the polling station, someone yelled out, "Are you going to sit up for the returns, Mr. President?" Truman responded, "No, I think I'll go to bed. I don't expect final results until tomorrow."[81]

According to Margaret, that afternoon her father "pulled his neatest trick of the campaign." He left with his Secret Service detail for a short drive to the Rockwood Country Club, a mile or two southwest of the city center on Maywood Avenue. There, the mayor of Independence hosted a luncheon for the president and thirty of his old friends. After lunch, Truman excused himself, supposedly to go to the men's room. Instead, he was whisked out the back door by three Secret Service agents and driven twenty-four miles north across a Missouri River bridge to the Elms Hotel in Excelsior Springs, a resort town known for its restorative mineral waters. Other than Margaret, Bess, his old friend Tom Evans, and the Secret Service, no one knew where the president had gone. When reporters returned from the club to the house on Delaware Street, "frantic" for information as to Truman's whereabouts, Margaret and Bess, who had been left to cope with them throughout that night, told them that Truman "was not in the house" but nothing else.[82]

After a Turkish bath and a massage, Truman retired to a room on the third floor at the end of a long hall. There, at about 6:30, he dined on a ham and cheese sandwich, drank a glass of buttermilk, and turned on the bedside radio to listen to early East Coast election returns and commentary. On that Tuesday night in November, the hotel was almost empty.

Why did the president choose to spend election night alone, leaving his wife and daughter to deal with the mob of reporters outside their house? In an undated longhand note written by Truman, his only explanation was that "I had had a strenuous summer and fall and was tired."[83] That was certainly true, but it must have been more than that. Deep down, in spite of his bravado, he likely had a flicker of doubt. If he should lose, he wanted to have time alone to compose himself before facing the media jackals and the American people.

As night fell, teletype reports from Truman's campaign staff in the presidential suite of the Muehlebach Hotel in Kansas City and Howard McGrath's DNC team at the Biltmore Hotel in New York indicated that Truman was leading in Chicago, Ohio was looking good, and the president was well on his way to winning in Virginia. However, Dewey was not only ahead of Truman in most of the Northeast; it had become apparent that he would carry both New York, his home state, and Maryland (a total of fifty-five electoral votes), states that FDR had won in 1944. In those states, Henry Wallace and his Progressive Party had drained enough votes away from Truman to make the difference.

By 9 p.m. Eastern Standard Time (8:00 in Missouri), the polls had closed in twelve of the forty-eight states. During the next hour or so, Dewey was declared the winner in New Jersey and Pennsylvania (a total of forty-one electoral votes), but Truman captured Massachusetts and Rhode Island (a total of twenty electoral votes), the only states that he won in New England.

While it had been predicted that Governor Dewey would win in Pennsylvania and most of the Northeast, he was worried about the farm vote, especially in Ohio (twenty-five electoral votes). The crucially important state was controlled by prominent Republicans and should have already been called in his favor. As the minutes ticked by, the race in the Buckeye State was tightening, way too close to call. Dewey retreated to a bedroom in his suite at the Roosevelt Hotel in New York, leaving his family in the living room watching TV. He wanted to be alone. There is no record of what he was thinking but he might have been brooding over the wisdom of his "above it all" campaign strategy of refusing to attack Truman head-on.

By all accounts, Truman was not worried. Confident that the farmers were with him and aware that he was pulling ahead in the popular vote, he turned off the radio at about 9:00 Central Time and fell asleep for the next three hours. An hour and fifteen minutes later, from Republican headquarters on the sixth floor of the Roosevelt Hotel in New York, Dewey's campaign manager, Herbert Brownell, issued a wildly optimistic statement: "I am convinced, as I stated earlier, the election of the Dewey–Warren Ticket is assured.... We conclude ... that Dewey and Warren are elected."[84]

Near midnight, Truman awoke. He tuned his radio to NBC in order to hear H. V. Kaltenborn, dean of radio commentators, predict that the president was "undoubtedly beaten," even though at that point he was ahead of Dewey by 1.2 million votes.[85] Kaltenborn reminded his audience that it was the electoral not the popular vote that counted. Truman went back to sleep. (At a white-tie dinner shortly after the election, Truman rendered a hilarious imitation of Kaltenborn's clipped diction and faint German accent as he predicted that Dewey was unbeatable.[86])

From the Muehlebach Hotel, Tom Evans, one of the very few who knew how to reach the president, placed a call to his room through the Elm Hotel's switchboard. It was 2:15 a.m. Evans excitedly informed Truman that based on the returns and the campaign experts in Kansas City and New York, he was positioned to win the election if he carried either Ohio, Illinois, or California. A win, Evans said, in just one of those three states would get Truman to 266 electoral votes. And since Ohio's returns would be counted earlier than those in Illinois because of the different time zones and California would take even longer, Evans told Truman that he needed to pay attention to the Ohio vote as it came in. According to Evans, Truman said, "That's good. I'm going to bed. Don't call me anymore." When Evans protested that Truman should stay up to follow Ohio and, if needed, Illinois, Truman replied, "I'm going to carry all three."[87] He turned over and went back to sleep again.

By 3 a.m. Kaltenborn admitted it was a "very close race" but he still thought Dewey had the best chance of winning.[88] To make that prediction, he had to be counting on Dewey prevailing in Ohio, Illinois, California, Oregon, the Dakotas, Nebraska, and Kansas, plus the states already called in his favor, which would have given him 267 electoral votes, one more than the 266 needed. On the other hand, Truman's analysts, by counting on most of the West and Midwest and even a good slice of the South, except California, Oregon, Michigan, Indiana, South Carolina, Alabama,

Mississippi, and Louisiana, believed they had 241 electoral votes in the bag and therefore needed only twenty-five to put Truman over the top.

At the Biltmore in New York at about 5:30 a.m., and an hour earlier in Missouri and Illinois, DNC chair Howard McGrath was on the phone with Colonel Jake Arvey, Democratic boss of Cook County. Arvey was in Chicago monitoring returns.[89] According to Jack Redding, who was in the room with McGrath when he was talking to Arvey, McGrath's face suddenly "brightened." He put the phone down. Arvey had said that "we've got Illinois!" hollered McGrath. "Close, but we've got [Illinois] for Truman."[90] With its twenty-eight electoral votes, this meant that Truman, by a slender margin in Illinois, had won the national election, assuming no miscounts or recounts in Illinois or elsewhere could change the outcome. McGrath promptly relayed this vital information to Matt Connelly at the Muehlebach Hotel in Kansas City. Connelly in turn alerted Secret Service agent Jim Rowley that he should inform the president immediately. Rowley, who had been up all night, knocked and went into the president's room. Truman woke up and reached for his glasses. Rowley gave him the word. "That's it," exclaimed Truman. "We've got 'em beat." Before getting dressed for the drive into Kansas City, Truman invited Rowley and two other agents to join him in toasting his victory with a shot or two of bourbon. When the president was suited up, fresh, and ready, he called to the Secret Service agents. "Harness the horses, boys"—meaning they should get the car. "We're in trouble for another four years."[91]

———

At the Muehlebach Hotel, wire service correspondent Bob Nixon had been up most of the night in the presidential suite, where teletype machines and typewriters had been set up for reporters covering the election. A little before 5 a.m., knowing that returns were trending toward the president, which meant that Truman would be coming to campaign headquarters at the hotel sometime later that morning, Nixon located a uniformed doorman in the lobby, slipped him a $20 bill, and told the man to call him the moment Truman arrived. An hour later, when Nixon was asleep in his room, the doorman called and told him that the president was just

entering the hotel. As Nixon later recounted to his interviewer, he threw
a trench coat over his pajamas, raced in his bedroom slippers to the elevator, and went up to the presidential suite on the seventeenth floor. When
he arrived, the door was open. The only one in the living room was the
president, who was sitting on a sofa talking on the telephone. He waved to
Nixon to come in. The reporter could tell from what he overheard that
Truman was talking to Bess, who was at home in Independence. "Tears
were streaming down his eyes," he recalled, while "he was telling her that
he had won," an intimate few moments to be sure. Nixon realized at once
that he had stumbled upon a real story. Once Truman put down the phone,
Nixon was able to spend several minutes alone with the newly elected
president. Exhausted campaign staffers and other reporters were either
napping on couches elsewhere in the suite or asleep in their own rooms.
Aside from questioning Truman about his immediate reaction to the election, Nixon recalled asking him whether he had ever lost faith in the outcome. "Bob," he responded, "I never . . . had any doubt *whatsoever* but that
I would win." Nixon, a hard-boiled reporter used to detecting white lies by
politicians, came away from his encounter that morning persuaded that
the president was sincere and "that it was his faith, as well as his fighting
spirit that carried him through" to victory.[92]

It wasn't long before reporters, staffers, and well-wishers from Independence and Kansas City filled every room in the suite and spilled outside
into the hall. With corks popping, the celebration was underway. World
War I buddies from Battery D showed up as did Eddie Jacobson, proprietor
of Westport Mens Wear. Truman sat on a couch accepting congratulations. At 8:30, a cheer went up when the razor-thin contest in Ohio was
called for Truman. An hour later he was declared the winner in California
and it became apparent that the Democrats would take back majorities in
the House and Senate.

About the time champagne arrived at DNC headquarters at the Biltmore, Chairman Howard McGrath was handed the phone. From Kansas
City, the president was on the line, thanking him for his hard work. With
a glass of champagne in hand and a gesture to the crowd in the room,
McGrath congratulated Truman and told him, "Your staff is drinking to
you . . . from the bottoms of our hearts we drink to you."[93] At that moment

India Edwards was standing next to McGrath. As she later recalled, Mc-Grath spoke into the phone to the president: "Now I want you to talk to the person who really had faith all the time, and who knew you were going to win." He handed the phone to Edwards. "I burst out crying," she recalled, "and I'm not a crying woman."[94] "I know I am tough," Edwards used to say, but on this occasion she was incoherent.[95] Perhaps it was due to a sudden release of tension or maybe because she had been up all night. But Truman understood. He remembered the conversation on the train when he told her that she was one of the only two who believed he could win. And he was grateful for all she had done—the women's vote, the Truman motion picture, the comic book titled *The Story of Harry S. Truman*, the mobile inflation trailers, and the bloodred beefsteak that she held up at the Democratic convention while blaming Republicans for the high cost.

At 11:15 a.m. in New York, 10:15 in Independence and Kansas City, Dewey gracefully conceded. Privately he said, "What do you know? The son of a bitch won."[96]

Truman won by capturing 303 electoral votes out of 531 electors from twenty-eight states to Dewey's 189 from sixteen states. Turnout was predictably low. Only 51.1 percent of those eligible voted. In the popular vote, Truman recorded 24,105,812 votes, 2.1 million more than Dewey but slightly less than 50 percent of the total vote. Of the two other major parties, Wallace received 1.1 million votes, half from New York City, and not a single electoral vote. Strom Thurmond, standard-bearer for the Dixiecrats, carried his home state of South Carolina and three other Deep South states with 1.2 million votes. And the four other presidential candidates, led by Socialist Norman Thomas, received almost three hundred thousand votes.

In the Senate, Democrats improved from a six-seat deficit to a surprising twelve-seat majority. In the House they picked up a whopping seventy-five seats for a ninety-two-seat majority. So much for the do-nothing Congress.

Truman's come-from-behind victory in 1948 was astonishing, arguably the most surprising in the history of presidential politics. Donald Trump's electoral win in 2016, though shocking to many, was not as surprising as Truman's. In the days leading up to Trump's election, virtually all pollsters concluded that Hillary Clinton's margin of victory had

narrowed considerably—more than Truman's—and that it was almost a
dead heat. By contrast, in Truman's case, none of the experts predicted
that he would come close enough in the popular or electoral votes in the
final days to actually pull off a win, particularly because the Democratic
Party was split three ways.

———————

T he next morning, Harry, Bess, and Margaret boarded the newly christened "Victory Special" for the trip back to Washington. At Union Station
in St. Louis, Truman, with a look on his face of sheer triumph, was photographed standing on the rear platform of the *Ferdinand Magellan* holding
aloft a two-day-old copy of the *Chicago Daily Tribune* bearing the headline
"DEWEY DEFEATS TRUMAN." In fairness to the newspaper's management, the limited "mail" edition brandished by Truman had to be printed
by early afternoon on Election Day because of an ongoing strike. Therefore, the overly optimistic editors—conservatives, by the way—chose to
call the election in Dewey's favor based on sketchy returns, polls, and
guesswork. Almost seventy years later, Ben Cosgrove of *Time* magazine
wrote that the iconic photograph—he called it the greatest political photo
ever made—is remembered not because of the erroneous headline itself.
Rather, it "endures because of the look of unabashed, in-your-face delight
in Truman's eyes."

Chapter 13

Liberator

Five days after the election, an ebullient Harry Truman left Washington for a vacation in the sun at Naval Station Key West, just outside the run-down village of old Key West. He was not alone. Joining him on the flight south were his physician, Dr. Wallace Graham, and twelve of his top advisers, including Clark Clifford, John Steelman, and Admiral Leahy. In separate planes and trains, Bess, Margaret, India Edwards (accompanied by her husband), and eleven more friends and advisers came and went during the ensuing two weeks. Security was provided to the president, his family, and his entourage by a fifteen-man Secret Service detail headed by Jim Rowley. With little breaking news to report, some fifty correspondents, radio broadcasters, photographers, and newsreel producers who were allowed to cover the so-called vacation were on their own, mixing at night with sailors and locals in Key West's cheap bars.

Sporting garish, untucked sports shirts colored with figures of swaying palm trees and pink flamingos—dubbed "Truman shirts"—the president and his friends frequented the small beach on the base, strolled into town, and played poker and watched movies most evenings. Many of the men went barefoot and did not shave for several days. Truman, with his glasses still on, swam sidestroke in the Atlantic Ocean while others enjoyed deep-sea fishing trips and junkets to Havana and the Dry Tortugas. Meals were usually served at the "Little White House," a frame dwelling built in 1890 in which the president and his closest aides were quartered. There, Truman often held court, entertaining his guests by reading letters from donors who claimed that their campaign contributions had been mailed late due to secretarial errors.

According to Robert Donovan, who interviewed many of those in Truman's entourage, "the election returns . . . gave Truman a feeling of being out from under the shadow of Roosevelt at last."[1]

When DNC chair Howard McGrath arrived in Key West on the morning of November 11, Truman and a few others, while having lunch or drinks before dinner, discussed with him the factors that had led to victory. Based on a memo from Philleo Nash, McGrath's view was that had it not been for the Black vote—more than 80 percent favoring Truman in "Negro districts" throughout the nation—Dewey would have won.[2] Others argued that it was the movement of the farm vote during the week before Election Day that had clinched the win for Truman. For his part, the president had already publicly credited the organizational muscle of the labor unions and the farm vote for his win, while curiously ignoring the contributions of African Americans. Historian Simon Topping claimed that Truman did this because he believed labor and farmers would be more "useful allies" than African Americans in the coming four years.[3] What the president might have revealed privately to McGrath during his one-day visit to Key West is unknown.

On the same day, George Elsey, a Roosevelt holdover who was Clifford's principal assistant, flew down to Key West to join the gathering of Truman's aides. A vacation, however, was far from Elsey's mind. He had heard from cabinet members that Truman planned to devote his January inaugural address to domestic issues. Elsey's mission—his reason for flying to Key West—was to convince Clifford and thereafter the president that instead of domestic issues Truman should confirm his role as leader of the free world by using his inaugural speech to lay out the principles of his foreign policy for the next four years.[4] Though it took him a few days,

Elsey's pitch was successful. He returned to Washington tasked with the job of producing an inaugural address devoted to foreign affairs. His initial move was to ask experts at the State Department to provide him with a draft. In due course, a draft speech arrived, but Elsey found it disappointing. It focused on three points that had already been publicized: continued support for the UN, the Marshall Plan for the recovery of Western Europe, and the defense alliance soon to be called NATO. There was nothing new and innovative to showcase Truman's world leadership. Fortunately, a fairly junior public affairs official in the State Department by the name of Ben Hardy contacted Elsey, whom he had never met, and asked to see him as soon as possible. When they got together in late December, Hardy proposed that the president should include in his inaugural address a "bold new program" whereby the U.S. would provide its technical assistance and know-how, but not in the form of money, to improve the growth of "underdeveloped areas" throughout the world.[5] Hardy explained that his idea had been scuttled by higher-ups at State and that he was risking his career by making an end run to the White House without permission from his bosses. When a draft speech including Hardy's idea was presented to Truman, the president's "enthusiasm" was immediate, wrote Elsey.[6]

The final act of the long yet unsteady transition of power from Franklin Roosevelt to Harry Truman took place on the east side of the Capitol at noon on January 20, 1949, when Truman was sworn in by Chief Justice Vinson. A few minutes later, under a dazzling sun and a cold north wind, the president began his inaugural address, the foreign policy speech written by George Elsey that introduced what became known as "the Point Four Program." Citing the threat to world peace by Communism, the first three points—unfaltering support of the UN, the Marshall Plan, and NATO—were vitally important, but not a surprise. It was the fourth point, however, that produced sustained applause, ignited the nation's imagination, and was acclaimed around the globe. Since more than half the world's population lived in poverty and misery, Truman declared, the U.S. must make available the inexhaustible "benefits of our scientific advances and industrial progress" to help the people living in underdeveloped countries "realize their aspirations for a better life."[7] Simply put, the essence of his fourth proposal, originated by Ben Hardy, was the distribution of knowledge and know-how, not money.

Truman was "enormously proud of Point Four," wrote Elsey.[8] However, the program was not enacted into law until June 1950 and, in the opinion of Truman, was underfunded by $10.5 million. Nonetheless, by the end of 1951, Point Four technical assistance had been provided to thirty-three countries. In his memoirs Truman devoted more pages (thirty-six) to touting Point Four and its accomplishments than to any other of his foreign policy initiatives.[9] It was a forerunner to today's Agency for International Development (AID) and the Peace Corps.

"Never before in the history of the world," wrote Jonathan Bingham, who had helped implement Point Four and later became a congressman, "had a government launched a large-scale effort to help peoples to whom it was bound by no special ties other than a common interest in the world's peace and prosperity."[10]

––––––––––

It was fitting that Truman's first and only inauguration featured an ambitious new program to lift people out of poverty in the underdeveloped world because it aligned with the most consequential actions of his presidency—initiatives designed to liberate the destitute and oppressed. Aided by George Marshall, Dean Acheson, George Kennan, and Arthur Vandenberg, to name a few, Truman, under the banner of the Truman Doctrine, had during his first term made bold and risky decisions that led to the liberation of millions of human beings in Western Europe, Western Germany, Berlin, and Japan. Moreover, by recognizing and supporting Israel, he had facilitated the establishment of a home for Holocaust survivors and other Jews, though at great cost to the lives of Palestinian Arabs. And in the U.S., the president's courageous civil rights agenda laid the groundwork for the movement in the 1960s toward eventual liberation of Black citizens from discrimination and denial of constitutional rights.

Whether measured by cold statistics or personal stories, Truman's decisions to authorize and aggressively support the Marshall Plan and its protective corollary, the NATO alliance, resulted in the liberation of countless Western Europeans from hunger, chaos, despair, and the attempted takeover of some of their governments by Communists. Referring in 1952 to the effect of these decisions, Winston Churchill, Truman's guest aboard the *Williamsburg*, said, "You more than any other man saved Western civilization."[11]

The agency that administered the Marshall Plan reported that by 1951 industrial production in Western Europe had increased to 43 percent above prewar levels and 64 percent above 1947. Steel production nearly doubled in less than four years. The standard of living throughout Western Europe had greatly improved and unemployment in most of the countries was low. Marshall Plan assistance resulted in the rebuilding of infrastructure such as dikes, dams, canals, power plants, and steelworks. But smaller projects that directly improved the lives of the people included, for example, shipments of thousands of gallons of orange juice for English youngsters, nets for Norwegian fishermen, looms for a weaving cooperative, and baby chicks to children in Vienna from an American 4-H Club.

In West Germany, which became eligible for Marshall Plan aid in 1948, it was discovered that less of its industrial capacity had been destroyed than previously thought. With Marshall Plan assistance, notably currency reform, together with West Germany's engineering know-how and skilled workforce, its recovery was so strong that the food ration for its citizens eventually exceeded that of the British occupation troops and their families. As Truman and those administering the Marshall Plan had hoped, West Germany rose to become Europe's economic engine—one of the world's strongest economies. Its stunningly rapid recovery was labeled "*Wirtschaftswunde*," or economic miracle. Since Truman served as president from the time the Nazis surrendered in 1945 through the rendering of Marshall Plan assistance to West Germany, he rightfully could be called a liberator of the millions of Germans who survived the carnage of World War II and benefited from the plan.

Ten days after Truman's inauguration, it became apparent that his firm stance on the Berlin Airlift had caused Stalin to back down. On that day, Stalin signaled a willingness to enter into talks to end the blockade. At a minute after midnight on May 12, 1949, the lights came on again for the more than two million resourceful West Berliners, who had been liberated from the 325-day siege. Joining the throng in the streets of Berlin, Edzard Reuter, son of the mayor of West Berlin, cried out, "Freedom has arrived!"[12] As Lucius Clay told Congress, "I saw in Berlin the spirit and soul of a people reborn."[13]

While the Marshall Plan was being implemented in Europe during the fall of 1948, orders governing the occupation of Japan that Truman had approved in 1945 were about to be changed but most of the political and social reforms that General MacArthur had put in place would remain. It was the economy that needed to be revived. MacArthur could not be blamed for the persistent stagnation. The original orders discouraged him from rehabilitating and strengthening the economy and urged him to break up the zaibatsu (family-owned oligopolies that controlled Japanese trade and industry); MacArthur had initially resisted going after the zaibatsu but since mid-1947 had been pursuing them with vigor.

The two individuals leading the movement to revive Japan's economy were General William Draper and George Kennan. Bill Draper was serving as undersecretary of the army; he had informed Truman, George Marshall, and members of Congress that Japan would collapse without perpetual support from U.S. taxpayers. He characterized Japan as an economic "morgue."[14] Kennan, head of policy planning at State, advocated a rebuilding of Japan's economy so that it could become "the linchpin of Washington's forward defense posture in East Asia."[15] Kennan's strategic objective dovetailed nicely with Draper's economic concerns.

On the evening of March 21, 1948, both Kennan and Draper, along with a group of big-business representatives, met with MacArthur at his headquarters in Tokyo. Draper told MacArthur that from Washington's standpoint, the occupation thus far had fulfilled its initial purpose but it had become clear that the "problem in Japan was one of economic recovery."[16] Members of Draper's group made it evident that a "break up the Zaibatsu firms" policy would undermine the recovery of Japan's economy.[17] Apparently, MacArthur did not push back. In *Mr. X and the Pacific*, East Asia expert Paul Heer wrote that MacArthur seemed to agree that the U.S.

should reassess its policy but his concurrence was "tentative," involving "little commitment on his part."[18]

In the ensuing months, both Draper and Kennan authored reports recommending a new emphasis—later called "reverse course"—on the economic revitalization of Japan, though most of the preexisting reforms would live on, notably those concerning women's right to vote, education, religious freedom, and the rights enumerated in the constitution. The Draper and Kennan reports were eventually distilled and merged into NSC 13/2, a landmark State Department document titled "Report by the National Security Council on Recommendations with Respect to United States Policy Toward Japan." At 11 a.m. on October 9, 1948, during a break in his whistle-stop tour, Truman received Secretary of State Marshall and Undersecretary Bob Lovett in the Oval Office. Having been briefed on NSC 13/2 in advance, Truman asked a few questions and then approved its recommendations. With the overall objective of reviving Japan's economy, 13/2 directed all relevant branches of the U.S. government to help develop the other country's "internal and external trade and industry," with particular focus on restoration of Japan's exports and merchant shipping. Mac-Arthur was advised not to introduce any further reform legislation nor to adopt additional reforms. This meant that his Deconstruction Law, which was the cornerstone of his campaign to dissolve the zaibatsu and his efforts to "purge" executives who had cooperated with the military government, were dead letters. The bottom-line message of 13/2 to the Japanese government was that the success of the recovery program was dependent on its efforts "to raise production and increase export levels" through hard work, a minimum of labor strikes, curbs on inflation, and a balanced budget.[19]

Knowing that MacArthur and his staff lacked economists and might prevaricate, Bill Draper recommended to the NSC and to Truman that an "economic czar" be appointed to implement the policies set forth in 13/2. His choice was Joseph Dodge, a Detroit banker who, as Lucius Clay's financial expert in Germany, had reorganized the banking system and developed plans for currency reform in the Western-occupied zones of Germany. Since Dodge was reluctant to take the post in Japan, Draper arranged for Truman to invite him to the White House. Draper recalled that the morning before seeing the president, Dodge "told me that he wasn't going to take the job." Nevertheless, after lunch with Truman, "he had taken the job."[20] During the meeting Truman assured Dodge that MacArthur was on board (by then he was), and the president pledged that he himself would fully support the plan to revitalize Japan's economy. [21]

Freshly confirmed Ambassador Dodge, soon to be known as "the imperial accountant," arrived in Tokyo in February 1949. His objective was to end the hyperinflation and put the country back on its feet as a self-sufficient market economy. Dodge was tough and unyielding. Within the next several months, he pressured the Japanese cabinet to adopt surplus budgets, cut off subsidies and loans from the U.S., undervalue the yen to encourage exports, restrict credit, and tighten up tax collections. The so-called Dodge Line demanded austerity in domestic consumption, restrictions on wage increases, layoffs of workers, and repression of labor activism.

The Dodge Line succeeded in liberating Japan's citizens from the scourge of rampant inflation. However, the austerity measures caused output to shrink. By the spring of 1950, a recession seemed inevitable. Fortunately for the Japanese people and their standard of living, Truman decided in June to send air and ground forces to Korea to prevent a takeover of the entire peninsula by the North Koreans. As a result, Japan became a convenient supply depot for war matériel and a nearby haven for armed forces R & R. Its economy boomed until the Korean War truce. Thereafter, with the departure of the U.S. occupiers, Japan's powerful Ministry of International Trade and Industry (MITI) took hold and guided the economy into the early 1990s, when it ranked second in the world—Japan's "economic miracle."

President Truman and his administration, including MacArthur, could not claim responsibility for the miraculous recovery that gradually liberated millions of Japanese from subsistence living. But during the last years of occupation, they certainly played a role in getting it started. Had it not been for Truman's approval and support of the "reverse course" policy in 1948, Japan's economy would have languished, dependent on loans and subsidies from the U.S. government. The reverse course authorized by the president was the first of several steps leading to Japan's economic miracle. Moreover, it must be remembered that most of the occupation reforms instituted by MacArthur from 1945 to 1947 and implicitly approved by Truman—namely voting rights, free and fair elections, land and education reforms, private property protections, and constitutional rights—liberated the citizens of Japan from the oppressive policies of their government during World War II.

———————

While domestic politics played a part in the president's decision to recognize Israel on May 15, 1948, the liberation of displaced Jews was definitely on his mind. As of the date of recognition, thousands of Holocaust survivors and other displaced Jews were still "living under [U.S. and British military] guard behind barbed-wire fences" in crude, overcrowded camps in Germany.[22] Since August 1945, when Truman vowed that this "misery could not be allowed to continue," his efforts to find a home for Jews in the U.S., Britain, and Palestine had failed.[23] Now, however, the president had another reason for recognizing Israel—the so-called temporary camps in Germany, as well as those in Austria and Italy, could be emptied by sending displaced Jews to Israel, where they would be welcomed. It appeared to be a win-win situation: the Jews loathed the thought of living among their persecutors and murderers, their presence would have been an "obstacle" to the development of the new West German state, and their emigration would relieve the U.S. and British armies of having to support and police the camps for the foreseeable future. In *Commentary*, Samuel Gringauz, a Dachau survivor and former president of the Council of Liberated Jews, wrote, "The resettlement of the Jewish DPs from West Germany must be seen as an integral part of our new American security policy, if not the very basis of its application in Germany."[24]

Almost immediately after Truman's recognition of the new state of Israel, the Israeli government, aided by funds from private sources and the resources of the U.S. Army, made arrangements to transport displaced persons from German camps, as well as from other such camps in Europe, to Palestine. Israel's policy was to accept every Jew who wished to immigrate. But given its need for Jewish men of "military age" to defend against the invasion of Arab armed forces from Egypt, Jordan, Syria, and Iraq, priority was given to displaced persons and volunteers who would fight or otherwise assist directly in Israel's war effort. During the nine-plus months of the Arab–Israeli War, approximately twenty-seven thousand Jewish displaced persons participated in the war, most as soldiers in combat.

By being the first to lead the way in recognizing and thus legitimizing the new state of Israel, Harry Truman triggered the largest migration in the history of modern Israel. For the first three and a half years of its existence, approximately 689,000 immigrants, including 332,000 Holocaust survivors and other Jews from Europe, Africa, and Asia, flocked to Israel's shores, an average of 200,000 per year. As a result, the Jewish population more than doubled.

Did the Holocaust survivors who emigrated from the displaced persons camps in Germany, Austria, and Italy to the new state of Israel feel liberated? Were they able to rebuild their lives and find happiness? Yes and no. Eliezer Ayalon, an eighty-year-old Holocaust survivor who had been in five concentration camps, recalled to an interviewer in 2008 that "the moment the boat arrived, Haifa and Mount Carmel looked like heaven. . . . Here began my new life in a country with the Jewish people. I felt that I had been saved." But after he had been in Israel for three years, he reflected, "It wasn't that easy because the absorption and integration into life was pretty difficult. The Jewish society at that time was not interested in listening to our stories [about the Holocaust] and helping us. We had to struggle on our own. They just saw us as people from a different world." Yet looking back, he was glad to have found a home. The fact that "I survived as a decent man and a believing Jew, that I can laugh and love and look on the world's bright side, is nothing less than magnificent. . . . Today I am the happiest man in the world."[25]

There are many happy-ending survivor stories like that of Mr. Ayalon. But what he and countless other displaced Jews tended to forget was that when they arrived in Israel shortly after its independence, they found the fledgling nation grappling with a deep economic crisis. In addition to financing an existential war against the Arabs, the government had to feed, house, absorb, and find employment for hundreds of thousands of migrants. Its chief problems were the lack of food and foreign currency. To address the crisis, Prime Minister David Ben-Gurion initiated a program of national austerity that involved the rationing of food. While most of the immigrants, like Mr. Ayalon, coped, some 10 percent of the new immigrants left the country within a few weeks or years. One of them, Yossel (Josef) Rosensaft, a displaced Jew who had been living in Germany's largest camp (Bergen-Belsen), traveled to Israel in April 1949 with the intention of emigrating with his wife, Hadassah, a dentist, and their one-year-old son, Menachem. According to Hadassah's memoir, Yossel found the conditions for incoming migrants "deplorable," with people "living in water-logged huts." Hadassah wrote that Yossel decided that he, and presumably his wife and child, "could not live in Israel" and that several of his friends from the Belsen displaced persons camp who had already emigrated to Israel wanted to return to Germany and emigrate to the U.S.[26] Mr. Rosensaft and his family eventually moved to Montreux, Switzerland, and after eight years to New York City, where he established a real estate business and built an art collection.

While Truman was gratified that his recognition decision resulted in a mass exodus of displaced persons from Europe into Israel, he was "rather disgusted," he said, with the way the new Israeli government reacted to the exodus of some 750,000 Palestinian Arabs who were forced out of their homes and businesses to places outside the boundaries of Israel (Gaza, the West Bank) or into neighboring states (Lebanon, Syria, Jordan).[27] This exodus out of Israel was called the "Nakba," an Arab word meaning "catastrophe" or "disaster." During the period from 1947 to 1949, which included the Arab–Israeli War, upwards of five hundred towns and villages that Palestinian Arabs had occupied for centuries were abandoned or destroyed and their businesses in Israeli cities were almost totally extinguished. Several respected historians, including Israelis, have concluded that the Palestinians were driven out by governmental expulsion, terrorism by Jewish gangs, psychological warfare, and resulting panic and fear. The Israeli government, however, has maintained to this day that it bears no responsibility. When Secretary of State George Marshall was informed by James McDonald, his special representative to Israel, that the Israeli government would not consider allowing the Palestinian refugees to return until the onset of peace negotiations with the Arabs, Marshall told him that the hard-core Israeli position prohibiting return would be an "obstacle" to any agreement to commence peace talks. He instructed McDonald to tell the leaders of Israel that they "would make a grave miscalculation if they thought callous treatment of this tragic issue could pass unnoticed by world opinion." To drive home the point that the refugee crisis was a matter of "life or death" and should be addressed, Marshall told McDonald that he had discussed the matter "with the President," and he agreed.[28]

Whether the president realized it or not, it was his recognition of Israel and his failure to restrain the Israel government that had the unintended consequence of displacing three-quarters of a million Arab Palestinians from their homes and businesses, a catastrophe that certainly did not go unnoticed. Since the Israeli government would not allow the Palestinians to return to their homes and businesses, the UN stepped in and assumed responsibility for providing humanitarian relief to the starving and dispossessed refugees. On March 24, 1949, Truman responded to the UN's call for member contributions by authorizing a donation by the U.S. of $16 million, half of the $32 million that would be contributed to a newly established UN relief fund. He followed up by authorizing $25.45 million for fiscal 1951 and requesting that Congress appropriate $50 million more for fiscal 1952, the last year of his presidency.

To justify the expenditures, Truman said he hoped that "before the relief money ran out, means will be devised for a permanent solution to the [Palestinian] refugee problem."[29] But hope was not enough. For the rest of Truman's presidency and far into the future, the Palestinian "refugee problem" could not be solved, though not for lack of trying. Over the past seven decades, dozens of "solutions" have been proposed, fruitless talks have been held, and billions have been spent on relief to the refugees and their descendants.

As of 2023 when this manuscript was finalized and the Israelis were well into their ground attack to crush Hamas, it was impossible to predict the fate of the Palestinians trapped in Gaza. One can only dream of a solution, perhaps two states, whereby Palestinians and Israelis would live side by side in peace.

In addition to the president's recognition decision, which led to the resettlement of displaced Jews in Israel, he had been trying since 1945 to ease U.S.

immigration policies so that they could find refuge and freedom in America. Since he could not increase quotas without legislation and Congress was unwilling to act, Truman issued an executive order three days before Christmas of 1945. That order mandated that "consular facilities" be quickly established in or near displaced persons camps in American occupation zones in Germany and Austria, where a large percentage were Jews who had fled from Eastern Europe. It further instructed that the eligibility of applicants for visas by Jews and non-Jews be expedited with special attention paid to orphaned children.[30] As it turned out, the order had minimal effect as far as Jews were concerned because the entire annual immigration quota was a tiny fraction of the numbers of Jews and non-Jews alike in the displaced persons camps.[31] Even so, the House Immigration Committee opposed Truman's directive. On August 16, 1946, and again in January and June of 1947, the president called on the 80th Congress to enact legislation to increase quotas and allow into the country an unspecified number of displaced persons who had fled to American camps; that group would have included a significant percentage of Jews. Privately, Truman expressed a desire for an annual quota of three hundred thousand displaced persons.

Senator Taft was, of course, aware that Truman was pushing for legislation to increase quotas for immigration of Eastern European displaced persons, especially Jews. One of his first moves after the GOP had seized control of Congress in 1947 was to task his Republican colleague, West Virginia senator Chapman ("Chappie") Revercomb, an anti-Semite, to "investigate" the admission of displaced persons into the U.S. If Taft's objective was to cripple Truman's plans, and it was, then Revercomb, the chair of the Judiciary Committee's Subcommittee on Immigration, was the perfect choice. He was on record as opposing any changes to America's draconian 1924 quota system, a system that discriminated against Eastern Europeans (think Jews).

Sensing that public opinion had shifted in favor of admitting displaced persons into the U.S. and that emergency legislation was likely to be introduced by another member of Congress, Senator Revercomb seized the initiative. He persuaded the Senate to pass a resolution authorizing his subcommittee to conduct a "full and complete investigation" of the nation's "entire immigration system."[32]

In the fall of 1947, Revercomb and his team of investigators visited displaced persons camps in Germany. His impressions were predictable. As part of a "Jewish conspiracy," he wrote, Polish Jews, with Communists hidden among them, had infiltrated displaced persons camps in Germany and had the capability to "gain entrance into the United States" by filing fraudulent documents to obtain visas. The Communists from Poland and other Eastern European nations were in a "dormant state," he reported, and their subversive "activities would not begin until they reach America."[33]

After returning from his fact-finding trip, Senator Revercomb and his colleagues, with Taft's implicit approval, drafted a "displaced persons bill" that employed an anti-Communism narrative to disguise their real objective—prevention of Eastern European displaced Jews from immigrating to the U.S. Though the bill was amended many times and reconciled with a House bill, its underlying discriminatory purpose emerged intact in the displaced persons legislation sent to the president in June 1948 without once mentioning the words "Jew" or "Jewish."

On its face, the DP legislation sent to Truman looked good because it appeared to allow two hundred thousand displaced persons, including Jews and non-Jews, to be admitted to the United States for the next two years. However, a poison pill for the Jews was the earlier insertion of an arbitrary date—December 22, 1945—into the bill. Inexplicably, that date, the date of Truman's 1945 executive order, determined the eligibility of displaced persons for visas to the United States. All DPs who had arrived in camps located in American zones in Germany, Austria, or Italy *before* December 22, 1945, would have been eligible for visas. Those who arrived *after* the twenty-second were not. Left unsaid was the fact that by late June 1948, when the amended and reconciled legislation would go into effect, virtually all Jews who had arrived before December 22, 1945, had already left for Palestine and other places, whereas the Jews who had arrived afterward—because they had been driven out of Eastern Europe and Soviet Russia by pogroms, persecution, and other forms of virulent antisemitism—were simply out of luck. In June 1948, they comprised 90 percent of the Jews in the American camps, which meant that only 10 percent of the Jews would be eligible for visas.

With the floor debate on the DP bill still going on, the summer recess of the 80th Congress was only a day away. Senator Revercomb refused to extend debate and called for a voice vote. Except for Jacob Javits (D-NY) and other Jewish members of Congress who all shouted no, even the skeptics added their yeas to the vote in favor of the reconciled bill. They reasoned that although the bill discriminated against Jews, it at least opened the doors to thousands of other displaced persons. In a blistering editorial, the *New York Times* labeled the legislation "a shameful victory for [the] school of bigotry." The president of the American Jewish Committee, Joseph Proskauer, called it "a betrayal of our basic American traditions."[34]

A few days after Congress adjourned, June 25, 1948, the president, with extreme reluctance, signed the Displaced Persons Act of 1948. In his accompanying statement, he said that if Congress had still been in session, he would have returned the bill without his approval because "it is flagrantly discriminatory" against "displaced persons of the Jewish faith."[35] However, he felt he had to sign the bill because it would not be right to deprive the main beneficiaries of the law—that is, the non-Jews who had arrived in the American camps before December 22, 1945, and were still there in significant numbers, plus the relatively few Jews who had also arrived before the twenty-second but had never left the camps to emigrate to Palestine and other places throughout the world.

Truman did not give up. At the Turnip Day special session in July 1948, he called upon Congress to amend the injustices of the DP Act but it was obvious to their leadership that inflation and housing were his top priorities, not immigration. They ignored his request. Then in August the president appointed three highly qualified liberals to a Displaced Persons Commission, whose task was to somehow get visas into the hands of two hundred thousand eligible refugees before the act was to expire in two years. By writing regulations that liberally interpreted the law's requirements and delegating Jewish, Protestant, and Catholic volunteer organizations to find sponsors, jobs, and housing in the U.S., as well as evidence (loosely defined) to establish that arrivals to the camps took place before December 22, 1945, the commissioners made slow but steady progress. In February 1949, "approximately 1700 Jewish Displaced Persons" sailed from Bremen to the U.S. Thereafter, departures "continued at an accelerated pace."[36]

In early June 1949, the House passed an amendment to the displaced persons law that had been drafted by the Truman administration, was supported by the president, and was "easily approved" by "voice vote" of a majority of Democrats in both houses.[37] The key provisions would allow an additional 179,000 displaced persons, Jews and non-Jews, to immigrate to America, provided they had arrived at the camps in Germany, Austria, or Italy before January 1, 1949 (instead of the old December 22, 1945, cutoff date). Since Senator Revercomb had been defeated and the Republicans lost the Senate in November 1948, the House bill was delivered to Democratic senator Patrick ("Pat") McCarran of Nevada, chairman of the Senate Judiciary Committee and its Subcommittee on Immigration. On immigration policy McCarran was even worse than Revercomb. In his opinion, the 1948 DP law did not discriminate against the Jews and therefore it did not need to be amended. McCarran was a virulent anti-Semite. He routinely opposed federal judicial nominees who were Jewish. He allegedly told his daughter, a nun, that the Jews in Palestine "tore down" the manger where Jesus was born and "sold it for firewood at a hundred percent profit."[38] McCarran refused to schedule hearings or propose an alternative DP bill. Instead, he departed to Europe on the *Queen Mary* for an intentionally lengthy investigation of how the Displaced Persons Act of 1948 was being implemented. He asked for a suspension of action in the Senate until he returned. In October, he reported that he had "found fraud in the workings" of the 1948 act and that it would be a "serious mistake" to liberalize it.[39] McCarran did not return to Washington until December.

After the second session of the 81st Congress was convened in January 1950, McCarran arranged for former employees of the Displaced Persons Commission to testify that it was almost always "the Jewish group" of displaced persons in the camps who forged documents that allowed them to emigrate to America.[40] McCarran claimed that such persons (he didn't have to say Jews) were being "used by the Soviet Government" to "destroy the very government that affords them the opportunity to come here."[41]

It was in fact true that many displaced Jews in the camps forged documents but not because they were part of a Soviet conspiracy. They did it, wrote David Nasaw in *The Last Million*, "because the 1948 law had made it impossible for them to get visas without these papers."[42]

One family that had to forge documents in order to become eligible for visas to America pursuant to the 1948 DP law was the Berger family— Rachel; her husband, Marcus; and their young son, Joey. Rachel and Marcus, originally Polish Jews, had spent much of the war working in the Soviet Union, where Joey was born. After the war they returned to their homeland but were forced to flee the country due to the panic caused by the July 1946 "Kielce pogrom," a bloody massacre of Jews in the city of Kielce. Fearing for their lives, Marcus paid smugglers to drive them to a DP camp on the outskirts of Munich. The family arrived in the winter of 1946–1947 and were assigned to a room in block eleven. There, they joined thousands of Holocaust survivors who had lived in forests and basements and Poles like themselves who had spent the war in Russia. As soon as the 1948 DP Act was passed, the only way for many in the camp to be eligible for visas was to forge documents establishing that they had arrived in or near the DP camp in Germany before December 22, 1945, the cutoff date. In addition, they had to destroy Joey's Russian birth certificate and anything else indicating that the family had spent time in the Soviet Union. According to Joe Berger's memoir, published in 2001, his mother told him, "If the Americans knew we had been in Russia during the war, they would not have let us come [to the U.S.] . . . We all made up false documents." In October 1948, all three members of the Berger family were approved. "We left behind the DP camp at Landsberg," wrote Joe, "and made our way to the port of Bremerhaven."[43]

Rachel found a tiny apartment on the West Side of Manhattan and Marcus soon found a job in Newark making asbestos covers for ironing board. Joe thrived in America. He became a *New York Times* reporter and editor and author of *Displaced Persons*, a memoir. Joe's parents spoke to him of their path to liberation but rarely to others outside the family.

Pat McCarran continued to make headlines with claims of fraud and conspiracy but he was outgunned by the influence of powerful American religious and ethnic organizations and respected individuals like Eleanor Roosevelt, Lucius Clay, and Jim Farley (a Democratic kingmaker in New York), who lobbied the Senate to pass an even more generous immigration bill. By the time the House and Senate bills were reconciled and approved by the conference committee, the bipartisan legislation would not only authorize visas to an additional 179,000 displaced persons from camps in Europe; it would also open the doors of America to ten thousand war orphans, ten thousand Greek refugees, 54,744 refugees and expellees of German origin, four thousand European refugees who had fled to the Far East to escape tyranny and now must leave because of a new tyranny, eighteen thousand veterans of the exiled Polish Army, and two thousand displaced persons in Trieste and Italy.

On June 16, 1950, President Truman, "with very great pleasure," signed the final bill, HR 4567, into law.[44] For the Jews remaining in the camps (142,000 had already departed to Israel and elsewhere), it was a victory even though only seventeen thousand immigrated to the U.S. under the new law. Still, it was a major triumph for Jewish and non-Jewish refugees all over the world. And a hard-fought success for Harry Truman, the liberator.

Epilogue

Grips to the Attic

Since Harry Truman had been elected by the votes of more than twenty-four million Americans, the shadow over his presidency cast by FDR had almost vanished. Sam Rosenman, who had worked closely with both FDR and Truman, recalled that after the election, when the latter made decisions, he would "no longer wonder what Roosevelt would have done."[1] The transition from death to rebirth, therefore, had come to an end.

With only three hours of sleep, Truman woke up in Blair House on the morning after his inauguration, January 21, 1949, to face his first and only full term as president in his own right. It was destined to be a troubled four years. We leave those years, however, to other historians and instead focus on the transition from FDR to Truman. Why does that particular time in history matter? Because, for the United States, it spawned the most consequential and productive events since the Civil War. During the period from 1944 to 1948, the U.S. defeated Germany, Italy, and Japan; liberated tens of millions of survivors in Europe, the Middle East, and Asia; and, with a monopoly on the atomic bomb at least for another year, emerged from the Second World War as the most powerful nation in the world, both militarily and economically. For national security and humanitarian reasons, America revived and reformed the economies of Western Europe and Japan. It provided relief to Greece and Turkey while moving to contain the aggressive designs of the Soviet Union in Berlin and elsewhere. In 1948, the U.S. was the first to recognize the new state of Israel, a haven for Holocaust survivors. At home, the economy boomed between 1945 and 1948, primarily due to a cut of more than 65 percent in government spending that spurred economic growth. Thousands of returning servicemen and -women went to college, thanks to the GI Bill. More than ten million vets and millions of other wartime workers found jobs. The average unemployment rate between September 1945 and December 1948 was only 3.5 percent. The U.S. opened its doors a crack to admit displaced Jews and it gave hope to Black citizens with its civil rights agenda. As to the social safety net, the 80th Congress refused to increase Social Security benefits and coverage but at least they remained the same until finally increased by the 81st in 1950.

The beginning of the long transition was rough because Roosevelt, who had been told that he would not survive a fourth term, did absolutely nothing to prepare his vice president. Truman, although far from blameless, had to have been frustrated, if not angered, by FDR's dereliction and he might have complained about it bitterly to his family and friends. But the only record of his reaction was a rather mild criticism contained in a diary note dated May 6, 1948. "Since I took over," he wrote, "I was handicapped by lack of knowledge of both foreign and domestic affairs—due principally to Mr. Roosevelt's inability to pass on responsibility. He was always careful to see that no credit went to anyone else for accomplishment."[2]

Though completely unplanned, the transition was seemingly providential. After Roosevelt's death, the Truman administration eventually developed and implemented a "get tough" foreign policy that contained the Soviet Union and promoted democracy around the world. For domestic consumption Truman updated FDR's New Deal progressive agenda and advocated civil rights. The two of them—one the inheritor, the other the deceased donor—made the transition work abroad and at home.

Except for people of color and the families of those killed in the war, the years from 1944 to 1948 for most Americans were best described by the title of the 1946 movie that won seven Academy Awards: *The Best Years of Our Lives.*

———

B y the time Truman's presidency was about to end after Dwight Eisenhower's landslide victory in November 1952, he was convinced by his own unhappy experience that he should plan, organize, and execute an orderly transition of power. It was to be the first formal presidential transition that had ever been attempted. His initial move toward that end, however, was not well received. On the morning after the election, Truman sent a five-sentence telegram to Eisenhower that began with a perfunctory "congratulations" on his victory, followed by a virtual command that the president-elect "should immediately" send a representative to confer on the 1954 budget, which was due on January 15. But it was the fifth and final sentence, a sarcastic dig by the president, that was calculated to infuriate Eisenhower: "The *Independence* [Truman's Douglas VC-118 airliner] will be at your disposal if you still desire to go to Korea."[3] During the 1952 campaign, Truman had publicly derided Eisenhower's dramatic pledge to make a trip to Korea after his election, which was coupled with a promise that he and only he could end the war. Truman's allusion to the trip in his telegram to Eisenhower doubled down on his conviction that Ike's planned trip was nothing more than a last-hour political stunt to win the election. Truman had to have known that his disingenuous offer to lend his plane would have been regarded by Ike as a petty, in-your-face insult. Later the same day, after Eisenhower had politely rebuffed the offer while making it clear that he "still" intended to go to Korea on a military transport plane, Truman sent to Ike a second telegram, which he should have sent in the first place: "I invite you," he wrote, to discuss "an orderly transfer of the business of the Executive branch . . . particularly in view of the international dangers and problems that confront this country and the whole free world."[4]

A week after Ike graciously accepted the invitation, Truman dispatched the heads of the CIA and the National Security Agency to Augusta, Georgia, to personally deliver to Eisenhower three top secret briefing books that included classified intelligence assessments on the world's danger spots and plans to be followed in the event of attacks by Communist countries. In addition, Truman sent him a one-page summary of foreign relations policy matters that required presidential consideration and decisions, including a "resolution pending on Korea in the UN"; delicate problems in Iran and Tunisia; and a "National Security Council problem regarding the allocation of resources." Notably, no mention was made of relations with the Soviet Union.[5]

Eisenhower arrived at the White House at 2 p.m. on November 18, accompanied by Joseph Dodge, Ike's personal liaison on the budget, and Senator Henry Cabot Lodge Jr. (R-MA), his liaison on all departments and agencies of the government except the Bureau of the Budget. Truman recalled that General Eisenhower was "unsmiling . . . looked tense."[6] He invited Eisenhower into the Oval Office for a private chat before meeting in the Cabinet Room with their respective aides. Describing the twenty-minute meeting, Truman wrote in his diary that the general entered the Oval "with a chip on his shoulder."[7] The reason? In October, while Truman had been out campaigning for Adlai Stevenson, who was the Democratic nominee for president, he called out Ike for appeasing Wisconsin senator Joe McCarthy and distancing himself for political reasons from George Marshall, his longtime friend and mentor. During a speech in Colorado Springs, Truman declared that Eisenhower's "moral blindness" branded him as "unfit to be President of the United States."[8] Truman also lambasted Eisenhower for endorsing Chapman Revercomb of West Virginia, who was making a comeback bid for the Senate in 1952. In a speech to the National Jewish Welfare Board, Truman tied Eisenhower to Revercomb's record of antisemitism by reminding the audience that Revercomb had done everything in his power to prevent Jewish refugees from immigrating to the United States. Truman declared that Eisenhower "cannot escape responsibility for his endorsements."[9]

During their one-on-one meeting, with Ike still seething, Truman gave the president-elect a good deal of advice on the different qualities that he should look for in appointing his key aides, namely his press, appointments, and correspondence secretaries, and made it clear that he had ordered his White House staff and cabinet secretaries to assist and cooperate in the transition of power at all levels. Asked by Eisenhower whether he had a chief of staff, Truman replied that Dr. John Steelman was the man who functioned as chief of staff for him, although his title was assistant to the president. Truman urged Steelman to stay on to help Eisenhower because, as he said, "the general doesn't know any more about the presidency and politics than a pig knows about Sunday."[10] Eisenhower eventually appointed Steelman.

Truman led Eisenhower into the Cabinet Room, where they were joined by Acheson, Lovett, Harriman, and Snyder as well as Lodge and Dodge from Ike's team. Truman made an opening statement stressing the need for a smooth transition that would show the world a national unity in foreign policy and keep the Kremlin from trying to exploit political divisions. After handing to Eisenhower a memo from John Snyder concerning issues to be confronted by the next treasury secretary, Truman asked Acheson to take the floor. The remainder of the seventy-five-minute meeting was devoted to foreign policy, with the bulk of the discussion focusing on a UN resolution supporting an armistice in Korea and the importance of continuing to provide economic and military assistance to Western Europe (meaning the Marshall Plan and NATO). Eisenhower made a point of asking Truman to provide him with briefing papers and a summary of the Cabinet Room meeting. Truman said he would be glad to do so.

Eisenhower's demeanor during the meeting, which Truman described as a "frozen grimness" and Acheson as "wary" and "taciturn," meant that Truman's hope for the beginning of a comprehensive transition, though well-intentioned, was doomed.[11] Eisenhower simply could not get past the president's personal attacks during the 1952 campaign. Nevertheless, in spite of the tensions between the incoming and outgoing presidents, Truman's initiative set the stage for more cordial transitions at the lower departmental levels of his administration. If FDR, or more likely his advisers, had set up a transition plan that even remotely resembled that which Truman offered to Eisenhower, Truman's confidence would have been boosted and the mistakes and gaffes he had made during his first two years might never have happened.

The last morning of Truman's seven years and nine months as president—Inauguration Day for Eisenhower—was cloudless and not too chilly. When the president-elect's motorcade pulled up to the North Portico of the White House at 11:30 a.m., Ike and his wife, Mamie, did not get out of their car. Eisenhower was still fuming because of Truman's remark at a recent news conference that Ike's planned trip to speak with troop commanders in Korea was "a piece of demagoguery." As a result, Eisenhower was not about to enter the White House while Truman was still there.[12] He had already rejected the traditional invitation to come in for coffee and a light lunch. The standoff was awkward, to say the least. It seemed longer, but within a couple of minutes, the doors opened and Harry and Bess appeared on the steps. At that point the Eisenhowers exited their car and the two couples greeted one another. Truman wrote in his diary that he rode to the Capitol "with Ike in car No. 1 along with Joe Martin [House Speaker] & Styles Bridges [Senate majority leader]." At first, the conversation in car No. 1 was general and innocuous—"the crowd, the pleasant day, the orderly turnover," recalled Truman.[13] Then, for some unknown reason, Eisenhower decided to explain why he did not attend Truman's inauguration in 1949. "Ike remarked that he had not come to [Truman's 1949] inauguration because he did not want to attract attention from the President," thus suggesting that the applause at the 1949 inauguration and parade would have been for him, not for the president. Truman icily responded, "You were not here [in 1949 at my inauguration] because I did not send for you. But if I had sent for you, you would have come."[14] In his diary that night, Truman wrote, "Bridges gasped and Joe Martin changed the subject."[15]

After the inauguration, Harry, Bess, and Margaret piled into a White House limousine on the south side of the Capitol. On the way to lunch at Dean Acheson's home in Georgetown, Margaret, who was sitting on the jump seat, looked directly at her dad and said, "Hello Mr. Truman." He and Bess got the joke. It was the first time in thirty years that he had lacked an official title. When they approached the old Acheson house on P Street, with its distinctive iron fence fashioned out of melted musket barrels from the Mexican–American war, a crowd of hundreds cheered "as if I were coming in instead of going out," wrote Truman.[16] Inside, they were greeted by the cabinet, the chief justice, and old friends. "It was a wonderful affair," wrote Margaret, "full of jokes and laughter and a few tears." After a nap for the ex-president at Matt Connelly's apartment, the threesome was driven to Union Station, where the *Ferdinand Magellan* (courtesy of Eisenhower) and an immense crowd on the concourse awaited them. Senators, ambassadors, judges, aides, and old friends crammed their way into the *Magellan* to shake Truman's hand. After an hour or so, Truman went out onto the rear platform to express his appreciation for the last time. "I'll never forget [my time as president] if I live to be a hundred," he said. "And that's just what I intend to do."[17] In three and a half months, he would be sixty-nine years old.

On the evening of January 21, Harry and Bess (Margaret had a commitment in New York) arrived in Independence, where they encountered a crowd of thousands at the train station and a mob of five hundred blocking the street in front of 219 North Delaware. Truman wrote that he and Bess "were overcome. It was the pay-off for thirty years of hell and hard work."[18] Asked by the mayor of Independence a few days later to describe the first thing he had done after settling in to begin his retirement, Harry said, "I took the grips up to the attic."[19]

Franklin Roosevelt, of course, did not live to enjoy retirement. However, he made several plans for his retirement years, two of which were the same as those of Truman: a presidential library and a lucrative book deal. Anticipating that he would retire at the end of his second term, as all two-term presidents had done since George Washington, Roosevelt began planning as early as 1937 to build with private funding a library to house his papers at the Roosevelt Hyde Park estate, which he would inherit from his mother. His idea was that as soon as he retired on January 20, 1941, he and Harry Hopkins would return to Hyde Park and use his papers to collaborate on writing a history of the New Deal; the library would eventually be donated to the public. In fact, in early January 1941, FDR signed a $75,000-a-year contract with *Collier's* to serialize the story of his eight years as president. In *Roosevelt and Hopkins: An Intimate History*, Robert Sherwood wrote that FDR had "financial reasons for wanting to return to private life—that his mother was digging into capital to keep the place at Hyde Park going."[20] After he decided to run for a third term, the completed library was dedicated just five months before Pearl Harbor; it was the first "presidential library" to be established under the National Archives system.[21]

For Truman, the construction and use of his library was one of the "great joys" of his "old age," wrote Margaret.[22] He was aware of FDR's library, having seen it for the first and only time in 1945, when he attended his predecessor's burial. On the second day of Truman's retirement, he drove in foul weather to the family farm in Grandview, thinking his library might be located there. But he changed his mind when the city of Independence offered a site at the north end of Delaware Street where it crossed U.S. Route 24. Truman was delighted with the location, a mile walk from the Truman house or a three-minute drive. The ex-president happily immersed himself in the details of the project, offering sketches of the building, hiring architects and a construction firm, raising $1.75 million in funds, and asking members of his administration to donate their papers.

Unlike the work on his library, Truman's memoirs project turned out to be a nightmare for him and his publishers, Life and Doubleday. Though he had signed a contract for a whopping $600,000, most of the money was paid in installments, beginning with submission of an acceptable manuscript and continuing thereafter until 1960. Because the manuscript Truman eventually submitted was late and almost twice the length specified in the contract, Doubleday was forced to severely cut and publish it in two volumes, the first in the fall of 1955 and the second in 1956. Meanwhile, Truman had to pay out-of-pocket expenses for office space, a handful of ghostwriters and researchers, typists, and so forth. He was the first to admit that he was "not a writer" and that he needed plenty of outside help.[23] Because of the expenses, the high marginal tax rate of that era, and the fact that his contract was for a flat sum, meaning no royalties, Truman netted little money, "only $37,000," he complained to House majority leader John McCormack.[24]

Compared to Truman's plans for retirement, Roosevelt's ideas for spending his remaining years ranged from the ambitious to the practical and the offbeat. As early as April 1943, FDR confided to cousin Daisy that after the war, he intended to resign and become "chairman of the peace organization" that he envisioned at the time, which was eventually to be

named the United Nations. He told her that the "org." should be run by
him and a "small staff half the year in an island, like Horta in the Azores."[25]
Almost a year later, Roosevelt repeated the same idea to Senator Claude
Pepper—that he would resign after the war and "be named head of the new
international organization" that he had sought to shape at Tehran.[26] Roosevelt apparently thought that running the UN after his years as president
would be a walk in the park.

Again confiding to Daisy, FDR more realistically envisioned a conventional retirement plan. After the end of his second term, he would live and
work on his memoirs and papers in Top Cottage, a small stone house that
he had designed and built for wheelchair accessibility on a hilltop above
Val-Kill (Eleanor's house). The place afforded majestic views of the mountains across the Hudson River and the wooded valley below. Moreover,
Top Cottage would serve as a refuge from Roosevelt's domineering mother,
who ruled Springwood, the big house in which he had grown up.

Roosevelt's offbeat retirement plan, cooked up in the months before
Pearl Harbor, was to build a "fishing retreat for Hopkins and himself" on
Channel Key "about half way from Key West to the mainland along the
Trestle," wrote Robert Sherwood. To protect against hurricanes, FDR
sketched an odd-looking "hurricane proof house" grounded with cables
that is reproduced in Sherwood's book. "I feel sure," wrote Sherwood, who
was very close to FDR, "that in the moment of his death Roosevelt was
determined to build that house and then pray for a hurricane to come
along and prove it practicable."[27]

If FDR had lived to retire, he and Eleanor would have had no worries
about a lack of money. Not so for Harry and Bess, who began retirement
feeling financially insecure. They returned to Independence without a
post-presidential salary or pension. Their only assets were Harry's one-
third share of the Grandview farm, his army pension of $113 per month, a
modest amount of government savings bonds, and Bess's inheritance from
her mother of $8,885. In the spring of 1953, she used the inherited cash to
buy out her three brothers, who owned quarter shares in the house at 219
North Delaware. Today, it would seem unusual, but until Bess's mother
died, she owned, lived in, and presided over the principal residence of
Harry and Bess (in Washington, DC, which they rented). In his fifty-three

years of marriage to Bess, Harry had never bought a house of his own. In this regard, Truman's living situation was similar to that of FDR. Until Sara Roosevelt died, she too owned and ruled Springbook, which Roosevelt regarded as his principal residence.

With modest savings from Truman's time as president, earnings from writing and speaking, and $73,000 from the sale in 1958 of 220 acres of the Grandview farm, Harry and Bess were able to live comfortably, if frugally, for the rest of their years. The only time they splurged was in the summer of 1953 when Harry, always a car lover, bought a Chrysler New Yorker. The two of them, with no security detail, took a three-week road trip to the East Coast and back, bunking with friends along the way and accepting an offer to stay at no cost in a suite at the Waldorf Astoria in New York City. Returning via the Pennsylvania Turnpike, they were stopped near Bedford by a state trooper for driving too slow in the left lane.

Truman's retirement lasted for almost twenty years. Throughout the first decade he remained active in presidential politics. In 1956, he made "a fool of himself" at the Democratic convention, said Bess to Tom Evans, because for a day or two he supported Averell Harriman, who didn't stand a chance.[28] During the 1960 campaign, Truman regarded Jack Kennedy as a rich playboy who lacked the maturity and experience to serve as president. On July 2, in a televised press conference at his library, Truman said he would not attend the convention as a delegate because Kennedy's people had it "rigged."[29] Nevertheless, after JFK was nominated and came to the Truman Library to make his case, Truman enthusiastically joined the campaign. At age seventy-six, he traveled by plane, train, and automobile to nine states to make speeches and conduct press conferences in support of Kennedy. It was his last campaign.

In Washington, on the morning of Kennedy's funeral in November 1963, Truman was shocked to receive a telephone call from estranged former president Dwight Eisenhower. He wanted to know if Mamie and he could pick Truman up at Blair House and take him and Margaret to the requiem mass at St. Matthews Cathedral. Truman could hardly believe what he was hearing. "Certainly," he replied. For the two ex-presidents, it was an overdue icebreaker. They sat together during the funeral. Afterward, they skipped the graveside service in Arlington and returned to Blair House for drinks and nonstop talking and reminiscing. According to Robert Dennison, Truman's former naval aide who was in the room, the conversation was "heartwarming" because his old boss and General Eisenhower "buried the hatchet." To the "horror of the secret service," recalled Dennison, when the Eisenhowers departed, Truman went with them and stood outside at the curb for several minutes while thanking Ike for taking the initiative.[30]

A year later, October 13, 1964, when Truman was eighty, Father Time caught up with him. As he entered the second-floor bathroom, he tripped on the sill and fell. As he was falling forward, his eyebrow and forehead slammed into the washbasin and then his exposed right side landed hard on the edge of the tub, thereby fracturing at least two ribs. A maid found him in a pool of blood, unconscious on the tile floor. He was rushed in an ambulance to the hospital. A couple of days later, with extremely painful ribs, Truman was sent home. He never fully recovered.

Though he had lost considerable weight and his face was drawn, Truman rallied when President Lyndon Johnson came to the Truman Library and in Truman's presence signed the Medicare bill into law on July 30, 1965. It was a magnanimous gesture for LBJ to have shared that moment with Truman, who had fought so hard during his presidency for universal health care. The last president Truman saw in person during his lifetime was Richard Nixon, whom he despised. Less than a month after his inauguration, Nixon asked to visit Truman. Bess felt they could not decline. A photo shows Truman leaning on his cane, looking down at Nixon, who was playing the "Missouri Waltz" on the same concert grand piano that Truman used to play when he was in the White House. Nixon had arranged to have that piano shipped to the Truman Library as a peace offering in advance of his visit. If he thought the piano and the song would help to achieve a reconciliation with the old ex-president, he was mistaken.

Sometime in his eighty-third or -fourth year, Truman ceased making regular outings to the library, where his office and secretary were located. Except for correspondence and occasional visits from neighbors and friends to the house, he began a slow withdrawal from the outside world.

He spent his days reading stacks of history books, especially those about the presidency, which he, with the assistance of Bess and their driver, borrowed from the local library. In July 1972 Truman was taken twice to the Research Hospital and Medical Center in Kansas City. The first time was after another fall at home and the second was due to a "lower gastrointestinal problem" that required a stay of nearly two weeks. Later that year, on the afternoon of December 5, the eighty-eight-year-old ex-president was rushed by ambulance to Research Hospital for the last time. A statement released by the hospital said that the preliminary diagnosis was "pulmonary congestion" and that his "condition is fair."[31] That night his condition was revised to "critical." For the next eighteen days. Truman continued to weaken as he suffered from bronchitis, kidney failure, heart irregularity, and fluctuating blood pressure. On December 23, just before he slipped into a coma, he saw and heard his beloved Bess for the last time.

The last day Franklin Roosevelt saw his wife, Eleanor, was on March 29, 1945. Because FDR was scheduled to leave for Warm Springs at 4:00 that afternoon and had a packed day ahead of time, he had breakfast with Eleanor and her houseguest, Margaret Fayerweather. Somehow Ms. Fayerweather turned the conversation to death and burial. In a lighthearted way, Roosevelt said he planned to be buried in the rose garden near Springwood, the place where "to his certain knowledge" were "buried an old mule, two horses, and a dozen or so of the family dogs."[32] Either when her husband had to leave breakfast for his first appointment in the Oval Office or at a moment later in the day, Eleanor "kissed Franklin good-bye [and] sent him on his way," knowing that his two cousins Daisy and Polly, who would be with him in Warm Springs, "would not bother him as I should by discussing questions of state."[33]

From Warm Springs on Saturday night, April 7, Franklin telephoned Eleanor when she was "half asleep" at Springwood in Hyde Park.[34] On this occasion she refrained from pestering him. Instead, they chatted as married couples do about the illness of one of their grandchildren, the weather in Warm Springs, and the tasks involved in opening up Springwood for the summer. In a letter to Franklin the next day, Eleanor wrote, "Much love to you dear . . . You sounded cheerful for the first time last night & I hope you'll weigh 170 lbs when you return." She was on her way to New Hamp-

shire in the morning but she'd be back in Washington "Wed. eve."[35] It was
their last conversation and the last letter that Eleanor sent to her husband.

––––––––

Pursuant to instructions that he wrote in 1937, Franklin Roosevelt's body
was buried "where the sundial stands" in the rose garden at Springwood.[36]
Eleanor Roosevelt was to be interred in the garden just south of her husband. With hat in hand, President Truman was among the three hundred
who attended the burial service on Sunday, April 15, 1945. He could hear
Chopin's funeral march played by the West Point band as the horse-drawn
caisson came up through the woods to the rose garden. "When they fired
3 volleys in the air," wrote Daisy, "Fala gave a sharp bark after each, an
unconscious salute of his own to his master."[37] Roosevelt's loyal companion would not be forgotten. The famous Scottie would be buried next to
FDR on April 5, 1952. Eleanor was laid to rest there on November 11, 1962.

Roosevelt's stone monument with no carvings or decorations was
made by the Vermont Marble Company. It bears a simple inscription:
"Franklin Delano Roosevelt 1882–1945." It was installed in the fall of 1945
but was far too heavy to be placed directly above the buried casket.

Truman could have lain in state at the Capitol in Washington and had
services there but he chose to have his funeral in Independence and his
burial in the courtyard of his library. On the morning of December 27,
1972, a private service for the family took place at Carson Chapel funeral
home. The flag-draped casket was then taken in a hearse through streets
lined with soldiers to the steps of the Truman Library, where an honor
guard placed it on a catafalque in the lobby. That afternoon President
Nixon and former President Johnson, Lady Bird, and their girls came to
the library to pay their respects. Throughout that night, twenty-six thousand people filed past the closed casket. After a thirty-minute Episcopal
service with no lengthy eulogies, at 2 p.m. the next day in the auditorium,
the crowd moved outside to the courtyard for the committal ceremony.
"Man, that is born of woman, hath but a short time to live," intoned the
Reverend John Lembcke. "He cometh up, and is cut down, like a flower."[38]
The service concluded with a twenty-one-gun salute from the Missouri
National Guard, a tribute to Captain Truman.

Unlike Roosevelt's, Truman's memorial was a long rectangular tablet made of Vermont granite that would be placed on the ground above his coffin. Its chiseled inscription reminds one of a résumé. It starts at the top with Truman's name and the dates of his birth, death, and marriage, plus the birth date of an unnamed "Daughter." The rest consists of a list of five official job titles together with dates of service, beginning with "Judge" and ending with "President." The grave marker Truman prescribed for Bess, with much less text, is elegant. Placed alongside Harry's, it bears the inscription "First Lady of the United States, 1945–1953."

———————

Chapter 14, verse 7 of the Book of Job speaks of death, rebirth, and transition: "For there is hope of a tree, if it be cut down, that it will sprout again and that the tender branch thereof will not cease." Franklin Roosevelt was like a giant American redwood who radiated hope and optimism as if he would live forever. When he was cut down, Harry Truman, a mere sprout, struggled but eventually his branches, tender but only at first, canopied the most powerful nation in the world. The transition of power from FDR to Truman was a remarkable success.

Acknowledgments

During September 2022, while I was in the midst of writing this book, I was shocked and saddened to learn that my New York literary agent, John Wayne Wright, passed away on his eighty-first birthday. For the previous ten years, John had been a constant presence in my life, not a close friend but a wise counselor, critic, witty conversationalist, and mentor. Were it not for my relationship with John, I would never have achieved modest success as a nonfiction writer.

It was Dick Moe, former president of the National Trust for Historic Preservation and a noted historian, who introduced me to John when I was thinking of writing a biography of General George C. Marshall. Even though Marshall had been the subject of several biographies, John took a chance and agreed to add me to his star-studded roster of nonfiction writers, which included the likes of Robert Dallek, Andrew Bacevich, Thomas Maier, and Tracy Campbell. For me, working with John to craft proposals to publishers for this book and the Marshall book were unique and often maddening experiences. For each book, John insisted that I spend months writing and rewriting a seventy-plus-page proposal according to his formula, which required a description of the core of the book in one or two pages, then in ten to twenty, and finally chapter headings and a layout of the entire book. When he was finally satisfied, his assessments were blunt, but he delivered them with warmth and conviction. I am told that editors at major publishing houses in Manhattan had huge respect for John because of his honesty and credibility.

Which brings me to my literary editor, Brent Howard. I don't know how he does it, but Brent is able to edit a four-hundred-page manuscript in less than a week, complete with deft comments, suggested deletions, and an uncanny ability to catch mistakes. He quickly responded to my many questions and I rarely questioned his judgment. After we had batted around title ideas for several days, it was Brent who came up with *Ascent to Power*, which in three words captures the theme of this book. Unfortunately for me and his many other authors, Brent resigned from Penguin Random House in late July 2023, although by then he had completed most of the editing of our book. My heartfelt thanks to Brent for all he has done for me and my best wishes for him wherever he lands next.

Luckily, the completion of this book was placed in the capable hands of Brent's successor, Grace Layer, and a talented copy editor. Grace made the production process go smoothly, while the traditionally nameless copy editor tried to teach me, without success, how to avoid my penchant for what he or she called "dangling modifying phrases." Also, kudos to Ella Kurki and Charlotte Peters for stepping in to solve a vexing computer problem that threatened to derail the manuscript.

Others whom I must single out for being of particular assistance in helping me research this book include: Patrick Fahy at the Franklin D. Roosevelt Library, who directed me to the Bruenn papers, the Boettiger diary, and several other sources, and Kevin Thomas, also at the FDRL, who located Eleanor's letter to May Craig; Randy Sowell and Brian Jolet of the Harry S. Truman Library, who helped me find the sources of quotes by Truman (Stalin "a little squirt") and his plucky mother ("you behave yourself"); Laurie Austin, also at the HSTL, who located several photos for the insert; Joan Leckie Salvas, at Rutherfurd Hall in New Jersey, who provided a rare photo of Lucy Mercer Rutherfurd for the insert; and last but by no means least, Lewis Wyman of the Manuscript Division of the Library of Congress, who pawed through the Joe Davies collection and found the document I was looking for.

Finally, a shout-out to my lovely and loving wife, Nancy, for tolerating the hundreds of hours I spent alone in the cluttered library of our ancient

Georgetown house, researching and writing on my old laptop. For the most part, she never complained. In fact, she encouraged me, always saying, "This is what you love to do," and she was right. Meanwhile, our daughter, Molly, a Peloton addict who works at a law firm in nearby Bethesda, and our son, Rich, a podcaster and bestselling author in Southern California, can't believe that their dad continues to live happily in the past.

Select Bibliography

★ Primary Sources ★

Author's note: During the pandemic, when I was conducting research for this book, the writing of which was under contract to be finished and the manuscript submitted by April of 2023, relevant archives were initially closed and thereafter many went on reduced hours because of staff shortages. The research rooms in the Truman and Roosevelt presidential libraries, the places where I had planned to do most of my research, were closed from March 2020 until early April 2022. As a consequence, I did not have the luxury of carefully searching through boxes of documents. Instead, I had to rely on accessing those primary source collections that had been digitized by early 2022, when I had to begin writing my manuscript. At that time, the extent of digitization varied from archive to archive (at the Truman Library in early 2022 it was less than 0.25 percent of its holdings, although "important" collections, of course, had priority).

The following identifies the primary source collections of documents that were available to me by early 2022 and described in the endnotes:

Selected collections, including oral histories, interviews, transcripts, speeches, letters, press conferences, and sound recordings, digitized at the Harry S. Truman Library, Independence, Missouri.

Selected collections, including notes taken during Big Three meetings abroad, oral histories, and letters, digitized at the Franklin D. Roosevelt Library, Hyde Park, New York.

Completely digitized public papers and addresses of the presidents of the United States. Franklin D. Roosevelt, 1933–1945, and Harry S. Truman, 1940–1953. Washington, DC: U.S. Government Printing Office, 1966. This includes all public speeches and press conferences.

Completely digitized daily White House appointment calendars of Presidents Roosevelt and Truman.

Completely digitized foreign relations of the United States, from 1943 to 1949, including Council of Foreign Ministers and conferences at Cairo, Tehran, Malta, Yalta, Quebec, Berlin (Potsdam), Near East, South Asia, and Africa.

Papers of Joseph Edward Davies, Manuscript Division, Library of Congress, Washington, DC.

Arthur Vandenberg papers, Bentley Historical Library, University of Michigan, Ann Arbor, Michigan.

Newspapers, magazines, and special collections at the Library of Congress.

Author interviews: Jean Kearny, Diana Hopkins Halsted, John Boettiger, Clifton Truman Daniel, and Joan Kennan.

✳   Books and Articles   ✳

Absolon, Peter. "The *Exodus* Affair: Hamburg 1947." *The Journal of Holocaust Education* 6, no. 3 (1997): 65–79.

Acacia, John. *Clark Clifford: The Wise Man of Washington.* Lexington: The University Press of Kentucky, 2009.

Acheson, Dean. *Present at the Creation: My Years in the State Department.* New York: W. W. Norton & Company, 1969.

Agnew, John, and Nicholas Entrikin, eds. *The Marshall Plan Today: Model and Metaphor.* New York: Routledge, 2016.

Allen, George. *Presidents Who Have Known Me.* London: Routledge Press, 2004.

Allen, Robert S., and William V. Shannon. *The Truman Merry-Go-Round.* New York: Vanguard, 1950.

Altschuler, Glenn C., and Stuart M. Blumin. *The GI Bill: A New Deal for Veterans.* New York: Oxford University Press, 2009.

Anderson, Carol. *Eyes off the Prize: The United Nations and the African American Struggle for Human Rights, 1944–1955.* London: Cambridge University Press, 2003.

Andrew, Christopher, and Vasili Mitrokihn. *The Sword and the Shield: The Mitrokhin Archives and the Secret History of the KGB*. New York: Basic Books, 1999.

Asada, Sadao. "The Shock of the Atomic Bomb and Japan's Decision to Surrender: A Reconsideration." In *Culture Shock and Japanese-American Relations*. Columbia: University of Missouri, 2011.

Asbell, Bernard, ed. *Mother and Daughter: The Letters of Eleanor and Anna Roosevelt*. New York: Fromm International Publishing Corporation, 1988.

———. *When F.D.R. Died*. New York: Holt, Rinehart and Winston, 1961.

Badash, Lawrence, Joseph O. Hirschfelder, and Herbert P. Broida, eds. *Reminiscences of Los Alamos, 1943–1945*. Boston: D. Reidel, 1980.

Baime, A. J. *White Lies: The Double Life of Walter F. White and America's Darkest Secret*. New York: Mariner Books, 2022.

Bainbridge, K. T. *Trinity*. Washington, DC: U.S. Energy Research and Development Administration, 1976.

Banac, Ivo, ed. *The Diary of Georgi Dimitrov, 1933–1949*. New Haven, CT: Yale University Press, 2003.

Batt, William L., Jr., and Robert Balducci. "Origin of the 1948 Turnip Day Session of Congress." *Presidential Studies Quarterly* 29, no. 1 (March 1, 1999): 80–3.

Bazna, Elyesa. *I Was Cicero*. New York: Harper & Row, 1962.

Berenbaum, Michael. Review of *Yesterday (My Story)*, by Hadassah Rosensaft. *Shofar* 26, no. 3 (Spring 2008): 169–71.

Berezhkov, Valentin. *History in the Making: Memoirs of World War II Diplomacy*. Moscow: Progress Publishers, 1983.

Berger, Joseph. *Displaced Persons: Growing Up American After the Holocaust*. New York: Washington Square Press, 2002.

Bernstein, Barton J. "Roosevelt, Truman, and the Atomic Bomb, 1941–45: A Reinterpretation." *Political Science Quarterly* 90, no. 1 (Spring 1975): 23–69.

Bernstein, Barton, and Allen J. Matusow, eds. *The Truman Administration: A Documentary History*, 57, excerpt from General Motors press release, December 29, 1945.

Beschloss, Michael. *The Conquerors: Roosevelt, Truman and the Destruction of Hitler's Germany, 1941–1945*. New York: Simon & Schuster, 2002.

Bingham, Jonathan B. *Shirt-Sleeve Diplomacy: Point 4 in Action*. New York: The John Day Company, 1954.

Bishop, Jim. *FDR's Last Year*. New York: William Morrow & Company, 1974.

Bland, Larry I., and Sharon Ritenour Stevens, eds. *The Papers of George Catlett Marshall*. Vol. 5. Baltimore: Johns Hopkins University Press, 2003.

Bland, Larry I., Mark A. Stoler, Sharon Ritenour Stevens, and Daniel D. Holt, eds. *The Papers of George Catlett Marshall.* Vol. 6. Baltimore: Johns Hopkins University Press, 2013.

Blum, Howard. *Night of the Assassins: The Untold Story of Hitler's Plot to Kill FDR, Churchill, and Stalin.* New York: Harper, 2020.

Blum, John Morton, ed. *The Price of Vision: The Diary of Henry A. Wallace, 1942–1946.* New York: Houghton Mifflin, 1973.

———. *Roosevelt and Morgenthau: A Revision and Condensation of From the Morgenthau Diaries.* Boston: Houghton Mifflin, 1970.

Boettiger, John R. *A Love in Shadow*: New York: W. W. Norton & Company, 1978.

Bohlen, Charles E. *Witness to History, 1929–1969.* New York: W. W. Norton & Company, 1973.

Bradley, Omar N. *A Soldier's Story.* New York: Holt, 1951.

Bradley, Omar N., and Clay Blair. *A General's Life.* New York: Simon & Schuster, 1983.

Breitman, Richard, and Allan J. Lichtman. *FDR and the Jews.* Cambridge, MA: The Belknap Press, 2013.

Broscious, S. David. "Longing for International Control, Banking on American Superiority." In *Cold War Statesmen Confront the Bomb: Nuclear Diplomacy Since 1945.* Edited by John Lewis Gaddis, Philip Gordon, Ernest May, and Jonathan Rosenberg, 15–38. New York: Oxford University Press, 1999.

Bruenn, Howard. "Clinical Notes on the Illness and Death of President Franklin D. Roosevelt." *Annals of Internal Medicine* 72, no. 4 (1970): 579–91.

Buhite, Russell D., and David W. Levy, eds. *FDR's Fireside Chats.* Norman: University of Oklahoma Press, 1992.

Bullitt, Orville H., ed. *For the President: Personal and Secret.* New York: Houghton Mifflin, 1972.

Bullitt, William C. "How We Won the War and Lost the Peace." *Life,* August 30, 1948.

Bullock, Alan. *Ernest Bevin: Foreign Secretary 1945–1951.* New York: W. W. Norton & Company, 1983.

Burnes, Brian. "Truman's Funeral." December 26, 2022. https://www.trumanlibraryinstitute.org/the-funeral-of-harry-s-truman/.

Busch, Andrew E. *Truman's Triumphs: The 1948 Election and the Making of Postwar America.* Lawrence: University Press of Kansas, 2012.

Butler, Susan, ed. *My Dear Mr. Stalin: The Complete Correspondence of Franklin D. Roosevelt and Joseph V. Stalin.* New Haven, CT: Yale University Press, 2005.

Byrnes, James F. *All in One Lifetime.* New York: Harper & Brothers, 1958.

——. "Restatement of Policy on Germany, Stuttgart, September 6, 1946." *Department of State Bulletin* 15 (September 15, 1946): 495–501.

——. *Speaking Frankly.* New York: Harper, 1947.

Campbell, John C. *The United States in World Affairs, 1945–1947.* New York: Harper, 1947.

Campbell, Kurt M., and James B. Steinberg. *Difficult Transitions: Foreign Policy Troubles at the Outset of Presidential Power.* Washington, DC: Brookings Institution Press, 2008.

Catledge, Turner. "Truman Nominated for Vice Presidency." *New York Times,* July 22, 1944.

Chace, James. *Acheson.* New York: Simon & Schuster, 1998.

Chandler, Aaron. "A Balance Statement: A Journal Posting on the Funding of the Truman–Dewey 1948 Presidential Election." *The Jackson County Historical Society Journal* 47, no. 2 (Autumn 2006): 16.

Chandler, Alfred D., Jr., ed. *Papers of Dwight David Eisenhower: The War Years.* Vol. 4. Baltimore: Johns Hopkins University Press, 1971.

Cherny, Andrei. "The Original October Surprise: Harry Truman and the Vinson Plan." *Atlantic,* October 11, 2012.

Churchill, Winston S. *The Second World War.* Vol. 5: *Closing the Ring.* Boston: Houghton Mifflin 1951.

——. *The Second World War.* Vol. 6: *Triumph and Tragedy.* Boston: Houghton Mifflin, 1953.

Clifford, Clark, and Richard Holbrooke. *Counsel to the President: A Memoir.* New York: Random House, 1991.

Cohen, Michael Joseph. *Truman and Israel.* Berkeley: University of California Press, 1990.

Collier, Richard. *Bridge Across the Sky: The Berlin Blockade and Airlift: 1948–49.* New York: McGraw-Hill, 1978.

Cook, Blanche Wiesen. *Eleanor Roosevelt.* Vol. 3: *The War Years and After, 1939–1962.* New York: Viking, 2016.

Craig, William. *The Fall of Japan.* Dial Press, 1967.

Dallek, Robert. *Franklin D. Roosevelt.* New York: Viking, 2017.

——. *The Lost Peace: Leadership in a Time of Horror and Hope, 1945–1953.* New York: Harper, 2010.

Dana, Rebecca, and Peter Carlson. "Harry Truman's Forgotten Diary." *The Washington Post,* July 11, 2003. https://www.washingtonpost.com/archive

/politics/2003/07/11/harry-trumans-forgotten-diary/97827dbd-e24f-49f6-a800
-2341a0688060/.

Danchev, Alex, and Daniel Todman, eds. *War Diaries 1939–1945: Field Marshal Alanbrooke*. Berkeley and Los Angeles: University of California Press, 2001.

Daniels, Jonathan. *Frontier on the Potomac*. New York: Macmillan, 1946.

———. *The Man of Independence*. New York: J. B. Lippincott, 1950.

Devine, Michael J., Robert P. Watson, and Robert J. Wolz, eds. *Israel and the Legacy of Harry S. Truman*. Kirksville, MO: Truman State University Press, 2008.

Dinnerstein, Leonard. *America and the Survivors of the Holocaust*. New York: Columbia University Press, 1982.

Dobbs, Michael. *Six Months in 1945: From World War to Cold War*. New York: Alfred A. Knopf, 2012.

Domarus, Max, ed. *Hitler, Speeches and Proclamations 1932–1945: The Chronicle of a Dictatorship*. Vol. 4: *The Years 1941 to 1945*. Wauconda, IL: Bolchazy-Carducci Publishers, 1977.

Donovan, Robert J. *Conflict & Crisis: The Presidency of Harry S. Truman, 1945–1948*. Columbia: University of Missouri Press, 1977.

———. *Tumultuous Years: The Presidency of Harry S. Truman, 1949–1953*. New York: W. W. Norton & Company, 1982.

Dower, John W. *Embracing Defeat: Japan in the Wake of World War II*. New York: W. W. Norton & Company, 1999.

Drummond, Steve. *The Watchdog: How the Truman Committee Battled Corruption and Helped Win World War Two*. Toronto: Hanover Square Press, 2023.

Drury, Allen. *A Senate Journal: 1943–1945*. New York: McGraw-Hill, 1963.

Eagleton, Thomas F., and Diane L. Duffin. "Bob Hannegan and Harry Truman's Vice Presidential Nomination." *Missouri Historical Review*, April 1996.

Eden, Anthony. *The Memoirs of Anthony Eden: The Reckoning*. Boston: Houghton Mifflin, 1965.

Eisenhower, Dwight D. *Crusade in Europe: A Personal Account of World War II*. New York: Harper & Brothers, 1950.

Elsey, George McKee. *An Unplanned Life*. Columbia: University of Missouri Press, 2005.

Erbelding, Rebecca. *Rescue Board: The Untold Story of America's Efforts to Save the Jews of Europe*. New York: Doubleday, 2018.

Feis, Herbert. *The Atomic Bomb and the End of World War II*. Princeton, NJ: Princeton University Press, 1966.

Fenby, Jonathan. *Alliance: The Inside Story of How Roosevelt, Stalin & Churchill Won One War & Began Another*. London: Simon & Schuster, 2006.

Ferrell, Robert H., ed. *The Autobiography of Harry S. Truman*. Boulder: Colorado Associated University Press, 1980.

———. *Choosing Truman: The Democratic Convention of 1944*. Columbia: University of Missouri Press, 1994.

———, ed. *Dear Bess: The Letters from Harry to Bess Truman, 1910–1959*. Columbia: University of Missouri Press, 1983.

———. *The Dying President*. Columbia: University of Missouri Press, 1998.

———. *Harry S. Truman: A Life*. Columbia: University of Missouri Press, 1994.

———, ed. *Off the Record: The Private Papers of Harry S. Truman*. Columbia: University of Missouri Press, 1997.

———, ed. *Truman in the White House: The Diary of Eben A. Ayers*. Columbia: University of Missouri Press, 1991.

———, ed. "A Visit to the White House, 1947: The Diary of Vic H. Housholder." *Missouri Historical Review* 78, no. 3 (1984): 311–36.

Fleming, Thomas. "Eight Days with Harry Truman," *American Heritage* 43, no. 4 (1992): 56.

Flynn, Edward J. *You're the Boss: My Story of a Life in Practical Politics*. New York: Viking, 1947.

Frank, Jeffrey. *The Trials of Harry S. Truman: The Extraordinary Presidency of an Ordinary Man, 1945–1953*. New York: Simon & Schuster, 2022.

Frank, Richard B. *Downfall: The End of the Imperial Japanese Empire*. New York: Penguin Books, 1999.

Freeland, Robert M. *The Truman Doctrine and the Origins of McCarthyism*. New York: New York University Press, 1985.

Freidel, Frank. *Franklin D. Roosevelt: A Rendezvous with Destiny*. New York: Little, Brown and Company, 1990.

Gaddis, John Lewis. *The Cold War: A New History*. New York: Penguin, 2007.

———. *George F. Kennan: An American Life*. New York: Penguin, 2011.

Gallicchio, Marc. *Unconditional: The Japanese Surrender in World War II*. New York: Oxford University Press, 2020.

Gardner, Michael R. *Harry Truman and Civil Rights*. Carbondale and Edwardsville: Southern Illinois University Press, 2002.

Geselbracht, Raymond H., ed. *The Civil Rights Legacy of Harry S. Truman*. Kirksville, MO: Truman State University Press, 2007.

Gilbert, Martin. *Winston S. Churchill.* Vol. 8: *Never Despair, 1945–1965.* London: William Heinemann Ltd., 1988.

Glass, Andrew. "Truman Approves Aid to Palestine, March 24, 1949." Politico, March 24, 2017. https://www.politico.com/story/2017/03/truman-approves-aid -to-palestine-march-24-1949-236260.

Goodwin, Doris Kearns. *No Ordinary Time: Franklin and Eleanor Roosevelt: The Home Front in World War II.* New York: Simon & Schuster, 1994.

Goulden, Joseph C. *The Best Years, 1945–1950.* New York: Atheneum, 1976.

Gregory, Ross. "America and Saudi Arabia, Act I: The Conference of Franklin D. Roosevelt and King Ibn Saud in February 1945." In *Presidents, Diplomats, and Other Mortals: Essays Honoring Robert H. Ferrell.* Edited by J. Garry Clifford and Theodore A. Wilson, 116–36. Columbia: University of Missouri Press, 2007.

Gringauz, Simon. "Our New German Policy and the DPs." *Commentary,* June 1948.

Groves, Leslie, M. *Now It Can Be Told: The Story of the Manhattan Project.* New York: Harper and Brothers, 1962.

Gruber, Ruth. *Witness: One of the Great Correspondents of the Twentieth Century Tells Her Story.* New York: Schocken, 2007.

Gunther, John. *Procession.* New York: Harper & Row, 1966.

———. *The Riddle of MacArthur.* New York: Harper & Row, 1951.

———. *Roosevelt in Retrospect: A Profile in History.* New York: Harper & Brothers, 1950.

Haas, Lawrence J. *Harry and Arthur: Truman and Vandenberg and the Partnership That Created the Free World.* Sterling, VA: Potomac Books, 2016.

Hagerty, James A. "Eisenhower Gaining Headway in Fight on Truman." *New York Times,* July 5, 1948.

Halamish, Aviva. *The Exodus Affair: Holocaust Survivors and the Struggle for Palestine.* Syracuse, NY: Syracuse University Press, 1998.

Hamby, Alonzo L. *Man of the People: A Life of Harry S. Truman.* New York: Oxford University Press. 1995.

Hamilton, Nigel. *War and Peace: FDR's Final Odyssey, D-Day to Yalta, 1943– 1945.* New York: Houghton Mifflin Harcourt, 2019.

Harriman, W. Averell, and Elie Abel. *Special Envoy to Churchill and Stalin, 1941– 1946.* New York: Random House, 1975.

Hasegawa, Tsuyoshi. *Racing the Enemy: Stalin, Truman, and the Surrender of Japan.* Cambridge, MA: The Belknap Press, 2005.

Hassett, William D. *Off the Record with FDR, 1942–1945.* New Brunswick, NJ: Rutgers University Press, 1958.

Hearings Before the Subcommittee on Education, Training, and Rehabilitation of the Committee on Veterans' Affairs, House of Representatives, Eightieth Congress, First Session on H.R. 2106, H.R. 2172, Bills Providing Educational and Loan Benefits for Widows and Children of Certain Deceased World War II Veterans, April 26 and 28 and June 6, 1947. Washington, DC: U.S. Government Printing Office, 1947.

Heer, Paul J. *Mr. X and the Pacific: George F. Kennan and American Policy in East Asia.* Ithaca, NY: Cornell University Press, 2018.

Henry, Laurin L. *Presidential Transitions.* Washington, DC: Brookings Institution Press, 1960.

Herf, Jeffrey. *Israel's Moment: International Support for and Opposition to Establishing the Jewish State, 1945–1949.* Cambridge, UK: Cambridge University Press, 2022.

Herken, Gregg. *Brotherhood of the Bomb: The Tangled Lives and Loyalties of Robert Oppenheimer, Ernest Lawrence, and Edward Teller.* New York: Holt Paperbacks, 2003.

Herman, Arthur. *Douglas MacArthur: American Warrior.* New York: Random House, 2016.

Hersey, John. *Hiroshima.* New York: Bantam Books, 1966.

Hill, Fiona, and Clifford G. Gaddy. *Mr. Putin: Operative in the Kremlin.* Washington, DC: Brookings Institution Press, 2013.

Hillman, William. *Mr. President.* New York: Farrar, Straus and Young, 1952.

Hornfischer, James D. *The Fleet at Flood Tide: America at Total War in the Pacific, 1944–1945.* New York: Bantam, 2016.

Hughes, Emmett John. *The Living Presidency: The Resources and Dilemmas of the American Presidential Office.* New York: Coward, McCann & Geoghegan, 1973.

Humphrey, Hubert H. *The Education of a Public Man: My Life and Politics.* New York: Doubleday, 1976.

Hurd, Charles. "The Veteran." *New York Times,* March 11, 1945.

Huston, John W., ed. *American Airpower Comes of Age: General Henry H. "Hap" Arnold's World War II Diaries.* Vol. 2. Maxwell Air Force Base, AL: Air University Press, 2002.

Isaacson, Walter, and Evan Thomas. *The Wise Men: Six Friends and the World They Made.* New York: Simon & Schuster, 1986.

Jähner, Harald. *Aftermath: Life in the Fallout of the Third Reich, 1945–1955.* New York: Alfred A. Knopf, 2022.

James, D. Clayton. *The Years of MacArthur.* Vol. 2: *1941–1945.* New York: Houghton Mifflin, 1975.

———. *The Years of MacArthur.* Vol. 3: *1945–1964.* New York: Houghton Mifflin, 1985.

Janken, Kenneth Robert. *White: The Biography of Walter White, Mr. NAACP.* New York: The New Press, 2003.

Jones, Bruce, ed. *The Marshall Plan and the Shaping of American Strategy.* Washington, DC: Brookings Institution Press, 2017.

Jones, Joseph Marion. *The Fifteen Weeks (February 21—June 5, 1947): An Inside Account of the Genesis of the Marshall Plan.* New York: Viking, 1955.

Jordan, David M. *FDR, Dewey, and the Election of 1944.* Bloomington: Indiana University Press, 2011.

Judis, John B. *Genesis: Truman, American Jews, and the Origins of the Arab/Israeli Conflict.* New York: Farrar, Straus and Giroux, 2014.

Judt, Tony. *Postwar: A History of Europe Since 1945.* New York: Penguin, 2006.

Karabell, Zachary. *The Last Campaign: How Harry Truman Won the 1948 Election.* New York: Alfred A. Knopf, 2000.

Kase, Toshikazu. *Journey to the Missouri.* New Haven, CT: Yale University Press, 1950.

Katamidze, Slava. *Loyal Comrades, Ruthless Killers: The Secret Services of the USSR, 1920 to the Present.* Miami: Lewis International, 2003.

Katznelson, Ira. *Fear Itself: The New Deal and the Origins of Our Time.* New York: Liveright, 2013.

Kennan, George F. "An Historian of Potsdam and His Readers." *America Slavic and East European Review* 20, no. 2 (April 1961): 289–94.

———. *Memoirs, 1925–1950.* Boston: Little, Brown and Company, 1967.

Key, V. O., Jr., and Alexander Heard. *Southern Politics in State and Nation.* New York: Alfred A. Knopf, 1949.

Kimball, Warren F. *Churchill and Roosevelt: The Complete Correspondence.* Vol. 1: *Alliance Emerging October 1933–November 1942.* Princeton, NJ: Princeton University Press, 1987.

———. *The Juggler: Franklin Roosevelt as Wartime Statesman.* Princeton, NJ: Princeton University Press, 1991.

Kort, Michael. *The Columbia Guide to Hiroshima and the Bomb.* New York: Columbia University Press, 2007.

Kurzman, Dan. *Ben-Gurion, Prophet of Fire*. New York: Simon & Schuster, 1983.

Ladd, Everett C. "The Trials of Election Polling: 1948 and Today." *The Public Perspective* 3, no. 4 (1992): 24–8.

Lash, Joseph P. *Eleanor and Franklin: The Story of Their Relationship*. New York: W. W. Norton & Company, 1971.

———. *Eleanor: The Years Alone*. New York: Smithmark Publishers, 1966.

———. *A World of Love: Eleanor Roosevelt and Her Friends, 1943–1962*. New York: Doubleday, 1984.

Laurence, William L. "Atomic Bombing of Nagasaki Told by Flight Member." *New York Times*, September 9, 1945.

Leahy, William D. *I Was There*. New York: McGraw-Hill, 1950.

Leffler, Melvn, and David Painter. eds. *Origins of the Cold War: An International History*. London, Routledge, 1994.

Lelyveld, Joseph. *His Final Battle: The Last Months of Franklin Roosevelt*. New York: Alfred A. Knopf, 2016.

Leuchtenburg, William E. *In the Shadow of FDR: From Harry Truman to Ronald Reagan*. Ithaca, NY: Cornell University Press, 1983.

———. "New Faces of 1946." *Smithsonian*, November 2006. https://www.smithsonianmag.com/history/new-faces-of-1946-135190660/.

Lilienthal, David E. *The Journals of David E. Lilienthal*. Vol. 2: *The Atomic Energy Years, 1945–1950*. New York: Harper & Row, 1964.

MacArthur, Douglas. *Reminiscences*, Annapolis, MD: Naval Institute Press, 1964.

Manchester, William. *American Caesar: Douglas MacArthur, 1880–1964*. Boston: Little, Brown and Company, 1978.

Manchester, William, and Paul Reid. *The Last Lion: Winston Spencer Churchill, Defender of the Realm, 1940–1965*. New York: Little, Brown and Company, 2012.

Maney, Patrick J. *The Roosevelt Presence: The Life and Legacy of FDR*. Berkeley: University of California Press, 1992.

Martin, Louis. "Million Dollar Truman Fund." *Chicago Defender*, August 7, 1948.

Masalha, Nur. *Palestine Nakba: Decolonising History, Narrating the Subaltern, Reclaiming Memory*. New York: Zed Books, 2012.

McCloy, John J. *The Challenge to American Foreign Policy*. Cambridge, MA: Harvard University Press, 1953.

McCoy, Donald R., and Richard T. Ruetten. *Quest and Response: Minority Rights and the Truman Administration*. Lawrence: University of Kansas Press, 2021.

McCrea, John L. *Captain McCrea's War.* New York: Skyhorse, 2016.

McCullough, David. *Truman.* New York: Simon & Schuster, 1992.

McFarland, Keith D., and David L. Roll. *Louis Johnson and the Arming of America: The Roosevelt and Truman Years.* Bloomington: Indiana University Press, 2005.

McIntire, Ross T. *White House Physician.* New York: Putnam's, 1946.

Mead, Walter Russell. *The Arc of a Covenant: The United States, Israel, and the Fate of the Jewish People.* New York: Alfred A. Knopf, 2022.

Mee, Charles L., Jr., *Meeting at Potsdam.* New York: M. Evans and Company, 1975.

Meijer, Hendrik. *Arthur Vandenberg: The Man in the Middle of the American Century.* Chicago: University of Chicago Press, 2017.

Meltzer, Brad, and Josh Mensch. *The Nazi Conspiracy: The Secret Plot to Kill Roosevelt, Stalin, and Churchill.* New York: Flatiron, 2023.

Michaeli, Ethan. *The Defender: How the Legendary Black Newspaper Changed America.* New York: Houghton Mifflin Harcourt, 2016.

Michaelis, David. *Eleanor.* New York: Simon & Schuster, 2020.

Miller, Loren. "The Negro Voters in the Far West." *The Journal of Negro Education* 26, no. 3 (Summer 1957): 267.

Miller, Merle. *Plain Speaking: An Oral Biography of Harry S. Truman.* New York: Berkley, 1974.

Millis, Walter, ed. *The Forrestal Diaries.* New York: Viking, 1951.

Milton, Giles. *Checkmate in Berlin: The Cold War Showdown That Shaped the Modern World.* New York: Henry Holt and Company, 2021.

Minkova, K. V. "Lend-Lease in Early Post-War Soviet–American Relations." *Vestnik of Saint Petersburg University, History, 2018* 63, no. 2 (June 2018): 614–35.

Miscamble, Wilson D. *From Roosevelt to Truman: Potsdam, Hiroshima, and the Cold War.* Cambridge, UK: Cambridge University Press, 2007.

———. *George F. Kennan and the Making of American Foreign Policy, 1947–1950.* Princeton, NJ: Princeton University Press, 1992.

Montefiore, Simon Sebag. *Stalin: The Court of the Red Tsar.* New York: Alfred A. Knopf, 2004.

Moran, Lord. *Churchill: Taken from the Diaries of Lord Moran.* Boston: Houghton Mifflin, 1966.

Morris, Seymour, Jr. *Supreme Commander: MacArthur's Triumph in Japan.* New York: Harper, 2014.

Murphy, Bruce Allen. *Wild Bill: The Legend and Life of William O. Douglas.* New York: Random House, 2003.

Murphy, Robert D. *Diplomat Among Warriors.* Garden City, NY: Doubleday, 1964.

Nasaw, David. *The Last Million: Europe's Displaced Persons from World War to Cold War.* New York: Penguin, 2020.

Neal, Steve, ed. *Eleanor and Harry: The Correspondence of Eleanor Roosevelt and Harry S. Truman.* New York: Scribner, 2002.

Nitze, Paul, Ann Smith, and Steven Rearden. *From Hiroshima to Glasnost: At the Center of Decision—A Memoir.* New York: Grove Weidenfeld, 1989.

Pappe, Ilan. *The Ethnic Cleansing of Palestine.* Oxford, UK: Oneworld Publications, 2006.

Patterson, James T. *Mr. Republican: A Biography of Robert A. Taft.* New York: Houghton Mifflin, 1972.

Pauley, Edwin W. "Life and Times of Edwin W. Pauley." Unpublished autobiography manuscript, The Harry S. Truman Presidential Library & Museum.

Pearson, Drew. "Woebegone Democrats Finally Come to Life; Drones 'Work or Else.'" *Radford* (VA) *News Journal,* September 18, 1948.

Persico, Joseph E. *Franklin and Lucy: President Roosevelt, Mrs. Rutherfurd, and the Other Remarkable Women in His Life.* New York: Random House, 2008.

Phillips, Cabell. *The Truman Presidency: The History of a Triumphant Succession.* New York: Macmillan, 1966.

Pick, Charles F., Jr., "Torpedo on the Starboard Beam." *Proceedings,* August 1970.

Plokhy, S. M. *Yalta: The Price of Peace.* New York: Viking, 2010.

Poen, Monte M., ed. *Letters Home by Harry Truman.* New York: Penguin, 1984.

Pogue, Forrest C. *George C. Marshall, Vol. 4: Statesman, 1945–1949.* New York: Viking, 1987.

"The President's Cardiologist." *Navy Magazine: A Magazine of Service,* March–April 1990.

"President Truman Did Not Understand." *U.S. News & World Report,* August 15, 1960.

Radosh, Allis, and Ronald Radosh. *A Safe Haven: Harry S. Truman and the Founding of Israel.* New York: HarperCollins, 2009.

Redding, John M. *Inside the Democratic Party.* New York: Bobbs-Merrill, 1958.

Reilly, Michael F. *Reilly of the White House.* New York: Simon and Schuster, 1947.

Reinsch, J. Leonard. *Getting Elected.* New York: Hippocrene, 1988.

Reston, James. *Deadline: A Memoir.* New York: Random House, 1992.

Reynolds, David. *From World War to Cold War: Churchill, Roosevelt, and the International History of the 1940s.* New York: Oxford University Press, 2006.

Rigdon, William McKinley. *White House Sailor.* New York: Doubleday, 1962.

Robertson, David. *Sly and Able: A Political Biography of James F. Byrnes.* New York: W. W. Norton & Company, 1994.

Roll, David L. *George Marshall: Defender of the Republic.* New York: Dutton, 2019.

———. *The Hopkins Touch: Harry Hopkins and the Forging of the Alliance to Defeat Hitler.* New York: Oxford University Press, 2015.

Roosevelt, Eleanor. *My Husband and I: Recalls Her Years With F.D.R.* Columbia, 1965, LP.

———. *This I Remember.* New York: Holtzbrinck, 1975.

Roosevelt, Franklin D. *Papers as Governor of New York, 1929–1932.* Hyde Park, NY: Franklin D. Roosevelt Library.

Rosenman, Sam, ed. *The Public Papers and Addresses of Franklin D. Roosevelt.* Vol 13: *1944–1945.* New York: Harper & Brothers, 1950.

———. *Working with Roosevelt.* New York: Harper & Brothers, 1956.

Rosensaft, Hadassah. *Yesterday (My Story).* Washington, DC: Vad Vashem and Holocaust Survivors' Memoirs, U.S. Holocaust Memorial Museum, 2005.

Ross, Dennis. *Doomed to Succeed: The U.S.–Israel Relationship from Truman to Obama.* New York: Farrar, Straus and Giroux, 2015.

Ross, Irwin. *The Loneliest Campaign: The Truman Victory of 1948.* New York: New American Library, 1968.

Safire, William. "Truman on Underdogs." *New York Times*, July 14, 2003. https://www.nytimes.com/2003/07/14/opinion/truman-on-underdogs .html.

Scanlon, Jennifer. *Until There Is Justice: The Life of Anna Arnold Hedgeman.* New York: Oxford University Press, 2016.

Schaller, Michael. *The American Occupation of Japan: The Origins of the Cold War in Asia.* New York: Oxford University Press, 1985.

Schauffler, Edward R. *Son of the Soil.* Kansas City, MO: Schauffler Publishing, 1947.

Schmitz, David F. *Henry L. Stimson: The First Wise Man.* Wilmington, DE: Scholarly Resources Inc., 2001.

Schonberger, Howard B. "Zaibatsu Dissolution and the American Restoration of Japan." *Bulletin of Concerned Asian Scholars 5, no. 2* (1973): 16–31, DOI: 10.1080 /14672715.1973.10406331.

Sengstacke, John H. "Let's Put Up or Shut Up." *Chicago Defender*, August 7, 1948.

Sheffer, Gabriel. *Moshe Sharett: Biography of a Political Moderate.* Oxford, UK: Oxford University Press, 1996.

Sherwood, Robert E. *Roosevelt and Hopkins: An Intimate History.* New York: Harper & Brothers, 1948.

Shogan, Robert T. *Harry Truman and the Struggle for Racial Justice.* Lawrence: University Press of Kansas, 2013.

Shoumatoff, Elizabeth. *FDR's Unfinished Portrait.* Pittsburgh: University of Pittsburgh Press, 1990.

Shtemenko, S. M. *The General Staff in the War Years.* Moscow: Voenizdat, 1989, http://militera.lib.ru/memo/russian/shtemenko/index.html.

Smith, Jean Edward. *Lucius D. Clay: An America Life.* New York: Henry Holt and Company, 1990.

———, ed. *The Papers of General Lucius D. Clay: Germany 1945–1949.* Vol. 2. Bloomington: Indiana University Press, 1975.

Smith, Richard Norton. *Thomas E. Dewey and His Times.* New York: Simon & Schuster, 1982.

Smith, Walter Bedell. *My Three Years in Moscow.* New York: Lippincott, 1950.

Steel, Ronald. *Walter Lippmann and the American Century.* New York: Little Brown and Company, 1980.

Steil, Benn. *The Marshall Plan: Dawn of the Cold War.* New York: Simon & Schuster, 2018.

Steinberg, Alfred. *The Man from Missouri: The Life and Times of Harry S. Truman.* New York: Putnam, 1962.

Stimson, Henry L., and McGeorge Bundy. *On Active Service in Peace and War.* New York: Harper & Brothers, 1948.

Stoler, Mark A., and Daniel D. Holt, eds. *The Papers of George Catlett Marshall.* Vol. 7. Baltimore: Johns Hopkins University Press, 2016.

Straight, Michael. "Turnip Day in Washington." *New Republic*, July 26, 1948.

Sudoplatov, Pavel, and Anatoli Sudoplatov with Jerrod L. and Leona P. Schechter. *Special Tasks: The Memoirs of an Unwanted Witness—A Soviet Spymaster.* Boston: Little, Brown and Company, 1994.

Sweeney, Charles W. *War's End: An Eyewitness Account of America's Last Atomic Mission.* New York: Avon Books, 1997.

Szilard, Gertrude Weiss, and Spencer R. Weant, eds. *Leo Szilard: His Version of the Facts: Selected Recollections and Correspondence.* Cambridge, MA: MIT Press, 1972.

Szilard, Leo. *Reminiscences.* Edited by Gertrude Weiss Szilard and Kathleen R. Windsor. *Perspectives in American History* 2 (1968).

Thomas, Evan. *Road to Surrender: Three Men and the Countdown to the End of World War II.* New York: Random House, 2023.

Topping, Simon. "Never Argue with the Gallup Polls: Thomas Dewey, Civil Rights and the Election of 1948." *Journal of American Studies* 38, no. 2 (August 2004): 179–98.

Trachtenberg, Marc. *A Constructed Peace: The Making of the European Settlement 1945–1963.* Princeton, NJ: Princeton University Press, 1999.

Tregaskis, Richard. *Invasion Diary.* New York: Random House, 1944.

Truman, Harry S. *Memoirs by Harry S. Truman.* Vol. 1: *Year of Decisions.* Garden City, NY: Doubleday, 1955.

———. *Memoirs by Harry S. Truman.* Vol. 2: *Years of Trial and Hope.* Garden City, NY: Doubleday, 1956.

———. *Public Papers and Addresses of the Presidents, Harry S. Truman, 1945– 1953.* Washington, DC: Government Printing Office, 1966.

Truman, Margaret. *Bess W. Truman.* New York: Macmillan, 1986.

———. *Harry S. Truman.* New York: William Morrow & Company, 1973.

———. *Souvenir.* New York: McGraw-Hill, 1956.

Vandenberg, Arthur, Jr., ed. *The Private Papers of Senator Vandenberg.* Boston: Houghton Mifflin, 1972.

Volganov, Dimitri. *Stalin: Triumph and Tragedy.* Translated by Harold Shukman. New York: Grove Press, 1988.

Walker, Frank C. *FDR's Quiet Confidant: The Autobiography of Frank C. Walker.* Denver: University Press of Colorado, 1997.

Wallace, Henry A. *Papers and Diary.* University of Iowa Library. Microfilm.

Ward, Geoffrey C., ed. *Closest Companion: The Unknown Story of the Intimate Friendship Between Franklin Roosevelt and Margaret Suckley.* New York: Simon & Schuster, 1995.

Watkins, T. M. *Righteous Pilgrim: The Life and Times of Harold Ickes, 1874–1952.* New York: Henry Holt and Company, 1990.

Weil, Martin. *A Pretty Good Club: The Founding Fathers of the U.S. Foreign Service.* New York: W. W. Norton & Company, 1978.

Weisberger, Bernard A. "An Exclusive Interview with Clark Clifford." *American Heritage* 28, no. 3 (April 1977). https://www.americanheritage.com/exclusive -interview-clark-clifford.

Weizmann, Chaim. *Trial and Error: The Autobiography of Chaim Weizmann.* New York: Harper, 1949.

Weizmann, Vera. *The Impossible Takes Longer.* New York: Harper & Row, 1967.

Wellerstein, Alex. "FDR and the Bomb." *The Nuclear Secrecy Blog*, September 30, 2016, nuclearsecrecy.com/2016/09/30/fdr-and-thebomb.

———. "The First Light of Trinity." *The New Yorker*, June 16, 2015. https://www .newyorker.com/tech/annals-of-technology/the-first-light-of-the-trinity-atomic -test.

Westad, Odd Arne. *The Cold War: A World History.* New York: Basic Books, 2017.

White, Walter. *A Man Called White: The Autobiography of Walter White.* New York: Viking Press, 1948.

White, William S. *The Taft Story.* New York: Harper & Row, 1954.

Whitney, Courtney. *MacArthur: His Rendezvous with History.* New York: Alfred A. Knopf, 1956.

Wilkerson, Isabel. *The Warmth of Other Suns: The Epic Story of America's Great Migration.* New York: Random House, 2010.

Willis, Resa. *FDR and Lucy: Lovers and Friends.* New York: Routledge, 2004.

Woolner, David B. *The Last 100 Days: FDR at War and at Peace.* New York: Basic Books, 2017.

Wyden, Peter. *Day One.* New York: Simon & Schuster, 1984.

Wyman, David S. *Abandonment of the Jews: America and the Holocaust, 1941–1945.* New York: New Press, 1984.

Yergin, Daniel. *Shattered Peace: The Origins of the Cold War.* New York: Penguin, 1990.

Notes

★ Abbreviations ★

FDR: Franklin Delano Roosevelt
FDRL: The Franklin D. Roosevelt Presidential Library & Museum
FRUS: The Foreign Relations of the United States series, 1940–1949
GCML: George C. Marshall Research Library
HSTL: The Harry S. Truman Presidential Library & Museum
PP, HST: Public Papers and Addresses of the Presidents of the United
   States; Harry S. Truman, 1945–1953

Prologue ★ Death and Rebirth

1. "'Common Man' Wins Praise of Neighbors," *New York Times*, December 28, 1972, 24.
2. Margaret Truman, *Harry S. Truman*, 167.
3. Sherwood, *Roosevelt and Hopkins*, 9.
4. Memorandum by Dr. Frank Lahey dated Monday, July 10, 1944, copies of which are at
   the Lahey Clinic in Boston and also in the hands of Dr. Harry Goldsmith. Dr. Lahey, a
   highly regarded surgeon who had examined the president, met with McIntire on Saturday afternoon, July 8, and recommended that Vice Admiral McIntire inform FDR
   that he would not survive a four-year term and that he had a "serious responsibility"
   to select his VP carefully. Lahey's memo states that "Admiral McIntire agrees with this
   and has, he states, so informed Mr. Roosevelt." Though the original of the memo has
   been lost or destroyed, there is every reason to believe that the copies are authentic and
   credible. See Harry S. Goldsmith, MD, *A Conspiracy of Silence: Impact on History*
   (Lincoln, NE: iUniverse, Inc., 2007), 171–2. See also Carey Goldberg (editor of Boston's
   WBUR-FM's CommonHealth section), "As Promised, Long-Lost Lahey Memo on
   FDR," April 11, 2011, https://www.wbur.org/news/2011/04/11/fdr-lahey-memo. Inexplicably, a copy of the Lahey memorandum is *not* archived at FDRL.
5. See e.g., Lelyveld, *His Final Battle*, 149–50, and Hamilton, *War and Peace*, 283.

6. Press and Radio Conference #961, July 11, 1944, 11:07 a.m., Press Conferences of President Franklin D. Roosevelt, 1933–1945, Series I: Press Conference Transcripts, FDRL.

7. Truman to Bess W. Truman, letter, July 12, 1944, Papers of Harry S. Truman Pertaining to Family, Business, and Personal Affairs, HSTL.

8. Miller, *Plain Speaking*, 408–9.

9. Freidel, *Franklin D. Roosevelt*, 36.

10. Truman, Pickwick Papers memos, HSTL. https://www.archives.gov/publications/prologue/2007/winter/proposal.html.

11. McCullough, *Truman*, 180.

12. FDR, radio address, April 7, 1932, *Papers as Governor of New York, 1929–1932*, 173.

13. Steinberg, *The Man from Missouri*, 132.

14. Ibid.; Phillips, *The Truman Presidency*, 26–7.

15. Steinberg, *The Man from Missouri*, 132.

16. Margaret Truman, *Harry S. Truman*, 118.

17. Harry Easley, oral history by J. R. Fuchs, August 24, 1967, 44–5, HSTL.

18. "Billion Dollar Watchdog," *Time*, March 8, 1943.

19. Ferrell, *Dear Bess*, 455.

20. It could be argued that the transition from presidents William McKinley to Theodore Roosevelt was even more productive and consequential because of TR's accomplishments during the seven and a half years of his presidency—the Panama Canal, a Nobel Peace Prize for diplomacy, leading the progressive movement, strengthening the navy, conservation, regulation of big business, and moving the U.S. toward global responsibility. These are truly impressive accomplishments but TR never faced major crises as Truman did—ending the war in Japan and the use of the bomb; reconversion of the U.S. economy; containing the Soviet Union; the Berlin Airlift; NATO; repelling the invasion of South Korea; firing MacArthur; crippling labor strikes; the revival of the economies of West Germany, Western Europe, and Japan. TR, a Republican, had a Republican Congress, whereas between 1947 and the beginning of 1949 Truman, a Democrat, had to deal with a House and Senate dominated by Republicans.

Chapter 1   ⋆   Over the Rainbow

1. In *War and Peace*, Nigel Hamilton inexplicably writes at page 13 that Roosevelt traveled on his train, the *Ferdinand Magellan*, from Washington to Newport News on the night of November 11 and at page 14 that he sailed on the USS *Potomac* that night from the Washington Navy Yard to Newport News. The White House log indicates that Roosevelt and his party traveled by automobile to the marine base at Quantico, where he and his party boarded the USS *Potomac*. See also Butler, *Roosevelt and Stalin*, 4.

2. McCrea, *Captain McCrea's War*, 179.

3. FDR to Marshal Stalin, November 8, 1943, *FRUS, Conferences at Cairo and Tehran*, 261.

4. "FDR to Churchill, November 11, 1943," *Franklin D. Roosevelt, Papers as President, Map Room Papers, 1941–1945*, Box 4, FDR–Churchill, November–December 1943, FDRL.

5. Blum, *Night of the Assassins*, 184, 195; Bazna, *I Was Cicero*, 42–67; Meltzer and Mensch, *The Nazi Conspiracy*, 236.

6. Blum, *Night of the Assassins*, 107.

7. Sherwood, *Roosevelt and Hopkins*, 227.

8. FDR diary (typed), "War Conferences in Cairo, Tehran, Malta, etc., November 11–December 17, 1943," *Franklin D. Roosevelt, Papers as President*, "The President's Official File, Part 1, 1933–945," 200-3-N, Box 64, FDRL.

9. Butler, *Roosevelt and Stalin,* 21–2; Pick, "Torpedo on the Starboard Beam," 90ff.; USS *Iowa* war diary, November 1943, NARA RG 38; USS *William D. Porter* war diary, November 1943, NARA RG 38; USS *Iowa* deck log, November 1943, NARA RG 24; *William D. Porter* deck log, November 1943 NARA RG 24; Rigdon, *White House Sailor,* 64.

10. McCrae, *Captain McCrea's War,* 186.

11. Ibid.

12. Rigdon, *White House Sailor,* 64; Arnold, *Global Mission,* 455.

13. "Minutes of Meeting Between the President and the Chiefs of Staff, Held on Board Ship in the President's Cabin, 15 November 1943, at 1400," *Franklin D. Roosevelt, Papers as President: Map Room Papers, 1941–1945,* 4, 5, Box 29, FDRL.

14. Sherwood, *Roosevelt and Hopkins,* 799; McIntire, *White House Physician,* 170–1.

15. William Bullitt to Roosevelt, January 29, 1943, Orville Bullitt, *For the President,* 578.

16. William Bullitt, "How We Won the War and Lost the Peace," *Life,* August 30, 1948.

17. Orville Bullitt, *For the President,* introduction by Kennan where he writes at page xiv that William Bullitt's letters "deserve a place among the major historical documents of the time."

18. Mark Clark, diary, November 13, 1943, Citadel, Box 64.

19. Tregaskis, *Invasion Diary,* 195.

20. Air Chief Marshal (Acting) and chief of Bomber Command Sir Arthur Harris's reply to a British "Secretary of State," The Pathfinders Archive, "Battle of Berlin," https://raf pathfinders.com.

21. Shtemenko, *The General Staff; Komsomolskaya Pravda,* May 7, 2007; *Lipetsk News,* April 11, 2007.

22. Banac, *The Diary of Georgi Dimitrov,* 145.

23. Volganov, *Stalin,* 498.

24. Blum, *Night of the Assassins,* 269–70, 277. In September, von Ortel, a heavy drinker, was training for the assassination mission in Ukraine. While being plied with drink, he told a Soviet agent who he thought was a fellow German that he was training with Otto Skorzeny for an important operation in the Middle East. Since Skorzeny was world-famous for rescuing Mussolini from a mountaintop in the Italian Alps, the Russian agent passed the information on to the NKVD, who alerted Soviet agents in Tehran that something big could happen in that city. Meltzer and Mensch, *The Nazi Conspiracy,* 242–3; Blum, *Night of the Assassins,* 162–3; Katamidze, *Loyal Comrades, Ruthless Killers,* 105; Sudoplatov et al., *Special Tasks,* 130.

25. Blum, *Night of the Assassins,* 208; Andrew and Mitrokihn, *The Sword and the Shield.*

26. Blum, *Night of the Assassins,* 275; Meltzer and Mensch, *The Nazi Conspiracy,* 285; Yuri Plutenko and Gevork Vartanian, "Tehran-43: Wrecking the Plan to Kill Stalin, Roosevelt and Churchill," RIA Novosti, October 16, 2007; Yuri Kuznets, *Tehran 43: Operation Long Jump* [43]; Alexander Lukin, "Operation Long Jump" [Lukin]; Victor Yegerov, *The Plot Against "Eureka"* [Eureka]; "Gevork Vartanian: Spy Who Helped Foil Hitler Death Plot," *The Independent,* December 1, 2012 [Foil]; "Gevork Vartanian, *The Telegraph,* January 11, 2012 [GV]. Words in brackets are shorthand for names of books in subsequent notes.

27. Blum, *Night of the Assassins,* 277–8; Bill Yenne, *Operation Long Jump,* 218–9 [Long Jump]; Havas, *Hitler's Plot to Kill the Big Three,* 220 [Plot]; Nikolai Dolgopolov, "How the Lion and the Bear Were Saved," *Rossiiskaya Gazeta,* November 29, 2007 [Saved]; Lukin; Eureka.

28. Harriman and Abel, *Special Envoy to Churchill and Stalin,* 164.

29. Moran, *Churchill at War,* 162–3.

30. Kimball, *The Complete Correspondence,* vol. 1. R-123/1 letter, FDR to Churchill, March 18, 1942, 421.

31. Reilly, *Reilly of the White House*, 178–9; Blum, *Night of the Assassins*, 302–3.

32. Bohlen, *Witness to History*, 139.

33. Fenby, *Alliance*, 226–7.

34. Harriman and Abel, *Special Envoy to Churchill and Stalin*, 265.

35. "Roosevelt–Stalin Meeting, November 28, 1943, 3 p.m., Roosevelt's Quarters, Soviet Embassy, Bohlen Minutes," *FRUS, Cairo and Tehran*, 483; Roll, *The Hopkins Touch*, 315.

36. Roosevelt–Stalin Meeting, November 28, 1943, *FRUS, Cairo and Tehran*, 483.

37. Ibid.

38. Ibid., 483–4.

39. Ibid., 484–5; Harriman and Abel, *Special Envoy to Churchill and Stalin*, 266.

40. "Roosevelt–Stalin Meeting, November 28, 1943," *FRUS, Cairo and Tehran*, 486.

41. Ibid.

42. Bohlen, *Witness to History*, 140–1.

43. "Roosevelt–Stalin Meeting, November 28, 1943," *FRUS, Cairo and Tehran*, 486.

44. Ibid., 487.

45. "First Plenary Session, November 28, 1943, 4 p.m., Soviet Embassy, Combined Chiefs of Staff Minutes," *FRUS, Cairo and Tehran*, 497.

46. Ibid.

47. Huston, *American Airpower Comes of Age*, 89.

48. "First Plenary Session, November 28, 1943, 4 p.m., Soviet Embassy, Bohlen Minutes," *FRUS, Cairo and Tehran*, 499.

49. Ibid.

50. Foreign Office to Moscow, outward telegram, October 26, 1943, UK National Archives (BNA).

51. "First Plenary Session, Combined Chiefs of Staff Minutes," *FRUS, Cairo and Tehran*, 499; "Roosevelt–Stalin Meeting, November 28, 1943," *FRUS, Cairo and Tehran*, 489.

52. "Roosevelt–Stalin Meeting, November 28, 1943," *FRUS, Cairo and Tehran*, 492.

53. Ibid., 494; "First Plenary Session, Combined Chiefs of Staff Minutes," *FRUS, Cairo and Tehran*, 505 (italics added).

54. "Roosevelt–Stalin Meeting, November 28, 1943," *FRUS, Cairo and Tehran*, 494.

55. "First Plenary Session, Combined Chiefs of Staff Minutes," 508.

56. Bohlen, *Witness to History*, 143–4.

57. Blum, *Night of the Assassins*, 304, 310–1, 314; Plot, 213, 218–9; Long Jump, 139–40; Foil; GV, 43; Eureka; Lukin; Saved.

58. Bohlen, *Witness to History*, 144.

59. Beria, *Beria, My Father: Inside Stalin's Kremlin*, 93.

60. Danchev and Todman, *War Diaries*, 485.

61. Moran, *Churchill at War*, 165 (entry of November 29, 1943).

62. "Roosevelt–Stalin Meeting, November 29, 1943, 2:45 p.m., Roosevelt's Quarters, Soviet Embassy, Bohlen Minutes," *FRUS, Cairo and Tehran*, 529–33, 622 (sketch).

63. Bohlen, *Witness to History*, 145.

64. "Roosevelt–Stalin Meeting, November 29, 1943, Bohlen Minutes," *FRUS, Cairo and Tehran*, 530–1.

65. Bohlen, *Witness to History*, 145.

66. Montefiore, *Stalin*, 468.

67. Moran, *Churchill at War*, 166 (entry of November 29, 1943).

68. "Roosevelt–Stalin Meeting, November 29, 1943, Soviet Embassy, 4 p.m., Combined Chiefs of Staff Minutes," *FRUS, Cairo and Tehran*, 540–1.

69. "Roosevelt–Stalin Meeting, November 29, 1943, Bohlen Minutes," *FRUS, Cairo and Tehran*, 535.

70. Leahy, *I Was There*, 208.

71. "Roosevelt–Stalin Meeting, November 29, 1943, Bohlen Minutes," *FRUS, Cairo and Tehran*, 538.

72. Bohlen, *Witness to History*, 146.

73. "Roosevelt–Stalin Meeting, November 29, 1943, Bohlen Minutes," *FRUS, Cairo and Tehran*, 539. For "conditions" specified, see Foreign Secretary Anthony Eden, October 27, 1943, CHAR 20/122/43, Churchill Archives Centre, Churchill College, Cambridge, UK.

74. "Roosevelt–Stalin Meeting, November 29, 1943, Combined Chiefs of Staff Minutes," *FRUS, Cairo and Tehran*, 552.

75. Eden, CHAR 20/122/43.

76. Bohlen, *Witness to History*, 146. See also "Tripartite Dinner Meeting, November 29, 8:30 p.m., Soviet Embassy, Bohlen Minutes," *FRUS, Cairo and Tehran*, 553–5.

77. Elliott Roosevelt, *As He Saw It*, 188.

78. Bohlen, *Witness to History*, 147.

79. Churchill, *Closing the Ring*, 374.

80. Ibid.

81. Bohlen, *Witness to History*, 146.

82. "Meeting of the Combined Chiefs of Staff, November 30, 1943, 9:30 a.m., Combined Chiefs of Staff Minutes," *FRUS, Cairo and Tehran*, 64 n10.

83. "Roosevelt–Churchill Luncheon Meeting, 1:30 p.m., Soviet Embassy, Bohlen Minutes," *FRUS, Cairo and Tehran*, 565.

84. Blum, *Night of the Assassins*, 315.

85. Danchev and Todman, *War Diaries*, 488.

86. Harriman and Abel, *Special Envoy to Churchill and Stalin*, 276.

87. Danchev and Todman, *War Diaries*, 486.

88. Fenby, *Alliance*, 252.

89. Bohlen, *Witness to History*, 149.

90. "Tripartite Dinner, November 30, 1943, 8:30 p.m., Boettiger Minutes," *FRUS, Cairo and Tehran*, 583. See also Roll, *The Hopkins Touch*, 324–5.

91. Harriman and Abel, *Special Envoy to Churchill and Stalin*, 277 (italics added).

92. "Tripartite Dinner, November 30, 1943," *FRUS, Cairo and Tehran*, 585.

93. Churchill, *Closing the Ring*, 388.

94. Bohlen, *Witness to History*, 149.

95. Blum, *Night of the Assassins*, 321; Plot, 233–5; Long Jump, 172–3; Eureka, 43; Saved; Foil; GV.

96. "Roosevelt–Stalin Meeting, December 1, 1943, 3:20 p.m., Roosevelt's Quarters, Bohlen Minutes," *FRUS, Cairo and Tehran*, 594–5.

97. Perkins, *The Roosevelt I Knew*, 83–5.

98. Gunther, *Roosevelt in Retrospect*, 17.

99. "Tripartite Political Meeting, December 1, 1943, 6 p.m., Soviet Embassy, Bohlen Minutes," *FRUS, Cairo and Tehran*, 597–9.

100. Bohlen, *Witness to History*, 152.

101. Eden, *The Memoirs of Anthony Eden: The Reckoning*, 496.

102. *FRUS, The Near East and Africa*, vol. 4, 414.

103. "Appendix D: Log of the President's Trip to Africa and the Middle East, November–December 1943," *Franklin D. Roosevelt, Papers as President, Map Room Papers, 1941–1945*, Box 24, FDRL. See also John Boettiger, *A Love in Shadow*, 250 ("took great pride . . . in having written the first draft").

104. Harriman and Abel, *Special Envoy*, 282.

105. "Appendix D," *Franklin D. Roosevelt, Papers as President, Map Room Papers, 1941–1945*, Box 24, FDRL.

106. Berezhkov, *History in the Making*, 474. See also, Fenby, *Alliance*, 260.

107. Sherwood, *Roosevelt and Hopkins*, 799.

108. Blum, *Night of the Assassins*, 327–30; Plot, 244; Long Jump, 179–80; Eureka, 43; Saved; Foil; GV.

109. Eisenhower, *Crusade in Europe*, 206–7.

110. Lash, *World of Love*, 98.

111. Rosenman, *Working with Roosevelt*, 411.

112. Press and Radio Conference #927, December 17, 1943, American Presidency Project.

113. Blum, *Night of the Assassins*, 333–4.

Chapter 2   ★   Go All Out for Truman

1. Canol Project: Testimony of General Brehon Somervell, December 20, 1943, Special Committee to Investigate the National Defense Program, United States Senate, NARA; White House Stenographer's Diary, December 20, 1943, Franklin D. Roosevelt, Day by Day, Project of Pare Lorentz Center, FDRL. See also, Drummond, *The Watchdog*, 299–302.

2. General Harry H. Vaughan, oral history, January 16, 1963, 71, HSTL.

3. Anna Boettiger to John Boettiger, December 19, 1943, Box 6, Boettiger Papers, FDRL.

4. Willis, *FDR and Lucy*, 122.

5. Boettiger, *A Love in Shadow*, 251 (Anna's words quoted by her son John).

6. Ibid., 254.

7. Persico, *Franklin and Lucy*, 281.

8. Anna Boettiger to John Boettiger, December 27, 1943, Box 6, Boettiger Papers, FDRL.

9. Ward, *Closest Companion*, 263.

10. McIntire, *White House Physician*, 180.

11. Buhite and Levy, *FDR's Fireside Chats*, 272–81.

12. Ward, *Closest Companion*, 264.

13. Press and Radio Conference #929, December 28, 1943, 4:07 p.m., Press Conferences of President Franklin D. Roosevelt, 1933–1945, Series 1: Press Conference Transcripts, FDRL.

14. *New York Herald Tribune*, January 2, 1944, II:1.

15. Ward, *Closest Companion*, 264 (the word "little" was underlined or otherwise given emphasis in Daisy's diary).

16. Entry of January 7, 1944, Harold D. Smith diary, Smith Papers, quoted in Ferrell, *The Dying President*, 30

17. Annual Message to Congress—State of the Union (speech file 1501), January 11, 1944, Franklin D. Roosevelt, Master Speech File, 1898–1945, Box 76, FDRL.

18. Rosenman, *Working with Roosevelt*, 427.

19. The White House log for January 20, 1944, indicates that Edward Flynn met with FDR at 12:45 p.m.; and the log indicates that on January 21, Frank Walker met with FDR at 1:50 p.m. and "members of the DNC" had tea with FDR and Eleanor Roosevelt at 5:35 p.m.

20. Ward, *Closest Companion*, 272–87.

21. Ibid., 286; Hassett, *Off the Record with FDR*, 239 (entry of March 24, 1944).

22. Press and Radio Conference #944, March 24, 1944, 11:09 a.m., Press Conferences of President Franklin D Roosevelt, 1933–1945, Series 1: Press Conference Transcripts, FDRL.

23. Asbell, *Mother and Daughter*, 177; Goodwin, *No Ordinary Time*, 493.

24. Ward, *Closest Companion*, 286 (entry of March 23, 1944).

25. Ward, *Closest Companion*, 288 (entry of March 26, 1944).

26. Ferrell, *The Dying President*, 37.

27. Ibid., 288 (entry of March 26, 1944).
28. Bishop, *FDR's Last Year*, 2.
29. Goodwin, interview with Dr. Howard Bruenn.
30. Interview with Jan K. Herman in "The President's Cardiologist," 6–13.
31. Bruenn, "Clinical Notes on the Illness and Death of President Franklin D. Roosevelt," 579–91.
32. Howard Bruenn, typewritten notes, undated, Howard Bruenn Papers, 1944–1946, FDRL.
33. "The President's Cardiologist," 9.
34. Ward, *Closest Companion*, 189 (entry of March 28, 1944).
35. Bruenn Folder, Small Collections, FDRL.
36. "The President's Cardiologist," 8.
37. Goodwin, *No Ordinary Time*, 495.
38. Bruenn, typewritten notes, Harold Bruenn Papers, FDRL.
39. Ibid.
40. Bishop, *FDR's Last Year*, 11.
41. Ibid., 18–9.
42. Rigdon, *White House Sailor*, 98.
43. Bishop, *FDR's Last Year*, 26.
44. Rigdon, *White House Sailor*, 98.
45. Joint Chiefs of Staff to MacArthur and Nimitz, March 12, 1944, quoted in Borneman, *MacArthur at War*, 365–6.
46. *New York Times*, April 29, 1944, 8.
47. Ward, *Closest Companion*, 294 (entry of March 4, 1944).
48. Ibid., 293 (entry of April 27, 1944).
49. Goodwin, interview with Dr. Howard Bruenn; FDR to Harry Hopkins, May 18, 1944, Harry Hopkins Papers, FDRL.
50. *Time*, May 15, 1944.
51. Wallace Diary, August 16, 1944, Wallace Papers and Diary, University of Iowa. The quote from the diary was omitted from John Blum, *The Price of Vision*, 380, after the second paragraph from the bottom ending with "even his family doesn't know anything about him . . ." Blum's book purported to quote from the August 16, 1944, diary but for some reason he deleted the quote that appeared in the original. Near the end of his life Truman said something quite similar: "He was the coldest man I ever met. He didn't give a damn personally for me or you or anyone else in the world as far as I could see." Thomas Fleming, "Eight Days with Harry Truman," *American Heritage* 43, no. 4 (1992): 56.
52. Anna Roosevelt Halsted, oral history, May 11, 1973, 55, Anna Roosevelt Halsted Papers, Box 12, FDRL. See also Richard H. Rovere interview, August 16, 1958, Richard H. Rovere Papers, Folder 1, Box 15, State Historical Society of Wisconsin, Madison.
53. Memorandum of conversation with Hannegan, May 25, 1946, by Robert E. Sherwood, correspondence, 122a, Sherwood Papers, Houghton Library, Harvard University, courtesy of Charles V. Reynolds Jr.; Flynn, *You're the Boss*, 181.
54. Pauley, "Life and Times of Edwin W. Pauley." See also Pauley, undated memorandum for Jonathan Daniels, Daniels Papers, HSTL [from Ferrell, *Choosing Truman*, 13].
55. Eagleton and Duffin, "Bob Hannegan and Harry Truman's Vice Presidential Nomination," 272.
56. Edwin W. Pauley with Richard English, "Why Truman Is President," undated, "The President," Box 30, White House Central Files, Confidential Files, HSTL.
57. Walker, *FDR's Quiet Confidant*, 142.
58. Lelyveld, *His Final Battle*, 166.

59. Pauley with English, "Why Truman Is President," 15.

60. Allen, *Presidents Who Have Known Me*, 128–9; Ferrell, *The Autobiography of Harry S. Truman*, 92; McCullough, *Truman*, 301; Blum, *The Price of Vision*, 364.

61. Ferrell, *The Autobiography of Harry S. Truman*, 89.

62. Blum, *The Price of Vision*, 364.

63. McCullough, *Truman*, 302.

64. Blum, *The Price of Vision*, 366–7; "Democratic National Conventions," President's Secretary's File, Box 129, FDRL.

65. Ferrell, *Choosing Truman*, 29–30.

66. Byrnes, *All in One Lifetime*, 222.

67. Ferrell, *Dear Bess*, 505.

68. Truman interview with Jonathan Daniels, November 12, 1949, 65, Daniels Papers, HSTL. In his memoir, Byrnes denied that he told Truman that it was the president who gave him the "go sign." Byrnes, *All in One Lifetime*, 226.

69. Margaret Truman, *Harry S. Truman*, 171.

70. Truman to Charles G. Ross, January 22, 1950, "Political—Vice Presidential Nomination—1944," President's Secretary's File, Box 321, HSTL. See also Margaret Truman, *Harry S. Truman*, 321.

71. Byrnes, *All in One Lifetime*, 223; Ferrell, *Choosing Truman*, 32.

72. Byrnes, *All in One Lifetime*, 224–5.

73. Ibid.

74. FDR to Robert Hannegan, July 14, 1944, HSTL.

75. Byrnes, *All in One Lifetime*, 226.

76. Ibid., 227.

77. Edward A. Harris, "Soothsayer from Lamar," 1–5, undated, enclosed in Harris to Revere, May 30, 1958, Folder 1, Box 15, Revere Papers, State Historical Society of Wisconsin, Madison.

78. Margaret Truman, *Bess W. Truman*, 272.

79. Ibid.

80. Walker autobiography, Frank C. Walker Papers, Archives of the University of Notre Dame, Hesburgh Library, South Bend, Indiana, 221.

81. Truman interview with Jonathan Daniels, November 12, 1949, 65, Daniels Papers, HSTL.

82. "Wallace Left to Delegates by Roosevelt," *New York Times*, July 18, 1944, 1.

83. Drury, *A Senate Journal*, 218.

84. James F. Byrnes Papers, letter dated July 19, 1944, from Byrnes to Senator Burnet Maybank, Folder 532, Cooper Memorial Library, Clemson University, Clemson, South Carolina; See also *New York Times*, July 25, 1944, 18.

85. *Chicago Tribune*, July 20, 1944, 1.

86. George Elsey, Notes, Ayers Papers, HSTL; Truman, *Memoirs*, vol. 1, 192–93; Truman interview with Daniels, November 29, 1949, 66, Daniels Papers, HSTL; Ferrell, *The Autobiography of Harry S. Truman*, 90.

87. Margaret Truman, *Souvenir*, 66.

88. James Roosevelt and Schalett, *Affectionately, F.D.R.*, 351–2; James Roosevelt, *My Parents: A Differing View*, 279.

89. *Time*, July 31, 1944.

90. *New York Times*, July 21, 1944, 8.

91. Walter Trohan, *Chicago Tribune*, August 4, 1944, 3.

92. Neale Roach, oral history by Jerry N. Hess, January 21, 1969, 24–5, HSTL.

93. Pauley, memorandum for Jonathan Daniels; Rensch, *Getting Elected*, 5–11.

94. David McCullough, interview of Claude D. Pepper.

95. Domarus, *Hitler: Speeches and Proclamations 1932–1945*, vol. 4, 2925, radio address, German News Bureau, July 20, 1944.

96. Manchester, *American Caesar*, 366. After saying he would lose, Manchester wrote that FDR "changed his mind" and said, "I'll beat that son of a bitch in Albany if it's the last thing I do."

97. "President Favors Truman, Douglas," *New York Times*, July 21, 1944, 10 (reporter James Hagerty quoting Ed Pauley).

98. Pauley with English, "Why Truman Is President," 24.

99. Catledge, "Truman Nominated for Vice Presidency," *New York Times*, July 22, 1944, 1.

100. Margaret Truman, *Bess W. Truman*, 230.

101. Catledge, "Truman Nominated for Vice Presidency."

102. *St. Louis Post-Dispatch*, July 22, 1944.

103. Margaret Truman, *Bess W. Truman*, 233.

Chapter 3   ⋆   Best He Could Do

1. Rosenman, *Working with Roosevelt*, 456.

2. Margaret Truman, *Bess W. Truman*, 234.

3. Rosenman, *Working with Roosevelt*, 456.

4. Ibid., 457.

5. MacArthur, *Reminiscences*, 199.

6. Manchester, *American Caesar*, 368.

7. James, *The Years of MacArthur*, vol. 2, 530.

8. Leahy, *I Was There*, 251.

9. Ibid., 250–1; James, *The Years of MacArthur*, vol. 2, 530; MacArthur, *Reminiscences*, 197.

10. Manchester, *American Caesar*, 368; Leahy, *I Was There*, 251.

11. Rosenman, *Working with Roosevelt*, 458–9.

12. Ibid., 459–60.

13. Ibid., 461.

14. Reilly, *Reilly of the White House*, 194.

15. Rosenman, *Working with Roosevelt*, 436.

16. Truman to Margaret Truman (probably dated August 3, 1944), quoted in Margaret Truman, *Harry S. Truman*, 184.

17. Truman to Bess W. Truman, letter, August 4, 1944, Papers of Harry S. Truman Pertaining to Family, Business, and Personal Affairs, Box 14, HSTL.

18. Ibid., August 11, 1944, HSTL.

19. Walter Hehmeyer, oral history, April 16, 1969, 84, HSTL.

20. *Pittsburgh Courier*, August 5, 1944.

21. Truman to Bess W. Truman, letter, August 18, 1944.

22. Harry Vaughan, oral history, January 16, 1963, HSTL.

23. Daniels, *The Man of Independence*, 259.

24. Truman to Bess W. Truman, letter, August 18, 1944.

25. Memorandum of conversation between FDR and Henry Morgenthau, May 15, 1942, Presidential Diary, p. 1093, Henry Morgenthau, Jr., Papers, FDRL; Kimball, *The Juggler*, 7 n1.

26. Truman to Bess W. Truman, letter, August 18, 1944, 509.

27. Ferrell, "A Visit to the White House, 1947: The Diary of Vic H. Housholder," 326. For a similar admission, see Charles G. Ross diary, April 19, 1946, Ross Papers and Diary, HSTL.

28. Tom L. Evans, oral history by J. R. Fuchs, 1962–1963, 450–4, HSTL; Leahy interview, August 31, 1949, by Jonathan Daniels, 13, HSTL; Truman, *Memoirs*, vol. 1, 10. According to Fred Canfil, interview, November 12, 1949, by Jonathan Daniels, 67, HSTL, and Byrnes, *All in One Lifetime*, 282, Truman knew of the nuclear bomb project generally through his Senate committee work, specifically from Canfil, one of the investigators who got into the Oak Ridge and Hanford facilities. See Ferrell, *Harry S. Truman*, 418 n37.

29. Hehmeyer, oral history, 93, HSTL.

30. Margaret Truman, *Harry S. Truman*, 186. In *Truman*, David McCullough writes at page 328 that the speech was given on "a steamy, full-moon night in front of the old red-brick courthouse in Lamar."

31. Text of Truman's acceptance speech, *New York Times*, September 1, 1944, 26. See also Audio Collection, HSTL.

32. "Truman of Missouri," *Life*, August 21, 1944, 75.

33. Ward, *Closest Companion*, 326 (entry of September 10, 1944).

34. *New York Times*, September 12, 1944, 56.

35. Lash, *World of Love*, 137; Esther Lape Papers, FDRL.

36. Eleanor Roosevelt to Esther Lape, September 22, 1944, Box 5, Esther Lape Papers, FDRL.

37. *New York Times*, September 12, 1944, 6.

38. Dallek, *Franklin D. Roosevelt*, 575.

39. *FRUS, Conference at Quebec*, 325. See also Moran, *Churchill at War*, 216–7.

40. *FRUS, Conference at Quebec*, 326. Roosevelt was quoting Stalin.

41. Ibid., 342.

42. Blum, *Roosevelt and Morgenthau*, 599.

43. *FRUS, Conference at Quebec*, 361–3.

44. Stimson and Bundy, *On Active Service in Peace and War*, 568–82.

45. Henry Stimson diary, October 3, 1944, Yale University.

46. James Byrnes memorandum of June 27, 1947, conversation with Stimson, Byrnes Papers, Clemson University; see also Stimson and Bundy, *On Active Service*, 581.

47. Stimson diary, FDR–Stimson, October 3, 1944, Yale University.

48. President Roosevelt's news conference #970, White House, September 19, 1944, 4, FDRL. See also Lacey, *Washington at War*, 462.

49. *Chicago Tribune*, October 17, 1944, 14.

50. "Truman Welcomed by His Home Town," *New York Times*, November 5, 1944, 38.

51. *Time*, October 2, 1944.

52. Rosenman, *The Public Papers and Addresses of Franklin D. Roosevelt*, vol. 13, 290.

53. *Time*, October 2, 1944, 22.

54. Bishop, *FDR's Last Year*, 157.

55. Ibid.

56. *St. Louis Post-Dispatch*, October 23, 1944, 1A.

57. Rosenman, *The Public Papers and Addresses of Franklin D. Roosevelt*, vol. 13, 414.

58. Margaret Truman, *Harry S. Truman*, 190.

59. *Boston Globe*, November, 9, 1944, 13.

60. Margaret Truman, *Harry S. Truman*, 193.

61. Harry Easeley, oral history by J. R. Fuchs, 99, August 24, 1967, HSTL.

62. Ibid., 190.

63. Eleanor Roosevelt interview, Graff Papers, FDRL.

64. Ward, *Closest Companion*, 344 (entry of November 15, 1944).

65. Sarah Churchill to Clementine Churchill, February 8, 1945, Papers of Sarah Churchill 1/1/8, Churchill Archives Centre, Churchill College, Cambridge, UK.

66. Leebaert, *Grand Improvisation*, 86.

67. John W. Snyder, oral history by Jerry N. Hess, 145, December 8, 1967, HSTL.

68. Rosenman, *Working with Roosevelt*, 516.

69. Margaret Truman, *Harry S. Truman*, 195.

70. Rosenman, *The Public Papers and Addresses of Franklin Delano Roosevelt*, vol. 13, 523–5 (FDR, fourth inaugural address, January 20, 1945).

71. Truman, *Memoirs*, vol. 1, 195.

72. "Harry Hopkins to Roosevelt, January 24, 1945," *FRUS, Conferences at Malta and Yalta*, 39–40.

73. Asbell, *Mother and Daughter*, 181.

74. Preston, *Eight Days at Yalta*, 147 ("Berlin radio"); *New York Times*, February 6, 1945 ("German radio").

75. Bishop, *FDR's Last Year*, 334.

76. William D. Leahy diary, February 7, 1945, Library of Congress.

77. "Section 7—'Poland,' Yalta Protocol," *FRUS, Conferences at Malta and Yalta*, 980; see also "Fifth Plenary Meeting, February 9, 1945, Bohlen Minutes," *FRUS, Conferences at Malta and Yalta*, 776–81.

78. "Declaration on Liberated Europe, Section 2 of the Protocol of Proceedings of the Crimea Conference," *FRUS, Conferences at Malta and Yalta*, 977–8.

79. Leahy, *I Was There*, 315–6.

80. Ibid., 321.

81. Ward, *Closest Companion*, 396 (letter from FDR to Daisy, February 18, 1945).

82. Leo Sack telegram to FDR and Israel Goldstein telegram to FDR, October 15, 1944—each in President's Personal File, 6j01, FDRL.

83. Robert N. Rosen, *Saving the Jews*, 209–10.

84. Jacob Blaustein to FDR, March 24, 1945, Office File, 76C, Box 9, FDRL; Campbell and Herring, *The Diaries of Edward R. Stettinius, Jr.*, 211.

85. Watkins, *Righteous Pilgrim*, 749 (quoting reknowned geologist Everett de Golyer).

86. Breitman and Lichtman, *FDR and the Jews*, 302.

87. William A. Eddy, *FDR Meets Ibn Saud*, original manuscript, 17–9, Eddy Papers, Box 14, Mudd Library, Princeton, NJ.

88. Ibid., 27–8.

89. *FRUS, The Near East and Africa*, vol. 8, 3; Breitman and Lichtman, *FDR and the Jews*, 303; Woolner, *The Last 100 Days*, 160; Gregory, "America and Saudi Arabia, Act I," 116–9.

90. Churchill, *The Second World War*, vol. 6, 393. See also Plokhy, *Yalta*, 316.

91. Margaret Truman, *Harry S. Truman*, 200.

92. Letter from Truman to his mother and sister (April 11, 1945), quoted in Margaret Truman, *Harry S. Truman*, 198.

93. Gunther, *Procession*, 256–7.

94. Edgar Hinde, oral history, 124–5, HSTL; Eddie McKim, oral history, 106, HSTL.

95. Miscamble, *From Roosevelt to Truman*, 31.

96. Rosenman, *The Public Papers and Addresses of Franklin D. Roosevelt*, vol. 13, doc. 138.

97. Rosenman, *Working with Roosevelt*, 480.

98. Rosenman, *The Public Papers and Addresses of Franklin D. Roosevelt*, vol. 13, doc. 138.

99. Butler, *My Dear Mr. Stalin* (FDR–Stalin, April 4, 1945), 313–5.

100. Ibid. (March 31, 1945), 310–2.

101. Jean Edward Smith, *Lucius D. Clay*, 215–6. See also Beschloss, *The Conquerors*, 202.

102. Hassett, *Off the Record with FDR*, 327–9.

103. Bruenn, "Clinical Notes on the Illness and Death of President Franklin D. Roosevelt," 590.

104. Shoumatoff, *FDR's Unfinished Portrait*, 100.

105. Butler, *My Dear Mr. Stalin* (FDR–Churchill, April 11, 1945, and FDR–Stalin, April 11, 1945,) 321–2.

106. Margaret Truman, *Harry S. Truman*, 206.

107. Ward, *Closest Companion*, 416.

108. Shoumatoff, *FDR's Unfinished Portrait*, 117.

109. Ward, *Closest Companion*, 418.

110. Shoumatoff, *FDR's Unfinished Portrait*, 118–9.

111. Ward, *Closest Companion*, 419–20.

Chapter 4 ⋆ Unprepared

1. Eleanor Roosevelt, *This I Remember*, 344.

2. Truman to Mary Jane Truman and Mary Ellen "Mattie" Truman, April 26, 1945, HSTL.

3. Steinberg, *Sam Rayburn*, 225.

4. Truman, *Memoirs*, vol. 1, 5.

5. Lash, *Eleanor and Franklin*, 720–1.

6. Eleanor Roosevelt, overseas cable, quoted in Asbell, *When F.D.R. Died*, 94.

7. Truman, *Memoirs*, vol. 1, 5.

8. Bishop, *FDR's Last Year*, 598.

9. Shoumatoff, *FDR's Unfinished Portrait*, 120.

10. *New York Times*, April 13, 1945, 18.

11. Churchill, *The Second World War*, vol. 6, 412; Harriman and Abel, *Special Envoy to Churchill and Stalin*, 440.

12. Margaret Truman, *Bess W. Truman*, 249–50; Margaret Truman, *Harry S. Truman*, 210.

13. Stimson diary, April 12, 1945.

14. Millis, *The Forrestal Diaries*, 42; Henry Morgenthau diaries, April 12, 1951, online, FDRL.

15. Daniels, *Frontier on the Potomac*, 11.

16. "Statement of the President After Taking the Oath of Office, April 12, 1945," HSTL.

17. Truman, *Memoirs*, vol. 1, 10; Truman diary, April 12, 1945, President's Secretary's Files, 1945–1953, Truman Papers, HSTL.

18. Margaret Truman, *Bess W. Truman*, 252.

19. Ibid., 253.

20. Jonathan Daniels, oral history, 58, HSTL.

21. Eben A. Ayers, oral history, 10, HSTL.

22. Truman, *Memoirs*, vol. 1, 14, 17.

23. Ibid., 18.

24. Stimson diary, April 13, 1945.

25. Vandenberg, *The Private Papers of Senator Vandenberg*, 167.

26. Robert J. Donovan, interview with Senator George D. Aiken, May 5, 1975.

27. Truman, *Memoirs*, vol. 1, 19.

28. Ibid.

29. Vandenberg, *The Private Papers of Senator Vandenberg*, 167.

30. Margaret Truman, *Harry S. Truman*, 218.

31. Truman, *Memoirs*, vol. 1, 23.

32. Margaret Truman, *Harry S. Truman*, 218.

33. Harold L. Ickes diary (April 29, 1945), Library of Congress.

34. Campbell and Herring, *The Diaries of Edward R. Stettinius, Jr.*, 318.

35. Truman, *Memoirs*, vol. 1, 25.

36. "The Ambassador in the Soviet Union (Harriman) to the Secretary of State, April 13, 1945," *FRUS, Diplomatic Papers, 1945, General: The United Nations*, vol. 1, 290.

37. J. B. West, *Upstairs at the White House*, 56. Doris Kearns Goodwin quoted this dialogue in *No Ordinary Time*, 613.

38. Ward, *Closest Companion*, 420–1.

39. Bishop, *FDR's Last Year*, 635.

40. Joseph Persico, interview of Curtis Roosevelt, November 15–16, 2005. This "author's interview" was referred to several times in Persico's book, *Franklin and Lucy* (2008), but it has not been published in its entirety. The phrase "drip disapproval," taken from Persico's interview, appears at page 346 of his book.

41. Joseph Lash, interview of Anna Roosevelt Halsted, October 29, 1968, Box 44, Papers of Joseph Lash, FDRL.

42. Lash, *World of Love*, 183.

43. Margaret Truman, *Harry S. Truman*, 222.

44. Truman, *Memoirs*, vol. 1, 32.

45. Sherwood, *Roosevelt and Hopkins*, 881.

46. Margaret Truman, *Harry S. Truman*, 224.

47. *Public Papers and Addresses of the Presidents of the United States. Harry S. Truman, 1945–1953*, Washington, DC, GPO, 1966, *PP, HST*, April 16, 1945, 2.

48. Hamby, *Man of the People*, 297.

49. Margaret Truman, *Harry S. Truman*, 225.

50. Ferrell, *Truman in the White House*, 11.

51. *New York Times*, April 18, 1945, 16.

52. *PP, HST*, April 17, 1945, 8–13.

53. Margaret Truman, *Harry S. Truman*, 226.

54. *Appendix to The Congressional Record*, 7-25-40, 4546.

55. Ferrell, *Truman in the White House*, 89.

56. *Appendix to The Congressional Record*, 7-25-40, 4546.

57. Margaret Truman, *Harry S. Truman*, 227–8; although Ms. Truman did not cite her source, it was almost certainly page 90 in by Edward R. Schauffler, a Kansas City newspaper reporter who was close to Truman and Charlie Ross.

58. "Memorandum of Conversation by Bohlen, April 20, 1945," *FRUS, 1945*, vol. 5, 231–2.

59. Memorandum of conversation, April 20, 1945, President's Secretary's Files, 1945–1953, Box 164, Truman Papers, HSTL.

60. "Memorandum of Conversation by Bohlen, April 20, 1945, *FRUS, 1945*, vol. 5, 231–2.

61. Ibid., 232–4.

62. Truman, *Memoirs*, vol. 1, 72.

63. Eden to Churchill, April 23, 1954 (telegram no. 2018), Foreign Office Records, Public Record Office, N 4511/6/G55.

64. Leahy, *I Was There*, 351.

65. "Memorandum of Truman–Molotov Conversation, April 23, 1945," *FRUS, 1945*, vol. 5, 256–7.

66. Bohlen, *Witness to History*, 213.

67. Truman, *Memoirs*, vol. 1, 82.

68. Yergin, *Shattered Peace*, 83.

69. Bohlen, *Witness to History*, 213.

70. Memorandum for the secretary of war, April 23, 1945, National Security Archives online.

71. J. Leonard Reinsch, oral history, quoted in Broscious, "Longing for International Control, Banking on American Superiority," 16.

72. In *The Conquerors* at page 225, Michael Beschloss quotes Truman as recalling in 1954 that Churchill "was very anxious for a surrender," suggesting that Churchill wanted to accept Himmler's proposal and that Truman was the one who insisted that the Germans must surrender to all three governments. The transcript of the telephone conversation is at odds with Truman's recollection and Beschloss's interpretation.

73. "Transcript of Trans-Atlantic Telephone Conversation Between President Truman and British Prime Minister Churchill, April 25, 1945," *FRUS, Diplomatic Papers, 1945, European Advisory Commission, Austria, Germany*, vol. 3, 763–8.

74. Address by President Harry S. Truman to the UN General Assembly, April 25, 1945, online.

75. Vandenberg, *The Private Papers of Senator Vandenberg* (Vandenberg diary, April 27, 1945), 182.

76. Boris Egorov, "Elbe Day: When Russians and Americans Embraced and Shook Hands in Friendship." *Russia Beyond*, April 25, 2019, https://www.rbth.com/history/330268 -elbe-day-soviet-us-friendship.

77. Statement by the President Announcing the Junction of the Anglo-American and Soviet Forces in Germany, April 27, 1945, https://www.trumanlibrary.org/publicpapers /viewpapers.php.pid=19.

78. Miscamble, *From Roosevelt to Truman*, 138, 140.

79. Bradley, *Soldier's Story*, 589.

80. Chandler, *Papers of Dwight David Eisenhower: The War Years*, vol. 4, 2696.

81. Truman, *Memoirs*, vol. 1, 219.

82. Margaret Truman, *Bess W. Truman*, 260.

83. Letter by Truman to his mother and sister quoted in Margaret Truman, *Harry S. Truman*, 341.

84. May 8, 1945, letter by Truman to his mother and sister quoted in Truman, *Memoirs*, vol. 1, 207.

85. Elsey, *An Unplanned Life*, 83.

86. *PP, HST, 1945*, May 8, 1945, 48–50.

87. Ibid., 50.

88. Truman, *Memoirs*, vol. 1, 438.

89. Fields, *My 21 Years in the White House*, 120.

Chapter 5 ★ Second Coming in Wrath

1. Hughes, *The Living Presidency*, 347.

2. Eden, *The Memoirs of Anthony Eden*, 621.

3. "Directive to Commander in Chief of United States Forces of Occupation Regarding the Military Government of Germany" (JCS 1067), signed by Truman on May 10, 1945, *FRUS, 1945*, vol. 3, 494.

4. Beschloss, *Conquerors*, 237 ("crazy plan"), citing transcript of interviews with aides, 1954, HSTL; Leffler, *Origins of the Cold War*, 64; Stimson to Truman, May 16, 1945 ("rehabilitation of Germany").

5. Truman, *Memoirs*, vol. 1, 255.

6. Memorandum of conversation, May 11, 1945, Papers of Joseph C. Grew, *Conversations*, vol. 7, Houghton Library, Harvard University.

7. "Memorandum by the Acting Secretary of State (Grew) and the Foreign Economic Administrator (Crowley) to President Truman, May 11, 1945," *FRUS, 1945*, vol. 5, 999–1000.

8. Minkova, "Lend-Lease in Early Post-War Soviet–American Relations," 628–30.

9. Sherwood, *Roosevelt and Hopkins*, 894, 896.

10. Davies to Truman, May 12, 1945, Joseph E. Davies Papers, Box 16, Library of Congress.

11. Davies diary, May 13, 1945, and Davies journal, May 13, 1945, Joseph E. Davies Papers, Box 16, Library of Congress.

12. Davies to Truman, May 12, 1945, Joseph E. Davies Papers, Box 16, Library of Congress.

13. Davies to Stalin (through Molotov), May 14, 1945, Joseph E. Davies Papers, Box 17, Library of Congress.

14. Sherwood, *Roosevelt and Hopkins*, 887.

15. "President Truman to Marshal Stalin, May 19, 1945," *FRUS, Conference of Berlin (The Potsdam Conference)*, vol. 1, 21–2.

16. Truman, *Memoirs*, vol. 1, 258–9.

17. Memo, May 23, 1945, Truman longhand notes—Presidential File, Harry S. Truman Papers, President's Secretary's File, Box 281, HSTL.

18. *FRUS, Conference of Berlin*, vol. 1, 35.

19. "Mr. Harry L. Hopkins, Adviser to President Truman, to the President, June 3, 1945," *FRUS, Europe*, vol. 5, 319.

20. Ibid.

21. "President Truman to Mr. Harry L. Hopkins, Adviser to the President, at Moscow, June 5, 1945," *FRUS, Europe*, vol. 5, 327.

22. "Churchill to Truman, June 4, 1945 (No. 72)," Char 20/220, Churchill Papers, Churchill Archives Centre, Churchill College, Cambridge, UK.

23. Bohlen, *Witness to History*, 220.

24. *PP, HST, 1945*, Truman press conference, June 13, 1945, 120–3.

25. "Success of Moscow Mission," *Times* (London), June 14, 1945, 4.

26. Allen and Shannon, *The Truman Merry-Go-Round*, 49.

27. *PP, HST, 1945*, address in San Francisco at the closing session of the United Nations Conference, June 26, 1945, 138–44.

28. Margaret Truman, *Harry S. Truman*, 253.

29. Eben Ayers's diary, September 14, 1945, HSTL.

30. Samuel I. Rosenman, oral history, October 15, 1968, 25, HSTL.

31. Beschloss, *The Conquerors*, 354, citing transcript of interviews with aides, 1954, HSTL.

32. Unsent letter to Jonathan Daniels, February 26, 1950, HSTL; Weil, *A Pretty Good Club*, 224.

33. The quote is from a March 25, 1945, letter from Albert Einstein to President Roosevelt seeking to arrange a meeting of his friend Szilard with Roosevelt and his cabinet members. Though Szilard had arranged through Mrs. Roosevelt to meet with FDR on May 8, 1945, the meeting obviously never took place because of FDR's death in April. The letter was left in White House files inherited by Truman and a copy plus Szilard's attached memo was presented by Szilard when he met with Matt Connelly, Truman's appointments secretary, on May 26, 1945.

34. Gertrude Szilard, *Reminiscences*, 68–71.

35. Leo Szilard, *His Vision*, 182–3.

36. Gertrude Szilard, *Reminiscences*, 125.

37. Leo Szilard, *His Vision*, 184

38. "A Petition to the President of the United States," July 17, 1945, U.S. National Archives, Record Group 77, Records of the Chief of Engineers, Manhattan Engineer District, Harrison–Bundy File, Folder 76. Szilard also signed on to the so-called Franck Report, a petition by several noted scientists urging the president to detonate an atomic bomb in an uninhabited area, which would allow the U.S. government "to take into account the public opinion of this country and of the other nations before deciding whether [atomic bombs] should be used against Japan. In this way, other nations may assume a share of the responsibility for such a fateful decision." The report was released on June 11, 1945, https://www.atomicheritage.org/key-documents/franck -report.nnt.

39. Gertrude Szilard, *Reminiscences*.

40. Notes of the Interim Committee Meeting, Thursday, May 31, 1945, HSTL.

41. Robertson, *Sly and Able*, 398.

42. Wyden, *Day One*, 161.

43. Notes of the Interim Committee Meetings of May 31 and June 1, 1945, HSTL.

44. Wyden, *Day One*, 163.

45. Bernstein, "Roosevelt, Truman, and the Atomic Bomb," 35.

46. Groves, *Now It Can Be Told*, 265.

47. Wellerstein, "FDR and the Bomb."

48. Ferrell, *Off the Record*, 40 (Truman diary, June 1, 1945).

49. "Minutes of Meeting, June 18, 1945," *FRUS, Conference of Berlin*, vol. 1, 905; see also "Minutes of Meeting Held at White House on 18 June 1945 at 1530," Xerox 1567, GCML.

50. See Frank, *Downfall*, 144–8.

51. "Minutes of Meeting, June 18, 1945," *FRUS, Conference of Berlin*, 909.

52. Ibid., 910.

53. Ibid.

54. See "McCloy on the A-Bomb," appendix in Reston, *Deadline*, 495–500; McCloy, *The Challenge to American Foreign Policy*, 41–3; Millis, *The Forrestal Diaries*, 70–1.

55. Ferrell, *Dear Bess*, 517.

56. "A Litany, IV The Trinity," www.luminarium.org/sevenlit/donne/litany.php.

57. Herken, *Brotherhood of the Bomb*, 129; Wellerstein, "The First Light of Trinity."

58. Bainbridge, *Trinity*, 39.

59. Ferrell, *Off the Record*, 49 (Truman diary, July 7, 1945); Ferrell, *Dear Bess*, 516–7; Truman to Martha Ellen Truman (mother) and Mary Jane Truman (sister), July 3, 1945, HSTL.

60. Ferrell, *Off the Record*, 49 (Truman diary, July 7, 1945).

61. Bohlen, *Witness to History*, 226.

62. Ferrell, *Dear Bess*, 517.

63. Log of President Harry S. Truman's trip to the Berlin Conference, Rose A. Conway's Papers, President Truman's Travel Logs, 1945, 11, HSTL.

64. Ibid., 13.

65. Ibid., 12.

66. Ibid., 13.

67. Ibid., 14.

68. Ibid., 15.

69. Beschloss, *The Conquerors*, 254, citing transcript of interviews with aides, 1954.

70. Letter from O. Müller-Grote to Truman, February 10, 1956, HSTL.

71. White House Map Room to Matthew J. Connelly, July 15, 1945, Staff Member and Office Files, Naval Aide to the President Files, Box 5, Truman Papers, HSTL.

72. Truman, *Memoirs*, vol. 1, 340.

73. Ferrell, *Off the Record*, 51 (Truman diary, July 7, 1945).
74. Mary Soames letter, July 16, 1945, quoted in Gilbert, *Winston S. Churchill*, vol. 8, 61.
75. Moran, *Churchill at War*, 336.
76. Mee, *Meeting at Potsdam*, 59.
77. Potsdam journal, July 16, 1945, Joseph E. Davies Papers, Box 18, Folder A, Library of Congress.
78. Truman, *Memoirs*, vol. 1, 341.
79. Notes by Harry S. Truman on the Potsdam Conference, July 16, 1945, The Decision to Drop the Atomic Bomb Collection, President's Secretary's File, HSTL.
80. "Acting Chairman of the Interim Committee (Harrison) to Secretary of War Stimson, July 16, 1945," *FRUS, Conference of Berlin*, vol. 2, document no. 1303, https://history.state.gov/historicaldocuments/frus1945Berlinv02/d1303.
81. Truman, *Memoirs*, vol. 1, 11. Truman wrote that Leahy said of the bomb, "This is the biggest fool thing we have ever done. The bomb will never go off, and I speak as an expert in explosives."
82. Memorandum for the president, "The Conduct of the War with Japan," July 16, 1945, Henry I. Stimson Papers, Yale University Library.
83. Memorandum for the president, "Trusteeship for Korea," July 16, 1945, Henry I. Stimson to Truman, *FRUS, Conference of Berlin*, vol 2, document no. 732.
84. Diary of Joseph E. Davies, July 19, 1945, Joseph E. Davies Papers, Box 18, Library of Congress.
85. Badash, Hirschfelder, and Broida, *Reminiscences of Los Alamos*, 7.
86. Memorandum for the secretary of war, July 18, 1945, General Leslie R. Groves, Truman Papers, HSTL.
87. Interview with J. Robert Oppenheimer, www.youtube.com/watch?v=QBYyUi-Nkts.
88. https://www.atomicheritage.org/profile/kenneth-bainbridge.
89. Ferrell, *Off the Record*, 53 (Truman diary, July 17, 1945).
90. *Decision: The Conflicts of Harry S. Truman*, a syndicated television series during the early 1960s that included narration by Truman, Film Collection, HSTL. In an unsent letter to Acheson dated March 15, 1957, Truman said of Stalin that he had "liked the little son of bitch," and also observed that the dictator was "a good six inches shorter than I am . . ." Ferrell, *Off the Record*, 349.
91. Ferrell, *Off the Record*, 53 (Truman diary, July 17, 1945); "Truman–Stalin Meeting, July 17, 1945, Bohlen Notes," *FRUS, Conference of Berlin*, vol. 2, unnumbered document following no. 710, with footnote identifying other accounts of the meetig, including Truman, *Memoirs*, vol. 1, 341–2.
92. Bohlen, *Witness to History*, 230.
93. Ferrell, *Off the Record*, 53 (Truman diary, July 17, 1945).
94. Truman, *Memoirs*, vol. 1, 341.
95. Sound recording of Truman interview, MP 2002-309, Screen Gems Collection, HSTL.
96. Ferrell, *Off the Record*, 53 (Truman diary, July 17, 1945).
97. Montefiore, *Stalin*, 498.
98. Gilbert, *Winston S. Churchill*, vol. 8, 63.
99. "Potsdam First Plenary Meeting, July 17, 1945, Ben Cohen," *FRUS, Conference of Berlin*, vol. 2, unnumbered after document no. 710
100. Modelski and Modelski, *Documenting Global Leadership*, 401.
101. Bohlen, *Witness to History*, 230.
102. "Groves Memorandum," July 18, 1945, *FRUS, Conference of Berlin*, vol. 2, document no. 1305. Groves's memo was so sensitive that he had it flown by special courier to Potsdam.

103. "Stimson Diary, July 21, 1945," attached as note 1 to "Groves Memorandum," *FRUS, Conference of Berlin*, vol. 2, document no. 1305.

104. Feis, *The Atomic Bomb and the End of World War II*, 87.

105. "Potsdam Declaration," July 26, 1945, *FRUS, Conference of Berlin*, vol. 2, document no. 1382, http://www.ndl.go.jp/constitution.e/etc/co6.html.

106. "Cable, July 23, 1945," *FRUS, Conference of Berlin*, vol. 2, document no. 1374.

107. "Stimson Diary, July 24, 1945," Yale University.

108. Longhand note, July, 25, 1945, Truman Papers, HSTL.

109. Longhand note by Truman for speech at Gridiron Club dinner on December 15, 1945, President's Secretary's Files, Speech Files, 1945–1953, HSTL.

110. Truman, *Memoirs*, vol. 1, 420–1. Stimson was responsible for ruling out Kyoto as a target.

111. "Potsdam Eighth Plenary Meeting, July 25, 1945, Ben Cohen," *FRUS, Conference of Berlin*, vol. 2, unnumbered following document no. 710.

112. Truman, *Memoirs*, vol. 1, 416.

113. Montefiore, *Stalin*, 497–500.

114. Hornfischer, *Fleet at Flood Tide*, 434. See also Mee, *Meeting at Potsdam*, 174.

115. Truman to Martha Ellen ("Mattie") Truman and Mary Jane Truman, July 29, 1945, HSTL.

116. The International Churchill Society attributes the quote to Clark Clifford, who heard it from Churchill in 1946 while traveling to Fulton, Missouri, where Churchill was to deliver his famous "iron curtain" speech.

117. Davies journal, July 28, 1945, Joseph E. Davies Papers, Box 19, Library of Congress.

118. "Protocol of the Proceedings of the Berlin Conference," *FRUS, Conference of Berlin*, vol. 2, 1479–98.

119. Byrnes, *Speaking Frankly*, 84–5.

120. "Eleventh Plenary Meeting, Department of State Minutes, July 31, 1945," *FRUS, Conference of Berlin*, vol. 2, 515.

121. "Twelfth Plenary Meeting, August 1, 1945, Thompson Notes," *FRUS, Conference of Berlin*, vol. 2, 567–8.

122. Samuel Lubell memo quoted in Mee, *Meeting at Potsdam*, 190.

123. Trachtenberg, *Constructed Peace*, 27.

124. Kennan, "An Historian of Potsdam and His Readers," 289.

125. "Protocol of the Proceedings of the Berlin Conference," *FRUS, Conference of Berlin*, vol. 2, 1479–95; "Communiqué, August 1, 1945," *FRUS, Conference of Berlin*, vol. 2, 1500–13.

126. "Cohen Notes, August 1, 1945," *FRUS, Conference of Berlin*, vol. 2, 602.

127. Elsey, *An Unplanned Life*, 90.

Chapter 6 ★ Bearing the Unbearable

1. Lt. William M. Rigdon, USN, "Log of the President's Trip to the Berlin Conference," 50 (August 6, 1945), HSTL; Leahy, *I Was There*, 432–3.

2. Cominch [Commander in Chief] & CNO [Chief of Naval Operations] to William D. Leahy, August 6, 1945, SMOF [Staff Member and Office Files], Naval Aide to the President Files, Box 6g, Truman Papers, HSTL.

3. Henry L. Stimson to Truman, SMOF, Naval Aide to the President Files, Box 6, Truman Papers, HSTL.

4. Rigdon, "Log of the President's Trip to the Berlin Conference," August 6, 1945.

5. "Truman Tells Warship Crew," *Los Angeles Times*, August 7, 1945, 2.

6. Transcript, August 6, 1945: "Statement by the President Announcing the Use of the A-Bomb at Hiroshima," *PP, HST*, 196–200.

7. Hersey, *Hiroshima*, 10. *Hiroshima* originally appeared in *The New Yorker* in 1946. The author is indebted to John Hersey for the account of Mrs. Nakamura and her children that is summarized in the text.

8. Ibid., 51.

9. Ibid., 115–6.

10. Ibid., 41–2 47–9, 51–9, 78.

11. Statement of Lieutenant General Seizo Arisue, Doc. No. 61411, Center for Military History, Washington, DC; Statement of Admiral Soemu Toyoda, August 29, 1949, Doc. No. 61340, May 7 and May 17, 1949, 30, Center for Military History, Washington, DC.

12. Asada, "The Shock of the Atomic Bomb and Japan's Decision to Surrender: A Reconsideration," in *Culture Shock and Japanese-American Relations*, 182.

13. "Soviet Declaration of War on Japan," August 8, 1945, Avalon Project, Yale Law School, Lillian Goldman Law Library, http://avalon.law.yale.edu/wwii/s4.asp.

14. Elsey, *An Unplanned Life*, 92.

15. Truman, *Memoirs*, vol. 1, 424.

16. President Truman's seventeenth news conference, held in his office at the White House at 3 p.m. on Wednesday, August 8, 1945. Fleet Admiral William D. Leahy and Secretary of State James F. Byrnes were special guests. The President's News Conference, August 8, 1945, HSTL.

17. Stimson diary, "Memorandum of Conference with the President, August 8, 1945, at 10:45 a.m."

18. Truman, *Memoirs*, vol. 1, 420–1 (directive by Thos. T. Handy to General Carl Spaatz, July 24, 1945).

19. William Laurence, "Atomic Bombing of Nagasaki Told by Flight Member," August 9, 1945, Atomic Heritage Foundation. Laurence was the *New York Times* science reporter who won a Pulitzer Prize in 1946 for his reporting on the development of the atomic bomb and the bombing of Nagasaki.

20. Sweeney, *War's End*, 219

21. Statement by Togo, May 17, 1949, 37, Center for Military History, Washington, DC.

22. Frank, *Downfall*, 289–90, citing *Daihon' ei Rikugun-Bu* 10, 431–2; IMTFE Kido 31, 172–4.

23. Frank, *Downfall*, 295, citing Daisaku Ikeda, "Minutes," 5.

24. Document E1, Emperor Hirohito's Surrender Decision, August 10, 1945, in Kort, *The Columbia Guide to Hiroshima and the Bomb*, 313. See also Robert J. C. Butow, *Japan's Decision to Surrender*, 175–6, cited in Frank, *Downfall*, 295.

25. *Japan's Struggle to End the War*, U.S. Strategic Bombing Survey, 9.

26. Truman, *Memoirs*, vol. 1, 427–8.

27. Hasegawa, *Racing the Enemy*, 220.

28. Millis, *The Forrestal Diaries*, 83.

29. Ferrell, *Off the Record*, 61 (Truman diary, August 10, 1945).

30. Truman, *Memoirs*, vol. 1, 429, 432.

31. To preempt demands by Molotov and Stalin to participate in decisions concerning occupation and surrender, Truman had decided, on or about August 8, the day he learned of the Soviet declaration of war, that he would appoint MacArthur to head the occupation of Japan and preside at the surrender. His decision was endorsed by Britain, China, and the Soviet Union. MacArthur was officially informed of his appointment on August 12. Truman approved the SCAP directive to MacArthur on August 13 and it was dispatched via courier on August 15. Bland and Stevens, *The Papers of George Catlett Marshall*, vol. 5, 268 n2.

32. Truman diary, August 11, 1945, 62, President's Secretary's Files, 1945–1953, Truman Papers, HSTL.

33. Truman, *Memoirs*, vol. 1, 433.

34. Margaret Truman, *Harry S. Truman*, 284.

35. The quotes are from a "reconstruction" of the emperor's words by Butow, *Japan's Decision to Surrender*, 207–8, as cited in Frank, *Downfall*, 315.

36. Statement of Lt. Col. Takeshita, June 11, 1949, Doc. No. 50025A, 5, Center for Military History; Statement of Saburo Hayashi, December 23, 1949, Doc. No. 61436, 6–7, 9–11, Center for Military History.

37. Frank, *Downfall*, 320.

38. Truman, news conference, 7 p.m. on August 14, 1945, American Presidency Project, Gerhard Peters and John T. Woolley, https://www.presidency.ucsb.edu/node/231067.

39. Neal, *Eleanor and Harry*, 37 (letter from Eleanor Roosevelt to Truman, August 15, 1945).

40. "President's Mother Says She's Glad That Harry Decided to End the War," *Christian Science Monitor*, August 15, 1945, 16.

41. Frederick R. Barkley, "President Joins Capital's Gaiety," *New York Times*, August 15, 1945, 3.

42. Stanton, *In Harm's Way*, 259, citing *New York Times*, August 15, 1945.

43. Emperor Hirohito, "The Jewel Voice Broadcast," August 15, 1945, The Atomic Heritage Foundation.

44. Message sent by Supreme Commander General MacArthur from Manila to Japanese General Headquarters in Tokyo on August 15, 1945. The Japanese responded promptly, sending a reply back to MacArthur, which he received on August 16. www.ibiblio.org/pha/policy/1945/1945-08-15b.html.

45. USSBS Interrogations of Japanese Officials, Nav No. 76, USSBS No. 379, Admiral Mitsumasa Yonai, IJN.

46. Whitney, *MacArthur*, 214; MacArthur, *Reminiscences*, 270; Manchester, *American Caesar*, 444.

47. Craig, *The Fall of Japan*, 292.

48. James, *The Years of MacArthur*, vol. 2, 785.

49. Truman, *Memoirs*, vol. 1, 451.

50. Directive by President Truman to the Supreme Commander for the Allied Powers in Japan (MacArthur), August 15, 1945. *FRUS, 1945*, vol. 7, Instrument for the surrender of Japan, General Order No 1.

51. Kase, *Journey to the Missouri*, 4.

52. Ibid., 7.

53. MacArthur, *Reminiscences*, 275.

54. Kase, *Journey to the Missouri*, 9.

55. MacArthur, *Reminiscences*, 275.

56. Ferrell, *Off the Record*, 47 (Truman diary, June 17, 1945).

57. Ibid., 60 (Truman diary, August 10, 1945).

58. Ickes diary, August 26, 1945.

59. "Chief of Staff (Marshall) to General of the Army Douglas MacArthur," *FRUS, 1945*, vol. 6, 717.

60. Ibid., 718–9.

61. MacArthur Memorial Archives, RG 10, Wood to MacArthur, September 4, 1945, quoted in Frazier Hunt, *The Untold Story of Douglas MacArthur*.

62. James, *The Years of MacArthur*, vol. 3, 18–9.

63. Gallicchio, *Unconditional*, 175.

64. "Acheson Sets Path," *New York Times*, September 20, 1945, 1.

65. MacArthur, *Reminiscences*, 306–7.

66. United States Initial Post-Surrender Policy for Japan, *FRUS, 1945*, vol. 6, Instructions to the General of the Army Douglas MacArthur (Message No. 1), September 6, 1945, document 491.

67. Gunther, *The Riddle of MacArthur*, xiii.

68. MacArthur, *Reminiscences*, 288.
69. Gallicchio, *Unconditional*, 179.
70. Chapter 1, Article I of the Japanese constitution reads as follows: "The Emperor shall be the symbol of the State and of the unity of the people, deriving his position from the will of the people with whom resides sovereign power," https://japan.kantei.go.jp /constitution_and_government_of_japan/constitution_e.html.

Chapter 7 ⋆ Had Enough?

1. Gridiron Club archives, December 16, 1945, Box 41, Library of Congress.
2. "The Birth of Pax Americana," *Wall Street Journal*, https://www.wsj.com/articles/the -birth-of-pax-americana-1482882200.
3. Ayers's diary, December 17, 1945, quoting Ferrell, *Truman in the White House*, 105.
4. Donovan, *Conflict & Crisis*, 107.
5. Executive Order 9599, August 18, 1945, www.presidency.ucsb.edu/documents/exeutive -order-9599-providing-for-assistance-expanded-production-and-continued.
6. Bernstein, "The Truman Administration and Its Reconversion Wage Policy," 214.
7. *Time*, October 29, 1945, 18–9.
8. Truman Papers, Executive Order 9651, amending Executive Order 9599. https://www .trumanlibrary.gov/library/executive-orders/9651/executive-order-9651.
9. Isaacson and Thomas, *The Wise Men*, 415.
10. *Wall Street Journal*, November 1, 1945, 1, 6.
11. *Washington Post*, November 2, 1945, 10.
12. Maney, *The Roosevelt Presence*, 190.
13. Hamby, *Man of the People*, 353.
14. Truman, *Memoirs*, vol. 1, 483.
15. Special Message to the Congress Presenting a 21-Point Program for the Reconversion Period, September 5, 1945, 16–37, https://www.trumanlibrary.gov/library/public-papers /128/special-message-congress-presenting-21-point-program-reconversion-period.
16. *Newsweek*, September 25, 1945, 30.
17. Truman, *Memoirs*, vol. 1, 482.
18. Ferrell, *Off the Record*, 71–2 (Truman to Martha Ellen [his mother] and Mary Jane Truman [his sister], October 23, 1945).
19. Public Law 346, 78th Congress, June 22, 1944.
20. "The Veteran," *New York Times*, March 11, 1945, 33.
21. Conference Report to Accompany H.R. 3749, Amendments to Servicemen's Readjustment Act of 1944, December 17, 1945, 79th Congress, House of Representatives, Report No. 1449.
22. Katznelson, *Fear Itself*, 15, 368.
23. *Hearings Before the Subcommittee on Education, Training, and Rehabilitation of the Committee on Veterans' Affairs*, 18.
24. Hamby, *Beyond the New Deal*, 67, citing *New York Times*, December 5, 1945, 9.
25. *PP, HST 1945*, 508.
26. Quoted in Bernstein and Matusow, eds., *The Truman Administration: A Documentary History*, 57, excerpt from General Motors press release, December 29, 1945.
27. Oscar Hammerstein II and Sigmund Romberg, songwriters.
28. Walter Brown diary, September 21, 1945, Folder 602, James F. Byrnes Papers, Cooper Library (Special Collections / Strom Thurmond Institute), Clemson University, Clemson, South Carolina.
29. Davies journal, December 18, 1945, Joseph E. Davies Papers, Box 22, Library of Congress.
30. Reminiscence by Howard Sachs, 1978, miscellaneous historical documents file, Box 10, document 312, HSTL.

31. Truman, *Memoirs*, vol. 1, 549.

32. *New York Times*, December 26, 1945, 1.

33. Ferrell, *Off the Record*, 75–6 (Truman to Bess, December 28, 1945).

34. Truman, *Memoirs*, vol. 1, 549.

35. Acheson, *Present at the Creation*, 136.

36. Telegram by Truman to Byrnes, President's Secretary's File, Presidential Appointment file, January 1946, Box 83, HSTL.

37. Acheson, *Present at the Creation*, 136.

38. Truman, *Memoirs*, vol. 1, 550.

39. Byrnes, *All in One Lifetime*, 345; James F. Byrnes Papers, Folder 573, Cooper Library (Special Collections / Strom Thurmond Institute), Clemson University, Clemson, South Carolina.

40. Acheson, *Present at the Creation*, 136.

41. The text of the letter to Byrnes, dated January 5, 1946, appears in Truman, *Memoirs*, vol. 1, 551–2, and Ferrell, *Off the Record*, 79–80. According to Eben Ayers, who was helping Truman with his papers, Truman told him, "I read that letter to Byrnes, right here in this office with him sitting right there where you are. I told him that I was not going to give him the letter but I wanted to read it to him. The President said that Byrnes' face was fiery red after the President finished." Ayers's diary, July 26, 1951, Ayers Papers, HSTL.

42. Hillman, *Mr. President*, 21–3.

43. Byrnes, *All in One Lifetime*, 402.

44. Ibid., 373.

45. Lash, *Eleanor: The Years Alone*, 36.

46. *PP, HST, 1946*, radio report to the American people on the status of the reconversion program, January 3, 1946. Trumanlibrary.gov/library/public-papers/2/radio-report-amercan-people-status-reconversion.

47. Goulden, *The Best Years*, 230.

48. Quote in interview by Robert J. Donovan with John W. Snyder, November 1, 1973, in Donovan, *Conflict & Crisis*, 167 n20.

49. Bowles, *Promises to Keep*, 140.

50. Pub. L 79-304 codified as 15 U.S.C. sec. 102.

51. *PP, HST, 1946*, 111.

52. *The Nation*, March 16, 1946, 303.

53. Speech delivered by J. V. Stalin at a meeting of voters of the Stalin Electoral District, Moscow, February 9, 1946. From the Pamphlet Collection, J. Stalin, *Speeches Delivered at Meetings of Voters of the Stalin Electoral District, Moscow* (Moscow: Foreign Languages Publishing House, 1950), 23 (translation from the latest Russian edition of the speeches published by Gospolitizdat, Moscow, 1946).

54. Millis, *The Forrestal Diaries*, 134.

55. Freeman Matthews to George Kennan, February 13, 1946 (861.00/2-1346), State Department Records, Central Decimal Files, NARA.

56. Kennan, *Memoirs*, 293.

57. Gaddis, *George F. Kennan*, 216.

58. "The Charge in the Soviet Union (Kennan) to the Secretary of State (861.00/2-2246: Telegram), February 22, 1946," *FRUS, 1946*, vol. 6, 696–701.

59. In 2003, George Elsey, curator of the Map Room in the White House, found a copy of Kennan's long telegram in his papers at the Truman Library. The copy had been initialed by Admiral Leahy and bore the letter "P," indicating that it had been read by or to the president. Elsey, *An Unplanned Life*, 137.

60. *Department of State Bulletin*, XIV (March 10, 1946), 355–8. Byrnes's speech was delivered on February 28, 1946, to the Overseas Press Club in New York City.

61. Gaddis, *Origins of the Cold War*, 304.

62. Clifford, *Counsel to the President*, 100–4.
63. Ibid., 102.
64. Ibid., 103.
65. As noted in Martin Gilbert's biography, Churchill showed a draft of his speech to Byrnes and Leahy a few days before the trip to Fulton and it is possible if not probable that Kennan's telegram was discussed. Gilbert, *Winston S. Churchill*, vol. 8, 196–7.
66. Winston Churchill, "The Sinews of Peace," March 5, 1946, Churchill Papers, Chur 5/4, Churchill Archives Centre, Churchill College, Cambridge, UK.
67. Winston S. Churchill, "The Sinews of Peace," speech in Fulton, March 5, 1946, http:// speeches-usa.com/transcripts/winston_churchill-ironcurtain.html.
68. "Churchill Speech Hailed in London; Call for Anglo–US Tie Is Applauded, but Remarks on Russia Bring Division," *New York Times*, March 6, 1946, 6.
69. *The Nation*, March 16, 1946, 303.
70. Steel, *Walter Lippmann and the American Century*, 428–9. See also Gilbert, *Winston S. Churchill*, vol. 8, 204–6.
71. Clifford, *Counsel to the President*, 101, 108.
72. *PP, HST, 1945*, March 8, 1945, 145.
73. Clifford, *Counsel to the President*, 108.
74. Ibid., 89.
75. Truman railroad speech draft, undelivered (italics added), Papers of Clark Clifford, HSTL.
76. Clark M. Clifford, oral history, April 12, 1971, 58, HSTL; Clifford, *Counsel to the President*, 88.
77. Clifford, *Counsel to the President*, 89.
78. Truman, radio address to the American people on the railroad strike emergency, May 24, 1945, broadcast from the White House at 10 p.m., https://www.trumanlibrary .gov/library/public-papers/124/radio-address-american-people-railroad-strike -emergency.
79. Clifford, *Counsel to the President*, 90.
80. Clifford, oral history, March 23, 1971, 63, HSTL (italics added), https://www.trumanli brary.gov/library/oral-histories/cliford1#11.
81. Special Message to the Congress Urging Legislation for Industrial Peace, May 25, 1946, HSTL, https://www.trumanlibrary.gov/library/public-papers/125/special-message -congress-urging-legislation-industrial-peace.
82. Clifford, *Counsel to the President*, 91.
83. Clifford, oral history, March 23, 1971, 64, HSTL.
84. Clifford, *Counsel to the President*, 91.
85. Ibid., 75.
86. McCullough, *Truman*, 509, based on author's unpublished interview.
87. "Text of Byrnes Report on Meeting of Foreign Ministers," *New York Times*, July 16, 1946, 4.
88. Medical report, Folder 617, James F. Byrnes Papers, Cooper Library (Special Collections / Strom Thurmond Institute), Clemson University, Clemson, South Carolina.
89. Roll, *George Marshall*, 398.
90. Ibid., 401 ("Marshall . . . made little if any progress in China during the exhausting summer of 1946. . . . 'For the moment,' wrote Marshall to Truman . . . 'I [am] stymied.'").
91. Special Message to the Congress upon Signing the Second Price Control Bill, July 25, 1946, https://www.trumanlibrary.gov/library/public-papers/179/special-message -congress-upon-signing-second-price-control-bill. Public Law 548, 79th Congress J (60 Stat. 664).
92. Clifford, *Counsel to the President*, 110.
93. Elsey, *An Unplanned Life*, 142.

94. Ibid., 144.

95. Margaret Truman, *Harry S. Truman*, 347.

96. Krock, *Memoirs*, 393–5, 449.

97. Clifford, *Counsel to the President*, 123.

98. Restatement of United States Foreign Policy on Germany: Address by the Secretary of State (Byrnes) at Stuttgart, Germany. September 6, 1946, Bulletin, September 15, 1946, 495–501.

99. Jean Edward Smith, *Lucius D. Clay*, 388.

100. Wallace account, Wallace diary, 612–3 ("page by page") in Blum, *The Price of Vision*; Ferrell, *Off the Record*, 94 (Truman diary, September 17, 1946; he said he had only three minutes to "skim through the [Wallace] speech").

101. *New York Times*, September 13, 1946, 1–2.

102. *PP, HST, 1946*, Truman press conference, September 12, 1946, 426–7.

103. Byrnes, *All in One Lifetime*, 375 (teletype record).

104. Ferrell, *Off the Record*, 95–6 (Truman to Martha Ellen and Mary Jane Truman, September 18, 1946).

105. Truman diary, September 19, 1945, President's Secretary's File, 1945–1953, Truman Papers, HSTL.

106. *PP, HST, 1946*, Truman to Martha Ellen and Mary Jane Truman, September 20, 1946, 431; Ferrell, *Off the Record*, 96–7.

107. William S. White, *The Taft Story*, 56.

108. Herman P. Kopplemann et al. to Truman, October 8, 1946, President's Secretary's Files, 1945–1953, General File "Meat" folder, HSTL.

109. *PP, HST, 1946*, Radio Report Announcing the Lifting of Major Price Controls, October 14, 1946, at 10 p.m., trumanlibrary.gov/library/public-papers/232/radio-report-nation -announcing-lifting-major-price-controls. Quote is in paragraphs 15 and 16; the sound recording of that report is SR 64-38 in the Sound Recording Collection, HSTL (contrary to *Conflict & Crisis*, 236, where Robert Donovan writes that Truman sounded "strained and tired," the recording conveys no such impression).

110. Margaret Truman, *Harry S. Truman*, 321.

111. McCullough, *Truman*, 524.

112. In the House, the American Labor Party held one seat (Vito Marcantonio of New York).

113. Leuchtenberg, "New Faces of 1946."

114. Margaret Truman, *Harry S. Truman*, 322.

115. Karl Inderfurth, *Harry and Dean*, a play posted by the Truman Library Institute in honor of the seventy-fifth anniversary of Truman's presidency, https://trumanlibrary institute.org/harry-dean-a-play-by-karl-inderfurth/.

116. Acheson, *Present at the Creation*, dedication page. See page 200 for Acheson's description of being the only one to greet Truman at Union Station the morning after the midterms.

117. Charles C. Ross to Ella Ross, November 13, 1946, Papers of Charles C. Ross, HSTL.

118. Truman to Bess Wallace Truman, November 18, 1946, Family, Business, File, Harry Truman Papers, HSTL.

119. "The Presidency: After Two Years," *Time*, April 7, 1947.

Chapter 8 ⋆ Transformation

1. Ferrel, *Off the Record*, 103–4 (Truman diary, December 11, 1946); McCullough, upublished interview of Clark Clifford.

2. Phillips, *The Truman Presidency*, 119.

3. As a pretext, Lewis claimed that the previous contract had been breached by the government and was therefore no longer valid. It was Lewis, however, who was attempting to nullify the contract so he could justify a strike. As noted in chapter 7, Lewis initially threatened to strike on November 1, four days before the midterm elections. However, the administration maneuvered to postpone his deadline until after the elections.

4. Clifford, *Counsel to the President*, 92–3.

5. For partial text (the substance) of Lewis's speech see *Newsweek*, December 16, 1946, 29.

6. Ibid.

7. Clifford, *Counsel to the President*, 95; Ayers's diary, December 7, 1946, quoting Ferrell, *Truman in the White House*, 163–4.

8. *United States v. United Mine Workers*, 330 US 258 (March 7, 1947).

9. Gridiron Club spring dinner, May 10, 1947, Gridiron Archives, Box 42, Library of Congress.

10. Executive Order 9808, Establishing the President's Committee on Civil Rights, https://trumanlibrary.gov/library/executive-orders/9808/executive-order-9808.

11. Truman to Tom Clark, September 20, 1946, Official File, Harry S. Truman Papers, HSTL.

12. Walter White, *A Man Called White*, 331.

13. Truman to Tom Clark, September 20, 1946, Official File, Harry S. Truman Papers, HSTL.

14. Shogan, *Harry S. Truman and the Struggle for Racial Justice*, 92.

15. Woody Guthrie, 1946, January 14, 2005, at the Wayback Machine, FortuneCity.

16. Shogan, *Harry Truman and the Struggle for Racial Justice*, 92.

17. Philleo Nash, oral history, August 17, 1966, 85, HSTL.

18. Ibid., February 1, 1967, 626–7.

19. Walter White, *A Man Called White*, 332.

20. Bland and Stevens, George Marshall to his aide Marshall (Pat) Carter, January 4, 1947, *The Papers of George Catlett Marshall*, vol. 5, 769.

21. Ferrell, *Off the Record*, 109 (Truman appointment sheet, February 18, 1946).

22. Acheson, *Present at the Creation*, 213.

23. Marshall interviews, 561–2, GCML.

24. Smith to Marshall, January 15, 1947, Papers of George C. Marshall, Folder 26, Box 137, GCML. See also Miscamble, *George F. Kennan and the Making of American Foreign Policy, 1947–1950*, 10.

25. "Taft Will Oppose Lilienthal," *New York Times*, March 22, 1947, 1.

26. Lilienthal, *The Atomic Energy Years*, 144.

27. Lilienthal nomination hearings, Lilienthal, *Journals*, vol. 2, appendix B, 646–8.

28. *FRUS, The Near East and Africa*, vol. 5, 32–7.

29. Truman, *Memoirs*, vol. 2, 101–2.

30. Acheson, *Present at the Creation*, 219.

31. Jones, *The Fifteen Weeks*, 139.

32. Acheson, *Present at the Creation*, 219.

33. Ibid.

34. Ibid.

35. Jones, *The Fifteen Weeks*, 142. In 1947 Jones was special assistant to the assistant secretary of public affairs in the State Department.

36. Vandenberg, *The Private Papers of Senator Vandenberg* (Vandenberg diary, June 6, 1947), 339.

37. Jones, *The Fifteen Weeks*, 142–4. In *Present at the Creation*, Acheson writes that Vandenberg expressed his "support" and that of others at the meeting on February 27, and Benn Steil in *The Marshall Plan* repeats Acheson's quote verbatim. This is inconsistent

with Vandenberg's later statement that no "commitments" were made. Moreover, it does not ring true. Given Vandenberg's history of needing to be courted and taking his time before favoring foreign policy initiatives proposed by the Truman administration, it is doubtful that he expressed his support and that of the other members of Congress at that meeting.

38. Isaacson and Thomas, *The Wise Men*, 395.
39. Jones, *The Fifteen Weeks*, 146.
40. Clifford, *Counsel to the President*, 136.
41. Acacia, *Clark Clifford*, 70.
42. Gaddis, *The United States and the Origins of the Cold War*, 350.
43. Steil, *The Marshall Plan*, 41.
44. Bohlen, *Witness to History*, 261.
45. Isaacson and Thomas, *The Wise Men*, 397–8.
46. President Truman's Special Message to the Congress on Greece and Turkey: The Truman Doctrine, 18:47 minutes, March 12, 1947, Sound Recording Collection, HSTL, https://www.trumanlibrary.gov/soundrecording-records/sr64-47-president-trumans-special-message-congress-greece-and-turkey-truman.
47. Acheson, *Present at the Creation*, 223.
48. *New York Times*, March 13, 1947, 1, 4.
49. Acheson, *Present at the Creation*, 223.
50. Donovan, *Conflict & Crisis*, 286.
51. Acheson, *Present at the Creation*, 224.
52. Excerpts from transcribed telephone conversation between James Forrestal and Carl Vinson, March 13, 1947, Papers of Clark Clifford, HSTL.
53. A photograph by Montgomery Foto Service, May 22, 1947, Accession No. 61-116-01, depicts Truman signing the bill at the Muehlebach Hotel. In his biography *Truman*, at pages 553–4, McCullough mistakenly writes that Truman signed the bill in the parlor at his mother's house in Grandview.
54. Judt, *Postwar*, 127.
55. "The Presidency: After Two Years," *Time*, April 7, 1947.
56. Ibid.
57. George Elsey, oral history, 32, HSTL.
58. Acheson, *Present at the Creation*, 730.
59. *FRUS, Council of Foreign Ministers, 1947*, vol. 2, 255–7.
60. Marshall quote in Walter Bedell Smith, *My Three Years in Moscow*, 226.
61. Quoted in Yergin, *Shattered Peace*, 300.
62. *FRUS, Council of Foreign Ministers, 1947*, vol. 2, 337–44.
63. Bohlen, *Witness to History*, 263.
64. Murphy, *Diplomat Among Warriors*, 307.
65. Bohlen, *Witness to History*, 263.
66. Truman, *Memoirs*, vol. 2, 112. For additional accounts of this meeting, see Bland et al., *The Papers of George Catlett Marshall*, vol. 6, 111–2.
67. Bland et al., *The Papers of George Catlett Marshall*, vol. 6, 113–21 (Marshall's national radio address, April 28, 1947).
68. Bohlen, *Witness to History*, 262–3; Forrest Pogue, *George C. Marshall*, 189–90; Kennan interview by Pogue, 6, GCML; Kennan interview by Harry Price, 1, GCML; Kennan, *Memoirs*, 325–6.
69. Truman, *Memoirs*, vol. 2, 113.
70. Speech by Dean Acheson, "The Requirements of Reconstruction," May 8, 1947, HSTL, https://www.trumanlibrary.gov/library/research-files/speech-dean-acheson-requirements-reconstruction?documentid=NA&pagenumber=1.

71. See dialogue between Reston and Acheson in Chace, *Acheson*, 172, and Mee, *Marshall Plan*, 95–6. Mee erroneously cites Leonard Miall's oral history at the Truman Library as a source.

72. "National Affairs: The Education of the Misters," *Time*, May 12, 1947; Hendrik Meijer, *Arthur Vandenberg*, 57.

73. Isaacson and Thomas, *The Wise Men*, 410, based on the authors' interview of Francis Wilcox, Vandenberg's chief aide.

74. Acheson, *Present at the Creation*, 230.

75. PPS/1: Policy with Respect to American Aid to Western Europe, May 23, 1947, III, 223–30 (italics in the original).

76. Nitze, *From Hiroshima to Glasnost*, 51–2.

77. "Clayton memorandum, 'The European Crisis,' May 27, 1947," *FRUS, 1947*, vol. 3, 230–2, italics added.

78. Freeland, *The Truman Doctrine and Origins of McCarthyism*, 17. See also, Roll, *Marshall*, 437–8,

79. Acheson, *Present at the Creation*, 232.

80. Agnew and Entrikin, *The Marshall Plan Today*, 10.

81. Kennan, *Memoirs*, 342.

82. Bohlen, oral history, Harry B. Price Papers, Box 3, Folder 32, HSTL; see "Summary of Discussion on Problems of Relief, Rehabilitation and Reconstruction of Europe, May 29, 1947," *FRUS, British Commonwealth, 1947*, vol. 3, 234–7.

83. Bland et al., *The Papers of George Catlett Marshall*, vol. 6, 149–50 (note).

84. Daily appointment sheet for President Harry S. Truman, June 2, 1947, HSTL, https://www.trumanlibrary.gov/library/truman-papers/daily-presidential-appointments-file-original-set-1945-52/daily-25.

85. Ibid., June 4, 1947.

86. Interview of Miall by Barbara Vandergrift, Marshal Foundation Librarian, September 19, 1977, GCML. See also oral history interview of Miall by Philip C. Brooks in London on June 17, 1964, HSTL.

87. The Marshall Plan Speech MP3, June 5, 1947, https://marshallfoundation.org/library/audio/mp3-marshall-plan-speech/.

88. *New York Times*, June 6, 1947, 1.

89. Leonard Miall, *American Commentary*, BBC broadcast, June 5, 1947.

90. Miall, oral history, 20, June 17, 1964, HSTL. See also, Bullock, *Ernest Bevin*, 405 (quoting speech by Bevin to the National Press Club, April 1, 1949) and interview of Miall by Vandergrift, September 19, 1977, 6 ("lifeline"), GCML.

91. Interview of Miall by Vandergrift, September 19, 1977, 6 ("Get me Marshall's speech"), GCML.

92. Acheson, *Present at the Creation*, 234.

93. Clifford, *Counsel to the President*, 144.

94. Vandenberg, *The Private Papers of Senator Vandenberg*, 374–5.

Chapter 9 ★ Lift Every Voice

1. Truman, *Memoirs*, vol. 2, 110.

2. Ibid.

3. Vandenberg, *The Private Papers of Senator Vandenberg*, 376.

4. Bland et al., *The Papers of George Catlett Marshall*, vol. 6, 153 (memorandum of interview with the president, June 16, 1947).

5. Acheson, *Present at the Creation*, 235.

6. "Membership of Committee on Foreign Aid," *Department of State Bulletin*, October 5, 1947, 696.

7. Haas, *Harry and Arthur*, 178.

8. Sudoplatov et al., *Special Tasks*, 231.

9. Harriman interview with Price, October 1, 1952, Price Collection, HSTL.

10. *PP, HST, 1947*, 288ff.

11. *Time*, June 30, 1947.

12. McCullough, *Truman*, 566, author's unpublished interview of Clark Clifford.

13. Leon H. Keyserling, oral history, May 10, 1971, 68, HSTL.

14. *Spokane Spokesman-Review*, January 4, 1945, 2.

15. *Time*, June 30, 1947.

16. Radio address to the American people on the veto of the Taft–Hartley Bill, American Presidency Project, https://www.presidency.ucsb.edu/documents/radio-address-the-american-people-the-veto-the-taft-hartley-bill.

17. *PP, HST, 1947*, 305.

18. Hamby, *Beyond the New Deal*, 185, citing James A. Wechsler, "New Law, New Crisis," *Progressive* XI, July 7, 1947, 1–2.

19. Walter White, *A Man Called White*, 347–8.

20. Memorandum to Matthew J. Connelly from David Niles, June 16, 1947, Clark Clifford File, HSTL.

21. "My Day," column by Eleanor Roosevelt, July 2, 1947, https://www2.gwu.edu/-erpapers/myday/displaydoc.cfm?_y=1947&_f=md000694.

22. Address before the National Association for the Advancement of Colored People, President Truman, Lincoln Memorial, Washington, DC, Sound Recording Collections, HSTL, https://www.trumanlibrary.gov/soundrecording-records/sr64-54-address-national-association-advancement-colored-people-president.

23. President Truman's address before the NAACP, Truman Library Institute, https://www.trumanlibraryinstitute.org/historic-speeches-naacp/ (italics added).

24. Walter White, *A Man Called White*, 348.

25. Letter to Mary Jane Truman, June 28, 1947, HSTL.

26. Speech of Harry S. Truman before the National Colored Association, Chicago, July 14, 1940, 2, HSTL.

27. Carol Anderson, *Eyes Off the Prize*, 155.

28. Executive Order 9980, Regulations Governing Fair Employment Practices, and Executive Order 9981, President's Committee on Equality of Treatment and Opportunity in the Armed Services.

29. Ferrell, *Harry S. Truman: A Life*, 297.

30. The President's Farewell Address to the American People (quote near the end), HSTL.

31. *FRUS, 1948, Germany and Austria*, vol. 2, JCS (Joint Chiefs of Staff) 1779, Directive to Commander-in-Chief of U.S. Forces of Occupation, Regarding the Military Government of Germany, July 11, 1947. JCS 1779 replaced JCS 1067.

32. Dana and Carlson, "Harry Truman's Forgotten Diary," quoting Sara J. Bloomfield, director of the U.S. Holocaust Memorial Museum.

33. Safire, "Truman on Underdogs."

34. Ferrell, *Dear Bess*, 548–9.

35. Ferrell, *Truman in the White House*, 187 (Saturday, July 26, 1947).

36. Ferrell, *Off the Record*, 275 (Truman diary, November 24, 1952).

37. *New York Times*, July 27, 1947, 1.

38. Margaret Truman, *Souvenir*, 174.

39. Diary, July 28, 1947, President's Secretary's Files, 1945–1953, Truman Papers, HSTL.

40. Remarks to reporters following the death of the resident's mother, August 1, 1947, HSTL.
41. "The Presidency: No. 1 Pollywog," *Time*, September 22, 1947.
42. *FRUS, 1947, The British Commonwealth; Europe*, vol. 3, 411–2.
43. See e.g., *New York Times*, September 8, 1947, 1; Absolon, "The *Exodus* Affair," 65–79.
44. Bland et al., *The Papers of George Catlett Marshall*, vol. 6, 213 (speech to the United Nations General Assembly, September 17, 1947).
45. Truman, *Memoirs*, vol. 2, 117; "The Immediate Need for Emergency Aid to Europe," September 29, 1947, HSTL, https://www.trumanlibrary.gov/library/research-files/im mediate-need-emergency-aid-europe?documentid=NA&pagenumber=1; see also "The President's News Conference Following a Meeting with Congressional Leaders," September 29, 1947, https://www.presidency.ucsb.edu/documents/the-presidents-news -conference-following-meeting-with-congressional-leaders.
46. Vandenberg, *The Private Papers of Senator Vandenberg*, 378.
47. Frank McNaughton to Don Bermingham, October 4, 1947, Folder "October 1947," Box 14, McNaughton Reports File, McNaughton Papers, HSTL.
48. Ferrell, *Dear Bess*, 550–1.
49. Marshall, oral interview, Price Collection, HSTL.
50. Steil, *The Marshall Plan*, 197.
51. Report of Herter Committee, May 1, 1948, prepared by the Executive Secretariat, International Cooperation Administration, September 15, 1956, GCML.
52. "Text of Taft's Speech Delivered Before the Ohio Society," *New York Times*, November 11, 1947, 20 (the speech was delivered on November 10).
53. Vandenberg, *The Private Papers of Senator Vandenberg*, 378–9.
54. Special message to the Congress on the first day of the Special Session, November 17, 1947, American Presidency Project, https://www.presidency.ucsb.edu/documents/spe cial-message-the-congress-the-first-day-the-special-session.
55. Campbell, *The United States in World Affairs: 1947–1948*, 505.
56. West Germany received assistance through the Government and Relief in Occupied Areas Program.
57. Truman, *Memoirs*, vol. 2, 160.
58. Eddie Jacobson to Truman, October 3, 1947, Eddie Jacobson Papers, HSTL.
59. Truman to Jacobson, October 8, 1947, Eddie Jacobson Papers, HSTL.
60. "Memorandum by Major General John H. Hilldring to the Secretary of State, October 9, 1947," *FRUS, 1947, The Near East and Africa*, vol. 5, document no. 816; the statement supporting partition was delivered to the Ad Hoc Committee by Ambassador Herschel Johnson on October 11, 1947. For text see *Department of State Bulletin*, October 19, 1947, 761.
61. Truman, *Memoirs*, vol. 2, 155.
62. *Department of State Bulletin*, October 19, 1947, 761.
63. "Memorandum by Mr. Gordon Knox to the Acting United States Representative at the United Nations (Johnson), October 3, 1947," *FRUS, 1947, The Near East and Africa*, vol. 5, 1174.
64. "King Abdul Aziz Ibn Saud to President Truman, October 26, 1947," *FRUS, 1947, The Near East and Africa*, vol. 5, 1212–3. Copies were sent by courier to Arab capitals and London. See also Bohlen, *Witness to History*, 203–4.
65. *FRUS 1947, The Near East and Africa*, vol. 5, 255–6.
66. Weizmann, *Trial and Error*, 458.
67. Clifford to Truman, November 19, 1947, Box 22, Clifford Papers (underlining of *Exodus* in the original), HSTL.
68. Sheffer, *Moshe Sharett*, 263.
69. *FRUS, Near East and Africa*, vol. 5, 1287–9.

70. "November 28, 1947," *FRUS, The Near East and Africa*, vol. 5, 1289–90.

71. Loy W. Henderson, oral history by Richard D. McKinzie, July 14, 1973, 137.

72. Gruber, *Witness*, 158.

73. *Newcastle Morning Herald and Miners' Advocate* (Australia), December 1, 1947.

74. "Jubilant Zionists Hold Rally Here," *New York Times*, December 3, 1947, 1.

75. Truman, *Memoirs*, vol. 2, 159.

76. Ibid., 157, 181.

77. Donovan, *Conflict & Crisis*, 332, quoting McCoy and Ruetten, *Quest and Response*, 94.

78. "To Secure These Rights," The Report of the President's Committee on Civil Rights, October 29, 1947, https://www.trumanlibrary.gov/library/to-secure-these-rights #139.

79. Walter White, *A Man Called White*, 333, 348.

80. Karabell, *The Last Campaign*, 48.

81. Elsey, *An Unplanned Life*, 154.

Chapter 10 ★ Politics of 1948

1. Truman, *Memoirs*, vol. 2, 171.

2. Ross, *The Loneliest Campaign*, 9, citing author's unpublished interview with Clark Clifford, September 14, 1965.

3. Clifford, *Counsel to the President*, 191.

4. Ibid., 193.

5. James H. Rowe, oral history, appendix B, "The Politics of 1948" (original memo by Rowe, September 19, 1947), HSTL; Clark Clifford, "The Politics of 1948" (memo to Harry S. Truman, November 19, 1947), Political File, Clifford Papers, HSTL.

6. Clifford, *Counsel to the President*, 195.

7. Truman, Annual Message to the Congress on the State of the Union, January 7, 1948, https://www.presidency.ucsb.edu/documents/annual-message-the-congress-the-state -the-union-14.

8. James Reston, "Truman Message Shows Lack of Cabinet Analysis," *New York Times*, January 8, 1948, 2, quoted by Clifford in *Counsel to the President*, 195–6.

9. Elsey, *An Unplanned Life*, 159.

10. *PP, HST, 1948*, 99, 101, 217.

11. Ibid., 101, 218, 219.

12. Clifford, *Counsel to the President*, 203.

13. *Morgan v. Virginia*, 328 U.S. 373 (June 3, 1946).

14. McCoy and Ruetten, *Quest and Response*, 52; Hillman, *Mr. President*, 134.

15. Key, *Southern Politics in State and Nation*, 330–1.

16. Clifford, *Counsel to the President*, 207.

17. "Democrats: Black Week," *Time*, March 1, 1948.

18. Frank, *The Trials of Harry S. Truman*, 156.

19. *PP, HST, 1948*, 147ff.

20. "Democrats: Black Week," *Time*, March 1, 1948.

21. Redding, *Inside the Democratic Party*, 136, 137.

22. *New York Times*, February 24, 1948, 1. See also Clifford, *Counsel to the President*, 207–8; Clifford, oral history, 52–4, 299, July 26, 1971, HSTL.

23. "Political Notes: They Voted Against Us," *Time*, May 1, 1948.

24. Redding, *Inside the Democratic Party*, 149.

25. *FRUS, The Near East, South Asia, and Africa*, vol. 5, pt. 2, 697, 680–1.

26. Ferrell, *Dear Bess*, 233.

27. Margaret Truman, *Harry S. Truman*, 387.

28. Jacobson to Dr. Josef Cohn, April 1, 1952, Weizmann Archives Records, Subject File, Relations Between the United States, Palestine, and Israel, HSTL. Instead of the phrase "son of a bitch," the typewritten letter contains a black line, but Jacobson and others who knew Truman believed these words were the swear words that Truman actually used. In *The Trials of Harry S. Truman*, Jeffrey Frank writes at page 162 that Jacobson's account is "more or less fiction," based on a 1969 oral history by A. J. Granoff in HSTL but that quote cannot be found.

29. Truman, *Memoirs*, vol. 2, 161.

30. Weizmann, *Trial and Error*, 472.

31. Truman, *Memoirs*, vol. 2, 161–2.

32. Ferrell, *Off the Record*, 127 (Truman diary, March 20, 1948).

33. Clifford quoted in Cohen, *Truman and Israel*, 193.

34. Bland et al., *The Papers of George Catlett Marshall*, vol. 6, 418 (memorandum by Marshall for Charles E. Bohlen, March 22, 1948).

35. *New York Times*, March 21, 1948, 8E (editorial).

36. "Foreign Relations: A Little Butter for His Bread," *Time*, April 5, 1948.

37. Ibid.

38. "The Position of the United States with Respect to Soviet-Dominated World Communism," NSC-7, March 30, 1948, Box NSC 1/1-33, Modern Military Branch, National Archives, Washington, DC.

39. Jean Edward Smith, *The Papers of General Lucius D. Clay*, vol. 2, 568–9 (Clay to Lieutenant General Stephen J. Chamberlin, March 5, 1948; italics added).

40. Millis, *The Forrestal Diaries*, 387.

41. Truman's handwritten note, March 5, 1948, President's Secretary's Files, 1945–1953, Truman Papers, Box 154, HSTL.

42. Jean Edward Smith, *The Papers of General Lucius D. Clay*, vol. 2, 569.

43. "Communiqué Issued at the Recess of the London Conference on Germany," *FRUS, Germany and Austria*, vol. 2, 142–3.

44. Kennan, *Memoirs*, 393.

45. Millis, *The Forrestal Diaries*, 394.

46. Steil, *The Marshall Plan*, 258.

47. Truman, "Special Message to the Congress on the Threat to the Freedom of Europe," March 17, 1948, https://www.trumanlibrary.gov/library/public-papers/52/special-message-congress-threat-freedom-europe.

48. St. Patrick's Day address in New York City, March 17, 1948, American Presidency Project, https://www.presidency.ucsb.edu/documents/st-patricks-day-address-new-york-city.

49. Hamby, *Beyond the New Deal*, 219.

50. "Truman Rejects Any Wallace Aid," *New York Times*, March 18, 1948, 30.

51. The Selective Service Act of 1948 was signed on June 24, 1948. It required all men eighteen and older to register for the draft. Under the act, all men eighteen to twenty-five became eligible to be drafted and serve for twenty-one months. Truman continued to urge passage of his Universal Military Training program but it never gained traction in Congress due to its expense and opposition by labor unions, churches, educators, and mothers.

52. Millis, *The Forrestal Diaries*, 407–9.

53. *PP, HST, 1948*, statement by the president upon signing the Foreign Assistance Act, April 3, 1948, 203.

54. *PP, HST, 1947*, remarks and question-and-answer period with the National Conference of Editorial Writers, October 17, 1947, 473.

55. Herf, *Israel's Moment*, 325.

56. Yegev, *Political and Diplomatic Documents*, companion volume no. 388, 25.

57. Ibid., no. 364, 588–90 (Weizmann to Truman, April 9, 1948).

58. Jacobson to Dr. Josef Cohn, April 1, 1952.

59. Weizmann, *The Impossible Takes Longer*, 231.

60. Mead, *The Arc of a Covenant*, 198–9.

61. Jean Edward Smith, *Lucius D. Clay*, 476.

62. Isaacson and Thomas, *The Wise Men*, 456.

63. Truman, "Special Message to the Congress on the Threat to the Freedom of Europe."

64. "Minutes of the Sixth Meeting of the United States–United Kingdom–Canada Security Conversations, April 1, 1948," *FRUS, 1948*, vol. 3, 71–6.

65. See George Elsey's "Western Union Chronology," April 13, 1948, Elsey Papers, Box 66, HSTL.

66. "Report by the Executive Secretary of the National Security Council (Souers) to the Council, NSC 9, April 13, 1948," *FRUS, Western Europe*, vol. 3, 85–8.

67. "The Director of the Policy Planning Staff (Kennan) to the Executive Secretary of the National Security Council (Souers), NSC 9/1, April 23, 1948" (which replaces paragraphs 8 to 14 of NSC 9), *FRUS, Western Europe*, vol. 3, 100–3.

68. Vandenberg, *The Private Papers of Senator Vandenberg*, 406.

69. Ibid., 406–7.

70. Steill, *The Marshall Plan*, 318.

71. Ibid.

72. Vandenberg, *The Private Papers of Senator Vandenberg*, 411.

73. Clifford, *Counsel to the President*, 5.

74. *FRUS, The Near East, South Asia, and Africa*, vol. 5, pt. 2, 906.

75. Clifford, *Counsel to the President*, 5–6.

76. Weisberger, "An Exclusive Interview with Clark Clifford."

77. Cohen, *Truman and Israel*, 279.

78. Truman letter to Clifford, May 9, 1948 (original in longhand), Shapell Manuscript Foundation (www.shapell.org).

79. *New York Times*, April 4, 1948, E3 (Arthur Krock).

80. Bland et al., *The Papers of George Catlett Marshall*, vol. 6, 449 (Marshall to Mrs. Truman, May 10, 1948, containing a written draft of Marshall's toast to the president).

81. Memo containing draft article from "Eddie Jones" (*Time* domestic correspondent) to "Don Bermingham" (*Time* U.S. and Canadian News Service correspondent), December 18, 1948, McNaughton Papers, HSTL.

82. Clifford, *Counsel to the President*, 3.

83. *FRUS, The Near East, South Asia, and Africa*, vol. 5, pt. 2, 973–4.

84. Clifford, *Counsel to the President*, 11.

85. Ibid., 11–2.

86. Clifford, letter to McCullough, quoting Deuteronomy 1:8, King James Version.

87. Clifford quoted in Cohen, *Truman and Israel*, 213.

88. Address by Clifford, American Ditchley Foundation, Ditchley Park, Oxfordshire, UK, April 4, 1984; McCullough, unpublished interview of Clifford.

89. *FRUS, The Near East, South Asia, and Africa*, vol. 5, pt. 2, 975.

90. Ibid. (italics added).

91. Clifford, *Counsel to the President*, 13, 15.

92. Ibid., 15; Clifford, oral history, 101–2, April 13, 1971, HSTL.

93. *FRUS, The Near East, South Asia, and Africa*, vol. 5, pt. 2, 1006 (italics added).

94. Clifford, *Counsel to the President*, 21.

95. Interview of Lovett by Isaacson and Thomas, in *The Wise Men*, 453 and n792.

96. *Official Gazette*, no. 1, of Iyar 5, 5708 (May 14, 1948).

97. Charles (Charlie) Ross, Alphabetical File, handwriting of Truman, HSTL.

98. Bland et al., *The Papers of George Catlett Marshall*, vol. 6, 457–8 and n1 (Mrs. Roosevelt to Marshall, May 18, 1948, and response by Marshall, May 18, 1948).

99. *FRUS, The Near East, South Asia, and Africa*, vol. 5, pt. 2, 1007.

100. Remarks at the Young Democrats Dinner, May 14, 1948, President's Secretary's Files, Box 74, HSTL, https://www.trumanlibrary.gov/library/public-papers/101/remarks-young-democrats-dinner.

101. Lowenthal Papers, May 15, 1948, University of Minnesota. See also Cohen, *Truman and Israel*, 22.

102. "Joseph Grew to William Moreland, March 24, 1945," *FRUS, The Near East and Africa*, vol. 8, 697.

103. *Time*, May 24, 1948.

104. Kurzman, *Ben-Gurion: Prophet of Fire*, 416. David Niles, who had worked closely with both Roosevelt and Truman, often expressed doubt that Israel would ever have come into existence if FDR had lived. Michael Benson, *Israel and the Legacy of Harry S. Truman* and *Harry S. Truman and the Founding of Israel*.

Chapter 11 ⋆ Pour It On, Harry

1. Redding, *Inside the Democratic Party*, 52–3.

2. Rowe, oral history, appendix B, "The Politics of 1948" (original memo by Rowe, September 19, 1947), HSTL; Clifford, "The Politics of 1948" (memo to Harry S. Truman, November 19, 1947), Political File, Clifford Papers, HSTL.

3. Clifford, *Counsel to the President*, 199.

4. Lash, *Eleanor: The Years Alone*, 146.

5. Neal, *Eleanor and Harry* (letter from Eleanor Roosevelt to Truman, March 26, 1948). 136–7.

6. Eleanor Roosevelt to May Craig, May 11, 1948, Box 1547, Folder: May 1948-1952, FDRL.

7. Humphrey, *Education of a Public Man*, 75.

8. Eleanor Roosevelt to Frances Perkins, October 4, 1948, Eleanor Roosevelt Papers Project, George Washington University.

9. *New York Times*, June 4, 1948, 1; *New York Herald Tribune*, June 4. 1948, 1.

10. Truman, *PP, HST, 1948*, rear platform remarks in Ohio and Indiana, June 4, 1948, 284–5.

11. *Omaha Morning World-Herald*, June 8, 1948, 1.

12. McKim, oral history, February 19, 1964, 149, HSTL.

13. Matthew J. Connelly, oral history, 1967–68 (transcript), 263, HSTL.

14. McKim, oral history, 149, HSTL.

15. This is a composite of a number of accounts that exist, including Donovan, *Conflict & Crisis*, 397–8; Karabell, *The Last Campaign*, 132; and Baime, *Dewey Defeats Truman*, 125.

16. Robert G. Nixon, oral history (transcript), October 30, 1970, 550, HSTL.

17. *Nation's Business*, June 1948, 29.

18. Truman, *PP, HST, 1948*, address at the stadium in Butte, Montana, 8:45 p.m., June 8, 1948, 304–7.

19. Ibid., rear platform and other remarks in Spokane, Washington, 8:40 a.m., June 9, 1948, 307–8.

20. Ibid., 308, 315.

21. Ibid., 309.

22. *Spokane Spokesman-Review*, June 10, 1948, 1.

23. *New York Times*, June 12, 1948, L7.

24. Redding, *Inside the Democratic Party*, 178–9.

25. Truman, *PP, HST, 1948*, 314–15 (informal remarks), 11:40 a.m., June 10, 1948.

26. Ibid., 318.

27. Ibid., 329.

28. Clifford, *Counsel to the President*, 201.

29. *Kansas City Star*, March 23, 1969, 18A.

30. Truman, *PP, HST, 1948*, rear platform remarks in Pocatello, Idaho, June 7, 1948, 7:50 a.m., 300. Actual words: "If they can prove it on you, you are in a bad fix indeed. They have never been able to prove it on me."

31. Ibid., rear platform and other remarks in Davis, California, June 12, 1948, 11:10 a.m., 335. Actual words: "You know, I am on a nonpolitical trip. I am going down here to Berkeley to get me a degree."

32. Charles S. Murphy, oral history, May 2, 1963, 18, HSTL.

33. Truman, *PP, HST, 1948*, rear platform and other remarks in Berkeley, California, June 12, 1948, 1:50 p.m., 335–6. Truman also got in a dig about Sproul's failed mission to Moscow in the fall of 1945. No one in the audience understood what Truman was talking about but Sproul certainly did.

34. Murphy, oral history, 18, HSTL.

35. Truman, *PP, HST, 1948*, commencement address at the University of California, Memorial Stadium, June 12, 1948, 4 p.m. 378–82.

36. Donovan, *Conflict & Crisis*, 401.

37. Ibid.

38. Truman, *PP, HST, 1948*, 289. In an address in Chicago on June 4 to the Swedish Centennial Association, Truman remarked that if "some of our people" are "arbitrarily denied the right to vote or deprived of other rights, and nothing is done about it, that is an invitation to communism."

39. Donovan, *Conflict & Crisis*, 401, unpublished interview by Donovan with Henry J. Nicholson, September 20, 1972. See also Howard McGrath, oral history, 12–4, HSTL.

40. Truman, *PP, HST, 1948*, 360.

41. Goulden, *The Best Years*, 371.

42. Yergin, *Shattered Peace*, 368.

43. Collier, *Bridge Across the Sky*, 48, based on eyewitness account by Margot Derigs, a newsroom employee at *Der Tag* (Berlin newspaper).

44. Hill and Gaddy, *Mr. Putin: Operative in the Kremlin*, 63–77.

45. Jean Edward Smith, *Lucius D. Clay*, 499.

46. Daily appointments of Harry S. Truman, Saturday, June 26, 1948, HSTL.

47. Berlin Airlift Historical Foundation, "What Was the Berlin Airlift?" http://www.spiritoffreedom.org/airlift.html.

48. Millis, *The Forrestal Diaries*, 454–5; see also Jean Edward Smith, *Lucius D. Clay*, 508.

49. Millis, *The Forrestal Diaries*, 455.

50. *PP, HST, 1948*, note at the end of the president's news conference of July 1, 1948, 394.

51. Hamby, *Man of the People*, 444.

52. Ferrell, *Off the Record*, 141 (Truman diary, July 6, 1948).

53. Hagerty, "Eisenhower Gaining Headway in Fight on Truman," 1.

54. *Newsweek*, July 19, 1948, 15.

55. Margaret Truman, *Harry S. Truman*, 7.

56. Interview with Alben W. Barkley, July 23, 1953, Alben W. Barkley Oral History Project, Louis B. Nunn Center for Oral History, University of Kentucky Libraries.

57. Truman, *Memoirs*, vol. 2, 190.

58. Murphy, *Wild Bill*, 264.

59. Ferrell, *Truman in the White House* (June 13, 1948), 265.

60. Ferrell, *Off the Record*, 141–2 (Truman diary, July 12, 1948). See also Margaret Truman, *Harry S. Truman*, 9.

61. Karabell, *The Last Campaign*, 156.

62. Ibid., 142.

63. Margaret Truman, *Harry S. Truman*, 11.

64. Clifford, *Counsel to the President*, 217.

65. The Moody amendment advocated for "the reserved powers of the states . . . to control and regulate local affairs and act in the exercise of police powers." Tom Clark, transcript of oral history by Jerry N. Hess, October 17, 1972, 185, HSTL.

66. Ferrell, *Off the Record*, 143.

67. Hubert Humphrey's 1948 Democratic Speech. https://www.americanrhetoric.com /speeches/huberthumphey1948dnc.html.

68. Ferrell, *Off the Record*, 143.

69. Ibid.

70. Clifford, *Counsel to the President*, 221.

71. Redding, *Inside the Democratic Party*, 196–7.

72. Margaret Truman, *Harry S. Truman*, 13.

73. Truman's Democratic Acceptance Speech, July 15, 1948, https://www.pbs.org/news hour/spc/character/links/truman_speech.html.

74. Margaret Truman, *Harry S. Truman*, 14.

75. "Should the President Call Congress Back?" June 29, 1948, 1948 Election Campaign, Papers of Samuel L. Rosenman, HSTL. It was this document that referred to Republican leaders as "Neanderthal." In addition to Batt, the members of the research team that worked on the memo were John Barriere, Kenneth Birkhead, Philip Dreyer, Johannes Hoeber, Frank Kelly, and David Lloyd. See Batt and Balducci, "Origin of the 1948 Turnip Day Session of Congress," 80–3.

76. Ferrell, *Off the Record*, 142 (Truman diary, July 16, 1948).

77. Straight, "Turnip Day in Washington."

78. *Hartford Courant*, July 18, 1948, 1.

79. "Thurmond and Wright Head Dixie Rights Ticket," *Atlanta Constitution*, July 18, 1948, 1.

80. McCullough, *Truman*, 645, quoting Steinberg, *The Man from Missouri*, 315.

81. "It's Wallace or War, Says Keynoter for New Party," *Washington Post*, July 24, 1948, 1.

82. "Text of Henry Wallace's Acceptance of Presidential Nomination," *Washington Post*, July 25, 1948, 28.

83. *Time*, August 9, 1948.

84. Clifford, *Counsel to the President*, 225.

85. Jean Edward Smith, *The Papers of General Lucius D. Clay*, vol. 2, 733–5.

86. Millis, *The Forrestal Diaries*, 459.

87. Ferrell, *Off the Record*, 145.

88. Ferrell, *Dear Bess*, 555.

89. Clay, *Decision in Germany*, 368.

90. Lucius Clay, oral history by Richard D. McKinzie, July 16, 1975, 39, HSTL.

91. Collier, *Bridge Across the Sky*, 91.

92. Clay, oral history, 39–40, HSTL; Collier, *Bridge Across the Sky*, 92.

93. Clay, oral history, 40, HSTL.

94. Nash, oral history, October 18, 1966, 346–48, HSTL.

95. Executive Order 9980, Regulations Governing Fair Employment Practices; and Executive Order 9981, President's Committee on Equality of Treatment and Opportunity in the Armed Services.

96. Gardner, *Harry Truman and Civil Rights*, 121 (paraphrase of statement by civil rights leader Dr. Dorothy Height).
97. Patterson, *Mr. Republican*, 422.
98. Clifford, *Counsel to the President*, 223.
99. Truman, *PP, HST, 1948*, 416.
100. Ibid., 419.
101. Ibid., 420.
102. Ibid., 449–50.
103. Ibid., 438.

Chapter 12 ⋆ Now It's My Fight

1. Ferrell, *Off The Record*, 146 (Truman diary, August 3, 1948); Margaret Truman, *Harry S. Truman*, 398; Truman to Mary Jane Truman, August 10, 1948, Papers of Harry S. Truman Pertaining to Family, Business, and Personal Affairs, Box 688, HSTL.
2. Margaret Truman, *Bess W. Truman*, 329.
3. Daily appointments of Harry S. Truman, off the record in the president's study, Thursday, July 22, 1948, HSTL. Persons who attended other than Truman: Tom Clark, Charles Sawyer, Oscar Ewing, Oscar Chapman, Les Biffle, William Pawley, William Hatch, Steve Early, Sam Rosenman, Matt Connelly.
4. Author interview with Jean Kearney (who worked closely with Johnson at the DNC), March 27, 2002.
5. Oscar L. Chapman, oral history, August 18, 1972, 321, HSTL.
6. Connelly, oral history, November 30, 1967, 290, HSTL.
7. President's Personal File: Political File D, Box 156, HSTL.
8. Telegram, August 31, 1948, McGrath Papers, Box 54, Finance Committee DNC, 1948, HSTL.
9. Pearson, "Woebegone Democrats Finally Come to Life," *Radford News Journal*, September 18, 1948.
10. Ibid.
11. Daily appointments of Harry S. Truman, off the record, September 10, 1948, 11:15 a.m., HSTL.
12. Neal Roach, oral history by Jerry N. Hess, October 2, 1969, 71, HSTL.
13. Samuel C. Brightman, oral history by Jerry N. Hess, December 7, 1966, 56, HSTL; see also Roach, oral history, 74.
14. Snyder, oral history by Hess, July 10, 1968, 763, HSTL.
15. Chandler, "A Balance Statement," 16.
16. Clifford, oral history by Hess, April 19, 1971, 137, HSTL.
17. Martin, "Million Dollar Truman Fund"; Sengstacke, "Let's Put Up or Shut Up."
18. Anna Arnold Hedgeman, "Untitled Talk," Box 150, Hedgeman Papers, National Afro-American Museum and Cultural Center, Wilberforce, Ohio.
19. Anna Arnold Hedgeman interview, transcript, 102, Black Women Oral History Project Interviews, 1976–1981, Harvard University.
20. Michaeli, *The Defender*, 289.
21. Miller, "The Negro Voters in the Far West," 267.
22. Shaffer, Helen B., "Women in Politics," Editorial Research Reports (February 20, 1956), vol. 1. http://library.cqpress.com/cqresearcher/cqresrre1956022000.
23. Brightman, oral history, 103, HSTL.
24. India Edwards, oral history by Hess, January 16, 1969, 61–2, HSTL.
25. "Mowing 'Em Down," *Time*, September 27, 1948.
26. Clark Clifford to Harry S. Truman, "Memorandum for the President: The 1948 Campaign," August 17, 1948, HSTL.

27. Drew Pearson, "The Washington Merry-Go-Round," August 15, 1948, quoting Truman expressing "confidence that he would carry much of the farm vote."

28. Truman not only flipped those three states; he also prevailed in Colorado and Wyoming, states that had a total of nine electoral votes, which could have been regarded as farm states. Dewey had won Colorado and Wyoming in 1944.

29. Charles S. Murphy, oral history, 136–9, May 21, 1969, HSTL. Murphy was not listed as an invitee in the White House log but he was flown down to the lower Potomac early Sunday morning, September 12, 1948.

30. *PP, HST, 1948*, 495, 497 (UMich/Hathi Trust pagination continues to be used the remainder of the PP cites).

31. Ibid., 504–8.

32. Darcy Maulsby, "Riding with Harry, 2016 Presidential Election Reflects Truman's Iowa Revival at 1948 Plowing Match in Dexter," https://www.darcymaulsby.com/blog/riding-with-harry-2016-presidential-election-reflects-trumans-iowa-revival-at-1948-plowing-match-in-dexter; Joy Neal Kidney, "President Truman and the 1948 National Plowing Match at Dexter, Iowa," https://joynealkidney.com/2018/09/13/president-truman-and-the-1948-national-plowing-match-at-dexter-iowa/.

33. Truman, *PP, HST, 1948*, 498.

34. Ross, *The Loneliest Campaign*, 193.

35. Edwards, oral history, 47–9 (emphasis in the original), HSTL.

36. Donovan, *Conflict & Crisis*, 422; Truman, *PP, HST, 1948*, 512.

37. Truman, *PP, HST, 1948*, 559.

38. Margaret Truman, *Harry S. Truman*, 31.

39. Ibid., 32.

40. McCullough, *Truman*, 675.

41. Margaret Truman, *Harry S. Truman*, 34.

42. Shogan, *Harry Truman and the Struggle for Racial Justice*, 139.

43. Clifford, *Counsel to the President*, 232–3.

44. Truman, *Memoirs*, vol. 2, 216.

45. Lovett interview by Forrest Pogue, Tape 120, Copy 2, August 28 and 29, 1973, 47, GCML.

46. Daniels, *The Man of Independence*, 29.

47. Goulden, *The Best Years*, 414.

48. Clifford, *Counsel to the President*, 233.

49. Cherny, "The Original October Surprise."

50. McCullough, *Truman*, 694.

51. *PP, HST, 1948*, 743, 747.

52. Clifford, *Counsel to the President*, 235.

53. Margaret Truman, *Harry S. Truman*, 21.

54. Clifford, *Counsel to the President*, 235.

55. McCullough, unpublished interview of Clifford.

56. Elsey, *An Unplanned Life*, 170.

57. Truman, *Memoirs*, vol. 2, 219. See Truman, *PP, HST, 1948*, address in Miami at the American Legion Convention, 815–8.

58. Truman, *PP, HST, 1948*, address at the state capitol, Raleigh, North Carolina, October 19, 1948, 821.

59. Millis, *The Forrestal Diaries*, 506–7.

60. Memorandum, President's Personal File 1920, October 21, 1948, HSTL, https://www.trumanlibrary.gov/library/research-files/summary-berlin-airlift-developments; Harry Truman to executive secretary, National Security Council, October 22, 1948, Harry S. Truman Papers, President's Secretary's Files, Box 178, HSTL.

61. *PP, HST, 1948*, address in Pittsburgh, Pennsylvania, October 23, 1948, 838–9.

62. Ibid., address in the Chicago Stadium, October 25, 1948, 848–53.

63. Busch, *Truman's Triumphs*, 152.

64. *PP, HST, 1948*, address in the Cleveland Municipal Auditorium, October 26, 1948, 863.

65. Wilkerson, *The Warmth of Other Suns*, 266.

66. Margaret Truman, *Harry S. Truman*, 30.

67. *PP, HST, 1948*, address at Mechanics Hall in Boston, October 27, 1948, 884, 886.

68. Ibid., address in Madison Square Garden, New York City, October 28, 1948, 913.

69. Nash, oral history, October 24, 1948, 387, HSTL.

70. Anna Hedgeman's biographer wrote that it is "not clear" whether Hedgeman organized the event "but it had all the markers of religion and race that she would have included." Plus, Hedgeman lived in Harlem for years and knew what a perfect setting it would make for Truman's only civil rights speech during the campaign. Scanlon, *Until There Is Justice*, 115.

71. Ibid., 398–400.

72. *PP, HST, 1948*, address in Harlem, New York, upon receiving the Franklin Roosevelt Award, October 29, 1948, 923–5 (italics added).

73. Nash, oral history, October 24, 1948, 404, HSTL.

74. Margaret Truman, *Harry S. Truman*, 38 (italics in the original).

75. Snyder, oral history, January 8, 1969, 936, HSTL.

76. *PP, HST, 1948*, address at the Kiel Auditorium, St. Louis, Missouri, October 30, 1948, 934–9.

77. Clifford, *Counsel to the President*, 237.

78. *New York Times*, November 1, 1948, 17.

79. Eleanor Roosevelt to Harry S. Truman, October 4, 1948, Eleanor Roosevelt Papers Project, Columbian College of Arts and Sciences.

80. Ladd, "The Trials of Election Polling."

81. *New York Times*, November 3, 1948, 7. See also Margaret Truman, *Harry S. Truman*, 39.

82. Margaret Truman, *Harry S. Truman*, 40.

83. Truman, handwritten note (November 1948) and transcript (November 2, 1948), https://www.trumanlibrary.gov/library/truman-papers/longhand-notes-presidential -file-1944-1953/ca-November-1948.

84. Statement by Herbert Brownell Jr. at 11:15 p.m., Thomas E. Dewey Papers, Series 2, Box 117, River Campus Libraries, University of Rochester (not online).

85. McCullough, *Truman*, 707.

86. "President Truman Imitates NBC Chief Newsman H. V. Kaltenborn 1948," https://www.youtube.com/watch?v=coxfmRl-34o; see also "Truman Mimics Broadcaster," https://www.budgetfilms.com/clip/15338/.

87. Tom L. Evans, oral history, September 18, 1963, 534–5, HSTL.

88. Donovan, *Conflict & Crisis*, 434.

89. Jacob Arvey's obituary, *New York Times*, August 26, 1977, D15.

90. Redding, *Inside the Democratic Party*, 21.

91. This is a composite of quotes from the following: Truman, handwritten note and transcript; "President Truman Imitates NBC Chief Newsman"; "Truman Mimics Broadcaster"; McCullough, *Truman*, 707; Donovan, *Crisis & Conflict*, 435; and Margaret Truman, *Harry S. Truman*, 41.

92. Nixon, oral history, 686–9 (emphasis in the original), HSTL.

93. Redding, *Inside the Democratic Party*, 23.

94. Edwards, oral history, 80–1, HSTL.

95. Ibid., 77.

96. Jack Hogan interview with Joseph Gasarch, January 24, 1980, cited in Richard Norton Smith, *Thomas E. Dewey and His Times*, 47.

Chapter 13   ⋆   Liberator

1. Donovan, *Tumultuous Years*, 17. See also William E. Leuchtenburg, *In the Shadow of FDR*, 1–40, and Miscamble, *From Roosevelt to Truman*, 323–5.
2. Letter from Philleo Nash to Harry S. Truman, November 6, 1948, 1948 Election Campaign, President's Secretary's Files, HSTL. Nash wrote, "Except in New York, the Wallace vote among Negro districts was insignificant." In Harlem, Truman received 65 percent of the combined vote. In Illinois, the average in all Negro districts was 78.8 percent for Truman.
3. Topping, "Never Argue with the Gallup Polls," 196–7.
4. Elsey, *An Unplanned Life*, 173 (paraphrase).
5. Ibid., 175, quoting excerpts from Elsey's talk at the U.S. Agency for International Development in 1999 on the fiftieth anniversary of Truman's inaugural address.
6. Ibid., 176. See also Christine Hardy Little, oral history, February 23, 1973, HSTL. Mrs. Little's husband was Ben Hardy, who died at age forty-five in a plane crash near Tehran on his way to discuss Point Four with the Iranians.
7. Truman, inaugural address, January 20, 1949, https://www.trumanlibrary.gov/library/public-papers/19/inaugural-address.
8. Elsey, *An Unplanned Life*, 276.
9. Truman, *Memoirs*, vol. 2, 226–39.
10. Bingham, *Shirt-Sleeve Diplomacy*, 11–2.
11. Margaret Truman, *Harry S. Truman*, 556, based on a recording by Joe Short, who was at the dinner, and the diary of Roger Tubby. McCullough, *Truman*, 874, and source notes, 1050.
12. Edzard Reuter, interview transcript, Kings College, London, Liddell Hart Centre for Military Archives, GBO99 Cold War.
13. General Lucius Clay, address (House), *Congressional Record*, May 17, 1949, 6339.
14. General William H. Draper Jr., oral history, January 11, 1972, 55, HSTL.
15. Heer, *Mr. X and the Pacific*, 51.
16. Miscamble, *George F. Kennan and the Making of American Foreign Policy*, 264.
17. Schonberger, "Zaibatsu Dissolution and the American Restoration of Japan," 27.
18. Heer, *Mr. X and the Pacific*, 72.
19. *FRUS, The Far East and Australasia*, vol. 6, 858–62.
20. Draper, oral history, 56–7, HSTL.
21. Schaller, *The American Occupation of Japan*, 138.
22. Harrison Report in Dinnerstein, *America and the Survivors of the Holocaust*, appendix B, 300–1.
23. Truman, *Memoirs*, vol. 2, 138–9. This was the president's reaction after reading the Harrison Report.
24. Gringauz, "Our New German Policy and the DPs," 508, 514.
25. "Survivors Speak About Their Lives After the Holocaust," https://www.yadvashem.org/artiahead.html
26. Rosensaft, *Yesterday (My Story)* 120–1.
27. "The President to Mark Ethridge, at Jerusalem, April 29, 1949," *FRUS, The Near East, South Asia, and Africa*, vol. 6, document 617.
28. "Marshall to McDonald, September 1, 1948," *FRUS, The Near East, South Asia, and Africa*, vol. 5, pt. 2, 1366–9.

29. Glass, "Truman Approves Aid to Palestine," Politico, March 24, 2017. Quote is from Senate Joint Resolution 26, March 24, 1949.

30. Statement and Directive by the President on Immigration to the United States of Certain Displaced Persons in Europe, December 22, 1945, Amerian Presidency Project, https://www.presidency.ucsb.edu/node/229546.

31. Dinnerstein, *America and the Survivors of the Holocaust*, 119. The annual quotas for Poland, Latvia, and Lithuania were 6,526, 246, and 386, respectively.

32. S. Res. 137, 80th Congress, 2nd Session, July 26, 1947.

33. Senate Committee on the Judiciary, *Displaced Persons in Europe*, 20.

34. *New York Times*, June 19, 1948, 14 (editorial); American Jewish Committee, Press Release, June 19.

35. Statement by the president upon signing the Displaced Persons Act, June 25, 1948, Trumanlibrary.gov/library/public-papers/142/statement-president-upon-signing-displaced-persons-act.

36. Nasaw, *The Last Million*, 447, citing Joint Distribution Committee Archives, New York Office, 1945–1954, Folder: Germany, Displaced Persons, 1–6; A. Haber, "Report on Activities . . . During the Month of February, 1949," March 22, 1949.

37. "Displaced Persons" in *CQ Almanac* 1949, 5th ed., 05-371–05–374, Washington, DC: *Congressional Quarterly*, 1950, http://library.cqpress.com/cqalmanac/cqal49-1400073.

38. Michael Green, Exhibit K, p. 2, Senate Committee on Government Affairs, March 17, 2017, https://www.leg.state.nv.us/Session/79th2017/Exhibits/Senate/GA/SGA4570K.pdf.

39. "M'Carran Charges Fraud in DP Set-Up," *New York Times*, October 8, 1949, 3.

40. Senate Committee on the Judiciary, "Displaced Persons," Hearings Before the Subcommittee on Amendments to the Displacement Act, 81st Congress, 1st and 2nd Sessions, 1950, 553.

41. 96 *Congressional Record* 96, part 2, 2420 (daily ed., February 28, 1950).

42. Nasaw, *The Last Million*, 489.

43. Berger, *Displaced Persons*, 279, 310–1.

44. *PP, HST, 1950*, statement by the president upon signing the bill amending the Displaced Persons Act, June 16, 1950, 483–4.

Epilogue ⋆ Grips to the Attic

1. Rosenman, oral history by Hess, October 15, 1968, 55, HSTL.

2. Ferrell, *Off the Record*, 134 (Truman diary, May 6, 1948).

3. Western Union telegram, November 5, 1952, to General Dwight D. Eisenhower, President's Secretary's Files, 1945–1953, Box 101, HSTL.

4. Truman, *Memoirs*, vol. 2, 505.

5. Letter from Truman to Eisenhower, November 6, 1952, President's Secretary's Files, 1945–1953, Box 101, HSTL.

6. Truman, *Memoirs*, vol. 2, 514.

7. Ferrell, *Off the Record*, 274 (Truman diary, November 20, 1952).

8. *PP, HST, 1952–1953*, 784–5.

9. Ibid., 862–3.

10. The Eisenhower Dispatch, "Ike and Truman's Strained and Tumultuous Relationship on Inauguration Day, 1953," January 5, 2021, National Park Service, https://www.nps.gov/eise/blogs/ike-and-trumans-strained-and-tumultuous-relationship-on-inauguration-day-1953.htm.

11. Truman, *Memoirs*, vol. 2, 521; Acheson, *Present at the Creation*, 706.

12. The President's news conference, December 11, 1952, HSTL.

13. Ferrell, *Off the Record*, 287 (Truman diary, January 20, 1953).

14. Margaret Truman, *Harry S. Truman*, 557. She paraphrased the substance of the exchange between her father and Eisenhower. Truman's attempt to replicate the conversation in his diary was somewhat garbled. See Ferrell, *Off the Record*, 287 (Truman diary, January 20, 1953).

15. Ferrell, *Off the Record*, 287 (Truman diary, January 20, 1953).

16. Ibid., 288.

17. "I'm Just Mr. Truman," *New York Times*, January 21, 1953, 16.

18. Ferrell, *Off the Record*, 288.

19. Poen, *Letters Home by Harry Truman*, 259.

20. Sherwood, *Roosevelt and Hopkins*, 94.

21. Hamby, *Man of the People: Harry S. Truman*, 629.

22. Margaret Truman, *Harry S. Truman*, 562.

23. McCullough, *Truman*, 947, quoting his unpublished interview with Francis Heller.

24. Ferrell, *Off the Record*, 347; Truman, letter to John W. McCormack, January 10, 1957, HSTL.

25. Ward, *Closest Companion*, 207 (entry of April 3, 1943).

26. *New York Daily News*, February 20, 1944, 87.

27. Sherwood, *Roosevelt and Hopkins*, 378–9.

28. Tom Evans, oral history, 687, HSTL.

29. Truman press conference, *New York Times*, July 3, 1960, 18.

30. Robert L. Dennison, oral history, November 2, 1971, 207–11, HSTL.

31. *New York Times*, December 6, 1972, 53. Wallace Graham, Truman's personal physician, was there and it was he who provided the diagnosis and condition ("fair").

32. Margaret Fayerweather, diary, March 28, 1945, Eleanor Roosevelt Papers, Box 1559, FDRL.

33. Eleanor Roosevelt, *My Husband and I*, two vinyl records, HSTL.

34. Lash, *World of Love*, 181–2.

35. Eleanor Roosevelt to Franklin D. Roosevelt, April 8, 1945, Eleanor Roosevelt Papers, FDRL.

36. Burial site of Franklin and Eleanor Roosevelt, National Park Service, https://www.nps.gov/places/burial-site-of-franklin-and-eleanor-roosevelt.htm.

37. Ward, *Closest Companion*, 422 (entry of April 15, 1945).

38. Brian Burnes, "Truman's Funeral," HSTL.

Index

About the Author

David L. Roll is the author of *George Marshall* and *The Hopkins Touch*, and coauthor of *Louis Johnson and the Arming of America*, a biography of Harry Truman's defense secretary. After serving as an assistant director in the Bureau of Competition at the FTC, Roll practiced law as a partner at Steptoe & Johnson LLP and founded the Lex Mundi Pro Bono Foundation, a public interest organization that provides pro bono legal services to social entrepreneurs around the world. He lives in Washington, DC.